WHAT GREAT MEN HAVE SAID ABOUT GREAT MEN

A DICTIONARY OF QUOTATIONS

BY

WILLIAM WALE

LONDON

SWAN SONNENSCHEIN & CO., LIM.

PATERNOSTER SQUARE

1902

REPUBLISHED BY GALE RESEARCH COMPANY, BOOK TOWER, DETROIT, 1968

Library of Congress Catalog Card
Number 68-17944

69– 8581

CONTENTS.

CONTENTS.

vii

viii CONTENTS.

Quote quotation on quotation.

—SWIFT.

The living words
Of our great men . . .
Pass not from door to door and out again,
But sit within the house.

—LORD TENNYSON.

Many are the sayings of the wise,
In ancient and in modern books enrolled.

—MILTON.

He rang'd his tropes, and preach'd up patience,
Back'd his opinion with quotations.

—PRIOR.

It often happens that the quotations constitute the most valuable part of a book.—
Dr. VICESIMUS KNOX.

A collection of good sentences resembles a string of pearls.—*Chinese Saying.*

By necessity, by proclivity, and by delight, we all quote. We quote not only books
and proverbs, but arts, sciences, religion, customs, and laws; nay, we quote temples and
houses, tables and chairs, by imitation.—EMERSON.

Every book is a quotation: and every house is a quotation out of all forests, and
mines, and stone-quarries; and every man is a quotation from all his ancestors.—*Idem.*

Peter Abelard.

French Scholastic Philosopher : 1079-1142.

The most eminent and the most orthodox Doctor of the eleventh century.—F. D. Maurice, *Mediæval Philosophy*.

Abelard was almost the first who awakened mankind in the ages of darkness to a sympathy with intellectual excellence. . . . Abelard was the first of recorded name, who taught the banks of the Seine to resound a tale of love; and it was of Eloise that he sang.—Hallam, *Student's Middle Ages*.

In the twelfth century was there any mind which shone more brightly, was there any eloquence which flowed more mightily, than that of Peter Abelard? Yet Abelard sank beneath the meanest of his scholastic contemporaries in the degradation of his career as much as he towered above the highest of them in the grandeur of his genius.—F. W. Farrar, *Seekers after God*.

Joseph Addison.

English Essayist and Dramatist : 1672-1719.

Thus Addison, by lords carest,
Was left in foreign lands distrest.

—Swift, *A Libel.*

On Addison's sweet lays attention waits
And silence guards the place while he repeats;
His Muse alike on every subject charms,
Whether he paints the God of Love, or Arms.

—Gay, *Epistle XIV.*

No whiter page than Addison remains.
—Pope, *Satires, etc., of Horace imitated.*

With graceful steps see Addison advance
The sweetest child of Attic elegance.
—Thomas Warton, *The Triumph of Isis.*

If Addison, or Rowe, or Prior write,
We study them with profit and delight.

—Congreve, *Of Pleasing.*

Guilt's chief foe in Addison is dead.

—Young, *Satire I.*

I

Our age demands correctness; Addison
And you this commendable hurt have done.

—YOUNG, *Epistle II.*

Urge on my soul, with no ignoble pride,
To woo the Muse, whom Addison enjoy'd,
See that bold swain to heaven sublimely soar,
Pursue at distance, and his steps adore.

—TICKELL, *Poem to the Lord Privy Seal.*

Every Muse was fond of Addison.

—*Id., Oxford : a Poem.*

Where Addison and Tickell lay inspir'd,
Inebriated, from the classic springs,
And tun'd to various-sounding harps the song,
Sublime or tender, humorous or grave,
Quaffing the Muses' nectar to their fill.

—THOMSON, *Progress of Sickness.*

In front of those came Addison. In him
Humour in holiday and sightly trim,
Sublimity and Attic taste combined,
To polish, furnish, and delight the mind.

—COWPER, *Table Talk.*

Every true critic—from the Stagyrite
To Schlegel and to Addison—hath won
His fame by serving a reflected light,
And clearing vapour from a clouded sun.

—LYTTON, *The True Critic.*

Whoever wishes to attain an English style, familiar, but not coarse,
and elegant, but not ostentatious, must give his days and nights to the
volumes of Addison.—DR. JOHNSON, *Lives of the Poets : Addison.*

The exquisite taste and fine observation of Addison.—LORD JEFFREY,
Essays.

It is the extremely moral and didactic tone of the *Spectator* which makes
us apt to think of Addison (according to Mandeville's sarcasm) as " a
parson in a tie-wig ".—HAZLITT, *Lectures on the English Comic Writers.*

No praise of Addison's style can exaggerate its merits. Its art is perfectly marvellous. No change of time can render the workmanship
obsolete. His style has that nameless urbanity in which we recognise
the perfection of manner—courteous, but not courtier-like ; so dignified,
yet so kindly ; so easy, yet so high-bred. Its form of English is fixed—a
safe and eternal model, of which all imitation pleases—to which all
approach is scholarship—like the Latin of the Augustan age.—LYTTON,
Miscellaneous Prose Works, Vol. III.

Joseph was of a cold nature, and needed perhaps the fire of wine to
warm his blood. If he was a parson, he wore a tye-wig, recollect. A
better and more Christian man scarcely ever breathed than Joseph
Addison. If he had not that little weakness for wine—why, we could
scarcely have found a fault with him, and could not have liked him as we

do. . . . He was a man's man, remember. The only woman he did know, he didn't write about. I take it there would not have been much humour in that story. . . . Is the glory of heaven to be sung only by gentlemen in black coats? Must the truth be only expounded in gown and surplice, and out of those two vestments can nobody preach it? Commend me to this dear preacher without orders—this parson in the tye-wig. When this man looks from the world, whose weaknesses he describes so benevolently, up to the Heaven which shines over us all, I can hardly fancy a human face lighted up with a more serene rapture : a human intellect thrilling with a purer love and adoration than Joseph Addison's.—THACKERAY, *English Humorists.*

To Addison himself we are bound by a sentiment as much like affection as any sentiment can be which is inspired by one who has been sleeping a hundred and twenty years in Westminster Abbey. . . . It is praise enough to say of a writer that, in a high department of literature, in which many eminent writers have distinguished themselves, he has had no equal; and this may with strict justice be said of Addison. . . . If we wish to find anything more vivid than Addison's best portraits, we must go either to Shakespeare or to Cervantes. . . . That which chiefly distinguishes Addison from Swift, from Voltaire, from almost all the other great masters of ridicule, is the grace, the nobleness, the moral purity, which we find even in his merriment.—MACAULAY, *Essays : Addison.*

Addison is as true as Truth itself.—RUSKIN, *Fors Clavigera.*

In Addison we discern the amenity and ideal grace of Raphael.—JAMES FERGUSON.

In every thousand of those who have been delighted with the papers of Addison, perhaps not more than one has seen the *Principia* of Newton. —DR. VICESIMUS KNOX, *Essays : on Essay Writing.*

To estimate Addison at his real value we must regard him as the chief Architect of Public Opinion in the eighteenth century. . . . The work of Addison consisted in building up a public opinion which, in spite of its durable solidity, seems, like the great Gothic cathedrals, to absorb into itself the individuality of the architect. A vigorous effort of thought is required to perceive how strong this individuality must have been.—W. J. COURTHOPE, *Addison.*

ÆSCHYLUS.

Greek Tragic Poet : B.C. 525-456.

Brave Æschylus and Sophocles, around
Whose sacred brows the tragic ivy twin'd.
—RICHARD GLOVER, London.

But, do you see my friend, that thus
You leave Saint Paul for Æschylus?
—Who made his Titan's arch-device
The giving men *blind hopes* to spice
The meal of life with.
—ROBERT BROWNING, Christmas Eve and Easter Day.

Are Æschylus and Sophocles and Euripides dead ?   No ; the wondrous
three are still in constellation.   Bright are they as when they first shone,
thousands of years ago, in the heavenly sky.   But which are they ?   In
what quarter of the region hang their golden lamps ?   Yonder.   You see
the glorious gems, enclosing as in a triangle a deep blue portion of stain-
less ether.   The apex-star is Æschylus—to the east is Sophocles—to the
west, Euripides !—JOHN WILSON, *Essays : Greek Drama.*

Æschylus, Shakespeare, and Schiller, three poetic worlds.—MAZZINI,
Life and Writings.

In Æschylus and Sophocles, in Pindar and Plato, you see conscience
asserting its sovereignty over the most sacred beliefs—instinctive reverence and piety struggling sometimes to express themselves under the
names and forms of the past, sometimes bursting out uncontrollably into
indignant abhorrence.—FROUDE, *Calvinism.*

That orthodox Christian and true Gospel preacher, Æschylus.—F. D.
MAURICE, *Life, Vol. II.*

All tragic poets, I presume, from Æschylus, the god-like father of them
all, to the last aspirant who may struggle after the traces of his steps,
have been poets before they were tragedians.—SWINBURNE, *A Study of
Shakespeare.*

Every character that is so much as touched by men, like Æschylus,
Homer, Dante, or Shakespeare, is by them held by the heart, and every
circumstance or sentence of their being, speaking, or seeming, is seized
by process from within, and is referred to that inner secret spring of which
the hold is never lost for an instant ; so that every sentence, as it has
been thought out from the heart, opens for us a way down to the heart,
leads us to the centre, and then leads us to gather what more we may.
It is the Open Sesame of a huge, obscure, endless cave, with inexhaustible
treasure of pure gold scattered in it ; the wandering about and gathering
the pieces may be left to any of us, all can accomplish that ; but the first
opening of that invisible door in the rock is of the imagination only.—
RUSKIN, *Modern Painters, Vol. II.*

As water, when heated to 100° C., is incapable of calorific increase, and
can rise no higher, so human thought attains in certain men its maximum
intensity.   Æschylus, Job, Phidias, Isaiah, St. Paul, Juvenal, Dante,
Michael Angelo, Rabelais, Cervantes, Shakespeare, Rembrandt, Beethoven, with some others, mark the 100° of genius. . . . Æschylus is
magnificent and powerful ; as though you saw him knitting his brows
beyond the sun.   He has two Cains, Eteocles and Polynices ; Genesis has
but one.   His swarm of sea monsters come and go in the dark sky, as a
flock of driven birds.   Æschylus has none of the known proportions.   He
is rough, abrupt, immoderate, incapable of smoothing the way, almost
ferocious, with a grace of his own which resembles the flowers in wild
places, less haunted by nymphs than by the Eumenides, of the faction of
the Titans, among goddesses choosing the sombre ones, and smiling
darkly at the Gorgons, a son of the earth like Othryx and Briareus, and
ready to attempt again the scaling of heaven against that *parvenu* Jupiter.
Æschylus is ancient mystery made man ; something like a pagan prophet.
His work, if we had it all, would be a kind of Greek Bible. . . . Æschylus
is up to his shoulders in the ashes of ages ; his head alone remains out of

that burying, and, like the giant of the desert, with his head alone he is as immense as all the neighbouring gods standing on their pedestals. Man passes before this unsubmergable wreck. Enough remains for an immense glory. What the darkness has taken adds the unknown to this greatness. Buried and eternal, his brow projecting from the grave, Æschylus looks at generations. . . . Æschylus is the ancient Shakespeare. . . . Whoever does not comprehend Æschylus is irremediably an ordinary mind. Intellects may be tried on Æschylus.—VICTOR HUGO, *William Shakespeare (transl.).*

As befits a demiurgic nature, Æschylus conceived and executed upon a stupendous scale. His outlines are huge; his figures are colossal; his style is broad and sweeping—like a river in its fulness and its might. Each of his plays might be compared to a gigantic statue, whereof the several parts, taken separately, are beautiful, while the whole is put together with some majestic harmony. But as the sculptor, in modelling a colossus, cannot afford to introduce the details which would grace a chimney ornament, so Æschylus was forced to sacrifice the working out of minor motives. His imagination, penetrated through and through with the spirit of his subject as a whole, was more employed in presenting a series of great situations, wrought together and combined into a single action, than in elaborating the minutiæ of characters and plots. The result has been that those students who delight in detail, have complained of a certain disproportion between his huge design and his insufficient execution. It has too frequently been implied that he could rough-hew like a Cyclops, but that he could not finish like a Praxiteles; that he was more capable of sketching in an outline than of filling up its parts.—J. ADDINGTON SYMONDS, *Studies of the Greek Poets, Second Series.*

The general spirit of Æschylus has been much misunderstood, owing to the external circumstance that his life came at the beginning of an age of rapid progress. The pioneer of 490 is mistaken for a reactionary of 404. Æschylus is in thought generally a precursor of the sophistic movement, as Euripides is the outcome of it. He is an enthusiastic democrat of the early type. Listen to the pæans about freedom in the *Persæ.* That is the very spirit recorded by Herodotus as having made Athens rise from a commonplace Ionian state to be the model and the leader of Hellas. And the *Persæ* is not isolated.—GILBERT MURRAY, *Ancient Greek Literature.*

MARK AKENSIDE.

English Poet: 1721-1770.

Th' Athenian Akenside may deign
To stamp me deathless with his pen.
        —CHRISTOPHER SMART, *Fable VII.*

His images are displayed with such luxuriance of expression, that they are hidden, like Butler's Moon, by a "Veil of Light"; they are forms fantastically lost under superfluity of dress.—DR. JOHNSON, *Lives of the Poets: Akenside.*

Akenside was one of the fiercest and most uncompromising of the young patriots out of Parliament. When he found that the change of administration had produced no change of system, he gave vent to his indignation in the " Epistle to Curio," the best poem that he ever wrote, a poem, indeed, which seems to indicate, that, if he had left lyric composition to Gray and Collins, and had employed his powers in grave and elevated satire, he might have disputed the pre-eminence of Dryden. —MACAULAY, *Essays : Walpole's Letters.*

Akenside attempted a sort of classical and philosophical rapture, which no elegance of language could easily have rendered popular, but which had merits of no vulgar order for those who could study it.—LORD JEFFREY, *Essays.*

ST. ALBAN.

Britain's Proto-Martyr.

Thus was Alban tried,
England's first martyr, whom no threats could shake ;
Self-offered victim, for his friend he died,
And for the faith—nor shall his name forsake
That hill, whose flowery platform seems to rise
By nature decked for holiest sacrifice.
—WORDSWORTH, *Persecution.*

LEONE BATTISTA ALBERTI.

Italian Poet, Painter, Architect : 1404-1484.

Leo Baptista Alberti was a man, who, if measured by the universality of his genius, may claim a place in the temple of glory he has not filled. —HALLAM, *Literature of the Middle Ages, Vol. I.*

ALEXANDER THE GREAT.

B.C. 356-323.

The storie of Alexandre is so commune
That every wight that hath discretioun
Hath herd somewhat or all of his fortune.
—CHAUCER, *Canterbury Tales : The Monkes Tale.*

'Twas at the royal feast, for Persia won
By Philip's warlike son :
Aloft in awful state
The godlike hero sate
On his imperial throne.

—DRYDEN, *Alexander's Feast.*

Children at toys, as men at titles, aim ;
And in effect both covet, but the same.
This Philip's son prov'd in revolving years ;
And first for rattles, then for worlds, shed tears.
—GARTH, *The Dispensary.*

Fathers, that, like so many Alexanders,
Have in these parts from morn till even fought,
And sheath'd their swords for lack of argument.

—SHAKSPERE, *King Henry V.*

Under the guidance of Alexander, the Greek spirit conquers and attempts to civilize the East. The parallel between Alexander and Achilles, as before hinted, is more than accidental. Trained in the study of Homer as we are in the study of the Bible, he compared his destinies with those of the great hero, and formed himself upon the type of Pelides. At Troy he pays peculiar reverence to the tomb of Patroclus. He celebrates Hephæstion's death with Homeric games and pyres up-piled to heaven. He carries Homer with him on war-marches, and consults the *Iliad* on occasions of doubt. Alexander's purpose was to fight out to the end the fight begun by Achilles between West and East, and to avenge Greece for the injuries of Asia. But it was not a merely military conquest which he executed. Battles were the means to higher ends. Alexander sought to subject the world to the Greek spirit, to stamp the customs, the thoughts, the language, and the culture of the Greeks upon surrounding nations. Poets and philosophers accompanied his armies. In the deserts of Bactria and Syria and Libya he founded Greek cities.
—J. ADDINGTON SYMONDS, *Studies of the Greek Poets.*

VITTORIO ALFIERI.

Italian Poet : 1749-1803.

So long as a ray of sunlight illumines her fields, Italy will reverence Alfieri as the first to give to tragedy a noble mission, to raise it from the dust in which it lay, and make of it the instructor of the people.—MAZZINI, *Life and Writings, Vol. II.*

Liberty was the Muse of Alfieri.—MACAULAY, *Essays : Moore's " Life of Byron ".*

ALFRED THE GREAT.

King of England : 849-901.

The crown
Of Saxon liberty that Alfred wore.

—WORDSWORTH, *The Warning.*

Behold a pupil of the monkish gown,
The pious Alfred, king to justice dear ;
Lord of the harp and liberating spear ;
Mirror of princes !

—*Id., Alfred.*

A thousand years the Earth cried, where are thou ?
And then the shadow of thy coming fell
On Saxon Alfred's olive-cinctured brow.

—SHELLEY, *Ode to Liberty.*

> I saw the spirit of Alfred;
> Alfred than whom no prince with loftier intellect gifted,
> Nor with a finer soul, nor in virtue more absolute, ever
> Made a throne twice-hallowed, and reign'd in the hearts of his people.
> —SOUTHEY, *Vision of Judgment.*

> What though the Danish raven spread
> Awhile his wings o'er English ground,
> The bird of prey funereal fled
> When Alfred call'd his peers around.
> —JOHN GILBERT COOPER, *The Genius of Britain.*

> A single gaol, in Alfred's golden reign,
> Could half the nation's criminals contain;
> Fair justice then, without constraint ador'd,
> Held high the steady scale, but sheath'd the sword.
> —DR. JOHNSON, *London.*

> 'Twas Alfred first, with letters and with laws,
> Adorn'd as he advanc'd his country's cause.
> —THOMAS WARTON, *The Triumph of Isis.*

> Soon illustrious Alfred came,
> And pitch'd fair wisdom's tent on Isis' plenteous plain.
> Alfred, on thee shall all the muses wait.
> —*Id., Ode to Music.*

> Here patriot Alfred, stain'd with Danish blood,
> Rear'd on one base, the king's, the people's good.
> —*Id., On the Marriage of the King, MDCCLXI.*

Tickler: "Napoleon and Alfred! The one is already dead, the other will live for ever. Alfred! the mighty warrior, who quelled and drove afar from him the terrible enemy that had baffled the prowess of all his predecessors; the Father of his people, who listened to all complaints, and redressed all wrongs; the philosopher who raised up a barbarous age towards the height of his own mind, and founded the civilisation of England; the legislator, whose laws, after a thousand years, make part of the liberties of his country!"—JOHN WILSON, *Noctes Ambrosianæ, Vol. III.*

In Alfred, in the Northmen, one may read the genius of the English society, namely, that private life is the place of honour.—EMERSON, *Character.*

Truth-teller was our own Alfred named.—F. W. FARRAR, *Social and Present-Day Questions.*

So stands the image of Alfred, shining brightly in the book of the world's history, never defaced by malice or ignorance, nor dimmed by his own errors. These he necessarily possessed, but they have been entirely forgotten in the blaze of his virtues, over which the lapse of centuries has cast no cloud. Severe trial and purifying cleansed him like a noble metal from all dross. Praise can never degenerate into flattery in the case of a great man whose strong sense of duty and exalted principles of morality have led him to employ his time in a truly noble manner. No king nor hero of antiquity or modern times can be compared with Alfred for so many distinguished qualities, and each so excellent. Princes more renowned for power and glory, and reigning over greater nations, have always had some defect in their moral character which forcibly contrasts with our high estimation of their mental qualities; and although by the side of Alfred, ruling in his narrow Wessex, their forms appear to tower high amongst the stars, yet his figure, in its smaller proportions, remains one of the most perfect ever held up by the hand of God as a mirror to the world and its rulers.—REINHOLD PAULI, *Life of Alfred the Great (transl.).*

Alfred, the unwilling author of these great changes, is the most perfect character in history. He is a singular instance of a prince who has become a hero of romance, who, as such, has had countless imaginary exploits attributed to him, but to whose character romance has done no more than justice, and who appears in exactly the same light in history and in fable. No other man on record has ever so thoroughly united all the virtues both of the ruler and of the private man. In no other man on record were so many virtues disfigured by so little alloy. A saint without superstition, a scholar without ostentation, a warrior all whose wars were fought in the defence of his country, a conqueror whose laurels were never stained by cruelty, a prince never cast down by adversity, never lifted up to insolence in the day of triumph—there is no other name in history to compare with his.—E. A. FREEMAN.

SAINT AMBROSE.

Bishop of Milan: 340-397.

Never, surely, was holier man
Than Ambrose, since the world began;
With diet spare and raiment thin,
He shielded himself from the father of sin;
With bed of iron and scourgings oft,
His heart to God's hand as wax made soft.
—J. R. LOWELL, *Poems: Ambrose.*

ANAXAGORAS.

Greek Philosopher: B.C. 499-428.

For Anaxagoras, long agone,
Saw hills, as well as you, i' th' moon,
And held the sun was but a piece
Of red-hot iron as big as Greece.
—SAMUEL BUTLER, *Hudibras, Part II., Canto III.*

LANCELOT ANDREWES.

Bishop successively of Chichester, Ely, Winchester: 1565-1626.

Andrewes, a man far more learned in patristic theology than any of the Elizabethan bishops.—HALLAM, *Literature of Europe.*

Whoever wishes to entertain himself with the quaintness of the old sermon writers, will find a fund of such entertainment as he seeks in the sermons of Bishop Andrewes, Barten, Halliday, Gataker, Donne, Saunderson, South, and many others of the last century.—Dr. VICESIMUS KNOX, *Essays.*

Andrewes claimed for the English Church its full interest and membership in the Church universal, from which Puritan and Romanist alike would cut off the island Church by a gulf as deep as the sea.—R. W. CHURCH, *Masters in English Theology.*

QUEEN ANNE.

Queen of Great Britain : 1665-1714.

At length great Anna said, " Let discord cease,"
She said, the world obey'd, and all was peace !
—POPE, Windsor Forest.

Hail, Anna, hail ! O may each muse divine
With wreaths eternal grace thy holy shrine !
Grav'd on thy tomb this sacred verse remain,
This verse, more sweet than conquest's sounding strain.
" She bade the rage of hostile nations cease,
The glorious arbitress of Europe's peace."
—LANGHORNE, Genius and Valour.

To Britain's queen the nations turn their eyes ;
On her resolves the western world relies ;
Confiding still, amidst its dire alarms,
In Anna's councils, and in Churchill's arms.
—ADDISON, The Campaign.

ST. ANSELM.

Archbishop of Canterbury : (?) 1033-1105.

Old Anselm, exiled Archbishop of Canterbury, one of the purest-minded " men of genius ".—CARLYLE.

Among the followers of Anselm are to be reckoned not merely the Doctors—Venerable, Invincible, Irrefragable, Angelical, and Seraphic— but a far greater than they, even Descartes himself.— SIR JAMES STEPHEN, *Essays in Ecclesiastical Biography.*

For Anselm was a philosopher, *the* philosopher of the 11th century.— F. D. MAURICE, *Mediæval Philosophy.*

Anselm, therefore, was a monk throughout, and in all his thoughts and ways, just as a soldier who is loyal to his profession can nowhere be uninfluenced by its rules and habits.   But he was much more than a monk. A great teacher, a great thinker, a great kindler of thought in others, he was also an example of gallant and unselfish public service, rendered without a thought of his own convenience or honour, to fulfil what seemed a plain duty, in itself very distasteful, and not difficult to evade, if he had wished to evade it.   Penetrated, too, as he was by the unflinching austerity of that hard and stern time, he was remembered among men, less as the great sage who had opened new paths to thought, or as the great archbishop who had not been afraid of the face of kings, or as the severe restorer of an uncompromising and high-aiming discipline, than as the loving and sympathising Christian brother, full of sweetness, full of affection, full of goodness, full of allowances and patience for others, whom men of all conditions liked to converse with, and whom neither high nor low ever found cold in his friendship, or unnatural and forced in his condescension. —R. W. CHURCH, *Anselm.*

MARCUS ANTONIUS.

Roman Triumvir : B.C. 83-30.

Out of Rome was sent a senatour
To conquerin relmis, and bring honour
Unto the toune of Rome, as was usaunce,
To have the worlde at her obëisaunce,
And, sothe to saie, Antonius was his name.
—CHAUCER, Legende of Cleopatra.

Oft has my soul with strong compassion strove,
To think of Anthony's ill-fated love.
—SAMUEL BOYSE, To Mrs. Oldfield.

I think it is not meet,
Mark Antony, so well belov'd of Cæsar,
Should outlive Cæsar : we will find of him
A shrewd contriver. <div align="right">—SHAKSPERE, <i>Julius Cæsar.</i></div>

Cæsar ? why, he's the Jupiter of men.
What's Antony ? The god of Jupiter.
—Id., Antony and Cleopatra.

THOMAS AQUINAS.

Scholastic Theologian : (?) 1224-1274.

What in Aquinas' bulky works are found,
Does not enlighten Reason, but confound.
—JOHN POMFRET, Reason : a Poem.

The Fifth Doctor of the Church.—POPE PIUS V.

The great lawgiver of the schools, Thomas Aquinas, whose opinions the Dominicans especially treat as almost infallible, went into the exaggerated principles of his age in favour of the See of Rome.—HALLAM, *Student's Middle Ages.*

Thomas Aquinas stands without a rival at the head of the scholastic theologians.—DR. VICESIMUS KNOX, *Essays.*

The " Angelical Doctor," standing in contrast with the " Seraphic Doctor," which is the title given to the Franciscan Bonaventura, denotes that the one was regarded as a pure Intelligence, the other as a being in whom the heart and affections were vastly predominant.—F. D. MAURICE, *Moral, etc., Philosophy.*

MADAME D'ARBLAY (*née* BURNEY).

English Novelist and Diarist : 1752-1840.

Miss Burney did for the English novel what Jeremy Collier did for the English drama ; and she did it in a better way.   She first showed that a tale might be written in which both the fashionable and the vulgar life of London might be exhibited with great force, and with broad comic humour, and which yet should not contain a single line inconsistent with rigid morality, or even with virgin delicacy.—MACAULAY, *Essays : D'Arblay.*

ARCHILOCHUS.

Greek Satiric Poet : fl. about B.C. 714-676.

The facts of the life of Archilochus are briefly these.   He was engaged to be married to Neobulé, daughter of Lycambes.   Her father retracted his consent to the marriage, having possibly discovered that the temper of his proposed son-in-law was a mixture of gall, wormwood, vinegar, verjuice, vitriol and nitric acid.   Thereupon, as Horace says :—
        "Archilochum proprio armavit iambo."
He made the Iambic metre his own, and sharpened it into a terrible weapon of attack.   Each verse he wrote was polished and pointed like an arrow-head.   Each line was steeped in the poison of hideous charges against his sweetheart, her sisters and her father.   The set of poems which he produced, and, as it would appear, recited publicly at the festival of Demeter, were so charged with wit and fire, that the country rang with them.   The daughters of Lycambes, tradition avers, went straightway and hanged themselves—unable to endure the flight of fiery serpents that had fallen on them : for, to quote the words of Browning, Archilochus had the art of writing verse that " bit into the live man's flesh like parchment," that sent him wandering, branded and for ever ashamed, about his native streets and fields.   After this murderous exhibition of his power Archilochus left Paros.
        "Away with Paros ! her figs and fishy life ! "
        —J. ADDINGTON SYMONDS, *Studies of the Greek Poets.*

ARCHIMEDES.

Greek Geometrician : B.C. 287-212.

Call Archimedes from his buried tomb
Upon the plain of vanished Syracuse,
And feelingly the sage shall make report
How insecure, how baseless in itself,
Is the philosophy, whose sway depends
On mere material instruments :—how weak
Those arts, and high inventions, if unpropped
By virtue.
                        —WORDSWORTH, *The Excursion.*

Thus Archimedes, in his crystal sphere,
Seem'd to correct the world's Artificer.
                        —DR. THOMAS YALDEN, *The Insect.*

O ! for an Archimedes new,
Of moral powers possess'd,
The world to move, and quite expel
That traitor from the breast.
—YOUNG, Resignation.

ARISTIDES THE JUST.

Athenian Archon : B.C. 489-468.

Then Aristides lifts his honest front ;
Spotless of heart, to whom th' unflattering voice
Of freedom gave the noblest name of Just ;
In pure majestic poverty rever'd.
—THOMSON, The Seasons : Winter.

O noblest, happiest age !
When Aristides rul'd, and Cimon fought.
—AKENSIDE, Ode XVIII.

Just Aristides here maintain'd the cause,
Whose sacred precepts shine through Solon's laws.
—FALCONER, The Shipwreck.

ARISTIPPUS.

Greek Philosopher : d. B.C. 380.

Sometimes with Aristippus, or St. Paul,
Indulge my candour, and grow all to all.
—POPE, Imitations of Horace.

ARISTOPHANES.

Greek Comic Dramatist : B.C. (?) 440-380.

The merry Greek, tart Aristophanes.
—BEN JONSON, To the Memory of Shakespeare.

Son of Philippos, Aristophanes
Surmounts his rivals now as heretofore,
Though stinted to mere sober prosy verse—
" Manners and men," so squeamish gets the world.
—ROBERT BROWNING, Aristophanes' Apology.

Aristophanes paints town-life with a suburb of gardens.—R. A. WILL-
MOTT, *Pleasures . . . of Literature.*

The brazen mask which crowns his theatre smiles indeed broadly,
serenely, as if its mirth embraced the universe ; but its hollow eye-sockets
suggest infinite possibilities of profoundest irony. Buffoonery carried
to the point of paradox, wisdom disguised as insanity, and gaiety con-
cealing the whole sum of human disappointment, sorrow, and disgust,
seem ready to escape from its open but rigid lips, which are moulded to
a proud perpetual laughter. It is a laughter which spares neither God
nor man, which climbs Olympus only to drag down the Immortals to its
scorn, and trails the pall of august humanity in the mire ; but which,
amid its mockery and blasphemy, seems everlastingly asserting, as by
paradox, that reverence of the soul which bends our knees to Heaven and

makes us respect our brothers.   There is nothing sinister or even serious
in Aristophanes.   He did not write in the sarcastic, cynical old age of
his nation or his era.   He is rather the voice of its superabundant youthfulness. . . . It is hard for the modern Christian world to tolerate his
freedom of speech and coarseness.   Of all the Greeks, essentially a rude
nation, he is the most naked, the most audacious in his revelation of all
that human nature is supposed to seek to hide.   The repugnance felt
of his ironical *insouciance* and for his profound indelicacy has prevented
us from properly valuing his poetry.   Critics begin their panegyrics of
him with apologies ; they lift their skirts and tread delicately, passing
over his broadest humour *sicco pede*, picking their way among his hetero-
geneous images, winking and blinking, hesitating and condoning, omitting
a passage here, attempting to soften an allusion there, until the real
Aristophanes has almost disappeared.—J. ADDINGTON SYMONDS, *Studies
of the Greek Poets.*

As a dramatist, Aristophanes is careless about construction ; but he
has so much "go" and lifting power that he makes the most absurd
situations credible.   He has a real gift for imposing on his audience's
credulity.   His indecency comes partly, no doubt, from that peculiarly
Greek *naïveté*, which is the result of simple and unaffected living ; partly
it has no excuse to urge except that it is not deliberately vicious.   It is
instructive to know that Plato liked Aristophanes. . . . The comedian's
speech in the *Symposium* shows the inner bond which united these two
great princes of imagination.   But only his own age could really stand
Aristophanes.   The next century wanted more refinement and character-
work, more plot and sentiment and sobriety.   It got what it wanted in
Menander.—GILBERT MURRAY, *Ancient Greek Literature.*

ARISTOTLE.

Greek Philosopher : B.C. 384-322.

The longest tyranny that ever sway'd,
Was that wherein our ancestors betray'd
Their free born reason to the Stagyrite,
And made his torch their universal light.
                         —DRYDEN, *Epistle II.: To Dr. Charleton.*

The mighty Stagyrite first left the shore,
Spread all his sails, and durst the deeps explore ;
He steer'd securely, and discover'd far,
Led by the light of the Mæonian star.
                         —POPE, *Essay on Criticism.*

Welcome, great Stagyrite ! and teach me now
All I was born to know :
Thy scholar's vict'ries thou dost far out-do ;
He conquer'd the earth, the whole world you.
                         —COWLEY, *The Motto.*

Great Stagyrite, the lost inquirer show
The spring whence motion did for ever flow ;
Since nothing of itself e'er moves or strives,
Tell what begins, what the first impulse gives.
                         —SIR RICHARD BLACKMORE, *Creation.*

The Stagyrite, who rules from nature drew,
Opinions gave, but gave his reasons too.
—Churchill, *The Apology.*

'Tis true, I love the ancients—but what then ?
Plato and Aristotle were but men.
I grant 'em wise—the wisest disagree,
And therefore no sufficient guide for me.
—Dodsley, *Modern Reasoning.*

All these things will be specified in time,
With strict regard to Aristotle's rules,
The *Vade Mecum* of the true sublime,
Which makes so many poets and some fools.
—Byron, *Don Juan, CCI.*

Aristotle hath the same authority in philosophy, that the Apostle Paul
hath in divinity.—Roger Bacon.

I do not think it possible that any one born an Aristotelian can become
a Platonist.—S. T. Coleridge, *Table Talk.*

The Aristotelian philosophy, even in the hands of the Master, was
like a barren tree that conceals its want of fruit by profusion of leaves.
—Hallam, *Student's Middle Ages,* *Chap. IX., Part II.*

Aristotle and Plato are reckoned the respective heads of two schools.
A wise man will see that Aristotle Platonizes.—Emerson, *Essays :
Circles.*

The robust Aristotelian method, with its breadth and adequateness,
shaming our sterile and leaner logic by its genial radiation, conversant
with series and degree, with effects and ends, skilful to discriminate
power from form, essence from accident, and opening, by its terminology
and definition, high roads into nature, had trained a race of athletic
philosophers.—Id., *Representative Men : Swedenborg.*

Were nothing else to be learnt from the *Rhetoric* and *Ethics* of Aristotle,
they should be studied by every educated Englishman as the best of commentaries on Shakespeare.—J. C. Hare, *Guesses at Truth.*

What a contrast is the style of Aristotle ! He sees nothing—he is
like a man groping in the dark about a room which he knows. He
hesitates and suggests ; proposes first one formula and then another ;
rejects both, gives a multitude of reasons, and ends at last with an
expression which he admits to be incorrect and an apologetic " let it
make no difference ". There are whole passages in his writings—the
discussion about Solon and happiness in the *Ethics,* is an instance—in
which he appears like a schoolboy who knows the answer to a sum, but
cannot get the figures to come to it.—Walter Bagehot, *Literary
Studies, Vol. II.*

The piercing sagacity of Aristotle.—W. E. Gladstone, *Gleanings,
Vol. VI.*

It is difficult to speak of Aristotle without exaggeration : he is felt to
be so mighty, and is known to be so wrong. History, surveying the
whole scope of his pretensions, gazes on him with wonder. Science,

challenging these separate pretensions, and testing their results, regards them with indifference; an indifference easily exasperated, into antagonism by the clamorous urgency of unauthenticated praise. It is difficult to direct the opposing streams of criticism into the broad equable current of a calm appreciation; because the splendour of his fame perpetuates the memory of his failure; and to be just we must appreciate both. His intellect was piercing and comprehensive; his attainments surpassed those of every known philosopher; his influence has only been exceeded by the great founders of religions; nevertheless, if we now estimate the product of his labours in the discovery of positive truths, it appears insignificant, when not erroneous. None of the great germinal discoveries in science are due to him, or to his disciples. His vast and active intellect gave an impulse to philosophy, and for twenty centuries held the world in awe. Then came a change; the long-murmuring spirit of rebellion grew strong enough to dethrone him. Ages of servility had raised him to an unexampled eminence; in the tumult of revolution this pedestal became a pillory.—G. H. LEWES, *Aristotle.*

It is said that metaphysics owe their name to the fact that, in Aristotle's works, questions of pure philosophy are dealt with immediately after those of physics. If so, the accident is happily symbolical of the essential relation of things; for metaphysical speculation follows as closely upon physical theory as black care upon the horseman.—HUXLEY, *Hume.*

As a physicist, Aristotle displayed what we should consider some of the worst attributes of a modern physical investigator—indistinctness of ideas, confusion of mind, and a confident use of language, which led to the delusive notion that he had really mastered his subject, while he had as yet failed to grasp even the elements of it. He put words in the place of things, subject in the place of object. He preached induction without practising it, inverting the true order of inquiry by passing from the general to the particular, instead of from the particular to the general. —TYNDALL, *Address before the British Association at Belfast,* 1874.

SIR RICHARD ARKWRIGHT.

Inventor of the Spinning Jenny: 1732-1792.

The gospel of Richard Arkwright once promulgated, no monk of the old sort is any longer possible in this world. . . . But Richard Arkwright too will have his monument, a thousand years hence: all Lancashire and Yorkshire, and how many other shires and countries, with their machineries and industries, for his monument.—CARLYLE, *Past and Present.*

Do not the constructive fingers of Watt, Fulton, Whitlemore, Arkwright, predict the fusible, hard and temperable texture of metals, the properties of stone, water and wood?—EMERSON *Essays: History.*

Watt, Arkwright, Crompton—these giants of intellectual power, whose discoveries have augmented tenfold, often a hundredfold, the productive powers of manufacturing labour—have been the worst enemies that the happiness and morals of the working manufacturers ever knew. —SIR ARCHIBALD ALISON, *Essays: Sismondi.*

Dr. Thomas Arnold.

Headmaster of Rugby School : 1795-1842.

The name of Dr. Arnold is a household word in England, not only as the great typical Christian schoolmaster, but as the leader of modern Liberal or Broad-Church theology.—W. M. Sinclair, *Leaders of Thought.*

Dr. Arnold . . . was a man whose whole study was to elevate the tone of common life to a Christian standard.—W. E. Gladstone, *Gleanings of Past Years, Vol. II.*

In the nineteenth century think how the sermons of Dr. Arnold tended to regenerate the spirit of public schools.—F. W. Farrar, *Social and Present-Day Questions.*

Since Laud there had been no such ecclesiastical statesman as Thomas Arnold.—A. I. Fitzroy, *Dogma and the Church of England.*

In plain truth, the English clergy must Arnold-ise, if they do not wish to go either to Rome or to the workhouse, before fifty years are out. There is, I do believe, an Arnold-ite spirit rising ; but most "laudant, non sequuntur". Decent Anglicanism, decent Evangelical Conservatism (or Evangelicalism) having become the majority, is now quite Conservative, and each party is playing Canute and the tide, as it can scramble in turn into the chair of authority. I would devote soul and body to get together an Arnold-ite party of young men.—Kingsley, *Letters and Memoirs, Vol. I.*

St. Augustin.

Monk : d. 605.

For ever hallowed be this morning fair,
Blest be the unconscious shore on which ye tread,
And blest the silver cross, which ye, instead
Of martial banner, in procession bear ;
The cross preceding Him who floats in air,
The pictured Saviour !—By Augustin led,
They come—and onward travel without dread,
Chanting in barbarous ears a tuneful prayer,
Sung for themselves, and those whom they would free !
                                   —Wordsworth, *Glad Tidings.*

St. Augustine.

Bishop of Hippo : 354-430.

As Saint Augustine in his fine confessions,
Which make the reader envy his transgressions.
                          —Byron, *Don Juan, XLVII.*

St. Augustine described the nature of God as a circle whose centre was everywhere, and its circumference nowhere. We are all our lifetime reading the copious sense of this first of forms.—Emerson, *Essays : Circles.*

The deepest spiritual natures that the world has ever known—St. Paul, Augustine, Luther, Pascal.—Dr. John Tulloch, *Beginning Life.*

Two names stand out conspicuous, and almost alone, as those of men who have told to the world the utter truth about themselves; they are the names of St. Augustine and Rousseau.—F. W. Farrar, *Social and Present-Day Questions.*

Augustine's Saviour is not the Saviour of the world. He is only the Saviour of the Church, and even in the Church itself the Saviour only of a mere handful of the elect, whom he saves only under strictly ecclesiastical conditions. It is the Church, not the living Christ, which becomes in the Augustinian system the one Mediator between God and man. . . . Augustine was so incessantly occupied with proving the countless errors of individuals and of sects, that he came to regard theology as a series of propositions as clear and as exactly definable as those of Euclid. The gate of the Church began to bristle with a fence-work of finely-articulated dogmas, many of them arrived at by pure sophistry, defended with hard intolerance, and enforced by sheer authority. In each of his chief controversies he mingled a great error with great truths.—*Id., Lives of the Fathers, Vol. II.*

We need only add here, to the appreciations of Augustine's personal character and literary genius which we have made from time to time as the occasion arose, that no human mind since that of St. Paul has so widely, deeply, permanently influenced the Church of Christ. The theology of the Western Church throughout the Middle Ages was deeply affected by his writings; the Reformers of the sixteenth century went back to them for their dogmatic theology; and we, perhaps, in the perplexities of our age, might do well to go back to the philosophical and doctrinal writings of the great thinker of the Western Church.—E. L. Cutts, *Augustine.*

In the *Confessions* of St. Augustine, passion, nature, human individuality only appear in order to be immolated to Divine grace. They are a history of a crisis of the soul, of a new birth, of a *Vita Nuova;* the *Saint* would have blushed to relate more than he has done of the life of the man, which he had quitted. With Rousseau the case is precisely the reverse; here grace is nothing, nature everything; nature dominant, triumphant, displaying herself with a daring freedom, which at times amounts to the distasteful—nay, to the disgusting.—Michelet, *Life of Luther* (transl.).

The ship of the Church never has been, and never will be " put about " by Augustines. This work must be done by rougher hands, and bolder tempers, and truer hearts. We say truer hearts, not as if Augustine and his company were not honest, or did not intend what they believed to be right; but integrity, using the word in an active sense, is a *force* which may be either that of a watch-spring maintaining a faithful whisper—a faint *tick, tick* from day to day; or it may be that of a coach-spring, sustaining a ton weight in the concussions of the roughest roads.—Isaac Taylor, *Introduction to Pfizer's " Luther ".*

The vehement temperament, the bold assertion, the ecstatic energy of men like St. Augustine or St. Paul, burn, so to speak, into the minds and memories of men, and remain there at once and for ever. Such men excel in the broad statement of great truths which flash at once with vivid evidence on the minds which receive them. The very words seem to glow with life; and even the sceptical reader is half awakened by them to a kindred and similar warmth. Such are the men who move the creeds of mankind, and stamp a likeness of themselves on ages that succeed them.—WALTER BAGEHOT, *Literary Studies, Vol. II.*

No Christian teacher since the days of the Apostles has influenced Christian thought so powerfully as St. Augustine. This influence has sometimes been, so to speak, imperial: the "Doctor of Grace" has reigned in the schools of theology; his Benedictine editors in the seventeenth century described him as "the oracle of the Church"; and, as Archbishop Trench has told us, a Spanish sermon was proverbially said to lack its best ingredient if it contained nothing out of Augustine.—DR. WILLIAM BRIGHT, *Three Great Fathers.*

JANE AUSTEN.

English Novelist: 1775-1817.

Shakespeare has had neither equal nor second. But among the writers who, in the point which we have noticed, have approached nearest to the manner of the great master, we have no hesitation in placing Jane Austen, a woman of whom England is justly proud. She has given us a multitude of characters, all in a certain sense, commonplace, as such as we meet every day. Yet they are all as perfectly discriminated from each other as if they were the most eccentric of human beings.—MACAULAY, *Essays: Madame D'Arblay.*

Read *Northanger Abbey;* worth all Dickens and Pliny together. Yet it was the work of a girl. She was certainly not more than twenty-six. Wonderful creature!—*Id., Life and Letters, Vol. II.*

JOHANN SEBASTIAN BACH.

German Musician: 1685-1750.

Are all men born to play Bach's fiddle-fugues?
—ROBERT BROWNING, *Mr. Sludge: "The Medium".*

Bach is the musical type of Protestantism.—FELIX MENDELSSOHN BARTHOLDY.

Every room in which Sebastian Bach is sung is transformed into a church.—*Id.*

FRANCIS, LORD BACON.

English Philosopher: 1561-1626.

If Bacon's eagle spirit had not leapt
Like lightning out of darkness—he compelled
The Proteus shape of Nature as it slept
To wake, and lead him to the caves that held
The treasure of the secrets of its reign.
—SHELLEY, *The Triumph of Life.*

If parts allure thee, think how Bacon shin'd,
The wisest, brightest, meanest of mankind!

—POPE, *Essay on Man.*

   This is the sixtieth year
Since Bacon, and thy lord was born, and here;
Son to the grave wise keeper of the seal,
Fame and foundation of the English weal.
What then his father was, that since is he,
Now with a title more to the degree;
England's High Chancellor: the destin'd heir
In his soft cradle to his father's chair;
Whose even thread the fates spin round and full,
Out of their choicest and their whitest wool.

—BEN JONSON, *Lord Bacon's Birthday.*

Among th' asserters of free reason's claim,
Our nation's not the least in worth or fame.
The world to Bacon does not only owe
Its present knowledge, but its future too.

—DRYDEN, *Epistle II.: To Dr. Charleton.*

Thine is a Bacon; hapless in his choice,
Unfit to stand the civil storm of state,
And through the smooth barbarity of courts,
With firm, but pliant virtue, forward still
To urge his course: him for the studious shade
Kind Nature form'd, deep, comprehensive, clear,
Exact, and elegant; in one rich soul,
Plato, the Stagyrite, and Tully join'd.
The great deliverer he! who from the gloom
Of cloister'd monks, and jargon-teaching schools,
Led forth the true philosophy, there long
Held in the magic chain of words and forms,
And definitions void: he led her forth,
Daughter of heaven! that slow-ascending still
Investigating sure the chain of things,
With radiant finger points to heaven again.

—THOMSON, *The Seasons: Summer.*

By truth inspir'd, *our* Bacon's force
Open'd the way to learning's source.

—CHURCHILL, *The Ghost, Bk. II.*

First Bacon usher'd in the dawning day,
And drove the mists of sophistry away;
Pervaded nature with amazing force
Following experience still throughout his course,
And finishing at length his destin'd way,
To Newton he bequeath'd the radiant lamp of day.
Illustrious souls!

—SOAME JENYNS, *On the Immortality of the Soul.*

Bacon, at last, a mighty man! arose.
Whom a wise King and Nature chose

Lord Chancellor of both their laws,
And boldly undertook the injured pupil's cause.
—Cowley, *Epistle : To the Royal Society.*

Bacon discovered new tracts of learning ; he gave directions to pursue them ; he banished hypothesis, and introduced experiment : he is deservedly the glory of our nation, as the restorer of true philosophy.—Dr. Vicesimus Knox, *Essays : On Essay Writing.*

Lord Bacon . . . might have been more emphatically the high priest of nature, if he had not been the chancellor of James I.—Hallam, *Introduction to the Literature of Europe, Vol. III.*

To give to the human mind a direction which it shall retain for ages is the rare prerogative of a few imperial spirits. It cannot, therefore, be uninteresting to inquire what was the moral and intellectual constitution which enabled Bacon to exercise so vast a benefit on society. . . . The art which Bacon taught was the art of inventing arts. The knowledge in which Bacon excelled all men was a knowledge of the mutual relations of all departments of knowledge.—Macaulay, *Essays : Lord Bacon.*

The prince of professed philosophers—the Lord Chancellor of Nature —Bacon.—Lytton, *Essays : On the Normal Clairvoyance.*

Bacon—Bacon, who served darkness in the hope that when he had raised himself to power his science would make the darkness light, the dupe of a dream of beneficent despotism, a warning to fastidious minds if they would work for the people to work with and by the people.— Goldwin Smith, *Three English Statesmen.*

But Bacon has a still greater place in English literature ; he first clearly set forth the claims of inductive philosophy as against the old methods of metaphysical speculation. He asserted that knowledge was to be found by careful investigation of nature, not by spinning cobwebs of the brain. He turned men from disputations of words to an observation of the world around them. Bacon's method was faulty, as was natural for a beginner ; but modern science has still to point to him as the man who first brought into due prominence the principles on which its method was to be founded.—Bishop Mandell Creighton, *The Age of Elizabeth.*

John Bacon.

English Sculptor : 1740-1799.

Bacon there
Gives more than female beauty to a stone.
—Cowper, *The Task : The Sofa.*

Sir Nicholas Bacon.

Lord Keeper : 1510-1579.

Sir Nicholas was no ordinary man. He belonged to a set of men whom it is easier to describe collectively than separately, whose minds were formed by one system of discipline, who belonged to one rank in society, to one university, to one party, to one sect, to one administration, and who resembled each other so much in talents, in opinions, in habits, in fortunes, that one character, we had almost said one life, may, to a considerable extent, serve for them all.—MACAULAY, *Essays: Lord Bacon.*

ROGER BACON.

English Philosopher: 1214-1294.

Bacon also was there, the marvellous Friar.
                         —SOUTHEY, *A Vision of Judgment.*

The mind of Roger Bacon was strangely compounded of almost prophetic gleams of the future course of science, and the best principles of the inductive philosophy.—HALLAM, *Literature of the Middle Ages, Vol. I.*

Bacon must be dearer to us than Duns can be. For he was an Englishman, not only in virtue of his birth-place, which no one disputes, but in virtue of gifts and of a character which we may boast of as specially national. Moreover, he was a martyr of science, and we should certainly be disposed to enlarge the canon which Anselm established in the case of another English divine by contending that the martyrs of science are the martyrs of God.—F. D. MAURICE, *Mediæval Philosophy.*

WALTER BAGEHOT.

English Economist: 1826-1877.

He was like a man that made you free of his house, not like a tradesman handing you goods over the counter. . . . His writings were an armoury against fools and pompous persons. . . . A man may print his private thoughts, but he does not speak them. . . . There is more meat on Bagehot's bones than on those of any other writer, and a deft cook makes them into a hundred dishes. . . . He was one of those men whose remarks never seem to have been made before. . . . He did not exactly revere business, but he spoke of it and other mundane matters, like the House of Lords, with respect tempered with amusement.—AUGUSTINE BIRRELL, *Lecture on Bagehot* (*Leighton House,* 14th March, 1901).

LORD BALMERINO.

Friend of Prince Charles Edward: 1688-1746.

To hold Balmerino's undying name,
Whose soul of fire, lighted at heaven's high flame,
Deserves the proudest wreath departed heroes claim.
                —BURNS, *Ode on the Birthday of Prince Charles Edward.*

DR. ISAAC BARROW.

English Theologian and Mathematician: 1630-1677.

I learned the little that I knew by this.
That is, some words of Spanish, Turk, and Greek,
Italian not at all, having no teachers:

Much English I cannot pretend to speak,
Learning that language chiefly from its preachers,
Barrow, South, Tillotson, whom every week
I study.

—BYRON, *Don Juan.*

Barrow's style,
Redundant and involv'd would soon oppress
Thy auditors.

—REV. RICHARD POLWHELE, *Pulpit Eloquence.*

These are the sermons which will ever live,
By these our Tonsons and our Knaptons thrive;
How such are read, and prais'd, and how they sell,
Let Barrow's, Clarke's, and Butler's sermons tell.
Preachers should either make us good or wise,
Him that does neither, who but must despise?

—DODSLEY, *The Art of Preaching.*

Barrow must be considered as closing the first great period of the English language.—S. T. COLERIDGE.

Isaac Barrow, a mighty genius, whose ardour was capable of accomplishing all it undertook. The tide of his eloquence flows with smooth yet irresistible rapidity. He treats his subject almost with mathematical precision, and never leaves it till he has exhausted it.—DR. VICESIMUS KNOX, *Essays: On Preaching and Sermon Writers.*

RICHARD BAXTER.

English Nonconformist Divine: 1615-1691.

In necessary things, unity; in doubtful things, liberty; in all things, charity.—*Richard Baxter's maxim.*

Barclay or Baxter, wherefore do we blame
For innovations, yet approve the same
In Wickliffe and in Luther? Why are these
Call'd wise reformers, those mad sectaries?

—DODSLEY, *The Art of Preaching.*

The Democritus and the Heraclitus of Nonconformity.—SIR JAMES STEPHEN, *Essays on Ecclesiastical Biography.*

Pray read with great attention Baxter's Life of himself. It is an inestimable work. . . . I could almost as soon doubt the Gospel verity as his veracity.—S. T. COLERIDGE, *Table Talk.*

It is impossible to read Baxter without hesitating which to admire most, the uncommon clearness (perspicuity and perspicacity) of his understanding, or the candour and charity of his spirit. Under such accursed persecutions he feels and reasons more like an angel than a man.—*Id., Notes on English Divines, Vol. II.*

No eminent chief of a party has ever passed through so many years of civil and religious dissension with more innocence than Richard Baxter.—MACAULAY, *History of England, Vol. I., Chapter IV.*

Richard, Richard, dost thou think we will let thee poison the court ? Richard, thou art an old knave. Thou hast written books enough to load a cart, and every book as full of sedition as an egg is full of meat. By the grace of God, I'll look after thee. I see a great many of your brotherhood waiting to know what will befal their mighty Don.—LORD GEORGE JEFFREYS, *Address at Baxter's Trial.*

Richard Baxter was the Paul of his century in manifold ways. . . . The epithets, "Venerable" for Bede, and "Judicious" (by which I suppose judicial is meant) for Hooker, are not more irreversible down the ages than is that of "Holy" applied to Richard Baxter. "The holy Baxter," says an able anonymous essayist, "is just the verdict which a seraph, 'full of eyes within and without,' might be expected to pronounce after having deliberately reviewed the whole history and work of the sage of Kidderminster".—A. B. GROSART, *Representative Nonconformists.*

To no times are Englishmen so deeply indebted for their civil and religious liberty as the times in which Baxter lived. To no body of men do they owe such an unpaid debt of gratitude as they do to that noble host, of which Baxter was a standard-bearer—I mean the Puritans. To no man among the Puritans are the lovers of religious freedom under such large obligations as they are to Richard Baxter.—BISHOP JOHN C. RYLE, *The Bishop, the Pastor, and the Preacher.*

EARL OF BEACONSFIELD.

English Statesman and Novelist : 1805-1881.

Keen must be the critical faculty which can nicely discern where the novelist ended and the statesman began in Benjamin Disraeli.— AUGUSTINE BIRRELL, *Obiter Dicta, First Series.*

The most remarkable feature in Disraeli's novels is the way in which they reflect his life and interpret his statesmanship. The magniloquence, the flash and the glitter of the early novels seem of a piece with the tales current regarding the author's manners and character, his dress designed to attract attention, and his opinions cut after the pattern of his dress. So in the *Coningsby* group we are struck with the forecast of the writer's future political action. His later policy seems to be just the realisation of his earlier dreams.—HUGH WALKER, *The Age of Tennyson.*

When the whole drama of his life shall be displayed to view ; when his relations with his colleagues and his opponents, with the Crown and the aristocracy, with friends and enemies, shall stand fully revealed to us ; when all the difficulties and all the jealousies which impeded him on the threshold of his career shall be clearly understood : then, indeed, we think that the life of Benjamin Disraeli will be recognised as one of the most "wondrous tales" which sober truth has ever told.—J. E. KEBBEL, *Beaconsfield.*

The professed creed of Disraeli was that of a "complete Jew," that is to say, he believed in "Him that had come " ; and "did not look for another ". To use his own words, he "believed in Calvary, as well as Sinai ".—SIR WILLIAM FRASER, *Disraeli and his Day.*

It was not merely by his great work in the Palace of Westminster that Lord Beaconsfield obtained his hold upon the feelings and the affections of the people of England. . . . But it was by his life in general, and by the interest which he took in all that was of interest to the people. . . . There was something about him at the moment of defeat which was great beyond description. The courage, the gaiety, the patience, with which he set himself to repair the disaster which might have befallen him, was a great example to statesmen and to his followers of every class and shade in society. And I say he had his reward, for no man more completely commanded the affections of the people of this country than Lord Beaconsfield.—THE EARL OF IDDESLEIGH.

FRANCIS BEAUMONT.

English Dramatist : 1585-1616.

How I do love thee Beaumont, and thy muse,
That unto me dost such religion use.
How I do fear myself, that am not worth
The least indulgent thought thy pen drops forth!
At once thou mak'st me happy, and unmak'st :
And giving largely to me, more thou tak'st.
—BEN JONSON, Epigram LV.

Witty Beaumont's poetry, and Fletcher's,
Who for a few misprisions of wit,
Are charg'd by those who ten times worse commit.
—SAMUEL BUTLER, Upon Critics.

Two men once united by friendship, and forever by fame, the Dioscuri of our zodiac, Beaumont and Fletcher, rose upon the horizon as the star of Shakespeare, though still in its fullest brightness, was declining in the sky.—HALLAM, *Introduction to the Literature of Europe, Vol. III.*

THOMAS BECKET.

Archbishop of Canterbury : 1118-1170.

King Henri wondede muche, to abbe men in offis
Mid him, that of conseil were god and wis.
Ercedekne of Kanterbury Sein Tomas tho was.
The king him made is chaunceler, at is wille it nout nas.
To him the king trust mest. Ne ther nas non so heye
That so muche wuste is priuite, ne that him were so ney.
—ROBERT OF GLOUCESTER.

As proud as Becket.   —TENNYSON, *Queen Mary.*

De Tracy : " Where is the Archbishop, Thomas Becket ? "
Becket :   " Here.
No traitor to the King, but Priest of God,
Primate of England."   *—Id., Becket.*

St. Thomas Becket then, which Rome did so much hery,
As to his christen'd name they added Canterbury;
There to whose sumptuous shrine the near-succeeding ages,
So mighty off'rings sent, and made such pilgrimages,
Concerning whom, the world since then hath spent much breath,
And many questions made both of his life and death:
If he were truly just, he hath his right; if no,
Those times were much to blame, that have him reckon'd so.
—DRAYTON, Polyolbion.

Saxon Becket spilt his life in Canterbury Cathedral, as Scottish Wallace did on Tower-Hill, and as generally a noble man and martyr has to do,—not for nothing; no, but for a divine something other than *he* had altogether calculated.—CARLYLE, *Past and Present.*

THE VENERABLE BEDE.

English Historian : 673 (?) -735.

Bede I beheld, who, humbly and holy,
Shone like a single star, serene in a night of darkness.
—SOUTHEY, A Vision of Judgment.

Certain Trolls or working brains, under the names of Alfred, Bede, Caxton, Bracton, Camden, Drake, Selden, Dugdale, Newton, Gibbon, Brindley, Watt, Wedgwood, dwell in the troll-mounts of Britain, and turn the sweat of their face to power and renown.—EMERSON, *English Traits : Ability.*

LUDWIG VON BEETHOVEN.

German Musician : 1770-1827.

Suppose, the spirit Beethoven wants to shed
New music he's brimful of; why he turns
The handle of this organ, grinds with Sludge,
And what he poured in at the mouth o' the mill
As a Thirty-third Sonata (fancy now !)
Comes from the hopper as bran-new Sludge, nought else.
—ROBERT BROWNING, Mr. Sludge: "The Medium".

Beethoven, Raphael, cannot reach
The charm which Homer, Shakespeare, teach.
—MATTHEW ARNOLD, Epilogue to Lessing's Laocoön.

JACOB BEHMEN.

German Mystic : 1575-1624.

As German Boehme never cared for plants
Until it happed, a-walking in the fields,
He noticed all at once that plants could speak,
Nay, turned with loosened tongue to talk with him.
—ROBERT BROWNING, Transcendentalism.

Jacob Behmen ! most obscurely wise.
—WALTER HARTE, An Essay on Satire.

Men like Behmen, Novalis, and Fourier, who can soar into the inner cloud-world of man's spirit, even though they lose their way there, dazzled by excess of wonder—men who, like Wordsworth, can give utterance to such subtle anthropologic wisdom as the *Ode on the Intimations of Immortality*, will for that very reason, most humbly and patiently " consider the lilies of the field, how they grow".—KINGSLEY, *Literary and General Lectures, etc.*

Such, then, is the track of Behmen's journeying across the speculative wilderness, following the fiery pillar of an imaginary illumination—a pillar, be it observed, much like that column of glory which, as we stand upon the sea-shore, descends to us from the setting sun,—a luminous line which moves as we move, and which, whatever point we occupy, glows from the ripples at our feet up to the fiery horizon beneath which day is sinking. Behmen's work was done chiefly among the educated. Had his mission been to the lower orders, we should probably have heard of him as the founder of a sect.—R. A. VAUGHAN, *Hours with the Mystics.*

The more a man originates, the less he needs to know ; and those who take the trouble to read such a writer as Jacob Boehme will not complain that he places before them little except the visions of his own brain, or rather of his own heart. A man's originality may occasionally consist in his power to interpret symbols—often, it may be, fancifully enough.—WILLIAM MACCALL, *The New Materialism.*

Why need I be afraid ? Say rather how dare I be ashamed of the Teutonic theosophist, Jacob Behmen ? Many, indeed, and gross were his delusions; and such as furnish frequent and ample occasion for the triumph of the learned over the poor ignorant shoemaker, who had dared think for himself. But while we remember that these delusions were such as might be anticipated from his utter want of all intellectual discipline, and from his ignorance of rational psychology, let it not be forgotten that the latter defect he had in common with the most learned theologians of his age. Neither with books nor with book-learned men was he conversant. A meek and shy quietist, his intellectual powers were never stimulated into feverous energy by crowds of proselytes, or by the ambition of proselyting. Jacob Behmen was an enthusiast in the strictest sense, as not merely distinguished, but as contra-distinguished, from a fanatic.—S. T. COLERIDGE, *Biographia Literaria.*

POPE BENEDICT XIV.

1675-1758.

Benedict the Fourteenth, the best and wisest of the two hundred and fifty successors of St. Peter.—MACAULAY, *Essays : Frederic the Great.*

JEREMY BENTHAM.

English Political Philosopher : 1747-1832.

I consider, then, that two series of causes conspired to produce Bentham —the one national, the other belonging to all Europe ; the same causes on the one hand which produced with us the Economists—the same causes on the other hand which produced in France, Helvetius, and

Diderot, Volney, Condorcet, and Voltaire. He combined what had not been yet done, the spirit of the Philanthropic with that of the Practical. He was the very Theseus of legislative reform, he not only pierced the labyrinth—he destroyed the monster.—LYTTON, *England and the English Intellectual Spirit.*

The writers of whom we speak have never been read by the multitude . . . but they have been the teachers of the teachers; there is hardly to be found in England an individual of any importance in the world of mind who (whatever opinions he may have afterwards adopted) did not first learn to think from one of these two ; and though their influences have but begun to diffuse themselves through these intermediate channels over society at large, there is already scarcely a publication of any consequence addressed to the educated classes, which, if these persons had not existed, would not have been different from what it is. These men are, Jeremy Bentham and Samuel Taylor Coleridge—the two great seminal minds of England in their age. . . . If we were asked to say, in the fewest possible words, what we conceive to be Bentham's place among these great intellectual benefactors of humanity . . . we should say—he was not a great philosopher, but he was a great reformer in philosophy. . . . It was not his opinions, in short, but his method, that constituted the novelty and the value of what he did ; a value beyond all price, even though we should reject the whole, as we unquestionably must a large part, of the opinions themselves.—JOHN STUART MILL, *Dissertations and Discussions.*

RICHARD BENTLEY.

English Classical Scholar : 1662-1742.

So diamonds take a lustre from their soil ;
And to a Bentley 'tis we owe a Boyle.
>   —GARTH, *The Dispensary.*

While Bentley, long to wrangling schools confin'd,
And, but by books, acquainted with mankind,
Dares, in the fulness of the pedants' pride,
Rhyme, tho' no genius ; though no judge, decide ;
Yet he, prime pattern of the captious art,
Out-tibbalding poor Tibbald, tops his part :
Holds high the scourge o'er each fam'd author's head ;
Nor are their graves a refuge for the dead.
>   —DAVID MALLET, *On Verbal Criticism.*

The greatest of English critics in this, or possibly any other age, Richard Bentley.—HALLAM, *Literature of the Middle Ages, Vol. IV.*

Those giants of ancient learning, Bentley and Parr.—CHANNING, *Remarks on Fénélon.*

GEORGE BERKELEY.

Irish Philosopher ; Bishop of Cloyne : 1684-1753.

And Berkeley angelic
Now in substance as soul, that kingdom enjoying where all things
Are what they seem, and the good and the beautiful there are eternal.
>   —SOUTHEY, *A Vision of Judgment.*

To Berkeley, every virtue under heaven.

—POPE, *Epilogue to the Satires.*

Such men as Berkeley, Butler and Paley, each according to his light, fought the battle fairly, on the common ground of reason and philosophy. —KINGSLEY, *Historical Lectures and Essays.*

Berkeley can only be confuted, or answered, by one sentence. His premises granted, the deduction is a chain of adamant.—S. T. COLERIDGE, *Table Talk.*

The idealism of Berkeley is only a crude statement of the idealism of Jesus.—EMERSON, *Essays : Circles.*

The idealism of Berkeley, though it has never organised a sect, has yet sensibly influenced the modes of thinking among metaphysicians ; and the coincidence of this system with the theory of certain Hindoo philosophers may lead us to suspect that it contains some great latent truth, of which the European and Hindoo intellect, so generally at variance, have caught a glimpse.—CHANNING, *On the Character of Milton.*

If any one chose to write in the antique style a debate between Philosophy, Tar-water and Laudanum, it would be almost enough to put in the mouth of Philosophy, " This gave me Berkeley and that deprived me of De Quincey ".—GEORGE SAINTSBURY, *Essays in English Literature.*

Berkeley, the strongest, the honestest thinker among our English metaphysicians—Berkeley, who loved truth with his whole heart and soul, and who, in pursuing it, was as humble as he was courageous. Berkeley, who, though he reasoned from narrow premises, and therefore never discovered the whole breadth and universality of the principles he sought after, yet was able, such was the spirituality of his intellect, even out of that narrow system, which conducted every one else who reasoned from it to materialism, to bring out the other and far more important side of truth. Berkeley, whose understanding. indeed, missed the " circumference," but who found the " centre " in his heart.—F. D. MAURICE, *Life by His Son, Vol. I.*

THOMAS BEWICK.

English Wood-engraver ; 1753-1828.

Oh, now that the genius of Bewick were mine,
And the skill which he learned on the banks of the Tyne !
Then the muses might deal with me just as they chose,
For I'd take my last leave both of verse and of prose.

What feats would I work with my magical hand !
Book-learning and books should be banished the land :
And, for hunger and thirst, and such troublesome calls,
Every alehouse should then have a feast on its walls.

—WORDSWORTH, *The Two Thieves.*

PRINCE BISMARCK.

German Chancellor : 1815-1898.

The resolute will and clear eye of Count Bismarck.—W. E. GLADSTONE, *Gleanings, Vol. IV.*

The greatest of War Ministers, Chatham, Bismarck.—LORD ROSEBERY, *Life of Pitt.*

If he has a military genius, like Belisarius, or administrative faculty, like Chatham or Bismarck, he is the king's king.—EMERSON, *Progress of Culture.*

Bismarck seems to me a genial, marvellous personification of Prussia. . . . A cool head controlling a warm heart—the maximum of ingenuity and audacity—Ulysses and Achilles in one; such will, to many besides ourselves, have appeared to be the solution of the enigma of Prince Bismarck's successes.—MORITZ BUSCH, *Our Chancellor (transl.), Vol. I.*

To the posterity of a hundred years hence Martin Luther and Prince Bismarck will undoubtedly be regarded as the Castor and Pollux of German history; and it is a remarkable coincidence that each of these greatest heroes of the German nation made his *début*, so to speak, as European actors on the very same obscure provincial stage.   It was in the University library of Erfurt that Luther first discovered the Bible, while it was in the church of the Augustines that he was consecrated and read his first mass; and it was in this identical church of the Augustines that Herr von Bismarck, as a member of the futile Union Parliament of 1850, first gave indication to his countrymen of how national unity could, or rather could not, be attained.—CHARLES LOWE, *Prince Bismarck, Vol. II.*

ROBERT BLAKE.

English Admiral : 1599-1657.

Ev'n in those troubled times, when dreadful Blake
Aw'd angry nations with the British name.

—THOMSON, Britannia.

O ever faithful, vigilant, and brave,
Thou bold asserter of Britannia's fame,
Unconquerable Blake.

—RICHARD GLOVER, London.

So like a Sailor Saint was he,
Our Sea King ; grave and sweet
In temper after victory,
And cheerful in defeat.
And men would leave their quiet home,
To follow in his wake,
And fight in fire, or float in foam,
For love of Robert Blake.
          .   .   .   .   .   .
Till she forget her old sea-fame,
Shall England honour him,
And keep the grave-grass from his name
Till her old eyes be dim.
And long as free waves folding round,
Brimful with blessing break,
At heart she holds him, calm and crown'd,
Immortal Robert Blake.

—GERALD MASSEY, Robert Blake.

Boadicea.

Queen of the Iceni : d. 61.

So the Queen Boadicea, standing loftily charioted,
Brandishing in her hand a dart and rolling glances lioness-like,
Yell'd and shriek'd between her daughters in her fierce volubility.
—TENNYSON, *Boadicea.*

When the British warrior Queen,
Bleeding from the Roman rods,
Sought, with an indignant mien,
Councils of her country's gods . . .
Regions Cæsar never knew
Thy posterity shall sway;
Where his eagles never flew,
None invincible as they.

—COWPER, *Boadicea.*

Nicolas Despreaux Boileau.

French Satirical Poet : 1636-1711.

Thence arts o'er all the northern world advance,
But critic-learning flourish'd most in France:
The rules a nation, born to serve, obeys;
And Boileau still in right of Horace sways.
—POPE, *Essay on Criticism.*

Here Boileau, strong in sense and sharp in wit,
Who, from the ancients, like the ancients writ,
Permission gain'd inferior vice to blame,
By flattering incense to his master's fame.
—LORD LYTTLETON, *To the Rev. Dr. Ayscough.*

Boileau had undoubtedly some of the qualities of a great critic. He
wanted imagination; but he had strong sense. His literary code was
formed on narrow principles; but in applying it, he showed great judgment and penetration. In mere style, abstracted from the ideas of which
style is the garb, his taste was excellent.—MACAULAY, *Essays : Addison.*

Anne Boleyn.

Queen of Henry VIII. : 1510 (?)-1536.

Wolsey : " Leave me awhile,—
It shall be to the duchess of Alençon,
The French king's sister; he shall marry her.—
Anne Bullen! No; I'll no Anne Bullens for him:
There's more in't than fair visage—Bullen!
No, we'll no Bullens—Speedily I wish
To hear from Rome."

—SHAKSPERE, *King Henry VIII.*

From a private gentlewoman you have made me first a marchioness, then a queen; and, as you can raise me no higher in this world, you are now sending me to be a saint in Heaven.—ANNE BOLEYN, *Last Message to Henry VIII.*

HENRY ST. JOHN, VISCOUNT BOLINGBROKE.

English Statesman and Writer : 1678-1751.

O, Bolingbroke ! O favourite of the skies,
O born to gifts by which the noblest rise,
Improv'd in arts by which the brightest please,
Intent to business, and polite for ease ;
Sublime in eloquence, where loud applause
Hath styl'd thee patron of a nation's cause.
                    —PARNELL, *Different Styles of Poetry.*

By different methods Bolingbroke shall raise
His growing honours and immortal praise.
He, fir'd with glory and the public good,
Betwixt the people and their danger stood :
Arm'd with convincing truths, he did appear ;
And all he said was sparkling, bright, and clear.
The listening senate with attention heard,
And some admired, while others trembling fear'd ;
Not from the tropes of formal eloquence,
But Demosthenic strength, and weight of sense,
Such as fond Oxford to her son supplied,
Design'd her own, as well as Britain's pride ;
Who, less beholden to the ancient strains,
Might shew a nobler blood in English veins,
Outdo whatever Homer sweetly sung
Of Nestor's counsels, or Ulysses' tongue.
Oh ! all ye nymphs, whilst time and youth allow,
Prepare the rose and lily for his brow.
Much he has done, but still has more in view ;
To Anna's interest and his country true.
More I could prophesy, but must refrain :
Such truths would make another mortal vain !
                    —WILLIAM KING, *Britain's Palladium.*

It is impossible to find lights and shades strong enough to paint the character of Lord Bolingbroke, who was a most mortifying instance of the violence of human passions, and of the most improved and exalted human reason. His virtues and his vices, his reason and his passions, did not blend themselves by a gradation of tints, but formed a shining and sudden contrast.—LORD CHESTERFIELD.

EDMUND BONNER.

Bishop of London : 1495-1569.

Gardiner out-Gardiners Gardiner in his heat,
Bonner cannot out-Bonner his own self—

Beast!—but they play with fire as children do,
And burn the house.
—TENNYSON, *Queen Mary.*

When persecuting zeal made royal sport
With tortured innocence in Mary's court,
And Bonner, blithe as shepherd at a wake,
Enjoy'd the show, and danced about the stake.
—COWPER, *Expostulation.*

We have not the smallest doubt that, when Bonner was in the Marshalsea, he thought it a very hard thing that a man should be locked up in a gaol for not being able to understand the words, "This is my body," in the same way with the lords of the council.—MACAULAY, *Essays : Sir James Mackintosh.*

JACQUES BÉNIGNE BOSSUET.

Bishop of Meaux : 1627-1704.

Bossuet, Fénélon and Massillon . . . worthy soldiers of the militia of Christ.—SIR ARCHIBALD ALISON, *Essays : Madame de Staël.*

Would not the man stamp himself as a barbarian who in French literature could not value the majesty of Bossuet ?—F. W. FARRAR, *Social and Present-Day Questions.*

Bossuet, however, required to be seen at the distance, as it were, of many miles ; and that, too, from a spot in which all irregularities might be reduced to a level. He was naturally moral and religious ; but bigotry converted his religion first into intolerance, and then into cruelty. —CHARLES BUCKE, *Anecdotes of Human Character.*

JAMES BOSWELL.

Biographer of Dr. Johnson : 1740-1795.

But could I like Montgomeries fight,
    Or gab like Boswell.
        —BURNS, *The Author's Earnest Cry and Prayer.*

Johnson found in James Boswell such a biographer as no man but himself ever had, or ever deserved to have. The performance, which chiefly resembles it in structure, is the life of the philosopher Demophon in Lucian ; but that slight sketch is far inferior in detail and in vivacity to Boswell's *Life of Johnson,* which, considering the eminent persons to whom it relates, the quantity of miscellaneous information and entertaining gossip which it brings together, may be termed, without exception, the best parlour-window book that ever was written.—SIR WALTER SCOTT, *Lives of the Novelists.*

Johnsons are rare ; yet, as has been asserted, Boswells perhaps still rarer—the more is the pity on both sides.—CARLYLE, *Hero-Worship.*

Jemmy had a sycophantish, but a sincere admiration of the genius, erudition and virtue of Ursa-Major, and in recording the noble growlings of the Great Bear, thought not of his own Scotch snivel.—JOHN WILSON, *Noctes Ambrosianæ, Vol. I.*

It is Boswell's eternal merit to have deeply reverenced the man whose littlenesses and asperities he could keenly discern, and has courageously depicted; and his work stands alone in Biography because he had this vision and this courage.　The image of Johnson is not defaced by these revelations; it only becomes more intelligible in becoming more human. —G. H. LEWES, *Introduction to Life of Dr. Johnson.*

The *Life of Johnson* is assuredly a great, a very great work.　Homer is not more decidedly the first of heroic poets, Shakespeare is not more decidedly the first of dramatists, Demosthenes is not more decidedly the first of orators, than Boswell is the first of biographers.　He has no second. . . . Eclipse is first, and the rest nowhere.—MACAULAY, *Essays : Boswell's " Life of Johnson ".*

Boswell's is one of the very few books which, after many years of familiarity, will still provoke a hearty laugh even in the solitude of a study ; and the laughter is of that kind which does one good.—LESLIE STEPHEN, *Hours in a Library, Second Series.*

Boswell has a little of the true Shakesperian secret.　He lets his characters show themselves without obtruding unnecessary comment. . . . Any one who will try to put down the pith of a brilliant conversation within the same space . . . will learn to appreciate Boswell's powers not only of memory but artistic representation.—*Id., Life of Johnson.*

No one, I presume, is ignorant how specially fortunate was Samuel Johnson in having Alexander Boswell the younger, of Auchinleck, Esq., for his biographer.　Could Boswell's *Life of Johnson* be expunged from English literature, the world would be poorer by the loss of one of the small number of books fit to live for ever.—J. ADDINGTON SYMONDS, *Ben Jonson.*

Boswell's book is an arch of triumph, through which, as we read, we see his hero passing into eternal fame, to take up his place with those—
> " Dead but sceptred sovereigns who still rule
> Our spirits from their urns."
> —AUGUSTINE BIRRELL, *Obiter Dicta, Second Series.*

ROBERT BOYLE.

English Philosopher : 1627-1691.

And now with lab'ring Boyle I trace
Nature through every winding maze ;
The latent qualities admire
Of vapours, water, air, and fire ;
With pleasing admiration see
Matter's surprising subtilty.
> —SOAME JENYNS, *An Epistle written in the Country.*

And noble Boyle, not less in nature seen,
Than his great brother read in states and men.
> —DRYDEN, *Epistle II. : To Dr. Charleton.*

So Locke the days of studious quiet spent ;
So Boyle in wisdom found divine content.
> —LORD LYTTLETON, *To the Rev. Dr. Ayscough.*

Boyle through the works of Nature ran.
> —CHURCHILL, *The Ghost, Bk. II.*

TYCHO BRAHE.

Danish Astronomer: 1546-1601.

In mathematics he was greater
Than Tycho Brahe or Erra Pater;
For he, by geometric scale,
Could take the size of pots of ale;
Resolve by sines and tangents straight
If bread or butter wanted weight.
> —SAMUEL BUTLER, *Hudibras.*

JOHN BRIGHT.

English Statesman: 1811-1889.

If rhetoric were poetry, John Bright would be a poet at least equal to John Milton.—SWINBURNE, *Studies in Prose and Poetry.*

So long as virtue, courage, and patriotism retain their significance, so long will these noble qualities continue to be associated with the name of John Bright.   He takes rank with the Pyms, the Hampdens, the Miltons, and other incorruptible great men of the past, who, in times of difficulty and of peril, have unswervingly fought the battle of freedom, and asserted the liberties of England.—G. BARNETT SMITH, *Life and Speeches of J. Bright.*

Bright was a man of less catholic temper, less comprehensive gifts [than Cobden].   But his singleness of aim, his combative spirit—it was wittily said of him that if he had not been a Quaker he must have been a prize-fighter—his superb eloquence—unsurpassed for purity and nobility of language, for spontaneous grace of gesture and native majesty of intonation, for pathos, for humour, and for a command of imagery at once simple and direct, and withal profoundly appropriate and impressive, his sympathetic insight into the sober, serious, righteous gravity of the English character, his noble scorn of wrong and his inflexible love of right made him an irresistible advocate and an indispensable ally.—J. R. THURSFIELD, *Life of Peel.*

JAMES BRINDLEY.

English Engineer: 1716-1772.

Ploughers, Spinners, Builders; Prophets, Poets, Kings; Brindleys and Goethes, Odins, and Arkwrights; all martyrs, and noble men, and gods are of one grand Host; immeasurable; marching ever forward since the beginnings of the world.—CARLYLE, *Past and Present: The Didactic.*

The rugged Brindley has little to say for himself; the rugged Brindley, when difficulties accumulate on him, retires silent, " generally to his bed "; retires "sometimes for three days together to his bed that he may be in perfect privacy there," and ascertain in his rough head how the difficulties may be overcome.   The ineloquent Brindley, behold he *has* chained seas together; his ships do visibly float over valleys, invisibly through the hearts of mountains; the Mersey and the Thames, the Humber and the Severn have shaken hands: Nature most audibly answers, yea!—*Id., Ibid.: The English.*

CHARLOTTE BRONTË.

English Novelist: 1816-1855.

It would hardly be safe to name Miss Austen, Miss Brontë, and George Eliot as the three greatest women novelists the United Kingdom can boast, and were one to go on and say that the alphabetical order of their names is also their order of merit, it would be necessary to seek police protection, and yet surely it is so.—AUGUSTINE BIRRELL, *Life of C. Brontë.*

Some portion of a faculty such as this, some touch of the same god-like and wonder-working might of imperious moral quality, some flush of the same divine and plenary inspiration, there was likewise in the noble genius and heroic instinct of Charlotte Brontë.   Some part of the power denied to many a writer of more keen and rare intelligence than even hers we feel "to the finest fibre of our nature" at the slight strong touch of her magnetic hand.—SWINBURNE, *Charlotte Brontë.*

Turning to the Brontës, does not one feel the very heartbeats of womanhood in those powerful utterances that seem to spring from some central emotional energy?—MATHILDE BLINDE, *George Eliot.*

Charlotte Brontë had, in the highest degree, that which Ruskin had called the "pathetic fallacy," the eye which beholds Nature coloured by the light of the inner soul.   In this quality she really reaches the level of fine poetry.   Her intense sympathy with her native moors and glens is akin to that of Wordsworth.   She almost never attempts to describe any scenery with which she is not deeply familiar.   But how wonderfully she catches the tone of her own moorland, skies, storm-winds, secluded hall or cottage. . . .   Charlotte Brontë is great in clouds, like a prose Shelley. . . .   Charlotte Brontë painted not the world, hardly a corner of the world, but the very soul of one proud and loving girl.   That is enough: we need ask no more.   It was done with consummate power. We feel that we know her life, from ill-used childhood to her proud matronhood; we know her home, her school, her professional duties, her loves and hates, her agonies and her joys, with that intense famili-arity and certainty of vision with which our own personal memories are graven on our brain.—FREDERIC HARRISON, *Early Victorian Literature.*

The most obvious of all remarks about Miss Brontë is the close con-nection between her life and her writings.   In no books is the author more completely incarnated.—LESLIE STEPHEN, *Hours in a Library, Vol. III.*

LORD BROUGHAM AND VAUX.

Lord Chancellor: 1779-1868.

In the picture of our century, as taken from life by History, this very man should have been a central figure; but now, owing to his want of steadfastness, there will be for ever a blur where Brougham should have been.—HARRIET MARTINEAU, *Biographical Sketches.*

Lord Chancellor Brougham has repeatedly declared, that he desired no other epitaph on his monument than that he was the founder of Universal English Education.—SIR ARCHIBALD ALISON, *Essays: The Old Scottish Parliament.*

With energies less dissipated and temper more controlled, Brougham's place in history, and even in literature, must have been very high. As it was, his life was a splendid failure.—T. F. TOUT, *Celebrities of the Century.*

Tickler: " Brougham is a volcano—an eruption—a devouring flame—a storm—a whirlwind—a cataract—a torrent—a sea—thunder and earthquake. You might apply the same terms, with the same truth, to a Billingsgate fishwife."
North: " Brougham's invective is formidable chiefly for its vulgarity. One hates, loathes, fears to be pelted with the mud and missiles of an infuriated demagogue—just as a gentleman declines the proffered combat with a carman, although conscious that in three rounds he would leave the ruffian senseless in the ring."
Tickler: " That sometimes occurs—as in the case of Canning."
North: " The straight hitting of the Foreign Secretary soon dorses your round-about hand-over-head millers, like Harry Brougham."
Tickler: " Yet how that outrageous violence and fury, arms aloft, eyes agog, cheeks convulsed, and lips quivering, passes with the multitude for demonstration of strength and science ! "
North: " Brougham never fights at points—he throws away his blows—and beyond all the other men, lays himself open to fatal punishment, although he has weight, length, and reach, and generally enters the ring in good condition, and after long and severe training, yet has he lost every battle. His backers are never confident—yet in a casual turn-up, it must be allowed that he is an ugly customer."—JOHN WILSON, *Noctes Ambrosianæ, Vol. I.*

Tickler: " Brougham in his robes ! Lord High Chancellor of England ! Stern face and stalwart frame—and his mind, people say, is gigantic. They name him with Bacon. Be it so; the minister he and interpreter of Nature ! Henry Brougham, in the eyes of his idolaters, is also an Edmund Burke. Be it so; at once the most imaginative and most philosophical of orators that ever sounded lament over the decline and fall of empires, while wisdom, listening to his lips, exclaimed :—
' Was ne'er prophetic sound so full of woe ! ' "
North: " Come—come, Tickler—none of your invidious eulogies on the Man of the People."
Tickler: " There he sits—a strong man—not about to run a race—"
North: " But who has run it, and distanced all competitors. There is something great, Tickler, in unconquerable and victorious energy—"
Tickler: " A man of many talents he—some of them seeming to be of the highest order. Sword-like acuteness—sun-like perspicacity—"
North: " And sledge-hammer-like power."
Tickler: " There is a wicked trouble in his keen grey eyes."
North: " No. Restless, but not unhappy."
Tickler: " Scorn has settled on that wide-nostril'd probo—"

North : " No.   It comes and goes—the nose is benevolent."
Tickler : " Do you say there is no brass on that hard forehead ? "
North : "I see but bone—and though the brain within is of intellect
' all compact,' the heart that feeds it burns with passions not unheroic."
Tickler : " King of them all—ambition."
North : " ' The last infirmity of noble minds ! ' "
Tickler : " No—you misunderstand—you misrepresent Milton.   He spoke
of the love of fame."
North : " So do I.   In Brougham—do him justice—the two passions are
one, and under its perpetual inspiration he has
                    ' Scorned delights, and lived laborious days,'
till with all his sins, by friend and foe, he is held to be, in his character
of statesman, the first man in England."—*Id., Ibid., Vol. III.*

Sir Thomas Browne.

English Physician and Author : 1605-1682.

The exclusive Sir Thomas-Browne-ness of all the fancies and modes of
illustration. . . . Strong feeling and an active intellect conjoined lead
almost necessarily, in the first stage of philosophising, to Spinozism.
Sir T. Browne was Spinozist without knowing it.   His own character
was a fine mixture of humourist, genius, and pedant.   A library was a
living world to him, and every book a man, absolute flesh and blood !
and the gravity with which he records contradictory opinions is exquisite.
—S. T. Coleridge, *Notes, Theological, Political, etc.*

Elizabeth Barrett Browning.

English Poetess : 1809-1861.

Miss Barrett . . . the most imaginative poetess that has appeared in
England, perhaps in Europe. . . . She is like an ultra-sensitive sister of
Alfred Tennyson.—Leigh Hunt, *Men, Women, and Books.*

The notes of Mrs. Browning's poetry are emotion, purity, pathos, intense
earnestness, sympathy with every form of suffering, with everything great
and good, hatred of everything evil, specially of all oppression.   Her
want of humour, a few rough and careless rhymes, an occasional forcing
of sense and phrase, have made some critics of word and style complain ;
but students may rely on it, that to know Mrs. Browning as she reveals
herself in her works is a liberal education, and to enter into her spirit
one of the most ennobling pursuits that a man can undertake.—F. J.
Furnivall, *Celebrities of the Century.*

Robert Browning.

English Poet : 1812-1889.

Well, any how here the story stays,
So far at least as I understand :
And, Robert Browning, you writer of plays,
Here's a subject made to your hand !
                    —Robert Browning, *A Light Woman.*

Shoddy : " The Brownings too ?
                    Give me a glossary—
Of English in frills and flounces, with a lot
Of cyclopedias, guide-books, catalogues,
To search out the allusions.   I'll read *them,*
And let the Brownings slide, if slide they will ! "
                    —Dr. Milo Mahan, *The Yorkshireman in Boston.*

I suppose, reader, that you see whereabouts among the poets I place
Robert Browning ; high among the poets of all time, and I scarce know
whether first, or second, in our own : and it is a bitter thing to me to see
the way in which he has been received by almost everybody.—William
Morris, *Oxford and Cambridge Magazine, March,* 1856.

If there is any great quality more perceptible than another in Mr.
Browning's intellect, it is his decisive and incisive faculty of thought,
his sureness and intensity of perception, his rapid and trenchant resolution of aim.   To charge him with obscurity is about as accurate as to
call Lynceus purblind, or complain of the sluggish action of the telegraph
wire.   He is something too much the reverse of obscure ; he is too
brilliant and subtle for the ready reader to follow with any certainty the
track of an intelligence which moves with such incessant rapidity. or
even to realise with what spider-like swiftness and sagacity his building
spirit leaps and lightens to and fro and backward and forward, as it lives
along the animated line of its labour, springs from thread to thread, and
darts from centre to circumference of the glittering and quivering web of
living thought, woven from the inexhaustible stores of his perception,
and kindled from the inexhaustible fire of his imagination.—Swinburne,
George Chapman.

When the news was flashed from Venice that Robert Browning had
died, men felt as of old they felt when a great king had passed away —
one who, at a time of change, had absorbed the new aims and thoughts
of his nation while they were yet unshaped, who had given them form in
himself, and sent them forth alive and fresh, to be loved and used by his
folk, and who, continuing to shape and reshape them with more and more
completeness, had himself quietly grown into such a power that he impressed the seal and spirit of his personality upon the character of his
people. . . . Song alone did not content him.   Music . . . claimed him,
and painting, and then the study of the great poets, in whom he " explored
passion and mind for the first time " ; till now his soul, fed at these great
springs, rose into keen life ; all his powers burst forth, and he gazed on
all things, and systems and schemes, and heard ineffable things unguessed
by man.   Then he vowed himself to liberty, to the new world that liberty
was to bring where
        " Men were to be as gods, and earth as heaven ".
All Plato entered into him ; it seemed he had the key to life ; his soul
rose to meet the glory he conceived.—Stopford Brooke.

Lovers of Browning are multiplying with great rapidity throughout
the land.   To claim to be his champion is to dress in rusty armour.
Writings in defence of Browning are as much out of date as pamphlets
on the Corn Laws.—Alex. Hill in *Browning Notes.*

There is no form of energy which to Browning seems so high, or on
which he dwells with such evident delight, as that which sums up in

itself all the vital faculties of man—which raises all his powers of resolve, of thought, of passion, of self-devotion, to the highest pitch of intensity— the energy of love ; the " infinite passion and the pain of finite hearts that yearn," the " moment which lets us through into eternity, our due ". —C. E. VAUGHAN in *Browning Notes.*

Through Nature, Wordsworth would lead the soul to rest. Through the spiritual struggles of the soul itself, Browning reveals the divine touch that discloses the true end of living and thinking.—G. D. BOYLE in *Browning Notes.*

Most thinkers write and speak of man ; Mr. Browning of men. With man as a species, with man as a society, he does not concern himself, but with individual man and man. Every man is for him an epitome of the universe, a centre of creation.—ARTHUR SYMONS, *Introduction to Browning.*

Mr. Browning evidently loves what we may call the realism, the gro- tesque realism, of orthodox Christianity. Many parts of it in which great divines have felt keen difficulties are quite pleasant to him. He must *see* his religion, he must have an " object-lesson " in believing. He must have a creed that will *take*, which wins and holds the miscellaneous world, which stout men will heed, which nice women will adore. The spare moments of solitary religion—the " obdurate questionings," the high " instincts," the " first affections," the " shadowy recollections,"

> " Which, do they what they may,
> Are yet the fountain-light of all our day—
> Are yet a master-light of all our seeing ; "

the great but vague faith—the unutterable tenets—seem to him worthless, visionary ; they are not enough immersed in matter ; they move about " in worlds not realised ". We wish he could be tried like the prophet once ; he would have found God in the earthquake and the storm ; he would have deciphered from them a bracing and a rough religion : he would have known that crude men and ignorant women felt them too, and he would accordingly have trusted them ; but he would have distrusted and disregarded the " still small voice " : he would have said it was " fancy " —a thing you thought you heard to-day, but were not sure you had heard to-morrow : he would call it a nice illusion, an immaterial prettiness ; he would ask triumphantly " How are you to get the mass of men to heed this little thing ? " he would have persevered and insisted " *My wife* did not hear it ".—WALTER BAGEHOT, *Literary Studies, Vol. II.*

Whatever we hold about the insight and imagination of Browning, no one can doubt that he often chose to be uncouth, crabbed, grotesque, and even clownish, when the humour was on him. There are high precedents for genius choosing its own instrument and making its own music. But whatever were Browning's latent powers of melody, his method when he chose to play upon the gong, or the ancient instrument of marrow-bone and cleavers, was the exact antithesis of Tennyson's ; and he set on edge the teeth of those who love the exquisite cadences of *In Memoriam* and *Maud.* Browning has left deep influence if not a school.—FREDERIC HARRISON, *Studies in Early Victorian Literature.*

Boldness of design then, and an even excessive opulence of intellect, were from the first the characteristics of Browning. He did not acquire them, they were his birthright. Carlyle stood out from among his contemporaries by virtue of conquests won through toil and pain, Browning entered into his inheritance at once and without effort. The one might have said, like the chief captain, " With a great sum obtained I this freedom "; and the other might have answered, with St. Paul, " But I was free born ".—HUGH WALKER, *The Age of Tennyson.*

ROBERT BRUCE.

King of Scotland : 1274-1329.

Where are the Muses fled that should produce
A drama worthy of the name of Bruce?
—Robert Bruce (Scott's Prologue.)

Scots! wha hae wi' Wallace bled,
Scots! wham Bruce has aften led,
Welcome to your gory bed,
     Or to victory!
Now's the day, and now's the hour;
See the front o' battle lour:
See approach proud Edward's power—
     Chains and slavery.
Id., Bruce's Address at Bannockburn.

Everything is interesting where Robert Bruce is the subject.—SIR WALTER SCOTT, *History of Scotland.*

Scotland recovered, during his administration, in a great measure, from the devastation that had preceded it; and the peasants, forgetting the stern warrior in the beneficent monarch, long remembered his sway, under the name of the " good King Robert's " reign. . . . In our national fondness, therefore, for the memory of Robert Bruce, the English should perceive the growth of those principles from which their own unequalled greatness has arisen; nor should they envy the glory of the field of Bannockburn, when we appeal to it as our best title to be quartered in their arms.—SIR ARCHIBALD ALISON, *Essays : Robert Bruce.*

MARCUS JUNIUS BRUTUS.

Cæsar's Chief Assassin : B.C. 85-42.

Alas, the lofty city! and alas,
The trebly hundred triumphs! and the day
When Brutus made the dagger's edge surpass
The conqueror's sword in bearing fame away!
— BYRON, *Childe Harold's Pilgrimage, LXXXII.*

Touch but a nerve—and Brutus is a slave;
A nerve, and Plato drivels! Was it mind,
Or soul, that taught the wise one in the cave,
The freeman in the wind?

     —LYTTON, *Mind and Soul.*

Suffolk : " A Roman sworder and banditto slave
Murder'd sweet Tully ; Brutus' bastard hand
Stabb'd Julius Cæsar ; savage islanders
Pompey the Great."

—SHAKSPERE, *King Henry VI., Part II.*

Cæsar : " *Et tu, Brute ?*—Then fall, Cæsar ! "

—*Id., Julius Cæsar.*

Stern Brutus was with too much horror good,
Holding his fasces stain'd with filial blood.

—PRIOR, *Carmen Seculare.*

Who speaks the truth stabs Falsehood to the heart,
And his mere word makes despots tremble more
Than ever Brutus with his dagger could.

—J. R. LOWELL, *L'Envoi.*

And thou, unhappy Brutus, kind of heart,
Whose steady arm, by awful virtue urg'd,
Lifted the Roman steel against thy friend.

—THOMSON, *The Seasons : Winter.*

O bluddy Brutus, rightly didst thou rew,
And thou Cassius justly came thy fall,
That with the swurd wherewith thou Cæsar slewe
Murdrest thy selfe, and rest thy life withall.
A myrrour let him be unto you all
That murderers be, of murder to your meede :
For murder crieth out vengeance on your seede.

—LORD BUCKHURST, *Complaynt of Henrye, Duke of Buckingham.*

JOHN BUNYAN : 1628-1688.

He rang'd his tropes, and preach'd up patience,
Back'd his opinion with quotations,
Divines and moralists ; and run ye on
Quite through from Seneca to Bunyan.

—PRIOR, *Pauls Purganti and his Wife.*

More to mankind is one page of the Bedford tinker, than all the banks
of the Rothschilds.—F. W. FARRAR, *Social and Present-Day Questions.*

I know of no book, the Bible excepted as above all comparison, which
I, according to my judgment and experience, could so safely recommend
as teaching and enforcing the whole saving truth according to the mind
that was in Christ Jesus, as the *Pilgrim's Progress.* It is, in my conviction, incomparably the best *summa theologiæ evangelicæ* ever produced by a writer not miraculously inspired.—S. T. COLERIDGE, *Table
Talk.*

The style of Bunyan is delightful to every reader, and invaluable as a
study to every person who wishes to obtain a wide command over the
English language. The vocabulary is the vocabulary of the common
people. There is not an expression, if we except a few technical terms
of theology, which would puzzle the rudest peasant. We have observed
several pages which do not contain a single word of more than two-

syllables. Yet no writer has said more exactly what he meant to say. For magnificence, for pathos, for vehement exhortation, for subtle disquisition, for every purpose of the poet, the orator and the divine, this homely dialect, the dialect of plain working men, was perfectly sufficient. There is no book in our literature on which we would so readily stake the fame of the old unpolluted English language, no book which shows so well how rich that language is in its own proper wealth, and how little it has been improved by all that it has borrowed.—MACAULAY, *Essays : John Bunyan.*

His is a homespun style, not a manufactured one : and what a difference is there between its homeliness and the flippant vulgarity of the Roger L'Estrange and Tom Brown school. If it is not a well of English undefiled, to which the poet as well as the philologist must repair, if they would drink of the living waters, it is a clear stream of current English, the vernacular speech of his age, sometimes indeed in its rusticity and coarseness, but always in its plainness and its strength. John Bunyan—the one man who has attained to write a successful prose allegory on a large scale, and to infuse true emotion into an exercise of ingenuity, and who probably owed less to study and training than any other of the great authors of the modern world. . . . Of Bunyan's character there can be but one opinion ; he was a truly Apostolic man. As no one's diction is more forcible, unadulterated Saxon, so no life has better expressed the sturdy, sterling virtues of the Englishman.—RICHARD GARNETT, *The Age of Dryden.*

Now in Bunyan there is a strong German (Albert Dürer) element which you must express, *viz.* (1) a tendency to the grotesque in imagination ; (2) a tendency to spiritual portraiture of the highest kind, in which an ideal character is brought out, not by abstracting all individual traits (the Academy plan), but by throwing in strong individual traits drawn from common life. . . . But there is another [element] of which Bunyan, as a Puritan tinker, was not conscious, though he had it in his heart, that is, classic grace and purity of form. He had it in his heart, as much as Spenser. His women, his Mr. Greatheart, his Faithful, his shepherds, can only be truly represented in a lofty and delicate outline, otherwise the ideal beauty which lifts them into a supernatural and eternal world is lost, and they become mere good folks of the seventeenth century. Some illustrators, feeling this, have tried to medievalize them—silly fellows. What has Bunyan to do with the Middle Age? He writes for all ages, he is full of an eternal humanity, and that eternal humanity can only be represented by something of the eternal form which you find in Greek statues.—KINGSLEY, *Life and Memories of his Life, Vol. II.*

A stranger, who admires and loves Bunyan, approaches Bedford as a poet or a divine would enter Smyrna ; the former thinking only of Homer, and the latter only of Polycarp ; and both trying how vividly they can realise the image of their favourite, amidst the scenes once consecrated by his presence, and still enshrined by his memory. I felt no difficulty, on entering Bedford, and walking around it, to associate everything with Bunyan, or to enshrine anything with his Pilgrim. The town, indeed, did not seem to me "the City of Destruction"; and the bridge was too good, and the water too clear, to allow the river to be regarded as "the Slough of Despond" : but it was hardly possible not to see Christian in every poor man who carried a burden, and Christina in every poor woman who carried a market-basket in one hand, and led a child with the other. One sweet-looking peasant girl, also, might have been Mercy's youngest sister. She would have been beautiful anywhere ; but she was enchanting upon the spot where Bunyan's Mercy (that finished portrait of female loveliness) had *walked and wept.* In like manner, any ragged urchin, if only robust and boisterous enough, and evidently the ringleader of fun or mischief, seemed the *boy* Bunyan himself, although only a few minutes before a venerable old man had seemed the very personification of the Baptist Minister of Bedford : but no one seemed to be the Glorious Dreamer, although many looked sleepy enough.—ROBERT PHILIP, *Life and Times of John Bunyan.*

EDMUND BURKE.

Irish Orator : 1729-1797.

Daddie Burke the plea was cookin'.
> —BURNS, *Lines written to a Gentleman.*

And Burke I beheld there,
Eloquent statesman and sage, who, though late, broke loose from his
    trammels,
Giving them to mankind what party too long had diverted.
> —SOUTHEY, *A Vision of Judgment*, X.

Yet never, Burke ! thou drank'st Corruption's bowl !
Thee stormy Pity and the cherished lure
Of Pomp, and proud Precipitance of soul
Wildered with meteor fires. Ah Spirit pure !
That error's mist had left thy purged eye :
So might I clasp thee with a Mother's joy !
> S. T. COLERIDGE, *Monody on the Death of Chatterton.*

If a man were to go by chance at the same time with Burke under a shed to shun a shower, he would say " this is an extraordinary man ".—DR. JOHNSON in BOSWELL, *Life of Johnson.*

Edmund Burke—and Sir Joshua—*par nobile Fratrum.*—JOHN WILSON, *Noctes Ambrosianæ, Vol. II.*

Burke spoke daggers, especially when he used none.—*Id., Homer and his Translators.*

Edmund Burke, one of the greatest men whom the United Kingdom has produced. With a fertility of fancy sufficient to make a poet of the rank of Milton, and a power of general reasoning which might have furnished a philosopher of the rank of Bacon, he devoted these rare gifts to political pursuits. He was not indeed the ivory paper-knife which Swift considers as the true measure of sharpness of intellect for a practical statesman, but was rather the razor to which Goldsmith compares him.—EARL RUSSELL, *Life of Charles Fox, Vol. III.*

The transcendent greatness of Burke.—SIR ARCHIBALD ALISON, *Essays : The Greek Drama.*

How much soever men may differ as to the soundness of Mr. Burke's doctrines, or the purity of his public conduct, there can be no hesitation in according to him a station among the most extraordinary persons that have ever appeared; nor is there now any diversity of opinion as to the place which it is fit to assign him.—LORD BROUGHAM, *Statesmen of the Time of George III.*

How are we to explain the notorious fact, that the speeches and writings of Edmund Burke are more interesting at the present day than they were found at the time of their first publication? . . . The satisfactory solution is, that Edmund Burke possessed and had sedulously sharpened that eye which sees all things, actions and events, in relation to the laws that determine their existence and circumscribe their possibility. He referred habitually to principles. He was a scientific statesman; and therefore a seer. For every principle contains in itself the germs of a prophecy.—S. T. COLERIDGE, *Biographia Literaria.*

Many of the passages to be found in Burke . . . shine by their own light, belong to no class, have neither equal nor counterpart, and of which we say that no one but the author could have written them!—HAZLITT, *Lectures on the English Comic Writers.*

Europe was conceived to be on the point of dissolution. Burke heard the death-watch, and rang the alarm. A hollow sound passed from nation to nation, like that which announces the splitting and breaking up of ice in the regions around the Pole. . . . Burke was a fine specimen of a *third-thoughted* man. So in our own times, consciously and professedly was Coleridge; who delighted in nothing more than in the revival of a dormant truth, and who ever looked over the level of the present age to the hills containing the sources and springs whereby that level is watered.—J. C. HARE, *Guesses at Truth, First Series.*

Often when we contemplate the mind and history of Edmund Burke—the plenitude of his knowledge, the profound wisdom of his intellect, the vast ken of his imaginative vision, the disinterestedness of his purpose, and the wide and watchful eye he kept on the progress of the human race everywhere, as well as the righteous and terrible anger which he felt at its oppressors—we are reminded less of a man, than of some benevolent angel or genie, incarnate in human flesh, for the purpose of furthering the great designs of God, and counteracting the machinations or the infuriated madness of infernal beings.— GEORGE GILFILLAN, *Dissertation, prefixed Shakespeare's Works.*

Burke's command of style is so great, that, as by some he was mistaken for Bolingbroke, so by others he has been identified with Junius.—LYTTON, *Essays: Style and Diction.*

The power to detach, and to magnify by detaching, is the essence of rhetoric in the hand of the orator and the poet. This rhetoric, or power to fix the momentary eminency of an object, so remarkable in Burke, in Byron, in Carlyle, the painter and sculptor exhibit in colour and in stone. —EMERSON, *Essays: Art.*

What I once heard a benevolent physician say of a madman! "Be sure you speak only the most direct truth to him; poor fellow, his mind is confused enough already with his own false impressions," is just the doctrine which Burke was preaching to the artificial world of the eighteenth century.—F. D. MAURICE, *Friendship of Books.*

The Arch-Whig Trumpeter, Mr. Burke.—LORD BEACONSFIELD.

The yet more venerable name of Burke.—W. E. GLADSTONE.

Burke is a name never to be mentioned without reverence ; not only because Burke was incomparably the greatest of all English political writers, and a standing refutation of the theory which couples rhetorical excellence with intellectual emptiness, but also because he was a man whose glowing hatred of all injustice and sympathy for all suffering never evaporated in empty words.—LESLIE STEPHEN, *Hours in a Library, Second Series.*

Burke, the Cobden of that era.—WALTER BAGEHOT, *Literary Studies, Vol. II.*

Apart from any systematic political speculation, it is difficult to name another publicist whose writings are so thickly studded with those unsystematic products of an acute, enlarged, and reflective mind, which are vaguely labelled as wisdom. Burke's mind was so vigorous, his acquired knowledge so large, and his opportunities of observation so wide, that the accumulation of this kind of wisdom in his pages, and the addition which he made to the human stock of so valuable a possession, appear no more than a natural result. In his wildest moment these sagacious apophthegms were present, green places in a wilderness of declamation. Many of them have got imbedded in the current phraseology, and men use Burke's maxims without knowing who is their teacher. His pages, as we turn them over, are bright with these luminous utterances.—JOHN MORLEY, *Edmund Burke.*

There are great personalities like Burke who march through history with voices like a clarion trumpet and something like the glitter of swords in their hands. They are as interesting as their work. Contact with them warms and kindles the mind.—*Id., Studies in Literature.*

I have often been struck with a resemblance, which I hope is not really fanciful, between the attitude of Burke's mind towards government and that of Cardinal Newman towards religion. Both these great men belong, by virtue of their imaginations, to the poetic order, and they both are to be found dwelling with amazing eloquence, detail, and wealth of illustration on the varied elements of society. Both seem as they write to have one hand on the pulse of the world, and to be forever alive to the throb of its action ; and Burke, as he regarded humanity swarming like bees into and out of their hives of industry, is ever asking himself, how are these men to be saved from anarchy ? whilst Newman puts to himself the question, how are these men to be saved from atheism ? Both saw the perils of free inquiry divorced from practical affairs.—AUGUSTINE BIRRELL, *Res Judicatæ.*

The meteoric mind of Burke.—LORD ROSEBERY, *Life of Pitt.*

WILLIAM CECIL, LORD BURLEIGH.

Lord High Treasurer : 1520-1598.

Elizabeth :   " But with Cecil's aid
And others, if our person be secured
From traitor stabs—we will make England great."
                              —TENNYSON, *Queen Mary.*

Burleigh, the subtlest builder of thy fame,—
The serpent craft of Walsingham.
—LYTTON, *The Last Days of Elizabeth.*

Cecil, the grave, the wise, the great, the good,
What is there more that can ennoble blood ?
The orphan's pillar, the true subject's shield,
The poor's full store-house, and just servant's field,
The only faithful watchman for the realm,
That in all tempests never quit the helm.
—BEN JONSON, *Epigram on William Lord Burleigh.*

And Cecil, whose wisdom
'Stablish'd the Church and State, Eliza's pillar of council.
—SOUTHEY, *A Vision of Judgment.*

Eliza first the sable scene withdrew,
And to the ancient world display'd the new ;
When Burleigh at the helm of state was seen,
The truest subject to the greatest queen.
—DR. WILLIAM KING, *Britain's Palladium.*

Wise Cecil, lov'd by people and by prince,
As often broke his word as any since.
—SOAME JENYNS, *First Epistle of Bk. II. of Horace imitated.*

Burleigh, like the old Marquess of Winchester, who preceded him in
the custody of the White Staff, was of the willow, and not of the oak.
He first rose into notice by defending the supremacy of Henry the
Eighth.—MACAULAY, *Essays : Burleigh and his Times.*

ROBERT BURNS.

Scottish Poet : 1759-1796.

While Terra firma, on her axis,
    Diurnal turns,
Count on a friend, in faith an' practice,
    In Robert Burns.
—BURNS, *To William Simpson.*

This wot ye all whom it concerns,
I, Rhymer Robin, *alias* Burns—
    October twenty-third—
A ne'er to be forgotten day—
Sae far I sprackled up the brae.
    I dinner'd wi' a Lord.
—*Id.*, *On Dining with Lord Daer.*

Him who walked in glory and joy
Following his plough, along the mountain-side,
By our own spirits are we deified :
We poets in our youth begin in gladness ;
But thereof comes in the end despondency and madness.
—WORDSWORTH, *Resolution and Independence.*

'Mid crowded obelisks and urns,
I sought the untimely grave of Burns;
Sons of the bard, my heart still mourns
   With sorrow true;
And more would grieve, but that it turns
   Trembling to you!
                    —*Id., To the Sons of Burns.*

The boast of Scotland, Robert Burns.
                    —Sir Walter Scott.

This mortal body of a thousand days
Now fills, O Burns, a space in thine own room,
Where thou didst dream alone on budded bays,
Happy and thoughtless of thy day of doom!
My pulse is warm with thine own Barley-bree,
My head is light with pledging a great soul,
My eyes are wandering, and I cannot see,
Fancy is dead and drunken at its goal;
Yet can I stamp my foot upon thy floor,
Yet can I ope thy window-sash to find
The meadow thou hast tramped o'er and o'er,—
Yet can I think of thee till thought is blind,—
Yet can I gulp a bumper to thy name,—
O smile among the shades, for this is fame!
          —Keats, *Sonnet written in Burns' Cottage, Alloway.*
Shakespeare was of us, Milton was for us,
Burns, Shelley, were with us,—they watch from their graves!
          —Robert Browning, *The Lost Leader.*

He spoke of Burns: men rude and rough
   Pressed round to hear the praise of one
Whose heart was made of manly, simple stuff,
   As homespun as their own.
          —J. R. Lowell, *An Incident in a Railroad Car.*

The lark of Scotia's morning sky!
   Whose voice may sing his praises?
With Heaven's own sunlight in his eye,
   He walked among the daisies,
Till through the cloud of fortune's wrong
   He soared to fields of glory;
But left his land her sweetest song
   And earth her saddest story.
          —Oliver Wendell Holmes, *For the Meeting of the
             Burns Club,* 1856.

I like full well the deep resounding swell
   Of mighty symphonies with cords inwoven;
But sometimes, too, a song of Burns,—don't you?
   After a solemn storm-blast of Beethoven.
          —*Id., How not to Settle it.*

Yes, there is such a human glow
Of life and love in Robin's breast;

Its warmth can melt the winter snow
  In Poverty's cold nest. . . .
And near or far, where Briton's band
To-day, the leal and true heart turns
Move fondly to the fatherland,
  For love of Robin Burns.

      —GERALD MASSEY, *Robin Burns.*

Search Scotland over, from the Pentland to the Solway, and there is not a cottage-hut so poor and wretched as to be without its Bible ; and hardly one that, on the same shelf, and next to it, does not treasure a Burns. Have the people degenerated since their adoption of this new manual ? Has their attachment to the Book of Books declined ? Are their hearts less firmly bound, than were their fathers', to the old faith and the old virtues ? I believe he that knows the most of the country will be the readiest to answer all these questions, as every lover of genius and virtue would desire to hear them answered. . . . Extraordinary . . . has been the inanity of his critics. While differing widely in their estimates of his character and *morale*, they have, without a single exception, expressed a lofty idea of his powers of mind and of the excellence of his poetry. Here, as on the subject of Shakespeare, and on scarcely any other, have Whigs and Tories, Infidels and Christians, bigoted Scotchmen and bigoted sons of John Bull, the high and the low, the rich and the poor, the prosaic and the enthusiastic lovers of poetry, the strait-laced and the morally lax, met and embraced each other.—LOCKHART, *Life of Burns.*

Scotland had lost that very year the great poet Burns—her glory and her shame.—*Id., Life of Sir W. Scott.*

Who has not a thousand times seen snow fall on the water ? Who has not watched it with a new feeling from the time that he has read Burns' comparison of sensual pleasure :

    " To snow that falls upon a river
    A moment white—then gone for ever ! "
      —S. T. COLERIDGE, *Biographia Literaria.*

The inspired Ploughman.—LEIGH HUNT, *Men, Women, and Books.*

Ay, for many a deep reason the Scottish people love their own Robert Burns. Never was the personal character of poet so strongly and endearingly exhibited in his song. They love him, because he loved his own order, nor ever desired for a single hour to quit it. They love him, because he loved the very humblest condition of humanity, where everything good was only the more commended to his manly mind by disadvantages of social position. They love him, because he saw with just anger, how much the judgments of " silly coward man " are determined by such accidents to the neglect or contempt of native worth. They love him for his independence. What wonder ! To be brought into contact with rank and wealth—a world inviting to ambition, and tempting to a thousand desires—and to choose rather to remain lowly and poor, than seek an easier or a brighter lot, by courting favour from the rich and great —was a legitimate ground of pride, if any ground of pride be legitimate. He gave a tongue to this pride, and the boast is inscribed in words of fire in the Manual of the Poor.—JOHN WILSON, *Speech at the Burns Festival.*

Burns, though conscious of the influences which formed him into a poet, was unable to tell how he trained his genius into art, yet *an artist* he indisputably was, and it is astonishing how marvellously correct, both in details and as wholes, most of the writings are. He is one of the most correct poets that the world has known.—LYTTON, *Essays: Gray's Works.*

Nevertheless, upon English soil, and among the mists of Scotland, arose the poetry most redundant in descriptive power; and for the last thirty years no country has produced poets who have understood the language of solitude, and transfused the very soul of nature, like Burns, Crabbe, and Wordsworth.—MAZZINI, *Life and Writings, Vol. II.*

Do you think Burns has had no influence on the life of men and women in Scotland, has opened no eyes and ears to the face of nature and the dignity of man and the charm and excellence of women?—EMERSON, *Poetry and Imagination.*

It was a curious phenomenon, in the withered unbelieving, second-hand Eighteenth Century, that of a Hero starting up, among the artificial, pasteboard figures and productions, in the guise of a Robert Burns. . . . One of the most considerable Saxon men of the eighteenth century was an Ayrshire Peasant named Robert Burns. Yes, I will say, here too was a piece of the right Saxon stuff: strong as the Harz-rock, rooted in the depths of the world;—rock, yet with wells of living softness in it! . . . Our peasant (Burns) showed himself among us, "a soul like an Æolian harp, in whose strings the vulgar wind, as it passed through them, changed itself into articulate melody".—CARLYLE, *Hero-Worship.*

The greatest Peasant—next perhaps to King David of the Jews, a peasant, a poet, a patriot, and a king—whom any age had produced.— CHARLES MACKAY, *Fifty Years' Recollections.*

To Sir Walter and Carlyle and Tennyson it has been revealed that life as sung by Burns is life indeed, that joy and change and death are, save for a few insignificant details, the same in the cottage as in the palace, and that whosoever has thrilled the heart of one honest man with his verse may thrill the whole world, and that the Laureate of toil is the Laureate of the human race.—P. ANDERSON GRAHAM, *Nature in Books.*

If ever there was a song-writer who could say with the most catholic comprehensiveness in the words of the old comedian, "*I am a man, and all things human are kin to me,*" it was Robert Burns. In this respect he is the Shakespeare of lyric poetry.—J. STUART BLACKIE, *Burns.*

In such poets as Burns and Tennyson, the element of what may be called *human reference* is always so decided that, though no poets describe nature more beautifully when they have occasion, it would still be improper to speak of them specially as descriptive poets. To borrow a distinction from the sister art, it may be said that, if Burns and Tennyson are more properly classed with the figure-painters, notwithstanding the extreme beauty and finish of their natural backgrounds, so, on the same principle, Wordsworth, whose skill in delineating the human subject is also admitted, may yet not erroneously be classed with the landscape-painters.—DAVID MASSON, *Wordsworth, Shelley, Keats.*

No wonder the peasantry of Scotland have loved Burns as perhaps never people loved a poet. He not only sympathised with the wants, the trials, the joys and sorrows of their obscure lot, but he interpreted these to themselves, and interpreted them to others, and this too in their own language made musical, and glorified by genius. He made the poorest ploughman proud of his station and his toil, since Robbie Burns had shared and sung them. He awoke a sympathy for them in many a heart that otherwise would never have known it. In looking up to him, the Scottish people have seen an impersonation of themselves on a large scale—of themselves, both in their virtues and in their vices.—J. C. Shairp, *Robert Burns*.

Robert Burton.

English Writer: 1576-1639.

The book, in my opinion, most useful to a man who wishes to acquire the reputation of being well read, with the least trouble, is Burton's *Anatomy of Melancholy*, the most amusing and instructive medley of quotations and classical anecdotes I ever perused. But a superficial reader must take care, or his intricacies will bewilder him. If, however, he has patience to go through his volumes, he will be more improved for literary conversation than by the perusal of any twenty other works with which I am acquainted, at least in the English language.—Byron in *Moore's Life of Byron*.

Burton's *Anatomy of Melancholy* is a valuable work. It is, perhaps, overloaded with quotation ; but there is a great spirit and great power in what Burton says, when he writes from his own mind. It is the only book that ever took me out of bed two hours sooner than I wished to rise.—Dr. Johnson.

Twenty lines of a poet, a dozen lines of a treatise on agriculture, a folio page of heraldry, a description of rare fishes, a paragraph of a sermon on patience, the record of the fever fits of hypochondria, the history of the particle *that*, a scrap of metaphysics,—that is what passes through his brain in a quarter of an hour ; it is a carnival of ideas and phrases—Greek, Latin, German, French, Italian, philosophical, geometrical, medical, poetical, astrological, musical, pedagogical, heaped one upon the other : an enormous medley, a prodigious mass of jumbled quotations, jostling thoughts, with the vivacity and the transport of a feast of unreason. He is never-ending ; words, phrases overflow, are heaped up, overlap each other, and flow on, carrying the reader along, deafened, stunned, half-drowned, unable to touch ground in the deluge. Burton is inexhaustible. There are no ideas which he does not iterate under fifty forms, and when he has exhausted his own, he pours out upon us other men's—the classics, the rarest authors known only to the *savants*—authors rarer still, known only to the learned : he borrows from all.—Henri Taine (*transl.*).

Dr. Richard Busby.

Head-Master of Westminster School: 1606-1695.

I laugh, and wish the hot-brain'd fustian fool
In Busby's hands, to be well lash'd at school.
                          —Earl of Rochester, *An Allusion*.

When Busby's skill, and judgment sage,
Repress'd the poet's frantic rage,
Cropt his luxuriance bold, and blended taught
The flow of numbers with the strength of thought.
   —ROBERT LLOYD, *Ode spoken at Westminster School.*

As we stood before Busby's tomb (in Westminster Abbey), the Knight (Sir Roger de Coverley) uttered himself again in the same manner, "Dr. Busby, a great man! he whipped my grandfather! a very great man! I should have gone to him myself, if I had not been a blockhead; a very great man ".—ADDISON, *The Spectator.*

JOSEPH BUTLER.

Bishop of Durham : 1692-1752.

Born in dissent, and in the school of schism
Bred, he withstood the withering influence
Of that unwholesome nurture. To the Church,
In strength of mind, nature and judgment clear,
A convert, in sincerity of heart
Seeking the truth, deliberately convinced,
And finding there the truth he sought, he came.
In honour must his high desert be held
While there is any virtue, any praise ;
For he it was whose gifted intellect
First apprehended, and developed first
The analogy connate, which in its course
And constitution Nature manifests
To the Creator's word and will divine ;
And in the depth of that great argument
Laying his firm foundation, built thereon
Proofs never to be shaken of the truths
Reveal'd from Heav'n in mercy to mankind ;
Allying thus Philosophy with Faith,
And finding in things seen and known, the type
And evidence of those within the veil.
   —SOUTHEY, *Epitaph on Butler in Bristol Cathedral* (ll. 8—end).

I have learned from four writers far beyond any, perhaps all, others—Butler, Aristotle, Dante, Saint Augustine, my four doctors.—W. E. GLADSTONE, *Life of Manning, Vol. II.*

The solid sense of Butler left the Deism of the Freethinkers not a leg to stand upon. Perhaps, however, he did not remember the wise saying that "a man seemeth right in his own cause, but another cometh after and judgeth him". Hume's Epicurean philosopher adopts the main arguments of the *Analogy*, but unfortunately drives them home to a conclusion of which the good Bishop would hardly have approved.—HUXLEY, *Hume.*

Ninety years subsequent to Gassendi the doctrine of bodily instruments, as it may be called, assumed immense importance in the hands of Bishop Butler, who, in his famous *Analogy of Religion*, developed, from his own point of view, and with consummate sagacity, a similar idea. The Bishop still influences superior minds. . . . This is the key of the Bishop's position; "our organised bodies are no more a part of ourselves than any other matter around us". In proof of this he calls attention to the use of glasses, which "prepare objects" for the percipient power exactly as the eye does. The eye itself is no more percipient than the glass; is quite as much the instrument of the true self, and also as foreign to the true self, as the glass is. "And if we see with our eyes only in the same manner as we do with glasses, the like may justly be concluded from analogy of all our senses."— TYNDALL, *Address before the British Association at Belfast*, 1874.

Now of the poetic religion there is nothing in Butler. No one could tell from his writings that the universe was beautiful. If the world were a Durham mine or an exact square, if no part of it were more expressive than a gravel-pit or a chalk-quarry, the teaching of Butler would be as true as it is now. A young poet, not a very wise one, once said, "he did not like the Bible, there was nothing about flowers in it". He might have said so of Butler with great truth; a most ugly and stupid world one would fancy his books were written in. But in turn and by way of compensation for this, there is a religion of another sort, a religion the source of which is within the mind, as the other's was found to be in the world without; the religion to which we have just now alluded as the religion (by an odd yet expressive way of speaking) of *superstition.*— WALTER BAGEHOT, *Literary Studies, Vol. II.*

Perhaps Butler has scarcely yet been sufficiently appreciated as the champion of "Human Nature". He cast to the winds, not in words exactly, but by implication in almost the whole course of his argument, that doctrine of its total depravity which was held, by some of the best men of his day, with whom on other grounds he would have gladly made common cause. . . . But not only does he recognise our natural affections as so many helps, not hindrances, to our due cultivation of goodwill to men, and our following the moral rule within us, but he holds that even our passions (using the word in its lower sense) may contribute to the same end if kept duly under control. "No passion that God has endowed us with can be in itself evil." Anger, in man's moral constitution, like pain in the natural world, is but an instance of the wisdom and goodness of Him who made us. How bold and wise are these words!— REV. W. L. COLLINS, *Joseph Butler.*

Butler was, I think, the only man of real genius, who, between the Restoration and the Revolution, showed a bitter enmity to the new philosophy, as it was then called.—MACAULAY, *History of England, Vol. I., ch.* 3, *n.*

SAMUEL BUTLER.

English Satirical Poet: 1612-1680.

Unmatch'd by all, save matchless Hudibras.

—BYRON.

Though Butler's wit, Pope's numbers, Prior's ease,
With all that fancy can invent to please
Adorn the polish'd periods as they fall,
One madrigal of theirs is worth them all.

—COWPER, *Table Talk.*

And though sometimes a lucky hit
May give a zest to Butler's wit;
Whatever makes the measure halt
Is beauty seldom, oft a fault.

—ROBERT LLOYD, *On Rhyme.*

But he enfranchis'd from his tutor's care,
Who places Butler near Cervantes' chair.

—DR. JOHN ARMSTRONG, *Taste.*

We grant that Butler ravishes the heart,
As Shakespeare soar'd beyond the reach of art.

—WALTER HARTE, *An Essay on Satire.*

Sir Hudibras talks Babylonian.

—R. A. WILLMOTT, *Advantages of Literature.*

If the French boast the learning of Rabelais, we need not be afraid of confronting them with Butler. If inexhaustible wit could give perpetual pleasure, no eye would ever leave half-read the work of Butler; for what poet has ever brought so many remote images so happily together? It is scarcely possible to peruse a page without finding some association of images that was never found before. By the first paragraph the reader is amused, by the next he is delighted, and by a few more strained to astonishment; but astonishment is a toilsome pleasure; he is soon weary of wondering, and longs to be diverted.—DR. JOHNSON, *Lives of the Poets: Butler.*

Hudibras is an Encyclopædia turned topsy-turvy—a large joking Geography—a Universal History, first reduced to its component parts, and then bound up again in the oddest possible style, and with all its pages awry.—REV. G. GILFILLAN, *Introduction to Butler's Works.*

The perpetual scintillation of Butler's wit is too dazzling to be delightful; and we can seldom read far in *Hudibras* without feeling more fatigue than pleasure. His fancy is employed with the profusion of a spendthrift, by whose eternal round of banqueting his guests are at length rather wearied out than regaled.—SIR WALTER SCOTT, *Prose Works, Vol. I.*

JOHN BYNG.

English Admiral, Executed for Error of Judgment: 1704-1757.

We think the punishment of the Admiral altogether unjust and absurd. Treachery, cowardice, ignorance, amounting to what lawyers have called *crassa ignorantia*, are fit objects of severe penal inflictions. But Byng was not found guilty of treachery, of cowardice, or of gross ignorance of his profession. He died for doing what the most loyal subject, the most intrepid warrior, the most experienced seaman, might have done. He died

for an error in judgment, an error such as the greatest commanders,
Frederic, Napoleon, Wellington, have often committed, and have often
acknowledged.—MACAULAY, *Essays : The Earl of Chatham.*

LORD BYRON.

English Poet : 1788-1824.

He is now at rest ;
And praise and blame fall on his ear alike,
Now dull in death.   Yes, Byron, thou art gone,
Gone like a star that through the firmament
Shot and was lost, in its eccentric course,
Dazzling, perplexing.   Yet thy heart, methinks,
Was generous, noble—noble in its scorn
Of all things low or little ; nothing there
Sordid or servile.

—SAMUEL ROGERS.

Byron ! how sadly sweet thy melody !
Attuning still the soul to tenderness,
As if soft Pity, with unusual stress,
Had touched her plaintive lute, and thou, being by,
Hadst caught the tones, nor suffered them to die.
O'ershading sorrow doth not make thee less
Delightful : thou thy griefs doth dress
With a bright halo, shining beamily,
As when a cloud the golden moon doth veil,
Its sides are tinged with a resplendent glow,
Through the dark robe oft amber rays prevail,
And like fair veins in sable marble flow ;
Still warble, dying swan ! still tell the tale,
The enchanting tale, the tale of pleasing woe.

—KEATS, *To Byron.*

When Byron's eyes were shut in death,
We bow'd our head and held our breath.
He taught us little ; but our soul
Had *felt* him like the thunder's roll.

—MATTHEW ARNOLD, *Memorial Verses.*

What helps it now, that Byron bore,
With haughty scorn which mock'd the smart,
Through Europe to the Æolian shore
The pageant of his bleeding heart ?
That thousands counted every groan,
And Europe made his woe her own ?

—*Id., Stanzas from the Grand Chartreuse.*

Nay, Byron, nay ! not under where we tread,
Dumb weight of stone, lies thine imperial head !
Into no vault lethargic, dark and dank
The splendid strength of thy swift spirit sank :

No narrow church in precincts cold and grey
Confines the plume that loved to breast the day;
Thy self-consuming, scathing heart of flame
Was quenched to feed no silent coffin's shame!
A fierce, glad fire in buoyant hearts art thou,
A radiance in auroral spirits now;
A stormy wind, an ever-sounding ocean;
A life, a power, a never-wearying motion!
Or deadly gloom, or terrible despair.
An earthquake-mockery of strong creeds that were
Assured possession of calm earth and sky,
Where doom-distraught pale souls took sanctuary,
As in strong temples. The same blocks shall build,
Iconoclast, the edifice you spilled,
More durable, more fair. O Scourge of God,
It was Himself who urged thee on thy road.
—RODEN NOEL, *Byron's Grave.*

Did not Byron's heart and soul overflow with all manly and humane affections, in spite of spite, and during the very disease of rancour? Is not one love-poem of his, breathed one hour, and forgotten by him the next, worth all the drivelling of you and all the other amiable characters in the kingdom, were you to drivel amatory effusions till the rheum ceased to flow from your over-aged eyes? What although he libelled his way through society, from the King upon the throne to the very meanest of his subjects? All the world loves his memory.—JOHN WILSON, *Essays: Streams.*

It is in this contrast between his august conceptions of man, and his contemptuous opinion of men, that much of the almost incomprehensible charm, and power, and enchantment of his poetry exists. We feel ourselves alternately sunk and elevated, as if the hand of an invisible being had command over us. At one time we are a little lower than the angels; in another, but little higher than the worms. We feel that our elevation and our disgrace are alike the lot of our nature; and hence the poetry of Byron . . . is read as a dark, but still a divine revelation.—*Id., Ibid.: Wordsworth.*

Byron hits the mark where I don't even pretend to fledge my arrow.—SIR WALTER SCOTT.

What Goethe has said of Byron I believe to be true, *viz.,* "He was essentially a born poet". He had very little art, very little of the ordinary knowledge which is essential to most writers, whether in prose or verse.—LYTTON, *Essays: Knowledge of the World.*

Lord Byron founded what may be called an esoteric Lake school; and all the readers of verse in England, we might say in Europe, hastened to sit at his feet. What Mr. Wordsworth had said like a recluse, Lord Byron said like a man of the world, with less profound feeling, but with more perspicuity, energy, and conciseness.—MACAULAY, *Essays: Moore's "Life of Lord Byron".*

The mass of sentimental literature, concerned with the analysis and description of emotion, headed by the poetry of Byron, is altogether of lower rank than the literature which merely describes what it saw. The

true Seer always feels as intensely as any one else ; but he does not much
describe his feelings.—RUSKIN, *Modern Painters, Vol. III.*

Among the many good-going gentlemen and ladies, Byron is generally
spoken of with horror—he is " so wicked," forsooth ; while poor Shelley,
" poor dear Shelley," is " very wrong, of course," but " so refined," " so
beautiful," " so tender "—a fallen angel, while Byron is a satyr and a devil.
We boldly deny the verdict.   Neither of the two are devils ; as for angels,
when we have seen one, we shall be better able to give an opinion ; at
present, Shelley is in our eyes far less like one of those old Hebrew and
Miltonic angels, fallen or unfallen, than Byron is.—KINGSLEY, *Literary
and General Lectures.*

His acute sensibility, intellectual independence, profound thought, and
giant soul, would have fitted Lord Byron to become the model of an
European poet, had not calumny, envy, and the lack of all response to his
own aspiration among the men of his time, driven him into the isolation
of despair.—MAZZINI, *Life and Writings, Vol. II.*

Under a thin disguise of name, country, and outward incident, they
[the poems] present us with the desires which actuated, the passions
which agitated, and the characters which were the ideals of the fashionable men and women of the earlier part of this century. Limited and
monotonous as they are in their essential nature, ringing perpetual changes
upon one passion and one phase of passion, the brilliance of their diction,
the voluptuous melody of their verse, the picturesque beauty of their
scenery, well enough represent that life of the richer classes, which chases
with outstretched arms all the Protean forms of pleasure, only to find the
subtle essence escape as soon as grasped, leaving behind in its place
weariness, disappointment, and joyless stagnation. . . . And so, into
whatever field the wide and restless energies of men like Lord Byron
carry them, they bring home no treasures that will endure—no marble of
which world-lasting statue or palace may be hewn or built—no iron, of
which world-subduing machines may be wrought.—GEORGE BRIMLEY,
Essays.

His passion for glory was not of the genuine stamp ; he thirsted not so
much for fame as for celebrity—celebrity at any price. This was the
true end and purpose of his life, though he here and there denies it. He
knew . . . only too well, that the eyes of the world were fixed upon him,
and he did his utmost to maintain the fascination. He stood before the
world as before a mirror, and the *pose* became at last a second nature ;
he lived, as it were, on the stage, and coquetted with the world. Although
he pretended to despise it, he could not live without its admiration, which
he claimed even for his faults.— KARL ELZE, *Life of Lord Byron.*

Byron lived longer and produced more than his brother poets. Yet he
was extinguished when his genius was still ascendant, when his swift and
fair creations were issuing like worlds from an archangel's hands.—
J. ADDINGTON SYMONDS, *Shelley.*

If it could be shown that all the evil things said of Byron fall short of
the truth, his writings would be no less delightful ; could he be proved to
have been as pious as Heber, his poetry would be none the better.—
J. CORDY JEAFFRESON, *The Real Lord Byron, Vol. II.*

Byron's mind was, like his own ocean, sublime in its yesty madness, beautiful in its glittering summer brightness, mighty in the lone magnificence of its waste of waters, gazed upon from the magic of its own nature, yet capable of representing, but as in a glass darkly, the natures of all others.—LORD BEACONSFIELD.

It was, I think, pure gain for Byron to be no mere bookman, hide-bound in calf, instead of human skin, and treating the universe as so much docile material for such as he to make pretty little things out of. He was a Berserker, whose wild spirit found vent in song, and his was a bleeding human heart, even though he made of it " a pageant ". What he does has the salt breath of impetuously moving sea, the thrill of warm-blooded life; his fervid voice has the living accent.—RODEN NOEL, *Life of Lord Byron.*

It was an easy thing for Lord Byron to be a great poet; it was merely indulging his nature; he was an eagle and must fly; but to have curbed his wilful humour, soothed his fretful discontent, and learned to behave like a reasonable being and a gentleman, that was a difficult matter, which he does not seem ever seriously to have attempted. His life, therefore, with all his genius, and fits of occasional sublimity, was, on the whole, a terrible failure, and a great warning to all who are willing to take a lesson.—J. STUART BLACKIE, *On Self-Culture.*

In the last great episode of his own career Byron was as lofty as the noblest side of his creed. The historic feeling for the unseen benefactors of old time was matched by vehemence of sympathy with the struggles for liberation of his own day. And for this, history will not forget him. Though he may have no place in our own Minster, he assuredly belongs to the band of far-shining men, of whom Pericles declared the whole world to be the tomb.—JOHN MORLEY, *Miscellanies, Vol. I.*

Byron has no relation to the master-minds whose works reflect a nation or an era, and who keep their own secrets. His verse and prose is alike biographical, and the inequalities of his style are those of his career. He lived in a glass case, and could not hide himself by his habit of burning blue lights. He was too great to do violence to his nature, which was not great enough to be really consistent. It was thus natural for him to pose as the spokesman of two ages—as a critic and as an author; and of two orders of society—as a peer, and as a poet of revolt. Sincere in both, he could never forget the one character in the other. To the last, he was an aristocrat in sentiment, a democrat in opinion. . . . This scion of a long line of lawless bloods—a Scandinavian Berserker, if there ever was one— the literary heir of the Eddas—was specially created to wage that war—to smite the conventionality which is the tyrant of England with the hammer of Thor, and to sear with the sarcasm of Mephistopheles the hollow hypocrisy—sham taste, sham morals, sham religion—of the society by which he was surrounded and infected, and which all but succeeded in seducing him. But for the ethereal essence,—

> The fount of fiery life
> Which served for that Titanic strife,

Byron would have been merely a more melodious Moore and a more accomplished Brummel. But the caged lion was only half tamed, and his continual growls were his redemption.—JOHN NICHOL, *Life of Byron.*

CAIUS JULIUS CÆSAR.

Roman Dictator : B.C. 100-44.

This Julius to the Capitolie wente
Upon a day, as he was wonte to gon,
And in the Capitolie anon him hente
This false Brutus and his other soon,
And stiked him with bodekins anon
With many a wound.

—CHAUCER, *The Monkes Tale.*

Antony : " O mighty Cæsar ! dost thou lie so low ?
Are all thy conquests, glories, triumphs, spoils,
Shrunk to this little measure ?   Fare thee well.
I know not, gentlemen, what you intend,
Who else must be let blood, who else is rank ;
If I myself, there is no hour so fit
As Cæsar's death-hour ; nor no instrument
Of half that worth as those your swords, made rich
With the most noble blood of all this world."

—SHAKESPERE, *Julius Cæsar.*

Antony : " Here was a Cæsar ! when comes such another ?
Never, never ! "

—*Id., Ibid.*

There Cæsar, grac'd with both Minervas, shone ;
Cæsar, the world's great master, and his own.

—POPE, *The Temple of Fame.*

The laurel wreaths were first by Cæsar worn,
And still they Cæsar's successors adorn :
One leaf of this is immortality,
And more of worth than all the world can buy.

—DRYDEN, *The Flower and the Leaf.*

That Julius, with ambitious thoughts,
Had virtues too, his foes could find ;
These equal him in all his faults,
But never in his noble mind.

—SHEFFIELD, DUKE OF BUCKINGHAMSHIRE, *Chorus III,*
in Marcus Brutus.

Or to the nobler Cæsar, on whose brow
O'er daring vice deluding virtue smil'd,
And who no less a vein superior scorn'd.
Both bled but bled in vain.

—THOMSON, *Liberty.*

When Cæsar in the senate fell,
Did not the sun eclips'd foretell,
And in resentment of his slaughter,
Look'd pale for almost a year after ?

—SAMUEL BUTLER, *Hudibras.*

Cæsar—the greatest man of ancient times.—LORD BROUGHAM, *Statesmen of the Time of George III., Vol II.*

Cæsar was endowed with every great and noble quality that could exalt human nature, and give a man the ascendant in society ; formed to excel in peace, as well as war ; provident in council ; fearless in action ; and executing what he had resolved with an amazing celerity ; generous beyond measure to his friends ; placable to his enemies ; and for parts, learning, eloquence, scarce inferior to any man.—DR. CONYERS MIDDLETON.

Did not Julius Cæsar show himself as much of a man in conducting his campaigns as in composing his Commentaries ?—HAZLITT, *Table Talk.*

In this class three men stand pre-eminent, Cæsar, Cromwell and Bonaparte. The highest place in this remarkable triumvirate belongs undoubtedly to Cæsar. He united the talents of Bonaparte to those of Cromwell ; and he possessed also, what neither Cromwell nor Bonaparte possessed, learning, taste, wit, eloquence, the sentiments and the manners of an accomplished gentleman.—MACAULAY, *Essays : Hallam's " Constitutional History ".*

CALIGULA.

Roman Emperor : 12-41.

So wise Caligula, in days of yore,
His helmet fill'd with pebbles on the shore,
Swore he had rifled ocean's richest spoils,
And claim'd a trophy for his martial toils.
—DAVID MALLET, Of Verbal Criticism.

The ladies prove averse,
And more untoward to be won
Than by Caligula the moon.
—SAMUEL BUTLER, Hudibras, Part III.

So th' Emperor Caligula,
That triumph'd o'er the British sea,
Took crabs and oysters prisoners,
And lobsters, 'stead of cuirassiers ;
Engag'd his legions in fierce bustles,
With periwinkles, prawns, and mussles,
And led his troops with furious gallops,
To charge whole regiments of scallops.

—Id., Ibid.

JOHN CALVIN.

Swiss Reformer : 1509-1564.

One thinks, on Calvin Heaven's own Spirit fell ;
Another deems him instrument of Hell.
If Calvin feel Heaven's blessing, or its rod,
This cries there is, and that, there is no, God.
—POPE, Essay on Man, Epistle IV.

But Calvin's dogma shall my lips deride?
In that stern faith my angel Mary died.
　　　　　—OLIVER WENDELL HOLMES, *A Rhymed Lesson.*

No one can suppose that Calvin did not deem that the angels smiled
approbation when he burned Servetus.—LYTTON, *Essays : Self-Control.*

Calvin was incomparably the wisest man that ever the French Church
enjoyed.—RICHARD HOOKER.

Calvin has been taxed with fierceness and bigotry. But his meekness
and benevolence were as eminent as the malice of his traducers is shame-
less.—TOPLADY.

Nevertheless, for hard times, hard men are needed, and intellects which
can pierce to the roots where truth and lies part company. It fares ill
with the soldiers of religion when " the accursed thing " is in their camp.
And this is to be said of Calvin, that so far as the state of knowledge
permitted, no eye could have detected more keenly the unsound spots in
the received creed of the Church, nor was there reformer in Europe so
resolute to exercise, tear our, and destroy what was distinctly seen to be
false—so resolute to establish what was true in its place, and make truth
to the last fibre of it the rule of practical life.—J. A. FROUDE, *Calvinism.*

Unless I can get from you some of your moderate and charitable and
two-sided notions, I shall begin to regard Calvin as a child of the Devil,
and Calvinism as the upas-tree, which Satan planted in the Lord's garden
at the Reformation to poison all with its shade. The influence of
Calvinism abroad seems to me to have been uniformly ruinous, destructive
equally of political and moral life, a blot and a scandal on the Reformation ;
and now that it has at last got the upper hand in England, can we say
much more for it ?—KINGSLEY, *Letter to F. D. Maurice.*

There was an infinite amount of what was good and noble about him,
despite his own ingenuous confession, to which the episode of Servetus
attaches force, that he was " a ferocious beast, animated by great and
numerous vices".—REV. F. ARNOLD, *Reminiscences of a Literary and
Clerical Life, Vol. I.*

History, as Döllinger has said, is no simple game of abstractions ; men
are more than doctrines. It is not a certain theory of grace that makes
the Reformation ; it is Luther, it is Calvin. Calvin shaped the mould in
which the bronze of Puritanism was cast. That commanding figure, of
such vast power yet somehow with so little lustre, by his unbending will,
his pride, his severity, his French spirit of system, his gift for government,
for legislation, for dialectic in every field, his incomparable industry and
persistence, had conquered a more than pontifical ascendancy in the
Protestant world. He meets us in England, as in Scotland, Holland,
France, Switzerland, and the rising England across the Atlantic. He
was dead (1564) a generation before Cromwell was born, but his influence
was still at its height. Nothing less than to create in man a new nature
was his far-reaching aim, to regenerate character, to simplify and con-
solidate religious faith. . . . It is a theory that might have been expected
to sink men crouching and paralysed into the blackest abysses of despair,
and it has in fact been answerable for much anguish in many a human
heart. Still Calvinism has proved itself a famous soil for rearing heroic

natures. Founded on St. Paul and on Augustine . . . Calvinism exalted its votaries to a pitch of heroic moral energy that has never been surpassed.
—JOHN MORLEY, *Oliver Cromwell.*

WILLIAM CAMDEN.

English Antiquary : 1551-1623.

Camden, most reverend head, to whom I owe
All that I am in arts, all that I know.
     —BEN JONSON, *Epigram to William Camden.*

Cambden ! the nourice of Antiquity,
And lanthorn unto late succeeding age,
To see the light of simple verity,
Buried in ruines, through the great outrage
Of her own people, led with warlike rage ;
Cambden ! though time all monuments obscure,
Yet thy just labours ever shall endure.
     —SPENSER, *The Ruines of Time.*

THOMAS CAMPBELL.

Scottish Poet : 1777-1844.

Why, how now, saucy Tom ?
If you thus must ramble,
I will publish some
Remarks on Mister Campbell.
     —BYRON, *Bowles and Campbell.*

Come forth, O Campbell ! give thy talents scope ;
Who dares aspire if thou must cease to hope.
     —*Id., English Bards and Scotch Reviewers.*

But many admire it, the English pentameter,
And Campbell, I think, wrote most commonly worse,
With less nerve, swing, and fire in the same kind of verse.
     —J. R. LOWELL, *A Fable for Critics.*

The lyric fire of Campbell.—SIR ARCHIBALD ALISON, *Essays : the Greek Drama.*

Campbell was himself a master in a distinct school of poetry, and distinguished by a very peculiar and fastidious style of composition.——LORD JEFFREY, *Essays.*

Thomas Campbell is the other pet poet—the last of all the flock. Ay —he, we allow, is a star that will know no setting ; but of this we can assure the world . . . that were Mr. Campbell's soul deified, and a star in the sky, and told by Apollo, who placed him in the blue region, that Scott and Byron were both buried somewhere between the Devil and the Deep Sea, he, the author of *Lochiel's Warning,* would either leap from heaven in disdain, or nsist on there being instanter one triple constellation. What to do with his friend Mr. Rogers, it might not be easy for Mr.

Campbell to imagine or propose at such a critical juncture; but we think it probable that he would hint to Apollo, on the appearance of his Lordship and the Baronet, that the Banker, with a few other pretty poets, might be permitted to scintillate away to all eternity as their—Tail.—JOHN WILSON, *Essays: Days Departed.*

What a pity it is that Campbell does not write more and oftener, and give full sweep to his genius! He has wings that would bear him to the skies; and he does, now and then, spread them grandly, but folds them up again, and resumes his perch, as if he was afraid to launch away.— SIR WALTER SCOTT, *Lockhart's Life, Vol. I.*

Campbell was greatly more of a poet in faculty than he was in fact and performance. Few men have approached nearer to a poet in the former respect than he did; and it was only his almost morbid delicacy of taste, of tact, and of ear, and his extreme fastidiousness, which prevented him from turning his powers to much greater practical results than he did. No man ever enjoyed so high and wide a poetical reputation upon so slender an amount of actual performance, and yet no man ever deserved his reputation more truly than Campbell did. Had it not been so, he would have done more; and, perhaps, have done better. But he had none of that vulgar hungering and hankering after fame which, write what they will to the contrary, no real poet ever felt as anything more than a momentary aspiration. Campbell knew and felt that he was a poet; and as the world in some sort assented to his own faith on this point, he was content "to know no more". . . . *Tom* Campbell was a very good fellow, and a very pleasant one withal; but he prevented Thomas Campbell from being a great poet, though not from doing great things in poetry.—P. G. PATMORE, *My Friends and Acquaintances, Vol. I.*

GEORGE CANNING.

English Prime Minister: 1770-1827.

Even this thy genius, Canning! may permit,
Who, bred a statesman, still wast born a wit,
And never, even in that dull House, couldst tame
To unleaven'd prose thine own poetic flame;
Our last, our best, our only orator,
Even I can praise thee—Tories do no more.
                              —BYRON, *The Age of Bronze.*

Or, like Canning, have silenced and charm'd a tumultuous Senate,
When to the height of his theme, the consummate Orator rising,
Makes our Catilines pale, and rejoices the friends of their country.
                              —ROBERT SOUTHEY, *A Vision of Judgment.*

I was bred under the shadow of the great name of Canning.—W. E. GLADSTONE.

The death of the Premier is announced—late George Canning—the witty, the accomplished, the ambitious; he who had toiled thirty years, and involved himself in the most harassing discussions, to attain this dizzy height; he who had held it for three months of intrigue and obloquy —and now a heap of dust, and that is all.—SIR WALTER SCOTT in LOCKHART, *Life of Scott.*

Canning's wit is infallible. It is never out of time or place, and is finely proportioned to its object. Has he a good-natured, gentlemanly, well-educated blockhead—say of the landed interest—to make ridiculous, he does it so pleasantly, that the Esquire joins in the general smile. Is it a coarse calculating dunce of the mercantile school, he suddenly hits him such a heavy blow on the organ of number, that the stunned economist is unable to sum up the total of the whole. Would some pert prig of the profession be facetious overmuch, Canning ventures to the very borders of vulgarity, and discomforts him with an old Joe. Doth some mouthing member of the mediocrity sport orator, and make use of a dead tongue, then the classical secretary runs him through and through with apt quotations, and before the member feels himself wounded, the whole House sees that he is a dead man.—JOHN WILSON, *Noctes Ambrosianæ*, *Vol. I.*

First Canning, and then Brougham, may be said, for a certain time, to have represented, more than any other individuals, the common Intellectual Spirit; and the interest usually devoted to the imaginative, was transferred to the real.—LYTTON, *England and the English: Intellectual Spirit.*

I never saw Mr. Canning but once, but I can recollect it but as yesterday, when I listened to almost the last accents—I may say the dying words—of that great man. I can recall the lightning flash of that eye, and the tumult of that ethereal brow ; still lingers in my ear the melody of that voice.—LORD BEACONSFIELD.

Canning, a great master of sparkling fancy and of playful sarcasm.— W. E. H. LECKY, *History of England, Vol. I.*

Men not measures—in these three words the political creed of George Canning is summed up. It mattered little to him whether a man was Whig or Tory, Papist or Protestant, provided that in seasons of crisis he knew how to mould circumstances to the best advantage, to inspire confidence in his followers, and to do battle against the common danger till it bites the dust. History teaches us that in this maxim of Canning there is no little truth.—A. C. EWALD, *Representative Statesmen, Vol. II.*

ANTONIO CANOVA.

Italian Sculptor: 1757-1822.

Thy decay
Is still impregnate with divinity,
Which gilds it with revivifying ray ;
Such as the great of yore, Canova is to-day.
                    —BYRON, *Childe Harold's Pilgrimage.*

CANUTE.

King of Denmark and England: 994-1035.

A pleasant music floats along the mere,
From monks in Ely chanting service high,
While as Canute the King is rowing by
" My oarsmen," quoth the mighty King, " draw near,
That we the sweet song of the monks may hear ".
                    —WORDSWORTH, *Canute.*

No:—the wild wave contemns your sceptred hand;—
It roll'd not back when Canute gave command.
—-CAMPBELL.

Now at Xerxes and Knut we all laugh, yet our foot
With the same wave is wet that mocked Xerxes and Knut.
—J. R. LOWELL, *A Fable for Critics.*

King Canute died.   Encoffined he was laid.
Of Aarhus came the Bishop prayers to say,
And sang a hymn upon his tomb, and held
That Canute was a saint—Canute the Great,
That from his memory breathed celestial perfume,
And that they saw him, they the priests, in glory,
Seated at God's right hand, a prophet crowned.
—VICTOR HUGO, *Poems collected by H. L. Williams.*

CARACTACUS.

King of the Silures : fl. 50.

All which his sonne Careticus awhile
Shall well defend and Saxons powre suppresse,
Untill a straunger king from unknowne soyle
Arriving, him with multitude oppresse.
—SPENSER, *The Faerie Queene.*

The spirit of Caractacus defends
The patriots, animates their glorious task :—
Amazement runs before the towering casque
Of Arthur, bearing through the stormy field
The Virgin sculptured on his Christian shield.
—WORDSWORTH, *Struggle of the Britons.*

THOMAS CARLYLE.

English Philosopher and Historian : 1795-1881.

To compare with Plato would be vastly fairer.
Carlyle's the more burly, but E. [Emerson] is the rarer.
—J. R. LOWELL, *A Fable for Critics.*

She is talking æsthetics, the dear clever creature ;
Upon man and his functions she speaks with a smile,
Her ideas are divine upon Art, upon Nature,
The Sublime, the Heroic, and Mr. Carlyle.
—OWEN MEREDITH (LORD LYTTON), *Midges.*

Gods spring from dust, and Hero-Worship wakes.
Out of that Past the humble Present makes.
—LYTTON, *The New Timon.*

Shoddy : " And mighty Carlyle, whose Cyclopean skull,
Encloses forges, and furnaces, and foundries
Of molten metallic thought."

5

Gas :   " Is he a poet ? "
Shoddy : " Aye Sir, a poet, a very Vesuvius,
A deep of song, an intellectual ocean,
Wherein Leviathan disports himself,
And at each breath snorts water-spouts of thought,
Clothed in hues of myriad-tinted rainbows ! "
Gas : " 'Tis true, he's a whole Typhos, hundred-headed,
Whose jerks and throes breed earthquakes ; but his style
Is rather addicted to hobbling. Is it not ? "
Shoddy : " 'Tis a divine and transcendental hobbling !
Rough, smoke-begrimed, and haggard like old Vulcan,
He has his charms, for Venus is his spouse,
And the three graces ever move around him.
His forged words are spears, and shields and swords,
And helmets terror-crested Gorgon-like :—
Meet armour for an age of heroic workers ! "
                    —MILO MAHAN, *Yorkshireman in Boston.*

The pure lightning of Carlyle. . . . I find Carlyle's stronger thinking colouring mine continually ; and should be very sorry if I did not ; otherwise I should have read him to little purpose.—RUSKIN, *Modern Painters, Vol. III.*

Carlyle was a man from his youth, an author who did not need to hide from his readers, and as absolute a man of the world, unknown and exiled on that hill-farm, as if holding on his own terms what is best in London. —EMERSON, *First Visit to England.*

As a representative author, a literary figure, no man else will bequeath to the future more significant hints of our stormy era, its fierce paradoxes, its din, and its struggling periods, than Carlyle. He belongs to our own branch of the stock, too ; neither Latin nor Greek, but altogether Gothic. Rugged, mountainous, volcanic, he was himself more a French Revolution than any of his volumes. . . . As launching into the self-complacent atmosphere of our days a rasping, questioning, dislocating agitation and shock, is Carlyle's final value.—WALT WHITMAN, *Specimen Days.*

No surer does the Auldgarth bridge, that his father helped to build, carry the traveller over the turbulent water beneath it, than Carlyle's books convey the reader over chasms and confusions, where before there was no way, or only an inadequate one.—JOHN BURROUGHS.

Carlyle is an old Hebrew prophet, who goes to prince and beggar, and says, " If you do this or that you will go to Hell, not the hell the priests talk of—but a hell on this earth ".—KINGSLEY, *Letters and Memoirs, Vol. I.*

St. Thomas Coprostom, late of Craigenputtock and Chelsea. . . . The Gospel according to St. Coprostom has the invaluable merit of pungent eccentricity and comparatively novel paradox. The evangelist of " golden silence "—whose own speech, it may be admitted, was " quite other " than " silvern "—is logically justified in his blatant but ineffable contempt for the dull old doctrines of mere mercy and righteousness, of liberty that knows no higher law than duty, of duty that depends for its existence on the existence of liberty.—SWINBURNE, *A Study of Victor Hugo.*

Thomas Carlyle, it is true, puts on the gloves with the ostensible and single purpose of covering the fair fame of a friend [Sterling]; but his foot once in the ring, his arm once fairly raised, and he thinks of nothing but punishing the foe. And what a foe! We may doubt the prudence of the undertaking, but who shall question the valour of the man who, single-handed, takes upon himself to thrash the whole world?—SAMUEL PHILLIPS, *Essays from " The Times "*.

Carlyle, the apostle of agnostic stoicism.—FRANCIS DE PRESSENSE, *Cardinal Manning*.

One of those enquiring minds, who are to history what excavators are to monuments—Thomas Carlyle.—LAMARTINE, *Celebrated Characters (transl.), Vol. II*.

Mr. Carlyle is no homœopathist; he never administers remedies for evil in infinitesimal doses; he never pollutes the sacredness of thought by out-ward concession or compromise with error. . . . There is profit for us in the very errors of a writer like Carlyle.—MAZZINI, *Life and Writings, Vol. IV*.

The most obvious of all remarks about Carlyle is one expressed (I think) by Sir Henry Taylor in the phrase that he was a " Calvinist who had lost his creed ". Rather we should say he was Calvinist who had dropped the dogmas out of his creed.—LESLIE STEPHEN, *Hours in a Library, Vol. III*.

Carlyle's dazzling effects of white light are frequently surrounded by the blackest gloom.—J. COTTER MORISON, *Life of Macaulay*.

Carlylism is the male of Byronism. It is Byronism with thew and sinew, bass pipe and shaggy bosom.—JOHN MORLEY, *Miscellanies, Vol. I*.

Carlyle's style is Carlylese. It would be the most affected of affectations for any one else to write in it. To him it was perfectly natural—as natural as the Miltonic style was to Milton. And that is its sufficient vindication. It was the only style in which he could deliver his prophetic message.—W. S. LILLY, *Four English Humourists*.

Carlyle cannot be killed by an epigram, nor can the many influences that moulded him be referred to any single source. The rich banquet his genius has spread for us is of many courses. . . . Carlyle's eye was indeed a terrible organ: he saw everything.—AUGUSTINE BIRRELL, *Obiter Dicta, First Series*.

Carlyle no doubt was a great talker—no man talked against talk or broke silence to praise it more eloquently than he, but unfortunately none of it is in evidence. All that is given us is a sort of Commination Service writ large. We soon weary of it. Man does not live by curses alone.—*Id., Ibid., Second Series*.

The dominant stratum of Carlyle's character was morality, hard Scotch granite, out of which the sweetest waters could break, and on whose top soil the tenderest seedlings could thrive—humour, pathos, poetry, the most subduing gentleness, all were there; but the main formation of his mind was all the same vehement sternness, with more than a touch of the Pharisaism that metes and judges, and swears by the law rather than the gospel. He had little love of music, no love of art, and considerable contempt for any poetry but the poetry of action.—W. J. Dawson, *Quest and Vision.*

Carlyle, if not the greatest prose master of our age, must be held to be, by virtue of his original genius and mass of stroke, the literary Dictator of Victorian prose. And, though we all know how wantonly he often misused his mighty gift, though no one would venture to imitate him even at a distance, and though Matthew Arnold was ever taking up his parable —"Flee Carlylese as the very Devil!"—we are sliding into Carlylese unconsciously from time to time, and even *Culture* itself fell into the trap in the very act of warning others.—Frederic Harrison, *Studies in Early Victorian Literature.*

Shelley works his will with language gracefully, as one guides a spirited steed; Carlyle with convulsive effort, as one hammers a red-hot bar, but in both cases the end is achieved. The two should be painted, like Plato and Verulam in the Palace of Art, as twin masters of speech, if such masters have pupils. But such power is not granted for the expression of vain and shallow thought, and whoever shares their gift will stand by their side. . . . But it is not as a man of letters that we would chiefly think of Carlyle, nor is it in his study that we would part with him. Great and deathless writer as he was, he will be honoured by posterity for his influence on human life, rather than for his supremacy as a literary artist. "The way to test how much he has left his country," says a great writer of another country, "were to consider, or try to consider, for a moment, the array of British thought, the resultant *ensemble* of the last fifty years, as existing to-day, but with Carlyle left out. It would be like an army with no artillery." The true legend for his monument is the dying witness of John Sterling: "Towards England no man has been and done like you".—Richard Garnett, *Carlyle.*

Carlyle adopted the stirring and dignified hypothesis, that the working of the universe is informed with purpose, that, come how it may, good in the end must be the final goal of ill; and if this be true, *Laborare est orare* is not the stern incredible creed it would appear.—P. Anderson Graham, *Nature in Books.*

In one sense, Carlyle was as a city set upon a hill, that cannot be hid; in another, he was an "open secret," hid by the very simplicity of his unconscious disguises, the frank perversities whose meaning could be known only by those close enough to hear the heart-beat beneath them; and many who have fancied that they had him rightly labelled with some moody utterance, or safely pigeon-holed in some outbreak of a soul acquainted with grief, will be found to have measured the oak by its mistletoe. . . . Graduation from "Carlyle Close," now a shamble, to the highest intellectual distinction of the nineteenth century implies the realization of several worlds dim to others. Out of a depth like this his voice will always go forth, and to it the deeps will always answer. The influence of Carlyle will never "stop": wherever shams are falling, his sturdy blows will still be heard; generations of the free will recognize that they are offspring of the fire in his heart, burning all fetters; and when the morning stars sing together of dawning days, when heroes of humanity replace nobles without nobility and bauble-crowned kings, his voice, so long a burden of pain, will be heard again rising into song. —Moncure Conway, *Thomas Carlyle.*

JOHN CARTERET, EARL OF GRANVILLE.

Lord-Lieutenant of Ireland : 1690-1763.

Go, Carteret, go ; and, with thee, go along
The nation's blessing, and the poet's song ;
Loud acclamations, with melodious rays,
The kindest wishes, and sincerest praise.
—AMBROSE PHILIPS, *To Lord Carteret.*

No public man of that age had greater courage, greater ambition, greater activity, greater talents for debate, or for declamation. No public man had such profound and extensive learning. He was familiar with the ancient writers, and loved to sit up till midnight discussing philological and metrical questions with Bentley. His knowledge of modern languages was prodigious. The privy council, when he was present, needed no interpreter. He spoke and wrote French, Italian, Spanish, Portuguese, German, even Swedish. . . . With all his learning, Carteret was far from being a pedant. His was not one of those cold spirits of which the fire is put out by the fuel. In council, in debate, in society, he was all life and energy.—MACAULAY, *Essays : Horace Walpole.*

CASSIUS LONGINUS.

Roman Tribune of the People : d. B.C. 42.

Cæsar : " Let me have men about me that are fat ;
Sleek-headed men, and such as sleep o' nights :
Yond Cassius has a lean and hungry look ;
He thinks too much : such men are dangerous."
Antony : " Fear him not, Cæsar ; he's not dangerous ;
He is a noble Roman, and well given."
Cæsar : " Would he were fatter ! but I fear him not :
Yet if my name were liable to fear,
I do not know the man I should avoid
So soon as that spare Cassius."
—SHAKESPEARE, *Julius Cæsar.*

Titinius : " But Cassius is no more. O setting sun,
As in thy red rays thou dost sink to-night,
So in his red blood Cassius' day is set,
The sun of Rome is set."

—*Id., Ibid.*

LORD ROBERT CASTLEREAGH.

English Statesman : 1769-1822.

Oh Castlereagh ! thou art a patriot now ;
Cato died for his country, so didst thou :
He perished rather than see Rome enslaved,
Thou cutt'st thy throat that Britain may be saved.
—LORD BYRON, *Epigram.*

And ne'er (enough) lamented Castlereagh,
Whose pen-knife slit a goose-quill t'other day.
                    —LORD BYRON, *The Age of Bronze.*

Lord Castlereagh is certainly the most striking example of the effects produced by our Parliamentary system of Government in most unjustly lowering the reputation of public men who happen not to succeed in debate.—LORD BROUGHAM, *Statesmen of the Time of George III., Vol. II.*

I would rather be Lord Castlereagh, as far as a sense of power is concerned (principle is out of the question), than such a man as Mr. Canning, who is a mere fluent sophist, and never knows the limits of discretion.—HAZLITT, *Table Talk.*

LUCIUS SERGIUS CATILINE.

Roman Patrician: B.C. 109-62.

Reason the bias turns to good from ill,
And Nero reigns a Titus if he will.
The fiery soul abhorr'd in Catiline,
In Decius charms, in Curtius is divine.
                         —POPE, *Essay on Man.*

Shall treason walk? shall proud oppression yoke
The neck of virtue! Lo the wretch abash'd,
Self-betray'd Catiline!
                    —DYER, *The Ruins of Rome.*

Waiting till discord havoc cries,
In hopes, like Catiline, to rise
On anarchy to pow'r!
                    —EDWARD MOORE, *The Discovery.*

MARCUS PORTIUS CATO.

Roman Philosopher: B.C. 95-46.

All that the sun surveys subdued,
   But Cato's mighty mind.
How grand! most true; yet far beneath
   The soul of the resign'd,

To more than kingdoms, more than worlds,
   To passion that gives law;
Its matchless empire could have kept
   Great Cato's pride in awe.
                    —YOUNG, *Resignation.*

Unconquer'd Cato, virtuous in extreme.
                    —THOMSON, *The Seasons: Winter.*

Describe his awful look, and God-like mind,
And Cæsar's power with Cato's virtue join'd.
                    —ADDISON, *Cato: A Tragedy.*

But where shall Cato's praise begin or end;
Inclin'd to melt, and yet untaught to bend,
The firmest patriot, and the gentlest friend?
How great his genius.
 —George Jeffreys, *Recommendatory Poem of Addison's " Cato ".*

And Cato, dying, seem'd to own he fear'd.
       —Prior, *Carmen Seculare.*

Had Cato bent beneath the conquering cause,
He might have liv'd to give new senates laws;
But on vile terms disdaining to be great,
He perish'd by his choice, and not his fate.
   —Lord Lansdowne, *Occasioned by the foregoing Verses.*

Once Cato's virtue did the gods oppose;
While they the victor, he the vanquish'd chose.
      —Dryden, *Epistle III.*

Even by the rule of that philosophy,
By which I did blame Cato for the death
Which he did give himself: I know not how,
But I do find it cowardly and vile.
     —Shakespeare, *Julius Cæsar.*

If we consider the character of Cato without prejudice, he was certainly a great and worthy man; a friend to truth, virtue, liberty; yet false by measuring all duty by the absurd vigour of the stoical rule, he was generally disappointed of the end which he sought by it, the happiness both of his private and public life. . . . The last act of his life was agreeable to his nature and philosophy: when he could no longer be what he had been; or when the ills of life overbalanced the good; which, by the principles of his sect, was a just cause for dying; he put an end to his life with a spirit and resolution which would make one imagine that he was glad to have found an occasion of dying in his proper character. On the whole, his life was rather admirable than amiable; fit to be praised, rather than imitated.—Dr. Conyers Middleton.

William Caxton.

Introducer of Printing into England: 1422-91.

Thy prayer was Light—more Light—while Time shall last!
 Thou sawest a glory growing on the night,
But not the shadows which that light would cast,
 Till shadows vanish in the Light of Light.
     —Tennyson, *Epitaph on Caxton.*

We submit that Caxton's press in Westminister Abbey, rude as it is, ought to be looked at with quite as much respect as the best constructed machinery that ever, in our time, impressed the clearest type on the finest paper.—Macaulay, *Essays: Sir James Mackintosh.*

Thank Heaven, such times are past; never, let us hope, to return! The printing press will save the world. Let us place the inventor of it, then,

at the head of mankind, after Memnon, the inventor of letters.—CHARLES
BUCKE, *Book of Human Character.*

MIGUEL DE CERVANTES-SAAVEDRA.

Spanish Novelist and Poet: 1547-1616.

The chymic secret which your pains would find,
Breaks out, unsought for, in Cervantes' mind;
And Quixote's wildness, like that king's of old,
Turns all he touches into pomp and gold.
—WALTER HARTE, *Essay on Satire.*

Till by the muses arm'd, in all the ire
Of wit, resistless as electric fire,
Forth rode La Mancha's knight; and sudden fled
Goblins and beauteous nymphs, and pagans dread,
As the delirious dream of sickness flies,
When health returning smiles from vernal skies.
—W. J. MICKLE, *Epistle from Lisbon.*

Don Quixote is the only book in the Spanish language which can now be
said to possess much of an European reputation.   It has, however, enjoyed
enough to compensate for the neglect of all the rest.—HALLAM, *Introduction to the Literature of Europe, Vol. III.*

Don Quixote and Sancho Panza can never have less than a world of
admirers and lovers.   Where they pass, there will ever be laughter and
sympathy—the first infallible, the other according to the capacity of the
reader.   The most ignorant person who is within the range of education
at all understands the allusions, of which all literature is full, to those two
personages and their ways; and those who are without that range have
perhaps a heartier delight still in the wonderful adventures which a child
can understand, though a wise man cannot exhaust them.—MRS. OLIPHANT,
Cervantes.

Cervantes is in the front rank of all imaginative creators, because he
has given birth to Don Quixote and Sancho Panza.—LESLIE STEPHEN,
Hours in a Library, First Series.

Hardly is there one immortal book the reading of which does not
provoke to sadness; the mirth of Cervantes himself ends in tears, like the
tragical fifth Act of Biography.—P. ANDERSON GRAHAM, *Nature in Books.*

Cervantes, as poet, has the three sovereign gifts; creation, which
produces types, and clothes ideas with flesh and bone; invention, which
hurls passions against events, makes man flash brightly over destiny, and
brings forth the drama; imagination, sun of the brain, which throws light
and shade everywhere, and, giving relievo, creates life.   Observation,
which is acquired, and which, in consequence, is a quality rather than a
gift, is included in creation.   If the miser was not observed, Harpagon
would not be created.   In Cervantes, a newcomer, glimpsed at in Rabelais,
puts in a decided appearance; it is common-sense.   You have caught
sight of it in Panurge, you see it plainly in Sancho Panza.   It arrives
like the Silenus of Plautus, and it may also say, "I am the god mounted
on an ass".—VICTOR HUGO, *William Shakespeare* (*transl.*).

Dr. Thomas Chalmers.

Scottish Clergyman and Natural Philosopher : 1780-1847.

A man whose name will always remain illustrious as perhaps the most distinguished son and greatest ornament of the Presbyterian system—I mean Dr. Chalmers.—W. E. Gladstone.

It was a smart saying of Robert Hall, that the mind of Chalmers seemed to "move on hinges, not on wheels. There is incessant motion, but no progress." Hall was more discursive in thought, and in style far more finished. But Chalmers knew what he was about, and secured the effect at which he aimed. He concentrated his force on one important truth at a time, turned it round and round in every light, and would not leave it till he had made full demonstration of it to those who heard him, and pressed it home upon them with all his energy. Till this was accomplished he would not, and could not, pass on to other matters. In this sense it may be admitted that he moved—he was born to move—on hinges, and not on wheels. And it must also be admitted that this, while it may arrest and convince an audience, may not suit so well the quiet examination of students. . . . Let Thomas Chalmers be remembered. Those who knew him need no such exhortation, those who were his students or his helpers cry with an air of triumph, "We were with Chalmers," as soldiers who had been in the Peninsular or at Waterloo used to say, "We were with Wellington".—Dr. Donald Fraser, *Thomas Chalmers.*

Dr. Chalmers was a ruler among men : this we know historically; this every man who came within his range felt at once. He was like Agamemnon, a native ἄναξ ἀνδρῶν, and with all his homeliness of feature and deportment, and his perfect simplicity of expression, there was about him "that divinity that doth hedge a king". You felt a power, in him, and going from him, drawing you to him in spite of yourself. He was in this respect a *solar* man, he drew after him his own firmament of planets. They, like all free agents, had their centrifugal forces acting ever towards an independent, solitary course, but the centripetal also was there, and they moved with and around their imperial sun,—gracefully or not, as the case might be, but there was no breaking loose : they again, in their own spheres of power, might have their attendant moons, but all were bound to the great massive luminary in the midst. . . . Dr. Chalmers would have made a sorry Balaam ; he was made of different stuff, and for other purposes. Your respectable men are ever doing their best to keep their status, to maintain their position. He never troubled himself about his status ; indeed, we would say *status* was not the word for him. He had a *sedes* on which he sat, and from which he spoke : he had an *imperium*, to and fro which he roamed as he listed : but a *status* was as little in his way as in that of a Mauritanian lion.—Dr. John Brown, *Horæ Subsecivæ, Second Series.*

Dr. William Ellery Channing.

American Unitarian : 1780-1842.

And Channing with his bland superior look,
Cool as a moonbeam on a frozen brook.
 —Oliver Wendell Holmes, *Vestigia Quinque Retrorsum.*

Farewell! good man, good angel now! this hand,
   Soon like thine own, shall lose its cunning, too;
Soon shall this soul, like thine, bewildered stand,
   Then leap to thread the free, unfathomed blue.
                         —J. R. LOWELL, *Channing.*

CHARLEMAGNE.

Emperor of the West: 742-814.

A sway surpassing that of Charlemagne.
                         —BYRON, *The Age of Bronze.*

Turn then to Pharamond and Charlemain,
And the long heroes of the Gallic strain;
Experienc'd chiefs, for hardy prowess known,
And bloody wreaths in venturous battles won.
                         —PRIOR, *Carmen Seculare.*

   Messengers of God and masters of men, five kings, in whose arms the
life of the world lay as a nursling babe. . . . Theodoric, Charlemagne,
Alfred, Canute, and the Confessor.—RUSKIN.

   Three Christain Kings, Henry the Fowler in Germany, Charlemagne
in France, and Alfred in England, typically represent the justice of
humanity, gradually forming the feudal system out of the ruined elements
of Roman luxury and law.—*Id., Fors Clavigera, Vol. II.*

   But, perhaps the greatest eulogy of Charlemagne is written in the dis-
graces of succeeding times and the miseries of Europe.   He stands alone,
like a beacon upon a waste, or a rock in the broad ocean.   His sceptre
was the bow of Ulysses, which could not be drawn by any weaker hand.
In the dark ages of European history the reign of Charlemagne affords a
solitary resting-place between two long periods of turbulence and ignominy.
—HALLAM, *The Student's Middle Ages.*

CHARLES I.

King of England: 1600-1649.

Strafford: " From this day begins
A new life, founded on a new belief
In Charles."
Hollis: " In Charles?   Rather believe in Pym ! "
                         —ROBERT BROWNING, *Strafford.*

King Charles, and who'll do him right now?
King Charles, and who's ripe for fight now?
Give a rouse: here's, in hell's despite now,
King Charles!
                         —*Id., Cavalier Tunes.*

Earth cannot check.   Oh, terrible excess
Of headstrong will!   Can this be pity?
No—some fierce maniac hath usurped her name,

And scourges England struggling to be free:
Her peace destroyed! her hopes a wilderness!
Her blessings cursed—her glory turned to shame!
                    —WORDSWORTH, *Troubles of Charles the First.*

Him I knew: and the Stuart, he who, serene in his meekness,
Bow'd his anointed head beneath the axe of rebellion,
Calm in that insolent hour, and over his fortune triumphant.
                    —SOUTHEY, *A Vision of Judgment.*

God save King Charles! God knows that pleasant knave
His grace will find it hard enough to save.
        —OLIVER WENDELL HOLMES, *Vestigia Quinque Retrorsum.*

The martyrs' blood was said, of old, to be
The seed from whence the church did grow:
The royal blood which dying Charles did sow,
Becomes no less the seed of royalty:
'Twas in dishonour sown,
We find it now in glory grown.
                    —COWLEY, *Odes, IX.*

How many books are still written and published about Charles the First and his times! Such is the fresh and enduring interest of that grand crisis of morals, religion and government!—S. T. COLERIDGE, *Table Talk.*

We detest the character of Charles; but a man ought not to be removed by a law *ex post facto*, even constitutionally procured, merely because he is detestable. He must also be very dangerous. We can scarcely conceive that any danger which a state can apprehend from any individual could justify the violent measures which were necessary to procure a sentence against Charles.—MACAULAY, *Essays: Hallam.*

The Evil Genius of the House of Stuart. . . . Charles acted at this conjuncture as he acted at every important conjuncture throughout his life. After oppressing, threatening, and blustering, he hesitated and failed. He was bold in the wrong place, and timid in the wrong place.—*Id., Ibid.: John Hampden.*

Charles I., with a person and countenance that, seen in the canvas of Vandyke, command our admiring interest, failed to conciliate or impose on those whom he addressed. . . . An ungracious and chilling manner, an imperfection of speech, a something about the living man which the painter has not transferred to the portrait, seem to have made him singularly unsuccessful wherever he relied on the effect of his presence. But of this he was insensible.—LYTTON, *Essays: Pym versus Falkland.*

We regard the death of Charles as an atrocious and abominable murder, vindicated by no reasons of expedience, authorised by no principle of justice, which has lowered for ever England to the level of the adjoining nations in the scale of crime; and which had it not been vindicated by subsequent loyalty and chivalrous feeling in the better part of the people, would long since have extinguished alike its liberties and its independence.—SIR ARCHIBALD ALISON, *Essays: Macaulay.*

King Charles I. was a prince whose conduct was grave and pure, and whose piety was acknowledged; and was diligent, learned and frugal, but little given to prodigality; reserved, yet not morose; dignified, yet not arrogant; he maintained order and decorum in his house; his whole demeanour announced a noble, upright mind; a friend of justice; his deportment and manners awed his courtiers and pleased his subjects, his virtues had gained him the esteem of all good people. But neither Charles nor the English knew how much they were estranged from each other, nor the causes at work, and growing into power to prevent them from mutually appreciating each other.—F. P. G. GUIZOT (*transl.*).

The blood of the Royal Martyr has been the seed of flunkeyism from that day to this. What man, what woman, feels any sentimental attachment to the memory of James II.? There would have been less attachment, if possible, to the memory of the weak and perfidious Charles, if his weakness and his perfidy had not been glorified by his death.—GOLDWIN SMITH, *Three English Statesmen.*

Charles had neither vision nor grasp. It is not enough to say that he was undone by his duplicity. There are unluckily far too many awkward cases in history where duplicity has come off triumphant. Charles was double, as a man of inferior understanding would be double who had much studied Bacon's essay on Simulation and Dissimulation, without digesting it or ever deeply marking its first sentence, that dissimulation is but a faint kind of policy or wisdom, for it asketh a strong wit and a strong heart to know when to tell truth and to do it; therefore it is the worst sort of politicians that are the great dissemblers. This pregnant truth Charles never took to heart. His fault—and no statesman can have a worse—was that he never saw things as they were. He had taste, imagination, logic, but he was a dreamer, an idealist, and a theoriser, in which there might have been good rather than evil if only his dreams, theories, and ideals had not been out of relation with the hard duties of a day of storm. . . . In other words, he was the Royal Egotist without the mask. . . .

This at least is certain, that the execution of Charles I. kindled and nursed for many generations a lasting flame of cant, flunkeyism, or whatever else be the right name of spurious and unmanly sentimentalism, more lively than is associated with any other business in our whole national history.

The two most sensible things to be said about the trial and execution of Charles I. have often been said before. One is that the proceeding was an act of war, and was just as defensible or just as assailable, and on the same grounds, as the war itself. The other remark, thought tolerably conclusive alike by Milton and by Voltaire, is that the regicides treated Charles precisely as Charles, if he had won the game, undoubtedly promised himself with law or without law that he would treat them. The author of the attempt upon the Five Members in 1642 was not entitled to plead punctilious demurrers to a revolutionary jurisdiction. From the first it had been *My head or thy head*, and Charles had lost.—JOHN MORLEY, *Oliver Cromwell.*

CHARLES II.

King of England : 1630-1685.

Who comes with rapture greeted, and caressed
With frantic love—his kingdom to regain?

Him virtue's nurse, adversity, in vain
Received, and fostered in her iron breast:
For all she taught of hardiest and of best,
Or would have taught, by discipline of pain
And long privation, now dissolves amain,
Or is remembered only to give zest
To wantonness.—Away, Circean revels!
Already stands our country on the brink
Of bigot rage, that all distinction levels
Of truth and falsehood, swallowing the good name,
And, with that draught, the life-blood, misery, shame,
By poets loathed; from which historians shrink!
> —WORDSWORTH, *Charles the Second.*

But when the second Charles assumed the sway,
And arts revived beneath a softer day,
Then, like a bow long forced into a curve,
The mind, released from too constrained a nerve,
Flew to its first position with a spring
That made the vaulted roofs of pleasure ring.
His court, the dissolute and hateful school
Of wantonness, where vice was taught by rule,
Swarm'd with a scribbling herd, as deep inlaid
With brutal lust as ever Circe made.
> —COWPER, *Table Talk.*

Here lies our sovereign lord the King,
Whose word no man relies on;
He never says a foolish thing,
Nor ever does a wise one.
> —EARL OF ROCHESTER, *Written on the Bed-Chamber
> Door of Charles II.*

Farewell, great Charles, monarch of blest renown,
The best good man that ever fill'd a throne:
Whom Nature as her highest pattern wrought,
And mix'd both sexes' virtues in one draught.
> —MONTAGUE, EARL OF HALIFAX, *On the Death of King Charles II.*

And if the second Charles brought in decay
  Of ancient virtue, if it well nigh wring
Souls that had broadened 'neath a nobler day,
  To see a losel, marketable king
Fearfully watering with his realm's best blood
Cromwell's quenched bolts.
> —J. R. LOWELL, *To John G. Palfrey.*

In private life, Charles II. was frugal to economy and meanness; in public affairs, thoughtless, negligent, and profuse. He cared not one single grain of dust where the money came from, as long as it came to him. In one respect he resembled his father; for, if viewed on one side, he was worthy the highest applause; if on the other, the most decided indignation.—CHARLES BUCKE, *Book of Human Character.*

That King of debauchees, Charles II.—WILLIAM HOWITT, *The Northern Heights of London.*

Charles II. was one of the most worthless of our monarchs, and the most beloved. The responsibility of all evils, troubles, or crimes, was laid upon his advisers, his mistresses, and any one but upon himself, by his loving subjects. His readiness of access, and good-humoured freedom of manner charmed all who came in contact with him. "Unthinkingness" was said by Halifax to be one of his characteristics, and Rochester used the expression, "Unthinking Charles"; yet this was more an apparent than a real characteristic. Like most indolent men, he tried to get his own way, and he was one of the earliest to find out that if the people are allowed their way when they are in earnest, they will let their governors do as they wish at other times. It has been said that the strongest resolve he ever formed was a determination not to go on his travels again; therefore he never opposed a strong popular movement.—H. B. WHEATLEY, *Samuel Pepys and the World he lived in.*

CHARLES IV.

Emperor of Germany : 1316-1378.

Charles IV. has been treated with more derision by his contemporaries, and consequently by later writers, than almost any prince in history; yet he was remarkably successful in the only objects which he seriously pursued. Deficient in personal courage, insensible of humiliation, bending without shame to the Pope, to the Italians, to the electors, so poor and so little reverenced as to be arrested by a butcher at Worms for want of paying his demand, Charles IV. affords a proof that a certain dexterity and cold-blooded perseverance may occasionally supply in a sovereign the want of more respectable qualities.—HALLAM, *The Student's Middle Ages, Chap. V.*

CHARLES V.

Emperor of Germany : 1500-1558.

The too much vaunted ages of Charles V., Leo X., and Louis XIV.— MAZZINI, *Life and Writings, Vol. II.*

Charles possessed, in the most eminent degree, the science which is of greatest importance to a monarch, that of knowing men and of adapting their talents to the various departments which he allotted to them. From the death of Chievres to the end of his reign, he employed no general in the field, no minister in the cabinet, no ambassador to a foreign court, no governor to a province, whose abilities were inadequate to the trust which he reposed in them.—WILLIAM ROBERTSON.

FRANÇOIS RENÉ DE CHATEAUBRIAND.

French Writer and Statesman : 1768-1848.

There Chateaubriand forms new books of martyrs;
And subtle Greeks intrigue for stupid Tartars.
                                        —BYRON, *The Age of Bronze.*

Fénélon and Chateaubriand are poets as much through sentiment as by the power of imagery.—LAMARTINE, *Celebrated Characters (transl.), Vol. II.*

Chateaubriand poured forth all its lustre in his resplendent descriptions. Strange, that when prose and poetry, in the hands of such masters, should all but put the colours on the canvas, painting itself, in the midst of such mighty allies, should still slumber on in comparative mediocrity.—SIR ARCHIBALD ALISON, *Essays : The British School of Painting.*

WILLIAM PITT, EARL OF CHATHAM.

English Statesman : 1708-1778.

Shall dastard tongues essay to blast the name
Of him whose meed exists in endless fame ?
When Pitt expired in plenitude of power,
Though ill success obscured his dying hour,
Pity her dewy wings before him spread,
For noble spirits " war not with the dead ".

—BYRON, On the Death of Mr. Fox.

A : Patriots, alas ! the few that have been found,
Where most they flourish upon English ground,
The country's need have scantily supplied ;
And the last left the scene when Chatham died.
B : Not so—the virtue still adorns our age,
Though the chief actor died upon the stage.
In him, Demosthenes was heard again ;
Liberty taught him her Athenian strain ;
She clothed him with authority and awe,
Spoke from his lips, and in his looks gave law,
His speech, his form, his action full of grace,
And all his country beaming in his face.
He stood, as some inimitable hand
Would strive to make a Paul or Tully stand,
No sycophant or slave that dared oppose
Her sacred cause, but trembled when he rose,
And every venal stickler for the yoke
Felt himself crush'd at the first word he spoke.
Such men are raised to station and command,
When Providence means mercy to a land.

—COWPER, Table Talk.

That Chatham's language was his mother-tongue,
And Wolfe's great name compatriot with his own.
Farewell those honours, and farewell with them
The hope of such hereafter. They have fallen
Each in his field of glory: one in arms,
And one in Council—Wolfe upon the lap
Of smiling Victory that moment won,
And Chatham, heart-sick of his country's shame !
They made us many soldiers. Chatham still
Consulting England's happiness at home,
Secured it by an unforgiving frown
If any wrong'd her.

—Id., The Task : The Time-Piece.

Or how our merry lads at hame,
In Britain's court, kept up the game;
How Royal George—the Lord leuk o'er him!—
Was managing St. Stephen's quorum;
If sleekit Chatham Will was livin',
Or glaikit Charlie got his nieve in.
—BURNS, *Lines Written to a Gentleman.*

Long had thy virtues mark'd thee out for fame,
Far, far superior to a cornet's name;
This generous Walpole saw, and griev'd to find
So mean a post disgrace that noble mind.
The servile standard from the freeborn hand
He took and bade thee lead the patriot band.
—LORD LYTTLETON, *To William Pitt.*

Or dine, when business would permit,
With that great statesman William Pitt.
—JAMES CAWTHORN, *Wit and Learning.*

From each low view of selfish factions free,
To think, to speak, to live, O Pitt, like thee.
—JOHN GILBERT COOPER, *The Genius of Britain.*

Or Pitt, can thy example be unknown,
While each fond father marks it to his son?
—PAUL WHITEHEAD, *Manners.*

Secure under Brunswick and heaven,
I trust the state vessel shall ride;
To Bute let the rudder be given,
Or Pitt, be permitted to guide.
—EDWARD LOVIBOND, *On Politics.*

O Pitt, while honour points thy liberal plan,
And o'er the minister exalts the man,
Isis congenial greets thy faithful sway,
Nor scorns to bid a statesman grace her lay.
—THOMAS WARTON, *On the Death of King George II.*

The pinnacle of glory to which the elder Pitt raised his country is a sufficient proof of the almost unequalled administrative genius which he displayed in the conduct of a war.—W. E. H. LECKY, *History of England, Vol. II.*

There is hardly any man in modern times, with the exception, perhaps, of Lord Somers, who fills so large a space in our history, and of whom we know so little, as Lord Chatham; and yet he is the person to whom every one would at once point, if desired to name the most successful statesman and most brilliant orator that this country ever produced. . . . As soon as Mr. Pitt took the helm, the steadiness of the hand that held it was instantly felt in every motion of the vessel.—LORD BROUGHAM.

Lord Chatham, who stands at the head, perhaps, of your orators and statesmen. . . . W. E. GLADSTONE, *Speeches, Vol. X.*

The greatest of War Ministers—Chatham, Bismarck.—EARL OF ROSE-BERY, *Life of Pitt.*

Behold Chatham's, Hampden's, Bayard's, Alfred's, Scipio's, Pericles's day,—day of all that are born of women.—EMERSON, *Literary Ethics.*

Yet with all his faults and affectations, Pitt had, in a very extraordinary degree, many of the elements of greatness. He had splendid talents, strong passions, quick sensibility, and vehement enthusiasm for the grand and the beautiful. There was something about him which ennobled tergiversation itself. . . . Pitt desired power, and he desired it, we really believe, from high and generous motives. He was, in the strict sense of the word, a patriot. He had none of that philanthropy which the great French writers of his time preached to all the nations of Europe. He loved England as an Athenian loved the City of the Violet Crown, as a Roman loved the City of the Seven Hills. He saw his country insulted and defeated. He saw the national spirit sinking. Yet he knew what the resources of the empire, vigorously employed, could effect; and he felt that he was the man to employ them vigorously. "My Lord," he said to the Duke of Devonshire, "I am sure that I can save my country, and that nobody else can."—MACAULAY, *Essays : Earl of Chatham.*

If the two men were to be compared in point of age, Fox seemed the wild boy, Pitt the matured man. . . . Pitt's great passion, no doubt, was the love of power, but it was made pure by its very intensity—a love that chastened itself by exalting the character of its object. To govern England, but to govern nobly, was the one end to which he devoted all the vigour of surpassing faculties, with that singleness of purpose which gives even to mediocrity successes that fail to genius, when genius renounces its own superiority of force by relaxing its discipline and scattering its troops.— LYTTON, *Essays : Pitt and Fox.*

Glorious was the eloquence of Mr. Pitt. Nations shook at the thunder of his voice.—DR. VICESIMUS KNOX, *Essays.*

Lord Chatham is a great and celebrated name ; a name that keeps the name of this country respectable in every other on the globe. It may be truly called—
> " Clarum et venerabile nomen
> Gentibus, et multum nostræ quod proderat urbi."

The venerable age of this great man, his merited rank, his superior eloquence, his splendid qualities, his eminent services, the vast space he fills in the eye of mankind, and, more than all the rest, his fall from power, which, like death, canonizes and sanctifies a greater character, will not suffer me to censure any part of his conduct. I am afraid to flatter him ; I am sure I am not disposed to blame him ; let those who have betrayed him by their adulation, insult him with their malevolence. But what I do not presume to censure, I may have leave to lament.— EDMUND BURKE.

As Walpole was essentially the Minister of Peace, so the haughty Chatham was essentially the Minister of War. . . . In his eyes the only means by which a people could command respect and maintain authority in the family of nations was by the display of a resolute warlike policy. He was the first of our parliamentary statesmen who believed in, and carried out, the maxim—If peace be sought after, prepare for war.—A. C. EWALD, *Representative Statesmen.*

6

Cromwell and Chatham, these are the two English statesmen the memory of whose sympathy America still cherished ; and were Cromwell and Chatham great un-Englishmen and traitors to their country?— GOLDWIN SMITH, *Three English Statesmen.*

THOMAS CHATTERTON.

The Boy Poet: 1752-1770.

I thought of Chatterton, the marvellous boy.
The sleepless soul that perished in his pride.
> —WORDSWORTH, *Resolution and Independence.*

The inheritors of unfulfilled renown
Rose from their thrones, built beyond mortal thought,
Far in the Unapparent.   Chatterton
Rose pale, his solemn agony had not
Yet faded from him.
> —SHELLEY, *Adonais, XLV.*

Here too, early lost and deplored, were the youths from the Muses
    sprinkled :
Mark'd for themselves at birth, and with dews from Castalia,
Chatterton first (for not to his affectionate spirit
Could the act of madness innate for guilt be accounted) :
Marvellous boy, whose antique songs and unhappy story
Shall by gentle hearts be in mournful memory cherish'd
Long as thy ancient towers endure, and the rocks of St. Vincent,
Bristol! my birth-place dear.
> —SOUTHEY, *A Vision of Judgment : The Young Spirits.*

Sweet Flower of Hope! free Nature's genial child!
That didst so fair disclose thy early bloom,
Filling the wide air with a rich perfume!
For thee in vain all heavenly aspects smiled ;
From the hard world brief respite could they win—
The frost nipped sharp without, the canker preyed within !
> —S. T. COLERIDGE, *Monody on the Death of Chatterton.*

O Chatterton! how very sad thy fate !
Dear child of sorrow—son of misery !
How soon the film of death obscured that eye,
When Genius mildly flashed, and high debate.
How soon that voice, majestic and elate,
Melted in dying numbers!   Oh! how nigh
Was night to thy fair morning.   Thou didst die
A half-blown flow'ret which cold blasts amate.
But this is past: thou art among the stars
Of highest Heaven: to the rolling spheres
Thou sweetly singest : nought thy hymning mars,
Above the ingrate world and human fears.
On earth the good man base detraction bars
From thy fair name, and waters it with tears.
> —KEATS, *To Chatterton.*

Strong derivative points are to be found in Keats and Coleridge from the study of Chatterton. . . . Not to know Chatterton is to be ignorant of the *true* day-spring of modern romantic poetry.—D. G. ROSSETTI in T. HALL CAINE's *Recollections of Rossetti.*

Where were ye, O ye friends to genius, when, stung with disappointment, distressed for food and raiment, with every frightful form of human misery painted on his fine imagination, poor Chatterton sunk in despair? Alas! ye knew him not then, and now it is too late,—

> For now he is dead;
> Gone to his deathbed,
> All under the willow tree.

So sang the sweet youth, in as tender an elegy as ever flowed from a feeling heart.—DR. VICESIMUS KNOX, *Essays: On the Poems attributed to Rowley.*

Nothing in Chatterton can be separated from Chatterton. His noblest flight, his sweetest strains, his grossest ribaldry, and his most commonplace imitations of the productions of magazines, were all the effervescences of the same ungovernable impulse, which, chameleon-like, imbibed the colours of all it looked on. It was Ossian, or a Saxon monk, or Gray, or Smollett, or Junius—and if it failed most in what it most affected to be, a poet of the fifteenth century, it was because it could not imitate what had not existed.—EARL OF ORFORD.

GEOFFREY CHAUCER.

The Father of English Poetry: 1340-1400.

Allas! my worthy maister honorable,
This londes verray tresour and richesse!
Dethe by thy dethe hath harm irreparable
Unto us done; hir vengeable duresse
Despoiled hath this lond of swetnesse
Of rhetoryk for unto Tullius
Was never man so like amonges us.
Also who was heyr [heir] in philosofye
To Aristotle in our tunge but thou?
The steppes of Virgile in poesye
Thou folwedst eke, men wote wel ynow.
She might have tarried hir vengeance a whyle
Til that some man had egal to thee be;
Nay, let be that! she knew wel that this yle
May never man bring forthe like to thee,
And hir office nedes do mote she:
God bade hir do so, I truste for the beste;
O maister, maister, God thy soule reste!
                    —THOMAS HOCCLEVE, *Lament for Chaucer.*

Dan Chaucer, the first warbler, whose sweet breath
Preluded those melodious bursts that fill
The spacious times of great Elizabeth
With sounds that echo still.
                    —TENNYSON, *A Dream of Fair Women.*

" Sweet is the holiness of youth "—so felt
Time-honoured Chaucer when he framed the lay
By which the prisoners beguiled the way,
And many a pilgrim's rugged heart did melt.
    —WORDSWORTH, *Edward VI.*

But let a portjon of ethereal dew
Fall on my head, and presently unmew
My soul ; that I may dare, in wayfaring,
To stammer where old Chaucer used to sing.
     —KEATS, *Endymion.*

But what old Chaucer's merry page befits,
The chaster muse of modern days omits.
    —COWPER, *Anti-Thelyphthora.*

Thee too, Father Chaucer ! I saw, and delighted to see thee,
At whose well undefiled I drank in my youth, and was strengthen'd :
With whose mind immortal so oft I have communed, partaking
All its manifold moods, and willingly moved at its pleasure.
  —SOUTHEY, *A Vision of Judgment : The Elder Worthies.*

Old Chaucer, like the morning star,
To us discovers day from far ;
His light those mists and clouds dissolv'd
Which our dark nation long involv'd ;
But he descending to the shades,
Darkness again the age invades.
    —SIR JOHN DENHAM, *On Mr. Cowley's Death.*

Thy genuine bards immortal Chaucer leads :
His hoary head o'erlooks the gazing quire,
And beams on all around celestial fire.
     —THOMAS WARTON.

But Chaucer (though he can but lewdely
On metres and on riming craftily)
Hath sayd him in swiche English as he can
Of olde time, as knoweth many a man.
    —CHAUCER, *The Man of Lawes Prologue.*

That noble Chaucer, in those former times,
The first enrich'd our English with his rhimes,
And was the first of ours that ever brake
Into the muses' treasure, and first spake
In weighty numbers, delving in the mine
Of perfect knowledge, which he could refine,
And coin for current, and as much as then
The English language could express to men,
He made it do ; and by his wondrous skill,
Gave us much light from his abundant quill.
    —DRAYTON, *Elegy to Henry Reynolds, Esq.*

Since Chaucer lived, who yet lives, and yet shall,
Though (which I grieve to say) but in his last.
Yet what a time hath he wrested from time,
And won upon mighty waste of days,

Upon th' immortal honour of our clime,
That by his means came first adorn'd with bays,
Unto the sacred relics of whose time,
We yet are bound in zeal to offer praise.
—SAMUEL DANIEL, *Musophilus.*

Such was the case when Chaucer's early toil
Founded the Muses' empire in our soil.
—DR. CHETWOOD, *To the Earl of Roscommon.*

Long had our dull forefathers slept supine,
Nor felt the raptures of the tuneful nine ;
Till Chaucer first, a merry bard, arose,
And many a story told in rhyme and prose.
But age has rusted what the poet writ,
Worn out his language, and obscur'd his wit.
—ADDISON, *An Account of the Greatest English Poets.*

The god of shepheards, Tityrus, is dead,
Who taught mee homely, as I can, to make :
Hee, whilst hee lived, was the sovereigne head
Of shepheards all that bene with love ytake :
Well couth hee waile his woes, and lightly slake
The flames which love within his heart had bredd,
And tell us merry tales to keepe us wake,
The while our sheepe about us safely fedde.
Now dead hee is, and lyeth wrapt in lead,
(O why should Death on him such outrage showe ?)
And all his passing skill with him is fledde,
The fame whereof doth daylie greater growe.
—SPENSER, *A Lament for Chaucer.*

But, could I chaunt, or rhyme, pardie,
Clear as Dan Chaucer, or as thee.
—PRIOR, *Erle Robert's Mice.*

There sprightly Chaucer charms our hours away
With stories quaint, and gentle roundelay.
Muse ! at that name each thought of pride recall,
Ah, think how soon the wise and glorious fall.
—ELIJAH FENTON, *To a Young Lady.*

Such was old Chaucer. Such the placid mien
Of him who first with harmony inform'd
The language of our fathers.
—AKENSIDE, *For a Statue of Chaucer.*

Not far from these, Dan Chaucer, ancient wight,
A lofty seat on Mount Parnassus held,
Who long had been the muses' chief delight ;
His reverend locks were silver'd o'er with eld ;
Grave was his visage, and his habit plain ;
And while he sang, fair nature he display'd,
In verse albeit uncouth, and simple strain.
—-ROBERT LLOYD, *The Progress of Envy.*

Yune Norman tymes, Turgotus and
Good Chaucer dydd excelle,

Then Stowe, the Bryghtstowe Carmelyte,
Dydd bare awaie the belle.
—CHATTERTON, *Song to Œlla.*

Vernal Chaucer, whose fresh words
Throb thick with merle and mavis all the year.
—J. R. LOWELL.

Humanity shines in Homer, in Chaucer, in Spenser, in Shakespeare, in Milton.   They are content with truth.   They use the positive degree.
—EMERSON, *Essays: The Over-Soul.*

The influence of Chaucer is conspicuous in all our early literature; and, more recently, not only Pope and Dryden have been beholden to him, but, in the whole society of English writers, a large unacknowledged debt is easily traced.   One is charmed with the opulence which feeds so many pensioners.—*Id., Ibid.: Shakespeare, or the Poet.*

I take unceasing delight in Chaucer.   His manly cheerfulness is especially delicious to me in my old age.—S. T. COLERIDGE, *Table Talk.*

Chaucer, "the poet of the dawn".   For in him there are many things significant of the age of transition in which he lived; in him the mixture of Frenchman and Englishman is still in a sense incomplete, as that of their language is in the diction of his poems.   His gaiety of heart is hardly English; nor is his willing (though to be sure, not invariably unquestioning) acceptance of forms into the inner meaning of which he does not greatly vex his soul by entering; nor his airy way of ridiculing what he has no intention of helping to overthrow; nor his light unconcern in the question whether he is, or is not, an immoral writer. . . . But he *is* English in his freedom and frankness of spirit; in his manliness of mind; in his preference for the good in things as they are to the good in things as they might be; in his loyalty, his piety, his truthfulness.—A. W. WARD, *Chaucer.*

Chaucer's humour is the most universally patent and easily recognised of his gifts.   The smile or laugh that he raises, by refined irony or by broad rough jest and incident, is conspicuously genial.   Mephistophelian mockery and Satanic grimness are not in his way.   This had nothing to do with his being the bright morning of English poetry—writing with the buoyancy of youth at a time when the struggle for existence was less fierce, when there was no bitter feeling between high and low, no envenomed warfare of civil or religious party.   There never has been age nor country in which the fierce spirit has wanted fuel for its fierceness.   It was simply the nature of the man to be genial,—"attempered and soft" as the climate of his gardens of Venus.   He would have been so in whatever age he had lived.—WILLIAM MINTO, *Characteristics of English Poets.*

Chaucer sparkles with the dew of morning.—J. C. HARE, *Guesses at Truth, First Series.*

THE EARL OF CHESTERFIELD.

English Statesman and Author: 1694-1773.

How can I Pult'ney, Chesterfield forget,
While Roman spirit charms, and Attic wit?
—POPE, *Epilogue to the Satires: Dialogue II.*

O, thou, whose wisdom, solid yet refin'd,
Whose patriot virtues, consummate skill
To touch the finer springs that move the world,
Join'd to whate'er the graces can bestow,
And all Apollo's animating fire,
Give thee, with pleasing dignity to shine
At once the guardian, ornament, and joy,
Of polish'd life ; permit the rural muse,
O Chesterfield, to grace with thee her song !
                              —THOMSON, *The Seasons : Winter.*

Hence, Chesterfield, that openness of heart,
And just disdain for that poor *mimic* art ;
Hence (manly praise !) that manner nobly free,
Which all admire, and I commend, in thee.
                              —YOUNG, *Love of Fame : Satire II.*

Lord Chesterfield stands much lower in the estimation of posterity than he would have done if his letters had never been published.—MACAULAY, *Essays : Horace Walpole.*

Chesterfield was specious, plausible, and penetrating ; with conversation not only brilliant, but frequently solid. His action, we are told, was dignified, and his eloquence mellifluent ; yet, occasionally deficient in argument ; therefore deficient in strength ; at times indicating a plausible and empty elegance, like double-distilled lavender water ; but he had not that pre-eminence of art, that could prompt him to enlist manners and conduct on the true side of virtue.—CHARLES BUCKE, *Book of Human Character.*

The late Lord Chesterfield, though justly decried as a moral instructor, is admired as a writer of peculiar elegance. No man more closely and successfully imitated the French in every circumstance. Like them, he writes with perspicuity, vivacity, and that gracefulness which is sure to please, and which he so strenuously recommends.—DR. VICESIMUS KNOX, *Cursory Thoughts on Epistolary Writers.*

The name of Chesterfield has become a synonym for good breeding and politeness. It is associated in our minds with all that is graceful in manner and cold in heart, attractive in appearance and unamiable in reality. The image it calls up is that of a man rather below the middle height, in a court suit and blue riband, with regular features, wearing an habitual expression of gentlemanlike ease. His address is insinuating, his bow perfect, his compliments rival those of *Le Grande Monarque* in delicacy : laughter is too demonstrative for him, but the smile of courtesy is ever on his lip ; and by the time he has gone through the circle, the avowed object of his daily ambition is accomplished—all the women are already half in love with him, and every man is desirous to be his friend.—ABRAHAM HAYWARD, *Biographical and Critical Essays, Vol. I.*

WILLIAM CHILLINGWORTH.

English Theologian : 1602-1643.

See Chillingworth the depths of doubt explore
And Selden ope the rolls of ancient lore.
                              —THOMAS WARTON, *The Triumph of Isis.*

He was called the immortal Chillingworth.—HALLAM, *Introduction to the Literature of Europe, Vol III.*

I should propose the constant reading of Chillingworth, who, by his example, will teach both perspicuity and the way of right reasoning, better than any book that I know: and therefore will deserve to be read upon that account over and over again; not to say anything of his argument.—LOCKE.

The wide fame of William Chillingworth may be said, with scarcely an exaggeration, to rest almost, if not altogether, on a single paragraph. It is, as its popularity has proved, telling and effective enough. He had been challenged to say what he meant when he said that the religion of Protestants was a safe way of salvation, and he accepted the challenge and replied, near the close of his great argument: " By the religion of Protestants I do not understand the doctrine of Luther, or Calvin, or Melancthon; nor the confession of Augusta (Augsburg), or Geneva; nor the Catechism of Heidelberg, nor the Articles of the Church of England; no, nor the harmony of Protestant confessions; but that wherein they all agree, and which they all subscribe with a greater harmony as a perfect rule of their faith and actions, that is, the BIBLE.   The Bible, I say, the *Bible* only, is the religion of Protestants." . . . Our last words of counsel for the student of religious thought, in relation to Chillingworth and the writings with which his name is identified, may well be, after the pattern of those which were spoken of old to the wavering disciple, " Let the dead bury their dead; but go thou and preach the Kingdom of God ". Let pamphleteer wrangle with pamphleteer; but go thou, and study, faithfully and patiently, boldly and yet reverentially, reverentially and yet boldly, the Books which have made Christendom what it is, and the Christendom which the Books have made.—DEAN PLUMPTRE, *Masters in English Theology.*

CHRISTINA.

Queen of Sweden : 1628-1689.

Christina, maiden of heroic mien !
Star of the North ! of northern stars the queen !
> —COWPER, *To Christina, Queen of Sweden.*

ST. JOHN CHRYSOSTOM.

Archbishop of Constantinople : 347-407.

Sermons he read, and lectures he endured,
    And homilies, and lives of all the saints:
To Jerome and to Chrysostom inured,
    He did not take such studies for restraints.
> —BYRON, *Don Juan, XLVII.*

A Chronicle of ancient standing;
A Chrysostom to smooth thy band in.
> —POPE, *The Happy Life of a Country Parson.*

But mostly Chrysostom engag'd his mind :
Great without labour, without art refin'd !
Now see his gentle elocution flows,
Soft as the flakes of heav'n—descending snows ;
Now see him, like th' impetuous torrent roll ;
Pure in his diction, purer in his soul :
By few men equall'd, and surpass'd by none ;
A Tully and Demosthenes in one !
> —WALTER HARTE, *Macarius ; or, The Confessor.*

CHARLES CHURCHILL.

English and Satiric Poet: 1731-1764.

I stood beside the grave of him who blazed
    The comet of a season, and I saw
The humblest of all sepulchres, and gazed
    With not the less of sorrow and of awe.
> —BYRON, *Churchill's Grave.*

Contemporaries all surpass'd, see one,
Short his career indeed, but ably run.
Churchill, himself unconscious of his powers,
In penury consumed his idle hours,
And like a scatter'd seed at random sown,
Was left to spring by vigour of his own.
Lifted at length, by dignity of thought
And dint of genius, to an affluent lot,
He laid his head in luxury's soft lap,
And took too often there his easy nap.
If brighter beams than all he threw not forth,
'Twas negligence in him, not want of worth.
Surly and slovenly, and bold and coarse,
Too proud for art, and trusting in mere force,
Spendthrift alike of money and of wit,
Always at speed, and never drawing bit,
He struck the lyre in such a careless mood,
And so disdain'd the rules he understood,
The laurel seem'd to wait on his command,
He snatch'd it rudely from the Muse's hand.
> —COWPER, *Table Talk.*

COLLEY CIBBER.

English Poet Laureate: 1671-1757.

With just desert enroll'd in endless fame,
Conscious of worth superior, Cibber came.
> —CHURCHILL, *The Rosciad.*

It wants a touch of Cibber's ease,
A higher kind of talk to please :
Such as your titled folks would choose,
And lords and ladyships might use.
> —ROBERT LLOYD, *A Familiar Epistle to G. Colman, Esq.*

Ye laughter-loving pow'rs, ye gods of mirth,
What! not regard my deputy on earth?
Whose chemic skill turns brass to gold with ease,
And out of Cibber forges Socrates.
                    —CHRISTOPHER SMART, *The Hilliad, Book I.*

MARIUS TULLIUS CICERO.

Roman Orator : B.C. 100-43.

I slept never on the Mount of Pernaso,
Ne lerned Marcus Tullius Cicero.
                    —CHAUCER, *The Frankeleine's Prologue.*

Calphurnia's cheek is pale; and Cicero
Looks with such ferret and such fiery eyes,
As we have seen him in the Capitol,
Being cross'd in conference by some senators.
                    —SHAKESPEARE, *Julius Cæsar.*

O come, that easy, Ciceronian style,
So Latin, yet so English all the while,
As, though the pride of Middleton and Bland,
All boys may read, and girls may understand!
                    —POPE, *Epilogue to the Satires : Dialogue I.*

Welcome learn'd Cicero! whose bless'd tongue and wit
Preserves Rome's greatness yet:
Thou art the first of orators; only he
Who best can praise thee next must be.
                    —COWLEY, *The Motto.*

            This, Cicero, is thy heart;
I hear it beating thro' each purple line.
                    —LYTTON, *The Souls of Books.*

This name [Cicero] represents not merely an orator, but eloquence itself.
—LAMARTINE, *Celebrated Characters* (transl.), *Vol. I.*

In the case of Cicero, we have the first eminent example (though he himself records some elder examples amongst his own countrymen) of a man's standing up manfully to support the pretensions of his mother-tongue. And this might be done in a mere spirit of pugnacious defiance to the arrogance of another nation—a spirit which finds matter of quarrel in a straw. But here also we find the first example of a statesman's seriously regarding a language in the light of a foremost jewel amongst the trophies of nationality.—DE QUINCEY, *Leaders in Literature.*

If Cato's virtue seems more splendid in theory, Cicero's will be found superior in practice; the one was romantic, the other rational; the one drawn from the refinements of the schools, the other from nature and social life; the one always unsuccessful, often hurtful; the other always beneficial, often salutary to the republic.—CONYERS MIDDLETON.

Cicero, the world's great model in the oratorical and the philosophical, is no less eminent in the epistolary style. He rivalled his great patterns, the Greeks, in eloquence and philosophy: and he excelled them in his letters.—DR. VICESIMUS KNOX.

GIOVANNI CIMABUE.

Italian Painter and Architect : 1240-1302.

Long slumber'd Painting in a stupid trance
Of heavy zeal, and Monkish ignorance :
(When faith itself for mere dispute was given,
Subtle was wise, and wranglers went to heav'n.)
Till glorious Cimabue restor'd her crown,
And dipp'd the pencil, studious of renown.
                    —WALTER HARTE, *An Essay on Painting.*

The early efforts of Cimabue and Giotto are the burning messages of prophecy, delivered by the stammering lips of infants.—RUSKIN, *Modern Painters, Vol. I.*

EARL OF CLARENDON.

English Statesman and Author : 1608-1674.

Clarendon had law and sense,
Clifford was fierce and brave.
                    —DRYDEN, *On the Young Statesmen.*

We suffer ourselves to be delighted by the keenness of Clarendon's observation, and by the sober majesty of his style, till we forget the oppressor and the bigot in the historian.—MACAULAY, *Essays : Lord Bacon.*

DR. SAMUEL CLARKE.

English Theologian and Philosopher : 1675-1729.

And Clarke's exactness, rigorous and precise,
Might vainly torture the protracted thought.
                    —REV. RICHARD POLWHELE, *Pulpit Eloquence.*

The subtle mind of Clarke, the champion of God Himself.—LYTTON, *England and the English : Survey of Education.*

By Dr. Clarke's death, the world was deprived of as bright a light, and masterly a teacher of truth and virtue, as ever yet appeared amongst us ; and his works must last as long as any language remains to convey them to future times.—BISHOP B. HOADLY.

THOMAS CLARKSON.

English Philanthropist : 1760-1846.

Clarkson ! it was an obstinate hill to climb :
How toilsome, nay, how dire it was, by thee
Is known,—by none, perhaps, so feelingly ;
But thou, who, starting in thy fervent prime,
Didst first lead forth this pilgrimage sublime,
Hast heard the constant voice its charge repeat,

Which, not of the young heart's oracular seat,
First roused thee.—Oh, true yoke—fellow of Time
With unabating effort, see the palm
Is won, and by all nations shall be worn!
The bloody writing is for ever torn,
And thou henceforth shalt have a good man's calm,
A great man's happiness; thy zeal shall find
Repose at length, firm friend of human kind!
    —WORDSWORTH, *To Thomas Clarkson.*

Clarkson, I answer'd, first; whom to have seen
And known in social hours may be my pride,
Such friendship being praise.
    —SOUTHEY, *The Poet's Pilgrimage : The Hopes of Man.*

' Mid the August and never-dying light
Of constellated spirits, who have gained
A throne in heaven, by power of heavenly acts,
And leave their names immortal and unchanged
On earth, even as the names of sun and moon,
Seest thou, my soul! 'mid all that radiant host
One worthier of thy love and reverence
Than He, the fearless spirit who went forth,
Mailed in the armour of invincible faith,
And bearing in his grasp the spear of truth,
Fit to destroy or save, went forth to wage,
Against the fierce array of bloody men,
Avarice and ignorance, cruelty and hate,
A holy warfare!
    —JOHN WILSON, *Lines written on Reading Mr. Clarkson's*
        History of the Abolition of the Slave Trade.

An institution is the lengthened shadow of one man; as Monachism, of the Hermit Antony; the Reformation, of Luther; Quakerism, of Fox; Methodism, of Wesley; Abolition, of Clarkson. Scipio Milton called "the height of Rome"; and all history resolves itself very easily into the biography of a few stout and earnest persons.—EMERSON, *Essays : Self-Reliance.*

CLEOPATRA.

Queen of Egypt : B.C. 69-30.

Yet sawe I more, howe in right pitous caas,
For Antony was slaine Cleopatras.
    —CHAUCER, *The Assemble of Ladies.*

High-minded Cleopatra, that with stroke
Of ashes sting her selfe did stoutly kill;
And thousands moe the like, that did that dongeon fill.
    —SPENSER, *The Faery Queene, Book I., Canto V.*

Age cannot wither her, nor custom stale
Her infinite variety.
    —SHAKESPEARE, *Antony and Cleopatra.*

Though Helen's form, and Cleopatra's charms,
The boast of fame, once kindled dire alarms:
Those dazzling lights the world no more must view,
And scarce would think the bright description true.

—JOHN HUGHES, Greenwich Park.

LORD CLIVE.

Indian Governor : 1725-1774.

To keep one lover's flame alive,
Requires the genius of a Clive.

—CHATTERTON, The Advice.

Clive, like most men who are born with strong passions and tried by strong temptations, committed great faults.   But every person who takes a fair and enlightened view of his whole career must admit that our island, so fertile in heroes and statesmen, has scarcely ever produced a man more truly great either in arms or in council.—MACAULAY, *Essays : Lord Clive.*

WILLIAM COBBETT.

English Political Writer : 1762-1835.

Imposing, undoubting, Cobbett-like manners.—S. T. COLERIDGE, *Table Talk.*

The late Lord Thurlow used to say that Cobbett was the only writer that deserved the name of a political reasoner. . . . People have about as substantial an idea of Cobbett as they have of Cribb. . . . He might be said to have the clearness of Swift, the naturalness of Defoe, and the picturesque satirical description of Mandeville.—HAZLITT, *Table Talk.*

One is slow to believe that a man is much in earnest, when he will not stand out and bear the brunt of the public gaze ; when he shrinks from avowing, *What I have written, I have written.*   Whereas a certain respect and deference is ever felt almost instinctively for the personality of another, when it is not impertinently obtruded : and it is pleasant to be reminded now and then that we are reading the words of a man not the words of a book. . . . This was one of the things which added to the power of Cobbett's style.   His readers knew who was talking to them.   They knew it was William Cobbett, not the *Times*, or the *Morning Chronicle*,—that the words proceeded from the breast of a man, not merely from the mouth of a print-ing-press.   It is only under his own shape, we all feel, that we can constrain Proteus to answer us, or rely on what he says.—J. C. HARE, *Guesses at Truth, First Series.*

It is worth while to read Cobbett, and especially the *Rural Rides*, not only to enjoy his fine homespun English, but to learn to know the man a little better.   Whatever the deserts or demerits of Cobbett as a political agitator, the true man was fully as much allied to modern Young England and the later type of conservatism as to the modern radical.   He hated the Scotch "feelosophers"—as he calls them—Parson Malthus, the political communists, the Manchester men, the men who would break up the old social system of the country, at the bottom of his heart.—LESLIE STEPHEN, *Hours in a Library, Vol. III.*

RICHARD COBDEN.

English Politician and Economist : 1804-1865.

Cobden believed that the real interests, of the individual, of the nation, and of all nations are identical ; and that these several interests are all in entire and necessary accord with the highest interests of morality. With this belief, an economic truth acquired with him the dignity and vitality of a moral law, and, instead of remaining a barren doctrine of the intellect, became a living force, to move the hearts and consciences of men.—SIR LOUIS MALLET, *Introductory Essay to Writings of Cobden.*

Cobden made his way to men's hearts by the union which they saw in him of simplicity, earnestness, and conviction, with a singular faculty of exposition.   This facility consisted in a remarkable power of apt and homely illustration, and a curious ingenuity, in framing the argument that happened to be wanted.   Besides his skill in thus hitting on the right argument, Cobden had the oratorical art of presenting it in the way that made its admission to the understanding of a listener easy and undenied. He always seemed to have made the right allowance for the difficulty with which men follow a speech, as compared with the ease of following the same argument on a printed page. . . . Then men were attracted by his mental alacrity, by the instant readiness, with which he turned round to grapple with a new objection. Prompt and confident, he was never at a loss, and he never hesitated. This is what Mr. Disraeli meant when he spoke of Cobden's sauciness.—JOHN MORLEY, *Life of Cobden, Vol. I.*

Cobden, must be looked on rather as a political missionary than as a statesman, as an agitator rather than as an administrator.—A. J. BALFOUR, *Essays and Addresses.*

SIR JOHN OLDCASTLE, LORD COBHAM.

English Soldier and Reformer : 1360-1417.

Why there ? they came to hear their preacher.   Then
Some cried on Cobham, on the good Lord Cobham :
Ay, for they love me ! but the king—nor voice
Nor finger raised against him—took and hang'd.
                    —TENNYSON, *Sir John Oldcastle, Lord Cobham.*

Sir John Oldcastle, Lord Cobham, was the most conspicuous of the first heretics, or, in other words, of the first who preferred death to insincerity, under the new law for burning heretics.—SIR JAMES MACKINTOSH, *History of England, Vol. I.*

Sir John Oldcastle, Lord Cobham, was a man whose virtue made him a reformer, whose valour made him a martyr.—HORACE WALPOLE.

DR. J. W. COLENSO.

Bishop of Natal and Biblical Critic : 1814-1883.

For our Essays and Reviews' debate
Begins to tell on the public mind,
And Colenso's words have weight.
                    —ROBERT BROWNING, *Gold Hair.*

SAMUEL TAYLOR COLERIDGE.

English Poet and Philosopher : 1772-1834.

Stop, Christian passer-by ; stop, child of God,
And read, with gentle breast. Beneath this sod
A poet lies, or that which once seemed he—
O, lift a prayer in thought for S. T. C.!
That he who many a year with toil of breath,
Found death in life, may here find life in death !
Mercy for praise—to be forgiven, for fame
He asked, and hoped through Christ. Do thou the same.
                —S. T. COLERIDGE, *Epitaph composed for Himself.*

You will see Coleridge ; he who sits obscure
In the exceeding lustre and the pure
Intense irradiation of a mind,
Which, with its own internal lustre blind ;
Flags wearily through darkness and despair—
A cloud-encircled meteor of the air,
A hooded eagle among blinking owls.
                —SHELLEY, *Letter to Maria Gisborne.*

And Coleridge, too, has lately taken wing,
But like a hawk encumber'd with his hood,
Explaining metaphysics to the nation—
I wish he would explain his explanation.
                —BYRON, *Don Juan, Canto I.*

Nor has the rolling year twice measured,
From sign to sign, its steadfast course,
Since every mortal power of Coleridge,
Was frozen at its marvellous source ;
The 'rapt One, of the godlike forehead,
The heavened-eyed creature sleeps in earth.
                —WORDSWORTH, *Extempore Effusion upon the Death
                of James Hogg.*

One whose fame is in all the churches. . . . Samuel Taylor Coleridge, logician, metaphysician, bard.—AUGUSTINE BIRRELL, *Obiter Dicta*, *First Series.*

Coleridge, a catholic mind, with a hunger for ideas, with eyes looking before and after to the highest bards and sages, and who wrote and spoke the only high criticism in his time, is one of those who save England from the reproach of no longer possessing the capacity to appreciate what rarest wit the island has yielded.—EMERSON, *English Traits : Literature.*

The magnificent imagery and the varied music of Coleridge and Shelley. —LORD MACAULAY, *Essays : Moore's Life of Lord Byron.*

This Manichean of poesy.—BYRON in MOORE'S *Life of Byron.*

Coleridge exerted so large an influence over so many of those minds which are in themselves reproductive, and yield in the sheaf what they receive in the germ, that if we were asked " What he had done in this life ? " it might be enough to answer, " he has lived ". We might almost suppress reference to his own writings, we might point to the writings of others.—LYTTON, *Essays: Charles Lamb.*

If it be true, as Lord Bacon affirms, that a knowledge of the speculative opinions of the men between twenty and thirty years of age is the great source of political prophecy, the existence of Coleridge will show itself by no slight or ambiguous traces in the coming history of our country ; for no one has contributed more to shape the opinions of those among its younger men, who can be said to have opinions at all. . . . He has been the great awakener in this country of the spirit of philosophy, within the bounds of traditional opinions. He has been, almost as truly as Bentham, "the great questioner of things established" ; for a questioner needs not necessarily be an enemy.—JOHN STUART MILL, *Dissertations and Discussions, Vol. I.*

"You can never say too much about Coleridge for me," Rossetti would write, "for I worship him on the right side of idolatry, and I perceive you know him well." Upon this one of my first remarks was that there was much in Coleridge's higher descriptive verse equivalent to the landscape art of Turner. The critical parallel Rossetti warmly approved of, adding however, that Coleridge, at his best as a pictorial artist, was a spiritualised Turner.—HALL CAINE, *Recollections of Dante Gabriel Rossetti.*

Coleridge sat on the brow of Highgate Hill in those years, looking down on London and its smoke-tumult, like a sage escaped from the inanity of life's battle ; attracting towards him the thoughts of innumerable brave souls still engaged there. His express contributions to poetry, philosophy, or any specific province of human literature or enlightenment, had been small and sadly intermittent ; but he had, especially among young inquiring men, a higher than literary, a kind of prophetic or magician character. He was thought to hold, he alone in England, the key of German and other Transcendentalisms ; knew the sublime secret of believing by "the reason" what "the understanding" had been obliged to fling out as incredible ; and could still, after Hume and Voltaire had done their best and worst with him, profess himself an orthodox Christian, and say and point to the Church of England, with its singular old rubrics and surplices at Allhallowtide, *Esto perpetua.* A sublime man ; who, alone in those dark days, had saved his crown of spiritual manhood ; escaping from the black materialisms, and revolutionary deluges, with "God, Freedom, Immortality" still his : a king of men.—CARLYLE, *Life of John Sterling.*

I have heard Coleridge. That man is entitled to speak on till Doomsday—or rather the genius within him—for he is inspired. Wind him up, and away he goes, discoursing most excellent music—without a discord—full, ample, inexhaustible, serious and divine !—JOHN WILSON, *Noctes Ambrosianæ, Vol. I.*

Coleridge, that rich-freighted Argosie tilting in sunshine over Imagination's Seas.—*Id., Ibid. : Old North and Young North.*

The Fakeer of Highgate.—KINGSLEY, *Literary and General Lectures.*

Coleridge's own imagination, too, enabled him to accompany all other poets in their boldest flights, and then to feel most truly in his element. Nor could anything be too profound or too subtle for his psychological analysis. In fact his chief failing as a critic was his fondness for seeking depth below depth, and knot within knot: and he would now and then try to dive, when the water did not come up to his ankles.—J. C. HARE, *Guesses at Truth, First Series.*

Coleridge's singular history may throw some light upon his teaching. Here we meet the hagiologist and the iconoclast, the twin plagues of the humble biographer. The hagiologist burns incense before his idol till it is difficult to distinguish any fixed outline through the clouds of gorgeously-tinted vapour. Coleridge thought himself to have certain failings. His relations fully agreed with him. His worshippers regard these meek confessions as mere illustrations of the good man's humility, and even manage to endow the poet and philosopher with all the homely virtues of the respectable and the solvent. To put forward such claims is to challenge the iconoclast. . . . To tell the story of Coleridge without the opium is to tell the story of Hamlet without mentioning the Ghost.— LESLIE STEPHEN, *Hours in a Library, Vol. III.*

WILLIAM COLLINS.

English Poet: 1720-1756.

Collins was simply a reed, cut short and notched by the great god Pan, for the production of enchanting flute-melodies at intervals; but for all other human purposes a vain and empty thing indeed.—E. W. GOSSE, *Gray.*

CHRISTOPHER COLUMBUS.

Discoverer of America: 1438-1506.

Spain once the most chivalric race on earth,
Spain then the mightiest, wealthiest realm of earth,
So made by me, may seek to unbury me,
To lay me in some shrine of this old Spain,
Or in that vaster Spain I leave to Spain.
Then someone standing by my grave will say,
" Behold the bones of Christopher Colòn "—
" Ay, but the chains, what do *they* mean—the chains ? "—
I sorrow for that kindly child of Spain
Who then will have to answer, " These same chains
Bound these same bones back thro' the Atlantic sea,
Which he unchain'd for all the world to come."
                              —TENNYSON, *Columbus.*

Remember whose and not how short it is !
It is God's day, it is Columbus's.
O lavish day ! One day, with life and heart,
Is more than time enough to find a world.
                              —J. R. LOWELL, *Columbus.*

Did great Columbus tame his eagle soul
To jostle with the daws that perch in courts ?
                              —*Id., L'Envoi.*

Who bid the stork, Columbus-like, explore
Heav'ns not his own, and worlds unknown before?
                    —POPE, *Essay on Man : Epistle III.*

Columbus was the first that shook his throne ;
And found a temperate in a torrid zone.
                    —DRYDEN, *Epistle II.: To Dr. Charleton.*

                    By the virtue led
Of Gama and Columbus.   The whole globe
Is now, of commerce, made the scene immense,
Which daring ships frequent, associated,
Like doves, or swallows, in th' ethereal flood,
Or, like the eagle, solitary seen.
                    —DYER, *The Fleece : Book IV.*

Columbus! scarce inferior fame
For thee to find, than heaven to frame
That womb of gold and gem : her wide domain,
An universe! her rivers seas !
Her fruits, both men and gods to please !
Heaven's fairest birth ! and, but for thee, in vain !
                    —YOUNG, *The Merchant : Strain IV.*

Columbus, boast of science, boast of man ;
Yet, by the great, the learned, and the wise,
Long held a visionary ; who, like thee
Could brook their scorn ; wait seven long years at court,
A selfish, sullen, dilatory court;
Yet never from thy purpos'd plan decline?
No god, no hero of poetic times,
In truth's fair annals may compare with thee !
                    —JAMES GRAINGER, *The Sugar Cane.*

Have we not lately, in the moon,
Found a new world, to th' old unknown?
Discover'd sea and land, Columbus
And Magellan cou'd never compass?
Made mountains with our tubes appear,
And cattle grazing on 'em there?
                    —SAMUEL BUTLER, *Hudibras, Part II., Canto* 3.

Still steer on, brave heart! though witlings laugh at thy emprize,
And though the helmsmen drop weary and nerveless their hands ;
Westward, westward still ! there land must emerge to the vision ;
There it lies in its light, dear to the eye of thy mind ;
Trust in the power that guides : press on o'er the convex of ocean :
What thou seekest—were it not—yet it would rise from the wave.
Nature with genius holds a pact that is fixt and eternal :
All that is promised by *this*, that never fails to perform.
                    —DR. WM. WHEWELL, *From Schiller's Columbus.*

   Columbus enriched kings with the wealth of a new hemisphere, and
Columbus came back in chains from the New World he had discovered.—
F. W. FARRAR, *Social and Present-Day Questions.*

Columbus found the New World in an undecked boat. It is curious to see the periodical disuse and perishing of means and machinery, which were introduced with loud laudation a few years or centuries before. The great genius returns to essential man.—EMERSON, *Essays: Self-Reliance*.

Columbus, too, read men sideways, as it were. No one has ever yet lived, whose career has had so great an effect on human affairs as Columbus; yet was he fated to die in ignorance of the grandeur of his own discovery.—CHARLES BUCKE, *Book of Human Character*.

Columbus had all the spirit of a crusader, and, at the same time, the investigating nature of a modern man of science. The Arabs have a proverb that a man is more the son of the age in which he lives than of his own father. This was not so with Columbus; he hardly seems to belong at all to his age. At a time when there was never more of worldliness and self-seeking; when Alexander Borgia was Pope; when Louis the Eleventh reigned in France, Henry the Seventh in England, and Ferdinand the Catholic in Arragon and Castile—about the three last men in the world to become Crusaders—Columbus was penetrated with the ideas of the twelfth century, and would have been a worthy companion of Saint Louis in that pious king's crusade.—SIR ARTHUR HELPS, *Life of Columbus*.

Like Joan of Arc, and other gifted beings who have been the instruments to work out great events, Columbus heard voices, which had the practical effect of rousing him from despondency and bracing him to his work. He has recorded two occasions on which this happened, but probably "the voices" made themselves heard at other critical turning-points of his life. Yet there was no danger of his becoming a mere missionary. His clear penetrating intellect saved him from that; and it was this unrivalled power, combined with a brilliant imagination, which constituted his genius. He prepared himself for his great work by long study, by the acquisition of vast experience, and by a minute knowledge of every detail of his profession. But this would not have sufficed. He added to these qualifications a master mind endowed with reasoning powers of a high order; and an ingenious, almost subtle, way of seizing upon and utilising every point which had a relation to the subject he was considering. His forecasts amount to precision. Assuredly the New World was no accident.—C. R. MARKHAM, *Life of Christopher Columbus*.

In Columbus were singularly combined the practical and the poetical. His mind had grasped all kinds of knowledge, whether procured by study or observation, which bore upon his theories; impatient of the scanty aliment of the day, "his impetuous ardour," as has well been observed, "threw him into the study of the fathers of the Church, the Arabian Jews, and the ancient geographers"; while his daring, but irregular genius, bursting from the limits of imperfect science, bore him to conclusions far beyond the intellectual vision of his contemporaries. If some of his conclusions were erroneous, they were at least ingenious and splendid; and their error resulted from the clouds which still hung over his peculiar path of enterprise. His own discoveries enlightened the ignorance of the age, guided conjecture to certainty, and dispelled that very darkness with which he had been obliged to struggle.—WASHINGTON IRVING, *Life and Voyages of Columbus, Vol. II*.

The men of that time justly deserving the title of innovators were those who foresaw the progress of civilization towards a vaster synthesis of the human race, and felt drawn nearer to God.   Their hot blood burned like fever in their veins ; their ideas changed with delirious rapidity : they were dominated by a superior force, impelling them across unknown seas to the discovery of unseen but truly imagined lands.   Of these men Christopher Columbus was the veritable type and exponent.   Rather than downright, genuine thinkers, they are champions of thought.   It is useless to ask them what they seek and whither they go.   They only know that they are pressing forward, and drawing the world after them in their course— nothing more.   Nor should we wonder at their unconsciousness, for it is their essential characteristic and merit.   They disperse the darkness, and cleave a passage for the new road, rather by force of will and faith, than by force of reason.   Theirs is the prophetic mind, the hero's heart, the martyr's fate.—Prof. Villari, *Life and Times of Savonarola* (*transl.*).

Philip de Comines.

French Historian and Statesman : 1445-1509.

If Froissart, by his picturesque descriptions, and fertility of historical *invention*, may be reckoned the Livy of France, she had her Tacitus in Philip de Comines.—Hallam, *Literature of the Middle Ages, Vol. I.*

Comines has made as many heretics in politics as Luther has in religion. —Catherine de Medici.

Auguste Comte.

French Philosopher : 1798-1857.

Let it by no means be supposed from all I have said, that I do not regard M. Comte's speculations as of great value.   True or untrue, his system as a whole, has doubtless produced important and salutary revolutions of thought in many minds ; and will doubtless do so in many more. . . . And he has done especial service by familiarizing men with the idea of a social science, based on the other sciences.—Herbert Spencer, *Philosophy of Comte.*

The most reverend prelate might dialectically hew M. Comte in pieces, as a modern Agag, and I should not attempt to stay his hand.   In so far as my study of what specially characterises the Positive Philosophy has led me, I find therein little or nothing of any scientific value, and a great deal which is as thoroughly antagonistic to the very essence of science as anything in ultramontane Catholicism.   In fact, M. Comte's philosophy, in practice, might be compendiously described as Catholicism *minus* Christianity.—Huxley, *Method and Results.*

A man wishing to build a house must indeed obey the law of universal gravitation, but it will help him little practically to have that law enunciated with the most convincing pomp of historical proof and the most rigid mathematical precision.   We are obliged to conclude, then, that positivism in M. Comte's hands, while pretending to take upon itself the regulation of human conduct, fails to furnish a guiding principle for either individuals or societies.   It sends us to sea with an admirable chart of the tides, currents, and winds ; instructs us how eminently modifiable these forces are by the rudder; but declines to provide us with a compass, or to say anything about the port for which we have to steer. All that can be done in such a case is to lie on one's back and look at the stars, or exercise an empirical prudence in selecting such a course as fancy or foresight may suggest. To drop metaphor, we must still have recourse to our celestial guides, or to our internal monitions, in our voyage along the stormy sea of life: for M. Comte provides us with no satisfactory substitute.—GEORGE BRIMLEY, *Essays*.

All Comte's books are dull. This Positivist Catechism is one of the dullest. And yet it is throughout abundantly entertaining. This may sound paradoxical; but the paradox at once vanishes if we consider that there is nothing more ludicrous even to the gravest than the gravity of a goose, an animal whose majestic strut along a common after it is tired of feeding is a familiar, but not, it must be confessed, an imposing, spectacle. M. Comte's pace and presence are kindred to those of this useful bird. And as destitute as the goose of humour, he provokes mirth by his solemn airs and by a ponderousness of speech which is meant for regal dignity.— WILLIAM MACCALL, *The Newest Materialism*.

CONFUCIUS.

Chinese Philosopher: B.C. 551-479.

Superior, and alone, Confucius stood,
Who taught that useful science,—to be good.
                    —POPE, *The Temple of Fame*.

And he talks in one breath of Confutzee, Cass, Zerduscht.
                    —J. R. LOWELL, *A Fable for Critics*.

Confucius perhaps displayed as much sagacity as benevolence, in making politeness one of his five cardinal virtues.—W. B. CHULOW.

What a pity their philosopher Confucius did not write poetry, with his precepts of mortality!—BYRON in MOORE's *Life of Byron*.

No great character in history can appeal more surely from the opinion of his contemporaries to the verdict of posterity than Confucius.—PROF. R. K. DOUGLAS, *Confucianism and Taouism*.

Confucius might well be the saint of modern Agnosticism.—C. L. BRACE, *Gesta Christi*.

WILLIAM CONGREVE.

English Dramatist and Poet: 1670-1729.

Did not the muses' other hope appear,
Harmonious Congreve, and forbid our fear:
Congreve, whose fancy's unexhausted store
Has given already much, and promis'd more.
Congreve shall still preserve thy fame alive,
And Dryden's music shall in his friend survive.
                    —ADDISON, *Account of the Greatest English Poets*.

The comic tone, inspir'd by Congreve, draws
At every word, loud laughter and applause.
                                    —ADDISON, *The Play House.*

No writers have injured the Comedy of England so deeply as Congreve
and Sheridan. Both were men of splendid wit and polished taste. Un-
happily they made all their characters in their own likeness. Their works
bear the same relation to the legitimate drama which a transparency bears
to a painting. There are no delicate touches, no hues imperceptibly fading
into each other: the whole is lighted up with an universal glare. Outlines
and tints are forgotten in the common blaze which illuminates all. The
flowers and fruits of the intellect abound; but it is the abundance of a
jungle, not a garden, unwholesome, bewildering, unprofitable from its very
plenty, rank from its very fragrance. Every fop, every boor, every valet,
is a man of wit.—MACAULAY, *Essays: Machiavelli.*

He formed a peculiar idea of comic excellence, which he supposed to
consist in gay remarks and unexpected answers; but that which he
endeavoured, he seldom failed of performing. His scenes exhibit not
much of humour, imagery, or passion: his personages are a kind of intellectual gladiators: every sentence is to ward or strike; the contest of
smartness is never intermitted; his wit is a meteor playing to and fro with
alternate coruscations.—DR. JOHNSON, *Lives of the Poets: Congreve.*

CAPTAIN JAMES COOK.

English Circumnavigator: 1728-1779.

When Cook—lamented, and with tears as just
As ever mingled with heroic dust,—
Steer'd Britain's oak into a world unknown,
And in his country's glory sought his own,
Wherever he found man, to nature true,
The rights of man were sacred in his view;
He soothed with gifts, and greeted with a smile,
The simple native of the new-found isle;
He spurn'd the wretch that slighted or withstood
The tender argument of kindred blood,
Nor would endure that any should control
His freeborn brethren of the southern pole.
But though some nobler minds a law respect,
That none shall with impunity neglect,
In baser souls unnumber'd evils meet,
To thwart its influence, and its end defeat.
While Cook is loved for savage lives he saved,
See Cortez odious for a world enslaved!
                                    —COWPER, *Charity.*

NICHOLAS COPERNICUS.

German Astronomer: 1473-1543.

The learned Scaliger complain'd
'Gainst what Copernicus maintain'd,
That in twelve hundred years and odd,

The sun had left its ancient road,
And nearer to the earth is come
'Bove fifty thousand miles from home.
　　　　—SAMUEL BUTLER, *Hudibras, Part II., Canto* 3.

If to the old you the new schools prefer,
And to the fam'd Copernicus adhere;
If you esteem that supposition best,
Which moves the earth, and leaves the sun at rest;
With a new veil your ignorance you hide,
Still is the knot as hard to be untied;
You change your scheme, but the old doubts remain,
And still you leave th' inquiring mind in pain.
　　　　—SIR RICHARD BLACKMORE, *Creation.*

The Founder of Modern Astronomy.—HALLAM, *Literature of the Middle Ages, Vol. I.*

Is it so bad, then, to be misunderstood? Pythagoras was misunderstood, and Socrates, and Jesus, and Luther, and Copernicus, and Galileo, and Newton, and every pure and wise spirit that ever took flesh. To be great is to be misunderstood.—EMERSON, *Essays: Self-Reliance.*

In 1543 the epoch-making work of Copernicus on the paths of the heavenly bodies appeared. The total crash of Aristotle's closed universe with the earth at its centre followed as a consequence, and "the earth moves!" became a kind of watchword among intellectual freemen. . . . In the last year of the life of Copernicus his book appeared: it is said that the old man received a copy of it a few days before his death, and then departed in peace.—TYNDALL, *Address before the British Association at Belfast,* 1874.

CHARLOTTE CORDAY.

Marat's Murderer: 1768-1793.

Judith and Charlotte Corday sacrificed themselves, but they sacrificed themselves even unto crime. . . . As for us, if we were to seek a name for this sublime saviour of her country, and generous murderess of tyranny, a name which should express equally the enthusiasm of our emotion for her, and the severity of our judgment on her act, we should create an expression which unites the two extremes of admiration and horror in human speech, and call her the Angel of Assassination.—LAMARTINE, *Celebrated Characters* (transl.), *Vol. II.*

Among the many heroic women of history there is not one whose name thrills us with as strange a mingling of admiration and repulsion as that of Charlotte Corday. We shudder when we think of the cool, deliberately-planned murder; but after studying her beautiful, womanly face, and tracing her life step by step, from innocent childhood to the unsullied girlhood full of noble dreams and unselfish desires, we learn first to understand and then to love her.—JEANETTE VAN ALSTYNE, *Charlotte Corday.*

ARCANGELO CORELLI.

Italian Musician : 1653-1713.

No charms are wanting to thy artful song,
Soft as Corelli, and as Virgil strong.
> —TICKELL, *To Mr. Addison.*

The country scraper, when he wakes his crowd,
And makes the tortur'd cat-gut squeak aloud,
Is often ravish'd, and in transport lost :
What more, my friend, can fam'd Corelli boast,
When harmony herself from heaven descends,
And on the artist's moving bow attends?
> —AMBROSE PHILLIPS, *Epistle : To a Friend.*

PIERRE CORNEILLE.

French Dramatist : 1606-1684.

How the big Roman soul shook, in Corneille,
The trembling stage.
> —THOMSON, *Liberty.*

Till late Corneille, with Lucan's spirit fir'd,
Breath'd the free strain, as Rome and he inspir'd.
> —COLLINS, *Epistle to Sir Thomas Hanmer.*

Exact Racine, and Corneille's noble fire,
Show'd us that France had something to admire!
> —POPE, *The First Epistle of the First Book of Horace.*

Our neighbour's stage-art too bare-fac'd betrays,
'Tis great Corneille at every scene we praise ;
On nature's surer aid Britannia calls,
None think of Shakespeare till the curtain falls.
> —YOUNG, *Epistle to Lord Landsdowne,* 1712.

Napoleon, at St. Helena, forgot the empire of the world on hearing, in the long evenings, the masterpieces of Corneille read aloud.—SIR ARCHIBALD ALISON, *Essays : The Greek Drama.*

ANTONIO ALLEGRI CORREGGIO.

Italian Painter : 1494-1534.

Correggio's softer line.
> —POPE, *Epistle to Mr. Jervas.*

And Parma's pride, the Jerome, let us add !
'Twere pleasant could Correggio's fleeting glow
Hang full in face of one where'er one roams,
Since he more than the others brings with him
Italy's self,—the marvellous Modenese !
> —ROBERT BROWNING, *Bishop Blougram's Apology.*

I know, Correggio loves to mass, in rifts
Of heaven, his angel faces, orb on orb
Breaking its outline, burning shades absorb.
>—ROBERT BROWNING, *A Face.*

The Correggiosity of Correggio.
>—RUSKIN, *On the Old Road, Vol. I.*

Like Euripides, Correggio was condemned to the misfortune of separating beauty from the idea, the body from the spirit. With them the forces inherent in the germs of their respective arts were exhausted. But those who rightly understand them must, we imagine, be prepared to accept with gratitude the existence of Correggio and Euripides, both as complementing Giotto and Æschylus, and also as accounting for the meridian splendour of Sophocles and Raphael. Without the cadence of Euripides the majestic aria of Sophocles would hardly be played out. By studying the Correggiosity of Correggio we comprehend how much of mere æsthetic beauty is held in solution in the work of Raphael. It is thus, as it were, that, like projectiles, arts describe their parabolas and end.—J. ADDINGTON SYMONDS, *Studies of Greek Poets.*

ABRAHAM COWLEY.

English Lyric Poet: 1618-1667.

Cowley blossomed soon, yet flourish.d long.
>—DRYDEN, *Epilogue to " Tamerlane the Great ".*

Time, which made their fame outlive,
To Cowley scarce did ripeness give.
To him no author was unknown,
Yet what he wrote was all his own.
>—SIR JOHN DENHAM, *On Cowley's Death and Burial.*

Who now reads Cowley ? if he pleases yet,
His moral pleases, not his pointed wit,
Forget his epic, nay Pindaric art !
But still I love the language of his heart.
>—POPE, *The First Epistle of the Second Book of Horace.*

Nor yet shall Waller yield to time,
Nor pensive Cowley's moral lay.
>—*Id., Imitations of Horace, Bk. IV., Ode* 9.

The Muses did young Cowley raise :
They stole thee from thy nurse's arms,
Fed thee with sacred love of praise,
And taught thee all their charms :
As if Apollo's self had been thy fire,
They daily rock'd thee on his lyre. . . .
Whatever Cowley writes must please ;
Sure, like the gods, he speaks all languages.
Whatever theme by Cowley's muse is dress'd,
Whatever he'll essay,
Or in the softer or the nobler way,
He still writes best.
>—SAMUEL WESLEY, *On Mr. Cowley's Juvenile Poems.*

Great Cowley then (a mighty genius) wrote;
O'er-run with wit, and lavish of his thought:
His turns too closely on the reader press:
He more had pleas'd us, had he pleas'd us less.
One glittering thought no sooner strikes our eyes
With silent wonder, but new wonders rise.
As in the milky-way a shining white
O'erflows the heavens with one continued light;
That not a single star can show his rays,
Whilst jointly all promote the common blaze.
> —ADDISON, *Account of the Greatest English Poets.*

How, in this toilsome age,
Didst thou, immortal man! when arts were overthrown,
When all the muses' garden was o'ergrown,
And whole Parnassus tumbled down,
Stand on its ruins, and erect a new one of thy own?
> —AARON HILL, *On Mr. Cowley's Introducing Pindaric Verse.*

Blest Cowley, too, who on the banks of Cam
So sweetly sighed his wrongs, and told his flame.
> —OLDHAM, *Pastoral on the Death of the Earl of Rochester.*

Cowley's verse keeps fair Orinda young.
> —PRIOR, *To the Countess of Exeter.*

In genius Cowley! and though now, reclaim'd
By modern lights from an erroneous taste,
I cannot but lament thy splendid wit
Entangled in the cobwebs of the schools:
I still revere thee, courtly though retired,
Though stretch'd at ease in Chertsey's silent bowers,
Not unemploy'd, and finding rich amends
For a lost world in solitude and verse.
> —COWPER, *The Task: The Winter Evening.*

The power of Cowley is not so much to move the affections, as to exercise the understanding. The *Chronicle* is a composition unrivalled and alone: such gaiety of fancy, such facility of expression, such varied similitude, such a succession of images, and such a dance of words, it is in vain to expect except from Cowley. His strength always appears in his agility; his volatility is not the flutter of a light, but the bound of an elastic mind. His levity never leaves his learning behind it; the moralist, the politician, and the critic, mingle their influence even in this airy frolic of genius.—DR. JOHNSON, *Lives of the Poets: Cowley.*

WILLIAM COWPER.

English Poet: 1731-1800.

What! must deserted Poesy still weep
Where her last hopes with pious Cowper sleep?
Unless, perchance, from his cold bier she turns
To deck the turf that wraps her minstrel, Burns?
> —BYRON, *English Bards and Scotch Reviewers.*

Cowper, thy lovely spirit was there, by death disenchanted
From that heavy spell which had bound it in sorrow and darkness,
Thou wert there, in the kingdom of peace and of light everlasting.
                    —SOUTHEY, *A Vision of Judgment.*

Shoddy : " How like you, then, the music unutterable
Of epic blank verse, Miltonian or Cowperian ? "
Gas : " Its merits, doubtless are unutterable !
To get it out, one has to mouth and lick it,
Like a she-bear, her charming cubs adorning
For a bear-dance on meteor-lighted snows
Of Lapland or Kamschatka ! "
                    —DR. MILO MAHAN, *The Yorkshireman in Boston, Sc. II.*

The Poet of Christianity, the Monitor of the world.—WILLIAM HAYLEY, *Life of Cowper.*

Is not *The Task* a glorious poem ? The religion of *The Task*, bating a few scraps of Calvinistic divinity, is the religion of God and nature, the religion that exalts, that ennobles man.—BURNS.

Religion was the muse of Cowper.—MACAULAY, *Essays : Moore's " Life of Byron ".*

I was brought up on Cowper.—BENJAMIN JOWETT in ABBOT ˙ and CAMPBELL'S *Life of Jowett.*

The Laureate of Evangelicism . . . Cowper was, *intus et in cute*, an Englishman and his poetry contains the refined essence of John Bullism. Its manliness, its clearness, its avoidance of mist and mysticism, its bluntness, its dogged sincerity, its prejudices, and its patriotic glow, are all characteristic of his native nook of earth ; and well might he indite that line, so noble in its simple strength—
      " England, with all thy faults, I love thee still ".
      —REV. GEORGE GILFILLAN, *Introduction to Cowper's Works.*

He read few books writ by man—but they were among the best—the books of his great native poets. His library was the Bible and the Book of Nature. We could prove that—but must not now. Moreover, in the art of poetry he is a consummate master. Teniers, Hogarth, Wilkie— each of them in his own art is a great master too ; but in conception, in comprehension, and in breadth and depth of colouring, Cowper was greater than them all three—could you conceive them all three in one ;—and then, what is painting compared with poetry ! So much by the way of a short imperfect notice of the greatest poet of the Poor.—JOHN WILSON, *Essays : Poetry of Ebenezer Elliott.*

In no natural struggle for existence would he have been the survivor, by no natural process of selection would he ever have been picked out as a vessel of honour. If the shield which for eighteen centuries Christ by His teaching and His death has spread over the weak things of this world should fail, and might should again become the title to existence and the measure of worth, Cowper will be cast aside as a specimen of despicable infirmity, and all who have said anything in his praise will be treated with the same scorn.—GOLDWIN SMITH, *Cowper.*

There is no more interesting poet than Cowper, and hardly one the area of whose influence was greater.   No man, it is unnecessary to say, courted popularity less, yet he threw a very wide net, and caught a great shoal of readers.   For twenty years after the publication of *The Task* in 1785, his general popularity never flagged, and even when in the eyes of the world it was eclipsed, when Cowper became, in the opinion of fierce Byronians, and moss-trooping Northerners, "a coddled Pope" and a milksop, our great, sober, Puritan middle-class took him to their warm firesides for two generations more.   Some amongst these were not, it must be owned, lovers of poetry at all; they liked Cowper because he is full of a peculiar kind of religious phraseology, just as some of Burns' countrymen love Burns because he is full of a peculiar kind of strong drink called whisky. —AUGUSTINE BIRRELL, *Res Judicatæ.*

GEORGE CRABBE.

Descriptive English Poet: 1754-1832.

With Crabbe it may be difficult to cope.

—BRYON, *Don Juan.*

The plebeian pathos of Crabbe.—LORD JEFFREY, *Essays.*

Read me some amusing thing—read me a bit of Crabbe.—SIR WALTER SCOTT in LOCKHART'S *Life of Scott.*

It is not purple patches that offend the reader in Crabbe, but the beads of clay strung at intervals upon the chain of pearls.—T. E. KEBBEL, *Life of George Crabbe.*

If Crabbe's verses retain rather too much of the earthly elements, he is capable of transmuting his minerals into genuine gold as well as of simply collecting them. . . . Though Crabbe may not prompt such outward and visible signs of emotion, I think that he produces a more distinct titillation of the lachrymatory glands than almost any poet of his time.— LESLIE STEPHEN, *Hours in a Library, Second Series.*

It has, I think, been observed, and if not the observation is obvious, that he has done with the pen for the neighbourhood of Aldborough and Glemham what Crome and Cotman have done for the neighbourhood of Norwich with the pencil. . . . You could play on Crabbe that odd trick which used, it is said, to be actually played on some mediæval verse chroniclers and unrhyme him—that is to say, put him into prose with the least possible changes—and his merits would, save in rare instances, remain very much as they are now.   You could put other words in the place of his words, keeping the verse, and it would not as a rule be much the worse.   You cannot do either of these things with poets who are poets. —GEORGE SAINTSBURY, *Essays in English Literature.*

THOMAS CRANMER.

Archbishop of Canterbury : 1489-1566.

King Henry : "Stand up, good Canterbury :
Thy truth, and thy integrity, is rooted
In us, thy friend.   Give me thy hand, stand up :

Pr'ythee, let's walk. Now, by my holy-dame,
What manner of man are you? My lord, I look'd
You would have given me your petition, that
I should have ta'en some pains to bring together
Yourself and your accusers; and to have heard you,
Without indurance, further."
Cranmer: "Most dread liege,
The good I stand on is my truth and honesty:
If they shall fail, I, with mine enemies,
Will triumph o'er my person; which I weigh not,
Being of those virtues vacant. I fear nothing
What can be said against me."
    —SHAKESPEARE, *King Henry VIII., Act V., Sc. I.*

Outstretching flame—ward his upbraided hand
(O God of mercy, may no earthly seat
Of judgment such presumptuous doom repeat!)
Amid the shuddering throng doth Cranmer stand;
Firm as the stake to which with iron band
His frame is tied; firm from the naked feet
To the bare head, the victory complete;
The shrouded body, to the soul's command,
Answering with more than Indian fortitude,
Through all her nerves with finer sense endued,
Till breath departs in blissful aspiration:
Then, 'mid the ghastly ruins of the fire,
Behold the unalterable heart entire,
Emblem of faith untouched, miraculous attestation.
    —WORDSWORTH, *Cranmer.*

Bearing the palm of martyrdom, Cranmer was there in his meekness
Holy name to be ever revered!
    —SOUTHEY, *A Vision of Judgment: The Elder Worthies.*

Mary: "Cranmer is head and father of these heresies,
New learning as they call it; yea may God
Forget me at most need when I forget
Her foul divorce—my sainted mother—
No!"
    —TENNYSON, *Queen Mary.*

Yes England! with all thy sins, thou holdest with fast devotion to the Faith, for which so many of thy sainted sons did perish in the fires of persecution. The smoke of those fierce faggots is dead; but, as that inspired man prophesied, while he held up his withered hand in the scorching flame —such a fire has been kindled as lights all the land, centuries after his martyred ashes were given to the heedless winds—and the names of Cranmer and Ridley are reverenced for ever more!—JOHN WILSON, *Essays: Old North and Young North.*

If we consider Cranmer merely as a statesman, he will not appear a much worse man than Wolsey, Gardiner, Cromwell, or Somerset. But, when an attempt is made to set him up as a saint, it is scarcely possible for any man of sense who knows the history of the times to preserve his gravity.—MACAULAY, *Essays: Henry Hallam.*

OLIVER CROMWELL.

Lord Protector of the Commonwealth of England : 1599-1658.

So Cromwell, with deep oaths and rows,
Swore all the Commons out o' th' House.
                    —SAMUEL BUTLER, *Hudibras, Part II., Canto* 2.

Cromwell, our chief of men, who through a cloud
Not of war only, but detractions rude,
Guided by faith, and matchless fortitude,
To peace and truth thy glorious way hast plough'd,
And on the neck of crowned Fortune proud
Hast rear'd God's trophies, and His work pursued,
While Darwen stream with blood of Scots imbrued,
And Dunbar field resounds thy praises loud,
And Worcester's laureat wreath.   Yet much remains
To conquer still ; Peace hath her victories
No less renown'd than war : new foes arise
Threat'ning to bind our souls with secular chains :
Help us to save free conscience from the paw
Of hireling wolves, whose gospel is their maw.
                    —MILTON, *To the Lord General Cromwell.*

Or ravish'd with the whistling of a name,
See Cromwell damn'd to everlasting fame !
                    —POPE, *Essay on Man : Epistle IV.*

So restless Cromwell could not cease
In the inglorious arts of peace,
        But through adventurous war
        Urgèd his active star :
And like the three-forked lightning first,
Breaking the clouds where it was nurst,
        Did through his own side
        His fiery way divide.

                                        —MARVELL.

When Cromwell fought for power, and while he reigned
The proud protector of the power he gain'd,
Religion, harsh, intolerant, austere,
Parent of manners like herself severe,
Drew a rough copy of the Christian face,
Without the smile, the sweetness, or the grace;
The dark and sullen humour of the time
Judged every effort of the Muse a crime ;
Verse, in the finest mould of fancy cast,
Was lumber in an age so void of taste.
                                —COWPER, *Table Talk.*

Sylla was first of victors ; but our own,
The sagest of usurpers, Cromwell !—he
Too swept off senates while he hew'd the throne
Down to a block—immortal rebel !   See
What crimes it cost to be a moment free

And famous through all ages !   But beneath
His fate the moral lurks of destiny ;
His day of double victory and death
Beheld him win two realms, and happier, yield his breath.
—BYRON, Childe Harold's Pilgrimage.

Power's the same imposing thing,
In Lord Protector, as in King.
—REV. JOHN DAVIES, Historic Prologues.

O Cromwell, we are fallen on evil times !
There was a day when England had wide room
For honest men as well as foolish kings ;
But now the uneasy stomach of the time
Turns squeamish at them both.
—J. R. LOWELL, A Glance behind the Curtain.

Man, friend, remain a Cromwell ! in thy name,
Rule, and if thy son be worthy, he and his,
So rule the rest for ages ! be it grander thus
To be a Cromwell than a Carolus.
—VICTOR HUGO, Milton's Appeal to Cromwell (transl.).

Behind, lo Cromwell looms, and dusks the land
With the swart shadow of his giant hand.
—LYTTON, The Last Days of Elizabeth.

The scourge and servant of the Lord,
This hand the Bible—that the sword—
The Phantom—Cromwell rides !
—Id., Cromwell's Dream.

         So Cromwell too
Was a great hero, and filled whole reams of paper
With thoughts chaotic,—the mightiest kind of thought—
The true sublime !   For what can be sublimer,
Than a dun lurid smoke, with fire-flakes flashing,
A dim fire-dappled mass, belched forth in volumes
From the depths of a bubbling bottomless abyss ?
The true sublime, sir, and the true heroic,
The great, the wonderful, the soul-enlarging,
The thing to worship, and to marvel at,
Stands ever in the chaotic.
—DR. MILO MAHAN, The Yorkshireman in Boston, Sc. IV.

Cromwell was a saint-like thief, who, under the double cloak of religion and patriotism, committed a burglary in the constitution, and robbed the people of their title to liberty.   He looked upon dissimulation as the only test of human wisdom, and made it the keystone of the arch on which he built his fortune.—EARL OF CHATHAM.

It was very fortunate for Cromwell, that he appeared upon the stage at the precise moment when the people were tired of Kings : and as un-fortunate for his son Richard, that he had to make good his pretensions, at a moment when the people were equally tired of Protectors.—VOLTAIRE.

Cromwell, the iron leader of English vengeance. . . . Without detracting from the well-earned fame of the Protector in this respect, it may safely be affirmed, that the main cause of his success in foreign transactions was, that he had got the means of making the English pay taxes. He levied them with the sabre and the bayonet. He had a standing army of forty thousand men for his tax gatherers.—SIR ARCHIBALD ALISON, *Essays: Macaulay.*

The unity which makes the whole life of an individual the manifestation of a potent hidden idea . . . that unity which is evinced in Cromwell and Bonaparte, as much as in Franklin and Washington.—MAZZINI, *Life and Writings, Vol. II.*

The inspiration of Scripture predominated, in 1600, over the three kingdoms. Cromwell, more imbued than any other with this sentiment, was neither a politician, nor an ambitious conqueror, nor an Octavius, nor a Cæsar. He was a Judge of the Old Testament.—LAMARTINE, *Celebrated Characters (transl.), Vol. II.*

If a French or Spanish army had invaded England, and if that army had been cut to pieces, as we have no doubt that it would have been, on the first day on which it came face to face with the soldiers of Preston and Dunbar, with Colonel Fight-the-good-Fight, and Captain Smite-them-hip-and-thigh, the House of Cromwell would probably now have been reigning in England. The nation would have forgotten all the misdeeds of the man who had cleared the soil of foreign invaders.—MACAULAY, *Essays: Sir James Mackintosh.*

Oliver Cromwell quitted his farming; undertook a Hercules' Labour and life-long wrestle with that Lernæan Hydra-coil, wide as England, hissing heaven-high through its thousand crowned, coroneted, shovel-patted quack-heads; and he did wrestle with it, the truest and terriblest wrestle I have heard of; and he wrestled it, and mowed and cut it down a good many stages, so that its hissing is ever since pitiful in comparison, and one can walk abroad in comparative peace from it.—CARLYLE, *Past and Present: Manchester Insurrection.*

Oliver Cromwell, whose body they hung on their Tyburn gallows because he had found the Christian Religion inexecutable in this country, remains to me by far the remarkablest Governor we have had here for the last five centuries or so. For the last five centuries, there has been no Governor among us with anything like similar talent—with an idea in the heart of him capable to inspiring similar talent, capable of co-existing therewith.—*Id., Ibid.: Sir Jabesh Windbag.*

The religion which teaches us our duty to others is not very likely to fail us in regard to ourselves. Watch Cromwell in any great crisis of his life, and judge whether the faith he held could have rested on any doubtful or insecure foundation. Take him at the moment of his greatest triumph, or in the hour of his darkest peril, and observe whether the one so unduly elates or the other so unworthily depresses him, as to cause him to lose the sense either of his own weakness or of his Creator's power, either of the littleness of time or of the greatness of eternity.—JOHN FORSTER, *Historical and Biographical Essays, Vol. I.*

God works by instruments; and if there is any one man who, in times past, has contributed more than another, more than all others, to the wonders of the present age, that man is . . . Oliver Cromwell. The existing greatness of England is but the realisation of the plan he had conceived.—MERLE D'AUBIGNÉ, *The Protector (transl.).*

Cromwell was, and felt himself to be, a dictator called in by the winning cause in a revolution to restore confidence and secure peace. He was, as he said frequently, "the Constable set to keep order in the Parish". Nor was he in any sense a military despot. He was no professional soldier; and he had no taste for arbitrary or martial rule. —FREDERIC HARRISON, *Cromwell.*

What may be fairly demanded alike of Cromwell's admirers and of his critics is that they shall fix their eyes upon him as a whole. To one of them he is the champion of liberty and peaceful progress, to another the forcible crusher of free institutions, to a third the defender of oppressed peoples, to a fourth the assertor of his country's right to dominion. Every one of the interpreters has something in which to base his conclusions. All the incongruities of human nature are to be traced somewhere or other in Cromwell's career. What is more remarkable is that this union of apparently contradictory forces is precisely that which is to be found in the English people, and has made England what she is at the present day. . . . With Cromwell's memory it has fared as with ourselves. Royalists painted him as a devil. Carlyle painted him as the masterful saint who suited his peculiar Valhalla. It is time for us to regard him as he really was, with all his physical and moral audacity, with all his tenderness and spiritual yearnings, in the world of action what Shakespeare was in the world of thought, the greatest because the most typical Englishmen of all time. This, in the most enduring sense, is Cromwell's place in history.—S. R. GARDINER, *Cromwell's Place in History.*

Cromwell was not only a religious man, he was a man to whom his religion was everything. To understand him, it is necessary to understand his religion and to sympathise with it. His life, which makes an impression on the world simply as a factor in the politics of the time, was to him a piece of work wrought under the great Taskmaster's eye, which could only be judged in relation to eternity.—R. F. HORTON, *Cromwell.*

Cromwell, at the beginning, probably sincere, was doubtless a dissembler from the hour at which he aspired to rule; but he had to deal with many bad men; and dissimulation was the weapon which they used. Cromwell took it up and vanquished them. Cromwell was a tyrant; but, of his personal ambition, this is truly to be said, that it was never seen but directed to the promotion of his country's greatness.—LORD NUGENT, *Some Memorials of John Hampden.*

In calm weather a small man may steer the ship of State safely through the rocks and shoals which always beset public life. But it is only the courageous and lofty spirits, such as Cromwell, Marlborough, Washington, Napoleon and Pitt, who can create the circumstances required for their own genius to work in. They alone can ride safely through the storms and upheavals which their policy necessarily occasions.—VISCOUNT WOLSELEY, *Life of Marlborough, Vol. I.*

As often as danger threatens us, the thought returns, not that we may have again a Marlborough or a Black Prince; but that the race which produced Cromwell may, at its need, produce his peer, and that the spirit

of the Great Usurper may once more stand forth in arms.—GOLDWIN
SMITH, *Three English Statesmen.*

What is the secret of this extraordinary power ? . . . There is one answer
I suppose everybody here would give — that the secret of Cromwell's
strength rested in his religious faith.   I discard that answer, because it
would be begging the question.   No, my answer is this—that he was a
practical mystic, the most formidable and terrible of all combinations.   A
man who combines inspiration apparently derived—in my judgment really
derived—from close communion with the supernatural and the celestial,
a man who has that inspiration and adds to it the energy of a mighty man
of action, such a man as that lives in communion on a Sinai of his own,
and when he pleases to come down to this world below seems armed with
no less than the terrors and decrees of the Almighty himself.—LORD
ROSEBERY, *Speech at the Cromwell Tercentenary,* 1899.

His rule was the rule of the sword.   Yet his name stands first, half
warrior, half saint, in the calendar of English-speaking democracy.—
JOHN MORLEY, *Oliver Cromwell.*

RICHARD CROMWELL.

Lord Protector (1658-9) *:* 1626-1712.

A man of timid, vacillating, and undecided character, with no religious or
political convictions or passions, Richard complacently acce̦ d the good
fortune which he inherited from his father, though he had ne er reckoned
upon it, and was no more disposed to sacrifice it than he was capable of
achieving it.   It would even appear that, during his father's lifetime, and
in the chambers of Whitehall, he had stated what the character of his
government should be, after the storms of the preceding administration—
" a golden mediocrity between a tripping head and a filthy tail " —GUIZOT,
Richard Cromwell (transl.).

WILLIAM AUGUSTUS, DUKE OF CUMBERLAND.

English Soldier, son of George II. : 1721-1765.

The bravery of the Duke of Cumberland was such as distinguished him
even among the princes of his brave house.   The indifference with which
he rode about midst musket balls and cannon balls was not the highest
proof of his fortitude.   Hopeless maladies, horrible surgical operations,
far from unmanning him, did not even discompose him.   With courage,
he had the virtues which are akin to courage.   He spoke the truth, was
open in enmity and friendship, and upright in all his dealings.   But his
nature was hard; and what seemed to him justice was rarely tempered
with mercy.   He was, therefore, during many years one of the most unpopular men in England.   The severity with which he had treated the
rebels after the battle of Culloden, had gained for him the name of the
Butcher.—MACAULAY, *Essays : The Earl of Chatham,* 1844.

ALLAN CUNNINGHAM.

Scottish Author and Critic : 1784-1842.

Allan, true child of Scotland, thou who art
So oft in spirit on thy native hills,

And yonder Solway shores, a poet thou,
Judge by thyself how strong the ties which bind
A poet to his home.

> —SOUTHEY, *Epistle to Allan Cunningham.*

The Right Poetical Allan Cunningham.—LEIGH HUNT.

JOHN PHILPOT CURRAN.

Irish Orator: 1750-1817.

Mr. Curran was something much better than a sayer of smart sayings. He was a lover of his country—and its fearless, its devoted, and indefatigable servant.—LORD JEFFREY, *Essays.*

I have met Curran at Holland House—he beats everybody ;—his imagination is beyond human, and his humour perfect. Then he has fifty faces, and twice as many voices, when he mimics—I never met his equal.—BYRON in MOORE'S *Life of Lord Byron.*

ALIGHIERI DANTE.

Italian Poet: 1265-1321.

Wel can the wise poet of Florence,
That highte Dante, speken of this sentence :
So in swiche maner rime is Dantes tale.

> —CHAUCER, *The Wif of Bathes Tale.*

Ungrateful Florence ! Dante sleeps afar,
Like Scipio, buried by the upbraiding shore ;
Thy factions, in their worse than civil war,
Proscribed the bard whose name for evermore
Their children's children would in vain adore
With the remorse of ages.

> —BYRON, *Childe Harold's Pilgrimage.*

For to thy mortal sight shall the Grave unshadow its secrets ;
Such as of yore the Florentine saw, Hell's perilous chambers
He who trod in his strength ; and the arduous Mountain of Penance,
And the regions of Paradise, sphere within sphere intercircled.

> —SOUTHEY, *A Vision of Judgment: The Trance.*

Hark, on the right with full piano tone
Old Dante's voice encircles all the air.

> —A. H. HALLAM.

Dante, pacer of the shore
Where glutted hill disgorgeth filthiest gloom,
Unbitten by its whirring sulphur-spume—
Or whence the grieved and obscure waters slope
Into a darkness quieted by hope.

> —ROBERT BROWNING, *Sordello.*

Dante who loved well because he hated,
Hated wickedness that hinders loving.
                              —ROBERT BROWNING, *One Word More.*

King, that hast reign'd six hundred years, and grown
In power, and ever growest, since thine own
Fair Florence honouring thy nativity.
Thy Florence now the crown of Italy,
Hath sought the tribute of a verse from me,
I, wearing but the garland of a day.
Cast at thy feet one flower that fades away.
                              —TENNYSON, *To Dante.*

Such wine as Dante poured.
                              —J. R. LOWELL, *The Cathedral.*

Dante was the first awakener of entranced Europe; he created a language, in itself music and persuasion, out of a chaos of inharmonious barbarisms. He was the congregator of those great spirits who presided over the resurrection of learning; the Lucifer of that starry flock, which, in the thirteenth century, shone forth from republican Italy, as from a heaven, into the darkness of the benighted world.—SHELLEY.

The *Divine Comedy* of Dante, the *Jerusalem Delivered* of Tasso, the *Paradise Lost* of Milton, are the *Iliads* and *Odysseys* of our theological system.—LAMARTINE, *Celebrated Characters* (*transl.*), *Vol. II.*

God created Dante and Italian literature together.—MAZZINI, *Life and Writings, Vol. II.*

Dante never stays too long.—MACAULAY, *Essays : Lord Bacon.*

There have been more editors and commentators (and imitators ultimately) of Dante than all their poets put together. *Not* a favourite! Why, they talk Dante—write Dante—and think and dream Dante at this moment to an excess which would be ridiculous, but that he deserves it. —BYRON in MOORE'S *Life of Byron.*

His verses are in the mouth of all who are torn by passion, gnawed by remorse, or tormented by apprehension; and how many are there in this scene of woe!—SIR ARCHIBALD ALISON, *Essays : Homer, Dante, and M. Angelo.*

Shakespeare and Dante are Saints of Poetry; really, if we will think of it, *canonised*, so that it is impiety to meddle with them. . . . Dante and Shakespeare are a peculiar two. They dwell apart, in a kind of royal solitude; none equal, none second to them: in the general feeling of the world, a certain transcendentalism, a glory as of complete perfection, invests these two. They are canonised though no Pope or Cardinals took hand in doing it! . . . The three kingdoms, *Inferno, Purgatorio, Paradiso*, look out on one another like compartments of a great edifice; a great supernatural world-cathedral, piled-up there, stern, solemn, awful; Dante's World of Souls ! It is, at bottom, the *sincerest* of all Poems.— CARLYLE, *Heroes and Hero-Worship.*

The *Divina Commedia* is one of the landmarks of history. More than a magnificent poem, more than the beginning of a language and the opening of a national literature, more than the inspirer of art, and the glory of a great people, it is one of those rare and solemn monuments of the mind's power, which measure and test what it can reach to, which rise up ineffaceably and for ever as time goes on, marking out its advance by grander divisions than its centuries, and adopted as epochs by the consent of all who come after. . . . It is the first Christian poem; and it opens European literature, as the *Iliad* did that of Greece and Rome. And, like the *Iliad*, it has never become out of date; it accompanies in undiminished freshness the literature which it began.—R. W. CHURCH, *Dante, and other Essays.*

As Byron said, there is no tenderness like Dante's, neither any intensity nor seriousness like his, such seriousness that it is incapable of perceiving that which is commonplace or ridiculous, but fuses all down into its own whitehot fire.—RUSKIN, *Modern Painters, Vol. II.*

Dante is not what Homer was, the father of poetry springing in the freshness and simplicity of childhood out of the arms of mother earth : he is rather, like Noah, the father of a second poetical world, to whom he pours out his prophetic song, fraught with the wisdom and the experience of the old world. Indeed he himself expresses this by representing himself as wandering on an awful pilgrimage under the guidance of Virgil.— J. C. HARE, *Guesses at Truth, First Series.*

That which Juvenal does for the Rome of the Cæsars, Dante does for the Rome of Popes ; but Dante is a more terrible judge than Juvenal. Juvenal whips with cutting thongs ; Dante scourges with flames. Juvenal condemns ; Dante damns. Woe to the living on whom this awful traveller fixes the unfathomable glare of his eyes !—VICTOR HUGO, *William Shakespeare (transl.).*

Doubt, says Dante, nestles at the root of truth, and no lesson more profound is to be learned among the many that have proceeded from that great and royal teacher.—W. E. GLADSTONE, *Gleanings, Vol. III.*

Dante bequeathed to his own nation a Bible, a Testament, a Book of Prophecy, which cannot be mute. Generations may rise and pass away. New creeds and politics may rule and perish. But the speech of Dante will still be fresh, for it is human—it proclaims immutable laws, which Zeus made not, but which stand for ever firm in the conscience and the soul of man.—J. ADDINGTON SYMONDS, *Study of Dante.*

GEORGE JAMES DANTON.

French Revolutionist : 1759-1794.

If any man can more than another be termed the author of the French Revolution, it is Danton.—LORD BROUGHAM, *Statesmen of the Time of George III., Vol. III.*

Danton was of the Herculean type of a Luther, though without Luther's deep vision of spiritual things ; or a Chatham, though without Chatham's august majesty of life ; or a Cromwell, though without Cromwell's calm steadfastness of patriotic purpose. His visage and port seemed to declare his character : dark overhanging brows ; eyes that had the gleam of lightning ; a savage mouth ; an immense head ; the voice of a Stentor. Madame Roland pictured him as a fiercer Sardanapalus. Artists called him Jove the Thunderer. His enemies saw in him the Satan of the *Paradise Lost.* He was no moral regenerator; the difference between him and Robespierre is typified in Danton's version of an old saying, that he who hates vices hates men. He was not free from that careless life-contemning desperation, which sometimes belongs to forcible natures. Danton cannot be called noble, because nobility implies a purity, an elevation, and a kind of seriousness which were not his.—John Morley, *Miscellanies, Vol. I.*

Charles Robert Darwin.

English Naturalist: 1809-1882.

Charles Darwin acted, nevertheless, the part of an immense and powerful accelerating energy. The impetus which he gave gained us at least fifty years of progress; it sent us at a bound from Copernicus to Newton; so far as ordinary minds were concerned, indeed, it transcended at a single leap the whole interval from Ptolemy to Herschel. The comparison is far from being a mere rhetorical one. A close analogy really exists between the two cases. . . . The Newton of Biology, he found the science of life a chaotic maze; he left it in an orderly system, with a definite plan and a recognisable meaning. Great men are not accidents; great works are not accomplished in a single day. Both are the product of adequate causes. The great man springs from an ancestry competent to produce him; he is the final flower and ultimate outcome of converging hereditary forces, that culminate at last in the full production of his splendid and exceptional personality.—Grant Allen, *Charles Darwin.*

If the proper study of mankind is man, Mr. Darwin has done more than any other human being to further the most desirable kind of learning, for it is through him that humanity in our generation has first been able to begin its response to the precept of antiquity—*Know thyself.*—G. J. Romanes in "*Nature*" *Memorial Notices of Darwin.*

For it was the *Origin of Species* which first clearly revealed to naturalists as a class, that it was the duty of their science to take as its motto, what is really the motto of natural science in general,

Felix qui potuit rerum cognoscere causas.

Not facts, then, or phenonema, but causes or principles, are the ultimate objects of scientific quest.

No one in this generation is able to imitate Darwin, either as an observer or a generalizer. But this does not hinder that we should all so far endeavour to follow his *method,* as always to draw a clear distinction, not merely between observation and deduction, but also between degrees of verification.—*Idem: Darwin and After Darwin, Vol. I.*

The Darwinian theory, even when carried out to its extreme logical conclusion, not only does not oppose, but lends a decided support to, a belief in the spiritual nature of man. It shows us how man's body may have been developed from that of a lower animal form under the law of natural selection; but it also teaches us that we possess intellectual and moral faculties which could not have been so developed, but must have had another origin; and for this origin we can only find an adequate cause in the unseen universe of S irit.—A. R. Wallace, *Darwinism.*

Darwinism has conferred upon philosophy and religion an inestimable benefit by showing us that we must choose between two alternatives: either God is everywhere present in Nature, or He is nowhere.—AUBREY MOORE, *Life and Letters of George Romanes*.

The glory of Charles Darwin, of which no change of view respecting his theories can rob him, is that he passed through the world with open eyes.—F. W. FARRAR, *Social and Present-Day Questions*.

In fine, the spirit of Mr. Darwin's teaching may be traced all through the literature of science, even in departments which he never himself entered. No branch of research has benefited more from the infusion of this spirit than geology. Time-honoured prejudices have been broken down, theories that seemed the most surely based have been reconsidered, and when found untenable, have been boldly discarded. That the Present must be taken as a guide to the Past, has been more fearlessly asserted than ever. And yet it has been recognised that the Present differs widely from the Past, that there has been a progress everywhere, that Evolution and not Uniformitarianism has been the law by which geological history has been governed. For the impetus with which these views have been advanced in every civilised country, we look up with reverence to the loved and immortal name of Charles Darwin. —ARCHIBALD GEIKIE in "*Nature*" *Memorial Notices of Darwin*.

One could not converse with Darwin without being reminded of Socrates. There was the same desire to find some one wiser than himself; the same belief in the sovereignty of reason; the same ready humour; the same sympathetic interest in all the ways and works of men. But instead of turning away from the problems of nature as hopelessly insoluble, our modern Philosopher devoted his whole life to attacking them in the spirit of Heraclitus and of Democritus, with results which are as the substance of which their speculations were anticipatory shadows. . . . None have fought better, and none have been more fortunate, than Charles Darwin. He found a great truth trodden under foot, reviled by bigots, and ridiculed by all the world; he lived long enough to see it, chiefly by his own efforts, irrefragably established in science, inseparably incorporated with the common thoughts of men, and only hated and feared by those who would revile, but dare not. What shall a man desire more than this? Once more the image of Socrates rises unbidden, and the noble peroration of the *Apology* rings in our ears as if it were Charles Darwin's farewell:—

" The hour of departure has arrived, and we go our ways—I to die, and you to live. Which is the better, God only knows."—HUXLEY in " *Nature*" *Memorial Notices of Darwin*.

This largeness of knowledge and readiness of resource render Mr. Darwin the most terrible of antagonists. Accomplished naturalists have levelled heavy and sustained criticisms against him—not always with the view of fairly weighing his theory, but with the express intention of exposing its weak points only. This does not irritate him. He treats every objection with a soberness and thoroughness which even Bishop Butler might be proud to imitate, surrounding each fact with its appropriate detail, placing it in its proper relations, and usually giving it a significance which, as long as it was kept isolated, failed to appear. This is done without a trace of ill-temper. He moves over the subject with the passionless strength of a glacier ; and the grinding of the rocks is not always without a counterpart in the logical pulverization of the objector. —TYNDALL, *Address before British Association at Belfast*, 1874.

SIR HUMPHREY DAVY.

English Chemist : 1778-1829.

Others came in that goodly band whom benigner fortune
Led into pleasanter ways on earth : the children of Science
Some, whose unerring pursuit would, but for death, have extended
O'er the unknown and material, Man's intellectual empire,
Such their intuitive power ; like Davy, disarming destruction
When it moves on the vapour. . . .
—SOUTHEY, *A Vision of Judgment : The Young Spirits.*

If Davy had not been the first Chemist, he would have been the first Poet of his age. . . . Sir Humphrey Davy, who may be said to have elevated the art of chemistry to the dignity of a science ; who has discovered that one common law is applicable to the mind and to the body, and who has enabled us to give a full and perfect Amen to the great axiom of Lord Bacon, that knowledge is power.—S. T. COLERIDGE.

DANIEL DEFOE.

Miscellaneous Writer : 1663-1731.

Perhaps there exists no book, either of instruction or entertainment, in the English language, which has been more generally read, and more universally admired, than the *Life and Adventures of Robinson Crusoe.* It is difficult to say in what the charm consists, by which persons of all classes and denominations are thus fascinated ; yet the majority of readers will recollect it as among the first works which awakened and interested their youthful attention ; and feel, even in advanced life, and in the maturity of their understanding, that there are still associated with *Robinson Crusoe*, the sentiments peculiar to that period, when all is new, all glittering in prospect, and when those visions are most bright, which the experience of after-life tends only to darken and destroy.—SIR WALTER SCOTT, *Prose Works, Vol. IV.*

I cannot understand the mania of some people about Defoe. They think him a man of the first order of genius, and a paragon of virtue. He certainly wrote an excellent book—the first part of *Robinson Crusoe*—one of those feats which can only be performed by the union of luck with ability. That awful solitude of a quarter of a century—that strange union of comfort, plenty, and security with the misery of loneliness—was my delight before I was five years old, and has been the delight of hundreds of thousands of boys. But what has Defoe done great except the first part of *Robinson Crusoe ?* The second part is poor in comparison. The *History of the Plague*, and the *Memoirs of a Cavalier*, are in one sense curious works of art. They are wonderfully like true histories ; but, considered as novels, which they are, there is not much in them. He had undoubtedly a knack at making fiction look like truth. But is such a knack much to

be admired ? . . . As a political writer Defoe is merely one of the crowd.
He seems to have been an unprincipled hack, ready to take any side of
any question. Of all writers he was the most unlucky in irony. Twice
he was prosecuted for what he meant to be ironical ; but he was so unskilful that everybody understood him literally. Some of his tracts are
worse than immoral ; quite beastly. Altogether I do not like him.—
MACAULAY, *Life and Letters, by Sir G. O. Trevelyan, Vol. II.*

But it will remain the chief distinction of Defoe to have been, in these
minor tales of English scenes and manners, the father of the illustrious
family of the English Novel. Swift directly copied from him ; Richardson
founded his style of minute narrative wholly upon him ; Fielding, Smollett,
Sterne and Goldsmith, — Godwin, Scott, Bulwer, and Dickens, — have
been more or less indebted to him. Shall we scruple to add, then, that
while he remains unapproached in his two great masterpieces, he has
been surpassed in his minor works by these his successors ? His language
is as easy and copious, but less elegant and harmonious ; his insight into
character is as penetrating, but not so penetrating into the heart ; his
wit and irony are as playful, but his humour is less genial and expansive ;
and he wants the delicate fancy, the richness of imagery, the sympathy,
the truth and depth of feeling, which will keep the later Masters of
our English Novel the delightful companions, the gentle monitors, the
welcome instructors, of future generations. So true it is, that every
great writer promotes the next great writer one step ; and in some cases
gets himself superseded by him.—JOHN FORSTER, *Historical and Biographical Essays, Vol. II.*

To Defoe, if we may imitate the language of the *Arabian Nights*, was
given a tongue to which no one could listen without believing every word
that he uttered—a qualification by the way which would serve its owner
far more effectually in this commonplace world than swords of sharpness
or cloaks of darkness, or other paraphernalia. In other words, he had the
most marvellous power ever known of giving verisimilitude to his fictions ;
or, in other words again, he had the most amazing talent on record for
telling lies.—LESLIE STEPHEN, *Hours in a Library, First Series.*

Defoe cannot be held up as an exemplar of moral conduct, yet if he is
judged by the measures that he laboured for, and not by the means that
he employed, few Englishmen have lived more deserving than he of their
country's gratitude. He may have been self-seeking and vain-glorious,
but in his political life self-seeking and vain-glory were elevated by their
alliance with higher and wider aims. Defoe was a wonderful mixture of
knave and patriot. Sometimes pure knave seems to be uppermost, sometimes pure patriot, but the mixture is so complex and the energy of the man
so restless, that it almost passes human skill to unravel the two elements.
The author of *Robinson Crusoe* is entitled to the benefit of every doubt.
—WILLIAM MINTO, *Daniel Defoe.*

Of *Robinson Crusoe* what necessity is there to speak ? Who is not
familiar with its pages ? What boy has not undergone a whipping for
leaving his lessons unstudied while he has been sitting in the Solitary's
hut, or spending an afternoon with " man Friday " ? How many in the
decline of life have over the leaves of that wonderful book grown young
again !—J. CORDY JEAFFRESON, *Novels and Novelists.*

DEMOSTHENES.

Athenian Orator and Statesman : B.C. 385-322.

Demosthenes has sanction'd the transaction,
In saying eloquence meant " Action, action ! "
> —LORD BYRON, *The Age of Bronze.*

Not from the tropes of formal eloquence,
But Demosthenic strength, and weight of sense.
> —DR. WILLIAM KING, *Britain's Palladium.*

Demosthenes can never be judged apart from his circumstances. He is no saint and no correct mediocrity. He is a man of genius and something of a hero ; a fanatic, too, no doubt, and always a politician. He represents his country in that combination of intellectual subtlety and practical driving-power with fervid idealism, that union of passion with art, and that invariable insistence on the moral side of actions, on the just and the noble, that characterises most of the great spirits of Greek literature. To say with Quintilian that Demosthenes was a " bad man," is like saying the same of Burke or even of Isaiah. It implies either that noble words and thoughts are not nobility, or else, what is hardly more plausible, that the greatest expressions of soul in literature can be produced artificially by a dodge.—GILBERT MURRAY, *History of Ancient Greek Literature.*

RENÉ DU PERROT DESCARTES.

French Philosopher : 1596-1650.

Deny Descartes his subtil matter,
You leave him neither fire nor water.
> —PRIOR, *Alma : or, The Progress of The Mind.*

Descartes abolished the dogma of authority.—MAZZINI, *Life and Writings, Vol. II.*

Dugald Stewart has given to Descartes a very proud title, " Father of the experimental philosophy of the human mind," as if he were to man what Bacon was to nature.—HALLAM, *Introduction to the Literature of Europe, Vol. III.*

These deeper questions cannot be treated in this short appendix to Descartes' life. They are mentioned here merely to show how he was to modern thought what Socrates was to Greek philosophy. Far. greater, too, was he than Socrates, in the range of his influence. In every department of his thinking—in his first philosophy, his theology, his physics, his psychology, his physiology—he sowed the dragons' teeth from which sprang hosts of armed men, to join in an intellectual conflict, internecine, let us trust, to their many errors and prejudices, but fraught with new life and energy to the intellectual progress of Europe.—J. P. MAHAFFY *Descartes.*

It was not uncommon, in the Middle Ages, for philosophers to deny, simply as philosophers, what they vindicated as theologians. And Descartes, with pretentious Pharisaism, with abject poltroonery, and probably with a keen sense of the comical, before entering scientifically on universal doubt, put the articles of theological faith aside as a sacred treasure. That we can at the same time believe and not believe the same thing—believe it as theologians, reject it as philosophers—looks a good deal like a juggle. —WILLIAM MACCALL, *The Newest Materialism.*

" I think, therefore I am," said Descartes. Only his own identity was sure to him ; and the development of this system would have led to an idealism in which the outer world would be resolved into a mere phenomenon of consciousness. Gassendi, one of Descartes' contemporaries, . . . quickly pointed out that the fact of personal existence would be proved as well by reference to any other act as to the act of thinking. I eat, therefore I am ; or I love, therefore I am, would be quite as conclusive. Lichtenburg showed that the very thing to be proved was inevitably postulated in the first two words " I think " ; and that no inference from the postulate could by any possibility be stronger than the postulate itself.— TYNDALL, *Address before the British Association at Belfast,* 1874.

CHARLES DICKENS.

English Novelist : 1812-1870.

Dickens, with preternatural apprehension of the language of manners, and the varieties of street life, with pathos and laughter, with patriotic and still enlarging generosity, writes London tracts. He is a painter of English details, like Hogarth ; local and temporary in his tints and style, and local in his aims.—EMERSON, *English Traits : Literature.*

Dickens . . . shows that life in its rudest forms may wear a tragic grandeur ; that amidst follies and sensual excesses, provoking laughter or scorn, the moral feelings do not wholly die ; and that the haunts of the blackest crimes are sometimes lighted up by the presence and influence of the noblest souls.—CHANNING, *On the Present Age.*

But she, the genius of Charles Dickens, how brilliant, how kindly, how beneficent she is ! dwelling by a fountain of laughter imperishable ; though there is something of an alien salt in the neighbouring fountain of tears. How poor the world of fancy would be, how " dispeopled of her dreams " if, in some ruin of the social system, the books of Dickens were lost.— ANDREW LANG.

Charles Dickens, the most popular novelist of the century and one of the greatest humourists that England has produced.—JOHN FORSTER.

The good, the gentle, high-gifted, ever-friendly, noble Dickens—every inch of him an Honest Man.—CARLYLE.

Many of his portraits excite pity, and suggest the existence of crying social sins ; but of almost all we are obliged to say that they border on and frequently reach caricature, of which the essence is to catch a striking likeness by exclusively selecting and exaggerating a peculiarity that marks the man but does not represent him. Dickens belongs in literature to the same class as his illustrator, Hablot Browne, in design, though he far surpasses the illustrator in range and power.—GEORGE BRIMLEY, *Essays.*

If we glance over the wit and satire of the popular writers of the day, we shall find that the *manner* of it, so far as it is distinctive, is always owing to Dickens ; and that out of his first exquisite ironies branched innumerable other forms of wit, varying with the disposition of the writers ; original in the matter and substance of them, yet never to have been expressed as they now are, but for Dickens.—JOHN RUSKIN, *Modern Painters*, *Vol. III.*

If this classification of men be admitted, there can be no hesitation in assigning to Mr. Dickens his place in it. His genius is essentially irregular and unsymmetrical. Hardly any English writer perhaps is much more so. His style is an example of it. It is descriptive, racy, and flowing ; it is instinct with new imagery and singular illustration ; but it does not indicate that due proportion of the faculties to one another which is a beauty in itself, and which cannot help diffusing beauty over every happy word and moulded clause.—WALTER BAGEHOT, *Literary Studies, Vol. II.*

In Dickens we have the Humourist as Democrat. . . . The ethical sentiment breathes throughout the pages of Dickens, and it may well cover a multitude of sins of taste. Whatever the judgment of posterity may be upon him, we may to-day take leave of him with that judgment of Carlyle, " Every inch of him an honest man ".—W. S. LILLY, *Four English Humourists.*

Of Charles Dickens' fame a grand feature is its universality. His name is as much a " Household Word " in every sequestered hamlet lying between the most extreme points of our *home* islands, as it is in the metropolis ; and he is as well known in the United States, Canada, and Australia, as he is in the city round St. Paul's. Wherever there are men of English origin, speaking the English tongue, there the genius of Charles Dickens is one of the important facts of life.

It would be a long task to say all that Dickens has done for the English novel. It would be easier to state what he has not done for it. Indeed the novel of this generation is so completely a work of his *re*-creation, that it would be mere ingratitude, backed up by stupidity, not to hail him as the immediate parent of it.—J. CORDY JEAFFRESON, *Novels and Novelists, Vol. II.*

The philosophy of Dickens certainly *is* the professed philosophy of kindliness, of a genial interest in all things great and small, of a light English joyousness, and a sunny universal benevolence.—DAVID MASSON, *British Novelists and their Styles.*

The characters of Dickens, then, are personified humours, his method is the method not of Shakespeare, but of Ben Jonson. Pecksniff is just another name for hypocrisy, Jonas Chuzzlewit for avarice, Quilp for cruelty. The result is excellent of its kind. The repetitions and catch-words are, within limits, highly effective. Sometimes they are genuinely illuminative ; but sometimes, on the other hand, they reveal nothing and are used to weariness.—HUGH WALKER, *The Age of Tennyson.*

Millions and millions of old and young love Charles Dickens, know his personages by heart, play at games with his incidents and names, and from the bottom of their souls believe that there never was such fun, and that there never will be conceived again such inimitable beings, as they find in his ever-fresh and ever-varied pages. This is by itself a very high title to honour : perhaps it is the chief jewel in the crown that rests on the head of Charles Dickens.—FREDERIC HARRISON, *Studies in Early Victorian Literature.*

Dickens is always a boy in his humour, and exaggerates his tragedy, as a man would who relies for his materials on imagination rather than experience; and, moreover, he seldom gives us any sense of intellectual resource.—W. J. DAWSON, *Quest and Vision.*

DENIS DIDEROT.

French Philosopher: 1713-1784.

Diderot . . . wrote things which, were we not assured to the contrary, we should insist were composed by two persons, not only differing in manners and morals, but even in age and country; for, though he aspired to the glory of Plato, as Barrière was accustomed to say, he did not blush to imitate Petronius.—CHARLES BUCKE, *Book of Human Character.*

DIOCLETIAN.

Emperor of Rome: 245-313.

In every Christian
Hourly tempestuous persecutions grow.
Temptations martyr us alive. A man
Is to himself a Diocletian.
> —DR. JOHN DONNE, *The Litany : The Confessors.*

Lament ! for Diocletian's fiery sword
Works busy as the lightning; but instinct
With malice ne'er to deadliest weapon linked,
Which God's ethereal storehouses afford ;
Against the followers of the incarnate Lord
It rages.
> —WORDSWORTH, *Persecution.*

The slave who sets his soul on worthless pelf,
Is a mere Diocletian to himself.
> —WALTER HARTE, *The Ascetic : or, Thomas à Kempis.*

DIONYSIUS.

Greek Historian and Critic : d. (?) B.C. 18.

See Dionysius Homer's thoughts refine,
And call new beauties forth from every line !
> —POPE, *Essay on Criticism.*

Though Dionysius' learned taste
Is very manly, just, and chaste,
Who, like a skilful, wise physician,
Dissects each part of composition,
And shows how beauty strikes the soul
From a just compact of the whole.
> —ROBERT LLOYD, *Epistle to J. B., Esq.,* 1757.

Dr. Philip Doddridge.

Nonconformist Divine: 1702-1751.

Philip Doddridge, one of those who have breathed most freely on earth the atmosphere of heaven.—Sir Jas. Stephen, *Essays in Ecclesiastical Biography*.

A comparison of the hymns of Doddridge, Watts, Ken, and Wesley would show that Doddridge rises above Watts from having caught the spirit of Ken ; and Wesley is deep and interior from having added to the Chrysostomian piety of Ken the experimental part of St. Augustine. Watts is a pure Calvinist ; Ken is as pure a Chrysostomian. Doddridge is induced to blend both, and the effect is valuable and interesting ; Wesley advances this union.—Alexander Knox.

Dr. John Donne.

Dean of St. Paul's: 1573-1631.

Can we not force from widow'd poetry,
Now thou art dead, Great Donne, one elegy
To crown thy hearse ? Why yet did we not crust,
Though with unkneaded dough—bak'd prose, thy dust ?

. . . The Muses' garden, with pedantic weeds
O'erspread, was purg'd by thee ; the lazy seeds
Of servile imitation thrown away,
And fresh invention planted ; thou didst pay
The debts of our penurious bankrupt age. . . .
　　　—Thomas Carew, *Elegy upon the Death of Dr. Donne*.

'Twas then plain Donne in honest vengeance rose,
His wit refulgent, though his rhyme was prose ;
He midst an age of puns and pedants wrote
With genuine sense, and Roman strength of thought.
　　　—Dr. Brown, *Essay on Satire*.

Donne, the delight of Phœbus and each Muse,
Who, to thy one, all other brains refuse ;
Whose every work, of thy most early wit,
Came forth example, and remains so yet ;
Longer a knowing than most wits do live,
And which no affection praise enough can give !
To it, thy language, letters, arts, best life,
Which might with half mankind maintain a strife ;
All which I meant to praise, and yet I would ;
But leave, because I cannot as I should !
　　　—Ben Jonson, *Epigram to John Donne*.

Who dares say thou art dead, when he doth see
Unburied yet this living part of thee ;
This part, that to thy being gives fresh flame,
And, tho' thou'rt Donne, yet will preserve thy name ?
　　　—Arthur Wilson, *Upon Mr. J. Donne and his Poems*.

. . . all the softnesses,
The Shadow, Light, the Air, and Life, of Love ;
The Sharpness of all Wit ; ev'n bitterness
Makes Satire Sweet ; all wit did God improve,
    'Twas flamed in him, 'Twas but warm upon
    His Embers ; He was more ; and it is Donne.
                —GEORGE DANIEL, *A Vindication of Poesy.*

Donne teem'd with wit, but all was maim'd and bruis'd,
The periods endless, and the sense confus'd.
                —WALTER HARTE, *An Essay on Satire.*

Is Donne, great Donne, deceased ? then, England, say
Thou hast lost a man wher't language chose to stay
And show its graceful power. I would not praise
That and his vast wit (which in these vain days
Make many proud) but as they serv'd to unlock
That Cabinet, his mind : where such a stock
Of knowledge was repos'd.
                —IZAAK WALTON, *An Elegy upon Dr. Donne.*

    . . . Donne . . .
Of stubborn thoughts a garland thought to twine ;
To his fair maid brought cabalistic posies,
And sung quaint ditties of metempsychosis ;
Twists iron pokers into true love-knots,
Coining hard words, not found in polyglots.
                —HARTLEY COLERIDGE, *Donne.*

    The vividness of the descriptions or declamations in Donne, or Dryden,
is as much and as often derived from the force and fervour of the describer,
as from the reflections, forms, or incidents which constitute their subject
and materials. The wheels take fire from the mere rapidity of their
motion.—COLERIDGE, *Bibliographia Literaria.*

SIR FRANCIS DRAKE.

English Admiral : 1540-1596.

Drake round the world his sovereign's honour spread,
Through straights and gulfs immense her fame convey'd ;
Nor rests inquiry here ; his curious eye
Descries new constellations in the sky.
                —WILLIAM KING, *Britain's Palladium.*

Immortal Drake, the British thunder drove,
Swift, as the bolt, hot-hissing from above ;
Wide o'er the main, the bright infection flew,
And flying, with tempestuous fury grew.
                —WILLIAM PATTISON, *Verses on the Fifth of November.*

JOHN DRYDEN.

English Poet : 1631-1700.

Here let me bend, great Dryden, at thy shrine,
Thou dearest name to all the tuneful nine.

What if some dull lines in cold order creep,
And with his theme the poet seems to sleep ?
Still, when his subject rises proud to view,
With equal strength the poet rises too :
With strong invention, noblest vigour fraught,
Thought still springs up and rises out of thought ;
Numbers, ennobling numbers in their course,
In varied sweetness flow, in varied force ;
The powers of genius and of judgment join,
And the whole Art of Poetry is thine.

—CHURCHILL, *The Apology.*

In the head of the gang, John Dryden appear'd,
That ancient grave wit so long lov'd and fear'd.
—EARL OF ROCHESTER, *A Trial of the Poets for the Bays.*

Let free, impartial men from Dryden learn
Mysterious secrets, of a high concern,
And weighty truths, solid convincing sense,
Explain'd by unaffected eloquence.
—EARL OF ROSCOMMON, *On Mr. Dryden's Religio Laici.*

But see where artful Dryden next appears,
Grown old in rhyme, but charming ev'n in years,
Great Dryden next, whose tuneful muse affords
The sweetest numbers, and the fittest words.
Whether in Comic sounds or Tragic airs
She forms her voice, she moves our smiles or tears.
If Satire or heroic strains she writes,
Her Hero pleases and her Satire bites.
From her no harsh unartful numbers fall,
She wears all dresses, and she charms in all.
—ADDISON, *An Account of the Greatest English Poets.*

How long, great Poet, shall thy sacred Lays
Provoke our Wonder, and transcend our Praise ?
Can neither injuries of Time, or Age,
Damp thy Poetic Heat, and quench thy Rage ? . . .
    Prevailing Warmth has still thy mind possest,
And second Youth is kindled in thy breast ;
Thou mak'st the beauties of the Romans known,
And England boasts of riches not her own ;
Thy lines have heighten'd Virgil's majesty,
And Homer wonders at himself in thee.
Thou teachest Persius to inform our isle
In smoother Numbers, and a clearer Style ;
And Juvenal, instructed in thy page,
Edges his Satire, and improves his Rage.
Thy Copy casts a fairer Light on all,
And still out-shines the bright Original.

—*Id., To Mr. Dryden.*

Pride, malice, folly, against Dryden rose,
In various shapes of parsons, critics, beaux :

But sense surviv'd, when merry jests were past ;
For rising merit will buoy up at last.
                    —POPE, *Essay on Criticism.*

Waller was smooth ; but Dryden taught to join
The varying verse, the full resounding line,
The long majestic march, and energy divine.
          —*Id., Imitations of Horace, Epistle I.*

Dryden is dead, Dryden alone could sing
The full grown glories of a future king.
     —DR. ISAAC WATTS, *On the Death of the Duke of Gloucester.*

Old Dryden, emulous of Cæsar's praise,
Cover'd his baldness with immortal bays ;
And death perhaps, to spoil poetic sport,
Unkindly cut an Alexandrine short.
          —ELIJAH FENTON, *An Epistle to Thomas Lambard, Esq.*

At length the matchless Dryden came,
To light the muses' clearer flame ;
To lofty numbers grace to lend,
And strength with melody to blend ;
To triumph in the bold career of song,
And roll th' unwearied energy along.
     —WARTON, *Ode on His Majesty's Birthday, June* 4, 1787.

     . . . Dryden in immortal strain,
Had raised the Table Round again,
But that a ribald King and Court
Bade him toil on, to make them sport ; . . .
The world defrauded of the high design,
Profaned the God-given strength, and marr'd the lofty line.
          —SCOTT, *Marmion, Introduction to Canto I.*

Like him great Dryden pour'd the tide of song,
In stream less smooth, indeed, but doubly strong.
          —BYRON, *English Bards and Scotch Reviewers.*

Chatting on deck was Dryden too,
The Bacon of the rhyming crew ;
None ever crosst our mystic sea
More richly stored with thought than he ;
Tho' never tender nor sublime,
He wrestles with and conquers Time.
                    —LANDOR, *To Wordsworth.*

     . . . Dryden, with imperial grace,
Gives to th' obedient lyre his rapid laws ;
Tones yet unheard, with touch divine, he draws,
The melting fall, the rising swell sublime,
And all the magic of melodious rhyme.
               —HAYLEY, *Essay on Epic Poetry, Ep. III.*

To Spenser much, to Milton much is due ;
But in great Dryden we preserve the two.
               —WALTER HARTE, *The Vision of Death.*

Behold where Dryden's less presumptuous car,
Wide o'er the fields of glory bear.
Two courses of ethereal race,
With necks in thunder cloth'd, and long resounding pace.
Hark, his hands the lyre explore!
Bright-eyed **Fancy** hovering o'er
Scatters from her pictured urn
Thoughts, that breathe, and words that burn.

      —Thomas Gray, *The Progress of Poesy.*

Dryden may be properly considered as the father of English criticism, as the writer who first taught us to determine upon principles the merit of composition.—Dr. Johnson, *Lives of the Poets : Dryden.*

The prose works of Dryden bear repeated evidence to his philosophical powers. His philosophy was not indeed of a formed and systematic character ; for he is often contented to leave the path of argument which must have conducted him to the fountain of truth, and to resort with indolence or indifference to the leaky cisterns which had been hewn out by former critics. But where his pride or his taste are interested, he shows evidently that it was not deficiency in the power of systematizing, but want of the time and patience necessary to form a system, which occasioned the discrepancy that we often notice in his critical and philological disquisitions. . . . The satirical powers of Dryden were of the highest order. He draws his arrow to the head, and dismisses it straight upon his object of aim. In this walk he wrought almost as great a reformation as upon versification in general.—Sir Walter Scott, *Life of Dryden.*

Dryden's genius was of that sort which catches fire by its own motion ; his chariot wheels *get* hot by driving fast.—Coleridge, *Table Talk.*

He (C. J. Fox) declared that he would use no word which was not to be found in Dryden.—Macaulay, *Essays : Sir James Mackintosh.*

Dryden too often violated his own admirable rule, that " an author is not to write all he can, only all he ought ". In his worst images, however, there is often a vividness that half excuses them. But it is a grotesque vividness, as from the flare of a bonfire. They do not flash into sudden lustre, as in the great poets, where the imaginations of poet and reader leap toward each other and meet half way. . . . But if he have not the potent alchemy that transmutes the lead of our commonplace associations into gold, as Shakespeare knows how to do so easily, yet his sense is always up to the sterling standard ; and though he has not added so much as some have done to the stock of bullion which others afterwards coin and put in circulation, there are few who have minted so many phrases that are still a part of our daily currency.—J. R. Lowell, *Among my Books.*

Dryden was a fine, bold, stout, strong, and sweeping satirist ; but, vacillating in his own principles and practice, in many of the highest affairs which a man has to discuss and settle with his own soul, " Glorious John," with the native strength of a giant, sometimes felt his own knees smiting against one another, his legs tottering, his footing unsure. . . . Dryden seems to have been a man of wavering principles, but warm and generous feelings ; so he had one of the best, and one of the worst qualities which a satirist can possess. But then, what an ear for music! . . . Even when the satire languishes, the poetry is magnificent: and you are brought back, with a refreshed appetite, to devour the castigation of the knave or fool whom you and the poet had for a while forgotten.—JOHN WILSON, *Essays: The Man of Ton.*

Dryden is always striving, and consciously striving, to find better literary forms, a better vocabulary, better metres, better constructions, better style. He may, in no one branch, have attained the entire and flawless perfection which distinguishes Pope as far as he goes. But the range of Dryden is to the range of Pope as that of a forest to a shrubbery, and in this case priority is everything, and the priority is on the side of Dryden. He is not our greatest poet; far from it. But there is one point in which the superlative may safely be applied to him. Considering what he started with, what he accomplished, and what advantages he left to his successors, he must be pronounced, without exception, the greatest craftsman in English letters, and as such he ought to be regarded with peculiar veneration by all who, in however humble a capacity, are connected with the craft.—GEORGE SAINTSBURY, *John Dryden.*

The moral defects of his writings, coarse licentiousness, unmeasured invective, and equally unmeasured adulation, belong to the age rather than to the man. On the whole, we may say that he was one whom we should probably have esteemed if we could have known him; but in whom, apart from his writings, we should not have discovered the first literary figure of his generation.—RICHARD GARNETT, *The Age of Dryden.*

No poetic style since can, in such respects, be compared to Dryden's. Pope's to his is feeble—and Byron's forced. He can say the strongest things in the swiftest way, and the most felicitous expressions seem to fall unconsciously from his lips. Had his matter, you say, but been equal to his manner, his thought in originality and imaginative power but commensurate with the boundless quantity, and no less admirable quality, of his words! His versification deserves a commendation scarcely inferior. It is "all ear," if we may so apply an expression of Shakespeare's. No studied rules,—no elaborate complication of harmonies,—it is the mere sinking and swelling of the wave of his thought, as it moves onward to the shore of his purpose. And, as in the sea, there are no furrows absolutely isolated from each other, but each leans on, or melts into each, and the subsidence of the one is the rise of the other—so with the versification of his better poetry.—REV. G. GILFILLAN, *Critical Dissertation prefixed to Dryden's Poetical Works, Vol. II.*

DUNS SCOTUS.

Scottish Philosopher: 1265-1308.

Who travels Scotus' swelling tomes shall find
A cloud of darkness rising on the mind.
                    —JOHN POMFRET, *Reason: A Poem.*

By Michael the Stammerer sent from the East,
And done into Latin by that Scottish beast,
Johannes Duns Scotus, who dares to maintain,
In the face of the truth, and error infernal,

That the universe is and must be eternal;
At first laying down, as a fact fundamental,
That nothing with God can be accidental;
Then asserting that God before the creation
Could not have existed, because it is plain
That, had he existed, he would have created;
Which is begging the question that should be debated,
And moveth me less to anger than laughter.
                    —LONGFELLOW, *The Golden Legend.*

ALBRECHT DÜRER.

Painter : 1471-1528.

Here, when Art was still religion, with a simple reverent heart,
Lived and laboured Albrecht Dürer, the Evangelist of Art. . . .
Not thy councils, not thy Kaisers, win for thee the world's regard;
But thy painter, Albrecht Dürer, and Hans Sachs, thy cobbler-bard.
                    —LONGFELLOW, *Nüremberg.*

Albrecht Dürer fills a large space in the history of art. So far as
Germany is concerned he is *facile princeps*, unrivalled even in his own
age by so great an artist as the young Hans Holbein, and towering
above all his successors, no one of whom can raise a head high enough
to look him in the face, with the exception perhaps of Adolf Menzel at
the present day. Wherever there are or will be students and lovers of
art, there must be a great majority in whom instinct and intellect will
be stimulated by the study of the works of Dürer, whether as painter,
engraver, philosopher, author, or merely as simple burgher citizen of
Nüremberg.—LIONEL CUST, *Albrecht Dürer.*

MARIA EDGEWORTH.

English Novelist : 1766-1849.

In short, she was a walking calculation,
Miss Edgeworth's novels stepping from their covers.
                    —BYRON, *Don Juan.*

If it were possible for reviewers to *envy* the authors who are brought
before them for judgment, we rather think we should be tempted to envy
Miss Edgeworth . . . for the delicate consciousness of having done more
good than any other writer, male or female, of her generation.—LORD
JEFFREY, *Essays.*

We owe also the popularity of the growing principle to the writings of
Miss Edgeworth and of Scott, who sought their characters among the
people, and who interested us by a picture of (and not a declamation
upon) their life and its humble vicissitudes, their errors and their virtues.
—LYTTON, *England and the English : Intellectual Spirit.*

Her novels have been described as a sort of essence of common sense,
and even more happily it has been said that it was her genius to be wise.
We must be content to take that which she can offer ; and since she offers
so much, why should we not be content? Miss Edgeworth wrote of

ordinary human life, and not of tremendous catastrophes or highly romantic incidents. Hers was no heated fancy; she had no comprehension of those fiery passions, those sensibilities that burn like tinder at contact with the feeblest spark; she does not believe in chance, that favourite of so many novelists; neither does she deal in ruined castles, underground galleries nor spectres, as was the fashion in her day.—HELEN ZIMMERN, *Maria Edgeworth.*

EDWARD THE CONFESSOR.

Saxon King of England: 1004-1066.

Edward was a royal anchorite, who, if he had been a professed recluse, or even a private man, might have been justly thought venerable or excusable, according to the various opinions and prepossessions of those who contemplated his character.—SIR J. MACKINTOSH, *History of England, Vol. I.*

EDWARD I.

King of England: 1239-1307.

Go, Edward, triumph now!
Cambria is fallen, and Scotland's strength is crush'd;
On Wallace, on Llewellyn's mangled limbs,
The fowls of heaven have fed.

Unrivall'd, unopposed,
Go Edward, full of glory to thy grave!
The weight of patriot blood upon thy soul,
Go, Edward, to thy God!
—SOUTHEY, *The Death of Wallace.*

So conspicuous a station at the head of the authentic history of our uninterrupted jurisprudence has contributed, more than his legislative acts, to procure for Edward the ambitious name of the English Justinian.— SIR J. MACKINTOSH, *History of England, Vol. I.*

Edward I. assisted the march of liberty; that is, he encouraged the march of the people in their path to power; but he did so because he thought it would operate as a check on the arrogance of the nobles and the bigotry of the clergy.—CHARLES BUCKE, *Book of Human Character.*

EDWARD III.

King of England: 1312-1377.

With Edward's acts adorn the shining page,
Stretch his long triumphs down through every age;
Draw monarchs chain'd and Cressy's glorious field,
The lilies blazing on the regal shield.
—POPE, *Windsor Forest.*

A more prosperous era began with Edward III., the father, as he may also be called, of English commerce, a title not indeed more glorious, but by which he may perhaps claim more of our gratitude than as the hero of Crécy.—HALLAM, *Student's Middle Ages, Chap. IX., Part II.*

Edward III., undoubtedly one of the greatest princes that ever swayed the sceptre of England; whether we respect him as a warrior, a law-giver, a monarch, or a man. He possessed all the romantic spirit of Alexander; the penetration, the fortitude, the polished manners of Julius; the liberality, the munificence, the wisdom, of Augustus Cæsar.—TOBIAS G. SMOLLETT.

EDWARD VI.

King of England: 1537-1553.

Now may that blessed edifice
Of public good be rear'd
Which holy Edward traced,
The spotless Tudor, he whom Death
Too early summon'd to his heavenly throne.

              —SOUTHEY, *Ode.*

" Sweet is the holiness of youth," so felt
Time-honoured Chaucer when he framed the lay
By which the prioress beguiled the way,
And many a pilgrim's rugged heart did melt.
Hadst thou, lov'd bard ! whose spirit often dwelt
In the clear land of vision, but foreseen
King, child, and seraph, blended in the mien
Of pious Edward kneeling as he knelt
In meek and simple infancy, what joy
For universal Christendom had thrilled
Thy heart ! what hopes inspired thy genius, skilled
(O great precursor, genuine morning star)
The lucid shafts of reason to employ,
Piercing the papal darkness from afar !

         —WORDSWORTH, *Edward VI.*

Henry VIII. was the Romulus, and Edward VI. the Numa Pompilius, of the English Reformation.—WILLIAM GUTHRIE.

JONATHAN EDWARDS.

American Divine: 1703-1758.

Who is this preacher our Northampton claims,
Whose rhetoric blazes with sulphureous flames
And torches stolen from Tartarean mines ?
Edwards, the salamander of divines.
       —OLIVER WENDELL HOLMES, *Vestigia Quinque Retrorsum.*

The greatest of New England reasoners, Jonathan Edwards, the Spinoza of Calvinism.—RICHARD GARNETT, *Life of Emerson.*

The peculiarity of Edwards' mind was, that the doctrine had thus been expanded along peculiar lines of thought, without equally affecting others. He is a kind of Spinoza-Mather ; he combines, that is, the logical keenness of the great metaphysician with the puerile superstitions of the New England divine; he sees God in all nature, and yet believes in the degrading supernaturalism of the Salem witches.—LESLIE STEPHEN, *Hours in a Library, Second Series.*

EARL OF ELDON.

Lord Chancellor of England: 1751-1838.

Lord Eldon, to great legal experience, and the most profound professional learning, united that thorough knowledge of men, which lawyers who practise in the courts, and especially the courts of common law, attain in a measure and with an accuracy hardly conceivable by those out of the profession.—LORD BROUGHAM, *Statesmen of the Time of George III., Vol. II.*

Lord Eldon might have carried any measure of legal reform as easily as the Duke of Wellington and Sir Robert Peel carried Catholic Emancipation. In his own court, he might have played the part of Hercules in the Augean stable; but he preferred to sit among the accumulations of dirt and rubbish, and looked with marked disfavour on all who approached to meddle with them. . . . It is going far enough to call Lord Eldon a great lawyer; but to call him a great man, or assign him the honours paid to those who have performed noble actions, produced immortal works, or conferred lasting benefits on mankind, is to degrade the general standard of excellence, to canker public virtue in the bud. There are rewards of a different order set apart for those who work for present objects and present pay. To a fair share of these he was entitled, and he had it. His earldom, his half-million, and the " one cheer more " of his biographer are enough in all conscience for such services as his, even if the " one cheer more " should not be caught up and echoed back by posterity.—A. HAYWARD, *Biographical and Historical Essays, Vol. I.*

" GEORGE ELIOT " (MARY ANN EVANS).

English Novelist: 1819-1880.

In George Eliot it is the most vivid and vital impulse which lends to her large intelligence the utmost it ever has of the spiritual breath and living blood of genius; and never had any such a gift more plainly and immediately as from the very heart of heaven.—SWINBURNE, *Charlotte Brontë.*

George Eliot loves to bathe her productions in the broad pitiless midday light, which leaves no room for illusion, but reveals all nature with uncompromising directness. . . . George Eliot, contemplative, observant, instinctively conservative, her imagination dearly loving to do "a little Toryism on the sly," is as yet the sole outcome of the modern positive spirit in imaginative literature —the sole novelist who has incorporated in an artistic form some of the leading ideas of Comte, of Mazzini, and of Darwin. In fact, underlying all her art there is the same rigorous teaching of the inexorable laws which govern the life of man. The teaching that not liberty but duty is the condition of existence; the teaching of the

incalculable effects of hereditary transmission, with the solemn responsi-
bilities it involves; the teaching of the inherent sadness and imperfection
in human nature, which render resignation the first virtue of man.—
MATHILDE BLIND, *George Eliot.*

Even in her best books we never quite get over the sense of almost
painful elaboration, of a powerful mind having rich gifts striving to produce
some rare music with an unfamiliar and uncongenial instrument. It
reminds us of Beethoven evolving his majestic sonatas on an untuned and
dilapidated old piano, the defects of which he could not himself hear. . . .
As the Gospel has it—"Which of you by taking thought can add one
cubit unto his stature?" George Eliot had not sufficiently meditated on
this subject. She too often supposed that by taking thought—by enormous
pains, profound thought, by putting this thought in exquisite and noble
words—she might produce an immortal romance, an immortal poem.—
FREDERIC HARRISON, *Studies in Early Victorian Literature.*

It is one of the minor lessons George Eliot is fond of teaching, that
faces can be masks as well as mirrors: it is the heart and not the face
that makes the traitor.—W. J. DAWSON, *Quest and Vision.*

In George Eliot, a reader with a conscience may be reminded of the
saying that when a man opens Tacitus he puts himself in the confessional.
—JOHN MORLEY, *Miscellanies, Vol. III.*

ELIZABETH.

Queen of England : 1533-1603.

Eliza then,
Amid these doubtful motions, steady, gave
The beam to fix.   She! like the secret eye
That never closes on a guarded world,
So sought, so mark'd, so seiz'd the public good,
That self-supported, without one ally,
She aw'd her inward, quell'd her circling foes.

　　　　　　　　　　　　　—THOMSON, *Liberty.*

Queen of the eagle eye, thou too, O matchless Eliza,
Excellent Queen, wert there! and thy brother's beautiful spirit!
O'er whose innocent head there hover'd a silvery halo,
Such as crowns the saint when his earthly warfare is ended.

　　　　　—SOUTHEY, *A Vision of Judgment : The Sovereigns.*

Hail, virgin queen! o'er many an envious bar
Triumphant—snatched from many a treacherous wile!
All hail, sage lady, whom a grateful isle
Hath blest, respiring from that dismal war
Stilled by thy voice!

　　　　　　　　　　　—WORDSWORTH, *Elizabeth.*

When great Eliza rul'd this state,
On English hearts she plac'd her throne,
And in their happiness her fate.

　　　　　　　—JOHN GILBERT COOPER, *The Genius of Britain.*

Let tyrants fear : I have always so behaved myself that, under God, I have placed my chiefest strength and safeguard in the loyal hearts and goodwill of my subjects.—QUEEN ELIZABETH.

I know I have but the body of a weak and feeble woman, but I have the heart of a king, and of a king of England too.—*Id.*

It may be said of Elizabeth, that if ever there was a monarch whose conduct seemed, according to the speech of the old heathen, to be governed alternately by two souls of a very different disposition and character, the supposition might be applied to her. Possessing more than masculine wisdom, magnanimity, and fortitude on most occasions, she betrayed, at some unhappy moments, even more than female weakness and malignity. —SIR WALTER SCOTT.

That this nation is what it is, and this Church is what it is, may without praise or blame, but only in acknowledgment of the fact, be owned due to Queen Elizabeth as much as to any human being that has ever in this island enjoyed or suffered the stern and bracing experience of life.—W. E. GLADSTONE, *Queen Elizabeth and the Church of England.*

Elizabeth made herself feared by the nobility, but beloved by the people. Wherefore ?—That she might make herself absolute.—CHARLES BUCKE, *Book of Human Character.*

What is England ? She is Elizabeth. There is no incarnation more complete. In admiring Elizabeth, England loves her own looking-glass. Proud and magnanimous with strange hypocrisies, great with pedantry, haughty with ability, prude with audacity, having favourites, but no masters, her own mistress, even in her bed, all-powerful queen, inaccessible woman, Elizabeth is a virgin as England is an island. Like England, she calls herself Empress of the sea, *Basilea maris.*—VICTOR HUGO, *William Shakespeare (transl.).*

With Elizabeth the heart never really spoke, and if the senses did, she had them under perfect control. And this was why she never loved or was loved, and never has been or will be regarded with enthusiasm by either man or woman.—E. S. BEESLY, *Queen Elizabeth.*

The wisdom of Elizabeth was shown in nothing so strongly as in her sagacity in the choice of ministers and her power of using men for her own purposes.—BISHOP MANDELL CREIGHTON, *The Age of Elizabeth.*

RALPH WALDO EMERSON.

American Essayist and Philosopher : 1803-1882.

Where in the realm of thought, whose air is song,
Does he, the Buddha of the West, belong ?
He seems a wingèd Franklin, sweetly wise,
Born to unlock the secrets of the skies ;
And which the nobler calling,—if 'tis fair
Terrestrial with celestial to compare,—
To guide the storm-cloud's elemental flame,
Or walk the chambers whence the lightning came,
Amidst the sources of its subtile fire,
And steal their effluence for his lips and lyre ?

If lost at times in vague aërial flights,
None treads with firmer footstep when he lights;
A soaring nature, ballasted with sense,
Wisdom without her wrinkles or pretence,
In every Bible he has faith to read,
And every altar helps to shape his creed.
Ask you what name this prisoned spirit bears
While with ourselves this fleeting breath it shares?
Till angels greet him with a sweeter one
In heaven, on earth we call him Emerson.
—OLIVER WENDELL HOLMES, *At the Saturday Club.*

There comes Emerson first, whose rich words, every one,
Are like gold nails in temples to hang trophies on.
—J. R. LOWELL, *A Fable for Critics.*

. . . in this book you'll find
Music from a prophet's mind.
Even when harsh the numbers be,
There's an inward melody;
And when sound is one with sense,
'Tis a bird's song—sweet, intense.
—R. W. GILDER, *To an English Friend, with Emerson's " Poems ".*

Emerson, to me, stands unmistakably at the head, but for the others I am at a loss where to give any precedence. Each illustrious, each rounded, each distinctive. Emerson for his sweet, vital-tasting melody, rhym'd philosophy, and poems as amber-clear as the honey of the wild bee he loves to sing.—WALT WHITMAN, *Specimen Days.*

Mr. Ruskin and Lord Tennyson have thought it worth their while to defend themselves from the charge of plagiarism. Emerson would never have taken the trouble to do such a thing. His mind was overflowing with thought as a river in the season of flood, and was full of floating fragments from an endless variety of sources. He drew ashore whatever he wanted that would serve his purpose. He makes no secret of his mode of writing, " I dot evermore in my endless journal, a line on every knowable in nature; but the arrangement loiters long, and I get a brick-kiln instead of a house ". . . . The natural purity and elevation of Emerson's character show themselves in all that he writes. His life corresponded to the ideal we form of him from his writings. This it was which made him invulnerable amidst all the fierce conflicts his gentle words excited. His white shield was so spotless that the least scrupulous combatants did not like to leave their defacing marks upon it. . . . His writings, whether in prose or verse, are worthy of admiration, but his manhood was the underlying quality which gave them their true value. It was in virtue of this that his rare genius acted on so many minds as a trumpet call to awaken them to the meaning and the privileges of this earthly existence with all its infinite promise. No matter of what he wrote or spoke, his words, his tones, his looks carried the evidence of a sincerity which pervaded them all and was to his eloquence and poetry like the water of crystallization; without which they would effervesce into mere rhetoric.
—OLIVER WENDELL HOLMES, *Life of R. W. Emerson.*

He delights to lavish his varied and brilliant resources upon some defiant paradox—and never more than when that paradox is engaged in behalf of an optimism extreme enough to provoke another Voltaire to write another *Candide*. He displays in its perfection the fantastic incoherence of the "God-intoxicated" man. . . . The Persian aspired to reach a divinity above him by self-conquest; the Amercian seeks to realise a divinity within him by self-will. Self-annihilation is the watchword of the one; self-assertion that of the other.—R. A. VAUGHAN, *Hours with the Mystics, Vol. II.*

Personally, like so many others, to Emerson I owe my freedom and emancipation from those Stocks of prejudice and those Pillories of public opinion which still make many sit in the world of thought like frightened criminals unable or afraid to stir.—REV. H. R. HAWEIS, *American Humorists.*

More than any of the other great writers of the age, he is a Voice. He is almost impersonal. He is pure from the taint of sect, clique, or party. He does not argue, but announces; he speaks when the Spirit moves him, and not longer. Better than any contemporary, he exhibits the might of the spoken word. . . . He would have been a light of the age of Buddha or of Solon, as well as of ours.—RICHARD GARNETT, *Life of Emerson.*

"Can you emit sparks?" said the cat to the ugly duckling in the fairy tale, and the poor abashed creature had to admit that it could not. Emerson could emit sparks with the most electrical of cats. He is all sparks and shocks. If one were required to name the most non-sequacious author one had ever read, I do not see how we could help nominating Emerson. . . . The unparalleled non-sequaciousness of Emerson is as certain as the Correggiosity of Correggio. You never know what he will be at. His sentences fall over you in glittering cascades, beautiful and bright, and for the moment refreshing, but after a very brief while the mind, having nothing to do on its own account but to remain wide open, and see what Emerson sends it, grows first restive and then torpid. Admiration gives way to astonishment, astonishment to bewilderment, and bewilderment to stupefaction.—AUGUSTINE BIRRELL, *Res Judicatæ.*

Though it is only the other day that Emerson walked the earth and was alive and among us, he is already one of the privileged few whom the reader approaches in the mood of settled respect, and whose names have surrounded themselves with an atmosphere of religion.—JOHN MORLEY, *Miscellanies, Vol. I.*

EMPEDOCLES.

Sicilian Philosopher and Poet : fl. about B.C. 450.

Even in his lifetime, and among contemporary Greeks, he swept the stage of life like a great tragic actor, and left to posterity the fame of genius as a poet, a physician, a patriot, and a philosopher. The well-known verses of Lucretius are enough to prove that the glory of Empedocles increased with age, and bore the test of time. Reading them, we cannot but regret that poems which so stirred the reverent enthusiasm of Rome's greatest singer have been scattered to the winds, and that what we now possess of their remains affords but a poor sample of their unimpaired magnificence. . . . In his comprehensive mind all the learning he had acquired from men, from books, from the world, and from reflection, was consolidated into one system, to which his double interest for mysticism and physics gave a double aspect. He was the first in Greece to reconcile Eleatic and Heraclitean speculations, the puzzle of plurality and unity, the antagonism of good and evil, in one theory, and to connect it with another which revealed a solemn view of human obligations and destinies, and required a life of social purity and self-restraint. The misfortune of Empedocles as a philosopher consisted in this—that he succeeded only in resuming the results of contemporary speculation, and of individual research, in a philosophy of indisputable originality, without anticipating the new direction which was about to be given to human thought by Socrates and Plato. He closed one period—the period of poetry and physical theories and mysticism. The period of prose, of logic, and of ethics, was about to begin.—J. Addington Symonds, *Studies of Greek Poets.*

EPICTETUS.

Greek Stoic Philosopher : 2nd cent.

For lofty and solid principles of practical ethics, we might safely match Epictetus and Antoninus with most of our modern speculators.—Lord Jeffrey, *Essays.*

The teaching of Epictetus, briefly expressed, is that man ought to be thankful to God for all things, and always content with that which happens, for what God chooses is better than what man can choose. His great merit as a teacher is that " he attempted to show that there is in man's nature and in the constitution of things sufficient reason for living a virtuous life ".—Geo. Long, *Introduction to Epictetus.*

Epictetus and Marcus Aurelius are not only the most clear-sighted moralists among ancient philosophers, but are also, with the single exception of Socrates, the best and holiest characters presented to us in the records of antiquity. . . . Epictetus was one of the few " in the very dust of whose thoughts was gold ". . . . Epictetus, like Seneca, is a preacher ; a preacher with less wealth of genius, less eloquence of expression, less width of culture, but with far more bravery, clearness, consistency, and grasp of his subject. His doctrine and his life were singularly homogeneous, and his views admit of brief expression, for they are not weakened by any fluctuations, or chequered with any lights and shades.—F. W. Farrar, *Seekers after God.*

Epictetus illustrates the difference of this age (A.D. 117-138) from that of Plato or also of Chrysippus, in that he practically abandons all speculation, and confines himself to dogmatic practical ethics. He accepts indeed, and hands on the speculative basis of morality as laid down by the earlier Stoics, but his real strength is in preaching and edification. He called his school a " *healing-place for diseased souls* ". Such a profession is slightly repellent ; but the breadth and concreteness of the teacher's conceptions, his sublimity of thought, and his humour, win the affection of most readers.—Gilbert Murray, *History of Ancient Greek Literature.*

EPICURUS.

Greek Philosopher: B.C. 342-270.

While Epicurus, blest with thought refin'd,
Makes the vast globe the pastime of the wind.
Were it not idle labour to confute
Notions so wild, unworthy of dispute?
I'd of the learned Epicurus ask,
If this were for the winds a proper task?
—Sir Richard Blackmore, *Creation.*

Even in the life-time of Epicurus his disciples and adherents were
numerous. His personal influence seems to have acted as a charm. Yet
probably his mind was one neither fitted for abstruse speculation nor sus-
ceptible of deep feeling and lofty sentiment. Everything seems to show
that he was as indifferent to the vocations of the scholar and the artist as
he confessedly was to the business and intrigues of political life. The
magic of his power lay in the bright and sweet humanity of his person and
character. His was a pre-eminently social nature, finding in friendly
communion the very salt without which life lost its savour. Women were
conspicuous among his friends; and without going so far as to call him a
ladies' man, one may say that he exhibited a decided taste for feminine
society; of deeper relations to the fair sex, however, there is no indication;
and it seems improbable that he should have felt a grand passion. His
nature was too calm and his affections too generically human for that.—
William Wallace, *Epicureanism.*

DESIDERIUS ERASMUS.

Dutch Reformer: 1467-1536.

A second deluge learning thus o'er-ran;
And the monks finished what the Goths began.
At length Erasmus, that great injur'd name,
(The glory of the priesthood, and the shame!)
Stemm'd the wild torrent of a barb'rous age,
And drove those holy Vandals off the stage.
—Pope, *An Essay on Criticism.*

But ah! Erasmus of Rotterdam,
He is the vilest miscreant
That ever walked this world below!
A Momus, making his mock and mow
At Papist and at Protestant,
Sneering at St. John and St. Paul,
At God and Man, at one and all;
And yet as hollow and false and drear,
As a cracked pitcher to the ear,
And ever growing worse and worse!
Whenever I pray, I pray for a curse
On Erasmus, the Insincere!
—Longfellow, *Martin Luther.*

On. thing was manifest, that he had greatly contributed to the success of the Reformation. It was said, that Erasmus had laid the egg,
and Luther had hatched it.—HALLAM, *Literature of the Middle Ages,
Vol. I.*

You cannot expect anything very deep from Erasmus.—COLERIDGE,
Table Talk.

Of the two imperial virtues, industry and self-denial, the literary character
of Erasmus was adorned by the first much more than by the second.—SIR
JAMES STEPHEN, *Essays in Ecclesiastical Biography.*

Erasmus sacrificed Truth to a love of Unity.   Luther sacrificed Unity to
a love of Truth.   The sacrifice of *self* to the love of both Truth and Unity
would have immortalized both, and have restored the Church.—BISHOP
CHRISTOPHER WORDSWORTH, *Erasmus and the Old Catholics.*

In a comparative estimate of genius, according to its kinds and degrees,
I should not hesitate to place Erasmus in the same class with Lucian.
There is, indeed, a seasoning of salt in all his writings, in which the
necessity of being grave did not forbid him to be facetious.—DR. VICESIMUS
KNOX, *Essays : On the Genius of Erasmus.*

Erasmus was a great literary precursor of the Reformation ; he armed
the hands of the Lutherans : but to call him, as some have done, a Reformer before the Reformation, seems hardly an appropriate description.
If, in our own day, those who are denominated Old Catholics had confined
themselves to urging the advisability of certain reforms, without disputing the authority of the Pope or proposing to secede from communion
with Rome, their position would have been analogous to that of Erasmus.
Viewed as a whole, his conduct was essentially consistent and independent.
His imperishable claim to the gratitude of the world, and especially of
the Teutonic peoples, rests on the part which he sustained in a contest of
even larger scope than that waged by Luther—in the great preliminary
conflict between the old and the new conception of knowledge, between
the bondage and the enfranchisement of the human mind, between a lifeless formalism in religion and the spirit of practical Christianity.   From
youth to old age, through many trials, he worked with indomitable energy
in the cause of light ; and it was his great reward, that, before he died, he
saw the dawn of a new age beginning for the nations of the north,—not
without clouds and storm, but with the assurance that the reign of darkness was past.—R. C. JEBB, *Erasmus.*

EUCLID.

Alexandrian Geometrician : B.C. 323-283.

Some people are unfortunately born scientific. . . . An aloofness and
abstractedness cleave to their greatness.   There is a coldness in their fame.
We think of Euclid as of fine ice ; we admire Newton as we admire the
Peak of Teneriffe.   Even the intensest labours, the most remote triumphs
of the abstract intellect, seem to carry us into a region different from our
own—to be in a *terra incognita* of pure reasoning, to cast a chill on human
glory.—WALTER BAGEHOT, *Literary Studies, Vol. II.*

EURIPIDES.

Greek Tragic Poet: B.C. 480-406.

Pella's bard, a magic name. —COLLINS, *Ode to Pity.*

He, the sweet Socratic sage,
Who steep'd in tears the wide Athenian stage.
                                —HAYLEY, *Ode to the Countess de Genlis.*

If in less stately mould thy thoughts were cast
    Than thy twin Masters of the Grecian stage,
Lone, 'mid the loftier wonders of the Past,
    Thou stand'st—more household to the Modern Age ;—
Thou mark'st that change in Manners when the frown
    Of the vast Titans vanish'd from the earth,
When a more soft Philosophy stole down
    From the dark heavens to man's familiar hearth.
Thy Phædra, and thy pale Medea, were
    The birth of that more subtle wisdom, which
Dawn'd in the world with Socrates, to bear
    Its last most precious offspring in the rich
And genial soul of Shakespeare.

                                —LYTTON, *Euripides.*

Our Euripides, the human,
    With his droppings of warm tears,
And his touches of things common
    Till they rose to touch the spheres !
                                —E. B. BROWNING, *Wine of Cyprus.*

Euripides was a Wordsworth, and Wordsworth is an Euripides.—
JOHN WILSON, *Essays: Greek Drama.*

For this reason, because he so exactly expressed the feelings and
opinions of his time, which feelings and opinions produced a permanent
national habit of mind, Euripides became the darling of posterity.
Æschylus was the Titanic product of a bygone period; Sophocles displayed the pure and perfect ideal; but Euripides was the artist who,
without improving on the spirit of his age, gave it a true and adequate
expression. The only wonder is, that during his lifetime Euripides was
not more popular at Athens. His comparative neglect proves him to
have been somewhat in advance of his century, and justifies Aristophanes
in the reproach that he anticipated the Athenians in the break-up of their
forms of thought.—JOHN ADDINGTON SYMONDS, *Studies of the Greek
Poets.*

In the end, perhaps this two-sidedness remains as the cardinal fact
about Euripides: he is a merciless realist; he is the greatest master of
imaginative music ever born in Attica. He analyses, probes, discusses
and shrinks from no sordidness ; then he turns right away from the world
and escapes " *to the caverns that the Sun's feet tread,*" or similar places,
where things are all beautiful and interesting, melancholy perhaps, like
the tears of the sisters of Phaethon, but not squalid or unhappy. . . .
Euripides was not essentially an artist. He was a man of extraordinary
brain-power, dramatic-craft, subtlety, sympathy, courage, imagination ;

he saw too deep into the world and took things too rebelliously to produce calm and successful poetry. Yet many will feel as Philemon did : *" If I were certain that the dead had consciousness, I would hang myself to see Euripides ".*— GILBERT MURRAY, *History of Ancient Greek Literature.*

JOHN EVELYN.

English Diarist : 1620-1706.

The memoirs of Evelyn and Pepys are the most obvious instances of works which derive their chief value from this source ; and which are read, not for any great interest we take in the fortunes of the writers, but for the sake of the anecdotes and notices of far more important personages and transactions which they so lavishly present us.—LORD JEFFREY, *Essays.*

LORD THOMAS FAIRFAX.

Parliamentary General : 1612-1671.

Fairfax, whose name in arms through Europe rings,
Filling each mouth with envy or with praise,
And all her jealous monarchs with amaze
And rumours loud, that daunt remotest kings
Thy firm unshaken virtue ever brings
Victory to home, though new rebellions raise
Their Hydra heads, and the false North displays
Her broken league to imp their serpent wings.
                    —MILTON, *To the Lord General Fairfax.*

VISCOUNT FALKLAND.

English Soldier : 1610-1643.

Callest thou thyself a Patriot ? On this field
Did Falkland fall, the blameless and the brave,
Beneath the banners of that Charles whom thou
Abhorrest for a Tyrant.
                    —SOUTHEY, *Inscription for a Column at Newbury.*

See Falkland dies, the virtuous and the just !
                    —POPE, *Essay on Man : Epistle IV.*

This man is no renegade, no apostate, but the purest of martyrs. . . . And such a martyr was Falkland !—DR. ARNOLD, *Introductory Lectures on Modern History.*

The charm with which the image of Falkland fascinates every purer eye. In that conflict of giants, each passion, each interest, finds its representative and type. Honour and Genius elect Falkland as their own. . . . That which pre-eminently distinguished Falkland amongst the actors of his time was his passion for justice. He was thus naturally the champion of the weak; he could not endure the sight of oppression. And by a consistency of character which bears down all the petty inconsistencies in detail from which no man of ardent temperament is free, the same tendencies that made him oppose Charles when powerful and oppressive—attracted him to Charles when feeble and oppressed.—LYTTON, *Essays: Pym versus Falkland.*

Falkland is commonly selected as the most respectable specimen of this class. He was indeed a man of great talents and of great virtues, but, we apprehend, infinitely too fastidious for public life. He did not perceive that, in such times as those on which his lot had fallen, the duty of a statesman is to choose the better cause and to stand by it, in spite of those excesses by which every cause, however good in itself, will be disgraced. The present evil always seemed to him the worst. He was always going backward and forward; but it should be remembered to his honour that it was always from the stronger to the weaker side that he deserted. While Charles was oppressing the people, Falkland was a resolute champion of liberty.—MACAULAY, *Essays: Hallam.*

MICHAEL FARADAY.

English Physicist and Chemist: 1791-1867.

Many readers remember that Sir Humphry Davy said, when he was praised for his important discoveries, "My best discovery was Michael Faraday".—EMERSON, *Greatness.*

You might not credit me were I to tell you how lightly I value the honour of being Faraday's successor compared with the honour of having been Faraday's friend. His friendship was energy and inspiration; his "mantle" is a burden almost too heavy to be borne. . . . Surely no memory could be more beautiful. He was equally rich in mind and heart. The fairest traits of a character sketched by Paul found in him perfect illustration. For he was "blameless, vigilant, sober, of good behaviour, apt to teach, not given to filthy lucre". . . . "Give me health and a day," says the brave Emerson, "and I will make the pomp of emperors ridiculous." In an eminent degree Faraday could say the same. What to him was the splendour of a palace compared with a thunderstorm upon Brighton Downs?—what among all the appliances of royalty to compare with the setting sun? I refer to a thunderstorm and a sunset, because these things excited a kind of ecstasy in his mind, and to a mind open to such ecstasy the pomps and pleasures of the world are usually of small account. Nature, not education, rendered Faraday strong and refined.—TYNDALL, *Faraday as a Discoverer.*

FRANÇOIS DE SALIGNAC DE LA MOTTE FÉNELON.

French Prelate: 1651-1715.

Of all modern men, Fénelon bears the strongest resemblance to the sages of antiquity. . . . Fénelon—Shall he not be called the Pythagoras, or Plato of France? . . . Fénelon was not only a poet, but also a political legislator; a modern Solon. . . . If genius acknowledged a sex, it might be said that Fénelon had the imagination of a woman to dream of heaven, and her soul to love the earth.—LAMARTINE, *Celebrated Characters (transl.), Vol. II.*

10

When we think of Fénelon in the palace of Louis XIV., it reminds us of a seraph sent on a divine commission into the abodes of the lost; and when we recollect that in that atmosphere he composed his *Telemachus,* we doubt whether the records of the world furnish stronger evidence of the power of a divine virtue to turn temptation into glory and strength, and to make even crowned and prosperous vice a means of triumph and exaltation.—CHANNING, *On the Character and Writings of Fénelon.*

Fénelon could not be approached too closely. He, at all times, appeared like a messenger from heaven.—CHARLES BUCKE, *Book of Human Character.*

JOHANN GOTTLIEB FICHTE.

German Philosopher: 1762-1814.

I cut and cut again!
First cut the Liquefaction, what comes last
But Fichte's clever cut at God Himself?
Experimentalise on sacred things!
                —BROWNING, *Bishop Blougram's Apology.*

There exists not now, there never did exist to any extent, a school of followers of Fichte; it may well be doubted if there are at present half-a-dozen students of his works. As a patriot, as representative of what seems noblest and loftiest in the German character, he lives, and will doubtless continue to live, in the grateful remembrance of his countrymen; as a metaphysician, he lives not at all beyond the learned pages of the historians of philosophy.—ROBERT ADAMSON, *Fichte.*

His unbelief proceeded rather from the despair of arriving at knowledge than from any voluntary choice of his own nature. . . . He who could forget the interests of personal comfort in his zeal to succour the sick and wounded [in 1813], and who by the hand of the pestilence could meet a heroic death, a martyr to his own unselfish devotion, is worthy to live in memory when his system of philosophy shall have crumbled in the dust, and shall stand as an eternal monument of that eternal truth, that man is greater than his opinions, and larger than the formula of his faith.— REV. GEORGE MATHESON, *Aids to the Study of German Theology.*

HENRY FIELDING.

English Novelist and Magistrate: 1707-1754.

What a master of composition Fielding was! Upon my word, I think the *Œdipus Tyrannus, The Alchemist,* and *Tom Jones,* the three most perfect plots ever planned. . . . How charming, how wholesome, Fielding always is!—COLERIDGE, *Table Talk.*

In the comic part of their writings, we have already said, Fielding is pre-eminent in grave irony, a Cervantic species of pleasantry in which Smollett is not equally successful.—SIR WALTER SCOTT, *Prose Works, Vol. III.*

Fielding, the *prose* Homer of human nature.—BYRON in MOORE'S *Life of Byron.*

I cannot offer or hope to make a hero of Henry Fielding. Why hide his faults? Why conceal his weaknesses in a cloud of periphrases? Why

not show him, like him as he is, not robed in a marble toga, and draped
and polished in an heroic attitude, but with inked ruffles, and claret-stains
on his tarnished laced coat, and on his manly face the marks of good-
fellowship, of illness, of kindness, of care, and wine. Stained as you see
him, and worn by care and dissipation, that man retains some of the most
precious and splendid human qualities and endowments. He has an admirable natural love of truth, the keenest instinctive antipathy to hypocrisy,
the happiest satirical gift of laughing it to scorn. His wit is wonderfully
wise and detective ; it flashes upon a rogue and lightens up a rascal like a
policeman's lantern. He is one of the manliest and kindliest of human
beings : in the midst of all his imperfections, he respects female innocence
and infantile tenderness as you would suppose such a great-hearted, courageous soul would respect and care for them. He could not be so brave,
generous, truth-telling as he is, were he not infinitely merciful, pitiful and
tender. He will give any man his purse—he can't help kindness and profusion. He may have low tastes, but not a mean mind ; he admires with
all his heart good and virtuous men, stoops to no flattery, bears no rancour,
disdains all disloyal arts, does his public duty uprightly, is fondly loved by
his family and dies at his work.—THACKERAY, *English Humourists of the
Eighteenth Century.*

If Fielding had painted pictures, it would have been in the style of the
Marriage à la Mode ; if Hogarth had written novels, they would have been
in the style of *Tom Jones. . . .* It may, nevertheless, be safely asserted
that there are few English novels of manners, written since Fielding's day,
which do not descend from him as from their fount and source ; and that
more than one of our modern masters betrays unmistakable signs of a
form and fashion studied minutely from his frank and manly ancestor.—
AUSTIN DOBSON *Life of Fielding.*

Regarded merely as writers, there can, I suppose, be no real rivalry between Fielding and Richardson. The superiority of Fielding is apparent
on every page. Wit, good humour, a superb lusty style which carries you
along like a pair of horses over a level moorland road, incidents, adventures,
inns, and all the glory of motion, high spirits, huge appetites, pretty women
—what a catalogue it makes ; of things no doubt smacking of this world
and the kingdom thereof, but none the less delightful on that account !
No wonder *Tom Jones* is still running ; where, I should like to know, is
the man bold enough to stop him ?—AUGUSTINE BIRRELL, *Res Judicatæ.*

Fielding, with all his faults and all his recklessness, was a manly, great-
hearted fellow, with more of the right heroic blood and true kingly talent
in him, though he did but occupy a police bench, and live by his wits,
than was to be found in the Austrian Hapsburgs, with whom he counted
kin.—DAVID MASSON, *British Novelists and their Styles.*

JOHN FISHER.

Bishop of Rochester : 1469-1535.

Supremacy from Heaven transmitted pure
As many hold ; and, therefore, to the tomb
Pass, some through fire—and by the scaffold some—
Like saintly Fisher, and unbending More.

" Lightly for both the bosom's lord did sit
Upon his throne " unsoftened, undismayed
By aught that mingled with the tragic scene
Of pity or fear.

—WORDSWORTH, *Apology.*

JOHN FLAXMAN, R.A.

English Sculptor : 1755-1826.

Nature, so prodigal to the English race in men of genius untutored, singular, and solitary, has given us but few seers who, in the quality of prolific invention, can be compared with Flaxman. For pure conceptive faculty, controlled by unerring sense of beauty, we have to think of Pheidias or Raphael before we find his equal. His powers were often employed on uncongenial subjects : nor had he, perhaps, a true notion of the limitations of his art ; else he would not have attempted to give sculpturesque form even in outline to many scenes from the *Divine Comedy.* . . . It may also be conceded that, to a large extent, his imagination, like a parasite flower, was obliged to bloom upon the branches of Greek art. What Flaxman would have been without the bas-reliefs, the vases, and the hand-mirrors of the ancients, it is difficult to conceive. . . . Whatever could be expressed according to the laws of bas-relief, embossed in metal, or hewn out of stone, or indicated in pure outline, he conveyed with a truth to nature, a grace of feeling, and an originality of conception, absolutely incomparable. Moreover, in this kind his genius was inexhaustible.—J. ADDINGTON SYMONDS, *Studies of the Greek Poets, Second Series.*

CHARLES JAMES FOX.

Orator and Statesman : 1749-1806.

When, lo a Hercules in Fox appear'd
Who for a time the ruin'd fabric rear'd.
He, too, is fall'n who Britain's loss supplied,
With him our fast-reviving hopes have died.
Not one great people only raise his urn,
All Europe's far-extended regions mourn.
" These feelings wide, let sense and truth unclue,
To give the palm where Justice points its due ; "
Yet let not canker'd Calumny assail,
Or round our statesman wind her gloomy veil.
Fox ! o'er whose corse a mourning world must weep,
Whose dear remains in honour'd marble sleep ;
For whom, at last, e'en hostile nations groan,
While friends and foes alike his talents own ;
Fox shall in Britain's future annals shine,
Nor e'en to Pitt the patriot's palm resign.

—BYRON, *On the Death of Mr. Fox.*

For the life of a Fox, of a Chatham the death,
What censure, what danger, what woe would I brave !

Their lives did not end when they yielded their breath ;
Their glory illumines the gloom of their grave.
　　　　　—BYRON, *Lines addressed to the Rev. J. T. Becher.*

Yon ill tongu'd tinkler, *Charlie Fox*,
May taunt you wi' his jeers an' mocks ;
But gie him't het, my hearty cocks !
　　　　　E'en cowe the cadie !
　　　　　　—BURNS, *The Author's Earnest Cry and Prayer.*

The mighty chiefs sleep side by side.
Drop upon Fox's grave the tear,
'Twill trickle on his rival's bier ;
O'er Pitt's the mournful requiem sound,
And Fox's shall the notes rebound.
The solemn echo seems to cry—
" Here let their discord with them die,"
Speak not for those a separate doom,
Whom Fate made brothers in the tomb.
But search the land of living men,
Where wilt thou find their like agen ?
　　　　　　—SIR WALTER SCOTT.

Charles James Fox, one of the greatest statesmen, had not his religion been party, and if not the greatest orator, certainly the most accomplished debater, that ever appeared upon the theatre of public affairs in any age of the world.—LORD BROUGHAM, *Statesmen of the Time of George III.*

The most Demosthenean speaker since Demosthenes. — SIR JAMES MACKINTOSH.

Mr. Fox united, in a most remarkable degree, the seemingly repugnant characters of the mildest of men and the most vehement of orators.—*Id.*

Fox and Sheridan, the English Demosthenes and the English Hyperides. —MACAULAY, *Essays : Warren Hastings.*

Fox had many noble and amiable qualities, which in private life shone forth in full lustre, and made him dear to his children, to his dependents, and to his friends ; but as a public man he had no title to esteem. In him the vices which were common to the whole school of Walpole appeared, not perhaps in their worst, but certainly in their most prominent form, for his parliamentary and official talents made all his faults conspicuous.— *Id., Essays : Earl of Chatham*, 1844.

Nature bestowed on Mr. Fox the qualities which are certain to command distinction in popular assemblies. He possessed in the highest degree the temperament of the orator, which, equal to the poet's in the intensity of feeling, is diametrically opposed to the poet's in the direction to which its instincts impel it. . . . In the union of natural passion with scholastic reasoning Mr. Fox excelled all who have dignified the English senate. He required no formal preparation beyond that which a mental review of the materials of a question in debate suggested to a mind rich in a copious variety of knowledge, and so charged with intellectual heat that it needed but collision to flash instantaneously into light.—LYTTON, *Essays : Pitt and Fox.*

In Fox, the heart warmed the genius ; in Pitt, the genius withered the heart.—NAPOLEON BONAPARTE.

In the most imperfect relics of Fox's speeches *the bones of a giant are to be discovered.*—LORD ERSKINE.

The sum of the whole character of Fox as a statesman is, that he was an ardent, consistent, and thorough lover of liberty. Whether in France or in America, whether in Ireland or in England, whether with reference to the Protestant or the Roman Catholic, whether to be applied to the white or the black man, the main and ruling passion of Fox's life was a love of liberty. For her cause, he was an orator ; for her cause, he was a statesman. He gave his life to the defence of English freedom ; he hastened his death by his exertions to abolish the African slave trade.— EARL RUSSELL, *Life of Charles Fox, Vol. III.*

As an orator, Fox's marked characteristic was his directness. He went straight to his goal with all the vigour of a mathematician working out a given problem. For this purpose he was content to sacrifice all that profuseness of ornament in which Burke indulged, and that accurate polish of diction which the younger Pitt affected. He never repeated himself; never went over a line of reasoning he had already traced ; never (to use Lord Brougham's expressive simile) went back upon a ground which he had utterly wasted and withered up by the tide of fire he had rolled over it. There was a steadiness and progressiveness of movement in his oratory which resembled the resistless march of Cromwell's Iron-sides.—W. H. DAVENPORT ADAMS, *English Party Leaders, etc., Vol. I.*

Fox, . . . a star of the first magnitude. . . . It may be said once for all that Fox was the greatest of all debaters, the most genial of all associates, the most honourable of all friends.—LORD ROSEBERY, *Life of Pitt.*

GEORGE FOX.

Founder of the Society of Friends : 1624-1690.

Quaker Fox, one of the founders of that pious and philosophic sect, who comprise all theology in charity.—LAMARTINE, *Celebrated Characters (transl.), Vol. II.*

Spinoza's ideal democracy was realised by a contemporary—not in a nation, for that is impossible, but in a sect—I mean by George Fox and his Quakers.—COLERIDGE, *Table Talk.*

He is a Cato-Howard. You see him in his early days, refusing to join in the festivities of the time called Christmas ; yet, if a stranger to the mirth, never to the mercy, of that kindly season.—REV. R. A. VAUGHAN, *Hours with the Mystics, Vol. II.*

George Fox was a man who had studied the Bible from cover to cover. It formed practically his sole education.—THOMAS HODGKIN.

It is difficult for a reader of the *Journal* not to feel that Fox is too confident of the absolute rightness of his own conduct, and the utter wickedness of all who oppose him. This is of course the usual note of the Prophet, and one of the things whereby he is most distinguished from the Philosopher, at least the true Philosopher. It is the spirit of Hosea rather than of Marcus Aurelius, and, paradoxical as it may sound, if Fox's education had been such as to give him a little less of the teaching of the Minor Prophets, and a little more—he probably had none—of the teaching of the best of the Greek philosophers, the result might have been a fuller manifestation of " the meekness and gentleness of Christ ".—*Id., Life of George Fox.*

FRANCIS D'ASSISI.

Founder of the Franciscan Order : 1182-1226.

But lest my language be not clearly seen,
Know, that in speaking of these lovers twain,
Francis and Poverty I mean.

—DANTE.

Clinging to the silent mother! Are we devils? are we men?
Sweet St. Francis of Assisi, would that he were here again!
—TENNYSON, *Locksley Hall, Sixty Years After.*

Yet hark--from Mantuan Albert making cease
The fierce ones, to St. Francis preaching peace,
Yonder! God's Truce—or trick to supersede
The very Use of Strength, is safe.
—ROBERT BROWNING, *Sordello.*

Francis had faith to see, and charity to love, even in the leprous, the imperishable traces of the Divine image in which man was created, and the brethren of the Divine sufferer by whom man was redeemed.—SIR JAMES STEPHEN, *Essays on Ecclesiastical Biography.*

Francis of Assisi may naturally lead us to the last mode in which the spirit of theological belief manifested itself; the confidence in a particular man, as the organ of a special divine illumination.—HALLAM, *Literature of the Middle Ages, Vol. I.*

It would be absurd to claim such men as St. Francis for one Church or religion more than another. They are the property of the universal human race. What was most beautiful in Jeremy Taylor, what was sweetest in Fénelon, what was profoundest in Jacob Boehme, what was purest in Oberlin, what was bravest in Chalmers, had so clearly the mark of God, that a sad and sinful thing would it be if the pride of sects were to make a monopoly thereof. God's apostles are for all the world; and let all the world bow down in honour, in gratitude, and in praise unto them.—WILLIAM MACCALL, *Foreign Biographies, Vol. I.*

Would you learn the might and majesty of self-sacrifice? Read of Francis of Assisi and Francis Xavier.—F. W. FARRAR, *Social and Present-Day Questions.*

Of all the men who have ever lived there is probably not one who has ever made it so absolutely his aim, as did St. Francis, to reproduce, in letter as well as in spirit, the very life of Christ. Among the hills and villages of Umbria he strove to live with his few first followers the very same life that our Lord had lived with His Apostles on the shores of Galilee and in the villages of Palestine.—*Id., Saintly Workers.*

At times when the conviction steals upon us that whatever Nature is, we are also, till we are ready with St. Francis to claim brotherhood with sun and wind, and hail even the last pale visitor as Sister Death ; when we believe with Darwin, as well as the poet, that every glistening little flower and green herb has its ego, its consciousness of pleasure and pain, then we may turn to Wordsworth as the supreme high priest of the mystery.—P. ANDERSON GRAHAM, *Nature in Books.*

When we read the *Fioretti di San Francesco,* we are well aware that the saint lived—his life is one of the chief realities of the thirteenth century ; but we perceive that the signs and wonders wrought by him proceed from the imagination of disciples ascribing to St. Francis what belongs partly to the ideal of his own character and partly to that of monastic sanctity in general.—J. A. SYMONDS, *Studies of the Greek Poets, Second Series.*

BENJAMIN FRANKLIN.

American Philosopher and Statesman : 1706-1790.

While Franklin's quiet memory climbs to heaven,
Calming the lightning which he thence hath riven.
Or drawing from the no less kindled earth
Freedom and peace to that which boasts his birth.
                              —BYRON, *The Age of Bronze.*

This self-taught American is the most rational perhaps of all philosophers.   He never loses sight of common sense in any of his speculations. . . . Upon the whole we look upon the life and writings of Dr. Franklin as affording a striking illustration of the incalculable value of a sound and well-directed understanding : and of the comparative uselessness of learning and laborious accomplishments.—LORD JEFFREY, *Essays.*

Franklin is, indeed, one of the very small class of men who can be said to have added something of real value to the art of living.—W. E. H. LECKY, *History of England, Vol. I.*

Where is the Master who could have instructed Franklin, or Washington, or Bacon, or Newton ?   Every great man is a unique.—EMERSON, *Essays : Self-Reliance.*

Franklin, who wrenched the lightning from heaven, and the sceptre from tyrants.—F. W. FARRAR, *Social and Present-Day Questions.*

SIR JOHN FRANKLIN.

English Arctic Explorer : 1786-1847.

Not here ! the white North has thy bones ; and thou heroic sailor-soul,
Art passing on thine happier voyage now toward no earthly pole.
                              —TENNYSON, *Sir John Franklin.*

We have only to look at one of our recent maps, as compared to those which were published fifty years ago, to see how much we owe to the courage and enterprise of Parry and Franklin, Park and Horneman, of Burckhardt and Lander.—SIR ARCHIBALD ALISON, *Essays : Humboldt.*

FREDERICK THE GREAT.

King of Prussia : 1712-1786.

The Justinian of the North.—LORD BROUGHAM, *Statesmen of the Time of George III.*

Frederick the Second, the ablest and most accomplished of the long line of German Cæsars.—MACAULAY, *Essays : Von Ranke.*

Most of the vices of Frederick's administration resolve themselves into one vice, the spirit of meddling. The indefatigable activity of his intellect, his dictatorial temper, his military habits, all inclined him to this great fault. He drilled his people as he drilled his grenadiers.—*Id., Ibid. : Frederick the Great.*

Frederick is by no means one of the perfect demigods : and there are various things to be said against him with good ground. To the last, a questionable hero ; with much in him which one could have wished not there, and much wanting which one could have wished. But there is one feature which strikes you at an early period of the inquiry : That in his way he is a Reality ; that he always means what he speaks ; grounds his actions, too, on what he recognises for the truth : and, in short, has nothing whatever of the Hypocrite or Phantasm. Which some readers will admit to be an extremely rare phenomenon.—CARLYLE, *History of Frederick II., Vol. I.*

It is a peculiarity of great men that they have a tendency to wreck the throne on which they sit. Take Frederick the Great—he led the life of a drill sergeant, of an estate steward, of a bureaucrat in one, making the details of every department of government centre in himself. He gradually absorbed everything, and nothing could be done without his sanction and knowledge. Such a man makes himself the mainspring of the machine, and when he withdraws the machine collapses and has to be constructed afresh.—LORD ROSEBERY, *Speech at the Cromwell Tercentenary, Queen's Hall, 14th Nov., 1899.*

ELIZABETH FRY.

English Prison Reformer : 1780-1845.

At Rome . . . Mrs. Fry would be foundress and first Superior of the Blessed Order of Sisters of the Gaols.—MACAULAY, *Essays : Von Ranke.*

THOMAS FULLER.

English Theologian : 1608-1661.

Fuller's language ! Grant me patience, Heaven ! A tithe of his beauties would be sold cheap for a whole library of our classical writers, from Addison to Johnson and Junius inclusive. And Bishop Nicolson !—a painstaking old charwoman of the Antiquarian and Rubbish Concern ! The venerable rust and dust of the whole firm are not worth an ounce of Fuller's earth !—S. T. COLERIDGE, *Notes, Theological, Political, etc.*

Next to Shakespeare, I am not certain whether Thomas Fuller, beyond all other writers, does not excite in me the sense and emotion of the marvellous ; the degree in which any given faculty or combination of faculties is possessed and manifested, so far surpassing what one would have thought possible in a single mind, as to give one's admiration the flavour and quality of wonder ! Wit was the stuff and substance of Fuller's intellect. It was the element, the earthen base, the material which he worked in, and this very circumstance has defrauded him of his due praise for the practical wisdom of the thoughts, for the beauty and variety of the truths, into which he shaped the stuff. . . . God bless thee, dear old man ! may I meet with thee ! which is tantamount to—may I go to heaven !—*Id.*, *Notes on English Divines*, *Vol. I.*

Thomas Fuller, one of the liveliest and yet, in the inmost heart of him, one of the most serious writers one can meet with. I speak of this writer partly because there is no one who is so resolute that we should treat him as a friend, and not as a solemn dictator. By some unexpected jest, or comical turn of expression, he disappoints your purpose of receiving his words as if they were fixed in print, and asserts his right to talk with you, and convey his subtle wisdom in his own quaint and peculiar dialect.—F. D. MAURICE, *Friendship of Books.*

Thomas Fuller often embroiders his history with sarcastic touches and humorous allusions; they fringe a sentence, or they slash it by a parenthesis ; they glitter on it, or they wind, like a button or a braid.—REV. R. A. VAUGHAN, *Essays and Remains*, *Vol. II.*

THOMAS GAINSBOROUGH.

English Painter : 1727-1788.

If Gainsborough did not look at nature with a poet's eye, it must be acknowledged that he saw her with the eye of a painter ; and gave a faithful, if not a poetical, representation of what he had before him.—SIR JOSHUA REYNOLDS.

If ever this nation should produce a genius sufficient to acquire to us the honourable distinction of an English School, the name of Gainsborough will be transmitted to posterity, in this history of the art, among the very first of that rising name.—*Id.*

Whatever may have been Gainsborough's failings, they vanished when he stood to his easel. If he was often wanting in judgment, he was always wise as an Artist, for he never attempted any style of work in which he was unable to succeed.—G. W. FULCHER, *Life of Thomas Gainsborough.*

Not so Gainsborough ; a great name his, whether of the English or any other school. The greatest colourist since Rubens, and the last, I think, of those who were fully acquainted with the power of their material.—RUSKIN, *Modern Painters*, *Vol. I.*

Supremely Gothic, Gainsborough.—*Idem.*

As a painter, Gainsborough was the artistic temperament made visible. It would be not rash to call him both the first and the best of the impressionists. In every task he set himself his aim was purely pictorial. He felt no temptation to be anecdotic, to be didactic, to be anything but artistic within the limits marked out by his own emotions and the materials he was using. His pictures are examples of pure reaction between object and subject, and their value depends more, perhaps, than in the case of any other man, on the quality of the senses of which they are so sincere an income. With Reynolds deliberation counted for much ; Gainsborough's good things are impromptus.—WALTER ARMSTRONG, *Thomas Gainsborough.*

CLAUDIUS GALEN.

Greek Physician : 131-201.

Worthy were Galen to be weighed in gold,
Whose help doth sweetest life and health uphold :
Yet by Saint Esculape he sollemne swore,
That for diseases they were never more,
Fees never lesse, never so little gaine,
Men give a groate, and aske the rest againe.
Groat's-worth of health can anie leech allot ?
Yet should he have no more than gives a groate.
—BISHOP J. HALL, Satire IV.

Only in this be no Galenist. To make
Courts hot ambitions wholesome, do not take
A dram of country's dulness ; do not add
Correctives, but as chemics purge the bad.
—DR. JOHN DONNE, To Sir Henry Wotton.

Who can this field of miracles survey
And not with Galen all in rapture say
Behold a God, adore him and obey !
—SIR RICHARD BLACKMORE, Creation.

That yellow blear-eyed wretch in chief
To whom the rest cringe low with feigned respect
Galen of Pergamos and hell—may speak
The tale, old man !
—BROWNING, Paracelsus.

GALILEI GALILEO.

Italian Astronomer : 1564-1642.

The starry Galileo with his woes.
—BYRON, Childe Harold's Pilgrimage, Canto IV.

That for which Galileo suffered hurt
Was light himself had seen and so might probe.
—ALFRED AUSTIN, Human Tragedy.

Galileo and Newton appear to us triumphing spirits. The sovereign and sole power of intellect swallowing up their life, appears to have something consecrating, in our estimation. We do not ask about the will of such men—perhaps we fear to do so, lest we should find a flaw, some evil lurking there that might bring down the starry Galileo from his throne in the skies, and show him, like ourselves, a child of dust.—JOHN WILSON, *Essays: Education of the People.*

Galileo, with an opera-glass, discovered a more splendid series of celestial phenomena than any one since.—EMERSON, *Essays: Self-Reliance.*

But what excuse can we devise for the humiliating confession and abjuration of Galileo? Why did this master-spirit of the age—this high-priest of the stars—this representative of science—this hoary sage, whose career of glory was near its consummation—why did he reject the crown of martyrdom which he had himself coveted, and which, plaited with immortal laurels, was about to descend upon his head? If, instead of disavowing the laws of Nature, and surrendering in his own person the intellectual dignity of his species, he had boldly asserted the truth of his opinions, and confided his character to posterity, and his cause to an all-ruling Providence, he would have strung up the hair-suspended sabre, and disarmed for ever the hostility which threatened to overwhelm him. The philosopher, however, was supported only by philosophy; and in the love of truth he found a miserable substitute for the hopes of the martyr. Galileo cowered under the fear of man, and his submission was the salvation of the Church. The sword of the Inquisition descended on his prostrate neck; and though its stroke was not physical, yet it fell with a moral influence fatal to the character of its victim, and to the dignity of science.—SIR DAVID BREWSTER, *Martyrs of Science.*

God is in nature; He is everywhere. Galileo saw Him in the farthest star.—F. W. FARRAR, *Social and Present-Day Questions.*

STEPHEN GARDINER.

Bishop of Winchester: 1483-1555.

Gardiner out-Gardiners Gardiner in his heat.—TENNYSON.

I look on Gardiner as canonisable compared with Sheldon.—COLERIDGE, *Notes on English Divines, Vol. II.*

GUISEPPI GARIBALDI.

Italian Patriot: 1807-1882.

This Garibaldi now, the Italian boys
Go mad to hear him—take to dying—take
To passion for ' the pure and high ';—God's sake.
　　　　　　　　—VICTOR HUGO, *Poems collected by H. L. Williams.*

He is the Helper that Italy wanted
To free her from fetters and cerements quite :
His is the great heart no dangers have daunted ;
His is the true hand to finish the fight.
Way, for a Man of the kingliest nature !
Scope, for a soul of the high Roman stature !
　　His great deeds have crowned him ;
　　His heroes are round him ;
On, on Garibaldi, for Freedom and Right.
　　　　　　　　—GERALD MASSEY, *Garibaldi.*

David Garrick.

English Dramatist and Actor: 1717-1779.

Here lies David Garrick, describe him who can ?
An abridgment of all that was pleasant in man ;
As an actor, confess'd without rival to shine ;
As a wit, if not first, in the very first line ;
Yet with talents like these, and an excellent heart,
The man had his failings, a dupe to his art ;
Like an ill-judging beauty his colours he spread,
And beplaster'd with rouge his own natural red.
On the stage he was natural, simple, affecting ;
'Twas only that when he was off he was acting.
                            —Goldsmith, *Retaliation.*

But when from nature's pure and genuine source,
These strokes of acting flow with gen'rous force ;
When in the features all the soul's portray'd ;
And passions, such as Garrick's, are display'd ;
To me they seem from quickest feelings caught :
Each start is nature ; and each pause is thought. . . .
If feelings which few hearts like his can know,
And which no face so well as his can show ;
Deserve the pref'rence ;—Garrick, take the chair ;
Nor quit it—till thou place an equal there.
                            —Churchill, *The Rosciad.*

So once were ranged the sons of ancient Rome,
O noble show ! while Roscius trod the stage ;
And so, while Garrick as renown'd as he,
The sons of Albion, fearing each to lose
Some note of Nature's music from his lips,
And covetous of Shakespeare's beauty seen
In every flash of his far-beaming eye.
                            —Cowper, *The Task : The Garden.*

Man praises man ; and Garrick's memory next,
When time hath somewhat mellow'd it, and made
The idol of our worship while he lived,
The god of our idolatry once more,
Shall have its altar ; and the world shall go
In pilgrimage to bow before his shrine, . . .
And strut and storm and straddle, stamp and stare,
To show the world how Garrick did not act.
For Garrick was a worshipper himself :
He drew the liturgy, and framed the rites
And solemn ceremonial of the day,
And call'd the world to worship on the banks
Of Avon famed in song.
                            —Id., Ibid. : *The Winter Walk at Noon.*

    Garrick who prefers a guinea
To all the eloquence of Pliny.
                            —James Cawthorn, *Wit and Learning.*

Poet and actor thus, with blended skill,
Mould all our passions to their instant will;
'Tis thus, when feeling Garrick treads the stage,
(The speaking comment of his Shakespeare's page)
Oft as I drink the words with greedy ears,
I shake with horror, or dissolve with tears.

—ROBERT LLOYD, *The Actor.*

So Shakespeare's page, the flower of poesy,
Ere Garrick rose had charms for every eye;
'Twas nature's genuine image wild and grand,
The strong-mark'd picture of a master's hand.
But when his Garrick, nature's Pallas, came,
The bard's bold painting burst into a flame:
Each part new force and vital warmth receiv'd.
As touch'd by heaven—and all the picture lived.

—W. J. MICKLE, *Stanzas on Mr. Garrick.*

JOHN GAY.

English Poet and Dramatist : 1688-1732.

Adieu to all but Gay alone,
   Whose soul, sincere and free,
Loves all mankind, but flatters none,
   And so may starve with me.

—POPE, *A Farewell to London.*

Of Manners gentle, of Affections mild;
In Wit, a Man; Simplicity, a Child:
With native Humour temp'ring virtuous Rage.
Form'd to delight at once and lash the age:
Above Temptation, in a low Estate,
And uncorrupted, ev'n among the great:
A safe Companion, and an easy Friend,
Unblam'd thro' Life, lamented in thy End.

—*Id., On Mr. Gay.*

I grieve to be outdone by Gay
In my own humorous biting way.

—SWIFT, *On the Death of Dr. Swift.*

These are thy honours! not that here thy bust
Is mix'd with heroes, or with kings thy dust;
But that the worthy and the good shall say,
Striking their pensive bosoms—Here lies Gay.

—*Id., On Mr. Gay.*

Thus Gay, the hare with many friends,
Twice seven long years the court attends:
Who, under tales conveying truth,
To virtue form'd a princely youth:
Who paid his courtship with the crowd
As far as modest pride allow'd;
Rejects a servile usher's place,
And leaves St. James's in disgrace.

—*Id., A Libel.*

The grinning hobbinals of Gay.—JOHN SCOTT.

Now, lend thy lug, and tent me, Gay,
Thy fate appears like flow'rs in May,
Fresh, flourishing, and lasting ay,
   Firm as the aik,
Which envious winds, when critics bray,
   Shall never shake.

Come, show your loof.—Ay, there's the line
Foretells thy verse shall ever shine,
Dowted, whilst living, by the nine,
   And a' the best,
And be, when past the mortal line,
   Of fame possest.

Immortal Pope, and skilfu' John,
The learned Leech from Caledon,
With mony a witty dame and don,
   O'er lang to name,
Are of your roundels very fon',
   And sound your fame.
   —ALLAN RAMSAY, *Epistle to Mr. John Gay.*

Gay is represented as a man easily incited to hope, and deeply depressed when his hopes were disappointed. This is not the character of a hero; but it may naturally imply something more generally welcome, a soft and civil companion.—DR. JOHNSON, *Lives of the Poets: Gay.*

GEORGE I.

King of Great Britain : 1660-1727.

There are stains on the portrait of the first George, and traits in it which none of us need admire; but, among the nobler features, are justice, courage, moderation—and these we may recognize ere we turn the picture to the wall.—THACKERAY, *The Four Georges.*

No shrewder men ever sat upon a throne than the first two Georges, monarchs of this realm.—AUGUSTINE BIRRELL, *Essays about Men, Women, and Books.*

GEORGE II.

King of Great Britain : 1683-1760.

If George the Second had been a more common man, instead of being Elector of Hanover and King of England, one might have said of him frankly enough that he was a person about as little to be admired as a man well could be who was not a coward or in the ordinary sense of the term a criminal. But because he was a crowned king, it was regarded as a patriotic duty then to make much of the departed monarch and to talk of him in the strain which would have been appropriate if he had been a Marcus Aurelius. The best, perhaps, that can be said of him is that, on the whole, all things considered, he might have been worse.—JUSTIN McCARTHY, *History of the Four Georges, Vol. II.*

There is George II., very like an unintellectual Voltaire.—KEATS in HOUGHTON'S *Life and Letters of John Keats.*

GEORGE III.

King of Great Britain : 1738-1820.

Still in prayers for King George, I most heartily join,
   The Queen and the rest of the gentry,
Be they wise, be they foolish, is nothing of mine ;
   Their title's avow'd by my country.
     —BURNS, *A Poetical Address to Mr. William Tytler.*

Ward of the law !—dread shadow of a king !
Whose realm had dwindled to one stately room ;
Whose universe was gloom immersed in gloom,
Darkness as thick as life o'er life could fling,
Save haply for some feeble glimmering
Of faith and hope ; if thou, by nature's doom,
Gently hast sunk into the quiet tomb,
Why should we bend in grief, to sorrow cling,
When thankfulness were best.
     —WORDSWORTH, *On the Death of His Majesty George III.*

George III. possessed much of the firmness of purpose which, being exhibited by men of contracted mind without any discrimination, and as pertinaciously when they are in the wrong as when they are in the right, lends to their characters an appearance of inflexible consistency, often mistaken for greatness of mind, and not seldom received as a substitute for honesty.—LORD BROUGHAM, *Statesmen of the Time of George III.*

Were a voice from heaven to proclaim aloud to us that there is another and a better world, in which virtue may expect its assured reward, the testimony of a miracle could not impress the awful truth more deeply upon the mind than the life and death of GEORGE the THIRD. . . . Known popularly and familiarly by the name of *Farmer George*, the British people at once loved him as a father, respected him as their sovereign, and re-garded even his peculiarities as something belonging to the character and humour of the nation, of whom he might be termed at once the king and the representative. . . . Old Farmer George's manly simplicity, modesty of expense, and domestic virtue saved this country at its most perilous crisis.—SIR WALTER SCOTT, *Edinburgh Weekly Journal*, 8th Feb., 1820.

The heart of Britain still beats kindly for George III., not because he was wise and just, but because he was pure in life, honest in intent, and because according to his lights he worshipped heaven.—W. M. THAC-KERAY, *The Four Georges.*

George III., who " gloried in the name of Briton," who obtained his initial popularity by being an Englishman born, and who, indeed, never travelled farther than York. was the German princelet of his day.—LORD ROSEBERY, *Life of Pitt.*

George IV.

King of Great Britain : 1762-1830.

To be the father of the fatherless,
To stretch the hand from the throne's height, and raise
His offspring, who expired in other days
To make thy sire's sway by a kingdom less,—
This is to be a monarch, and repress
Envy into unutterable praise.
—Byron, *Sonnet to George the Fourth.*

It was the good fortune of George IV. to wield the English sceptre during the most glorious period in our annals ; yet no monarch ever owed less to his own wisdom or exertions.—Sir Archibald Alison, *Epitome of the History of Europe.*

The iron age of George IV.—Gladstone, *Gleanings, Vol. VI.*

Edward Gibbon.

English Historian : 1737-1794.

A far greater historian—the greatest our literature can boast—Gibbon. —John G. Lockhart.

Gibbon's autobiography is the most perfect account of an eminent man's life, from his own hand, which exists in any language.—Sir Archibald Alison, *Essays : Autobiography.*

That it is not hopeless to look for such a mind is evident to all who recollect how Gibbon has painted the still wider expanse, and traced the longer story, of *The Decline and Fall of the Roman Empire* ; but how often in a century does a Gibbon appear in the world !—*Id., Ibid. : Michelet's France.*

Grave, tranquil, decorous pageantry is a part, as it were, of the essence of the last age. There is nothing more characteristic of Gibbon. A kind of pomp pervades him. He is never out of livery. He ever selects for narration those themes which look most like a levee : grave chamberlains seem to stand throughout ; life is a vast ceremony, the historian at once the dignitary and the scribe. The very language of Gibbon shows these qualities. Its majestic march has been the admiration—its rather pompous cadence the sport of all perusers. It has the greatest merit of an historical style : it is always going on ; you feel no doubt of its continuing in motion.—Walter Bagehot, *Literary Studies, Vol. II.*

It is Gibbon's triumph that he made his thoughts acts. He is not exactly what you call a pious writer, but he is provocative of at least one pious feeling. A sabbatical calm results from the contemplation of his labours. Succeeding scholars have read his history and pronounced it good. It is likewise finished. Hence this feeling of surprise.—Augustine Birrell, *Res Judicatæ.*

William Gifford.

English Critic and Poet: 1757-1826.

Where could you find a bitterer, more venomous body, than old Gifford ? Yet he is universally respected, for his bitterness changed many a scribbling block-head into an inoffensive man, and he spat his venom chiefly on corroded Cockneys, whom it was pleasant to see writhing in the dead-thraws. His friends know him to be one of the best of enlightened and religious men ; and as his Quarterly accounts have long been found correct, so will his accounts of all sorts pass at the last general audit.—John Wilson, *Essays: Streams.*

Giotto.

Italian Painter and Architect: 1276-1336.

Works done least rapidly, Art most cherishes.
Thyself shalt afford the example, Giotto !
Thy one work, not to decrease or diminish,
Done at a stroke, was just (was it not ?) " O ! "
The great Campanile is still to finish.
                    —Browning, *Old Pictures in Florence.*

William Ewart Gladstone.

English Statesman: 1809-1898.

The two Pitts and Mr. Gladstone are the three examples of speakers of transcendent power exercising for a considerable time a commanding influence over English politics.—W. E. H. Lecky, *History of England, Vol. I.*

Mr. Gladstone seems to us to be, in many respects, exceedingly well qualified for philosophical investigation. His mind is of large grasp ; nor is he deficient in dialectical skill. But he does not give his intellect fair play. There is no want of light, but a great want of what Bacon would have called dry light. Whatever Mr. Gladstone sees is refracted and distorted by a false medium of passions and prejudices. His style bears a remarkable analogy to his mode of thinking, and indeed exercises great influence on his mode of thinking. His rhetoric, though often good of its kind, darkens and perplexes the logic which it should illustrate. Half his acuteness and diligence, with a barren imagination and a scanty vocabulary, would have saved him from almost all his mistakes. He has one gift most dangerous to a speculator, a vast command of a kind of language, grave and majestic, but of a vague and uncertain import.—Macaulay, *Essays: Gladstone on Church and State (April,* 1839).

His choice of language was unbounded. It has been said of Lord Holland and his illustrious son, Charles James Fox, that from the very wealth of their vocabulary there arose a tendency to hesitation. But the wealth of vocabulary which was at Mr. Gladstone's command never produced that effect. His flow of words was not that of the mountain-stream which comes tumbling down helter-skelter. It was that of the river with an immense volume of water, whose downward course is as regular as it is stately. He never gabbled. He never drawled. . . . He was a living thesaurus or "Gradus," containing synonym after synonym; and it was this extraordinary wealth of words which laid him open to the charge, not without reason, of being verbose. Diffuseness at times led to discursiveness; and in this connection I am reminded of a remark made once by Mr. Bright on Mr. Gladstone's style of speaking: "I sail," said Mr. Bright, "or endeavour to sail, from headland to headland. Gladstone, making for the same point, sails round the coast, and whenever he comes to a navigable river he cannot resist the temptation of tracing it to its source." Mr. Gladstone's sentences were often very long; and one sometimes wondered how he would ever extricate himself from the maze of words. But there was nothing faulty in the construction of a sentence. There were parentheses, and occasionally even parentheses within parentheses; but no sentence was ever ungrammatical or unfinished.—Sir E. W. Hamilton, *Mr. Gladstone: a Monograph.*

Mr. Gladstone has fascinated two generations, not merely in pellucid and sparkling statement, but in those rolling and interminable sentences, which come thundering in mighty succession like the Atlantic waves on the Biscayan coast,—sentences, which other men have "neither the understanding to form nor the vigour to utter".—Lord Rosebery, *Life of Pitt.*

Johann Wolfgang von Goethe.

German Poet: 1749-1832.

And quiet Weimar, hush'd of look and staid,
  As if she knew the passing stranger came,
  Drawn to her by the splendour and the fame
Of her two mighty sons, whose dust is laid
Within her bosom side by side. And she
  Covers their ashes still with flowers that bind
  Mortals to all the high Immortals. He,
Goethe—a sea without one waft of wind;
Schiller—the river yearning for that sea,
  High, pure and restless, with an upward mind.
  So let her keep her sacred dust. For through
The march of ages as they sweep along,
  Will rise the potent voices of these two—
  The ocean and the river of her song.
            —Alexander Anderson, *Sonnets to a Friend, V.*

Faced by fulfilled Ideals, he aspired
To win the perished secret of their grace,—
To dower the earnest children of a race
Toil never tamed, nor acquisition tired,
  With Freedom born of Beauty!—and for them
      His Titan soul combined
      The passions of the mind,
  Which blood and time so long had held apart,
  Till the white blossom of the Grecian Art
The world saw shine once more, upon a Gothic stem!
            —Bayard Taylor, *Goethe.*

Goethe, raised o'er joy and strife,
Drew the firm lines of Fate and Life,
And brought Olympian wisdom down
To court and mart, to gown and town ;
Stooping, his finger wrote in clay
The open secret of to-day.

       —EMERSON, *Solution.*

. . . Goethe, with that reaching eye
His soul reached out from, far and high,
And fell from inner entity.

    —E. B. BROWNING, *A Vision of Poets.*

When Goethe's death was told, we said :
Sunk, then, is Europe's sagest head.
Physician of the iron age,
Goethe has done his pilgrimage.

    —MATTHEW ARNOLD, *Memorial Verses.*

And Goethe's course few sons of men
May think to emulate.
For he pursued a lonely road,
His eyes on Nature's plan ;
Neither made man too much a God,
Nor God too much a man.

    —*Id., In Memory of the Author of Obermann.*

Wordsworth's world is not Goethe's world: the Wordsworthian star,
like that of Jove itself, "so beautiful and large," is not like the star
Goethe. Both are the brightest of the bright ; but the breath of peace
envelops the one, with " an ampler ether, a diviner air "—at its height,
the other often looks troubled, and seems to reel in its sphere, with a
lurid but still celestial light.—JOHN WILSON, *Noctes Ambrosianæ, Vol. IV.*

Goethe has been likened to a cupola lighted from below.—LYTTON,
Essays : Charles Lamb and some of his Companions.

It seems to me that, among modern poets, Goethe ranks next to Shakespeare, at however wide an interval, in the combination of abstract, metaphysical speculation, and genial, easy, clement knowledge of the actual
world.—*Ibid., Knowledge of the World.*

Goethe was the philosopher of this multiplicity ; hundred-handed,
Argus-eyed, able and happy to cope with this rolling miscellany of facts
and sciences, and, by his own versatility, to dispose of them with ease ;
a manly mind, unembarrassed by the variety of coats of convention, with
which life had yet incrusted. . . . Goethe, the head and body of the
German nation, does not speak from talent, but the truth shines through :
he is very wise, though his talent often veils his wisdom.—EMERSON,
Goethe ; or the Writer.

This perception of the worth of the vulgar is fruitful in discoveries.
Goethe, in this very thing the most modern of the moderns, has shown
us, as none ever did, the genius of the ancients.—*Id., The American
Scholar.*

The cosmopolitan many-sidedness of Goethe. Goethe worked in the mornings, and husbanded that costly thing emotion. Schiller, who lived in the region of the ideal, was a man of large historic view, and strongly moved by the events of his day. Goethe, who lived in the actual, regarded the striving multitudes of men with a philosophic smile. For the outer world of Schiller was Humanity ; the outer world of Goethe, Nature. Goethe scrutinised nature with the man of science, and hence the accuracy of his delineation. He watched it lovingly with the man of taste, and hence the comprehensiveness and the judgment displayed in his descriptions. He had seen far more of nature than Schiller, and seen to better purpose every object within that wide range. Schiller makes nature speak his language ; Goethe forgets himself that he may interpret hers. As a word-painter of landscape, the superiority of Goethe will be readily acknowledged. Yet the descriptive power of Schiller was in reality more rare and wonderful.—R. A. VAUGHAN, *Essays and Remains, Vol. II.*

His great philosophic power, endless variety of fancy, and breadth of vision, render Goethe the master mind of the epoch.—JOSEPH MAZZINI.

In virtue of a genius such as modern times have only seen equalled once or twice, Goethe deserves the epithet of great ; unless we believe a great genius can belong to a small mind. Nor is it in virtue of genius alone that he deserves the name. Merck said of him that what he lived was more beautiful than what he wrote ; and his life, amid all its weaknesses and all its errors, presents a picture of a certain grandeur of soul, which cannot be contemplated unmoved.—G. H. LEWES, *Life and Works of Goethe, Vol. I.*

The man who can read Goethe's works and not perceive in them a spirit deeply religious, must limit the word religion to the designation of his own doctrines ; and the man who, reading them, discovers that Goethe was not orthodox, is discovering the sun at midday. Orthodox he never pretended to be. His religious experiences had begun early, and his doubts began with them. There are those who regard Doubt as criminal in itself ; but no human soul that has once struggled, that has once been perplexed with baffling thoughts which it has been too sincere to puddle away and stifle in precipitate conclusions, dreading to face the consequences of doubt, will speak thus harshly and unworthily of it.—*Id., Ibid., Vol. II.*

" Goethe," observes Madame de Staël, " should not be criticised as an author good in one kind of composition and bad in another. He rather resembles nature, which produces all and *of* all ; and we can prefer in him his climate of the south to his climate of the north, without disregarding in him the talents which harmonise with these different regions of the soul." In whichever of these regions we encounter him, we recognise a master mind ; and without pretending to fix his precise place amongst the greatest poets, we do not hesitate to declare him the most splendid specimen of cultivated intellect ever manifested to the world.—A. HAYWARD, *Life of Goethe.*

If we look back upon the course of Goethe's long life, it is impossible not to be struck with admiration when we think of the extraordinary range of his activity. There are few departments of intellectual life into which he did not penetrate, and in everything which, as a thinker, he undertook, he displayed the highest order of mental power. As a man of science, he ranks among the foremost investigators of his age. He had no sooner begun to reflect seriously on scientific problems than he placed himself in what proved to be the central current of modern thought. . . . It is only, indeed, since the law of evolution was detected, that the world has recognised the full meaning and importance of his contributions to scientific progress.—JAMES SIME, *Life of Goethe.*

The analogy between the history of a race so undisturbed in its development as the Greek, and the life of a man, is not altogether fanciful. A man like Goethe, beautiful in soul and body, exceedingly strong and swift and active and inquisitive in all the movements of his spirit, first lives the life of the senses and of physical enjoyment. His soul, "immersed in rich foreshadowings of the world," has scarcely begun to think consciously in the first period. But he feels the glory of existence, the strivings of inexhaustible energy, the desire of infinite expansion. The second period is one of *Sturm und Drang.* New things are learned: much of the beautiful physical activity is sacrificed; he discovers that life involves care and responsibility as well as pleasure; he concentrates his mental faculty on hard and baffling study, in which at first he halts and falters. Then he goes forth to the world, and wins great fame, and does the deeds and thinks the thoughts by which he shall be known to all posterity. His physical and mental faculties are now in perfect harmony; together they offer him the noblest and most enduring pleasures. But after a while his productiveness begins to dwindle. He has put forth his force, has fully expressed himself, has matured his principles, has formed his theory of the world. Our fourth period corresponds to the early old age of such a man's life. He now applies his principles, propagates his philosophy, subordinates his fancy, produces less, enjoys with more sobriety and less exhilaration, bears burdens, suffers disappointments, yet still, as Solon says, "learns always as he grows in years". Then comes the fifth stage. He who was so vigorous and splendid, now has but little joy in physical life; his brain is dry and withering; he dwells on his old thoughts, and has no faculty for generating new ones: yet his soul contains deep mines of wisdom; he gives counsel and frames laws for younger generations. And so he gradually sinks into the grave. His acts remain: his life is written.—J. ADDINGTON SYMONDS, *Studies of the Greek Poets.*

All the reformation that was done in England by Wordsworth was done at the same time for Germany by Goethe. It was done not indeed more faithfully and in the face of less opposition; but it was done with far wider intelligence, and with far profounder results. But that it should have been done at all, adds another great title to those high and varied pretensions which Goethe puts forward. The Shakespeare was at the same time the Wordsworth. . . . To Goethe, reality is almost the sole source of poetry; in his works so much poetry, so much experience. . . . Goethe is a perfect Solomon for proverbs; they pour from him in floods. —SIR J. R. SEELEY, *Goethe reviewed after Sixty Years.*

OLIVER GOLDSMITH.

Irish Poet and Novelist: 1728-1774.

And tender Goldsmith crowned with deathless praise.
                              —WORDSWORTH, *Seathwaite Chapel.*

Child, *thou*, sweet bard of Auburn!—Child! what then?
A child inspired, and worth a world of men.
—LYTTON, St. Stephen's, Part II.

. . . Goldsmith . . .
Whose verse shall live in every British mind,
Though sweet, yet strong; though nervous, yet refined.
—HARTLEY COLERIDGE, Young and his Contemporaries.

Who wanders not with Erin's wandering bard?
Who sits not down with Auburn's pastor mild
To take upon his knee the shyest child?
These in all hearts will find a kindred place,
And live the last of our poetic race.
—LANDOR, Goldsmith and Gray.

No man was more foolish when he had not a pen in his hand, or more wise when he had.—DR. JOHNSON.

The wreath of Goldsmith is unsullied; he wrote to exalt virtue and expose vice; and he accomplished his task in a manner which raised him to the highest rank among British authors.—SIR WALTER SCOTT, *Prose Works, Vol. III.*

Goldsmith's poetry enjoys a calm and steady popularity. It inspires us, indeed, with no admiration of daring design, or of fertile invention; but it presents, within its narrow limits, a distinct and unbroken view of poetical delightfulness.—CAMPBELL.

If Goldsmith had never written anything but the two or three first chapters of the *Vicar of Wakefield*, or the character of a Village-School-master, they would have stamped him a man of genius.—HAZLITT, *Table Talk.*

A king might refuse Goldsmith a pension, as a publisher might keep his masterpiece and the delight of all the world in his desk for two years; but it was a mistake, and not ill-will. Noble and illustrious names of Swift, and Pope, and Addison! dear and honoured memories of Gold-smith and Fielding! kind friends, teachers, benefactors! who shall say that our country, which continues to bring you such an unceasing tribute of applause, admiration, love, sympathy, does not do honour to the literary calling in the honour which it bestows upon *you!*—THACKERAY, *English Humourists of the Eighteenth Century.*

The works of Goldsmith are distinguished by the chastest simplicity; yet his character may be described best by his dress; which not only Boswell, but Northcote, represent as having been exceedingly tawdry.—CHARLES BUCKE, *Book of Human Character.*

Goldsmith is one of those characters whom the present generation has rightly determined to love, and foolishly resolved to cover with unqualified praise. . . . But Goldsmith is one of those distinguished writers with respect to whom a plain line of distinction can be drawn between their private lives and their positions as artists. As a mere citizen, Goldsmith was a blunder; from the beginning to the end his life was a failure—a series of unhappy experiences, humiliations, and grave errors; as an artist he was as nearly perfect as it is possible to conceive a poor human being striving to describe an ideal world, too beautiful to be painted by the pauper hieroglyphics of language, to be.—J. CORDY JEAFFRESON, *Novels and Novelists, Vol. I.*

" Innocently to amuse the imagination in this dream of life is wisdom." So wrote Oliver Goldsmith ; and surely among those who have earned the world's gratitude by this ministration he must be accorded a conspicuous place.—WILLIAM BLACK, *Life of Goldsmith.*

GENERAL CHARLES GEORGE GORDON.

English Soldier : 1833-1885.

Warrior of God, man's friend, and tyrant's foe,
  Now somewhere dead far in the waste Soudan,
Thou livest in all hearts, for all men know
  This earth has never borne a nobler man.
                    —TENNYSON, *General Gordon.*

Some men live near to God, as my right arm
Is near to me ; and thus they walk about.
Mailed in full proof of faith, and bear a charm
That mocks at fear, and bars the door on doubt,
And dares the impossible. So, Gordon, thou,
Through the hot stir of this distracted time,
Dost hold thy course, a flaming witness how
To go and dare, and make our lives sublime
As God's campaigners.

                    —J. STUART BLACKIE.

  Poor fellow ! I wonder if he has entered upon the larger sphere of action which he told me was reserved for him in case of such a trifling accident as death. Of all the people whom I have met with in my life, he and Darwin are the two in whom I have found something bigger than ordinary humanity, an unequalled simplicity and directness of purpose—a sublime unselfishness. Horrible as it to us, I imagine that the manner of his death was not unwelcome to himself. Better wear out than rust out, and better break than wear out.—HUXLEY, *Letter to Donnelly* (on hearing of Gordon's death) *in his Life and Letters, Vol. II.*

HENRY GRATTAN.

Irish Orator : 1746-1820.

Ever glorious Grattan ! the best of the good !
So simple in heart, so sublime in the rest !
With all which Demosthenes wanted endued,
And his rival or victor in all he possess'd.
Ere Tully arose in the zenith of Rome,
Though unequall'd, preceded, the task was begun,
But Grattan sprang up like a god from the tomb
Of ages, the first, last, the saviour, the *one !*
                    —BYRON, *The Irish Avatar.*

Thomas Gray.

English Lyric Poet: 1716-1771.

No bard divine! For many a care beguil'd
  By the sweet magic of thy soothing lay,
For many a raptur'd thought, and vision wild,
  To thee this strain of gratitude I pay.
                    —Thomas Warton, *To Mr. Gray.*

. . . Gray's unlaboured art
Soothes, melts, alarms, and ravishes the heart;
While the lone wanderer's sweet complainings flow
In simple majesty of manly woe;
Or while, sublime, on eagle pinion driven,
He soars Pindaric heights, and sails the waste of heaven.
          —Beattie, *On the Report of a Monument, etc.*

Or pour, with Gray, the moving flow
              Warm on the heart.
                    —Burns, *The Vision, II.*

In his "Elegy written in a Country Churchyard," Gray has caught, concentrated, and turned into a fine essence, the substance of a thousand meditations among the tombs.—Rev. George Gilfillan, *Dissertation prefixed to Gray's Poetical Works.*

Gray's *style* in prose, as exhibited in his correspondence, is confessedly delightful. Though somewhat quaint, it is an easy quaintness. He was infinitely more natural in prose than verse. Horace Walpole lets us into the secret of this. "Gray," says that piercing reader of such characters as came within the scope of his actual observation, "*never wrote anything easily but things of humour*"; and humour, his natural gift, is the characteristic of his correspondence. If not the best letter-writer in the language, he is the best letter-writer of all the professed *scholars.*—Lytton, *Essays: Gray's Works.*

Gray, as a poet of the lyre, appears to me to be more uniformly grand and majestic. The mind is elevated by him to ethereal regions, and soars with eagle flight, without being forced to fall from its eminence, like the son of Dædalus. Gray wings his way on high like a glorious luminary, all stately, all regularly magnificent.—Dr. Vicesimus Knox, *Winter Evenings: Evening C.*

Lady Jane Grey.

Queen of England (ten days): 1537-1554.

Bagenhall: "No—murder fathers murder: but I say
There is no man—there was one woman with us—
It was a sin to love her married, dead
I cannot choose but love her."
Stafford: "Lady Jane?"
                    —Tennyson, *Queen Mary.*

FRANÇOIS P. G. GUIZOT.

French Statesman and Historian : 1787-1874.

He is not, properly speaking, a historian ; his vocation and object were different. He is a great discourser on history. If ever the philosophy of history was embodied in a human being, it is in M. Guizot.—SIR ARCHIBALD ALISON, *Essays : Guizot.*

JOHN GUTENBERG.

Supposed Inventor of Movable Types for Printing : 1400-1468.

Gutenberg has given the world a soul.—LAMARTINE, *Celebrated Characters (transl.), Vol. II.*

The multiplication of readers is the multiplication of loaves. On the day when Christ created that symbol, he caught a glimpse of printing. His miracle is this marvel. Behold a book. I will nourish with it five thousand souls, a hundred thousand souls—a million souls—all humanity. In the action of Christ bringing forth the loaves, there is Gutenberg bringing forth books. One sower heralds the other. . . . Gutenberg, in the fifteenth century emerges from the awful obscurity, bringing out of the darkness that ransomed captive the human mind. Gutenberg is for ever the auxiliary of life ; he is the permanent fellow-workman in the great work of civilisation. Nothing is done without him. He has marked the transition of the man-slave to the free-man. Try and deprive civilisation of him, you become Egypt. The decrease of the liberty of the press is enough to diminish the stature of a people. . . . A Gutenberg discovering the method for the sowing of civilisation and the means for the ubiquity of thought, will be followed by a Christopher Columbus discovering a new field. A Christopher Columbus discovering a world will be followed by a Luther discovering a liberty. After Luther, innovator in the dogma, will come Shakespeare, innovator in art. One genius completes the other. —VICTOR HUGO, *William Shakespeare (transl.).*

JEANNE MARIA BOUVIER DE LA MOTTE GUYON.

French Mystic : 1648-1717.

Madame Guyon was gifted by nature with beauty of a dreamy and melancholy order, a passionate soul, and an imagination so exalted that earth could not satisfy it ; but seeking for love it mounted to heaven.— LAMARTINE, *Celebrated Characters (transl.), Vol. II.*

The ecstatic prophetess Madame de Guyon.—DR. J. IGNATIUS VON DÖLLINGER, *Studies in European History (transl.).*

As contrasted with the mysticism of St. Theresa, that of Madame Guyon appears to great advantage. She guards her readers against attempting to form any image of God. She aspires to an intellectual elevation—a spiritual intuition, above the sensuous region of theurgy, of visions, and of dreams. She saw no Jesuits in heaven bearing white banners among the heavenly throng of the redeemed. She beheld no Devil, "like a little negro" sitting on her breviary. She did not see the

Saviour in an ecstasy, drawing the nail out of His hand. She felt no large white dove fluttering above her head. But she did not spend her days in founding convents—a slave to the interests of the clergy. So they made a saint of Theresa, and a confessor of Madame Guyon.—R. A. VAUGHAN, *Hours with the Mystics, Vol. II.*

ARTHUR HENRY HALLAM.

Son of the Historian : 1811-1838.

Thus it is, that to teach one of us the death of Arthur Hallam—his thoughts and affections—his views of God, of our relations to Him, of duty, of the meaning and worth of this world and the next—where he now is, have an individual significance. He is bound up in our bundle of life ; we must be the better or the worse ₁of having known what manner of man he was ; and in a sense less peculiar, but not less true, each of us may say :—

> —" The tender grace of a day that is dead
> Will never come back to me."

> " A life that all the Muses deck'd
> With gifts of grace, that might express
> All comprehensive tenderness,
> All-subtilising intellect."

> —" Oh for the touch of a vanished hand,
> And the sound of a voice that is still ! "
> —DR. JOHN BROWN, *Horæ Subsecivæ, First Series.*

HENRY HALLAM.

English Historian : 1777-1859.

By the death of Mr. Hallam we have lost an eminent representative of a class of men, few in number, but inestimable in value at present—the scholar—author—the Working Man of Letters.—HARRIET MARTINEAU, *Biographical Sketches.*

Almost all the distinguished writers who have treated of English history are advocates. Mr. Hallam and Sir James Mackintosh alone are entitled to be judges. But the extreme austerity of Mr. Hallam takes away something from the pleasure of reading his learned, eloquent, and judicious writings. He is a judge, but a hanging judge, the Page or Buller of the High Court of Literary Justice. His black cap is in constant requisition. In the long calendar of those whom he has tried, there is hardly one who has not, in spite of evidence to character and recommendations to mercy, been sentenced and left for execution.—MACAULAY, *Essays : Sir James Mackintosh.*

We manage these things better in England. Sir Walter Scott gives us a novel ; Mr. Hallam a critical and argumentative history. Both are occupied with the same matter. But the former looks at it with the eye of a sculptor. His intention is to give an express and lively image of its external form. The latter is an anatomist. His task is to dissect the subject of its inmost recesses, and to lay bare before us all the springs of motion and all the causes of decay.—*Id., Ibid. : Hallam.*

Sir William Hamilton.

Scottish Philosopher: 1788-1856.

Hamilton . . .—the Scottish Stagyrite, the metaphysician of recent Europe.—DAVID MASSON, *British Novelists, etc.*

As Mill's is a *sweated* mind, often entangled in the sudorific blankets, when wanting to move, and incapable of walking, though a splendid rider —of hobbies—so Sir William Hamilton's was a swollen mind. The good Sir William was the Daniel Lambert of Philosophy. He had the shark's, the ostrich's enormous appetite, with no more power of discrimination than the ostrich or the shark. Quantity was everything, quality nothing. Blending the shark and the ostrich, he could make a decent meal of bricks, empty barrels, copper bolts, and tenpenny nails. He is almost the only learned man that Scotland has had since George Buchanan, and there are no signs that Scotland will ever have a learned man again. But his learning was a pedantic plethora, an apoplectic monstrosity, an asthmatic ventriloquism squeaking and growling through layers and convolutions of fat. It would be difficult to say whether Sir William Hamilton devoured books and systems, or was devoured by them. The result, at all events, was chaotic conglomeration. Little would it have mattered how many books or systems Sir William Hamilton had swallowed, if he had not been tormented by the unhappy yearning to be a creator of systems himself.—WILLIAM MACCALL, *The New Materialism.*

John Hampden.

English Patriot: 1594-1643.

A Hampden too is thine, illustrious land,
Wise, strenuous, firm, of unsubmitting soul,
Who stem'd the torrent of a downward age
To slavery prone, and bade thee rise again,
In all thy native pomp of freedom bold.
Bright, at his call, thy age of *men* effulg'd,
Of men on whom late time a kindling eye
Shall turn, and tyrants tremble while they read.
—THOMSON, The Seasons: Summer.

See Roman fire in Hampden's bosom swell.
—THOMAS CAMPBELL.

Dost thou boast
Of loyalty ? The field is not far off
Where in rebellious arms against his king
Hampden was kill'd, that Hampden at whose name
The heart of many an honest Englishman
Beats with congenial pride.
—SOUTHEY, Inscription for a Column at Newbury.

Like Hampden struggling in his country's cause,
The first, the foremost to obey the laws,
The last to brook oppression ! On he moves,

Careless of blame while his own heart approves,
Careless of ruin—(" For the general good,
'Tis not the first time I have shed my blood ".)
—SAMUEL ROGERS.

In Hampden, and in Hampden alone, were united all the qualities which, at such a crisis, were necessary to save the state, the valour and energy of Cromwell, the discernment and eloquence of Vane, the humanity and moderation of Manchester, the stern integrity of Hale, the ardent public spirit of Sydney. Others might possess the qualities which were necessary to save the popular party in the crisis of danger ; he alone had both the power and the inclination to restrain its excesses in the hour of triumph. Others could conquer ; he alone could reconcile. A heart as bold as his brought up the cuirassiers who turned the tide of battle on Marston Moor.—MACAULAY, *Essays : John Hampden.*

Of the Revolution in all countries and times, John Hampden is the perfect symbol.—RUSKIN.

GEORGE FREDERICK HÄNDEL.

German Musician and Composer : 1684-1759.

Some say that Signior Bononcini,
Compar'd to Handel's a mere ninny :
Others aver that to him Handel
Is scarcely fit to hold a candle.
Strange ! that such difference should be
'Twixt Tweedledum and Tweedledee !
—SWIFT, *Directions for Making a Birthday Song.*

There Handel strikes the strings, the melting strain
Transports the soul, and thrills through every vein.
—JOHN GAY, *Trivia.*

While love shall live, and rapture shall rejoice,
Fed by the notes of Handel, Arne and Boyce.
—CHRISTOPHER SMART, *The Hilliad.*

Remember Handel ? Who that was not born
Deaf as the dead to harmony, forgets,
Or can, the more than Homer of his age ?
Yes, we remember him ; and while we praise
A talent so divine, remember too
That His most holy Book from whom it came
Was never meant, was never used before,
To buckram out the memory of a man.
—COWPER, *The Task : The Winter Walk at Noon.*

The mighty musician of Germany, ours by adoption,
Who beheld in the king his munificent pupil and patron.
—SOUTHEY, *A Vision of Judgment.*

While men of sense, with Handel's happier skill,
Correct the taste, and harmonise the will ;

Teach their affections like his notes to flow,
Not rais'd too high, nor ever sunk too low.
    —James Cawthorn, *Life Unhappy, because we use it Improperly.*

From tyrant Handel rends the imperial bay,
And guards the Magna Charta of—Sol-fa.
                    —Paul Whitehead, *Honour.*

                    Yet, Handel, raise,
Yet wake to higher strains thy sacred lyre:
The name of ages, the supreme of things,
The great Messiah asks it; he whose hand
Stretch'd o'er the wilds of space this beauteous ball,
Whose spirit breathes through all his smiling works
Music and love—yet Handel raise the strain.
Hark! what angelic sounds, what voice divine
Breathes through the ravish'd air! my rapt ear feels
The harmony of heaven. . . .
Seraphic Handel! how shall words describe
Thy music's countless graces, nameless powers!
    —Dr. John Langhorne, *A Poem, To the Memory of Mr. Handel.*

Does not the eye of the human embryo predict the light? the ear of Handel predict the witch-craft of harmonic sound?—Emerson, *Essays: History.*

"Of what use," answers Madame de Staël, "is the Apollo Belvidere, or the poetry of Milton; the paintings of Raphael, or the strains of Handel? Of what use is the rose or the eglantine; the colours of autumn or the setting sun?" And yet what object ever moved the heart as they have done, and ever will do? Of what use is all that is sublime or beautiful in nature, if not to the soul itself?—Sir Archibald Alison, *Essays: The Crusades.*

Of Handel, and of Handel alone, can we say that the most splendid inspirations of Hebrew poetry gain an added glory from his music, and that thousands exist for whom passages of Scripture which have for eighteen centuries been very near the heart of Christendom acquire a yet deeper meaning, a yet more spiritual power, through the strains with which his genius has inseparably associated them.—A. J. Balfour, *Essays and Addresses.*

It may sound like an anachronism to call Handel a contemporary; and yet he seems so constantly with us, that at times we can hardly believe that he has passed away. We are surrounded by his effigies; no living face is more familiar—no modern minstrel more beloved than he who has now lain quietly in the great Abbey for some one hundred and ten years. —Rev. H. R. Haweis, *Music and Morals.*

Why, Handel was the most incorrigible dreamer, the most irrepressible romancist, that ever lived: and every note he wrote proves it. But, beneath his dreams, there was a fund of practical good sense, without which he would never have completed the work which has immortalised him. We read, in certain old-world stories, of dreams which work their own fulfilment. His dreams were of that order. He never neglected the means. Because kind Nature had endowed him with genius, he did not throw himself with the less ardour into the study of Counterpoint. . . . Should the " plagiarisms " ever be clearly proved, Handel will stand forth not only as the greatest constructor of Music that ever lived, but also as so skilful an adapter of other men's ideas to purposes of his own, that, in his hands " filched " thoughts were as great as original ones, and " pebbles " as brilliant as " diamonds ".—W. S. ROCKSTRO, *Life of G. F. Handel*.

Grandeur is the distinctive characteristic which dominates over all the compositions of Handel. Even in the exquisite gracefulness of *Acis and Galatea* there is a latent vigour, a certain solemnity of style, which elevates whilst it chains the mind. Every one is struck with this. So true is it, that critics, biographers, friends, and enemies all concur in speaking of him as a " colossus," a " giant," a " man mountain ". His atmosphere is the Immensity resplendent with the sun. Like Corneille, he lived in the sublime. . . . Handel has treated all styles, and has excelled in all, whether the subject be gay or serious, light or solemn, profane or sacred. He would be the Shakespeare of music if he were not the Michael Angelo. . . . In that musical Olympus the most divine masters have given to Handel the place of Jupiter Tonans. " He is the father of us all," exclaimed the patriarchal Haydn. " Handel," said the dogmatic Mozart, " knows better than any one of us what is capable of producing a great effect ; when he chooses he can strike like a thunderbolt." The lyrical Beethoven called him " the monarch of the musical kingdom. He was the greatest composer that ever lived," said he to Mr. Moscheles. " I would uncover my head, and kneel before his tomb."—VICTOR SCHOELCHER, *Life of Handel (transl.)*.

HANNIBAL.

Carthaginian General : B.C. 247-183.

Or, if dire Hannibal thy model be,
Dread lest, like him, thou bear the thunder *home !*
Perchance ev'n now a Scipio dawns for thee,
Thou doomest Carthage while thou smitest Rome—
    Write, write " Let carnage cease ! "
           —LYTTON, *Napoleon at Isola Bella*.

At his name the heart of the patriot has thrilled through every subsequent age. To celebrate his virtues, genius and learning have striven in every succeeding country ; and the greatest praise which the world can yet bestow on warriors is to compare them to Hannibal. No name, even in the majestic annals of Roman victors, stand forth with lustre equal to that of the Carthaginian hero. These were made by their countrymen, but his countrymen were made by him. . . . Of Hannibal's political wisdom and far-seeing sagacity, ancient history is full. Alone of all his contemporaries, he clearly, and from his very infancy, perceived the extent of the danger which threatened his country from the insatiable ambition and growing power of the Romans ; alone he pointed out the only mode in which it could be successfully combated. He was at once the Burke, the Pitt, and the Wellington of his country.—SIR ARCHIBALD ALISON, *Essays : Hannibal*.

VISCOUNT HARCOURT.

Lord Chancellor of England : 1660-1727.

Harcourt I see, for eloquence renown'd,
The mouth of justice, oracle of law !
Another Simon is beside him found,
Another Simon, like as straw to straw.
—GAY, *Epistle VI. : To Mr. Pope.*

And Harcourt's knowledge, equitably shown,
Makes justice call his firm decrees her own.
—PARNELL, *On Queen Anne's Peace.*

ROBERT HARLEY, EARL OF OXFORD.

Lord Treasurer of England : 1661-1724.

On Britain Europe's safety lies ;
Britain is lost if Harley dies :
Harley depends upon your skill ;
Think what you save, or what you kill.
—SWIFT, *Epigram Extempore.*

DR. WILLIAM HARVEY.

Discoverer of the Circulation of the Blood : 1578-1657.

Thus Harvey sought for truth in Truth's own book,
The creatures, which by God Himself was writ ;
And wisely thought 'twas fit
Not to read comments only upon it,
But on the original itself to look. . . .
Had Harvey to this road confin'd his wit,
His noble Circle of the blood had been untrodden yet.
Great Doctor ! the art of curing's cured by thee ;
We now thy patient, Physic, see
From all inveterate diseases free,
Purg'd of old errors by thy care,
New-dieted, put forth to clearer air.
—COWLEY, *Ode Upon Dr. Harvey.*

The circling streams, once thought but pools, of blood
(Whether life's fuel, or the body's food)
From dark oblivion Harvey's name shall save
While Ent keeps all the honour that he gave.
—DRYDEN, *Epistle II. : To Dr. Charleton.*

WARREN HASTINGS.

Governor-General of British India : 1732-1818.

Hastings ! I knew thee young, and of a mind
While young, humane, conversable, and kind ;
Nor can I well believe thee, gentle then,

Now grown a villain, and the worst of men :
But rather some suspect, who have oppress'd
And worried thee, as not themselves the best.
—COWPER, *To Warren Hastings, Esq.*

Here, where wrongs are forgiven, was the injured Hastings beside him :
Strong in his high deserts, and in innocence happy, though injured,
He, in his good old age, outlived persecution and malice.
—SOUTHEY, *A Vision of Judgment.*

The just fame of Hastings rises still higher, when we reflect that he was not bred a statesman ; that he was sent from school to a counting-house ; and that he was employed during the prime of his manhood as a commercial agent, far from all intellectual society.—MACAULAY, *Essays : Warren Hastings.*

It is no wonder that among the sundry and manifold difficulties of such a period, a man of his training and temper should have occasionally done things that are hard to justify and easy to condemn, or that his public acts should have brought him to the verge of private ruin. For he was undoubtedly cast in the type, so constantly recurrent in political history, of the sons of Zeruiah, and he very nearly earned their historical reward.
—SIR ALFRED LYALL, *Life of Warren Hastings.*

SIR HENRY HAVELOCK.

English Soldier : 1795-1857.

Honour to Henry Havelock ! tho' not of kingly blood,
He wore the double royalty of being great and good.
He rose and reacht the topmost height ; our Hero lowly born :
So from the lowly grass hath grown the proud embattled Corn !
He rose up in our cruel need, and towering on he trod ;
Bearing his brow to battle bold, as humbly to his God.
He did his work nor thought of nations ringing with his name,
He walkt with God, and talkt with God, nor cared if following Fame
Should find him toiling in the field, or sleeping underground ;
Nor did he mind what resting-place, with heaven embracing round.
—GERALD MASSEY, *Havelock's March.*

Havelock's religion underlay his whole character, of which it formed the stamina. For thirty-five years of his life religion was the ruling principle which pervaded his mind and regulated all his conduct. It was this which enabled him to overcome the innate defects of his character, and to become distinguished for qualities which nature had denied him. In all circumstances he was the bold and unflinching champion of Christian truth, though he never obtruded his religious views on others. . . . It was his constant aim to adorn his religious profession, and to demonstrate that spiritual-mindedness was not incompatible with the energetic pursuit of a secular calling—that " a saint could be a soldier ". More than any other chief did he appear to combine the great military talents of the generals of the Commonwealth with the fervour—though not the fanaticism—of their religious feelings ; and it is, perhaps, owing in a great measure to this identity of character, that the name of Havelock is so warmly cherished by his fellow countrymen.—J. C. MARSHMAN, *Memoirs of Sir Henry Havelock.*

12

Sir John Hawkwood.

English Soldier of Fortune : 1394.

Hawkwood appears to me the first real general of modern times: the earliest master, however imperfect, in the science of Turenne and Wellington.   Every contemporary Italian historian speaks with admiration of his skilful tactics in battle, his stratagems, his well-conducted retreats. . . . Hawkwood was not only the greatest but the last of the foreign condottieri, or captains of mercenary bands.—HALLAM, *Student's Middle Ages, Chap. III., Part II.*

Nathaniel Hawthorne.

American Novelist and Poet : 1804-1864.

There is Hawthorne, with genius so shrinking and rare
That you hardly at first see the strength that is there:
A frame so robust, with a nature so sweet,
So earnest, so graceful, so solid, so fleet,
Is worth a descent from Olympus to meet.
                    —J. R. Lowell, *A Fable for Critics.*

Should you ask me, Who is Hawthorne?
Who this Hawthorne that you mention?
I should answer, I should tell you,
" He's a Yankee, who has written
Many books you must have heard of;
For he wrote *The Scarlet Letter*
And *The House of Seven Gables,*
Wrote, too, *Rappacini's Daughter,*
And a lot of other stories ;—
Some are long, and some are shorter .
Some are good, and some are better.
And this Hawthorne is a Consul,
Sitting in a dismal office,—
Dark and dirty, dingy office,
Full of mates, and full of captains,
Full of sailors and of niggers,—
And he lords it over Yankees." . . .
Do you ask me, " Tell me further
Of this Consul, of this Hawthorne? "
I would say, " He is a sinner,—
Never goes inside a chapel,
Only sees outsides of chapels,
Says his prayers without a chapel!
I would say that he is lazy,
Very lazy, good for nothing;
Hardly ever goes to dinners,
Never goes to balls or soirées:
Thinks one friend worth twenty friendly ;
Cares for love, but not for liking;
Hardly knows a dozen people."
                    —Henry Bright, *Song of Consul Hawthorne.*

There are few authors with whom the world is more intimate than the one supposed to have most shunned its intimacy. But Nathaniel Hawthorne, though his peculiar sensibility shrank from men, loved mankind, and described his earliest writings as "attempts to open an intercourse with the world". In his works he has occasionally taken the world into his confidence in matters which most men of the world would veil—as in the opening chapter of *The Scarlet Letter*. Like his own Hilda, in *Transformation*, he was spiritually compelled to descend from his aerial hermitage, and unburden his heart in the world's confessional.—DR. MONCURE CONWAY, *Life of Nathaniel Hawthorne.*

We may hope that, though America may never produce another Hawthorne, yet other American writers may arise who will apply some of his principles of art, and develop the fineness of observation and delicate sense of artistic propriety for which he was so conspicuous. On that matter, at least, we can have no jealousies ; and if our cousins raise more Hawthornes, we may possibly feel more grateful than for some of their other productions.—LESLIE STEPHEN, *Hours in a Library, First Series.*

FRANZ JOSEPH HAYDN.

German Musical Composer : 1732-1809.

In Haydn's oratorios, the notes present to the imagination, not only motions, as of the snake, the stag, and the elephant, but colours also ; as the green grass. The law of harmonic sounds reappears in the harmonic colours.—EMERSON, *Miscellanies : Nature.*

We can assert with confidence that without Haydn we should not have the Mozart we know; that without Mozart we should not have the Beethoven we know; and that without Beethoven the whole musical history of the nineteenth century would have been utterly different from what it is.—A. J. BALFOUR, *Essays and Addresses.*

BENJAMIN ROBERT HAYDON.

English Historical Painter : 1786-1846.

Haydon was exactly the vulgar idea of a man of genius. He had all the morbid peculiarities which are supposed by fools to belong to intellectual superiority,—eccentricity, jealous caprice, infinite disdain for other men ; and yet he was as poor, commonplace, a creature as any in the world. He painted signs, and gave himself more airs than if he had painted the Cartoons. . . . Whether you struck him or stroked him, starved him or fed him, he snapped at your hand in just the same way. He would beg you in piteous accents to buy an acre and a half of canvas that he had spoiled. Some good-natured Lord asks the price. Haydon demands a hundred guineas. His Lordship gives the money out of mere charity, and is rewarded by some such entry as this in Haydon's journal: "A hundred guineas, and for such a work ! I expected that, for very shame, he would have made it a thousand. But he is a mean, sordid wretch." In the meantime the purchaser is looking out for the most retired spot in his house to hide the huge daub which he has bought, for ten times its value, out of mere compassion.—MACAULAY, *Life and Letters, Vol. II.*

WILLIAM HAZLITT.

English Critic : 1778-1830.

Hazlitt's brilliancy is seen chiefly in separate splinterings of phrase or image which throw upon the eye a vitreous scintillation for a moment, but spread no deep suffusions of colour, and distribute no masses of mighty shadow. A flash, a solitary flash, and all is gone. Rhetoric, according to its quality, stands in many degrees of relation to the per-manencies of truth; and all rhetoric, like all flesh, is partly unreal, and the glory of both is fleeting. . . . Some fireworks require an hour's duration for the expansion of their glory ; others, as if formed from ful-minating powder, expire in the very act of birth. Precisely on that scale of duration and of power stand the glitterings of rhetoric that are not worked into the texture, but washed on from the outside. Hazlitt's thoughts were of the same fractured and discontinuous order as his illus-trative images—seldom or never self-diffusive; and *that* is a sufficient argument that he had never cultivated philosophic thinking.—THOMAS DE QUINCEY, *Leaders in Literature.*

That spiritual essence, Hazlitt himself.—JOHN WILSON, *Essays : Streams.*

Hazlitt was, even by nature, but by circumstances still more so, *a lone man,* living, moving, and having his being, for and to himself exclusively ; as utterly cut off from fulfilling and exercising the ordinary pursuits and affections of his kind, and of his nature, as if he had been bound hand and foot in a dungeon, or banished to a desert. And so, indeed, he was—bound in the gloomiest of all dungeons—that built for us by our own unbridled passions—banished to that dreariest of all deserts, spread out for us by seared hopes and blighted affections.—P. G. PATMORE, *My Friends and Acquaintances, Vol. II.*

Hazlitt harps a good deal on one string ; but that string vibrates forcibly. His best passages are generally an accumulation of short, pithy sentences, shaped in strong feeling, and coloured by picturesque association ; but re-peating, rather than corroborating, each other. The last blow goes home, but each falls on the same place. He varies the phrase more than the thought ; and sometimes he becomes obscure, because he is so absorbed in his own feelings that he forgets the very existence of strangers who require explanation.—LESLIE STEPHEN, *Hours in a Library, Second Series.*

There never was such an epicure of his moods as Hazlitt.—A. T. QUILLER-COUCH, *Adventures in Criticism.*

There may be others who, in different parts of their work, are more un-equal than he is ; but with him the inequality is pervading, and shows itself in his finest passages, in those where he is most at home, as much as in his hastiest and most uncongenial task-work. It could not, indeed, be otherwise, because the inequality itself is due less to an intellectual than to a moral defect. The clear sunshine of Hazlitt's admirably acute intellect is always there ; but it is constantly obscured by driving clouds of furious prejudice. Even as the clouds pass, the light may be seen on distant and scattered parts of the landscape ; but wherever their influence extends, there is nothing but thick darkness, gusty wind and drenching rain. And the two phenomena, the abiding intellectual light, and the fits and squalls of moral darkness, appear to be totally independent of each other, or of any single will or cause of any kind.—GEORGE SAINTSBURY, *Essays in English Literature*.

For an author to fare better dead than alive is good proof of his literary vivacity and charm. The rare merit of Hazlitt's writing was recognised in his lifetime by good judges, but his fame was obscured by the unpopularity of many of his opinions, and the venom he was too apt to instil into his personal reminiscences. He was not a safe man to confide in. He had a forked crest which he sometimes lifted. Because they both wrote essays and were fond of the Elizabethans, it became the fashion to link Hazlitt's name with Lamb's. Hazlitt suffered by the comparison. . . . William Hazlitt had to take a thrashing from life. He took it standing up like a man, not lying down like a cur; but take it he had to do. He died on 18th September, 1830, tired out, discomfited, defeated. Nobody reviewing the facts of his life can say it was well spent. There is nothing in it of encouragement. He reaped what he sowed, and it proved a sorry harvest.—AUGUSTINE BIRRELL, *Res Judicatæ*.

REGINALD HEBER.

Bishop of Calcutta : 1783-1826.

Yes, to the Christian, to the Heathen world,
Heber, thou art not dead, . . . thou canst not die!
Nor can I think of thee as lost.
A little portion of this little isle
At first divided us; then half the globe:
The same earth held us still; but when,
O Reginald, wert thou so near as now!
　　　　—SOUTHEY, *Ode on the Portrait of Bishop Heber*.

Praise! for yet one more name, with power endow'd
　To cheer and guide us onward as we press;
Yet one more image, on the heart bestow'd,
　To dwell there—beautiful in holiness!
Thine, Heber, thine! whose mem'ry from the dead
Shines as the star which to the Saviour led.
　　　　—FELICIA HEMANS.

We have no bishops on our establishment; and have been accustomed to think that we are better without them. But, if we could persuade ourselves that bishops in general were at all like Bishop Heber, we should tremble for our Presbyterian orthodoxy; and feel not only veneration, but something very like envy, for a communion which could number many such men among its ministers.—LORD JEFFREY, *Essays*.

Heber stands alone as the one English gentleman—rector and squire, poet and scholar—who gave himself in early life to the missionary enterprise when the Church of England was reproached by its own son, Southey, for that hostility which Henry Martyn was even then beginning to convert into devotion to the cause. What Heber, representing Oxford, as Martyn inspired Cambridge, did " to elevate the Church of England," to use Mr. Gladstone's happy phrase, in the first twenty years of the

century, by his gracious character, broad charity, deep spirituality, parish
work, cultured preaching, genial learning, missionary enthusiasm, and
sacred gift of song, he crowned in the last three by his statesman-like
administration of the vastest of all Episcopal dioceses, and by his martyr-
like death.—GEORGE SMITH, *Life of Bishop Heber.*

GEORG W. F. HEGEL.

German Philosopher: 1770-1831.

As Socrates was compared to those figures of Silenus which were contained within the image of an Olympic god, so it may be said that in
Hegel we find an idealist, for whom truth is poetry and religion one with
philosophy, in the dress of a punctual and orderly civil servant of the
Prussian Government. . . . To him, therefore, the great aphorism, in
which the Christian ethics and theology may be said to be summed up,
that " he that saveth his life shall lose it, and he that loseth his life shall
save it," is no mere epigrammatic saying, whose self-contradiction is not
to be regarded too closely ; it is rather the first distinct, though as yet
undeveloped, expression of the exact truth as to the nature of the spirit.
—EDWARD CAIRD, *Life of Hegel.*

Perhaps no primordial thinker, no man of a piercing and puissant
brain, ever talked so much hollow and high-sounding nonsense as Hegel,
though the more unintelligible he was to himself and to others the more
his ardent acolytes celebrated him as the Messiah of philosophy. It
would be juster to delineate him as the Archimimus in Philosophy's
funeral procession. No Materialist, Hegel yet scattered the seeds of
loathsome materialisms, which now rankly flourish. Enlightened in his
political views, he yet glorified the contemptible Prussian bureaucracy,
taught it to be scientifically cruel where before it had simply displayed
the coarse cruelty of routine. Despising the mob he yet heralded the
silliest of democracies, a democracy unanimously condemned by Europe,
a dozen years ago, a democracy compared with which Red Republicanism
in France and elsewhere was wise and worthy. The self-appointed
renovator of moral as of metaphysical science, Hegel yet perfected lotos-
eating into an art for the benefit of a nation of lotos-eaters. Such is the
man before whom—a clever Vera—many accomplished students would
have us bow down.—WILLIAM MACCALL, *The New Materialism.*

HEINRICH HEINE.

German Poet: 1797-1856.

Heine for songs; for kisses, how ?

> —BROWNING, *Dis aliter visum.*

What, then, so harsh and malign,
Heine ! distils from thy life ?
Poisons the peace of thy grave ? . . .
The Spirit of the world
Beholding the absurdity of men—

Their vaunts, their feats—let a sardonic smile,
For one short moment, wander o'er his lips.
That smile was Heine!
> —MATTHEW ARNOLD, *Heine's Grave.*

The moonlight witchery of Heine's song.
> —ALEXANDER ANDERSON, *Sonnets to a Friend, II.*

This was a singer, a poet bold,
Compact of Fire and Rainbow Gold:
Compact of Rainbow Gold and of Fire,
Of sorrow and sin and of heart's desire—
Of good and of evil and things unknown,
A merciless poet who cut to the bone.
He sounded the depths of our grief and our gladness,
He laughed at our mirth and he wept at our madness;
He knew all the joy of the world, all the strife,
He knew, and he knew not, the meaning of life.
> —WALTER HERRIES POLLOCK, *Heinrich Heine.*

The exuberance of Heine's heart, as has been well said, was only equalled by the dryness of his spirit; a real enthusiasm was blended with an unquenchable love of satire; "his exquisite dilettantism made him adore the gods and goddesses of Greece at the expense even of Christianity". In short, qualities scarcely ever found in combination, were combined in him; in one weak, suffering body two distinct and opposite natures, each equally mighty, were united. Perhaps the best name ever applied to him is that of the "Julian of poetry".—E. A. BOWRING, *Sketch of Heine's Life* (prefixed to his *Poems*).

Heine passed as a drifting cloud: but his songs remain like stars in the heaven of poetry.—WILLIAM SHARP, *Life of Heinrich Heine.*

The cynicism of Heine, which is, after all, only sentimentalism soured. —J. R. LOWELL, *Among my Books.*

FELICIA DOROTHEA HEMANS.

English Poet: 1791-1835.

Gone is she
Who shrouded *Casabianca*, she who cast
The iron mould of *Ivan*, yet whose song
Was soft and varied as the nightingale's,
And heard above all others.
> —LANDOR, *The Heroines of England.*

Perhaps she shuddered while the world's cold hand her brow was wreathing,
But never wronged that mystic breath which breathed in all her breathing,
Which drew from rocky earth and man, abstractions high and moving,
Beauty, if not the beautiful, and love, if not the loving. . . .
Be happy, crowned and living One! and as thy dust decayeth
May thine own England say for thee what now for Her it sayeth—
"Albeit softly in our ears her silver song was ringing,
The foot-fall of her parting soul is softer than her singing."
> —ELIZABETH BARRETT BROWNING, *Felicia Hemans.*

The genius of Felicia Hemans, beautiful and lofty as Christian fame, we have ever loved, and admired, and honoured.—JOHN WILSON, *Essays: The Loves of the Poets.*

HENRY IV.

King of France: 1553-1610.

Take, for example, the best French sovereign, Henry IV., a king who restored order, terminated a terrible civil war, brought the finances into an excellent condition, made his country respected throughout Europe, and endeared himself to the great body of the people whom he ruled. Yet this man was twice a Huguenot, and twice a Papist. He was, as Davila hints, strongly suspected as having no religion at all in theory; and was certainly not much under religious restraints in his practice.— MACAULAY, *Essays: Gladstone on Church and State.*

HENRY V.

King of England: 1388-1422.

O for a muse of fire, that would ascend
The brightest heaven of invention !
A kingdom for a stage, princes to act,
And monarchs to behold the swelling scene !
Then should the warlike Harry, like himself,
Assume the port of Mars : and at his heels,
Leash'd in like hounds, should famine, sword, and fire,
Crouch for employment.
> —SHAKSPERE, *King Henry V.*

King Henry the Fifth, too famous to live long !
England ne'er lost a king of so much worth. . . .
Henry the Fifth ! thy ghost I invocate ;
Prosper this realm, keep it from evil broils !
Combat with adverse planets in the heavens !
A far more glorious star thy soul will make,
Than Julius Cæsar, or bright—. . . .
That ever-living man of memory,
Henry the Fifth.
> —*Id., King Henry VI., Act I., Sc. I.*

Henry the Fifth, that man made out of fire.
> —DRAYTON, *The Battle of Agincourt.*

HENRY VIII.

King of England: 1491-1547.

The imperial stature, the colossal stride,
Are yet before me ; yet do I behold
The broad full visage, chest of amplest mould,
The vestments broidered with barbaric pride :
And lo ! a poniard, at the monarch's side,

Hangs ready to be grasped in sympathy
With the keen threatenings of that fulgent eye,
Below the white-rimmed bonnet, far descried.
Who trembles now at thy capricious mood ?
' Mid those surrounding worthies, haughty king !
We rather think, with grateful mind sedate,
How Providence educeth, from the spring
Of lawless will, unlooked-for streams of good,
Which neither force shall check nor time abate.
>   —WORDSWORTH, *Sonnet on Henry VIII.*

Henry the Eighth, the Caligula of England.—LAMARTINE.

Henry VIII. perhaps approached as nearly to the ideal standard of perfect wickedness as the infirmities of human nature would allow.—SIR JAMES MACKINTOSH.

It can hardly be a matter of surprise that Henry VIII. should be taken by some persons to have been " our first Protestant King ". Nevertheless, it is a great mistake: Henry's mission was not to *build*, but to *destroy*. It is a wonderful fact that in the last fourteen years of his reign he accomplished the two remarkable exploits, of separating his kingdom from the Church of Rome, and of clearing monasticism out of England. To accomplish these two great achievements a man of remarkable kind was needed. He must be a man of strong will and of a strong right arm. His chief characteristic must be that which was seen in the Eighth Henry throughout. It was, says Bishop Short, " want of self-restraint ".—ROBERT BENTON SEELEY, *England's Training.*

GEORGE HERBERT.

English Parson and Poet: 1593-1632.

Of lyrics, he, the utmost fame
Has gain'd ; and how they vail, to hear him sing ;
Bocace in voice, and Casimire in wing.
>   —G. DANIEL, *An Ode upon " The Temple ".*

Two centuries have vanished since thy day,
    And yet that venerable Temple stands
Untouched by time, impervious to decay :
    But thou, blest builder, livest in other lands—
In other mansions, fashioned not of clay,
    Or man's device—thy " house not made with hands ".
>   —GEORGE MORINE, *George Herbert's " Temple ".*

Such as the Heaven-taught skill of Herbert drew.
>   —WORDSWORTH.

What Quarles's poetry was and is to more plebeian Christians, and to those fond of " strong meat " in theology, the same was and has been Herbert's " Temple " to Christians of more aristocratic breeding or of milder theological tastes.—DAVID MASSON, *The Life of Milton, Vol. I.*

HERODOTUS.

Greek Historian : B.C. 484-408.

Herodotus is all sweetness.—DR. VICESIMUS KNOX, *Essays : Cursory Thoughts on Biography.*

As the general father of prose composition, Herodotus is nearly related to all literature whatsoever, modern not less than ancient ; and as the father of what may be called ethnographical geography, as a man who speculated most ably on all the *humanities* of science—that is, on all the scientific questions which naturally interest our human sensibilities in this great temple which we look up to, the pavilion of the sky, the sun, the moon, the atmosphere, with its climates and its winds ; or in this home which we inherit, the earth, with its hills and rivers—Herodotus ought least of all to be classed amongst historians: that is but a secondary title for *him ;* he deserves to be rated as the leader amongst philosophical polyhistors, which is the nearest designation to that of encyclopedist current in the Greek literature. . . . We hold that Herodotus furnishes by much the largest basis for vast commentaries revealing the archæologics of the human race : whilst, as the eldest of prose writers, he justifies his majestic station as a brotherly assessor on the same throne with Homer.—DE QUINCEY, *Leaders in Literature.*

Herodotus does not expect to be pinned to conclusions. As Plutarch angrily puts it, he cares for accuracy, in such points "no more than Hippocleides"! . . . To Plutarch the age Herodotus treated is an age of giants, of sages and heroes in full dress, with surprising gifts for apothegm and repartee, and he sees all their deeds in a glow of adoring humility. He hates, he rejects their meaner side ; and he cannot bear the tolerant gossiping realism of Herodotus. Yet it is this power of truthfulness in the man, combined with his tragic grasp and his wide sympathy—this way of seeing men's hearts just as they are with all their greatness and their failure, that causes a critic who weighs his every word, to claim that "no other Greek writer has covered so large a world with so full a population of living and immortal men and women as Herodotus" [Macan, LXXIII.], and to place his work opposite Homer's, "irremovably and irreplaceably" at the fountain-head of European prose literature.—GILBERT MURRAY, *History of Ancient Greek Literature.*

ROBERT HERRICK.

English Poet : 1591-1674.

We cry, we laugh ; ah, life is half and half,
  Now bright and joyous as a song of Herrick's,
Then chill and bare as funeral-minded Blair ;
  As fickle as a female in hysterics.
          —OLIVER WENDELL HOLMES, *How not to settle it.*

Brief as thy lyrics, Herrick, are,
And polished as the bosom of a star.

          —T. B. ALDRICH, *Hesperides.*

Hayrick some do spell thy name,
And thy verse approves the same ;
For 'tis like fresh-scented hay,—
With country lasses in 't at play.
—W. ALLINGHAM, *To the Author of " Hesperides ".*

Fresh with all airs of woodland brooks
    And scents of showers,
Take to your haunt of holy books
    This saint of flowers.

When meadows burn with budding May,
    And heaven is blue,
Before his shrine our prayers we say,—
    Saint Robin true.
—E. W. GOSSE, *With a copy of Herrick.*

The most amorous, and among the best of our amorous poets was
Robert Herrick. . . . Herrick has as much variety as the poetry of kisses
can well have.—HALLAM, *Introduction to the Literature of Europe, Vol. III.*

Herrick is, in my mind, fully entitled to the reputation he has ; and yet
I scarcely wonder that many of his readers should overlook the golden
side of his shield, and persist in estimating him by the reverse—I fear we
must not call it silver. One cause of this is the arrangement, or rather *no*
arrangement, of the poems in the *Hesperides ;* where the coarsest epigram
is perhaps followed by half a dozen graceful verses, full of tender feeling ;
or a worthless imitation of Martial or Ovid by a solemn prayer for the
success of King Charles. They remind one of some quaint old Roman
Catholic procession, in which shaven friars and morris-dancers, saintly
relics and frisking dragons, follow each other in the happiest confusion.—
R. J. KING, *Sketches and Studies.*

DR. THOMAS HERRING.

Archbishop of Canterbury : 1693-1757.

But who like Herring or like Hoadly shine,
Must with great learning real virtue join.
—DODSLEY, *The Art of Preaching.*

JAMES HERVEY.

English Parson and Author : 1714-1758.

To form the taste, and raise the nobler part,
To mend the morals, and to warn the heart ;
To trace the genial source we nature call,
And prove the God of nature, friend of all ;
Hervey for this his mental landscape drew,
And sketch'd the whole creation out to view.
—DR. NATHANIEL COTTON, *To the Rev. James Hervey.*

I venture to think it would be well for the Church of our day, if we had a few more hard students and careful writers of the stamp of James Hervey. I therefore boldly claim for him a high place among the spiritual heroes of the last century. Let us admire Whitfield and Wesley; but let us not grudge Hervey his crown. He deserves to be had in remembrance.—BISHOP J. C. RYLE, *Christian Leaders of the Last Century.*

HESIOD.

Greek Poet : fl. about B.C. 870.

That Ascræan bard, whose fame now rings
Through the wide world.
—SPENSER, *Virgil's Gnat.*

Homer strung his lyre in the halls of princes who loved to dwell on the great deeds of their god-descended ancestors. Hesiod utters a weaker and more subdued note to the tillers of the ground and the watchers of the seasons. In Homer we see the radiant heroes expiring with a smile upon their lips as on the Æginetan pediment. In Hesiod we hear the low sad outcry of humanity. The inner life, the daily loss and profit, the duties and the cares of men are his concern.—J. ADDINGTON SYMONDS, *Studies of the Greek Poets.*

ST. HILDEBRAND.

Pope Gregory VII. : 1013-1085.

Hildebrand, the very impersonation of Papal Arrogance and of Spiritual Despotism.—SIR JAMES STEPHEN, *Essays in Ecclesiastical Biography.*

The last words of Gregory—"I have loved righteousness and hated iniquity"—were no more than the truth. He had no selfish or sordid aims ; the moral purification of the Church, its organisation as a great spiritual empire under one supreme head, and its emancipation, for this purpose, from all secular control—this was the ideal for which he lived. The dying words of one of our archbishops, "*Pro ecclesiâ Dei, pro ecclesiâ Dei,*" might well stand as the motto of Gregory's life ; the victories of the Church were his joys, her defeats his sorrows.—W. R. W. STEPHENS, *Hildebrand and His Times.*

REV. ROWLAND HILL.

Dissenting Minister : 1744-1833.

Rector of Surrey Chapel, Vicar of Wotton-under-Edge, and Curate of all the fields and commons throughout England and Wales.—REV. ROWLAND HILL.

I go to hear Rowland Hill, because his ideas come red-hot from the heart.—SHERIDAN.

At his [Whitfield's] death there was only one young man to be found who had caught the fire of his zeal, possessed similar powers of eloquence, and was actuated by the same self-denying and disinterested spirit. This was Mr. Rowland Hill, who appeared in many respects to have been cast in the same mould. His doctrines, his preaching talents, his popularity, his want of any definite system, were all Whitfield again.—REV. EDWIN SIDNEY, *Life of the Rev. Rowland Hill.*

SIR ROWLAND HILL.

Originator of the Cheap Postage System : 1795-1879.

So long as men keep warm feelings, and the name of home has still its charm ; so long as there are sorrowful partings and hearts that need comforting ; so long as our high aim is towards peace on earth, good-will toward men, Rowland Hill is not likely to be forgotten. For he has done almost more than any other man to bring near those who are far off, to bind the nations together, and to make the whole world kin.—G. B. HILL, *Life of Sir Rowland Hill, Vol. II.*

THOMAS HOBBES.

English Philosopher : 1588-1679.

Thou great Columbus of the golden lands of new philosophies,
Thy task was harder much than his,
For thy learn'd America is
Not only found out first by thee,
And rudely left to future industry,
But thy eloquence and thy wit
Has planted, peopled, built, and civilized it.
　　　　　　　　　—COWLEY, *To Mr. Hobbes.*

Th' envenom'd stream that flows from Toland's quill,
And the rank dregs of Hobbes and Mandeville.
Detested names ! yet sentenc'd ne'er to die :
Snatch'd from oblivion's grave by infamy !
　　　　　　　　　—DR. JOHN BROWN, *On Honour.*

Thus Hobbes on one dear system fix'd his eyes,
And prov'd his nature wretched—to be wise.
Each zealot thus, elate with ghostly pride,
Adores his God, and hates the world beside.
　　　　　　—DR. JOHN LANGHORNE, *The Enlargement of the Mind.*

Hobbes is perhaps the first of whom we can say that he is a good English writer.—HALLAM, *Introduction to the Literature of the Middle Ages, Vol. IV.*

Hobbes was perfect in the " noble vulgar speech ".—EMERSON, *English Traits : Literature.*

Hobbes was a thinker and writer of marvellous power, and, take him altogether, is probably the greatest of English philosophers.—HUXLEY, *Method and Results.*

WILLIAM HOGARTH.

English Painter: 1697-1764.

Farewell, great painter of mankind,
  Who reach'd the noblest point of art ;
Whose pictur'd morals charm the mind,
  And through the eye correct the heart!
If genius fire thee, reader, stay ;
  If nature touch thee, drop a tear :—
If neither move thee, turn away,
  For Hogarth's honour'd dust lies here.
          —DAVID GARRICK, *Epitaph on William Hogarth.*

That praise be Hogarth's ; freely let him wear
The wreath which genius wove, and planted there.
Foe as I am, should envy tear it down,
Myself would labour to replace the crown.
Hogarth unrivall'd stands, and shall engage
Unrivall'd praise to the most distant age.
          —CHURCHILL, *An Epistle to William Hogarth.*

But O for Hogarth's magic pow'r
To show Sir Bardy's willyart glowr !
          —BURNS, *On Dining with Lord Daer.*

        And Hogarth, who follow'd no master,
Nor by pupil shall e'er be approached, alone in his greatness.
          —SOUTHEY, *A Vision of Judgment.*

Thy Hogarth first of every clime
For humour keen, or strong sublime,
And hail him from his fire and spirit,
The child of genius and merit.
          —ROBERT LLOYD, *Genius, Envy, and Time.*

  I count those persons fools who think it a pity Hogarth did not succeed
better in serious subjects.—HAZLITT, *Table Talk.*

  It is not hazarding too much to assert that he [Hogarth] was one of the
greatest comic geniuses that ever lived, and he was certainly one of the
most extraordinary men this country has produced. Criticism has not
done him justice, though public opinion has. His works have received a
sanction which it would be vain to dispute, in the universal delight and
admiration with which they have been regarded, from their first appearance
to the present moment. . . . They stimulate the faculties as well as
soothe them. " Other pictures we see, Hogarth's we read."—*Id.,*
Lectures on the English Comic Writers : Hogarth.

  It is the fashion with those who cry up the great Historical School in
this country, at the head of which Sir Joshua Reynolds is placed, to exclude
Hogarth from that school, as an artist of an inferior and vulgar class.
Those persons seem to me to confound the painting of subjects in common
or vulgar life with the being a vulgar artist.   The quantity of thought which
Hogarth crowds into every picture would alone *unvulgarise* every subject
which he might choose.—CHARLES LAMB.

I very much doubt whether the sermons of a Tillotson ever dissuaded so efficaciously from lust, cruelty, and intemperance, as the prints of a Hogarth.—Dr. VICESIMUS KNOX, *Essays : On the Moral Effects of Painting and Prints.*

The true ideal is not opposed to the real, nor is it any artificial heightening thereof, but lies *in* it, and blessed are the eyes that find it ! It is the *mens divinior* which hides within the actual, transfiguring matter-of-fact into matter-of-meaning for him who has the gift of second sight. In this sense Hogarth is often more truly ideal than Raphael, Shakespeare often more truly so than the Greeks.—J. R. LOWELL, *Among My Books.*

What has been said of Rabelais applies with even greater force to Hogarth, whose absolute sincerity is as great as that of Aristophanes, but who is never light and careless. His coarseness is the product of a coarse nature, of coarse manners, of a period of national coarseness. We tolerate it because of the moral earnestness beneath : the artist is striving diligently to teach us by warning us of vice. This is hardly ever the case with Aristophanes. When he is coarse, we pardon him for very different reasons. In his wilful degradation of humanity to the level of animals we recognize a portion of the Weltvernichtungsidee.—JOHN ADDINGTON SYMONDS, *Studies of the Greek Poets.*

It is neither as engraver, draughtsman, nor painter that William Hogarth claims pre-eminence among English artists ; it was as a wit, a humorist, a satirist upon canvas. To take some social blot, some fashionable vice, and hold it up sternly to " hard hearts " ; to imagine it vividly and dramatically, and body it forth with all the resources of unshrinking realism ; to tear away its trappings of convention and prescription, to probe it to the quick, and lay bare all its secret shameful workings to their inevitable end ; to play upon it with inexhaustible invention, with the keenest and happiest humour ; to decorate it with the utmost prodigality of fanciful accessory and allusive suggestion ; to be conscious at his gravest how the grotesque in life elbows the terrible, and the strange grating laugh of Mephistopheles is heard through the sorriest story :—these were his gifts, and this was his vocation—a vocation in which he has never yet been rivalled.—AUSTIN DOBSON, *Life of Hogarth.*

JAMES HOGG.

The Ettrick Shepherd, Poet : 1772-1835.

You will see Hogg, and I cannot express
His virtues, though I know they are great,
Because he locks, then barricades, the gate
Within which they inhabit ;—of his wit
And wisdom, you'll cry out when you are bit.
He is a pearl within an oyster shell,
One of the richest of the deep.
                    —SHELLEY, *Letter to Maria Gisborne.*

In pace requiescat. There will never be such an Ettrick Shepherd again. —LOCKHART, *Life of Scott.*

Next to Robert Burns, the Ettrick Shepherd is unquestionably the most distinguished of Scottish bards sprung from the ranks of the people : in the region of the supernatural he stands alone.—REV. CHARLES ROGERS, *Memoir prefixed to Tales and Sketches by the Ettrick Shepherd.*

Towards the last he occupied a very curious position, never I think quite paralleled elsewhere—the position of a Boswell who would fain be a Boswell and is not allowed to be, who has wild notions that he is really a greater man than Johnson and occasionally blasphemes against his idol, but who in the intervals is truly Boswellian.—SAINTSBURY, *Essays in English Literature.*

LORD HOLLAND.

English Statesman and Author : 1773-1840.

It may be doubted if any man in any age ever had so few enemies, so many attached friends, as Lord Holland; and no man could better deserve the universal affection of which he was the object.—LORD BROUGHAM, *Statesmen of the Time of George III., Vol. II.*

Lord Holland is the most agreeable man I ever knew ; in criticism, in poetry, he beats those whose whole study they have been. No man in England has a more thorough knowledge of English authors, and he expresses himself so well that his language illustrates and adorns his thoughts, as light streaming through coloured glass heightens the brilliancy of the objects it falls upon.—SIR WALTER SCOTT in LOCKHART'S *Life of Scott.*

OLIVER WENDELL HOLMES.

American Poet and Essayist : 1809-1894.

His still the keen analysis
   Of men and moods, electric wit,
Free play of mirth, and tenderness
   To heal the slightest wound from it.

And his the pathos touching all
   Life's sins and sorrows and regrets,
Its hopes and fears, its final call
   And rest beneath the violets.

            —WHITTIER, *Our Autocrat.*

There's Holmes, who is matchless among you for wit,
A Leyden-jar always full-charged, from which flit
The electrical jingles of hit after hit.
            —J. R. LOWELL, *A Fable for Critics.*

Master alike in speech and song
   Of fame's great antiseptic—Style,
You with the classic few belong
   Who tempered wisdom with a smile.
            —Id., *To Holmes on his Seventy-fifth Birthday.*

HENRY HOME, LORD KAMES.

Scottish Judge and Philosopher: 1696-1782.

The truth seems to be that the soil of Scotland is most happily adapted for the cultivation of philosophical criticism. There was old Kames, though flawed and cracked, a diamond almost of the first water. Hold up his *Elements* between your eye and the firmament, and you see the blue and the clouds. To speak sensibly, he was the very first person produced by this island of ours entitled to the character of a philosophical inquirer into the principles of poetical composition. He is the father of such criticism in this country—the Scottish—not the Irish—Stagyrite. He is ours—let the English show their Aristotle. That his blunders are as plentiful as blackberries, is most true ; but that they are so is neither wonder nor pity—for so are Burke's ; yet is his treatise on the Sublime and Beautiful, juvenile as it is, full of truth and wisdom. Change the image ; and fling Kames' *Elements of Criticism* into the fanners of Wordsworth's wrath ; and after the air has been darkened for a while with chaff, the barn-floor will be like a granary rich in heaps of the finest white wheat which, baked into bolted bread, is tasteful and nutritive sustenance even for a Lake poet.—JOHN WILSON, *Essays : Homer and His Translators.*

HOMER.

Early Greek Poet.

So from one Homer all the holy fire
That ever did the hidden heat inspire
In each true Muse came clearly sparkling down,
And must for him compose one flaming crown.
> —CHAPMAN, *Epistle Dedicatory to Robert, Earl of Somerset.*

None like Homer hath the world ensphered,
  Earth, seas, and heaven, fix'd in his verse, and moving ;
Whom all times' wisest men have held unpeer'd.
> —Id., *Sonnet to the Earl of Salisbury.*

I can no more believe old Homer blind
Than those who say the Sun hath never shin'd ;
The age wherein he liv'd was dark, but he
Could not want sight, who taught the world to see :
They who Minerva from Jove's head derive,
Might make old Homer's Skull the Muses' Hive ;
And from his Brain that Helicon distil
Whose Racy Liquor did his offspring fill.
> —DENHAM, *The Progress of Learning.*

              And as the prince
Of poets, Homer, sung long since,
A skilful leech is better far
Than half a hundred men of war.
> —SAMUEL BUTLER, *Hudibras, Part I., Canto II.*

Blind Homer's Muse and Virgil's stately verse,
While any live, shall never need a hearse.
> —SUCKLING, *An Answer to some Verses made in his Praise.*

High on the first the mighty Homer shone,
Eternal adamant compos'd his throne;
Father of verse! in holy fillets drest,
His silver beard wav'd gently o'er his breast;
Though blind, a boldness in his looks appears:
In years he seem'd, but not impair'd by years.

—POPE, *The Temple of Fame.*

Be Homer's works your study and delight,
Read them by day, and meditate by night;
Thence form your judgment, thence your maxims bring,
And trace the muses upward to their spring. . . .
Those oft are stratagems which errors seem,
Nor is it Homer nods, but we that dream.

—*Id., Essay on Criticism.*

Read Homer once, and you can read no more,
For all books else appear so mean, so poor,
Verse will seem prose; but still persist to read,
And Homer will be all the books you need.

—DUKE OF BUCKINGHAM, *An Essay on Poetry.*

Hang Homer and Virgil! their meaning to seek,
A man must have pok'd into Latin and Greek;
Those who love their own tongue, we have reason to hope,
Have read them translated by Dryden and Pope.

—PRIOR, *Down-Hall, A Ballad.*

Where are they?—Homer's reverend page
Holds empire to the thirtieth age,
And tongues and climes obey.

—AKENSIDE, *Ode VII., On the Use of Poetry.*

Great Homer too appears, of daring wing,
Parent of song!

—THOMSON, *The Seasons: Winter.*

            The Fountain Bard,
Whence each poetic stream derives its course.

—*Id., Liberty, Part II. (Greece).*

The great Mæonian, sire of tuneful song,
And prototype of all that soar'd sublime.

—SHENSTONE, *Economy.*

Aye on the shores of darkness there is light
   And precipices show untrodden green,
There is a budding morrow in midnight,
   There is a triple sight in blindness keen;
Such seeing hadst thou, as it once befel
To Dian, Queen of Earth, and Heaven, and Hell.

—KEATS, *To Homer.*

Homer the great Thunderer.

—WORDSWORTH, *The Prelude, Book V.*

Twice is almighty Homer far above
Troy and her towers, Olympus and his Jove.
First, when the God-led Priam bends before
Him sprung from Thetis, dark with Hector's gore :
A second time, when both alike have bled,
And Agamemnon speaks among the dead.
—LANDOR, *Miscellaneous Poems, CXVI.*

The strong-wing'd music of Homer.
—TENNYSON, *On Translations of Homer.*

. . . Homer, with the broad suspense
Of thunderous brows, and lips intense
Of garrulous god-innocence.
—E. B. BROWNING, *A Vision of Poets.*

That wit and joy might find a tongue,
And earth grow civil, Homer sung.

—EMERSON, *Solution.*

Beethoven, Raphael, cannot reach
The charm which Homer, Shakespeare, teach.
To these, to these, their thankful race
Gives, then, the first, the fairest place :
And brightest is their glory's sheen,
For greatest hath their labour been.
—MATTHEW ARNOLD, *Epilogue to Lessing's Laocoön.*

Sometimes come pauses of calm, when the rapt bard, holding his heart back,
Over his deep mind muses, as when o'er awe-stricken ocean
Poises a heapt cloud luridly, ripening the gale and the thunder :
Slow rolls onward the verse with a long swell heaving and swinging,
Seeming to wait till, gradually wid'ning from far-off horizons,
Piling the deeps up, heaping the glad-hearted surges before it,
Gathers the thought as a strong wind darkening and cresting the tumult.
—J. R. LOWELL, *Impressions of Homer.*

Homer's poem is intellectual, and full of affections; it would go as near to make a philosopher as a soldier. I should say that war appears as the business of Homer's heroes, not often a matter of pure enjoyment. One would conceive, that if there could be found anywhere, in language, the real breathing spirit of lust for fight, which is in some nations, there would be conceptions, and passion of blood-thirst, which are not in Homer. There are flashes of it in Æschylus.—JOHN WILSON, *Noctes Ambrosianæ, Vol. I.*

Every novel is a debtor to Homer.—EMERSON, *Uses of Great Men.*

Homer lies in sunshine.—*Id., Shakespeare ; or the Poet.*

A man may have a high Intellect with little or no Imagination ; but he cannot have a high Imagination with little or no Intellect. The Intellect of Homer, Dante, Milton and Shakespeare, was higher than that of Aristotle, Newton and Bacon. When elevated by feeling into Imagination, their intellect became transcendent—and thus were they poets—the noblest name by far and away that belongs to any of the children of men. —JOHN WILSON, *Noctes Ambrosianæ, Vol. II.*

Oh! call not Greek a dead language, if you have a soul to be saved! The bard who created, and the heroes who fought in the *Iliad*, are therein not entombed, but enshrined; and their spirits will continue to breathe and burn there, till the stars are cast from the firmament, and there is an end to what we here call Life.—*Id., Essays : Homer and his Translators.*

Milton strove to raise earth to heaven : Homer brought down heaven to earth. The latter attempt was a much easier one than the former ; it was more consonant to human frailty ; and, therefore, it has met with more success. No one can doubt that Homer was endowed with the true poetic spirit, and yet there is very little of what we now call poetry in his writings. There is neither sentiment nor declamation—painting nor reflection. He is neither descriptive nor didactic. With great powers for portraying nature, as the exquisite choice of his epithets and the occasional force of his similes prove, he never makes any laboured attempt to delineate her features. He had the eye of a great painter ; but his pictorial talents are employed, almost unconsciously, in the fervour of narrating events, or the animation of giving utterance to thoughts. He painted by an epithet or a line. . . . There never was a greater painter of nature than Homer ; there never was a man who aimed less at being so.—SIR ARCHIBALD ALISON, *Essays : Homer, Dante, etc.*

That "Greek Gazette," the *Iliad* of Homer.—GEORGE GILFILLAN, *Dissertation prefixed to the Poetical Works of John Dryden, Vol. II.*

Without doubt, in his influence over future mankind, Homer is eminently the Greek of Greeks : if I were to associate any one with him it would be Herodotus. . . . But Homer is the great type, and the more notable one because of his influence on Virgil, and, through him, on Dante, and all the after ages.—RUSKIN, *Modern Painters, Vol. III.*

Homer is the huge poet-child. The world is born, Homer sings. He is the bird of this aurora. Homer has the holy sincerity of the early dawn. He almost ignores shadow. . . . Homer to the Greeks, was God ; he had priests, the Homerides. Alcibiades gave a bombastic orator a cuff for boasting that he had never read Homer. The divinity of Homer has survived paganism. Michael Angelo said, " *When I read Homer, I look at myself to see if I am not twenty feet high* ". . . . If anything is greater than God seen in the sun, it is God seen in Homer.—VICTOR HUGO, *William Shakespeare (transl.).*

I take Homer and Herodotus as two men who, while separated in time by a number of centuries even greater than the four which the historian allows, were both of them, according to the lights and opportunities of their day, pious men. But how far stronger, more familiar, and more vivid, is the sense of a providence truly divine, of the *theos* and *theoi* quite apart from polytheistic limitations, in Homer than in Herodotus !—W. E. GLADSTONE, *On the Ancient Beliefs in a Future State.*

The Greek mind, which became one of the main factors of the civilised life of Christendom, cannot be fully comprehended without the study of Homer, and is nowhere so vividly or so sincerely exhibited as in his works.

He has a world of his own, into which, upon his strong wing, he carries us. There we find ourselves amidst a system of ideas, feelings and actions different from what are to be found anywhere else, and forming a new and distinct standard of humanity. Many among them seem as if they were then shortly about to be buried under a mass of ruins, in order that they might subsequently reappear, bright and fresh for application, among later generations of men. Others of them almost carry us back to the early morning of our race, the hours of its greater simplicity and purity, and more free intercourse with God. In much that this Homeric world exhibits, we see the taint of sin at work, but far, as yet, from its perfect work and its ripeness; it stands between Paradise and the vices of later heathenism, far from both, from the latter as well as the former, and if among all earthly knowledge the knowledge of man be that which we should chiefly court, and if to be genuine it should be founded upon experience, how is it possible to over-value this primitive representative of the human race in a form complete, distinct and separate, with its own religion, ethics, policy, history, arts, manners, fresh and true to the standard of its nature, like the form of an infant from the hand of the Creator, yet mature, full and finished, in its own sense, after its own laws, like some master-piece of the sculptor's art.—W. E. GLADSTONE, *Studies on Homer and the Homeric Age.*

In Achilles, Homer summed up and fixed for ever the ideal of the Greek character. He presented an imperishable picture of their national youthfulness, and of their ardent genius, to the Greeks. The " beautiful human heroism " of Achilles, his strong personality, his fierce passions controlled and tempered by divine wisdom, his intense friendship and love that passed the love of woman, above all, the splendour of his youthful life in death made perfect, hovered like a dream above the imagination of the Greeks, and insensibly determined their subsequent development. At a later age this ideal was destined to be realised in Alexander. The reality fell below the ideal: for *rien n'est si beau que la fable si triste que la verité.* But the life of Alexander is the most convincing proof of the importance of Achilles in the history of the Greek race.—J. ADDINGTON SYMONDS, *Studies of the Greek Poets.*

DR. WALTER FARQUHAR HOOK.

Dean of Chichester, Author: 1798-1875.

Christian is my name, Catholic my surname. —DEAN HOOK.

RICHARD HOOKER.

Theologian: 1553-1600.

But if in Hooker, Sprat, or Tillotson,
A thought unworthy of themselves is shown,
I grieve to see it; but 'tis no surprise,
The greatest men are not at all times wise.
                    —DODSLEY, *The Art of Preaching.*

The " Ecclesiastical Polity " of Hooker is a monument of real learning, n profane as well as theological antiquity.—HALLAM, *Literature of the Middle Ages, Vol. II.*

Hooker was truly judicious—the consummate *synthesis* of understanding and sense. . . . Doubtless, Hooker was a theological Talus, with a club of iron against opponents with pasteboard helmets, and armed only with crabsticks.—COLERIDGE, *Notes on English Divines, Vol. I.*

In Hooker—more (I think) than in many great theologians who succeeded him—we find, under some archaism of form, the enunciation of the true principles, which must always guide the believer ; whenever, with the beacon-light or the revelation of Christ before his eyes, he sees new cross-lights breaking in on every side—lights which, if they be true, he will neither quench nor ignore—lights of which, if they be ever so true, yet none is sufficient to be his guide.—BISHOP BARRY, *Masters in English Theology.*

Hooker, a thinker of transcending compass, sweeping in the range of his imperial mind the whole circumference of Christian speculation—rising with the wings of boldness to the heights of the Divine government, and yet folding them with the sweetest reverence before the throne.—DR. JOHN TULLOCH, *Beginning Life.*

QUINTUS HORATIUS FLACCUS.

Latin Poet and Critic : B.C. 65-8.

Horace's lofty Genius boldlier rear'd
His manly Head, and through all Nature steer'd ;
Her richest Pleasures in his Verse refin'd,
And wrought 'em to the Relish of the Mind.
He lash'd with a true Poet's fearless Rage,
The Villainies and Follies of the Age.
　　—OTWAY, *Prologue to " The History and Fall of Caius Marius ".*

Serene, and clear, Harmonious Horace flows,
With sweetness not to be exprest in Prose.
　　　　　　　　—ROSCOMMON, *Essay on Translated Verse.*

Horace still charms with graceful negligence,
And without method talks us into sense,
Will, like a friend, familiarly convey
The truest notions in the easiest way.
　　　　　　　　　　—POPE, *Essay on Criticism.*

Here happy Horace tun'd th' Ausonian lyre
To sweeter sounds, and temper'd Pindar's fire :
Pleas'd with Alcæus' manly rage t' infuse
The softer spirit of the Sapphic Muse.
　　　　　　　　　—*Id., The Temple of Fame.*

Then farewell Horace : whom I hated so,
Not for thy faults, but mine ; it is a curse
To understand, not feel thy lyric flow,
To comprehend, but never love thy verse,
Although no deeper Moralist rehearse
Our little life, nor Bard prescribe his art,

Nor livelier Satirist the conscience pierce,
Awakening without wounding the touch'd heart,
Yet fare thee well—upon Soracte's ridge we part.
　　　　　　　—BYRON, *Childe Harold's Pilgrimage.*

Horace and Virgil, in whose mighty lines
Immortal wit, and solid learning, shines.
　　　　　　　　　—JOHN POMFRET, *The Choice.*

　　　　　Above all rivals, fit
To win the palm of gaiety and wit.
　　　　　　　　　—WORDSWORTH, *Liberty.*

Horace, singing yet
Of love, regret,
　　And flowers ;
This Roman rose is ours.
　　　　　　　—F. D. SHERMAN, *The Garland.*

Horace, the ailing lord,
Of plaster palaces and hollow groves,
Absorbed in half-a-hundred tiny arts,
Master of none.
　　　—A. C. BENSON, *The Professor and other Poems.*

　　Horace, the politest writer whom the world ever produced, adopted satirical writing, and succeeded in it, though there is every reason to believe that his natural disposition was not severe. The truth is, he was a man of the world as well as a man of reflection, and wrote his remarks on men and things in careless verse ; not without censuring them indeed, but without indulging the asperity of sarcasm. He probed every wound with so gentle a hand, that the patient smiled under the operation.—DR. VICESIMUS KNOX, *Essays : Cursory Thoughts on Satire and Satirists.*

　　Horace certainly wrote plenty of good moral sentiment and patriotism of the sort possible under a despotism of the modern French type ; but he will always be for us the little fat man who loved and lived with various Lalages, and made them, we feel perfectly assured, of more account in his existence than the great " nephew of his uncle," his prime minister Mæcenas, or even, we fear, than the Palatine Apollo himself, and that Jupiter Optimus Maximus who half frightened the little sceptic with summer thunder.—GEORGE BRIMLEY, *Essays.*

DR. JOHN HOUGH.

Bishop of Worcester : 1651-1743.

Such as on Hough's unsullied mitre shine.
　　　　　　　　—POPE, *Epilogue to the Satires.*

So good, so blest th' illustrious Hough we find,
Whose image dwells with pleasure on my mind ;
The mitre's glory, freedom's constant friend,
In times which ask'd a champion to defend ;
Who after near a hundred virtuous years,

His senses perfect, free from pains and fears,
Replete with life, with honours, and with age,
Like an applauded actor left the stage.
　　　　—SOAME JENYNS, *On the Immortality of the Soul, Book II.*

A Bishop by his neighbours hated
Has cause to wish himself translated.
But why should Hough desire translation,
Lov'd and esteem'd by all the nation?

　　　　　　　　　　　　　　　　　　　　—SWIFT.

RICHARD MONCKTON MILNES, LORD HOUGHTON.

English Poet: 1809-1885.

Adieu, dear Yorkshire Milnes! we think not now
Of coronet or laurel on thy brow;
The kindest, faithfullest of friends wast thou.

　　　　　　　　　　　　　　　　—W. ALLINGHAM.

Of Houghton himself it may be said, in the words of Landor, that he "warmed both hands before the fire of life". But this also may be truly claimed for him by his biographer, that from first to last no object was dearer to him than the sharing of the pleasures and the blessings which he himself relished so keenly with those who were less happily placed. "Other people," he once said to a neighbour at Fryston, "like to give their friends bread; I like to give them cake." And the whimsical saying was absolutely true. He never stinted his deeds of kindness and goodwill, even when prudence might have led him to do so. It was his greatest delight to give, not the savourless bread of charity, but the rich fruits of sympathy and love to all who stood in need of them. "Write me as one that loved his fellow-men" was an epitaph he would never have thought of claiming for himself; for cant and the affectation of virtue were alike hateful to him. But it may justly be claimed for him by his friends; and if those words had been written upon his tomb, for once an epitaph would not have lied.
—SIR T. WEMYSS REID, *Life, Letters, and Friendships of R. M. Milnes, First Lord Houghton, Vol. II.*

JOHN HOWARD.

English Philanthropist: 1726-1790.

I may alarm thee, but I fear the shame
(Charity chosen as my theme and aim)
I must incur, forgetting HOWARD's name.
Blest with all wealth can give thee, to resign
Joys doubly sweet to feelings quick as thine,
To quit the bliss thy rural scenes bestow,
To seek a nobler amidst scenes of woe,
To traverse seas, range kingdoms, and bring home,
Not the proud monuments of Greece or Rome,
But knowledge such as only dungeons teach,
And only sympathy like thine could reach.
　　　　　　　　　　　　　　　　—COWPER, *Charity.*

The name of Howard is a great name. When the preacher wishes to freight a precept, or the writer to round a phrase, no name occurs more readily to the mind. Howard stands for benevolence. With the religious public his name is a shining light : it is dear to the patriot, it is sacred to the philanthropist. Yet the man himself is little more than a myth. Except among a certain class of earnest enthusiasts, his form and figure, his presence in the world, and his influence on the age in which he lived, are well-nigh forgotten. The cause of this is not far to seek. Howard does not belong to literature ; his work lay apart. He did not talk with Johnson, or dine with Fox. Reynolds never painted his portrait, and he passed through life unnoticed by Gibbon.—W. HEPWORTH DIXON, *John Howard.*

There was more than *humanity* in his conduct. *Charity* better describes it. It was the energy of holiness, actuated by love. He went about doing good, because he had practically learned the precept, " That he who loveth God, loves his brother also ".—REV. J. FIELD, *Life of John Howard.*

Of Mr. Howard's heroic philanthropy the world wants no monument more honourable than the loud plaudits of his own countrymen.—DR. VICESIMUS KNOX, *Winter Evenings : Evening LXIV.*

Conceive a Puritan of the sternest days of Cromwell, dressed in the simple and austere garb of his order, armed resolutely for battle, resolved upon victory, and fighting less for personal triumph than for the glory of God. You have then a picture of John Howard. But remember that the weapons are not of steel, and that the glory by no means consists in the shedding of blood. Howard assailed inhumanity as the Roundhead battled against Royalty ; in either case it was war to the extremity, and the prosecution of work in the spirit of a divinely appointed missionary. . . . Measure him by the vulgar standard, and all the elements of heroism are missing in his composition. Judge him in his own peculiar light, and you may search the annals of heroism in vain for one more illustrious than he. —SAMUEL PHILLIPS, *Essays from " The Times ".*

Would you learn how " the high desire that others may be blessed savours of heaven " ? Read of John Howard, and Elizabeth Fry, and Father Damien.—F. W. FARRAR, *Social and Present-Day Questions.*

VICTOR HUGO.

French Poet, Dramatist, and Novelist : 1802-1885.

Victor in Drama, Victor in Romance,
Cloud-weaver of phantasmal hopes and fears,
French of the French, and Lord of human tears ;
Child-lover ; Bard whose fame-lit laurels glance
Darkening the wreaths of all that would advance.
                    —TENNYSON, *To Victor Hugo.*

He set the trumpet to his lips, and lo !
The clash of waves, the roar of winds that blow,
The strife and stress of Nature's warring things,
Rose like a storm-cloud, upon angry wings.

He set the reed-pipe to his lips and lo!
The wreck of landscape took a rosy glow,
And life, and love, and gladness that love brings
Laughed in the music, like a child that sings.

Master of each, Arch-Master! We that still
Wait in the verge and outskirt of the Hill
Look upward lonely—lonely to the height
Where thou hast climbed, for ever, out of sight!
                          —AUSTIN DOBSON, *Victor Hugo.*

Sun, that hast not seen a loftier head wax hoary,
    Earth, which hast not shown the sun a nobler birth,
Time, that hast not on thy scroll defiled and gory
    One man's name writ brighter in its whole wide girth,
Witness, till the final years fulfil their story,
    Till the stars break off the music of their mirth,
What among the sons of men was this man's glory,
    What the vesture of his soul revealed on earth.
                          —SWINBURNE, *The Statue of Victor Hugo.*

O light of song, whose fire is perfect light!
        No speech, no voice, no thought,
        No love, avails us aught
For service of thanksgiving in his sight
        Who hath given us all for ever
        Such gifts that man gave never
So many and great since first Time's wings took flight.
        Man may not praise a spirit above
Man's: life and death shall praise him: we can only love.

Life, everlasting while the worlds endure,
        Death, self-abased before a power more high,
Shall bear one witness, and their word stand sure,
        That not till time be dead shall this man die.
Love, like a bird, comes loyal to his lure;
        Fame flies before him, wingless else to fly.
A child's heart towards his kind is not more pure,
        An eagle's toward the sun no lordlier eye.
        Awe sweet as love and proud
        As fame, though hushed and bowed,
Yearns toward him silent as his face goes by:

        All crowns before his crown
        Triumphantly bow down,
For pride that one more great than all draws nigh:
        All souls applaud, all hearts acclaim,
One heart benign, one soul supreme, one conquering name.
                          —*Id., A New-Year Ode to Victor Hugo.*

Victor Hugo is always fine, always a master-spirit.—MAZZINI, *Life and Writings, Vol. II.*

Hugo, undoubtedly, was a much greater lyrical poet than Dryden, and was enkindled by spontaneous inspirations which never visited Dryden; yet the two are essentially of the same genus; the differences between

them are rather characteristic of their eras than of themselves; and while
Hugo's imagination would have pined in the seventeenth century, Dryden's
intellect and Dryden's modesty would have been highly serviceable to Hugo
in the nineteenth.— DR. RICHARD GARNETT, *The Age of Dryden.*

There are some men round whose name and fame and work it would
almost seem as if human opinion were destined to range in never-ending
strife. Such a man was Victor Hugo. For upwards of sixty years he remained conspicuous among his contemporaries, an object of passionate
admiration, and almost equally passionate dislike. During the earlier
portion of that period he stood in the forefront of the great battle between
the Romantic and Classical schools in French literature. To his followers
he was the man of men, the " impeccable master," the genius of his age,
a kind of sun-god dispelling the drear darkness of poetic routine and ancient
night. To his adversaries he was a mere savage, a monster, rudely violat-
ing his mother tongue, and setting all sane traditions at defiance. Then,
when that battle had in a measure fought itself out, came even fiercer
warfare in the world of politics.—FRANK T. MARZIALS, *Life of Victor
Hugo.*

But if for the Latin peoples generally Hugo is a typical hero, representing fully their sharp scorn of conventions, their distrust of governing
classes, and their deep sense of universal right—for France he is all that
and something more. In him all Frenchmen find the proof that France
has been the support of liberal and humanitarian ideas in the century of
their birth ; to them he is the sign, as Renan puts it, that liberalism is the
national work of France. . . . He completes the ideal of modern France
as Cæsar did that of Roman conquest, or Nelson that of England's
supremacy on the seas. That is why Frenchmen of all ranks and opinions
—even those, and they were many, who distrusted and dreaded his
utterances while he lived—gratefully accord him unprecedented national
honours now that he is dead.—JAMES CAPPON, *Victor Hugo : A Memoir
and a Study.*

Poet, dramatist, novelist, historian, philosopher, and patriot, the spiritual
sovereign of the nineteenth century was before all things, and above all
things a poet. Throughout all the various and ambitious attempts of his
marvellous boyhood—criticism, drama, satire, elegy, epigram, and romance
—the dominant vein is poetic. His example will stand for ever as the
crowning disproof of the doubtless more than plausible opinion that the
most amazing precocity of power is a sign of ensuing impotence and premature decay. There was never a more brilliant boy than Victor Hugo :
but there has never been a greater man. . . . But from the first, without
knowing it, he was on the road to Damascus : if not to be struck down by
sudden miracle, yet by no less inevitable a process to undergo a no less
unquestionable conversion. . . . Hugo, for all his dramatic and narrative
mastery of effect, will always probably remind men rather of such poets
as Dante or Isaiah than of such poets as Sophocles or Shakespeare. We
cannot of course imagine the Florentine or the Hebrew endowed with
his infinite variety of sympathies, of interests, and of powers ; but as
little can we imagine in the Athenian such height and depth of passion,
in the Englishman such unquenchable and sleepless fire of moral and
prophetic faith.—SWINBURNE, *A Study of Victor Hugo.*

Friedrich H. A. von Humboldt.

Prussian Naturalist and Geographer: 1769-1859.

Humboldt, " the first of travellers," but not
The last, if late accounts be accurate,
Invented, by some name I have forgot,
As well as the sublime discovery's date,
An airy instrument, with which he sought
To ascertain the atmospheric state,
By measuring the " *intensity of blue* ".
　　　　　　　—Byron, *Don Juan, Canto the Fourth.*

Humboldt is, in many respects, and perhaps upon the whole, at the head of the list. He unites, in a degree that perhaps has never before been witnessed, the most varied qualities, and which, from the opposite characters of mind which they require, are rarely found in unison. A profound philosopher, an accurate observer of nature, an unwearied statist, he is at the same time an eloquent writer, an incomparable describer, and an ardent friend of social improvement. Science owes to his indefatigable industry some of her most valuable acquisitions; geography, to his intrepid perseverance, many of its most important discoveries; the arts to his poetic eye and fervid eloquence, not a few of their brightest pictures. He unites the austere grandeur of the exact sciences to the bewitching charm of the fine arts. . . . There are few Humboldts either in the reading or thinking world.—Sir Archibald Alison, *Essays: Lamartine.*

With all Humboldt's great and transcendent merits, he is a child of Adam, and therefore not without his faults. The principal of these is the want of arrangement.—*Id., Ibid.: Humboldt.*

Almost every man of science in Germany who has found his place has been conducted to it by Humboldt . . . the Monarch of Science.

Wellington never showed more studious skill in the arrangement of his forces, nor Napoleon a more efficient will in the distribution of the sceptres of European empires, than Humboldt to the very last, in disposing his forces, and conferring crowns in the interests of the kingdoms of the higher realm of Nature.—Harriet Martineau, *Biographical Sketches.*

Humboldt, the Encyclopædia of Science.—Emerson, *Society and Solitude: Old Age.*

Perfect symmetry never produces the effect of vastness. It is only by studying the details that we comprehend the character of the whole. Humboldt, however, may be termed the Father of Physical Geography, and the suggester, if not the discoverer, of that system of the distribution of plants and animals which opens to our view another field of that Divine Order, manifested in the visible world. He strove to grasp those secrets, which, perhaps, no single mind will ever be able to comprehend —the aggregate of the laws which underlie the mysteries of Creation, Growth, and Decay; and though he fell short of the sublime aim, he was at least able to say, like Kepler, when he discovered the mathematical harmonies of the solar system, " Oh, Almighty God, I think Thy thoughts after Thee! "—Bayard Taylor, *Introduction to the Life, Travels, and Books of Alexander Von Humboldt.*

DAVID HUME.

Scottish Historian and Philosopher: 1711-1776.

There nations yet unborn shall trace
In Hume's perspicuous page,
How Britain rose, and through what storms attain'd
Her eminence of power.
—SOUTHEY, *Ode written after the King's Visit to Scotland.*

Hume, from whose fascinating narrative the great mass of the reading public are still contented to take their opinions, hated religion so much that he hated liberty for having been allied with religion, and has pleaded the cause of tyranny with the dexterity of an advocate, while affecting the impartiality of a judge.—MACAULAY, *Essays: Milton.*

Hume seems to have had but two hearty dislikes: the one to the English nation, and the other to all professors of dogmatic theology. The one aversion he vented only privately to his friends; but, if he is ever bitter in his public utterances, it is against priests in general and theological enthusiasts and fanatics in particular; if he ever seems insincere, it is when he wishes to insult theologians by a parade of sarcastic respect.—HUXLEY, *Hume.*

It is assuredly one of Hume's greatest merits that he clearly recognised the fact that philosophy is based upon psychology; and that the inquiry into the contents and the operations of the mind must be conducted upon the same principles as a physical investigation, if what he calls the "moral philosopher" would attain results of as firm and definite a character as those which reward the "natural philosopher". . . . For kindly David Hume, "the damnation of one man is an infinitely greater evil in the universe than the subversion of a thousand million of kingdoms". And he would have felt with his countryman Burns, that even "auld Nickie Ben" should "hae a chance".—*Id., Ibid.*

In David Hume, however, our British Philosophy reached the most significant crisis it has as yet passed through, mainly because of the thoroughness and consistency with which he developed to its furthest issues the doctrine of *Experience*, on which that philosophy had been founded by Bacon, expanded by Hobbes, and wrought out by Locke. He saw, with consummate clearness, the logical result of a system of which Experience is the alpha and omega; and his destructive criticism has been quite as helpful to the progress of the human mind, as the constructive efforts which it overthrew, chiefly because it cleared the atmosphere of mist.—WILLIAM KNIGHT, *Life of Hume.*

LEIGH HUNT.

English Poet and Essayist: 1784-1859.

You will see Hunt; one of those happy souls
Which are the salt of the earth, and without whom
This world would smell like what it is—a tomb;
Who is, what others seem:—his room no doubt

Is still adorned by many a cast from Shout,
With graceful flowers, tastefully placed about;
And coronals of bay from ribbons hung.
And brighter wreaths in neat disorder flung,
The gifts of the most learned among some dozens
Of female friends, sisters-in-law, and cousins.
And there is he with his eternal puns,
Which beat the dullest brain for smiles, like duns
Thundering for money at a poet's door;
Alas! it is no use to say, " I'm poor!"
Or oft in graver mood, when he will look
Things wiser than were ever said in book,
Except in Shakespeare's wisest tenderness.

      —SHELLEY, *Letter to Maria Gisborne.*

What though, for showing truth to flatter'd state,
    Kind Hunt was shut in prison, yet has he,
    In his immortal spirit, been as free
As the sky-searching lark, and as elate.
Minion of Grandeur! think you he did wait?
    Think you he nought but prison-walls did see,
    Till, so unwilling, thou unturn'dst the key?
Ah, no! far happier, nobler was his fate!
In Spenser's halls he stray'd, and bowers fair,
    Culling enchanted flowers; and he flew
With daring Milton through the fields of air:
    To regions of his own his genius true
Took happy flights. Who shall his fame impair
When thou art dead, and all thy wretched crew?

      —KEATS, *Written on the Day that Mr. Leigh Hunt Left Prison.*

Leigh Hunt, the bloom I name for thine
Is pretty, pointed Eglantine;
Flusht with the gentlest garden hue,
Yet with a wilding freshness too;
With fragment breath in fine flower-lips,
And fragrance to green finger-tips;
And all its sweetness sweeter yet,
With dews or showery droppings wet.
For not in blossom books alone
Thy Poetry and Love are shown;
And tearful trials of this earth
But draw their richest essence forth.

      —WILLIAM ALLINGHAM, *Poets and Flowers.*

We have a kindness for Mr. Leigh Hunt. We form our judgment of him, indeed, only from events of universal notoriety, from his own works, and from the works of other writers, who have generally abused him in the most rancorous manner. But, unless we are greatly mistaken, he is a very clever, a very honest, and a very good-natured man. We can clearly discern together with many merits, many faults both in his writings and in his conduct. But we really think that there is hardly a man living whose merits have been so grudgingly allowed, and whose faults have been so cruelly expiated.—MACAULAY, *Essays: Leigh Hunt.*

To pass from Hazlitt to Leigh Hunt is like passing from a rough landscape sketch by Salvator, in which, according to Coleridge, the rocks take vague likeness of the human figure, to a garden scene by Lancret, with a group seated round a fountain engaged in dining off peaches, and listening to a gentle shepherd who is playing a guitar or telling a pleasant story.   Leigh Hunt is as constitutionally gay as Hazlitt is constitutionally saturnine.—LYTTON, *Essays : Charles Lamb and some of his Companions.*

Something not to be replaced would be struck out of the gentler literature of our century, could the mind of Leigh Hunt cease to speak to us in a book.—*Id., Ibid.*

Though Leigh Hunt's character was simple and his gifts distinct, he is not easy to class either as an author or a man.   His literary pretentions were well summed up by Charles Lamb in the couplet :—

> " Wit, poet, proseman, partyman, translator,
> Hunt, thy best title yet is Indicator."

With a nature filled with poetry, but yet most faulty as a poet; learned beyond the average, but hardly a scholar ; full of sweet thoughts, but no thinker ; vivacious and sportive to an extraordinary degree, yet falling short of supreme qualities as a humorist, Leigh Hunt scarcely attained to the first rank of writers, except as a sentimentalist, an anthologist, and a gossip, yet he so nearly touched it at so many points, and there is such a special quality in almost everything he wrote, that one hesitates to set him in a duller circle.—COSMO MONKHOUSE, *Life of Leigh Hunt.*

Leigh Hunt, if " Ariel " be in some respects too complimentary a name for him, is at any rate a most tricksy spirit.   The finest taste in some ways, contrasting with what can only be called the most horrible vulgarity in others ; a light hand tediously boring again and again at obviously miscomprehended questions of religion, philosophy, and politics ; a keen appetite for humour condescending to thin and repeated jests ; a reviler of kings going out of his way laboriously to beslaver royalty ; a man of letters, of talent almost touching genius, who seldom writes a dozen consecutive good pages :—these are only some of the inconsistencies that meet us in Leigh Hunt.—GEORGE SAINTSBURY, *Essays in English Literature.*

DR. JOHN HUNTER.

Scottish Surgeon : 1728-1793.

John Hunter was a great man—*that* any one might see without the smallest skill in surgery.   His style and manner showed the man.   He would set about cutting up the carcass of a whale with the same greatness of *gusto* that Michael Angelo would have hewn a block of marble.— HAZLITT, *Table Talk.*

It is impossible to include in one view the multitudinous forms of Hunter's work : you cannot see the wood for the trees.   He was anatomist, biologist, naturalist, physician, surgeon, and pathologist, all at once, and all in the highest.—STEPHEN PAGET, *Life of John Hunter.*

SELINA, COUNTESS OF HUNTINGDON.

Founder of the Calvinistic Methodists: 1707-1791.

The chief perfection of both sexes joined,
With neither's vice nor vanity combined;
Of this our age the wonder, love, and care,
The example of the following, and despair;
Such beauty, that from all hearts love must flow,
Such majesty, that none durst tell her so;
A wisdom of so large and potent sway,
Rome's Senate might have wished, her Conclave may:
Which did to earthly thoughts so seldom bow,
Alive she scarce was less in heaven than now;
So void of the least pride, to her alone
These radiant excellencies seemed unknown;
Such once there was; but let thy grief appear,
Reader, there is not: HUNTINGDON lies here.
　　　　　—LORD FALKLAND, *An Epitaph on the Excellent Countess of Huntingdon.*

At Rome the Countess of Huntingdon would have a place in the calendar as St. Selina.—MACAULAY, *Essays : Von Ranke.*

That grim but grand old Mother in Israel, Selina, Countess of Huntingdon.—[G. W. E. RUSSELL], *Collections and Recollections.*

As long as Christ has a Church on earth, and disciples animated with zeal for the glory of His Name, the Countess of Huntingdon will live, and enjoy a distinguished niche in the Temple of God.　The world has its heroes, whom it holds up to universal admiration in the page of history —here the Church of Christ presents to us one of hers.—"A MEMBER OF THE HOUSES OF SHIRLEY AND HASTINGS," *Life and Times of Selina, Countess of Huntingdon.*

JOHN HUSS.

Bohemian Reformer: 1373-1415.

In the streets of Constance was heard the shout,
" Masters! bring the arch-heretic out ! "
The stake had been planted, the faggots spread,
And the tongues of the torches flickered red.
" Huss to the flames " they fiercely cried:
And the gates of the Convent opened wide.
　　　　　— ALFRED AUSTIN, *Soliloquies in Song.*

Huss did not die in vain; his arguments against religious persecution remain on record unanswered and unanswerable for ever; and the more civilized and the more highly regarded a nation is in the polity of the world, the more fully will it be found to have accepted his two grand principles of the supremacy of the conscience in the individual life and soul, and of the scriptures in the common life of the Church and in matters of faith.—A. H. WRATISLAW, *Life of John Huss.*

Huss died, not as an anabaptist, but as a Christian. He offers an example of Christian frailty, but at the same time there was roused in his soul a power as from God which sustained him. The struggle between the flesh and the spirit, with Christ and with Huss, is beautiful to behold. Constance is now a poor wretched city. I believe that God has thus punished it. John Huss was burnt, and I believe that I shall, if it please God, be also slain. Huss weeded from out of Christ's vineyard a few thorns, in attacking only the scandalous doings of the papists; whereas I, doctor Martin Luther, found myself upon a well-tilled and already black mould—I attacked the doctrine of the pope, and I overthrew it.—MARTIN LUTHER (*transl.*).

ELIZABETH INCHBALD.

English Authoress: 1753-1821.

If Mrs. Radcliffe touched the trembling chords of the imagination, making wild music there, Mrs. Inchbald has no less power over the springs of the heart. She not only moves the affections but melts us into "all the luxury of woe". . . . Mrs. Inchbald is an instance to confute the assertion of Rousseau, that women fail wherever they attempt to describe the passion of love.—HAZLITT, *Lectures on the English Comic Writers: Lect. VI., On the English Novelists.*

EDWARD IRVING.

Scottish Clergyman: 1792-1834.

Amongst the frequent visitors of Coleridge was Edward Irving, who, himself a great preacher and teacher of religion, used to sit at the feet of Coleridge as at those of Gamaliel, meekly listening. Amongst all his admiring auditors, Coleridge never had a nobler and more Christian one than Edward Irving. . . . He continued persecuted, meek, loving, and forgiving to the last. Since the days of his great prototype and Saviour, we know of no man who so much resembled Him in patient, loving, and unresentful faith.—WILLIAM HOWITT, *The Northern Heights of London.*

Irving shows the other side of Carlyle's Puritanism. He was utterly and purely a theologian; God was all in all to him. From God he must begin. And how to establish a relation between God and mankind on the Calvinistic hypothesis, which he nobly determined not to abandon for any Arminian or semi-Arminian compromises; this was the problem in trying to solve which he gave up his fame and his life.—F. D. MAURICE, *Life of F. D. Maurice by His Son, Vol. II.*

WASHINGTON IRVING.

American Author: 1783-1859.

Perhaps, of all American writers, in Washington Irving the polite air of the man of the European world is the most seen; but then, of all American writers, Washington Irving is the one who most sedulously imitated, and most happily caught, the spirit of European writers, formed under aristocratic as well as popular influences;—of all American writers he is thus the least American.—LYTTON, *Essays: Knowledge of the World.*

14

JAMES I.

King of England : 1566-1625.

As when their ancestors *be-versed,*
That glorious STUART, JAMES the FIRST.
—ROBERT LLOYD, *The Poetry Professors.*

In a word, James the Sixth was an example that neither high rank, nor shrewd sense, nor ready wit, nor a deep acquaintance with the learning of the age, can acquire respectability for a man timid both by moral and physical causes, and incapable of acting upon suiting occasion, with total carelessness to his own comforts, for his own safety, or, if the case calls for it, his own life.—SIR WALTER SCOTT, *History of Scotland, Vol. II.*

Of James the First, as of John, it may be said that, if his administration had been able and splendid, it would probably have been fatal to our country, and that we owe more to his weakness and meanness than to the wisdom and courage of much better sovereigns.—MACAULAY, *History of England, Vol. I.*

The most ridiculous weaknesses seemed to meet in the wretched Solomon of Whitehall, pedantry, buffoonery, garrulity, low-curiosity, the most contemptible personal cowardice. Nature and education had done their best to produce a finished specimen of all that a king ought not to be. His awkward figure, his rolling eye, his rickety walk, his nervous tremblings, his slobbering mouth, his broad Scotch accent, were imperfections which might have been found in the best and greatest man. Their effect, however, was to make James and his office objects of contempt, and to dissolve those associations which had been created by the noble bearing of preceding monarchs, and which were in themselves no inconsiderable fence to royalty.—*Id.*, *Essays : John Hampden.*

The wisest fool in Christendom.—SULLY *(transl.).*

JAMES II.

King of England : 1633-1701.

And James his brother reigned in his stead.
But such a reign—so glaring an offence
In ev'ry step 'gainst freedom, law, and sense,
'Gainst all the rights of nature's gen'ral plan,
'Gainst all which constitutes an Englishman.
—CHURCHILL, *Gotham : Book II.*

JEANNE D'ARC.

The Maid of Orleans, Deliverer of France : 1412-1431.

No longer in Saint Dennis will we cry,
But Joan la Pucelle shall be France's saint.
—SHAKSPERE, *King Henry VI.*

No; misconceived Joan of Arc hath been
A virgin from her tender infancy,
Chaste and immaculate in every thought;

Whose maiden blood, thus vigorously effus'd,
Will cry for vengeance at the gates of heaven.
—SHAKSPERE, *King Henry VI.*

Or Joan de Pucelle's braver name,
Our right to arms and conduct claim;
Who, though a spinster, yet was able
To serve France for a Grand Constable.
—SAMUEL BUTLER, *Hudibras.*

Soon as the saintly sword is found,
Long time entombed in holy ground,
Armed cap-à-pie, Joan takes the field,
Celestial agency her shield.
—REV. JOHN DAVIES, *Historic Prologues.*

First in the ranks see Joan of Arc advance,
The scourge of England, and the boast of France!
Though burnt by wicked Bedford for a witch,
Behold her statue placed in glory's niche.
—BYRON, *English Bards and Scotch Reviewers.*

So as he spake approaching, cried the chief,
" Well hast thou proved thy mission, as by words
And miracles attested when dismay'd
The grave theologists dismiss'd their doubts,
So in the field of battle now confirm'd."
—SOUTHEY, *Joan of Arc.*

Joan of Arc,
A light of ancient France.
—TENNYSON, *A Dream of Fair Women.*

The history of Joan of Arc is as mysterious as it is remarkable. That she believed herself inspired, few will deny; that she was inspired, no one will venture to assert; and it is difficult to believe that she was herself imposed upon by Charles and Dunois.—SOUTHEY, *Preface to Joan of Arc.*

Joan of Arc, the prophetess, the heroine, and the saint of French patriotism, the glory, the deliverance, and equally the shame of her country. . . . Angel, maiden, warrior—she has become a fit blazon for the soldier's banner.—LAMARTINE, *Celebrated Characters (transl.).*

We cannot pretend to explain the surprising story of the Maid of Orleans; for, however easy it may be to suppose that a heated and enthusiastic imagination produced her own visions, it is a much greater problem to account for the credit they obtained, and for the success that attended her.—HALLAM, *Student's Middle Ages.*

But the military desolation of France, this it was that woke the faith of Joanna in her own heavenly mission of deliverance. It was the attitude of her prostrate country, crying night and day for purification from blood, and not from feudal oppression, that swallowed up the thoughts of the impassioned girl. But *that* was not the cry that uttered itself afterwards in the French Revolution. In Joanna's days, the first step towards rest for France was by expulsion of the foreigner. Independence of a foreign yoke, liberation as between people and people, was the one ransom to be paid for French honour and peace. *That* debt settled, there might come a time for thinking of civil liberties. But this time was not within the prospects of the poor shepherdess. The field—the area of her sympathies —never coincided with that of the revolutionary period.—DE QUINCEY, *Leaders in Literature.*

The Maid of Orleans—a creature as noble and pure minded as any that the Church has ever canonised.—DR. REINHOLD PAULI, *Pictures of Old England (transl.).*

FRANCIS, LORD JEFFREY.

Scottish Lawyer, Critic, and Essayist : 1773-1850.

Health to immortal Jeffrey ! once, in name,
England could boast a judge almost the same ;
In soul so like, so merciful, so just,
Some think that Satan has resign'd his trust,
And given the spirit to the world again,
To sentence letters as he sentenced men.
—BYRON, *English Bards and Scotch Reviewers.*

Mightiest of all Dunedin's beasts of chase !
For thee my Pegasus would mend his pace.
Arise my Jeffrey ! or my inkless pen
Shall never blunt its edge on meaner men.
—*Id., Hints from Horace.*

Mr. Jeffrey said so, who must certainly know,
    For he was the Edinburgh Prophet.
They all of them knew Mr. Jeffrey's Review,
Which with Holy Writ ought to be reckon'd :
It was through thick and thin to its party true ;
    Its back was buff, and its sides were blue,
            Morbleu ! Parbleu !
It served them for Law and for Gospel too.
—SOUTHEY, *The March from Moscow.*

LORD GEORGE JEFFREYS.

Lord Chancellor of England : 1648-1689.

And murderous rage itself, in Jeffreys' form.
—THOMSON, *Liberty.*

The person selected was Sir George Jeffreys, Chief Justice of the Court of Queen's Bench. The depravity of this man has passed into a proverb. —MACAULAY, *History of England, Vol. I., Chap. IV.*

DR. EDWARD JENNER.

Discoverer of Vaccination : 1749-1823.

Jenner ! for ever shall thy honour'd name
Among the children of mankind be blest,

Who by thy skill hast taught us how to tame
One dire disease, the lamentable pest
Which Africa sent forth to scourge the West.
　　　　　　—SOUTHEY, *A Tale of Paraguay, Canto I.*

Jenner introduced vaccination ; we admire him for it, and we shall
continue to admire him for it, although some still safer and more agreeable preservative should be discovered.—MACAULAY, *Essays : Sir James
Mackintosh.*

JEROME OF PRAGUE.

Bohemian Reformer : 1378-1416.

Jerome of Prague, the friend and disciple of John Huss, has hitherto
held the position of a mere shadow of his greater master, until, after that
master's martyrdom, he passes once for all across the stage in a blaze of
light in the eloquent letter of Poggio Bracciolini.—REV. A. H. WRATIS-
LAW, *Life of John Huss.*

DR. JOHN JEWEL.

Bishop of Salisbury : 1522-1571.

Concerning our bishop it may be said "*nomen omen*". Jewel was his
name, and precious were his virtues. So that if the like ambition led us
Englishmen as doth foreigners, specially to render our surnames in Greek
or Latin, he may be termed Johannes Gemma, or better account than
Gemma Frisius entitled himself thereunto.—DR. THOMAS FULLER.

JOHN.

King of England : 1166-1216.

John rests below. A man more infamous
Never hath held the sceptre of these realms,
And bruised beneath the iron rod of Power
The oppressed men of England. Englishman !
Curse not his memory. Murderer as he was,
Coward and slave, yet he it was who sign'd
That charter which should make thee morn and night
Be thankful for thy birth-place ; Englishman !
That holy charter, which, shouldst thou permit
Force to destroy or Fraud to undermine,
Thy children's groans will persecute thy soul.
For they must bear the burthen of thy crime.
　　　　　　—SOUTHEY, *Epitaph on King John.*

Lo ! John self-stripped of his insignia ;—
Sceptre and mantle, sword and ring, laid down
At a proud legate's feet. The spears that line
Baronial halls, the opprobrious insult feel ;
And angry ocean roars a vain appeal.
　　　　　　—WORDSWORTH, *Papal Abuses.*

John of Gaunt.

Son of Edward III.: 1340-1399.

Old John of Gaunt, time-honoured Lancaster.
　　　—Shakspere, *King Richard II., Act I., Scene I.*

K. Richard. "What comfort, man? How is't with aged Gaunt?"
Gaunt. "O, how that name befits my composition!
Old Gaunt, indeed; and gaunt in being old:
Within me grief hath kept a tedious fast;
And who abstains from meat, that is not gaunt?
For sleeping England longtime have I watch'd;
Watching breeds leanness, leanness is all gaunt:
The pleasure that some fathers feed upon,
Is my strict fast,—I mean my children's looks;
And therein fasting hast thou made me gaunt:
Gaunt am I for the grave, gaunt as a grave."
　　　—*Id., Ibid., Act II., Scene I.*

Dr. Samuel Johnson.

Lexicographer and Miscellaneous Writer: 1709-1784.

Here Johnson lies, a sage by all allow'd,
Whom to have bred, may well make England proud;
Whose prose was eloquence, by Wisdom taught,
The graceful vehicle of virtuous thought;
Whose verse may claim, grave, masculine and strong,
Superior praise to the mere poet's song;
Who many a noble gift from heaven possess'd,
And faith at last, alone worth all the rest.
O man, immortal by a double prize,
By fame on earth, by glory in the skies!
　　　—Cowper, *Epitaph on Dr. Johnson.*

If manly Johnson, with satiric rage,
Lash the dull follies of a trifling age,
If his strong muse with genuine strength aspire,
Glows not the reader with the poet's fire?
His the true fire, where creep the witling fry
To warm themselves, and light their rushlights by.
　　　—Robert Lloyd, *An Epistle to C. Churchill.*

If from the tongue the period round
Fall into style, and swell to sound,
'Tis nature which herself displays,
And Johnson speaks a Johnson's phrase.
But can you hear, without a smile,
The formal coxcomb ape his style?
　　　—*Id., A Familiar Epistle.*

Here Johnson comes—unblest with outward grace,
His rigid morals stamp'd upon his face,
While strong conceptions struggle in his brain

(For even wit is brought to bed with pain).
To view him, porters with their loads would rest,
And babes cling frighted to their nurse's breast.
—CUTHBERT SHAW, *The Race.*

And oft it chances, that the true heroic
In man or spirit is undiscerned for ages
Till some great mind discovers, and brings it out.
Thus whoe'er thought that Johnson was a hero
For knocking a bookseller down with a dictionary,
Till Carlyle saw it ?
—DR. MILO MAHAN, *The Yorkshireman in Boston.*

Johnson to be sure, has a roughness in his manner ; but no man alive has a more tender heart.—OLIVER GOLDSMITH.

Of all the men distinguished in this or any other age, Dr. Johnson has left upon posterity the strongest and most vivid impression, so far as person, manners, disposition and conversation are concerned. We do but name him, or open a book which he has written, and the sound and action recall to the imagination at once his form, his merits, his peculiarities, nay, the very uncouthness of his gestures, and the deep, impressive tone of his voice. We learn, not only what he said, but form an idea how he said it ; and have, at the same time, a shrewd guess of the secret motive why he did so, and whether he spoke in sport or in anger, in the desire of conviction, or for the love of debate. . . . When we consider the rank which Dr. Johnson held, not only in literature but in society, we cannot help figuring him to ourselves as the benevolent giant of some fairy tale, whose kindness and courtesies are still mingled with a part of the rugged ferocity imputed to the fabulous sons of Anak ; or rather, perhaps, like a Roman dictator, fetched from his farm, whose wisdom and heroism still relished of his rustic occupation.—SIR WALTER SCOTT, *Lives of the Novelists.*

I am not here saying that Dr. Johnson was a man without originality, compared with the ordinary run of men's minds, but he was not a man of original thought or genius, in the sense in which Montaigne or Lord Bacon was. He opened no new vein of precious ore, nor did he light upon any single pebbles of uncommon size and unrivalled lustre.— HAZLITT, *Lectures on the English Comic Writers, Lect. V.: On the Periodical Essayists.*

Old Sam—a jewel rough set, yet shining like a star ; and though sand-blind by nature, and bigoted by education, one of the truly great men of England, and "her men are of men the chief," alike in the dominions of the understanding, the reason, the passions, and the imagination. No prig shall ever persuade me that *Rasselas* is not a noble performance—in design and in execution. Never were the expenses of a mother's funeral more gloriously defrayed by son, than the funeral of Samuel Johnson's mother by the price of *Rasselas*, written for the pious purpose of laying her head decently and honourably in the dust.—JOHN WILSON, *Noctes Ambrosianæ, Vol. II.*

The Johnsonian magniloquence. . . . Johnson had neither eye nor ear ; for nature, therefore, he cared, as he knew, nothing. His knowledge of town life was minute; but even that was imperfect.—COLERIDGE, *Table Talk*.

He was a good man, as he was a great man; and he had so firm a regard for virtue that he wisely set much greater store by his worth than by his fame.—LORD BROUGHAM, *Men of Letters, etc., Vol. II*.

The mighty intellect, the eloquent morality and lofty style of Dr. Johnson.—LORD JEFFREY, *Essays*.

No critic can say that Johnson and Gibbon are obscure; their meaning is much plainer than that of many a writer who prefers a colloquial diction. Not only in spite of the fault, but because of the fault we impute to their styles, Johnson and Gibbon are—Johnson and Gibbon.—LYTTON, *Essays : Rhythm in Prose*.

Boswell's *Life of Johnson* is in everybody's hands; you will hear the pithy sayings, the admirable reflections, the sagacious remarks it contains, from one end of the world to the other. The secret of this astonishing success is to be found in the caustic tone, sententious brevity, and sterling good sense of Johnson, and the inimitable accuracy, faithful memory, and almost infantile simplicity of his biographer.—SIR ARCHIBALD ALISON, *Essays : Autobiography*.

There is something in Archimedes or in Luther or Samuel Johnson that needs no protection. There is something in the true scholar which he cannot be laughed out of, nor be terrified or bought off from. —EMERSON, *Greatness*.

As for Johnson, I have always considered him to be, by nature, one of our great English souls. A strong and noble man; so much left undeveloped in him to the last: in a kindlier element what might he not have been,—Poet, Priest, sovereign Ruler ! . . . Johnson was a Prophet to his people; preached a Gospel to them—as all like him always do. The highest Gospel he preached we may describe as a kind of Moral Prudence : " in a world where much is to be done, and little is to be known," see how you will *do* it. A thing well worth preaching. . . . Brave old Samuel : *ultimus Romanorum !* . . . Old Samuel Johnson, the greatest soul in England in his day, was not ambitious. " Corsica Boswell" flaunted at public shows with printed ribbons round his hat; but the great old Samuel stayed at home. The world-wide soul wrapt-up in its thoughts, in its sorrows ;—what could paradings, and ribbons in the hat, do for it ? . . . Had Johnson left nothing but his *Dictionary*, one might have traced there a great intellect, a genuine man. Looking to its clearness of definition, its general solidity, honesty, insight, and successful method, it may be called the best of all Dictionaries. There is in it a kind of architectural nobleness ; it stands there like a great solid square-built edifice, finished, symmetrically complete : you judge that a true Builder did it. —CARLYLE, *On Heroes and Hero-Worship*.

King Samuel has had no successor : nobody since his day, and that of his contemporary Voltaire, has sat on a throne of literature either in England or in France.—G. L. CRAIK, *Sketches of the History of Literature and Learning in England*.

The names of many greater writers are inscribed upon the walls of Westminster Abbey; but scarcely any one lies there whose heart was more acutely responsive during life to the deepest and tenderest of human emotions. In visiting that strange gathering of departed heroes and statesmen and philanthropists and poets, there are many whose words and deeds have a far greater influence upon our imaginations; but there are very few whom, when all has been said, we can love so heartily as Samuel Johnson.—LESLIE STEPHEN, *Life of Johnson*.

The second great Dictator of literary London who bore the name of Johnson.—SWINBURNE, *A Study of Ben Jonson*.

The great and dingy Reality of the eighteenth century, the Immortal.—AUGUSTINE BIRRELL, *Obiter Dicta, First Series*.

A hundred years can make no difference to a character like Johnson's, or to a biography like Boswell's.—*Id., Ibid., Second Series*.

INIGO JONES.

English Architect: 1573-1652.

The admirers of Inigo Jones have always maintained that his works are inferior to those of Sir Christopher Wren, only because the great fire of London gave Wren such a field for the display of his powers as no architect in the history of the world ever possessed.—MACAULAY, *Essays: Henry Hallam*.

BENJAMIN JONSON.

English Dramatist: 1574-1637.

O rare Ben Jonson!
　　　　—SIR JOHN YOUNG, *Epitaph in Westminster Abbey*.

Too nicely Jonson knew the critic's part;
Nature in him was almost lost in art.
　　　　—COLLINS, *An Epistle addressed to Sir T. Hanmer*.

Then shall we see that these two names are one,
Jonson and Poetry, which now are gone.
　　　　—WILLIAM CARTWRIGHT, *In Memory of Ben Jonson*.

After the rare arch-poet Jonson died,
The sock grew loathsome, and the buskin's pride,
Together with the stage's glory, stood
Each like a poor and pitied womanhood.
The cirque profaned was; and all postures racked;
For men did strut and stride and stare, not act.
The temper flew from words; and men did squeak,
Look red, and blow and bluster, but not speak.
　　　　—HERRICK, *Upon Mr. Ben Jonson, An Epigram*.

Here lies Jonson with the rest
Of the poets; but the best.
Reader, wouldst thou more have known?
Ask his story, but not this stone.
That will speak what this can't tell
Of his glory. So farewell.
　　　　—*Id., Upon Ben Jonson*.

Drawn to the life of every line and limb,
He (in his truth of art, and that in him)
Lives yet, and will, whilst letters can be read ;
The loss is ours ; now hope of life is dead.
Great men, and worthy of report, must fall
Into their earth, and sleeping there sleep all :
Since he, whose pen in every strain did use
To drop a verse, and every verse a muse,
Is vowed to heaven : as having with fair glory,
Sung thanks of honour, or some nobler story.
The court, the university, the heat
Of theatres, with what can else beget
Belief, and admiration, clearly prove
Our Poet first in merit, as in love :
Yet if he do not at his full appear,
Survey him in his Works, and know him there.
> —FORD, *On the Best of English Poets, Ben Jonson.*

Look up ! where Seneca and Sophocles,
Quick Plautus and sharp Aristophanes,
Enlighten yon bright orb ! Doth not your eye,
Among them, one far larger fire, descry
At which their lights grow pale ? 'Tis Jonson.
> —W. HABINGTON, *Upon the Death of Ben Jonson.*

In ancient learning train'd,
His rigid judgment Fancy's flights restrain'd ;
Correctly pruned each wild luxuriant thought,
Mark'd out her course, nor spared a glorious fault :
The book of man he read with nicest art,
And ransack'd all the secrets of the heart ;
Exerted penetration's utmost force,
And traced each passion to its proper source ;
Then, strongly mark'd, in liveliest colours drew,
And brought each foible forth to public view :
The coxcomb felt a lash in every word,
And fools, hung out, their brother fools deterr'd.
His comic humour kept the world in awe,
And laughter frighten'd folly more than law.
> —CHURCHILL, *The Rosciad.*

Great Jonson did by strength of judgment please ;
Yet, doubling Fletcher's force, he wants his ease.
In different talents both adorn'd their age ;
One for the study, t'other for the stage.
> —DRYDEN, *Epistle X., To my dear Friend, Mr. Congreve.*

Then Jonson came, instructed from the school,
To please by method, and invent by rule.
His studious patience, and laborious art,
With regular approach assay'd the heart :
Cold approbation gave the ling'ring bays,
For they who durst not censure, scarce could praise.
> —DR. JOHNSON, *Prologue spoken by Mr. Garrick.*

The greatest man of the last age, Ben Jonson, was willing to give place to the classics in all things: he was not only a professed imitator of Horace, but a learned plagiary of all the others; you track him everywhere in their snow. If Horace, Lucan, Petronius Arbiter, Seneca, and Juvenal had their own from him, there are few serious thoughts which are new in him. But he has done his robberies so openly, that one may see he fears not to be taxed by any law. He invades authors like a monarch; and what would be theft in other poets is only victory in him. —DRYDEN, *Prose Works, Vol. III.*

Ben Jonson is a great borrower from the works of others, and a plagiarist even from nature; so little freedom is there in his imitations of her, and he appears to receive her bounty like an alms. . . . There are people who cannot taste olives—and I cannot much relish Ben Jonson, though I have taken some pains to do it, and went to the task with every sort of goodwill. . . . He wears out a jest to the last shred and coarsest grain. His imagination fastens instinctively on some one mark or sign by which he designates the individual, and never lets it go, for fear of not meeting with any other means to express himself by. . . . His portraits are caricatures by dint of their very likeness, being extravagant tautologies of themselves.—HAZLITT, *Lectures on the English Comic Writers, Lect. II.: On Shakespeare and Ben Jonson.*

In Ben Jonson you have an intense and burning art.—COLERIDGE, *Table Talk.*

He held the prose writers and poets of antiquity in solution in his spacious memory. He did not need to dove-tail or weld his borrowings into one another: but rather, having fused them in his own mind, poured them plastically forth into the mould of thought. Therefore, unless we are happy to recognise the originals on which he has been drawing, we shall fancy that he is speaking from his own stores. This kind of looting from classical treasuries of wit and wisdom was accounted no robbery in that age; and Jonson's panegyrists praised him as a conqueror who spoiled the empires of the past like Alexander. . . . So many points of close resemblance between Ben Jonson and Samuel Johnson, as regards mind, person, character and habits, present themselves unsought, that it would argue affectation to ignore them. Both were confirmed Londoners; both felt the town to be their element. Both were huge, unwieldy, unhealthy men. Both possessed vast memories and mighty erudition, and were of a stamp to have been eminent in many branches of human activity, if circumstance had not made them authors. Both, as characters, were greater and more influential even than as men of letters. Both as it happens, made short journeys into France and Scotland; and each found in a Scotchman his biographer. . . . Those who have most deeply studied Jonson and most truly felt his power, will hesitate the longest before pronouncing a decisive judgment on the place he occupies among the foremost poets of our literature. One thing, however, can be considered as certain in any estimate which we may form. His throne is not with the Olympians but with the Titans; not with those who share the divine gifts of creative imagination and inevitable instinct, but with those who compel our admiration by their untiring energy and giant strength of intellectual muscle. What we most marvel at in his writings, is the prodigious brainwork of the man,

the stuff of constant and inexhaustible cerebration they contain.—J.
ADDINGTON SYMONDS, *Ben Jonson.*

If poets may be divided into two exhaustive but not exclusive classes—
the gods of harmony and creation, the giants of energy and invention—the
supremacy of Shakespeare among the gods of English verse is not more
unquestionable than the supremacy of Jonson among its giants. Shakespeare himself stands no higher above Milton and Shelley than Jonson
above Dryden and Byron. Beside the towering figure of this Enceladus
the stature of Dryden seems but that of an ordinary man, the stature of
Byron—who indeed can only be classed among giants by a somewhat
licentious or audacious use of metaphor—seems little higher than a
dwarf's. . . . No giant ever came so near to the ranks of the gods:
were it possible for one not born a god to become divine by dint of
ambition and devotion, this glory would have crowned the Titanic
labours of Ben Jonson. . . . There is much in the work of Ben Jonson
which may seem strange and perplexing to the most devout and rapturous
admirer of his genius: there is nothing so singular, so quaint, so inexplicable, as his selection of Horace for a sponsor or a patron saint. The
affinity between Virgil and Tennyson, between Shelley and Lucretius, is
patent and palpable: but when Jonson assumes the mask of Horace we
can only wonder what would have been the sensation on Olympus if
Pluto had suddenly proposed to play the part of Cupid, or if Vulcan had
obligingly offered to run on the errands of Mercury.—SWINBURNE, *A
Study of Ben Jonson.*

DECIMUS JUNIUS JUVENALIS.

Roman Satirist : 42-120.

I read to-day a Poet dead
    In old Rome, centuries ago ;
Once more returned the days long fled,
    The dried-up waters seemed to flow.

Once more the keen tongue known in youth
    Lashed the gross vices of the time,
Portraying with a dreadful truth
    The sloughs of sense, the deeps of crime.
                    —LEWIS MORRIS, *From Juvenal.*

Juvenal is the ancient free spirit of the dead republics ; in him there is
a Rome, in the bronze of which Athens and Sparta are cast. Thence in
his poetry something of Aristophanes and something of Lycurgus. Take
care of him ; he is severe. Not a chord is wanting to his lyre or to the
lash he uses. He is lofty, rigid, austere, thundering, violent, grave, just,
inexhaustible in imagery, harshly gracious when he chooses. His
cynicism is the indignation of modesty. His grace, thoroughly independent and a true figure of liberty, has talons ; it appears all at once,
enlivening, we cannot tell what supple and spirited undulations, the well-
formed majesty of his hexameter. You may imagine that you see the
Cat of Corinth roaming on the frieze of the Parthenon. There is the
epic in his satire : that which Juvenal has in his hand is the sceptre
of gold with which Ulysses beat Thersites.—VICTOR HUGO, *William
Shakespeare (transl).*

Immanuel Kant.

German Philosopher: 1724-1804.

The Devil then sent to Leipsic fair
For Born's translation of Kant's book;
A world of words, tail foremost, where
Right, wrong—false, true—and foul and fair—
As in a lottery-wheel are shook.
—Shelley, *Peter Bell the Third, Part VI.*

A dunce may talk on the subject of the Kantian philosophy with great impunity: if he opened his lips on any other, he might be found out.—Hazlitt, *Table Talk.*

A modification was introduced into Rationalism by the Philosophy of one of the most celebrated Metaphysicians at the close of the last century. It was the fundamental principle of that Philosophy—the Philosophy of Kant—that Human Reason is not sufficient to discover what was divine. It even professed a desire to make common cause with Christianity.—Bishop Christopher Wordsworth, *Miscellanies: Kant's Influence on Biblical Interpretations.*

Every man his own doctor, every man his own lawyer, every man his own priest—that was the ideal of Kant. . . . Kant left behind him no *system*, but he threw out suggestions of matchless fertility, and marked out with the instinct of genius the true form of philosophic problems. His philosophy is not, indeed, disconnected or self-contradictory, but its foundations are not sufficiently deep. At every step he carries us beyond his own lines, and hints at a systematic unity which might carry us over the breaks in his thought. These hints were followed out with various success by the succeeding systems of Fichte, Schelling, and Hegel. They were his children, though he disowned them, and though they, like Schopenhauer, and with more reason and courtesy, spoke hardly of their father. . . . But in many ways Kant is honoured. Kant-philology even is better than the half-ignorant worship of a few Kantian phrases. For those who have learned Kant, many questions have ceased to trouble: many are bright with a light unknown before: and others are at least placed in a fair way for further solution.—William Wallace, *Kant for English Readers.*

The revolution achieved by Kant, vigorously grasped, without completely solving, the ethical problems which had perplexed the philosopher's predecessors. Kant repeated the blunder of Socrates. He maintained that the moral law is authoritative, that the principle of virtue is imperative and independent. Yet he confessed that the idea of happiness could not be divorced from either of them, and that to reconcile the idea of happiness with the principle of virtue, and the moral law, the belief in God and in immortality was indispensable; assertions surely not a little contradictory.—William Maccall, *The Newest Materialism.*

John Keats.

English Poet: 1795-1821.

I weep for Adonais—he is dead!
Oh! weep for Adonais, though our tears

Thaw not the frost which binds so deara head!
And thou, sad Hour, selected from all years
To mourn our loss, rouse thy obscure compeers,
And teach them thine own sorrow! Say: " With me
Died Adonais!" Till the future dares
Forget the past, his fate and fame shall be
An echo and a light unto eternity.
> —SHELLEY, *Elegy on the Death of John Keats.*

Who kill'd John Keats?
" I," says the Quarterly,
So savage and Tartarly;
" 'Twas one of my feats."

Who shot the arrow?
" The poet-priest Milman
(So ready to kill man),
Or Southey, or Barrow."
> —BYRON, *John Keats.*

Keats, the Gods' own young historian of Gods.
> —LEIGH HUNT, *The Feast of the Poets (Postscript).*

Keats, that sad name, which time shall write in tears.
> —E. ELLIOT, *The Village Patriarch, Book IV., II.*

Poesy breath'd over *him*, breath'd constantly, tenderly, freshly.
> —LANDOR, *English Hexameters.*

By Keats' soul, the man who never stepped
In gradual progress like another man,
But, turning grandly on his central self,
Ensphered himself in twenty perfect years
And died, not young (the life of a long life
Distilled to a mere drop, falling like a tear
Upon the world's cold cheek to make it burn
For ever).
> —ELIZABETH BARRETT BROWNING, *Aurora Leigh.*

Meek child of earth! thou wilt not shame
The sweet, dead poet's holy name;
The God of music gave thee birth,
Called from the crimson-spotted earth,
Where, sobbing his young life away,
His own fair Hyacinthus lay.
> —OLIVER WENDELL HOLMES, *After a Lecture on Keats.*

Great soul. thou sittest with me in my room,
Uplifting me with thy vast, quiet eyes,
On whose full orbs, with kindly lustre, lies
The twilight warmth of ruddy ember-gloom:
Thy clear, strong tones will oft bring sudden bloom
Of hope secure, to him who lonely cries,
Wrestling with the young poet's agonies,
Neglect and scorn, which seem a certain doom:
Yes! the few words which, like great thunder-drops,
Thy large heart down to earth shook doubtfully.

Thrilled by the inward lightning of its might.
Serene and pure, like gushing joy of light.
Shall track the eternal chords of Destiny.
After the moon-led pulse of ocean stops.
                    —J. R. LOWELL, *To the Spirit of Keats.*

No richer more equable eye,
No tongue or more musical art
Conversed with the Gods on high,
Among all the minstrels who made
Sweetness 'tween Etna and Alp :
        Nor was any laid
With such music and tears in the tomb.
                    —F. T. PALGRAVE, *Two Graves at Rome.*

O sweetest lips since those of Mitylene !
O poet-painter of our English Land !
Thy name was writ in water—it shall stand :
And tears like mine will keep thy memory green,
As Isabella did her Basil-tree.
                    —OSCAR WILDE, *The Grave of Keats.*

The epithet (Cockney School) proved too much for one of the writers in question, and stuck like a barbed arrow in his heart. Poor Keats ! What was sport to the town, was death to him. . . . Young, sensitive, delicate, he was like
            " A bud bit by an envious worm,
            Ere he could spread his sweet leaves to the air,
            Or dedicate his beauty to the sun."
                    —HAZLITT, *Table Talk.*

Keats was a rare and great genius. He had, I think, the finest and richest fancy that has been since Shakespeare, and his imagination gave promise of an equal development. Ought we to sorrow for his early death or to be glad that we have in his works an eternal dawn of poesy, as in Shakespeare we have early morning and full day ?—J. R. LOWELL.

Past question, Keats started grandly, and has left us a monument of Cyclopean architecture in verse almost impeccable—a Stonehenge of reverberance ; he has made us feel that his elder gods were profoundly primeval, powers so august and abstract-natured as to have become already obsolete in the days of Zeus and Hades : his Titans, too, were so vast and muscular that no feat would have been difficult to them except that of interesting us.—W. M. ROSSETTI, *Life of Keats.*

As of Keats' character, so of his poetry, enjoyment is the primary element, the perpetual undertone : his very melancholy is the luxury of sadness, his despair the drained and reversed cup of ecstasy. Enjoyment as the soul of the work, profusion as its body ; consummate niceties of art as its adornment. The spirit of art was always vividly near and precious to Keats. He fashioned it exuberantly into a thousand shapes, now of gem-like exquisiteness, now mere sightly or showy trinkets ; and of these the scrupulous taste will even pronounce the cheapest, and rightly pronounce them, to be trumpery. Still, there is the feeling of art, however provoking its masquerade ; recognisable here as clearly as it is in the formative fine art, wrought by a cunning hand, in a period of great and overblown development and impending decadence—such as the late cinquecents or the earlier French rococo. . . . Keats, youthful and prodigal, the magician of unnumbered beauties which neither author nor reader can think of counting or assessing, is the Keats of our affections. Mature him, and he would be a more perfect planner and executant, and promoted to yet loftier office among the immortals; but he could not win upon us more,—could not leave us a more lovely memory, nor so priceless a treasure of regret.—W. M. ROSSETTI, *Critical Memoir prefixed to the Poetical Works of Keats.*

John Keats was born under an unlucky star. He was beset with evil influences from the moment that he felt his own strength. Had he been suffered to walk alone, unaided but by the might of his spirit, he would never have been struck down on the way by the fury of men who were waging war to the death against his associates. Keats at starting was the victim of a quarrel between parties who, like most antagonists, were wrong and were right in their respective grounds of opposition. . . . Keats might have sung as an angel, and his voice would have made no impression upon ears that listened to nothing but the promptings of an internal and most vindictive rage. . . . It is the spirit of Keats that at the present moment hovers over the best of our national poesy, and inspires the poetic genius—such as it is—of our unpoetic age. Had he lived, he would eventually have towered over his contemporaries; dying before he was twenty-six years of age, he took his place at once amongst the examples whom he so passionately loved, and the models he so successfully imitated, and so closely approached.—SAMUEL PHILLIPS, *Essays from " The Times," Vol I.*

In Keats, on the contrary, the originality in the use of his scanty materials, his expansion of them to the proportions of his own imagination, and, above all, his field of diction and expression extending so far beyond his knowledge of literature, is quite inexplicable to any of the ordinary processes of mental education. If his classical learning had been deeper, his seizure of the full spirit of Grecian beauty would have been less surprising; if his English reading had been more extensive, his inexhaustible vocabulary of picturesque and mimetic words could more easily be accounted for; but here is a surgeon's apprentice, with the ordinary culture of the middle classes, rivalling, in æsthetic perceptions of antique life and thought, the most careful scholars of his time and country, and reproducing these impressions in a phraseology as complete and unconventional as if he had mastered the whole history and the frequent variations of the English tongue, and elaborated a mode of utterance commensurate with his vast ideas. . . . Let us never forget, that wonderful as are the poems of Keats, yet, after all, they are rather the records of a poetical education than the accomplished work of the mature artist. This is in truth the chief interest of these pages; this is what these letters so vividly exhibit. Day by day, his imagination is extended, his fancy enriched, his taste purified; every fresh acquaintance with the motive minds of past generations leads him a step onwards in knowledge and in power; the elements of ancient genius become his own; the skill of faculties long spent revives in him; ever, like Nature herself, he gladly receives and energetically reproduces.—LORD HOUGHTON, *Life of Keats.*

From the height to which the genius of Keats arose during the brief period between its first effervescence and its exhaustion—from the glowing humanity of his own nature, and the completeness with which, by the

testimony alike of his own consciousness and his friend's experience, he was accustomed to live in the lives of others—from the gleams of true greatness of mind which shine not only in his poetry, but equally amid the gossip and pleasantry of his familiar letters—from all our evidences, in a word, as to what he was as well as from what he did—I think it probable that by power, as well as by temperament and by aim, he was the most Shakespearian spirit that has lived since Shakespeare; the true Marcellus, as his first biographer has called him, of the realm of English song; and that in his premature death our literature has sustained its greatest loss.
—SIDNEY COLVIN, *Life of Keats.*

In the soul of Keats, if ever in a human soul at all, there was a portion of the real poetic essence—the real faculty divine. . . . His most obvious characteristic, I repeat, is the universality of his sensuousness. And this it is, added to his exquisite mastery in language and verse, that makes it such a luxury to read him.—DAVID MASSON, *Wordsworth, Shelley, and Keats.*

Keats is the very minister of sensuous beauty, the thrilling voice that sings from the lattices of
> Magic casements opening on the foam,
> Of perilous seas in faery lands forlorn.
> > —W. J. DAWSON, *Quest and Vision.*

JOHN KEBLE.

English Theologian and Poet: 1792-1866.

> For its golden fraught
> Of prayer and praise, of dream and thought,
> Where poesy finds fitting voice
> For all who hope, fear, grieve, rejoice,
> Long have I loved, and studied long,
> The pious minstrel's varied song.
> > —PRAED, *To Helen, with Keble's " Christian Year ".*

High Churchmanship had been hitherto dry and formal; Keble carried into it the emotions of Evangelicalism while he avoided angry collision with Evangelical opinions. Thus all parties could find much to admire in him, and little to suspect. English religious poetry was generally weak —was not, indeed, poetry at all. Here was something which in its kind was excellent; and every one who was really religious, or wished to be religious, or even outwardly and from habit professed himself and believed himself to be a Christian, found Keble's verses chime in his heart like church bells.—J. A. FROUDE, *Short Studies on Great Subjects, Vol. IV.*

Mr. Keble, the " sweet singer of Israel," and a true saint, if this generation has seen one.—W. E. GLADSTONE, *A Chapter of Autobiography.*

JOHN KEPLER.

German Astronomer: 1571-1630.

Kepler asserts these wonders may be done
By the magnetic virtue of the sun,

Which he, to gain his end, thinks fit to place
Full in the centre of that mighty space.
                    —SIR RICHARD BLACKMORE, *Creation.*

Galileo was a great genius, and so was Newton ; but it would take two
or three Galileos and Newtons to make one Kepler.—S. T. COLERIDGE,
Table Talk.

No man was more unassuming than Kepler, but he wrote in reference
to his great discoveries, and the neglect they at first met with, " I may
well be a century without a reader, since God Almighty has been six
thousand years without such an observer as I ".—SIR ARCHIBALD ALISON,
Essays : Autobiography.

Kepler was the wildest of guessers.—HUXLEY, *Method and Results.*

The great astronomer, Kepler, said that two things filled him with
wonder ; the starry heavens above and the moral law within the soul.—
DR. SILVANUS P. THOMPSON.

CHARLES KINGSLEY.

Canon of Westminster, Author, Social Reformer : 1819-1875.

Never shall I forget the moment when for the last time I gazed upon
the manly features of Charles Kingsley, features which death had rendered
calm, grand, sublime.   The constant struggle that in life seemed to allow
no rest to his expression, the spirit, like a caged lion, shaking the bars of
his prison, the mind striving for utterance, the soul wearying for loving
response—all that was over.   There remained only the satisfied expression
of triumph and peace, as of a soldier who had fought a good fight, and
who, while sinking into the stillness of the slumber of death, listens to
the distant sounds of music and to the shouts of victory.   One saw the
ideal man, as nature had meant him to be, and one felt that there is no
greater sculptor than Death.—MAX MÜLLER in *Charles Kingsley : His
Letters and Memories of His Life, By His Widow, Vol. II.*

In England, Kingsley has been loved and revered for many years as a
writer and a poet.   But he has been much more than that.   He formed
part and parcel of the people ; nay, one might say he formed part of the
English conscience.   He was one of the men of whom one thought at
once, whenever a social or a religious, or a great political question stirred
the people.—*Id., Biographical Essays.*

Kingsley was not exactly the founder of a new school, but he helped in
forming a new school of the Prophets, a new order of truth-seeking and
truth-speaking young clerics, whose distinctive characteristic is *clergy-
manliness,* who in directness, spontaneity, and earnest simplicity which
avoids the sanctimonious tone, but looks to true sanctity as the aim of
all Christian teaching and life, are more or less influenced by the example
of what Sir Mountstuart E. Grant Duff calls the *open-airness* in the tone
and teaching of Charles Kingsley.—REV. M. KAUFMAN, *Charles Kingsley,
Christian Socialist and Social Reformer.*

Kingsley's exuberant faith in his own message showed the high spirits
of youth rather than a profound insight into the conditions of the great
problems which he solved so fluently.   At the time, however, this youth-

ful zeal was contagious. If not an authority to obey, he was a fellow-worker in whom to trust heartily and rejoice unreservedly.—LESLIE STEPHEN, *Hours in a Library, Vol. III.*

Certainly no intelligent reader ever rose from a perusal of Kingsley's books without feeling himself a stronger, more natural, more sympathetic human being, or without an increased sense of that faith in God and nature which was always at the centre of Kingsley's thought.—DEAN CHAS. WM. STUBBS, *Charles Kingsley and the Christian Social Movement.*

Kingsley's three masters were—in poetry, Tennyson; in social philosophy, Carlyle; in things moral and spiritual, Frederick D. Maurice. He had far more of genius than had Maurice; he was a much more passionate reformer than Tennyson; he was far more genial and social than Carlyle. Not that he imitated any of the three.—FREDERIC HARRISON, *Studies in Early Victorian Literature.*

SIR GODFREY KNELLER.

German Painter : 1648-1723.

What god, what genius did the pencil move,
When Kneller painted these?
'Twas friendship—warm as Phœbus, kind as love,
And strong as Hercules.
> —POPE, *On Sir Godfrey Kneller's painting for the Author the Statues of Apollo, Venus, and Hercules.*

Kneller, by Heaven, and not a master taught,
Whose art was nature, and whose pictures thought;
Now for two ages having snatch'd from fate
Whate'er was beauteous, or whate'er was great,
Lies crown'd with princes' honours, poets' lays,
Due to his merit, and brave thirst of praise.
Living, great nature fear'd he might outvie
Her works; and dying, fears herself may die.
> —*Id., Epitaph on Sir Godfrey Kneller.*

Such are thy pictures, Kneller; such thy skill,
That nature seems obedient to thy will;
Comes out, and meets thy pencil in the draught;
Lives there, and wants but words to speak her thought.
> —DRYDEN, *To Sir Godfrey Kneller.*

Thou, Kneller, long with noble pride,
The foremost of thy art, hast vied
With nature in a generous strife,
And touch'd the canvas into life.
> —ADDISON, *To Sir Godfrey Kneller.*

When Kneller's works of various grace
Were to fair Venus shown,
The goddess spied in every face
Some features of her own.
> —PRIOR, *The Judgment of Venus.*

I yield, O Kneller! to superior skill,
Thy pencil triumphs o'er the poet's quill:
If yet my vanquish'd muse exerts her lays,
It is no more to rival thee, but praise.
　　　　　　　　—CONGREVE, *To Sir Godfrey Kneller.*

O Kneller! like thy pictures were my song,
Clear like thy paint, and like thy pencil strong;
These matchless beauties should recorded be,
Immortal in my verse, as in thy gallery.
　　　　　　　—LORD LANSDOWNE, *The Progress of Beauty.*

Kneller with animated art, could trace,
The magic wonders of a lovely face;
His nice creating fancy could impart,
Fire to each charm, and flames to ev'ry heart.
　　　　　—WILLIAM PATTISON, *To an Old Lady that used to Paint.*

You know they paint the great man's soul as like,
As can his features Kneller or Vandyke.
　　　—SOAME JENYNS, *The First Epistle of Book II. of Horace imitated.*

It is said that the hasty and rapacious Kneller used to send away the ladies who sate to him as soon as he had sketched their faces, and to paint the figure and hands from his housemaid.—MACAULAY, *Essays: Horace Walpole.*

THOMAS KEN.

Bishop of Bath and Wells: 1637-1711.

As for my religion, I die in the Holy Catholic and Apostolic Faith, professed by the whole Church before the disunion of the East and the West; more particularly, I die in the communion of the Church of England, as it stands distinguished from all Papal and Puritan innovations, and as it adheres to the doctrine of the Cross.—BISHOP KEN, *Part of His Will that relates to Religion.*

Who was this father of the Church,
　　So secret in his glory?
In vain might antiquarians search
　　For record of his story;
But preciously tradition keeps
　　The fame of holy men;
So there the Christian smiles or weeps
　　For love of Bishop Ken.
A name his country once forsook,
　　But now with joy inherits,
Confessor in the Church's book
　　And martyr in the Spirit's!
That dared with royal power to cope,
　　In peaceful faith persisting,
A braver Becket—who could hope
　　To conquer unresisting.
　　　　　　　—LORD HOUGHTON, *Lines on Ken's Grave.*

The life of Ken presents an almost, if not altogether, unique instance of a man who, while continually writing poetry, probably from early manhood to the very close of life, reserved all that he had written, the three Hymns for Morning, Evening, and Midnight excepted, for posthumous publication. The fact seems to me singularly suggestive. If I understand his character rightly, he was one of those who find, in writing verse, what Keble in his *Prælectiones* calls the *vis medica* of the poetic art. He wrote to relieve his mind from emotions, which otherwise would have been too strong for him, from thoughts, for which other men might have found utterance in sermons or controversial treatises.—DEAN PLUMTRE, *Life of Thomas Ken, Vol. II.*

When the Ahaz of England would have combined an altar of Damascus with one of higher origin and purer design, Dr. Ken appeared there as the Prophet of the English Church, to plead for civil and religious liberty. Before that time he had boldly rebuked royal vice. " I must go and hear little Ken tell me of my faults," said Charles the Second with what for him may have been a melancholy smile. The monarch knew his man. He remembered why and when his Chaplain had said " Not for his kingdom ". . . . It is evident that Ken's knowledge was compacted and accessible. The grosser particles of his learning were fused and clarified by the fires of thought, of feeling, and of prayer. In this he stands almost alone among our elder divines. But with Ken the dogma is simple and catholic, the devotion tender and ardent, and the dogma and the devotion are one. With most orthodox theologians dogma is like an armour, necessary indeed, but cumbrous ; with Ken the armour becomes wingèd, and lifts him from the earth. . . . By loving contemporaries he was called " the seraphic Ken ". But while his heart was rapt in the ardours of devotion before the altar, his grave and serious intellect was on its guard. His words were wise as well as burning—explained or modified, if misunderstood. If he never " evaporated " the Sacrament into a " metaphor," he never materialised the presence which he confessed. . . . One gift was bestowed upon Ken in no ordinary measure—the gift of producing prayers which can really be used. If we measure the value of products by their rarity, then such prayers are the most precious of all products. They are not compositions. They are not rhapsodies. They are effusions. The press teems with Manuals of Devotion. But to-day they are, to-morrow are cast into the oven. Monarchs, senates, convocations, may order forms of prayer. They may get speeches to be spoken upward by people on their knees. But prayers which have the one condition of peccability they can no more command than they can order a new Cologne Cathedral or a new epic poem. . . . Ken, with Wesley's impatience, out upon a theological campaign, might have rent the Church of England in sunder. With himself and his friends he would have carried away from the National Establishment the acorn in which lay folded the Church Revival.—ARCH-BISHOP W. ALEXANDER, *Ibid.*

JOHN KNOX.

Scottish Reformer : 1505-1572.

Orthodox ! orthodox !—
Wha believe in John Knox.

—BURNS, *The Kirk's Alarm.*

As if you had carried sour John Knox
To the play-house at Paris, Vienna or Munich,
Fastened him into a front-row box,
And danced off the ballet with trousers and tunic.
                    —BROWNING, *Garden Fancies.*

John Knox, a man of a fearless heart and a fluent eloquence; violent, indeed, and sometimes coarse, but the better fitted to obtain influence in a coarse and turbulent age, capable at once of reasoning with the wiser nobility, and inspiring with his own spirit and zeal the fierce populace. Toleration, and that species of candour which makes allowance for the prejudices of birth or situation, were unknown to his uncompromising mind: and this deficiency made him the more fit to play the distinguished part to which he was called.—SIR WALTER SCOTT, *History of Scotland.*

We must spare a few words for Knox; himself a brave and remarkable man; but still more important as Chief Priest and Founder, which one may consider him to be, of the Faith that became Scotland's, New England's, Oliver Cromwell's. . . . This that Knox did for his Nation, I say, we may really call a resurrection as from death. It was not a smooth business; but it was welcome surely, and cheap at that price, had it been far rougher. On the whole, cheap at any price;—as life is. The people began to *live :* they needed first of all to do that, at what cost and costs soever. Scotch Literature and Thought, Scotch Industry; James Watt, David Hume, Walter Scott, Robert Burns: I find Knox and the Reformation acting in the heart's core of every one of these persons and phenomena; I find that without the Reformation they would not have been.—CARLYLE, *On Heroes and Hero-Worship.*

It may surprise many a reader, if we designate John Knox as a " Man of Genius ": and truly it was not with what we call "Literature," and its harmonies and symmetries, addressed to man's Imagination, that Knox was ever for an hour concerned ; but with practical truths alone, addressed to man's inmost Belief, with immutable Facts, accepted by him, if he is of loyal heart, as the daily voices of the Eternal—even such in all degrees of them. It is, therefore, a still higher title than " Man of Genius " that will belong to Knox; that of a heaven-inspired seer and heroic leader of men. But by whatever name we call it, Knox's spiritual endowment is of the most distinguished class; intrinsically capable of whatever is noblest in literature and in far higher things.—*Id., An Essay on the Portraits of John Knox.*

Without Knox, humanly speaking, the Reformation would not have been at all, or at least would not have been what it actually became. He had not the lyric thrill of genius that vibrates in the songs of Robert Burns; but in his own way and to his own tune he sang, " A man's a man for a' that," two hundred years before the Ayrshire bard was born. . . . He had the near sight which sees what is closest to it with admirable distinctness, and the far sight which descries with equal accuracy what is distant, and with these he combined the philosophic spirit which marked very correctly the connection between the two. He was a true patriot, and ever willing to sacrifice himself in the welfare of his country. And all these qualities in him were raised to the white heat of enthusiasm, and fused into the unity of holiness by his devotion to the God and Father of his Saviour the Lord Jesus Christ. He spoke, and wrote, and acted as ever in His sight. This was the secret of his courage, the root of his inflexibility, and the source of his power. As a Reformer he had in him the boldness of Luther, combined with some of the qualities of Calvin, and though as a whole he was inferior to both, yet more than either he reminds us of a Hebrew prophet. When we see him before Queen Mary, we think at once of Elijah before Ahab, and more appropriately perhaps than any other man in modern history he might have taken for the motto of his life the oft-repeated asseveration of the Tishbite, "As the Lord God of Israel liveth, *before whom I stand*".—W. M. TAYLOR, *Life of John Knox.*

Of the Reformation in all countries and times, John Knox is the perfect symbol.—RUSKIN.

No one in England or Scotland who values liberty, national, civil, or religious, can speak of Knox without reverence or gratitude.—SIR W. S. MAXWELL, *Miscellaneous Essays and Addresses, Vol. VI.*

Broadly viewed, the true worth of Knox was that in a measure beyond any of his countrymen he revealed the heart and mind of the nation to itself, and thus made clear its precise vocation among the peoples. Among the great personages of the past it would be difficult to name one who in the same degree has vitalised and dominated the collective energies of his countrymen. . . . What has been said of all religion when it takes full possession of man's nature is eminently true of the religion of Knox: it was something "savage and bare, but infinitely strong". It was the religion of St. Columba, who rushed knee-deep into the sea after a sacrilegious robber, pursuing him with curses; of St. Bernard, who believed that the slaying of an infidel was a service to God. . . . As the exaggerated type of his own countrymen, Knox, like Voltaire and Dr. Johnson, necessarily repels men of other nations; while his own people, even those who differ most widely from his religious and political teaching, regard even his asperities with the kindly allowance that is made for family idiosyncrasies.—P. HUME BROWN, *John Knox: A Biography, Vol. II.*

LOUIS KOSSUTH.

Hungarian Patriot and Statesman : 1806-1894.

I Kossuth am: O Future, thou
That clear'st the just and blott'st the vile,
O'er this small dust in reverence bow,
Remembering what I was erewhile.

—J. R. LOWELL, *Kossuth.*

GILBERT MOTIER, MARQUIS DE LA FAYETTE.

French General and Politician : 1757-1834.

Thou Fayette! who didst wake with startling voice
Life's better sun from that long wintry night,
Thus in thy Country's triumphs shalt rejoice,

And mock with raptures high the dungeon's might:
For lo! the morning struggles into day,
And Slavery's spectres shriek and vanish from the ray!
—S. T. COLERIDGE, Sonnet VIII.

Lafayette's inflexible integrity.
It was the great and rare praise of Lafayette—a praise hardly shared by him with any other revolutionary chief—that he both bore a forward part in the scenes of two Revolutions, and refused steadily to move one step farther in either than his principles justified, or his conscientious opinion of the public good allowed.—LORD BROUGHAM, *Statesmen of the Time of George III.*

Lafayette—the purest, the most temperate, and therefore the most inflexible friend of rational liberty in France.—LORD JEFFREY, *Essays.*

There was something aristocratic even in the Revolution, so long as the white steed and lofty plume of Lafayette were visible amid the riot, rolling back the carnage.—LYTTON, *Essays : The Reign of Terror.*

ALPHONSE DE LAMARTINE.

French Poet and Historian : 1792-1869.

Who says thy day is o'er?   Control,
My heart, that bitter first emotion ;
While men shall reverence the steadfast soul,
The heart in silent self-devotion
Breaking, the mild, heroic mien,
Thou'll need no prop of marble, Lamartine.
—J. R. LOWELL, Lamartine.

Honour to Alphonse Lamartine for his knowledge of the heart in that moment which saved the dignity of France and the peace of Europe, no matter what were his defects in the knowledge of the world—defects by which rulers destined to replace him learned to profit! Honour to that one triumph of poetry put into action.—LYTTON, *Essays : Knowledge of the World.*

CHARLES LAMB.

English Essayist and Poet : 1775-1834.

Genius triumphed over seeming wrong,
And poured out truth in works by thoughtful love
Inspired—works potent over smiles and tears.
And as round mountain-tops the lightning plays,
Thus innocently sported, breaking forth
As from a cloud of some grave sympathy,
Humour and wild instinctive wit, and all
The vivid flashes of his spoken words.
—WORDSWORTH, Written after the Death of Charles Lamb.

And Lamb, the frolic and the gentle,
Has vanished from his lonely hearth.
—Id., Extempore Effusion.

Steadfast and rooted in the heavenly Muse,
And washed and sanctified to Poesy.
—S. T. COLERIDGE, *To a Friend who had declared his intention
of writing no more Poetry.*

Cordial old man! what youth was in thy years,
What wisdom in thy levity, what truth
In every utterance of that purest soul!
Few are the spirits of the glorified
I'd spring to earlier at the gate of heaven.
—LANDOR, *Miscellaneous Poems*, *CCLXXXVI.*

Beloved beyond all names of English birth,
More dear than mightier memories; gentlest name
That ever clothed itself with flower-sweet fame,
Or linked itself with loftiest names of old
　　By right and might of loving. . . .
—SWINBURNE, *On Lamb's Specimens of Dramatic Poets, I.*

Charles Lamb, if any ever *was*, is amongst the class here contemplated;
he, if any ever *has*, ranks amongst writers whose works are destined to be
for ever unpopular, and yet for ever interesting; interesting, moreover, by
means of those very qualities which guarantee their non-popularity. The
same qualities which will be found forbidding to the world and the thoughtless, which will be found insipid to many even amongst robust and powerful minds, are exactly those which will continue to command a select
audience in every generation. The prose essays, under the signature of
Elia, form the most delightful section amongst Lamb's works. They
traverse a peculiar field of observation, sequestered from general interest;
and they are composed in a spirit too delicate and unobtrusive to catch
the ear of the noisy crowd, clamouring for strong sensations. But this
retiring delicacy itself, the pensiveness chequered by gleams of the fanciful,
and the humour that is touched with cross lights of pathos, together with
the picturesque quaintness of the objects casually described, whether men,
or things, or usages, and, in the rear of all this, the constant recurrence to
ancient recollections and to decaying forms of household life, as things
retiring before the tumult of new and revolutionary generations; these
traits in combination communicate to the papers a grace and strength of
originality which nothing in any literature approaches, whether for degree
or kind of excellence, except the most felicitous papers of Addison, such
as those on Sir Roger de Coverly, and some others in the same vein of
composition. They resemble Addison's papers also in the diction, which
is natural and idiomatic, even to carelessness. . . . The syllables lurk up
and down the writings of Lamb which decipher his eccentric nature. His
character lies there dispersed in anagram; and to any attentive reader the
regathering and restoration of the total word from its scattered parts is
inevitable without an effort. . . . Charles Lamb is gone; his life was a
continued struggle in the service of love the purest, and within a sphere
visited by little of contemporary applause. Even his intellectual displays
won but a narrow sympathy at any time, and in his earlier period were
saluted with positive derision and contumely on the few occasions when
they were not oppressed by entire neglect. But slowly all things right
themselves. All merit, which is founded in truth, and is strong enough,
reaches by sweet exhalations in the end a higher sensory; reaches higher

organs of discernment, lodged in a selecter audience. But the original obtuseness or vulgarity of feeling that thwarted all just estimation of Lamb in life, will continue to thwart its popular diffusion. There are even some that continue to regard him with the old hostility, and the old unmitigated scorn. And we, therefore, standing by the side of Lamb's grave, seemed to hear, on one side (but in abated tones), strains of the ancient malice— "This man, that thought himself to be somebody, is dead—is buried—is forgotten!" and, on the other side, seemed to hear ascending as with the solemnity of a saintly requiem—"This man, that thought himself to be nobody, is dead—is buried; his life has been searched; and his memory hallowed for ever!"—DE QUINCEY, *Leaders in Literature.*

Charles and Mary Lamb! what recollections, pleasant and painful, do these twin names recall. Well do I remember, the first time I met this most delightful couple, and the kindness with which I was received and greeted by this twin union in partition; now, alas! for a short time separated. No man that I have ever known was so well fitted to attract and engage the sympathies, the love, the affectionate regards, and the respect of ingenious natures.—S. T. COLERIDGE, *Letters, Conversations, and Recollections.*

Charles Lamb ought really not to abuse Scotland in the pleasant way he so often does in the sylvan shades of Enfield; for Scotland loves Charles Lamb; but he is wayward and wilful in his wisdom, and conceits that many a Cockney is a better man even than Christopher North. But what will not Christopher forgive to genius and goodness? Even Lamb bleating libels on his native land. Nay, he learns lessons of humanity, even from the mild malice of Elia, and breathes a blessing on him and his household in their Bower of Rest.—JOHN WILSON, *Essays: Anglomania.*

Charles Lamb had a head worthy of Aristotle, with as fine a heart as ever beat in human bosom, and limbs very fragile to sustain it.—LEIGH HUNT, *Autobiography.*

Lamb is one of those rare favourites of the Graces on whom the gift of *charm* is bestowed—a gift not indeed denied to Hunt, but much more sparingly granted to him and much more alloyed in its nature. . . . Humour in itself is among the most popular gifts of genius; amiable humour among the most lovable. The humour of Charles Lamb is at once pure and genial; it has no malice in its smile. His keenest sarcasm is but his archest pleasantry.—LYTTON, *Essays: Charles Lamb and some of his Companions.*

In Charles Lamb's instance, the quaintness of the dress fits with the quaintness of the mind. Through this cloudy medium of language which always hangs as a curtain between reader and author, we see glimpses of the real man—his shape and colour, even his gait and manner. He takes the reader by the button, as he would his friend, and pours out upon him a current of delightful humours, and fine mental oddities, almost too delicate to be seen by vulgar eye. He is the Montaigne of English essayists, and has all the engaging confidence of the Frenchman. Yet never does he slide into an offensive familiarity, which is sure to be the case when the lower journeyman of letters begins to talk with the same freedom. He, in truth, seems to be only thinking aloud, and we are behind the tapestry listening. . . . Yet with all his quaintness and disorderly current of thought, the mere "English" of Lamb is wonderful. In this apparent no-art, there is everywhere an abundant artfulness. Those little "dashes" which he used so profusely are disposed with the nicest harmony both for eye and ear. Somehow it has always seemed to me, that he extracts a new force out of italics, which he used very sparingly. He has charming little forms of his own, which fit him, and him only. They are truly Lambesque, if we may use the word.—PERCY FITZGERALD, *Charles Lamb ; His Friends, His Haunts, and His Books.*

As an Essayist, Charles Lamb will be remembered, in years to come, with Rabelais and Montaigne, with Sir Thomas Browne, with Steele, and with Addison. He unites many of the finest characteristics of these several writers. He has wisdom and wit of the highest order, exquisite humour, a genuine and cordial vein of pleasantry, and the most heart-touching pathos. In the largest acceptation of the word he is a humanist. No one of the great family of authors past or present has shown in matters the most important or the most trivial so delicate and extreme a sense of all that is human. . . . We know of no inquisition more curious, no speculation more lofty, than may be found in the Essays of Charles Lamb. We know no place where conventional absurdities receive so little quarter ; where stale evasions are so plainly exposed ; where the barriers between names and things are at times so completely flung down. And how indeed could it be otherwise ? For it is truth that plays upon his writings like a genial and divine atmosphere.—JOHN FORSTER.

Charles Lamb, the most supremely competent judge and exquisite critic of lyrical and dramatic art that we have ever had.—SWINBURNE, *William Blake : A Critical Essay.*

In short, to sum up the case as paradoxically as we have been tempted, from the peculiar nature of the theme, to commence and carry it on, Charles Lamb's face, like his other attributes, amounts to a "contradiction in terms," with this special qualification in every particular of the case, that the contradiction is invariably in favour of right, of truth, and of good, wherever these are brought into momentary contention with their opposites. —P. G. PATMORE, *My Friends and Acquaintance, Vol. I.*

He did more than recall attention to certain forgotten writers. He flashed a light from himself upon them, not only heightening every charm and deepening every truth, but making even their eccentricities beautiful and lovable. And in doing this he has linked his name for ever with theirs. When we think of the sweetest names, and which carry a perfume in the mention—Kit Marlowe, Drayton, Drummond of Hawthornden, and Cowley—then the thought of Charles Lamb will never be far off. His name, too, has a perfume in the mention. "There are some reputations," wrote Southey to Caroline Bowles, "which will not keep, but Lamb's is not of that kind. His memory will retain his fragrance as long as the best spice that ever was expended upon one of the Pharaohs."— CANON ALFRED AINGER, *Life of Charles Lamb.*

We want Lambs, not Coleridges. The verdict to be striven for is not "Well guessed," but "well done". . . . I believe, however, I run no great risk in asserting that, of all English authors, Charles Lamb is the one loved most warmly and emotionally by his admirers.—AUGUSTINE BIRRELL, *Obiter Dicta, First Series.*

Lamb's letters from first to last are full of the philosophy of life; he was as sensible a man as Dr. Johnson.   One grows sick of the expression, "poor Charles Lamb," as if he were one of those grown-up children of the Leigh Hunt type, who are perpetually begging and borrowing through the round of every man's acquaintance.   Charles Lamb earned his own living, paid his own way, was the helper, not the helped; a man who was beholden to no one, who always came with gifts in his hand, a shrewd man capable of advice, strong in council.   Poor Lamb indeed!—AUGUSTINE BIRRELL, *Obiter Dicta, Second Series.*

There are certain people whose biographies *ought* to be long.   Who could learn too much concerning Lamb?—A. T. QUILLER-COUCH, *Adventures in Criticism.*

ROBERT DE LAMENNAIS.

French Abbé and Philosopher: 1782-1854.

Lamennais was gifted by nature with far more of the temperament of the martyr than of the sectary of public applause.—MAZZINI, *Life and Writings, Vol. VI.*

There is, and will always be, an irresistible attraction in the story of those lives that have described vast parabola, that have known great sorrows, and made great sacrifices.   The story of a Lamennais has passionately affected our contemporaries, beginning with faith, or at least with the steep will of faith, imposed by main force on himself and others, and ending in the most grievous of shipwrecks, and in that gloomy isolation of a Titan, crushed by the thunderbolt, able indeed to renounce Christ, but not to shake off his priest's robe.—FRANCIS DE PRESSENSÉ, *Cardinal Manning (transl.).*

Lamennais, the greatest genius of the French clergy of his day.— GLADSTONE, *Gleanings, Vol. III.*

WALTER SAVAGE LANDOR.

English Poet and Essayist: 1775-1864.

High from his throne in heaven Simonides,
    Crowned with wild aureole of memorial tears
That the everlasting sun of all time sees
    All golden, molten from the forge of years,
Smiled, as the gift was laid upon his knees
    Of songs that hang like pearls in mourners' ears,
Mild as the murmuring of Hymettian bees
    And honeyed as their harvest, that endears
        The toil of flowery days;
        And smiling perfect praise
Hailed his one brother mateless else of peers: . . .

The mightiest heart since Milton's leapt,
The gentlest since the gentlest heart of Shakespeare slept. . . .

All sweet, all sacred, all heroic things,
    All generous names and loyal, and all wise,

With all his heart in all its wayfarings
  He sought, and worshipped, seeing them with his eyes
In very present glory, clothed with wings
  Of words and deeds and dreams immortal, rise
Visible more than living slaves and kings,
  Audible more than actual vows and lies. . . .
    —SWINBURNE, *Song for the Centenary of Walter Savage Landor.*

We pour the Greek honey, grown blander,
    Of Landor.
                    —AUSTIN DOBSON,' *Jocosa Lyra.*

O, old man eloquent, your place is sure,
  Your place, how high, amid thought's sceptred kings.
                    —W. C. BENNETT, *Sonnet XIX.*

Another flaring beacon of the rock, on which great wits are often
wrecked for want of a little kindly culture of unselfishness, is Walter
Savage Landor, the most finished master of style, perhaps, that ever used
the English tongue ; but a person at the same time so imperiously wilful,
and so majestically cross-grained, that, with all his polished style and
pointed thought, he was constantly living on the verge of insanity.—J.
STUART BLACKIE, *On Self-Culture.*

Landor was not one of our modern dressing-gown-and-slippers kind of
authors.   He always took pains to be splendid, and preferred stately
magnificence to chatty familiarity.—AUGUSTINE BIRRELL, *Obiter Dicta,*
Second Series.

HUGH LATIMER.

Bishop of Worcester, Martyr : 1490-1555.

Old Latimer preaching did fairly describe
A bishop, who rul'd all the rest of his tribe :
And who is this bishop ? and where does he dwell ?
Why truly 'tis Satan, archbishop of hell.
And he was a primate and he wore a mitre
Surrounded with jewels of sulphur and nitre.
                    —SWIFT, *On the Irish Bishops,* 1731.

How fast the Marian death-list is unrolled !
See Latimer and Ridley in the might
Of faith stand coupled for a common flight !
One (like those prophets whom God sent of old)
Transfigured, from this kindling hath foretold
A torch of inextinguishable light ;
The other gains a confidence as bold ;
And thus they foil their enemy's despite.
The penal instruments, the shows of crime,
Are glorified while this once-mitred pair
Of saintly friends, the " murtherer's chain partake,
Corded, and burning at the social stake : "
Earth never witnessed object more sublime
In constancy, in fellowship more fair !
                    —WORDSWORTH, *Latimer and Ridley.*

Here Latimer and Ridley in the flames
Bore witness to the truth.　If thou hast walk'd
Uprightly through the world, just thoughts of joy
May fill thy breast in contemplating here
Congenial virtue.

　　　　　—ROBERT SOUTHEY, *For a Monument at Oxford.*

He was the Cobbett of the Reformation, with more honesty than
Cobbett, and more courage; but very like him in the character of his
understanding.—MACAULAY, *Life and Letters, Vol. II.*

Would that every age had its own Latimer!—ARCHDEACON W. M.
SINCLAIR, *Leaders of Thought, etc.*

DR. WILLIAM LAUD.

Archbishop of Canterbury : 1573-1645.

Prejudged by foes determined not to spare,
An old weak man for vengeance thrown aside,
Laud, " in the painful art of dying " tried,
(Like a poor bird entangled in a snare
Whose heart still flutters, though his wings forbear
To stir in useless struggle) hath relied
On hope that conscious innocence supplied,
And in his prison breathes celestial air.

　　　　　　—WORDSWORTH, *Laud.*

　　　　　　　　Oh, thank Laud!
You know when Laud once gets on Church affairs
The case is desperate.

　　　　　　—BROWNING, *Strafford.*

Laud was not exactly a Papist, to be sure ; but he was on the road
with the Church with him to a point, where declared popery would have
been inevitable.—S. T. COLERIDGE, *Table Talk.*

Poor Laud seems to me to have been weak and ill-starred, not dis-
honest; an unfortunate Pedant, rather than anything worse.　His
" Dreams " and superstitions, at which they laugh so, have an affectionate, lovable kind of character.　He is like a College-Tutor, whose whole
world is forms, College-rules ; whose notion is that these are the life and
safety of the world.—CARLYLE, *On Heroes and Hero-Worship.*

Of all the prelates of the Anglican Church, Laud had departed farthest
from the principle of the Reformation, and had drawn nearest to Rome.
His theology was more remote than even that of the Dutch Arminians
from the theology of the Calvinists.—MACAULAY, *History of England,
Vol. I., Chap. I.*

Like many a mischief-maker before and since, Laud pulled the house
upon his own head.　He raised a storm at length before which the
Church, the Throne, and the Bishops, all went down together, and in the
midst of which he himself was put on his trial and lost his life.—BISHOP
RYLE, *The Bishop, the Pastor, and the Preacher.*

One would fain think and speak with some respect of any man who has been beheaded ; much more of one who was beheaded for a cause to which he had conscientiously devoted his life, and which thousands of his countrymen, two centuries after his death, still adhere to, still expound, still uphold, albeit with the difference, incalculable to themselves, of all that time has flung between. But it is impossible to like or admire Laud. The nearer we get to him, the more all soft illusion falls off, and the more distinctly we have before us the hard reality, as D'Ewes and others saw it, of a "little, low, red-faced man," bustling by the side of that king of the narrow forehead and the melancholy Vandyke air, or pressing his notions with a raspy voice at the council-board till Weston became peevish and Cottington wickedly solemn, or bowing his head in churches not very gracefully.—DAVID MASSON, *Life of Milton, Vol. I.*

SIR HENRY LAWRENCE.

Indian Administrator : 1806-1857.

" Never surrender, I charge you, but every man die at his post ! "
Voice of the death whom we loved, our Lawrence the best of the brave :
Cold were his brows when we kiss'd him—we laid him that night in his grave.
— TENNYSON, *The Defence of Lucknow.*

Lawrence, who feared man so little because he feared God so much !
—F. W. FARRAR, *Social and Present-Day Questions.*

GOTTFRIED W. LEIBNITZ.

German Philosopher : 1646-1716.

But, in a point obscure and dark,
We fight as Leibnitz did with Clarke ;
And, when no reason we can show,
Why matters this or that way go,
The shortest way the thing we try,
And what we know not, we deny.
— PRIOR, *Alma, Canto III.*

The pith of all we would say about Leibnitz, even if we had time or wish to write a long dissertation, is, that he was a man of cyclopædic perspicacity, not of catholic vision ; of immense faculty, unwarmed, unleavened, unfecundated by genius. What looks like genius in his works is nothing more than capricious analogy hammering the incongruous into the symmetrical through the brave blows of a most imperious will. Pantheism spiritualises all matter ; materialism denies spirit; the dualism, which is a distinguishing feature, as it has been a most effective weapon, of Christianity, separates matter from spirit by a gulf deep as the Infinite. Leibnitz does nothing of all this, but transforms the universe and Deity Himself into a dead and ghastly mechanism. With his optimism, his monadalogy, his pre-established harmony and his other jargons and crotchets, we hold that Liebnitz has been absolutely barren in philosophy itself, while he will have a large and abiding renown as a primordial harmoniser of metaphysical idealism with that physical science which at this hour, for good or for evil, is the chief conqueror of the earth.—
WILLIAM MACCALL, *Foreign Biographies, Vol. II.*

Gotthold Ephraim Lessing.

German Poet and Critic : 1729-1781.

Neither Schiller's nor Goethe's prose style approaches to Lessing's, whose writings, for *manner*, are absolutely perfect.—S. T. Coleridge, *Table Talk.*

Well does Heine exclaim, that "Lessing was the literary Arminius, who freed the German theatre from every foreign domination". Nor the theatre alone—all German Art was embraced by the vast range of his criticism and the stalwart vigour of his genius. It is impossible to over-rate the excellence of Lessing's intellectual nature, and the noble tendencies of his ambition.—Lytton, *Life of Schiller, Chapter II.*

There is that life in Lessing's thought which engenders life, and not only thinks for us, but makes us think. Not sceptical, but for ever testing and inquiring, it is out of the cloud of his own doubt that the flash comes at last with sudden and vivid illumination. Flashes they are indeed, his finest intuitions, and of very different quality from the equable north-light of the artist. He felt it, and said it of himself, "Ever so many flashes of lightning do not make daylight".—J. R. Lowell, *Among My Books.*

Abraham Lincoln.

President of the United States : 1809-1865.

Abraham Lincoln . . . leaves for America's history and biography, so far, not only its most dramatic reminiscence—he leaves, in my opinion, the greatest, best, most characteristic, artistic, moral personality. Not but that he had faults, and showed them in the presidency; but honesty, goodness, shrewdness, conscience, and (a new virtue, unknown to other lands, and hardly yet really known here, but the foundation and tie of all, as the future will grandly develop), Unionism, in its truest and amplest sense, formed the hard-pan of his character. These he sealed with his life. The tragic splendour of his death, purging, illuminating all, throws round his form, his head, an aureole that will remain and will grow brighter through time, while history lives, and love of country lasts.—Walt Whitman, *Specimen Days.*

Carl von Linnæus.

Swedish Naturalist: 1707-1778.

And oft we search'd Linnæus' page ;
The Scanian sage, whose wondrous toil
Had class'd the vegetable race.
> —John Scott, *Ode XII., To a Friend.*

Linnæus worshipped Him in the humblest flower.—F. W. Farrar, *Social and Present-Day Questions.*

David Livingstone.

English Missionary : 1813-1873.

Livingstone, whose name cannot be mentioned . . . anywhere, without awakening the sympathy of all Christian men.—Cardinal Manning, *Purcell's Life of Manning, Vol. II.*

John Locke.

English Philosopher : 1632-1704.

Locke hath a soul wide as the sea,
Calm as the night, bright as the day,
There may his vast ideas play,
Nor feel a thought confin'd.
> —Isaac Watts, *To John Locke, Esq.*

Locke, who made the whole internal world his own.
> —Thomson, *The Seasons : Summer.*

Long had the mind of man with curious art,
Search'd nature's wond'rous plan through every part,
Measur'd each tract of ocean, earth and sky,
And number'd all the rolling orbs on high ;
Yet still, so learn'd herself she little knew,
Till Locke's unerring pen the portrait drew.
> —Soame Jenyns, *Written on Mr. Locke's " Essay on Human Understanding ".*

See Locke lead Reason, his majestic bride.
> —Thomas Warton, *The Triumph of Isis.*

When Locke walk'd musing forth ! e'en now I view
Majestic Wisdom thron'd upon his brow ;
View Candour smile upon his modest cheek,
And from his eye all Judgment's radiance break.
> —William Mason, *Isis : An Elegy.*

A French lady, who had married an Englishman who said little, excused him by saying, " He is always thinking of Locke and Newton ".—Hazlitt, *Table Talk.*

No quality more remarkably distinguishes Locke than his love of truth.—Hallam, *Literature of the Middle Ages, Vol. IV.*

Locke is as surely the influx of decomposition and of prose, as Bacon and Platonists, of growth.—Emerson, *English Traits : Literature.*

In metaphysical knowledge, England has not advanced since Locke. . . . The philosophy of Locke is still the *system* of the English, and all their new additions to his morality are saturated with his spirit.—Lytton, *England and the English : Survey of Education.*

The name of John Locke is familiar to every scholar. He rendered distinguished service to the philosophy of the human mind ; nor is this his highest praise. His writings on government and toleration contributed more than those of any other individual to the diffusion of free and generous sentiments through Europe and America; and perhaps Bishop Watson was not guilty of great exaggeration when he said, " This great man has done more for the establishment of pure Christianity than any author I am acquainted with ".—DR. W. E. CHANNING, *Unitarian Christianity*.

Whether as public patriot or private friend, Locke appears " a spirit without spot," and his resolute temper, his intellectual ardour, and his brilliant achievements, effectually preserve him from the insipidity which so frequently mars the moral physiognomies of good men. His countenance indeed is not illumined by the spirituality of a Channing; but the robuster virtues stand forth in even bolder relief, and his apparent exemption from the minor failings which beset even a Newton, is the more remarkable as he wanted neither for enemies nor biographers.—RICHARD GARNETT, *The Age of Dryden*.

The conqueror of a new world is not to be blamed for not at once mastering every inch of its territory, or endeavouring to quell, in anticipation, any insurrections that may afterwards arise in it. That Locke did conquer his new world, far more thoroughly than Columbus conquered his, and showed how prosperous colonies might be planted in it, albeit to contend with one another until one grand empire should be constructed out of them under the sway of truth alone, was praise enough. To pursue his conquest he found it necessary almost to invent, out of the rusted materials handed down from the days of Aristotle, with much new and bright material of his own unearthing, the art of logic. Then, having shown, according to his light, what ideas are, and how words are to be used as their weapons, he showed what use is to be made of them in the acquisition of knowledge.—H. R. FOX BOURNE, *Life of John Locke, Vol. II.*

Locke's writings, which everywhere express his character, have made his intellectual and moral features not less familiar to Englishmen than his countenance has been made by Kneller. . . . " I can no more know anything by another man's understanding," he would say, " than I can see by another man's eyes. The knowledge which one man possesses cannot be lent to another." Reluctance to believe in the dark, on blindly accepted authority, instead of faith sustained in the judgment by self-evident or demonstrative reason, or by good probable evidence, runs through his life. He is the typically English philosopher in his love for concrete exemplifications of the abstractions in which more speculative minds delight; in his reverence for facts—facts in nature, or facts in conscious life; in indifference to speculation on its own account; in aversion to verbal reasonings; in suspicion of mystical enthusiasm; in calm reasonableness, and ready admission to truth, even when the truth could not be reduced to system by a human understanding; and in the honest originality which stamped the features of his intellect and character upon all that he wrote. —A. C. FRASER, *Biography and Philosophy of John Locke*.

But far more important than their specific influence on other writers, or even on the development of the subjects with which they deal, has been the effect of Locke's writings on the history of progress and civilization. In an age of excitement and prejudice, he set men the example of thinking calmly and clearly. When philosophy was almost synonymous with the arid discussion of scholastic subtleties, he wrote so as to interest statesmen and men of the world. At a time when the chains of dogma were far tighter, and the penalties of attempting to loosen them far more stringent, than it is now easy to conceive, he raised questions which stirred the very depths of human thought. And all this he did in a spirit so candid, so tolerant, so liberal, and so unselfish, that he seemed to be writing not for his own party or his own times, but for the future of knowledge and of mankind.—THOMAS FOWLER, *Life of John Locke.*

HENRY WADSWORTH LONGFELLOW.

American Poet : 1807-1882.

With loving breath of all the winds his name
Is blown about the world.
> —J. R. LOWELL, *To H. W. Longfellow.*

Surely if skill in song the shears may stay
  And of its purpose cheat the charmed abyss,
If our poor life be lengthened by a lay,
He shall not go, although his presence may,
  And the next age in praise shall double this.
> —*Id., To H. W. L., on his Birthday.*

Kind, soft-voiced, gentle, in his eye there shines
The ray serene that filled Evangeline's,
  Modest he seems, not shy ; content to wait
Amid the noisy clamour of debate
The looked-for moment when a peaceful word
Smooths the rough ripples louder tongues have stirred.
In every tone I mark his tender grace
And all his poems hinted in his face ;
What tranquil joy his friendly presence gives !
How could I think him dead ? He lives ! He lives !
> —O. W. HOLMES, *At the Saturday Club.*

Of Cambridge's dear poet was our talk,
Who gave Evangeline with us to dwell,
  And wild, sweet Indian visions to our eyes,
With their strange beauty, which we love so well.
> —W. C. BENNETT, *Sonnet VI.*

Lie calm, O white and laureate head !
Lie calm, O Dead, thou art not dead,
  Since from the voiceless grave,
Thy voice shall speak to old and young
While song yet speaks an English tongue
  By Charles' or Thamis' wave !
> —AUSTIN DOBSON, *Henry Wadsworth Longfellow.*

Longfellow for rich colour, graceful forms and incidents—all that makes life beautiful and love refined—competing with the singers of Europe on their own ground, and, with one exception, better and finer work than that of any of them.—WALT WHITMAN, *Specimen Days.*

Longfellow was content to be humanity's city missionary, so long as the common people heard him gladly. Although he was not of heroic mould, he was at least twenty times a nobler man than Poe, with a fund of miscellaneous culture, and a knowledge of human nature that in the long run more than compensated for any inferiority his imagination presented in comparison with Poe's brightest inspirations. He had not the keenness of Poe's artistic sensibility, yet it can at least be said of him that he would have scorned the atrocious, if rare, faults that so disfigure Poe's writings in verse. The same width of learning in matters of general culture, to which allusion has just been made, gave Longfellow an appeal to far larger audiences than those that Whittier can attract ; and by his gracious choice of subjects, and his treatment of these in almost every form of verse dear to the people, Longfellow has of course laid himself out—and successfully—to win a hearing where Whitman, with all his boasted feeling for democracy, is looked upon as an intellectual Coriolanus contemptuous and uncouth.—ERIC S. ROBERTSON, *Life of Henry Wadsworth Longfellow.*

Longfellow is exactly the antithesis of Poe, who, with all his science of verse and ghostly skill, has no humanity, or puts none of it into his lines. One is the poet of Life, and every-day life ; the other is the poet of Death, and of *bizarre* shapes of death, from which Heaven deliver us !—ANDREW LANG, *Letters on Literature.*

The place that Longfellow claims is the place of a singer in the great temple, and if his voice has not the resonant volume of the great masters, it has the delightful flute-like freshness of the choir-boy's unspoiled alto. . . . It is one of the distinctive charms of Longfellow that he is the children's poet ; the fresh grace, the agile hope, the dew-like purity of the child's heart and mind perpetually fascinate him. More than once he takes a little child and sets him in the midst of the world's feverish circle, preaching by the child's innocence the highest of all lessons. – W. J. DAWSON, *Quest and Vision.*

LOUIS IX.

King of France : 1215-1270.

The noblest and holiest of monarchs, Louis the Ninth.—DR. THOMAS ARNOLD, *Introductory Lectures on Modern History.*

Louis XI. had methods of preserving his ascendancy very different from military prowess. That excellent prince was perhaps the most eminent pattern of unswerving probity and Christian strictness of conscience that ever held the sceptre in any country. There is a peculiar beauty in the reign of St. Louis, because it shows the inestimable benefit which a virtuous king may confer on his people, without possessing any distinguishable genius.—HALLAM, *Student's Middle Ages, Chap. I., Part I.*

LOUIS XIV.

King of France : 1638-1715.

Louis the Fourteenth must be looked upon as an exception to everything, even to humanity itself. This king must not be judged like other kings ; he seems to have had a conscience, a virtue, a God, apart from the rest of mortals.—LAMARTINE, *Celebrated Characters* (transl.), *Vol. II.*

Louis the Fourteenth is justly censured for trying to dragoon his subjects to heaven.—MACAULAY, *Essays : Sir James Mackintosh.*

M. Guizot well observes, at the close of the reign of Louis XIV., monarchy was as decrepit as the monarch. The splendid progress of art and mind which characterised that noble reign, announced the anomaly which always ends in gigantic innovation—*viz.*, a restless population and a stationary government.—LYTTON, *Essays: The Reign of Terror.*

The French Revolution is perpetually sounded in our ears as a warning against the lawlessness of the people. But whence came this Revolution ? Who were the regicides ? Who beheaded Louis the Sixteenth ? You tell me the Jacobins ; but history tells a different tale. I will show you the beheaders of Louis the Sixteenth. They were Louis the Fourteenth, and the Regent who followed him, and Louis the Fifteenth. These brought their descendant to the guillotine.—DR. W. E. CHANNING, *On the Present Age.*

In the seventeenth century there were but two men : Louis XIV., and Oliver Cromwell ; the former representing absolutism and Roman Catholicism ; the latter, evangelical Christianity and liberty. There were certainly in that age other important personages ; and the name of the generous Gustavus Adolphus immediately recurs to every mind. But the two chief figures are Louis and Oliver. Between them—between their systems, if not between their persons—the struggle was fought ; and the victory, although slow and long disputed, particularly in France, remained with Oliver. They are the representatives of two principles, of two worlds. These two gigantic figures are each raised on a lofty pedestal ; and their shadows fall not only on their own age, but extend over all future times. —J. H. MERLE D'AUBIGNÉ, *The Protector (transl.).*

Probably there are not five historical personages upon whom the world's judgment is so irreconcilably divided, so sharply at variance, as upon Louis XIV. . . . The reign of Louis XIV. afforded the most brilliant, imposing spectacle of pure monarchy that the world had yet seen. The consciousness of royalty was developed in him to the highest degree ; he possessed, to the greatest perfection, the art of playing the king.--J. I. VON DÖLLINGER, *Studies in European History (transl.).*

LOUIS XVI.

King of France : 1754-1793.

Of all the monarchs who ever sat on the French throne, Louis XVI. was the least calculated either to provoke or to subdue a revolution.—SIR ARCHIBALD ALISON.

Had Louis XVI. shown half the courage and firmness of Charles I. he would have triumphed.—NAPOLEON BONAPARTE.

By a people contented with Reforms, such a king would have been adored. For Louis XVI. was by nature a Reformer—and happy had it been for France had her population possessed half the virtues of her king. But amongst a people less desirous to reform than eager to destroy, the safety of the ruler depends little on the qualities that beget affection, unless he has also those which inspire awe. Louis was never more insecure than in those periods of his reign when he was most popular.— LYTTON, *Essays : The Reign of Terror.*

Had the French aristocracy been less strong and less odious, Louis XVI. would not have fallen a victim to that fearful glamoury which conjured a scaffold from a throne.　That unfortunate king may justly be called a martyr;—he was a martyr to the vices of his *noblesse !*—LYTTON, *England and the English : A View of Our Political State.*

JAMES RUSSELL LOWELL.

American Poet : 1819-1891.

There's Lowell who's striving Parnassus to climb,
With a whole bale of *isms* tied together in rhyme.
He might get on alone, spite of brambles and boulders,
But he can't with that bundle he has on his shoulders.
The top of the hill he will ne'er come nigh reaching,
Till he learns the distinction between singing and preaching.
His lyre has some chords that would ring pretty well,
But he'd rather by half make a drum of the shell,
And rattle away till he's old as Methusalem,
At the head of a march to the last new Jerusalem.
　　　　　　　　—J. R. LOWELL, *A Fable for Critics.*

This singer whom we long have held so dear
　　Was Nature's darling, shapely strong, and fair ;
Of keenest wit, of judgment crystal-clear,
　　Easy of converse, courteous, debonair, . . .
Peace to thy slumber in the forest shade !
　　Poet and patriot, every gift was thine ;
Thy name shall live while summers bloom and fade,
　　And grateful Memory guard thy leafy shrine !
　　　　　　　—O. W. HOLMES, *James Russell Lowell.*

Lowell : the labours of your noble life,
Your state-craft, and your high poetic skill
Were aye a force that made for union, till
The peace now reigning hushed the ancient strife
Between the mighty land that gave you life,
And that whose kinship distance could not kill.
I think your death has drawn us nearer still !
Now with your praise our island home is rife,
While rings your continent with equal praise ;
And here, as there, we sadly quote your lays.
　　　　　　　—J. K. STEPHEN, *J. R. Lowell.*

DR. ROBERT LOWTH.

Bishop of Durham : 1710-1787.

Boast we *true critics* in their proper right,
While LOWTH and Learning, HURD and Taste unite.
Hail sacred names !　O guard the Muse's page,
Save your lov'd mistress from a ruffian's rage.
　　　　　　　—ROBERT LLOYD, *An Epistle to C. Churchill.*

For Providence, that seems concerned to exempt
The hallowed bench from absolute contempt,
In spite of all the wrigglers into place,
Still keeps a seat or two for worth and grace ;
And therefore 'tis, that though the sight be rare,
We sometimes see a Lowth or Bagot there.

—COWPER, *Tirocinium.*

IGNATIUS LOYOLA.

Founder of the Jesuit Order : 1491-1556.

Who hath not heard Loyola's sainted name,
Before whom Kings and Nations bow'd the knee ?

—SOUTHEY, *A Tale of Paraguay.*

The course prescribed by Loyola led his disciples not to solitude, but to the world. They became the associates and counsellors, as well as the confessors of the great. They had to wield the powers of the earth for the service of heaven.—HALLAM, *Introduction to the Literature of Europe, Vol. III.*

It is Loyola who has shown the world what might be meant by the phrase " Spiritual Polity " : it is he who has shown how to smelt soul ore into one mass—a mass uniformly crystallised, and shining on its surface, and mathematical in its figure, and thoroughly malleable and ductile, and a good conductor of sounds : it is he who has brought to perfection the process—often attempted—of forging hundreds of individual wills into so true a continuity of substance that the volitions of single mind should pass, like galvanic currents, through the whole, and become intelligible and effective at the remotest distances. . . . His biographers assure us that he was accustomed frequently to cast his eyes heaven-ward ; yet he was neither the mystic nor the contemplatist :—his Institute is all earthward-bent. Spiritualism would have been to him idleness ; he could occupy himself with nothing that had no product. The depths which he fathomed were not those abysses of the moral world whereinto sombre and solitary meditation plunges ; but those near-at-hand deeps of human nature which a few minds are gifted to reach, as at a step, by intuition of the way. As our Shakespeare knew human nature to paint it truly in all its moods, so Loyola knew it to rule it absolutely in all those moods. . . . Loyola could never have been the reformer of established systems ; for he worshipped every shred of the ecclesiastical tatters of past ages. But he was the inventor of a scheme essentially his own, and with marvellous sagacity, and a tact fertile in resources, he contrived to lodge the prodigious novelty—the Society of Jesus—within the very adytum of the old system, and to do so, without noise, without any displacement of parts, or the breaking off even of a moulding ! By his hands a house was built within a house ; yet none had heard the din of the builder's tools while it was in progress.—ISAAC TAYLOR, *Loyola and Jesuitism in its Rudiments.*

If there be in any of our universities a professor of moral philosophy initiating his pupils into the science of human nature, let him study the constitutions of Ignatius Loyola.—SIR JAMES STEPHEN, *Essays in Ecclesiastical Biography.*

Ignatius Loyola upstayed a falling Church by genuine devotion; but the Jesuits, adopting the ambitious machinery, forgetting the true self-denials, became the curse and the shame of Rome.—F. W. FARRAR, *Social and Present-Day Questions.*

Compared with St. Francis the life of Ignatius is poor in vision and in miracle. But his relics have since made him ample amends.—R. A. VAUGHAN, *Hours with the Mystics, Vol. II.*

LUCAN.

Roman Poet: 39-65.

The great poet Dan Lucan,
And on his shoulders bare up then,
As high as that I might see,
The fame of Julius, and Pompey.
                    —CHAUCER, *The House of Fame, Book III.*

It makes me ravish'd with just wonder, cry,
What muse, or rather god of harmony,
Taught Lucan these true moods? replies my sense,
What gods, but those of arts, in eloquence?
          —BEN JONSON, *To my chosen Friend, the learned Translator of Lucan, Thomas May, Esq.*

LUCIAN.

Greek Satirist: 120-200.

The greatest of the second-century Sophists was Lucian. He and Plutarch are the only writers of the period who possess a real importance to the world, who talk as no one else can talk, and who continue to attract readers on their own merits. Lucian has been compared to Erasmus in general cast of mind. He is learned, keen-eyed, before all things humorous; too anxious for honesty, too critical, and too little inspired, to be carried into the main currents of his time. He lived through the great reformation and literary revival of Marcus, but he seems not to have shared in it. He read philosophy deeply and widely, but always as an outsider and with an amused interest in its eccentricities.—GILBERT MURRAY, *History of Ancient Greek Literature.*

CARUS TITUS LUCRETIUS.

Roman Philosopher and Poet: B.C. 95-51.

He soared beyond our utmost sphere,
And other worlds discovered there.
His boundless and unruly wit,
To Nature does no bounds permit;
But boldly has removed those bars
Of heaven and earth and seas and stars,
By which she was before supposed,

By moderate wits, to be enclosed,
Till his free muse threw down the pale,
And did at once dispark them all.
    —WALLER, *To Master Evelyn.*

Come from thy niche, Lucretius! Thou didst give
Man the black creed of Nothing in the tomb!
    —LYTTON, *The Souls of Books.*

Lucretius, nobler than his mood,
Who dropped his plummet down the broad
Deep universe and said " No God "—

Finding no bottom : he denied
Divinely the divine, and died
Chief poet on the Tiber-side

By grace of God : his face is stern
As one compelled, in spite of scorn,
To teach a truth he would not learn.
    —E. B. BROWNING, *A Vision of Poets.*

 That Lucretius had a strong scientific imagination the foregoing references prove. A fine illustration of his power in this respect is his explanation of the apparent rest of bodies whose atoms are in motion. He employs the image of a flock of sheep with skipping lambs, which, seen from a distance, present simply a white patch upon a green hill, the jumping of the individual lambs being quite invisible.—JOHN TYNDALL, *Address before the British Association,* 1874.

MARTIN LUTHER.

German Reformer : 1483-1546.

Still in thy heart, heroic England! long
May Luther's voice and Luther's spirit live
Unsilenced and unshamed.
    —ROBERT MONTGOMERY.

Thou huntress swifter than the Moon! thou terror
Of the world's wolves! thou bearer of the quiver,
Whose sunlike shafts pierce tempest-winged Error,
As light may pierce the clouds when they dissever
In the calm regions of the orient day!
 Luther caught thy wakening glance,
 Like lightning, from his leaden lance
Reflected, it dissolved the visions of the trance
In which, as in a tomb, the nations lay.
    —SHELLEY, *Ode to Liberty.*

Thence the flame, long and hardly preserved, was to Luther transmitted
Mighty soul, and he lifted his torch, and enlighten'd the nations.
  —SOUTHEY, *A Vision of Judgment : The Elder Worthies.*

Grand rough old Martin Luther.   —BROWNING, *The Twins.*

Why, to be Luther— that's a life to lead,
Incomparably better than my own.
He comes, reclaims God's earth for God, he says,
Sets up God's rule again by simple means,
Re-opens a shut book, and all is done.
He flared out in the flaring of mankind;
Such Luther's luck was: how shall such be mine?
—BROWNING, Bishop Blougram's Apology.

Well done! Thy words are great and bold;
At times they seem to me,
Like Luther's in the days of old,
Half-battles for the free.
—LONGFELLOW, To W. E. Channing.

What! shall one monk, scarce known beyond his cell,
Front Rome's far-reaching bolts, and scorn her frown?
Brave Luther answered YES; that thunder's swell
Rocked Europe, and discharmed the triple crown.
—J. R. LOWELL, To W. L. Garrison.

Luther is, in parts, the most evangelical writer I know, after the apostles and apostolic men. . . . All Germany, England, Scotland and other countries, started like giants out of their sleep at the first blast of Luther's trumpet. The only fit commentator on Paul was Luther—not by any means such a gentleman as the Apostle, but almost as great a genius.—S. T. COLERIDGE, *Table Talk.*

Notwithstanding the great things he had performed, he gave himself no air of grandeur or importance. He seemed to consider himself as a common man among common men. He was doctor Martin Luther, and nothing more. There was a simplicity and commonness in his habits and conversation which contrasts wonderfully with the mighty revolution he brought about. This simplicity, we were going to say, shows his native greatness, but we correct ourselves, and add, that it exhibits that apostolic frame of mind which all the messengers of God, from Moses downwards, have displayed. Such men are moulded at once by the hand that sends them. The accidents of this world have no power (as they have upon others) to change or modify their moral conformation. There is a oneness, a wholeness, an uncompoundedness of character in these elect instruments: on their moral frame is chiselled by the Divine finger one idea, and one only—and that external to their worldly condition. Hence was begotten the simplicity and homeliness of Luther's walk in life. Had he acted the great man, he would have proved that he was not the apostle.—WM. HAZLITT, Jun., *Introduction to Michelet's Life of Luther.*

I will call this Luther a true Great Man; great in intellect, in courage, affection and integrity; one of our most lovable and precious men. Great, not as a hewn obelisk; but as an Alpine mountain;—so simple, honest, spontaneous, not setting up to be great at all; there for quite another purpose than being great!—CARLYLE, *On Heroes and Hero-Worship.*

In the primal and restless consciousness of the new spirit, Luther appealed to the people—the first, since Christ, who so adventured. From that moment all the codes of classic dogmatists were worthless—the expired leases to an estate just let to new tenants, and upon new conditions.—LYTTON, *England and the English : A View*, etc.

It is not, therefore, inexact to say that Luther was in point of fact, the restorer of liberty to the ages which followed his era. He denied it theoretically, indeed, but he established it in practice ; if he did not absolutely create, he at least courageously signed his name to the great revolution which legalised in Europe the right of free examination. To him it is, in great measure, owing that we of the present day exercise in its plenitude that first great right of the human understanding, to which all the rest are annexed, without which all the rest are naught. We cannot think, speak, write, read, for a single moment, without gratefully recalling to mind this enormous benefit of intellectual enfranchisement. The very lines I here trace, to whom do I owe it that I am able to send them forth, if not to the liberator of modern thought ? . . . Saxon Luther was the Arminius of modern Germany.—JULES MICHELET, *Life of Martin Luther (transl.)*.

Luther, moreover, though eminently a revolutionist, rejected all other weapons than words.—MAZZINI, *Life and Writings, Vol. II.*

There is an Apostolical Succession. It is not the power of God conveyed by physical contact, it is not a line of priests ; it is a succession of prophets, a broken, scattered one, but a real one. John was the successor of Elias' spirit. In the spiritual birth Luther was the offspring of the mind of St. Paul. Mind acts on mind, whether by ideas or character : herein is the spiritual succession.—F. W. ROBERTSON, *Life and Letters, Vol. II.*

If any such pseudo-scientific method were adopted and applied to the instances of Martin Luther and of Ignatius Loyola, it might be easy to shed upon our theme a glare of philosophic splendour. Thus this pair of worthies might he held up to view as binary stars, revolving round a common centre, and exhibiting the counter-active forces, moral and religious, of the sixteenth century ! Each, it might be said, and each, as related to the other, was the necessary consequence of the conflicting ferments of that stirring age. Each of these great men came forth, we might be told, when he came, and each was what he was, and each did what he did, in obedience to certain occult forces which from the depth of ages, had been working themselves up to the surface of European civilisation ! The one was "an Idea" proper to Germany ; the other "an Idea" proper to Spain ; and the two were simultaneously evolved by a silent energy of the moral system, then struggling into light, and asking to be defined, and to be uttered aloud, and to be defended, and to be consigned to future ages ! Luther, according to some such theory, was the spokesman of the Teutonic idea of Christianity ; Loyola, of the Spanish ; and thus we should have before us the philosophy of the religious movements of the sixteenth century ; that is to say, of the Reformation throughout the northern, and of the Catholic reaction throughout the southern nations of Europe.—ISAAC TAYLOR, *Loyola and Jesuitism.*

Perhaps there is no one in the whole history of the world, against whom such a host of implacable prejudices and antipathies have been permanently arrayed as against Luther. For the contest in which he engaged is the most momentous ever waged by a single man : it had been secretly preparing for centuries ; and its issue is still pending. Even in our days the dark, terrible power, which Luther assailed and cast down, has been lifting itself up in renewed vigour: Dagon has been set up again in the very presence of the ark of God; and all they who are fighting for Dagon, who are upholding the cause attacked by Luther, cannot possibly be just to Luther, whose whole life and character, his heart and soul and mind, are identified and one with his great work, in a manner very different from what we see in other men. . . . Luther, apart from the Reformation, would cease to be Luther. His work was not something external to him, like Saturn's ring, on which he shone, and within which he revolved: it was his own very self, that grew out of him, while he grew out of his work. . . . Luther, if we take the two masses of his writings, those in Latin, and those in his own tongue, which display different characters of style, according to the persons and objects they are designed for, in the highest qualities of excellence, in the faculty of presenting grand truths, moral and spiritual ideas, clearly, vividly, in words which elevate and enlighten men's minds, and stir their hearts, and control their wills, seem incomparably superior to Bossuet, almost as superior as Shakespeare to Racine, or as Ulswater to the Serpentine. In fact, when turning from one to the other, I have felt at times as if I were passing out of a gorgeous, crowded drawing-room, with its artificial lights and dizzying sounds, to run up a hill at sunrise. . . . Verily Luther is a strange sort of Antino-mian. Yea, he belongs to that great Antinomian multitude, which com-prises the glorious company of the Apostles, and the goodly fellowship of the Prophets and the noble army of martyrs. Day by day he rose up to wield the sword of the gospel, almost single-handed, against all the force and fraud of a corrupt and lying Church, which had cast its fetters over the mind, and breathed its rottenness into the heart of Christendom. Day by day, too, he turned from this grand conflict, to refresh himself by relieving the simplest and deepest wants of the poor and ignorant, by teaching them their duty to God and man, by explaining the mysteries of the Gospel to them in the plainest, homeliest speech, by telling them what they were to pray for, and by putting words into their mouths to pray with. . . . A *No* has little power, unless it be the rebound of a *Yes*, the thunderclap following the lightning-flash. Erasmus's *No*, Voltaire's *No*, merely awakened echoing *Noes* in the hollow caverns of men's hearts, and, the latter at least, gnawed at men's hearts, dried up the fountains of tears, and turned their smiles into sneers. Luther's shook the world, but shook it in order to steady it. It burst the chains of death, to set free the spirit of life.—J. C. HARE, *Vindication of Luther.*

There came upon Christendom, initiated by the bravery of Luther, a powerful impulse, which passed into a mighty struggle. —GLADSTONE, *Gleanings, Vol. III.*

Luther told the Papacy to stand out of the world's light, to give free course to whatever sunbeams might be struggling down to cheer us. . . . The printing-press is the most puissant agency that ever gave wings to thought, or turned ideas into forces. It has a speciality of interest in connection with the revolution inaugurated by Luther. In this instance, *for the first time* did it show its full power. Luther without his printing-press would have been Moses without his rod. Luther was the first, and to this hour he continues the greatest, of those tribunes of the people who have addressed their audience through the press. It is the grandest of all the mechanical implements of Democracy; and Luther, whether he

would have liked to be told so or not, initiated modern Democracy.—
PETER BAYNE, *Life and Work of Martin Luther, Vol. I.*

Not unjustly might Luther be named the last of the scholastics. Luther's awful remorse, the curse of his cloister, the burden and the pang which he bore till he died, was the heritage of a time when the idolatry of Aristotle was at once the confession of guilt and the atonement for it. If Luther, as a monk, had not been harassed by the perplexities which were both the crucifixion and the crown of the mediæval philosophy, he would never have been a reformer. But Luther and the Reformation overlooked the principal element of that philosophy, its relation to the religious life.—WILLIAM MACCALL, *The Newest Materialism.*

Luther himself was one of the grandest men that ever lived on earth. Never was any one more loyal to the light that was in him, braver, truer, or wider minded in the noblest sense of the word. The share of the work which fell to him Luther accomplished most perfectly. But he was exceptionally fortunate in one way, that in Saxony he had his sovereign on his side, and the enemy, however furious, could not reach him with fleshly weapons, and could but grind his teeth and curse.—J. A. FROUDE, *Calvinism.*

There are some men whose greatness no person of common sense thinks of disputing. They tower above the rest of mankind like the Pyramids, the Parthenon, and the Colosseum, among buildings. Such men were Luther and Augustine, Gustavus Adolphus and George Washington, Columbus and Sir Isaac Newton. He who questions *their* greatness, must be content to be thought very ignorant, very prejudiced, or very eccentric.—BISHOP RYLE, *The Bishop, the Pastor, and the Preacher.*

Of all our historic names, no single one ever exerted an influence so broad and lasting as that of Martin Luther. The revolution which he inaugurated still progresses ; the Christian world goes on divided. Perhaps it need not have been so ; at all events it is so. That single united body of Christians which recognised Rome as its head, was doubtless the most intelligent, the strongest coalition of men the world ever saw. That it could have been disintegrated by the efforts of one man is something remarkable. We may go on explaining it all, still the presence of that superior manhood confronts us ; unerring, resolute, fearless, he flung back the gates that resisted John Huss, and through them men are walking to this day.—JOHN H. TREADWELL, *Life of Martin Luther.*

The German Apostle of Light and Freedom.—LORD ROSEBERY, *Life of Pitt.*

Two hundred and fifty years afterwards, another gifted mind, in looking back, took much the same view that Erasmus had taken in looking forward. Goethe deplored Luther's violence. But Luther might have quoted Ajax. To dream that such evils could be cured by the gentle magic of literature was indeed to chant incantations over a malady that craved the surgeon's knife.—SIR R. C. JEBB, *Erasmus.*

EDWARD BULWER, LORD LYTTON.

English Novelist, Poet, Dramatist : 1806-1873.

Bulwer is, in every point of view, a highly distinguished writer. His work on England and the English is a brilliant performance, abounding

with sparkling observations, containing many profound ones, and particularly interesting to the multitude of persons to whom foreign travelling
has rendered the comparison of English and French character and institutions an object of interest. The great defects of this work, in a
political point of view, is that he does not assign sufficient weight to the
agency of a superintending Providence, and the laboured attempt to
exculpate the errors, and screen the vices, and draw a veil over the
perils of democratic government.—Sir Archibald Alison, *Essays : The
Athenian Democracy.*

Bulwer, an industrious writer, with occasional ability, is distinguished
for his reverence of intellect as a temporality, and appeals to the worldly
ambition of the student.—Emerson, *English Traits : Literature.*

Lord Macaulay.

English Historian, Critic, Poet : 1800-1859.

The dreary rhymer's measured snore
Falls heavy on our ears no more ;
And by long strides are left behind
The dear delights of woman-kind,
Who win their battles like their loves,
In satin waistcoats and kid gloves,
And have achieved the crowning work
When they have truss'd and skewer'd a Turk.
Another comes with stouter tread,
And stalks among the statelier dead :
He rushes on, and hails by turns
High-crested Scott, broad-breasted Burns ;
And shows the British youth, who ne'er
Will lag behind, what Romans were,
When all the Tuscans and their Lars
Shouted, and shook the towers of Mars.

—Landor, *To Macaulay.*

I wish I were only as sure about any one thing as Macaulay is about
every thing.—Lord Melbourne.

The son of the Saint, who seems himself to be something of a reviewer,
is insidious as a serpent, but fangless as the slow-worm.—John Wilson,
Noctes Ambrosianæ, Vol. II.

What ! Poetry from Macaulay ? Ay, and why not ? The House
hushes itself to hear him, even though Stanley is the cry ! If he be not
the first of critics (spare our blushes), who is ? Name the young Poet
who could have written the *Armada.* The Young Poets all want fire ;
Macaulay is full of fire. The Young Poets are somewhat weakly ; he is
strong. The Young Poets are rather ignorant ; his knowledge is great.
The Young Poets mumble books ; he devours them. The Young Poets
dally with their subject ; he strikes its heart. The Young Poets are still
their own heroes ; he sees but the chiefs he celebrates. The Young Poets
weave dreams with shadows transitory as clouds without substance ; he
builds realities lasting as rocks. The Young Poets steal from all and

sundry, and deny their thefts; he robs in the face of day. Whom? Homer.
—JOHN WILSON, *Blackwood's Magazine*, 1847.

Macaulay can afford to smile at all reviewers who affect to possess more than his own gigantic stores of information. . . . Macaulay's style, like other original things, has already produced a school of imitators. Its influence may distinctly be traced, both in the periodical and daily literature of the day. Its great characteristic is the shortness of the sentences, which often equals that of Tacitus himself, and the rapidity with which new and distinct ideas or facts succeed each other in his richly-stored pages. He is the Pope of English prose: he often gives two sentiments or facts in a single line. No preceding writer in prose, in any modern language with which we are acquainted, has carried this art of abbreviation, or rather cramming of ideas, to such a length: and to its felicitous use much of the celebrity which he has acquired is to be ascribed.—SIR ARCHIBALD ALISON, *Essays : Macaulay*.

The brilliant Macaulay, who expresses the tone of the English governing classes of the day, explicitly teaches that *good* means good to eat, good to wear, material commodity; that the glory of modern philosophy is its direction on " fruit "; to yield economical inventions: and that its merit is to avoid ideas, and avoid morals.—EMERSON, *English Traits : Literature*.

I hear that Mr. Macaulay is to be returned. If he speaks half as well as he writes, the House will be in fashion again.—LORD BEACONSFIELD, *The Young Duke*.

The fancy tires, if you appeal only to the fancy; the understanding is aware of its dulness, if you appeal only to the understanding: the curiosity is soon satiated unless you pique it with variety. This is the very opportunity for Macaulay. He has fancy, sense, abundance; he appeals to both fancy and understanding. There is no sense of effort. His books read like an elastic dream. There is a continual sense of instruction: for who had an idea of the transactions before? The emotions, too, which he appeals to are the easy admiration, the cool disapprobation, the gentle worldly curiosity, which quietly excite us, never fatigue us, which we could bear for ever. To read Macaulay for a day, would be to pass a day of easy thought, of pleasant placid emotion.—WALTER BAGEHOT, *Literary Studies, Vol. II.*

What his violins were to Stradivarius, and his fresco to Leonardo, and his campaigns to Napoleon, that was his *History* to Macaulay. How fully it occupied his thoughts did not appear in his conversation; for he steadily and successively resisted any inclination to that most subtle form of selfishness, which often renders the period of literary creation one long penance to all members of an author's family. But none the less his book was always in his mind: and seldom indeed did he pass a day or turn over a volume without lighting upon a suggestion which could be turned to useful purpose.—SIR GEORGE O. TREVELYAN, *Life and Letters of Lord Macaulay.*

Lord Macaulay lived a life of no more than fifty-nine years and three months. But it was an extraordinarily full life, of sustained exertion; a high table-land, without depressions. . . . The laboriousness of Macaulay as an author demands our gratitude. . . . It is delightful to find, that the most successful prose-writer of the day was also the most painstaking.— GLADSTONE, *Gleanings, Vol. II.*

Macaulay's knowledge was not only very wide, it was both thoroughly accurate and instantly ready. For this stream of apt illustrations he was indebted to his extraordinary memory, and his rapid eye for contrasts and analogies. They come to the end of his pen as he writes; they are not laboriously hunted out in indexes, and then added by way of after-thought and extraneous interpolation. Hence quotations and references that in a writer even of equal knowledge, but with his wits less promptly about him, would seem mechanical and awkward, find their place in a page of Macaulay as if by a delightful process of complete assimilation and spontaneous fusion. . . . Macaulay is like the military king who never suffered himself to be seen, even by the attendants in his bed-chamber, until he had had time to put on his uniform and jack-boots. His severity of eye is very wholesome; it makes his writing firm, and firmness is certainly one of the first qualities that writing must have.—JOHN MORLEY, *Miscellanies, Vol. I.*

From Eton and Harrow down to an elementary school in St. Giles's or Bethnal Green, Macaulay's *Essays* are a text-book. At home and in the colonies, they are on every shelf between Shakespeare and the Bible.— *Id., Ibid., Vol. III.*

I recall no writer who is Macaulay's equal in this art of covering his larger surfaces with minute work which is never out of place. Like the delicate sculpture on the sandals of Athene in the Parthenon, it detracts nothing from the grandeur of the statue. Or, to take a more appropriate figure, it resembles a richly decorated Gothic porch, in which every stone is curiously carved, and yet does its duty in bearing the weight of the mighty arch as well as if it were perfectly plain.—J. COTTER MORISON, *Life of Macaulay.*

Macaulay is brilliant and emphatic, but we weary at last of his ever-lasting *staccato* on the trumpet. . . . Macaulay turned his back on social problems and disdained any kind of gospel. He had no mission to tell the world how bad it is: on the contrary, he was never wearied with his proofs that it ought to be well satisfied with its lot and its vast superiority in all things to its ancestors. . . . Macaulay has conferred most memorable services on the readers of English throughout the world. He stands between philosophic historians and the public very much as journals and periodicals stand between the masses and great libraries. Macaulay is a glorified journalist and reviewer, who brings the matured results of scholars to the man in the street in a form that he can remember and enjoy, when he could not make use of a merely learned book.—FREDERIC HARRISON, *Studies in Early Victorian Literature.*

In several respects Macaulay is the natural antithesis to Carlyle: to some extent they may even be regarded as complementary. We may correct the excess of the one by the opposite excess of the other. Macaulay was an optimist, Carlyle a pessimist; Macaulay was the panegyrist of his own time, Carlyle was its merciless critic; Macaulay devoutly believed all the formulas of the Whig creed and had great faith in Reform Bills and improvements in parliamentary machinery, Carlyle accepted no formulas whatsoever, and set small store by any reforms that were merely parliamentary; Macaulay was orthodox in his literary tastes and methods, Carlyle was revolutionary and scornful of rule.—HUGH WALKER, *The Age of Tennyson.*

We do well to be proud of Macaulay.—AUGUSTINE BIRRELL, *Obiter Dicta, First Series.*

Lord Macaulay was a royal eclectic, and was quite out of sympathy with the majority of that brotherhood who are content to tone down their contradictories to the dull level of ineptitudes. Macaulay never toned down his contradictories, but, heightening everything all round, went on his sublime way, rejoicing like a strong man to run a race, and well knowing that he could give anybody five yards in fifty and win easily.—*Id., Ibid., Second Series.*

NICHOLAS MACHIAVELLI.

Florentine Historian and Political Writer : 1467-1527.

One great luminary, however, appeared at this time, though, as has been usually deemed, rather a sinister meteor, than a benignant star. It is easy to anticipate the name of Nicholas Machiavel.—HALLAM, *Literature of the Middle Ages, Vol. I.*

The subtle observant intelligence of Machiavelli.—GLADSTONE, *Gleanings, Vol. VI.*

Machiavelli, a man whose public conduct was upright and honourable, whose views of morality, where they differed from those of the persons around him, seemed to have differed for the better, and whose only fault was, that, having adopted some of the maxims then generally received, he arranged them more luminously, and expressed them more forcibly, than any other writer.—MACAULAY, *Essays : Machiavelli.*

SIR JAMES MACKINTOSH.

British Statesman and Historian : 1765-1832.

Sir James Mackintosh was fitted to have been the Guizot of English history. His mind was essentially didactic. Reflection, not action, was both the bent of his disposition and the theatre of his glory.—SIR ARCHIBALD ALISON, *Essays : Macaulay.*

Sir James Mackintosh is the king of the men of talent. He is a most elegant converser.—S. T. COLERIDGE, *Table Talk.*

We will venture to say that Sir James Mackintosh often did more for religious liberty and for parliamentary reform in a quarter of an hour than most of those zealots who are in the habit of depreciating him have done or will do in the whole course of their lives. . . . Whatever was valuable in the compositions of Sir James Mackintosh was the ripe fruit of study and of meditation. It was the same with his conversation. In his most familiar talk there was no wildness, no inconsistency, no amusing nonsense, no exaggeration for the sake of momentary effect. His mind was a vast magazine, admirably arranged. Everything was there; and everything

17

was in its place. His judgments on men, on sects, on books, had been often and carefully tested and weighed, and had then been committed, each to its proper receptacle, in the most capacious and accurately constructed memory that any human being ever possessed. It would have been strange indeed if you had asked for anything that was not to be found in that immense storehouse. The article which you required was not only there. It was ready.—MACAULAY, *Essays : Sir James Mackintosh.*

MAHOMET.

Apostle of Islam : 571-632.

The moon of Mahomet
Arose, and it shall not set :
While, blazoned as on heaven's immortal noon,
The Cross leads generations on.

—SHELLEY, *Hellas.*

Utter the song, O my soul! the flight and return of Mohammed,
Prophet and priest, who scatter'd abroad both evil and blessing,
Huge wasteful empires founded and hallow'd slow persecution,
Soul-withering, but crush'd the blasphemous rites of the Pagan
And idolatrous Christians—For veiling the Gospel of Jesus,
They, the best corrupting, had made it worse than the vilest.
Wherefore Heaven decreed th' enthusiast warrior of Mecca,
Choosing good from iniquity rather than evil from goodness.

—S. T. COLERIDGE, *Mahomet.*

It is probably true of Mohammed himself, it is certainly true of such men as Loyola and George Fox, that a vein of insanity which ran through their natures, was one great element of their power.—W. E. H. LECKY, *History of England, Vol. I.*

The sensual and sanguinary creed of Mahomet.—LORD JEFFREY, *Essays.*

Mahomet said that he experienced more difficulty in persuading his four wives of his divine mission than all the rest of the world besides ; and this, says Gibbon, was not surprising, for they knew best his weaknesses as a man.—SIR ARCHIBALD ALISON, *Essays : Autobiography.*

Moses and Mahomet were not men of speculation, but men of action ; and it is the stress they laid upon the latter that has given them the power they wield over the destinies of mankind.—ERNEST RENAN (*transl.*).

I like Mahomet for his total freedom from cant. He is a rough self-helping son of the wilderness; does not pretend to be what he is not. There is no ostentatious pride in him ; but neither does he go much upon humility : he is there as he can be, in cloak and shoes of his own clouting ; speaks plainly to all manner of Persian kings, Greek emperors, what it is they are bound to do ; knows well enough, about himself, " the respect due unto thee ".—CARLYLE, *On Heroes and Hero-Worship.*

The message of Mahomet, when he first unfolded the green banner, was one of the most simple. There is no god but God: God is King, and you must and shall obey His will. This was Islam, as it was first offered at the sword's point to people who had lost the power of understanding any other argument. Your images are wood and stone ; your metaphysics are words without understanding; the world lies in wickedness because you have forgotten the statutes of your Master, and you shall go back to those; you shall fulfil the purpose for which you were set to live upon the earth, or you shall not live at all. Tremendous inroad upon the liberties of conscience!—J. A. FROUDE, *Calvinism.*

Mahomet arose in a barbarous country, and with no human aid so great as his own indomitable will abolished the outward expression of a cherished idolatry in his native land, bowed to himself the hearts of his countrymen, and finally gave to the world that creed which has exercised so tremendous an influence on its destiny. In the man, no one can fail to see elements of power and human greatness, which compel our wonder, if not our admiration ; but in that Islam which he founded, history recognises, in its ultimate effects, one of the greatest evils which have afflicted humanity, arising both from its hostility to the purer faith of Christianity, and also from its essential antagonism to progress, civilisation, and the truth.—J. W. H. STOBART, *Islam and its Founder.*

COUNT DE MAISTRE.

Italian Statesman and Writer: 1754-1821.

The name of the Count de Maistre has become one of European celebrity. He is one of the writers who have had the very largest share in shaping the modern tendencies of the devout and energetic portion of the Roman Catholics of Western Europe.—GLADSTONE, *Gleanings, Vol. V.*

NICHOLAS DE MALEBRANCHE.

French Priest and Philosopher: 1638-1715.

And Malebranche has an odd conceit,
As ever enter'd Frenchman's pate :
Says he, so little can our mind
Of matter or of spirit find
That we by guess at least may gather
Something, which may be both, or neither.
—PRIOR, *Alma, Canto III.*

Perhaps France has never had but one real metaphysician—Malebranche. —WILLIAM MACCALL, *The Newest Materialism.*

In Malebranche there is a less overpowering sense of religion ; his eye roams unblenched in the light, before which that of Pascal had been veiled in awe.—HALLAM, *Literature of the Middle Ages, Vol IV.*

We are not surprised to be told that a fly interested Malebranche more than all the Greek and Roman history.—R. A. WILLMOTT, *Advantages of Literature.*

HENRY EDWARD MANNING.

Cardinal of the Roman Church: 1808-1892.

Ecce sacerdos magnus—that is the conclusion to which from every point we come when we review the various aspects of Manning's life and work.

Whatever we find, either to praise or perhaps to blame, it is always a characteristic of a great and good priest. Those to whom the idea of the Catholic priesthood is altogether unwelcome, and who regard it as the very incarnation of evil on this earth, can hardly be expected therefore to admire a man who was always and before all things a priest. But yet it is true that, whatever may be the inevitable tendency of the teachings of Catholicism towards intellectual obscurantism, it yet remains, and is likely long to remain, the greatest social force for good that the world possesses; and it is true that, whatever may be the moral shortcomings of a small percentage of its priesthood, and although no man penetrated with modern ideas can permanently remain in its service without a consciousness of intellectual dishonesty which must sooner or later be fatal to the moral sense, the Catholic priesthood is far away the greatest organisation that exists on earth of good and able men working for the moral welfare of the human race.—A. W. HUTTON, *Cardinal Manning.*

WILLIAM MURRAY, EARL OF MANSFIELD.

Scottish Judge : 1705-1793.

And burning with the glorious flame
Of public virtue, Mansfield came.
> —CHURCHILL, *The Ghost, Book IV.*

Eclipse great Mansfield's strong meridian light.
> —FALCONER, *The Demagogue.*

And Mansfield the just and intrepid;
Wise Judge, by the craft of the Law ne'er seduced from its purpose;
And when the misled multitude raged like the winds in their madness,
Not to be moved from his rightful resolves.
> —SOUTHEY, *A Vision of Judgment.*

Dost not know that old Mansfield, who writes like the Bible,
Says—the more 'tis a truth, sir, the more 'tis a libel?
> —BURNS, *On the Window of an Inn at Stirling.*

O for thy spirit, MANSFIELD! at thy name
What bosom glows not with an active flame?
Alone from jargon born to rescue law,
From precedent, grave hum, and formal saw!
To strip chican'ry of its vain pretence,
And marry common law to common sense!
> —ROBERT LLOYD, *The Law Student.*

Young lawyers copy Murray where they can.
> —ROBERT DODSLEY, *The Art of Preaching.*

Two men, little, if at all, inferior to Pitt in powers of mind, held, like him, subordinate offices in the government. One of these, Murray, was successively Solicitor-General and Attorney-General. This distinguished person far surpassed Pitt in correctness of taste, in power of reasoning, in depth and variety of knowledge. His parliamentary eloquence never blazed into sudden flashes of dazzling brilliancy; but its clear, placid, and mellow splendour was never for an instant over-clouded. Intellectually he was, we believe, fully equal to Pitt; but he was deficient in the moral qualities.

to which Pitt owed most of his success. Murray wanted the energy, the courage, the all-grasping and all-risking ambition, which make men great in stirring times.—MACAULAY, *Essays : Earl of Chatham*, 1834.

Nature and education prepared William Murray for the very highest forensic distinction, and his career is chiefly remarkable for the certain, though gradual, steps by which he reached it. His success was the legitimate and logical result of the means sedulously taken to obtain it. Had William Murray failed to win his race, it would have been because he had dropped down dead on the course, or violent hands had forbidden his progress. The conditions of victory were secured at starting in his own person, let the competitors be whom they might.—SAMUEL PHILLIPS, *Essays from " The Times "*.

JEAN PAUL MARAT.

French Revolutionist : 1744-1793.

Yes, this was Marat!—And in him appeared the friend of the populace (*peuple*), because the true son of the populace. This rickety, bilious, scrofulous, diseased victim of the neglect, the ailments, and the vices of his parents, represented in himself the squalid masses who formed the procession of Jourdain Couptête, or filled the gloomy pandemonium of the Jacobin Club. But beneath all this external debasement moved the iron springs of an indomitable, dogged, frantic energy ; a spirit of blood and vengeance which made a virtue of crime, so honest was it, so sincere. Marat shrieking day after day for 300,000 heads—Marat emerging from cave and garret into a power that shook alike court and temple—the Arch Alecto starting from the rags and decrepitude in which the fury had been a while concealed—Marat was as willing to be the martyr as the hangman : those filthy hands would have spurned the gold that sullied the ruffles of the corrupt Danton. Nothing could soften, nothing humanize, but nothing could intimidate, nothing bribe. For a time Marat was the *peuple* and the *peuple* Marat.—LYTTON, *Essays : The Reign of Terror.*

MARCUS AURELIUS ANTONINUS.

Emperor of Rome : 121-180.

And wise Aurelius, in whose well-taught mind
With boundless pow'r unbounded virtue join'd ;
His own strict judge, and patron of mankind.
                    —POPE, *The Temple of Fame.*

The disadvantage of being known to posterity by general commendation, instead of discriminating description, is common to Alfred with Marcus Aurelius.—SIR JAMES MACKINTOSH, *History of England, Vol. I.*

It is more delightful to speak of Marcus Aurelius than of any man in history ; for if there is any sublime human virtue it is his. He was certainly the noblest character of his time, and I know no other man who combined such unaffected kindness, mildness, and humility, with such conscientiousness and severity towards himself. We possess innumerable busts of him, for every Roman of his time was anxious to possess his portrait, and if there is anywhere an expression of virtue it is in the heavenly features of Marcus Aurelius.—BARTHOLD GEORG NIEBUHR (*transl.*).

As Epictetus gives a higher tone to the theology of the school (Stoic), so the writings of M. Aurelius manifest an improvement in its ethical teaching. The manifold opportunities of his position would cherish in an emperor naturally humane and sensitive wider sympathies than were possible to a lame old man born and bred a slave, whom cruel treatment had estranged from his kind and who was still further isolated by his bodily infirmity. At all events it is in this point, and perhaps in this alone, that the meditations of M. Aurelius impress us more favourably than the discourses of Epictetus. As a conscious witness of God and a stern preacher of righteousness, the Phrygian slave holds a higher place : but as a kindly philanthropist, conscientiously alive to the claims of all men far and near, the Roman emperor commands deeper respect.—BISHOP JOSEPH B. LIGHTFOOT, *Epistle to the Philippians.*

A Stoic in Marcus Aurelius gave a passing dignity to the dishonoured purple.—J. A. FROUDE, *Calvinism.*

In the texture and whole bent of his mind Marcus Aurelius was far more of a Greek than a Roman, of a philosopher than a ruler. In his campaigns he was surrounded by a train of philosophers ; in the camp he composed his *Meditations*, one of the most remarkable books in the Greek language, the mature fruit of a mind strengthened and ennobled by severe self-discipline.—JOHN I. VON DÖLLINGER, *Studies in European History* (*transl.*).

The *Meditations* of Marcus Aurelius were in fact his private diary ; they are a noble soliloquy with his own heart, an honest examination of his own conscience ; there is not the slightest trace of their having been intended for any eye but his own. In them he was acting on the principle of St. Augustine : " Go up into the tribunal of thy conscience, and set thyself before thyself ". He was ever bearing about—

> " A silent court of justice in himself,
> Himself the judge and jury, and himself
> The prisoner at the bar."
> —F. W. FARRAR, *Seekers after God.*

We may reasonably hold that the most perfect man would live the life of Christ in obedience to the maxims of the Roman Emperor, and that Christianity provides us with precisely what was wanting in the Aurelian system. Stoicism stood in need of a criterion. What is reason ? what is the true character of truth and goodness ? Christianity appears with a criterion which approves itself to our intuitive apprehension. The life of Christ is the perfect life. Learn that, and follow that, and you will reach the height of human nature. To live in harmony with the universe is to live as Christ lived. It is the wrong done in the name of Christ, the figments falsely stamped with Christ's superscription, the follies of Bibliolatry and dogmatic orthodoxy, that must be abjured ; and I maintain that in our present mood the best hope of not casting away the wheat together with the chaff, of retaining what is fit for human use in Christianity, consists in first assuming the scientific standpoint of Aurelius.—J. ADDINGTON SYMONDS, *Studies of the Greek Poets, Second Series.*

Among philosophers, Marcus is neither prophet, law-giver, nor scribe ; he is not a teacher expounding a creed, confirming doubters or controverting opponents. He is a diarist conversing with himself, not claiming even for the doctrines of his school, much less for his own judgments, any absolute infallibility, or certitude. There is no pretence to completeness, little even to method, in the handling of ethical topics. . . . Marcus Aurelius Antoninus survives as perhaps the loftiest exemplar of unassisted duty whom history records—unalterably loyal to the noblest hypothesis of life he knew. For him, life was indeed more like wrestling than dancing, yet " in his patience he won his soul ". He lived when national virtue was dead, and almost buried ; yet by integrity, by industry, and by mere fairness of mind, he helped not a little to make Roman Law the mother of codes and the saviour of society. War was to him a hateful " hunting of Sarmatians," yet " duty made him a great Captain," and he stayed the barbarian till Western civilization was Christian and safe. Intellectually, he had neither genius nor learning, and wrote only for relief of sleeplessness and solitude, yet the centuries still turn to him for wisdom ; and the *Thoughts* remain imperishable, dignifying duty, shaming weakness, and rebuking discontent.—G. H. RENDALL, *Marcus Aurelius to Himself.*

Picturesque as the external circumstances of Epictetus are, they are dimmed by comparison with those which make the figure of Marcus Aurelius so uniquely fascinating. And the clear, strong style of the professional lecturer does not attain that extraordinary power of appeal which underlies the emperor's awkward *Communings with Himself.* With Marcus, as with so many great souls, everything depends on whether you love him or not. If the first three chapters win you, every word he writes seems precious ; but many people, not necessarily narrow-minded or vicious in taste, will find the whole book dreary and unmeaning. It would be hard to deny, however, that the ethical teaching of the old Stoa, as expounded by these two men, is one of the very highest, the most spiritual, and the most rational ever reached by the human intellect.— GILBERT MURRAY, *History of Ancient Greek Literature.*

MARIE ANTOINETTE.

Queen of France: 1755 1793.

Marie Antoinette . . . suffered on the same spot where her husband perished, with a firmness and Christian hope worthy of the daughter of the Cæsars. Few human beings have passed, in a life of thirty-nine years, through more awful vicissitudes, and her character passed pure and unsullied through the revolutionary furnace.—SIR ARCHIBALD ALISON.

To the trials of that stern inquisitress adversity, Marie Antoinette was fully exposed in her later years ; and not only did she rise above them, but the more terrible and unexampled they were, the more conspicuous was the superiority of her mind to fortune. It is no exaggeration to say that the history of the whole world has preserved no record of greater heroism, in either sex, than was shown by Marie Antoinette during the closing years of her life. No courage was ever put to the proof by such a variety and such an accumulation of dangers and miseries ; and no one ever came out of an encounter with even far inferior calamities with greater glory.—C. D. YONGE, *Life of Marie Antoinette.*

Is there a man's heart that thinks without pity of those long months and years of slow wasting ignominy ; of thy birth, self-cradled in imperial

Schonbrunn, the winds of heaven not to visit thy face too roughly, thy foot to light on softness, thy eye on splendour; and then of thy death, or hundred deaths, to which the guillotine and Fouquier Tinville's judgment-bar was but the merciful end!　Look *there*, O man born of woman!　The bloom of that fair face is wasted, the hair is grey with care; the brightness of those eyes is quenched, their lids hang drooping, the face is stony pale, as of one living in death.　Mean weeds, which her own hand has mended, attire the Queen of the World.　The death-hurdle where thou sittest pale, motionless, which only curses environ, has to stop; a people, drunk with vengeance, will drink it again in full draught looking at thee there.　Far as the eye reaches, a multitudinous sea of maniac heads, the air deaf with their triumph-yell!　The living-dead must shudder with yet one other pang; her startled blood yet again suffuses with the hue of agony that pale face, which she hides with her hands.　There is there *no* heart to say God pity thee!　O think not of these; think of HIM whom thou wor-shippest, the crucified—who also treading the winepress *alone*, fronted sorrow still deeper; and triumphed over it and made it holy, and built of it a " sanctuary of sorrow " for thee and all the wretched!　Thy path of thorns is nigh ended, one long last look at the Tuileries, where thy step was once so light—where thy children shall not dwell.　The head is on the block; the axe rushes—dumb lies the world; that wild-yelling world, and all its madness is behind thee.—CARLYLE, *History of the French Revolution.*

JOHN CHURCHILL, DUKE OF MARLBOROUGH.

English General: 1650-1722.

Marlborough's exploits appear divinely bright,
And proudly shine in their own native light;
Rais'd of themselves, their genuine charms they boast,
And those who paint them truest praise them most.
>　　　　　　　　—ADDISON, *The Campaign.*

Dost thou recall to mind with joy, or grief,
Great Marlborough's actions; that immortal chief,
Whose slightest trophy rais'd in each campaign,
More than suffic'd to signalize a reign?
>　　　　　—CONGREVE, *A Letter to Lord Viscount Cobham*, 1729.

Though in your life ten thousand summers roll,
And though you compass earth from pole to pole,
Where'er men talk of war and martial fame,
They'll mention Marlborough's and Cæsar's name.
>　　　　　　　　　　—GAY, *Epistle V.*

From Marlb'rough's eyes the streams of dotage flow.
>　　　　—DR. JOHNSON, *The Vanity of Human Wishes.*

Marlborough and Alexander vie for fame
With glorious competition ; equal both
In valour and in fortune: but their praise
Be different, for with different views they fought;
This to *subdue*, and that to *free* mankind.
>　　　　　　　　—LORD LYTTLETON, *Blenheim.*

The present century was growing blind
To the great Marlborough's skill in giving knocks,
Until his late Life by Archdeacon Coxe.
                              —BYRON, *Don Juan.*

Marlborough, wise in council as in field.
          —SOUTHEY, *Ode written during the War with America.*

And the Victor of Blenheim, alike in all virtues accomplish'd,
Public or private, he; the perfect soldier and statesman,
England's reproach and her pride; her pride for his noble achievements,
Her reproach for the wrongs he endured.
          —*Id., A Vision of Judgment: The Elder Worthies.*

With all his weaknesses, or rather with his one great weakness, of always playing to win, Marlborough had in perhaps the greatest measure of any Englishman every great practical quality of the English character, except unflinching honesty and truth. His covetousness, though not his parsimony, can, it is to be feared hardly be set down as altogether un-English. But the entire absence of vainglory and *forfanterie* in him, the intense business-like energy with which he set about his work, the complete freedom from flightiness and fidgetiness with which he carried it out, the thoroughness with which he put the final touches to it, are all examples, on the greatest scale, of qualities on which Englishmen especially pride themselves. In Marlborough's fashion of war-making there was emphatically no nonsense. He never wasted a man or a movement; he never executed a single manœuvre for show; he never, either in words or deeds, indulged in the least gasconading. Probably no man ever had such a superhuman business as he had put on his shoulders in the business of at once fighting half Europe and keeping the other half in fighting order. . . . A slight, if not a reproach, of centuries was rolled away from the nation in the course of those ten years. It is for this, first of all, that Englishmen ought to reverence the memory, stained as it is, and even if it were worse stained than it is, of Jack of Marlborough.— GEORGE SAINTSBURY, *Life of Marlborough.*

Marlborough had many failings, and great as he was, it is not easy to love his memory as we all love that of Nelson, nor to respect it as we do that of Wellington. Yet still there is something so attractive about the man's personality that we feel drawn towards him in spite of his faults. He was no saint, and he was too fond of money, but throughout his whole life he displayed a simplicity and gentleness of disposition, a touching sympathy with grief and sorrow, and a loathing of cruelty and injustice, that go far to counterbalance his many faults. Mercy was always in his thoughts, and if in action he smote hard, he always sheathed his sword with unaffected pleasure, and upon any good excuse. . . . It must be admitted that the reputation of our army only dates from Marlborough's victories. His wars first proved to modern Europe that Great Britain could produce not only stalwart soldiers as hard to beat as the victors of Creçy and Agincourt, but able commanders also; and that England possessed a native army officered by English gentlemen and led by an English General before which no other army of equal number could hold its own. It was Marlborough who first taught us to be proud of our standing army as a national institution, and the spirit of confidence which pervaded

Wellington's army in the Peninsular, and to a still more remarkable degree shows itself now in Queen Victoria's army, may be said to have been born at Blenheim, baptized at Ramillies, and confirmed at Oudenarde.—LORD WOLSELEY, *Life of Marlborough, Vol. I.*

CHRISTOPHER MARLOWE.

English Dramatist : 1564-1593.

Neat Marlowe bathed in the Thespian springs,
Had in him those brave translunary things,
That the first poets had, his raptures were,
All air, and fire, which made his verses clear,
For that fine madness still he did retain,
Which rightly should possess a poet's brain.
> —DRAYTON, *Elegy to Henry Reynolds, Esq.*

Marlowe, renown'd for his rare art and wit. . . .
> —T. HEYWOOD, *The Hierarchy of the Blessed Angels, IV.*

" If all the pens that ever poets held
  Had fed the feeling of their masters' thoughts,"
  And as with rush of hurtling chariots
The flight of all their spirits were impelled
  Toward one great end, thy glory—nay, not then,
Not yet might'st thou be praised enough of men.
> —SWINBURNE, *Christopher Marlowe.*

Marlowe of all our fathers first beheld
  Beyond the tidal ebb and flow of things
The tideless depth and height of souls, impelled
  By thought or passion, borne on waves or wings,
Beyond all flight or sight but song's : and he
First gave our song a sound that matched our sea.
> —*Id., Inscriptions for a Pedestal.*

For thou, if ever godlike foot there trod
These fields of ours, wert surely like a god.
Who knows what splendour of strange dreams was shed
With sacred shadow and glimmer of gold and red
From hallowed windows, over stone and sod,
On thine unbowed bright insubmissive head ?
The shadow stayed not, but the splendour stays,
Our brother, till the last of English days.
No day nor night on English earth shall be
For ever, spring nor summer, Junes nor Mays,
But somewhat as a sound or gleam of thee
Shall come on us like morning from the sea.
> —*Id., In the Bay, XVIII., XIX.*

'Tis Marlowe falls ! That last lunge rent asunder
  Our lyre of spirit and flesh, wild Marlowe's life,
  Whose chords seemed strung by earth and heav'n at strife,
Yet ever strung to beauty above or under !
Heav'n kens of Man, but still the stars can blunder

If Fate's hand guided yonder villain's knife
Through that rare brain, so teeming, daring, rife
With all that makes us sing, our love and wonder.
Or was it Chance ?—Shakespeare—who art supreme
  O'er man and men, yet sharest Marlowe's sight
  To pierce the clouds that hide the inhuman height
Where man and men and gods and all that seem
Are Nature's mutterings in her changeful dream—
  Come read the runes these bloody rivulets write !
                —THEODORE WATTS, *The Death of Marlowe.*

When Christopher Marlowe came up to London from Cambridge, a boy
in years, a man in genius, and a god in ambition, he found the stage which
he was born to transfigure and re-create by the might and masterdom of
his genius, encumbered with a litter of rude rhyming farces and tragedies
which the first wave of his imperial hand swept so utterly out of sight and
hearing that hardly by piecing together such fragments of that buried
rubbish as it is now possible to unearth can we rebuild in imagination so
much of the rough and crumbling walls that fell before the trumpet-blast
of *Tamburlaine* as may give us some conception of the rabble dynasty of
rhymers whom he overthrew—of the citadel of dramatic barbarism which
was stormed and sacked at the first charge of the young conqueror who
came to lead English audiences and to deliver English poetry.—SWIN-
BURNE, *A Study of Shakespeare.*

The sweetest names, and which carry a perfume in the mention, are Kit
Marlowe, Drayton, Drummond of Hawthornden, and Cowley.—CHARLES
LAMB.

ANDREW MARVELL.

English Politician, Poet and Satirist : 1620-1678.

In those worst of times,
The hardy poet raised his honest rhymes
To dread rebuke, and bade Controlment speak.
In guilty blushes on the villain's cheek ;
Bade Power turn pale, kept mighty rogues in awe,
And made them fear the Muse, who fear'd not law.
                —CHURCHILL, *The Author.*

Marvell, wit, patriot, and poet, who knew
How to give, both at once, Charles and Cromwell their due.
                —LEIGH HUNT, *To Charles Lamb.*

          As Marvell stood,
Loyal to Truth dethroned, nor could be wooed
To trust the playful tiger's velvet paws.
                —J. R. LOWELL, *To John G, Palfrey.*

We read the verses of one of the great English poets, of Chaucer, of
Marvell, of Dryden, with the most modern joy—with a pleasure, I mean,
which is in great part caused by the abstraction of all *time* from their
verses.   There is some awe mixed with the joy of our surprise, when this
poet, who lived in some past world, two or three hundred years ago, says

that which lies close to my own soul, that which I also had well nigh thought and said.—EMERSON, *The American Scholar.*

It was a prophetic coincidence that named him a—Marvel.   Rare are the men of this divine stamp!   In a most debased and demoralised age Marvell stood poor—willingly, voluntarily poor and incorruptible.   Like the angel Abdiel, he stood

Among the faithless, faithful only he.

Witty beyond most of his age; the friend of Milton, and one of the first to discern and proclaim the magnificent genius of *Paradise Lost*, express-ing his amazement at it in those fine lines, beginning

When I beheld the poet blind, yet bold;

learned and accomplished by study and travel; having a wonderful in-fluence in the House of Commons; capable by his talents and personal suavity of reaching the highest honours of the state, he preferred to be the unshaken friend of England, liberty, and Magna Charta; the advocate of justice and virtue, and the terror of the evil and corrupt, who never felt safe till, having missed him with the dagger of the assassin, they de-spatched him with poison. . . . God's true Nobleman. — WILLIAM HOWITT, *The Northern Heights of London.*

MARY I.

Queen of England : 1516-1558.

Mary's horrid days
To fancy bleeding rose, and the dire glare
Of Smithfield lighten'd in its eyes anew.

—THOMSON, *Liberty.*

Still amourous, and fond, and billing,
Like Philip and Mary on a shilling.
—SAMUEL BUTLER, *Hudibras, Part III., Canto I.*

When persecuting zeal made royal sport
With tortured innocence in Mary's court.
—COWPER, *Expostulation.*

Queen Mary's saying serves for me—
(When fortune's malice
Lost her—Calais)
Open my heart and you will see
Graved inside of it, " Italy ".
—BROWNING, " *De Gustibus—*"

Mary.   " Calais !
Our one point on the main, the gate of France !
I am the Queen of England ; take mine eyes, mine heart,
But do not lose me Calais. . . ."
Mary.   " I am a byword.   Heretic and rebel
Point at me and make merry.   Philip gone !
And Calais gone !   Time that I were gone too ! "
—TENNYSON, *Queen Mary.*

Of the first Mary, long and too deservedly known by the title of " Bloody Mary," . . . we confess we can never think without commiseration.— LEIGH HUNT, *Men, Women, and Books.*

Queen Mary left none to lament her, and there was not the semblance of sorrow for her loss. She died in the morning; in the afternoon the bells of all the churches in London were rung for the accession of Elizabeth, and at night bonfires were made, and tables set out in the streets, at which the citizens caroused.—SOUTHEY.

The reign of Mary the Bigot is stigmatised, and justly, for the enormity of religious persecutions. She is, therefore, almost universally believed to have united the three pestilent vices of avarice, pride and revenge; chastened only by the affection which she entertained for a worthless husband. During her reign two hundred and seventy-seven persons died at the stake; but it ought not to be forgotten, that if Mary was attached to the stake, Elizabeth seems to have been equally attached to the halter; for in her reign one hundred and sixty-eight persons were executed for being priests, for harbouring priests, or for being converts.—CHARLES BUCKE, *Book of Human Character.*

MARY STUART.

Queen of Scots : 1542-1587.

O for a Shakespeare or an Otway scene,
To paint the lovely, hapless Scottish Queen !
Vain ev'n the omnipotence of female charms
'Gainst headlong, ruthless, mad rebellion's arms.
                    —BURNS, *Scots Prologue.*

The meanest hind in fair Scotland
  May rove their sweets amang ;
But I, the Queen of a' Scotland,
  Maun lie in prison strang !
I was the Queen o' bonie France,
  Where happy I hae been ;
Fu' lightly rase I in the morn,
  As blythe lay down at e'en :
And I'm the Sovereign of Scotland,
  And mony a traitor there ;
Yet here I lie in foreign bands,
  And never-ending care.
                    —*Id., Lament of Mary, Queen of Scots.*

Hark ! the death-note of the year
  Sounded by the castle clock !
From her sunk eyes a stagnant tear
  Stole forth, unsettled by the shock ;
But oft the woods renewed their green,
Ere the tired head of Scotland's queen
Reposed upon the block !
                    —WORDSWORTH, *Lament of Mary, Queen of Scots.*

Falsehood unmask'd withdraws her ugly train,
  And Mary's virtues all illustrious shine—
Yes, thou hast friends, the godlike and humane
  Of latest ages, injur'd queen, are thine.
—W. J. MICKLE, *Mary, Queen of Scots.*

This may be truly said, that if a life of exile and misery, endured with almost saintly patience, from the 15th of June, 1567, until the day of her death, upon the 8th of February, 1587, could atone for crimes and errors of the class imputed to her, no such penalty was ever more fully discharged than by Mary Stuart.—SIR WALTER SCOTT, *History of Scotland.*

Yet in the darkest hours of her existence, even when she hailed the prospect of a scaffold as a blessed relief from her protracted sufferings, she never once expressed a doubt as to the verdict that would be finally pronounced between her and her enemies. " The theatre of the world," she calmly reminded her judges at Fotheringay, " is wider than the realm of England." She appealed from the tyranny of her persecutors to the whole human race ; and she has not appealed in vain. The history of no woman that ever lived approaches in interest to that of Mary Stuart ; and so long as beauty and intellect, a kindly spirit in prosperity and matchless heroism in misfortune, attract the sympathies of men, this illustrious victim of sectarian violence and barbarous statecraft will ever occupy the most prominent place in the annals of her sex.—JOHN HOSACK, *Life of Mary, Queen of Scots.*

PHILIP MASSINGER.

English Dramatist : 1584-1640.

Grave and great-hearted Massinger, thy face
High melancholy lights with loftier grace
  Than gilds the brows of revel : sad and wise,
The spirit of thought that moved thy deeper song,
Sorrow serene in soft calm scorn of wrong,
  Speaks patience yet from thy majestic eyes.
—SWINBURNE, *Philip Massinger.*

The richer genius of Massinger, whose main fault, perhaps, lies in an over-fondness for metaphysical research in the creation of exceptional characters influenced by exceptional motives, and a lavish beauty of expression, which is often inharmonious to the displeasing nature of the action.—LYTTON, *Essays : Knowledge of the World.*

Massinger reminds us of the intricacies of Sansovino, Shakespeare of Gothic aisles or heaven's cathedral, Fletcher of the sylvan architecture of wild greenwoods, Ford of glittering Corinthian colonnades, Webster of vaulted crypts, Heywood of homely manor-houses on our English countryside, Marlowe of masoned clouds, and Marston, in his better moments, of the fragmentary vigour of a Roman.—J. A. SYMONDS, *Ben Jonson: A Memoir.*

FREDERICK DENISON MAURICE.

English Clergyman and Author : 1805-1872.

Come, Maurice, come : the lawn as yet
Is hoar with rime, or spongy wet ;

But when the wreath of March has blossom'd,
Crocus, anemone, violet.

—TENNYSON, *To the Rev. F. D. Maurice.*

The most beautiful human soul whom God has ever in His great mercy allowed me most unworthy to meet with on this earth; the man who of all men I have seen approached nearest to my conception of St. John, the Apostle of Love.—KINGSLEY, *Life of F. D. Maurice by his Son, Vol. II.*

It is hardly too much to say that it was the doctrine of Maurice rather than that of Pusey or Newman, which for forty years—Maurice began his work in 1835; he died in 1872—" kept the whole of his forward movement in the social and political life of the English people in union with God and identified with religion," a doctrine which, idealized and transfigured in the two great poets of the century, Tennyson and Browning, . . . has, during this last decade of the century, turned so wisely the current of our English Christianity to the consideration of the great social problems of the age, and is at this moment so profoundly affecting, moulding, inspiring, transfusing the social ideals of the present.—DEAN C. W. STUBBS, *Charles Kingsley and the Christian Social Movement.*

GIULIO MAZARIN.

Italian Cardinal and Statesman: 1602-1661.

Fox-Mazarin.

—VICTOR HUGO.

Veil'd in the Roman purple, preys
   The canker-worm within;
And more than Bourbon's sceptre, sways
   The crook of Mazarin.

—LYTTON, *Mazarin.*

Amongst those bad men who have had some fine qualities, may be ranked Cardinal Mazarin. Envy, ingratitude, deception, ignorance of legislation, obliquity, hypocrisy, insatiable avarice; these are some of the qualities by which he was dishonoured. "Alike insensible to injuries and to favours," says Deformaux, "he knew not how to punish or to reward. Hence favours, the best deserved, were only forced from him by threats, or by working on his fears." Yet had this very cardinal many virtues, arising from grace of action and sweetness of temper.—CHARLES BUCKE, *Book of Human Character.*

JOSEPH]MAZZINI.

Italian Patriot; 1808-1872.

I think Mazzini has done a very noble work for his country, and that his watchword " God and the people " is one which all nations must be the better for : one which is the truest possible testimony against the intellectual liberalism which seems to abhor God and the people.—F. D. MAURICE in *Life of F. D. Maurice by his Son.*

PHILIP MELANCHTHON.

German Reformer: 1497-1560.

Philip Melanchthon! thou alone
Faithful among the faithless known,
Thee I hail, and only thee!
Behold the record of us three!
   Res et verba Philippus,
   Res sine verbis Lutherus ;
   Erasmus verba sine re!
My Philip, prayest thou for me?
Lifted above all earthly care,
From these high regions of the air,
Among the birds that day and night
Upon the branches of tall trees
Sing their lauds and litanies,
Praising God with all their might,
My Philip, unto thee I write.

My Philip! thou who knowest best
All that is passing in this breast ;
The spiritual agonies,
The inward deaths, the inward hell,
And the divine new births as well,
That surely follow after these,
As after winter follows spring ;
My Philip, in the night-time sing
This song of the Lord I send to thee,
And I will sing it for thy sake,
Until our answering voices make
A glorious antiphony,
And choral chant of victory!

       —LONGFELLOW, *Martin Luther.*

MELEAGER.

Greek Epigrammatist: fl. B.C. 60

    While reading his verse, it is impossible to avoid laying down the book and pausing to exclaim : How modern is the phrase, how true the passion, how unique the style! Though Meleager's voice has been mute a score of centuries, it yet rings clear and vivid in our ears ; because the man was a real poet, feeling intensely, expressing forcibly and beautifully, steeping his style in the fountain of tender sentiment which is eternal. We find in him none of the cynicism which defiles Straton, or of the voluptuary's despair which gives to Agathias the morbid splendour of decay, the colours of corruption. All is simple, lively, fresh with joyous experience in his verse. . . . The first great merit of Meleager as a poet is limpidity. A crystal is not more transparent than his style ; but the crystal to which we compare it must be coloured with the softest flush of beryl or of amethyst.—J. ADDINGTON SYMONDS, *Studies of the Greek Poets.*

MENANDER.

Chief Poet of the (Greek) New Comedy : B.C. 342-29?

Thou [William Wycherley], whom the Nine with Plautus' wit inspire,
The art of Terence, and Menander's fire;
Whose sense instructs us, and whose humour charms,
Whose judgment sways us, and whose spirit warms!
—POPE, *Pastorals.*

If we were to judge by the fragments transmitted to us, we should have to say that Menander's comedy was ethical philosophy in verse; so mature is their wisdom, so weighty their language, and so grave their tone. The brightness of the beautiful Greek spirit is sobered down in him almost to sadness. Middle age, with its maturity, has been substituted for youth with its passionate intensity. Taking Menander for our guide, we cannot cry: "You Greeks are always children". . . . There is something even almost awful in the placid acquiescence of Menander. He has come to the end of passions and pleasures: he expects pain and is prepared to endure it; his happiness consists in tranquil contemplation of life, from which he no longer hopes for more than what Balzac calls the *à peu près* of felicity. This tranquillity does not diminish but rather increases his power of enjoyment and the clearness of his vision. He combines the exact knowledge of the scientific analyst with judicial impartiality; and yet his worldly wisdom is not cold or dry. To make selections from fragments, every word whereof is golden, would be weary work; nor is it possible to preserve in translation the peculiar savour of this Attic salt. Menander should be spared this profanation. Before we leave him, let us remember what Goethe, a man as like Menander as a modern man can be, has said of him: "He is thoroughly pure, noble, great, and cheerful, and his grace is unattainable. It is to be lamented that we possess so little of him, but that little is invaluable."—J. ADDINGTON SYMONDS, *Studies of the Greek Poets, Second Series.*

FELIX MENDELSSOHN-BARTHOLDY,

German Musical Composer : 1809-1847.

The fame of this illustrious musician may, and probably will, reach into future ages: but a knowledge of the qualities which distinguished him as a man, can never be adequately communicated to posterity. Those only who possessed the blessed privilege of calling him friend, can either know or feel *how* much of virtue, genius, and charm of character, was extinguished in the person of that miracle of humanity, Felix Mendelssohn!—SIR JULIUS BENEDICT, *Sketch of the Life and Works of the late Felix Mendelssohn-Bartholdy.*

In this age of mercenary musical manufacture and art degradation, Mendelssohn towers above his contemporaries like a moral lighthouse in the midst of a dark and troubled sea. His light always shone strong and pure. The winds of heaven were about his head, and the "STILL SMALL VOICE" was in his heart.—REV. H. R. HAWEIS, *Music and Morals.*

18

No man ever wrote more in the presence of his public and less in the seclusion of his study than Mendelssohn.—Rev. H. R. HAWEIS, *Contemporary Review*, 1870.

Mendelssohn, whose music uplifts the soul as on dovelike wings.—F. W. FARRAR, *Social and Present-Day Questions.*

PRINCE VON METTERNICH.

Austrian Statesman : 1773-1859.

There Metternich, power's foremost parasite,
Cajoles.   —BYRON, *The Age of Bronze.*

The life of Metternich, which is the real thread of Austrian history from the beginning of the century—a thread now and then snapped or worn, but knotted together again, for more pearls of policy to be strung on.— HARRIET MARTINEAU, *Biographical Sketches.*

JACOB MEYERBEER.

German Musical Composer : 1791-1864.

In a period of transition like our own, we may not expect the High Priest of the music of the future to appear amongst us ; but Meyerbeer is the precursor spirit, sent to announce his coming.—MAZZINI, *Life and Writings, Vol. IV.*

MICHELANGELO BUONARROTI.

Italian Painter, Sculptor, Architect, Poet : 1474-1563.

Michael Angelo has exercised an influence on modern art little, if at all, inferior to that produced on the realms of thought by Homer and Dante. . . . Michael Angelo was, in one sense, the painter of the Old Testament, as his bold and aspiring genius aimed at delineating the events of warfare, passion, or suffering, chronicled in the records of the Jews, rather than the scenes of love, affection, and benevolence, depicted in the gospels. But his mind was not formed merely on the events recorded in antiquity : it is no world doubtful of the immortality of the soul which he depicts.—SIR ARCHIBALD ALISON, *Essays : Homer, Dante, and Michael Angelo.*

We still feel the force of Michel Angelo, wearing the four crowns of architecture, sculpture, painting, and poetry.—EMERSON, *Society and Solitude : Old Age.*

Let none presume to measure the irregularities of Michel Angelo and Socrates by village scales.—*Id., Plato : New Readings.*

Michel Angelo was the conscience of Italy. We grow free with his name, and find it ornamental now ; but in his own days, his friends were few.—*Id., Progress of Culture.*

Michael Angelo, the creator of gigantic and preternatural powers.— LYTTON, *England and the English : Intellectual Spirit.*

I believe there is nearly as much occasion, at the present day, for advocacy of Michael Angelo against the pettiness of the moderns, as there is for support of Turner against the conventionalities of the ancients. For, though the names of the fathers of sacred art are on all our lips, our faith in them is much like that of the great world in its religion—nominal, but dead.—RUSKIN, *Modern Painters, Vol. I.*

Michael Angelo, in whose hands the marble was said to be flexible.— W. E. CHANNING, *Character and Writings of Milton.*

Michelangelo, then, as Carlyle might have put it, is the Hero as Artist. When we have admitted this, all dregs and sediments of the analytic alembic sink to the bottom, leaving a clear crystalline elixir of the spirit. About the quality of his genius opinions may, will, and ought to differ. It is so pronounced, so peculiar, so repulsive to one man, so attractive to another, that, like his own dread statue of Lorenzo de' Medici, "it fascinates and is intolerable". There are few, I take it, who can feel at home with him in all the length and breadth and dark depths of the regions that he traversed. The world of thoughts and forms in which he lived habitually is too arid, like an extinct planet, tenanted by mighty elementary beings with little human left to them but visionary Titan-shapes, too vast and void for common minds to dwell in pleasurably. The sweetness that emerges from his strength, the beauty which blooms rarely, strangely in unhomely wise, upon the awful crowd of his conceptions, are only to be apprehended by some innate sympathy or by long incubation of the brooding intellect. . . . Each supreme artist whom God hath sent into the world with inspiration and a particle of the imperishable fire, is a law to himself, an universe, a revelation of the divine life under one of its innumerable attributes. We cannot therefore classify Michelangelo with any of his peers throughout the long procession of the ages. Of each and all of them it must be said in Ariosto's words, "Nature made him, and then broke the mould". Yet if we seek Michelangelo's affinities, we find them in Lucretius and Beethoven, not in Sophocles and Mozart. He belongs to the genus of deep, violent, colossal, passionately striving natures; not, like Raffaello, to the smooth, serene, broad, exquisitely finished, calmly perfect tribe.—J. ADDINGTON SYMONDS, *Life of Michelangelo Buonarroti, Vol. II.*

The stern, sad spirit of Michael Angelo.—F. W. FARRAR, *Social and Present-Day Questions.*

JOHN STUART MILL.

English Philosopher and Economist: 1806-1873.

Mr. Mill's more popular writings are remarkable for a lofty earnestness, more stern than genial, and which rather flagellates or shames men out of wrong, than allures them to the right. Perhaps this is the style most natural to a man of deep moral convictions, writing in an age and in a state of society like that in which we live. But it seems, also, to be congenial to the character of his own mind; for he appears, on most occasions, much more strongly alive to the evil of what is evil in our destiny, than to the good of what is good. He rather warns us against the errors that tend to make us miserable, than affords us the belief that by any means we can attain to much positive happiness. He does not hope enough from human nature—something despondent and unelevating clings round his estimate of its powers. He saddens the Present by a reference to the Past—he does not console it by any alluring anticipations of the Future ; —he rather discontents us with vice than kindles our enthusiasm for virtue.—LYTTON, *England and the English, Appendix C.*

Mill laid up in his capacious mind a variety of things; but, with all his getting, he got this special understanding—the understanding of principles. If you wanted, at any time, to commend yourself to his favourable regards, you had but to start a doctrinal discussion—to bring a new *logos* to his view. . . . Who shall sum up Mill's collective influence as an instructor in Politics, Logic, and Metaphysics ? No calculus can integrate the innumerable little pulses of knowledge and of thought that he has made to vibrate in the minds of his generation.—ALEXANDER BAIN, *John Stuart Mill : A Criticism.*

I used familiarly to call him the Saint of Rationalism, a phrase roughly and partially expressing what I now mean. Of all the motives, stings, and stimulants that reach men through their egoism in Parliament, no part could move or even touch him. His conduct and his language were, in this respect, a sermon. Again, though he was a philosopher, he was not, I think, a man of crotchets.—W. E. GLADSTONE.

He was the natural leader of Liberal thought ; not in the House, but out of it. "Saint of Rationalism," however, in Mr. Gladstone's happy phrase, he remained. He had been declared to be Adam Smith and Petrarch rolled into one ; and if he thus combined sentimentalism with the doctrines of political economy, he equally exhibited the cold clearness of the Rationalistic thinker, tempered by the emotional warmth of high moral ideas.—W. L. COURTNEY, *Life of John Stuart Mill.*

Himself pervadingly an intellectual machine, Mr. Mill seems to have interest in his countrymen only to the extent that they can be made intellectual machines too. His faith appears to be boundless in the omnipotence of the alphabet : his test of merit and of fitness is wholly mental. . . . Mr. Mill, by the inexorable directness and the faultless limpidity of his speech, forces back to reality the brain which has been bewildered by a vapoury, chaotic pictorialism. He is the Priessnitz of Literature, and much is a Priessnitz of Literature needed when there has been a reckless revel in furibond and fantastic phrases. If, then, you know any one who has been ensnared of the Carlyle apes—for whom, however, the great and good man they outrageously imitate should not be held responsible—send him to the physician Mill. . . . The physician Mill, though he gives us water in abundance, furnishes us with rather scanty fare ; and those of us who have a good appetite are obliged to go elsewhither. . . . The works of Mr. Mill, masterpieces under more than one aspect, reveal to us a mind cultivated, disciplined to excess ; a mind trained like the body of a boxer, *sweated* like the body of a jockey. Never was a more perfect thinking and calculating machine. And by thinking and calculating machines alone has Mr. Mill in his studies been attracted. If ever Mr. Mill deserts for a moment his own province, it is from an artificial taste.—WILLIAM MACCALL, *The Newest Materialism.*

JOHN MILTON.

English Poet and Writer : 1608-1674.

Three poets, in three distant ages born,
Greece, Italy and England did adorn.
The first in loftiness of thought surpass'd ;
The next in majesty : in both the last.
The force of Nature could no further go ;
To make a third she joined the former two.
> —DRYDEN, *Under Mr. Milton's Picture.*

I ope thy pages, Milton, and, behold,
Thy spirit meets me in the haunted ground !
> —*Id., The Souls of Books.*

Our wives read Milton, and our daughters plays.
> —POPE, *The First Epistle of the Second Book of Horace.*

Milton . . . with high and haughty stalks,
Unfettered in majestic numbers walks ;
No vulgar hero can his Muse engage ;
Nor earth's wide scene confine his hallow'd rage.
See ! see, he upward springs, and tow'ring high
Spurns the dull province of mortality,
Shakes heav'n's eternal throne with dire alarms,
And sets th' Almighty thunderer in arms.
Whate'er his pen describes I more than see,
Whilst ev'ry verse, array'd in majesty,
Bold, and sublime, my whole attention draws,
And seems above the critic's nicer laws.
> —ADDISON, *An Account of the Greatest English Poets.*

So mark thou Milton's name ;
And add, " Thus differs from the throng
The spirit which inform'd thy awful song,
Which bade thy potent voice protect thy country's fame ".
> —AKENSIDE, *Ode XVIII.. To the Earl of Huntingdon.*

Is not each great, each amiable Muse
Of classic ages in thy Milton met ?
A genius universal as his theme ;
Astonishing as chaos, as the bloom
Of blowing Eden fair, as heaven sublime.
> —THOMSON, *The Seasons : Summer.*

There Milton dwells : The mortal sung
Themes not presum'd by mortal tongue ;
New terrors, or new glories shine
In every page, and flying scenes divine
Surprise the wondering sense, and draw our souls along.
> —ISAAC WATTS, *The Adventurous Muse.*

Then Milton had indeed a poet's charms :
New to my taste, his Paradise surpass'd
The struggling efforts of my boyish tongue
To speak its excellence : I danced for joy.

I marvell'd much that, at so ripe an age
As twice seven years, his beauties had then first
Engaged my wonder, and admiring still,
And still admiring, with regret supposed
The joy half lost because not sooner found.
                    —COWPER, *The Task : The Winter Evening.*

Milton, whose genius had angelic wings,
And fed on manna.
                    —Id., Ibid., The Garden.

Ages elapsed ere Homer's lamp appear'd,
And ages ere the Mantuan swan was heard ;
To carry nature lengths unknown before,
To give a Milton birth, ask'd ages more.
                    —Id., Table Talk.

In Homer's craft Jock Milton thrives.
                    —BURNS, *Poem on Pastoral Poetry.*

If, fallen in evil days on evil tongues,
Milton appeal'd to the Avenger, Time,
If Time, the Avenger, execrates his wrongs,
And makes the word " Miltonic " mean *sublime*,
He deign'd not to belie his soul in songs,
Nor turn his very talent to a crime, . . .
Milton's the prince of poets—so we say ;
A little heavy, but no less divine :
An independent being in his day—
Learn'd, pious, temperate in love and wine ;
But his Life falling into Johnson's way,
We're told this great high priest of all the Nine
Was whipt at college—a harsh sire—odd spouse,
For the first Mrs. Milton left his house.
                    —BYRON, *Don Juan.*

The immortal wars which gods and angels wage,
Are they not shown in Milton's sacred page ?
His strain will teach what numbers best belong
To themes celestial told in epic song.
                    —*Id., Hints from Horace.*

He died,
Who was the Sire of an immortal strain,
Blind, old and lonely, when his country's pride,
The priest, the slave and the liberticide,
Trampled and mocked with many a loathèd rite
Of lust and blood ; he went, unterrified,
Into the gulf of death ; but his clear Sprite
Yet reigns o'er earth ; the third among the sons of light.
                    —SHELLEY, *Adonais, IV.*

Chief of organic numbers !
   Old scholar of the Spheres !
Thy spirit never slumbers,

But rolls about our ears
For ever and for ever!

. . . . .

How heavenward thou soundest!
    Live Temple of sweet noise,
And Discord unconfoundest,
    Giving Delight new joys.
And Pleasure nobler pinions:
O where are thy dominions?

—KEATS, *To Milton.*

    . . . He, that rode sublime
Upon the seraph wings of ecstasy,
The secrets of th' abyss to spy.
He pass'd the flaming bounds of Place and Time:
The living Throne, the sapphire-blaze,
Where Angels tremble, while they gaze.

—GRAY, *Progress of Poesy.*

Milton's severer shade I saw, and in reverence humbled
Gazed on that soul sublime: of passion now as of blindness
Heal'd and no longer here to Kings and to Hierarchs hostile,
He was assoil'd from taint of the fatal fruit; and in Eden
Not again to be lost, consorted and equal with Angels.

—SOUTHEY, *A Vision of Judgment: The Elder Worthies.*

            Milton's mind
Shall dwell with us, an influence and a power.

—*Id., Oliver Newman: The Voyage.*

        That mighty orb of song,
The divine Milton.

—WORDSWORTH, *The Excursion, Book I.*

Thy soul was like a star, and dwelt apart:
Thou hadst a voice whose sound was like the sea:
Pure as the naked heavens, majestic, free,
So didst thou travel on life's common way,
In cheerful godliness; and yet thy heart
The lowliest duties on herself did lay.

—*Id., London,* 1802.

And dart, like Milton, an unerring eye
Through the dim curtains of Futurity. . . .
And Milton's self (at that thrice-honoured name,
Well may we glow—as men, we share his fame)
And Milton's self, apart with beaming eye,
Planning he knows not what—that shall not die!

—ROGERS, *Human Life.*

Homer and Milton,—can we call them blind?—
Of godlike sight, the vision of the mind.

—J. G. SAXE, *The Library.*

When, where yon beech tree veil'd the soft'ning ray,
On violet banks young Milton dreaming lay.

For him the earth below, the heaven above,
  Doubled each charm in the clear glass of youth;
And the vague spirit of unsettled love
  Rov'd thro' the visions that precede the truth,
While Poesy's low voice so hymn'd thro' all
That ev'n the very air was musical.

> —LYTTON, *Milton.*

The mighty man who open'd Paradise,
Harmonious far above Homeric song,
Or any song that human ears shall hear. . . .

> —LANDOR, *To the Author of Festus.*

O mighty-mouth'd inventor of harmonies,
O skill'd to sing of Time or Eternity,
God-gifted organ-voice of England,
Milton, a name to resound for ages.

> —TENNYSON, *Milton.*

Nor shall the grateful Muse forget to tell,
That—not the least among his many claims
To deathless honour—he was Milton's friend.

> —J. R. LOWELL.

I pace the sounding sea-beach and behold
  How the voluminous billows roll and run,
  Upheaving and subsiding, while the sun
  Shines through their sheeted emerald far unrolled,
And the ninth wave, slow gathering fold by fold
  All its loose-flowing garments into one,
Plunges upon the shore, and floods the dun
  Pale reach of sands, and changes them to gold.
  So in majestic cadence rise and fall
  The mighty undulations of thy song,
  O sightless bard, England's Mæonides!
And ever and anon, high over all
  Uplifted, a ninth wave, superb and strong,
  Floods all the soul with its melodious seas.

> —LONGFELLOW, *Milton.*

              No later song
Has soar'd, as wide-winged, to the diadem'd thrones
That, in their inmost heaven, the Muses high
Set for the sons of immortality.

> —F. T. PALGRAVE, *The Poet's Euthanasia.*

High the chant of Paradise and Hell
Rose, when the soul of Milton gave it wings.

> —SWINBURNE, *A New Year's Ode to Victor Hugo.*

With whatever faculties we are born, and to whatever studies our genius may direct us, *studies* they must still be. I am persuaded that Milton did not write his *Paradise Lost*, nor Homer his *Iliad*, nor Newton his *Principia*, without immense labour.—COWPER.

Milton was a great poet; but a bad divine, and a miserable politician.— JOHN WILSON, *Noctes Ambrosianæ, Vol. I.*

What moral man in majestic wisdom of moral imagination—that is, "in the vision and the faculty *divine*," ever equalled Milton?—JOHN WILSON, *Noctes Ambrosianæ, Vol. IV*.

The worst you can say of Milton is that he was a regicide; yet was he, like his own Adam, the first of men.—*Id., Essays: The Loves of the Poets*.

Milton spoke historical pictures in the *Paradise Lost.*—SIR ARCHIBALD ALISON, *Essays: The British School of Painting*.

The genius of Milton, more particularly in respect to its span in immensity, calculated him by a sort of birth-right for such an argument as the *Paradise Lost*. He had an exquisite passion for what is properly, in the sense of ease and pleasure, poetical luxury; and with that, it appears to me, he would fain have been content, if he could, so doing, preserve his self-respect and feeling of duty performed; but there was working in him, as it were, that same sort of thing which operates in the great world to the end of a prophecy's being accomplished. Therefore he devoted himself rather to the ardours than the pleasures of song, solacing himself, at intervals, with cups of old wine; and those are, with some exceptions, the finest parts of the poem. With some exceptions; for the spirit of mounting and adventure can never be unfruitful nor unrewarded. Had he not broken through the clouds which envelop so deliciously the Elysian fields of verse, and committed himself to the extreme, we should never have seen Satan as described. . . . Milton has put vales in Heaven and Hell with the very utter affection and yearning of a great Poet. It is a sort of Delphic abstraction, a beautiful thing made more beautiful by being reflected and put in a mist. . . . Milton in many instances pursues his imagination to the utmost, he is " sagacious of his quarry," he sees beauty on the wing, pounces upon it, and gorges it to the producing his essential verse.—KEATS in HOUGHTON'S *Life and Letters of John Keats*.

Milton almost requires a solemn service of music to be played before you enter upon him. But he brings his music, to which who listens had need bring docile thoughts, and purged ears.—LAMB, *Essays of Elia and Eliana*.

A purpose of the same nature is answered by the higher literature, *viz.*, the literature of power. What do you learn from *Paradise Lost?* Nothing at all. What do you learn from a cookery-book? Something new—something that you did not know before, in every paragraph. But would you therefore put the wretched cookery-book on a higher level of estimation than the divine poem? What you owe to Milton is not any knowledge, of which a million separate items are still but a million of advancing steps on the same earthly level; what you owe, is *power*, that is, exercise and expansion to your own latent capacity of sympathy with the infinite, where every pulse and each separate influx is a step upwards —a step ascending as upon a Jacob's ladder from earth to mysterious altitudes above the earth. *All* the steps of knowledge, from first to last, carry you further on the same plane, but could never raise you one foot above your ancient level of earth: whereas, the very *first* step in power is a flight—is an ascending movement into another element where earth is forgotten.—DE QUINCEY, *Leaders in Literature*.

I think that it would take many Newtons to make one Milton. . . . John Milton himself is in every line of the *Paradise Lost*. . . . Milton is the deity of prescience; he stands *ab extra*, and drives a fiery chariot and four, making the horses feel the iron curb which holds them in.—S. T. COLERIDGE, *Table Talk*.

In Milton there may be traced obligations to several minor English poets: but his genius had too great a supremacy to belong to any school. . . . If we call diction the garb of thought, Milton in his style may be said to wear the costume of sovereignty.—CAMPBELL.

As the needle turns away from the rising sun, from the meridian, from the occidental, from regions of fragrancy and gold and gems, and moves with unerring impulse to the frosts and deserts of the north, so Milton and some few others, in politics, philosophy, and religion, walk through the busy multitude, wave aside the importunate trader, and, after a momentary oscillation from eternal agency, are found in the twilight and in the storm, pointing with certain index to the pole-star of immutable truth.—LANDOR.

Milton is one of the three great Christian poets who were to the theogony of the Middle Ages what Homer was to the Olympus of paganism. . . . The immortal name of the great poet Milton, the English Dante.—LAMARTINE, *Celebrated Characters (transl.), Vol. II.*

Goethe compares the joy of the poet to the joy of the bird; the bird sings because it is its nature to sing, not because it is to be praised for singing. But Milton's joy was high beyond the bird's, it was the joy of a sublime human soul, the joy of lifting himself above man's judgment, as a great soul ever seeks to do, high above the evil days, the dangers and the darkness, with which he was encompassed round.—LYTTON, *Essays: Posthumous Reputation.*

I suspect that every great writer of a nation a little corrupts its tongue. His knowledge suggests additions and graces from other tongues: his genius applies and makes them popular. Milton was the greatest poet of our country, and there is scarcely an English idiom which he has not violated, or a foreign one which he has not borrowed.—*Id., England and the English.*

We turn for a short time from the topics of the day, to commemorate, in all love and reverence, the genius and virtues of John Milton, the poet, the statesman, the philosopher, the glory of English literature, the champion and the martyr of English liberty. . . . Milton did not strictly belong to any of the classes which we have described. He was not a Puritan. He was not a free thinker. He was not a Royalist. In his character the noblest qualities of every party were combined in harmonious union. From the parliament and from the court, from the conventicle and from the Gothic cloister, from the gloomy and sepulchral circles of the Roundheads, and from the Christmas revel of the hospital cavalier, his nature selected and drew to itself whatever was great and good, while it rejected all the base and pernicious ingredients by which those finer elements were defiled. . . . It is to be regretted that the prose writings of Milton should, in our time, be so little read. As compositions, they deserve the attention of every man who wishes to become acquainted with the full power of the English language. They abound with passages compared with which the finest declamations of Burke sink into insignificance. They are a perfect field of cloth of gold. The style is stiff with gorgeous embroidery. . . . It is, to borrow his own majestic language, " a sevenfold chorus of hallelujahs and harping symphonies ".—MACAULAY, *Essays : Milton.*

Did you ever read *Paradise Lost ?* If not, I would advise you to read it now ; for it is the best commentary that I know on the Prometheus. There was a great resemblance between the genius of Æschylus and the genius of Milton ; and this appears most strikingly in those two wonderful creations of the imagination, Prometheus and Satan. I do not believe that Milton borrowed Satan from the Greek drama. For though he was an excellent scholar after the fashion of his time, Æschylus was, I suspect, a little beyond him.—*Id., Life and Letters, Vol. II.*

But when we adhere to the ideal of the poet, we have our difficulties even with Milton and Homer. Milton is too literary, and Homer too literal and historical.—EMERSON, *Essays : The Poet.*

Milton, who was the stair or high table-land to let down the English genius from the summits of Shakespeare.—*Id., English Traits : Literature.*

In delineating Milton's character as a poet, we are saved the necessity of looking far for its distinguishing attributes. His name is almost identified with sublimity. He is in truth the sublimest of men. He rises, not by effort or discipline, but by a native tendency and a godlike instinct, to the contemplation of objects of grandeur and awfulness. He always moves with a conscious energy. There is no subject so vast or terrific as to repel or intimidate him. The overpowering grandeur of a theme kindles and attracts him. . . . We should not fulfil our duty were we not to say one word on what has been justly celebrated, the harmony of Milton's versification. His numbers have the prime charm of expressiveness. They vary with, and answer to, the depth, or tenderness, or sublimity of his conceptions, and hold intimate alliance with the soul. Like Michael Angelo, in whose hands the marble was said to be flexible, he bends our language, which foreigners reproach with hardness, into whatever forms the subject demands. All the treasures of sweet and solemn sound are at his command. Words, harsh and discordant in the writings of less gifted men, flow through his poetry in a full stream of harmony. This power over language is not to be ascribed to Milton's musical ear. It belongs to the soul.—W. E. CHANNING, *On the Character and Writings of Milton.*

Milton is saved from making total shipwreck of his large-utteranced genius on the desolate Noman's Land of a religious epic only by the lucky help of Satan and his colleagues, with whom, as foiled rebels and republicans, he cannot conceal his sympathy. . . . Milton sets everywhere his little pitfalls of bookish association for the memory. I know that Milton's manner is very grand. It is slow, it is stately, moving as if in triumphal procession, with music, with historic banners, with spoils from every time and every region ; and captive epithets, like huge Sicambrians, thrust their broad shoulders between us and the thought whose pomp they decorate.—J. R. LOWELL, *Among My Books.*

Milton glows with orient light. One might almost fancy that he had gazed himself blind, and had then been raised to the sky, and there stood and waited, like " blind Orion hungering for the morn ". So abundantly

had he stored his mind with visions of natural beauty, that, when all without became dark, he was still most rich in his inward treasure, and " Ceast
not to wander where the Muses haunt clear spring, or shady grove, or
sunny hill ". . . . When Milton lost his eyes, Poetry lost hers.—J. C.
HARE, *Guesses at Truth.*

I do not know any one who makes us feel more than Milton does the
grandeur of the ends which we ought to keep always before us, and therefore our own pettiness and want of courage and nobleness in pursuing them.
I believe he failed to discern many of the intermediate relations which
God has established between Himself and us; but I know no one who
teaches us more habitually that disobedience to the Divine will is the seat
of all misery to men.—F. D. MAURICE, *The Friendship of Books.*

Milton's diction is the elaborated outcome of all the best words of all
antecedent poetry, not by a process of recollected reading and storage, but
by the same mental habit by which we learn to speak our mother tongue.
Only, in the case of the poet, the vocabulary acquired has a new meaning
superadded to the words, from the occasion on which they have been
previously employed by others. . . . If Milton resembled a Roman republican in the severe and stoic elevation of his character, he also shared
the aristocratic intellectualism of the classical type. He is in marked
contrast to the levelling hatred of excellence, the Christian trades-unionism
of the model Catholic of the mould of S. Francis de Sales, whose maxim
of life is *marchons avec la troupe de nos frères et compagnons, doucement,
paisiblement, et aimablement.*—MARK PATTISON, *Life of Milton.*

Milton—a man than whom England never produced another more
worthy of her pride—a man raised by his endowments almost above the
level and the lot of humanity—in whom a genius that resembled inspiration,
and attainments which might have been thought too various and extensive
for human capacity, were sanctified by the grace of God, and devoted to
the freedom, the advancement, and the happiness of man. – C. R. EDMONDS,
Life of John Milton.

Milton played on his metre like his organ. He brings out with a daring
finger every grand and various note, sometimes—with wonderful effect—
striking a momentary crash of discord into the full swell of the music.—
R. A. WILMOTT, *Advantages of Literature.*

Had it been otherwise—had that pure, courageous youth, who, two hundred and thirty years ago, stood dubious by the threshold, but crossed the
black marble line and advanced into the sacred vestibule and the aisles
beyond—what might the result not have been ! Milton, as an ecclesiastic,
would have been Milton still; such an archbishop, mitred or unmitred, as
England has never had. The tread of such a foot across the sacred floor,
what it might have trampled into extinction; the magnanimity of such a
soul, breathed into the counsels of the Church through that approaching
revolution when Church as well as State was to be riven asunder for
repair, how it might have affected these counsels while yet the future
model was in doubt, and only the site and the materials solicited the
architect ! But it was not so to be.—DAVID MASSON, *Life of Milton, Vol. I.*

It is possible to dislike Milton. Men have been found able to do so, and
women too; amongst these latter his daughters, or one of them at least,
must even be included. But there is nothing sickening about his biography,

for it is the life of one who early consecrated himself to the service of the highest Muses, who took labour and intent study as his portion, who aspired himself to be a noble poem, who, Republican though he became, is what Carlyle called him, the moral king of English literature.—AUGUSTINE BIRRELL, *Obiter Dicta, Second Series.*

COMTE DE MIRABEAU.

French Orator and Revolutionist: 1749-1791.

That Mirabeau understood how to act with others, and by others—this was his genius, this was his originality, this was his greatness.—GOETHE.

"There is but one step," roared Mirabeau from his stormy tribune, "from the Capitol to the Tarpeian Rock!" And on that step stood, from the taking of the Bastille till the fall of Robespierre, all the philosophers, legislators, dreamers; with the certainty that for him who lost the Capitol, there was no destiny but the rock. . . . There is indeed, to a vulgar gaze, something almost captivating in this Mirabeau of the Mob, despite his horrible excesses. He was free from all personal vindictiveness, he was not naturally cruel; he spilt blood in torrents, but always for a purpose and from policy; he could not be sanguinary in detail; he had no coward in him, no envy. About his character was a large rough good-nature; he was affectionate and loyal to those he loved (for he did love and he was loved, this master butcher who could order the massacre of 2,000 prisoners in cold blood). He had no religion, even of atheism, for atheism is not like scepticism, lukewarm and hesitating, but is ardent and intolerant in its creed; he laughed at the Goddess of Reason: he had therefore no vestige of hypocrisy or cant. Frankly he confessed his total infidelity, candidly he owned his theories of Revolutions, " things not made with rose-water," in which (as he said) " the boldest scoundrel was the most successful actor ". He was profligate, lustful, and corrupt in money matters, but he was all these so undisguisedly, that the vulgar, who like a frank villain, ranked them amongst his merits.—LYTTON, *Essays: The Reign of Terror.*

MARY RUSSELL MITFORD.

English Poet and Novelist: 1786-1855.

North. . . . " Miss Mitford has not, in my opinion, either the pathos or humour of Washington Irving; but she excels him in vigorous conception of character, and in the truth of her pictures of English life and manners. Her writings breathe a sound, pure, and healthy morality, and are pervaded by a genuine rural spirit—the spirit of merry England. Every line bespeaks the lady."

Shepherd. " I admire Miss Mitford just excessively. I dinna wunner at her being able to write sae weel as she does about drawing-rooms wi' sofas and settees, and about the fine folk in them seein' themsels in lookin'-glasses frae tap to tae; but what puzzles the like o' me, is her pictures o' poachers, and tinklers, and pottery-trampers, and ither ne'er-do-weels, and o' huts and hovels without riggin' by the wayside, and the cottages o' honest puir men, and byres, and barns, and stack-yards; and merry-makin's at winter-ingles, and courtship aneath trees, and at the gable-ends o' farmhouses, atween lads and lasses as laigh in life as the servants in her father's ha'. That's the puzzle, and that's the praise. But ae word explains a'—Genius—Genius—wull a' the metaphizzians in the warld ever expound that mysterious monysyllable ?"—JOHN WILSON, *Noctes Ambrosianæ, Vol. I.*

JEAN BAPTISTE MOLIÈRE.

French Dramatist and Poet : 1622-1673.

How Molière's scene,
Chastis'd and regular, with well-judg'd wit,
Not scatter'd wild, and native humour, grac'd,
Was life itself.
—THOMSON, *Liberty.*

Here Molière, first of comic wits, excell'd
Whate'er Athenian theatres beheld ;
By keen, yet decent, satire skill'd to please,
With morals mirth uniting, strength with ease.
—LORD LYTTLETON, *To the Rev. Dr. Ayscough.*

Molière is perhaps, of all French writers, the one whom his country has most uniformly admired, and in whom her critics are most unwilling to acknowledge faults.—HALLAM, *Literature of the Middle Ages, Vol. IV.*

Molière is one of that rarest order of poets whose very faults become sacred in the eyes of admirers. He is not only revered as a master, but beloved by us as a friend. Of all the French dramatists, he is the only one whose genius is as conspicuous to foreign nations as it is to his own. Like Shakespeare he is for all time and for all races. A piercing observer of the society around him, he selects from that society types the least socially conventional. His very men of fashion are never out of the fashion.—LYTTON, *Essays : Knowledge of the World.*

Of Molière I think very differently. Living in the blindest period of the world's history, in the most luxurious city, and the most corrupted court, of the time, he yet manifests through all his writings an exquisite natural wisdom ; a capacity for the most simple enjoyment ; a high sense of all nobleness, honour, and purity, variously marked throughout his slighter work, but distinctly made the theme of his two perfect plays—the *Tartuffe* and *Misanthrope ;* and in all that he says of art or science he has an un-erring instinct for what is useful and sincere, and uses his whole power to defend it, with as keen a hatred of everything affected and vain.— RUSKIN, *Modern Painters, Vol. III.*

COUNT VON MOLTKE.

Prussian Field-Marshal : 1800-1891.

A Moltke in council, on the eve of a great battle which is to shift the centre of gravity of our western political system, is only acting on a maxim of practical wisdom that requires to be applied with as much discrimina-tion, tact, and delicacy, by the provost of a provincial town, planning a water-bill or a tax for the improvement of the city.—J. STUART BLACKIE, *On Self-Culture.*

MICHEL EYQUÈM DE MONTAIGNE.

French Philosopher and Essayist: 1533-1592.

For't has been held by many, that
As Montaigne, playing with his cat,
Complains she thought him but an ass,
Much more she would Sir Hudibras.
—SAMUEL BUTLER, *Hudibras, Part I., Canto I.*

I love to pour out all myself, as plain
As downright Shippen, or as old Montaigne:
In them, as certain to be lov'd as seen,
The soul stood forth, nor kept a thought within.
—POPE, *Satires and Epistles of Horace imitated.*

Montaigne is the earliest classical writer in the French language, the first whom a gentleman is ashamed not to have read.—HALLAM, *Literature of the Middle Ages, Vol. II.*

Montaigne is the frankest and honestest of all writers. His French freedom runs into grossness; but he has anticipated all censure by the bounty of his own confessions. In his time, books were written to one sex only, and almost all were written in Latin; so that, in a humorist, a certain nakedness of statement was permitted, which our manners of a literature addressed equally to both sexes do not allow. But though a Biblical plainness, coupled with a most uncanonical levity, may shut his pages to many sensitive readers, yet the offence is superficial.—EMERSON, *Montaigne, or the Sceptic.*

The Father of Modern Essay. . . . Montaigne is the antipodes to Shakespeare, inasmuch as he is intensely subjective, obtrusively personal. So, as a narrator of his own personal experiences and opinions, he ought to have been; just as Shakespeare, where a dramatist, could not have been obtrusively personal, even where writing his own most haunting thoughts. But where Montaigne is to be likened to Shakespeare is in the similar result at which through so antagonistic a process he arrives. Though apparently only studying himself, he himself has a nature so large that it comprehends mankind. Never did one man in his egotism more faithfully represent the greatest number of attributes common to the greatest number of men. His grasp comprehends materials for thought that it might task a thousand sages to work up into systems. His fineness of vision seizes on subtleties in character and mysteries, in feeling that might open new views of the human heart to a thousand poets.—LYTTON, *Essays: Knowledge of the World.*

CHARLES DE SECONDAT, BARON DE MONTESQUIEU.

French Jurist and Philosopher: 1689-1755.

Montesquieu—an author who frequently appears profound when he is only paradoxical, and seems to have studied with great success the art of hiding a desultory and fantastical style of reasoning in imposing aphorisms and epigrams of considerable effect.—LORD JEFFREY, *Essays.*

Montesquieu errs, because he has a fine thing to say, and is resolved to say it. If the phenomena which lie before him will not suit his purpose, all history must be ransacked. If nothing established by authentic testimony can be racked or chipped to suit his Procrustean hypothesis, he puts up with some monstrous fable about Siam, or Bantam, or Japan, told by writers compared with whom Lucian and Gulliver were veracious, liars by a double right, as travellers and as Jesuits.—MACAULAY, *Essays: Machiavelli.*

THOMAS MOORE.

Irish Poet: 1779-1852.

My boat is on the shore,
And my bark is on the sea;
But before I go, Tom Moore,
Here's a double health to thee!
—BYRON, *To Thomas Moore.*

From her wilds Ierne sent
  The sweetest lyrist of her saddest wrong,
And love taught grief to fall like music from his tongue.
—SHELLEY, *Adonais, XXX.*

The falling of fountains—the slight summer rain—
The voice of the dove, were less sweet than thy strain ;
Till stirred with delight, would her exquisite wings
Beat time on the west wind, to echo thy strings. . . .
Thy song has its sunshine—perhaps to that sun
It owes half the loveliest wreaths it has won.
It still lofty hopes and sad thoughts has betrayed—
Where on earth is the sunshine that flingeth no shade ?
—L. E. LANDON, *Thomas Moore, Esq.*

The land where the staff of Saint Patrick was planted,
Where the shamrock grows green from the cliffs to the shore,
The land of fair maidens and heroes undaunted,
Shall wreathe her bright harp with the garlands of Moore!
—OLIVER WENDELL HOLMES, *For the Moore Centennial.*

Moore has a peculiarity of talent, or rather talents—poetry, music, voice, all his own; and an expression in each, which never was, nor will be, possessed by another. But he is capable of still higher flights in poetry. By the by, what humour, what—everything, in the "Post-Bag!" There is nothing Moore may not do, if he will but seriously set about it. In society, he is gentlemanly, gentle, and altogether more pleasing than any individual with whom I am acquainted. For his honour, principle, and independence, his conduct to . . . speaks "trumpet tongued". He has but one fault—and that one I daily regret—he is not *here.*—BYRON in MOORE's *Life of Byron.*

Mr. Moore's poetry is the thornless rose, its touch is velvet, its hue vermilion, and its graceful form is cast in beauty's mould.—LORD JEFFREY, *Essays.*

As a satirist Moore stands at the head of his class, and as constructor and embellisher of metrical romances he is the cleverest of the poets. It is, in truth, a reproach to him to have been too clever, to have been too little of an inspired bard, and too much of a man of letters. He could have excelled in anything demanded by the taste of his day; the one distinctively poetical endowment which he really possessed was an inexhaustible fount of melody. . . . Intellectually, Moore's defect is a certain smallness. He has excellent sense and spirit, but when measured, even by himself, against any contemporary of much distinction, he invariably appears the shorter. . . . If he was less distinctively a poet than a man of letters, the same may be said of his contemporary, adversary, and yet in many respects counterpart, Robert Southey. The poetry of both survives, and will survive, yet their better title to fame is their brilliant versatility in many and various fields of literature.—RICHARD GARNETT, *Introduction to " Thomas Moore : Anecdotes "*.

Of Moore's character not much need be said, nor need what is said be otherwise than favourable. Not only to modern tastes, but to the sturdier tastes of his own day, and even of the days immediately before his, there was a little too much of the parasite and the hanger-on about him. It is easy to say that a man of his talents, when he had once obtained a start, might surely have gone his own way and lived his own life, without taking up the position of a kind of superior gamekeeper or steward at rich men's gates. But race, fashion, and a good many other things have to be taken into account; and it is fair to Moore to remember that he was, as it were from the first, bound to the chariot-wheels of "the great," and could hardly liberate himself from them without churlishness and violence. Moreover it cannot possibly be denied by any fair critic that if he accepted to some extent the awkward position of led-poet, he showed in it as much independence as was compatible with the function.—SAINTSBURY, *Essays in English Literature*.

SIR THOMAS MORE.

English Statesman : 1480-1535.

Cromwell. " The next is, that Sir Thomas More is chosen
Lord Chancellor in your place."
Wolsey. " That's somewhat sudden :
But he's a learnèd man. May he continue
Long in his highness' favour, and do justice
For truth's sake, and his conscience; that his bones,
When he has run his course and sleeps in blessings,
May have a tomb of orphans' tears wept on them."
—SHAKSPERE, *King Henry VIII., Act III., Scene II.*

Where learnèd More and Gardiner I met,
Men in those times immatchable for wit,
Able that were the dullest spirit to whet,
And did my humour excellently fit.
—DRAYTON, *Legend of Thomas Cromwell, Earl of Essex.*

In statesmen thou,
And patriots fertile. Thine a steady More,
Who, with a generous, though mistaken zeal,

Withstood a brutal tyrant's useful rage,
Like Cato firm, like Aristides just,
Like rigid Cincinnatus nobly poor,
A dauntless soul erect, who smil'd on death.
                        —Thomson, *The Seasons : Summer.*

            Unsoftened, undismayed
By aught that mingled with the tragic scene
Of pity or fear; and More's gay genius played
With the inoffensive sword of native wit,
Than the bare axe more luminous and keen.
                        —Wordsworth, *Apology.*

When we reflect that Sir Thomas More was ready to die for the doctrine of transubstantiation, we cannot but feel some doubt whether the doctrine of transubstantiation may not triumph over all opposition. More was a man of eminent talents. He had all the information on the subject that we have, or that, while the world lasts, any human being will have. The text, " This is my body," was in his New Testament as it is in ours. The absurdity of the literal interpretation was as great and as obvious in the sixteenth century as it is now. No progress that science has made, or will make, can add to what seems to us the overwhelming force of the argument against the real presence. We are, therefore, unable to understand why what Sir Thomas More believed respecting transubstantiation may not be believed to the end of time by men equal in abilities and honesty to Sir Thomas More. But Sir Thomas More is one of the choice specimens of human wisdom and virtue; and the doctrine of transubstantiation is a kind of proof charge. A faith which stands that test will stand any test.—Macaulay, *Essays: Von Ranke.*

No estimate of More's life would be satisfactory which did not consider his position and his influence in relation to the great movements of his age. Posterity will here rank him at least as highly as did his contemporaries. No one who reverences the heritage of faith bequeathed to the Christian Church will remember him without gratitude. He was placed suddenly in face of a critical question. He answered it as his successors in the English Church would not now answer. But it would be difficult to find in his writings any formal statement of doctrine which the English Church since his day has ever formally abandoned. It would be idle indeed to dispute with Roman hagiologists their right to revere him as a martyr of their own; but no true theological estimate would deny that he belongs to the historic and continuous Church of England. A close study of his religious writings, as of his life, shows that More was a saint of whom England may still be proud.—W. H. Hutton, *Life of Sir Thomas More.*

William Morris.

English Poet: 1834-1896.

Morris, our sweet and simple Chaucer's child,
Dear heritor of Spenser's tuneful reed,
With soft and sylvan pipe hast oft beguiled
The weary soul of man in troublous need,

And from the far and flowerless fields of ice
Hast brought fair flowers to make an earthly paradise.
—OSCAR WILDE, *The Garden of Eros.*

Glory lends unto thy name
All the lustre that is fame ; . . .
God such singers wills to us,
High above the world's poor fuss
To lift up our rarer thought
Where the airs of heaven are caught, ...
Lo, a new creation thou
Willest, wondrous singer, now,
Now and always, while go by
Generations born to die ;
Thou, Columbus, from the night
Hast a new world sunned to sight,
Peopled full of shapes that awe,
Kin to those that Homer saw ;
Brother thou, the fit eye sees,
Unto blind Mæonides : . . .
Life with Spenser through the years,
Virgil, Milton, thy high peers ;
In our memory shalt thou dwell
When of Dante's Dream we tell. . . .
—W. C. BENNETT, *To William Morris (written in " Sigurd
the Volsung ").*

William Morris has a sunny slope of Parnassus all to himself.—AUGUS-
TINE BIRRELL, *Obiter Dicta, First Series.*

J. C. W. T. MOZART.

German Musical Composer : 1756-1791.

Such multitudes of heavenly strains
As from the kings of sound are blown,
Mozart, Beethoven, Mendelssohn.
—MATTHEW ARNOLD, *Epilogue to Lessing's Laocoön.*

The bewitching melody of Mozart . . . will captivate mankind to the
end of the world.—SIR ARCHIBALD ALISON, *Essays : The British Theatre.*

True composition is inexplicable. No one can explain how the notes
of a Mozart melody, or the folds of a piece of Titian's drapery, produce
their essential effects on each other. If you do not feel it, no one can by
reasoning make you feel it.—RUSKIN, *Modern Painters, Vol. V.*

Music could no longer be called a *terra incognita.* When Mozart
died, all its great mines, as far as we can see, had at least been opened.
—H. R. HAWEIS, *Music and Morals.*

NAPOLEON I.

Emperor of the French : 1769-1821.

I grieved for Bonaparte, with a vain
And an unthinking grief ! for, who aspires

To genuine greatness but from just desires,
And knowledge such as *he* could never gain ?

—WORDSWORTH, 1801.

'Tis done--but yesterday a King !
And arm'd with Kings to strive—
And now thou art a nameless thing :
So abject—yet alive !
Is this the man of thousand thrones,
Who strew'd our earth with hostile bones,
And can he thus survive ?
Since he, miscall'd the Morning Star,
Nor man nor fiend hath fallen so far.

—BYRON, *Napoleon.*

He teaches them the lesson taught so long,
So oft, so vainly—learn to do no wrong !
A single step into the right had made
This man the Washington of worlds betray'd :
A single step into the wrong has given
His name a doubt to all the winds of heaven ;
The reed of Fortune, and of thrones the rod,
Of Fame the Moloch or the demigod ;
His country's Cæsar, Europe's Hannibal,
Without their decent dignity of fall.

—*Id., The Age of Bronze.*

" Fall'n, as Napoleon fell."—I felt my cheek
Alter, to see the shadow pass away
Whose grasp had left the giant world so weak.

—SHELLEY, *The Triumph of Life.*

Such was the danger when that Man of Blood
Burst from the iron Isle, and brought again,
Like Satan rising from the sulphurous flood,
His impious legions to the battle plain.

—SOUTHEY, *The Poet's Pilgrimage : The Journey.*

You, the Earth-shakers from whose right hands, war
Far, as from Jove's the thunderbolt, obey ;
Gaul's sceptic Cæsar had his guardian star,
Stout Cromwell's iron creed its chosen day,
'Tis in proportion as men's lives are great
That, fates themselves,—they glass the shades of fate.

—LYTTON, *Forebodings.*

—Be a Napoleon, and yet disbelieve—
Why, the man's mad, friend, take his light away !
What's the vague good o' the world, for which you dare
With comfort to yourself blow millions up ?

—ROBERT BROWNING, *Bishop Blougram's Apology.*

What strange tidings from that Anakim of anarchy—Buonaparte ! Ever
since I defended my bust of him at Harrow against the rascally time-
servers, when the war broke out in 1803, he has been a " Héros de Roman "
of mine—on the Continent ; I don't want him here. But I don't like those

same flights—leaving of armies, etc., etc. I am sure when I fought for his bust at school, I did not think he would run away from himself.—BYRON in MOORE'S "*Life of Byron*".

Napoleon will live when Paris is in ruins; his deeds will survive the dome of the Invalides: no man can show the tomb of Alexander!—SIR ARCHIBALD ALISON.

There never were monarchs who mowed down the population and wasted the resources of France like Napoleon and Louis XIV.; but as long as they were successful, and kept open the career of elevation to the people, they commanded their universal attachment. It was when they grew unfortunate, and could call them only to discharge the mournful duties of adversity, that they became the objects of universal execration. The revolution has ever been true to its polar star—worldly success.—*Id., Essays: The Fall of the Throne of the Barricades.*

Napoleon said truly, that he was so long successful because he always marched with the opinions of five millions of men.—*Id., Ibid.: The Copyright Question.*

No man ever surpassed the French Emperor in the clearness of his ideas, or the stretch of his glance into the depths of futurity. But he was often misled by the vigour of his conceptions, and mistook the dazzling brilliancy of his own genius for the steady light of truth.—*Id., Ibid.: Wellington.*

Bonaparte—a name that *will* go down to posterity, and of whom it is not yet clear, perhaps, how posterity will judge. The greatest of conquerors, in an age when great conquests appeared no longer possible—the most splendid of usurpers, where usurpation had not been heard of for centuries—who entered in triumph almost all the capitals of continental Europe; and led, at last, to his bed, the daughter of her proudest sovereign —who set up kings and put them down at his pleasure, and for sixteen years defied alike the swords of his foreign enemies and the daggers of his domestic factions!—LORD JEFFREY, *Essays.*

What a fine iron binding Buonaparte had round his face, as if it had been cased in steel!—HAZLITT, *Table Talk.*

Buonaparte was only above his competitors, but under his age!—S. T. COLERIDGE, *Table Talk.*

Napoleon Buonaparte, certainly the most extraordinary person who has appeared in modern times, and to whom, in some respects, no parallel can be found, if we search the whole annals of the human race. . . . It is quite certain that the mighty genius of Napoleon was of the highest order; he was one of the greatest masters of the art of war; he is to be ranked among the generals of the highest class, if indeed there be any but Hannibal who can be placed on a level with him.—LORD BROUGHAM, *Statesmen of the Time of George III., Vol. III.*

It is very true that I have said that I considered Napoleon's presence in the field equal to forty thousand men in the balance. This is a very loose way of talking; but the idea is a very different one from that of his presence at a battle being equal to a reinforcement of forty thousand men.—DUKE OF WELLINGTON.

Napoleon has words in him which are like Austerlitz Battles. . . . Napoleon does by no means seem to me so great a man as Cromwell. His enormous victories which reached over all Europe, while Cromwell abode mainly in our little England, are but as the high *stilts* on which the man is seen standing; the stature of the man is not altered thereby. I find in him no such *sincerity* as in Cromwell; only a far inferior sort. No silent walking through long years, with the Awful Unnameable of this Universe; "walking with God," as he called it; and faith and strength in that alone: *latent* thought and valour, content to lie latent, then burst out as in blaze of Heaven's lightning! Napoleon lived in an age when God was no longer believed; the meaning of all Silence, Latency, was thought to be Nonentity: he had to begin not out of the Puritan Bible, but out of poor Sceptical Encyclopedies. . . .—CARLYLE, *On Heroes and Hero-Worship.*

The three names of Bonaparte, Byron and Greece suggest poetry enough for ten generations.—MAZZINI, *Life and Writings, Vol. II.*

Put Napoleon in an island prison, let his faculties find no men to act on, no Alps to climb, no stake to play for, and he would beat the air and appear stupid. Transport him to large countries, dense populations, complex interests, and antagonist power, and you shall see that the man Napoleon, bounded, that is, by such a profile and outline, is not the virtual Napoleon.—EMERSON, *Essays: History.*

Every one of the million readers of anecdotes, or memoirs, or lives of Napoleon, delights in the page, because he studies in it his own history. Napoleon is thoroughly modern, and, at the highest point of his fortunes, has the very spirit of the newspaper. He is no saint,—to use his own word, "no capuchin,"—and he is no hero in the high sense. The man in the street finds in him the qualities and powers of other men in the street. He finds him, like himself, by birth a citizen, who, by very intelligible merits, arrived at such a commanding position, that he could indulge all those tastes which the common man possesses, but is obliged to conceal and deny.—*Id., Napoleon, or the Man of the World.*

Bonaparte obeyed that law of progress to which the highest minds are peculiarly subjected; and acquisition inflamed, instead of appeasing, the spirit of dominion. He had long proposed to himself the conquest of Europe, of the world: and the title of Emperor added intenseness to this purpose. Did we not fear that by repetition we might impair the conviction which we are most anxious to impress, we would enlarge on the enormity of the guilt involved in the project of universal empire. Napoleon knew distinctly the price which he must pay for the eminence which he coveted. He knew that the path to it lay over wounded and slaughtered millions, over putrefying heaps of his fellow-creatures, over ravaged fields, smoking ruins, pillaged cities. He knew that his steps would be followed by the groans of widowed mothers and famished orphans: of bereaved friendship and despairing love; and that, in addition to this amount of misery, he would create an equal amount of crime, by multiplying indefinitely the instruments and participators of his rapine and fraud. He knew the price and resolved to pay it. . . . Henceforth, to rule was not enough for Bonaparte. He wanted to amaze, to dazzle, to overpower men's souls, by striking, bold, magnificent, and unanticipated results. To govern ever so absolutely would not have satisfied him, if he must have governed silently.

He wanted to reign through wonder and awe, by the grandeur and terror of his name, by displays of power which would rivet on him every eye, and make him the theme of every tongue. Power was his supreme object, but a power which should be gazed at as well as felt, which should strike men as a prodigy, which should shake old thrones as an earthquake, and, by the suddenness of his new creations, should awaken something of the submissive wonder which miraculous agency inspires.—W. E. CHANNING, *On the Life and Character of Napoleon Bonaparte.*

Napoleon had a great genius for war; Wellington, great military talent. —ARCHBISHOP R. C. TRENCH, *Letters and Memorials.*

Napoleon I. ruthlessly destroyed, in the municipality and the commune, the remaining depositories of public spirit, responsibility, and manhood.— W. E. GLADSTONE.

Many know man well who do not know men; many know men who do not know man. To know man well without knowing men well is to overrate the human race; to know men well without knowing man is to underrate him. Napoleon knew men well, but not man. Men he needed as tools, and man he despised. Scott, with his genial nature and broad sympathies, knew man and men equally well; and painted no less faithfully than vividly.—WILLIAM MACCALL, *The Newest Materialism.*

The first Napoleon, in his thunderous career over our western world, was a notable example of superhuman force in a human shape, without any real human greatness.—J. STUART BLACKIE, *On Self-Culture.*

I am convinced that with the perfidy and rapine of Bonaparte no peace could be made, that the struggle with him was a struggle for the independence of all nations against the armed and disciplined hordes of a conqueror as cruel and as barbarous as Attila. The outward mask of civilization Bonaparte wore, and he could use political and social ideas for the purposes of his ambition as dexterously as cannon; but in character he was a Corsican and as savage as any bandit of his isle. If utter selfishness, if the reckless sacrifice of humanity to your own interest and passions be vileness, history has no viler name.—GOLDWIN SMITH, *Three English Statesmen.*

Such a worshipper of self, ready for self's sake to deluge the world in blood and steep his conscience in crime, was Bonaparte.—F. W. FARRAR, *Social and Present-Day Questions.*

What we complain of in Napoleon Bonaparte, for instance, is not that he sought power, but that he sought it in the interests of a coarse, brutal, and essentially unmeaning personal ambition.—JOHN MORLEY, *Miscellanies, Vol. I.*

The series of Napoleon's successes is absolutely the most marvellous in history. No one can question that he leaves far behind him the Turennes, Marlboroughs, and Fredericks; and when we bring up for comparison an Alexander, a Hannibal, a Cæsar, a Charles, we find in the single point of marvellousness Napoleon surpassing them all. Every one of those heroes was born to a position of exceptional advantage. Two of them inherited thrones; Hannibal inherited a position royal in all but name; Cæsar inherited an eminent position in a great empire. But Napoleon, who rose as high as any of them, began life as an obscure provincial, almost as a

man without a country. It is this marvellousness which paralyses our judgment. We seem to see at once a genius beyond all estimate, and a fortune
utterly unaccountable. . . . The Napoleon who was *himself*, who executed
his plans with almost unlimited power, has no monument. All that he
built, at such a cost of blood and tears, was swept away before he himself
ended his short life.—Sir J. R. Seeley, *Napoleon the First.*

The Man of Miracles himself, the one *unique* man, perhaps, in the
history of the human race. Napoleon is the greatest of Frenchmen, or
the greatest of Italians, according to the fancy of his historian.—K.
Waliszewski, *Life of Peter the Great (transl.), Vol. I.*

It is very difficult, by any process of criticism, to define the impression
of splendour and of glory which the character of Achilles leaves upon the
mind. There is in him a kind of magnetic fascination, something incom-
mensurable and indescribable, a quality like that which Goethe defined
as dæmonic. They are not always the most noble or the most admirable
natures which exert this influence over their fellow-creatures. The
Emperor Napoleon and our own Byron had each, perhaps, a portion of
this Achilleian personality. Men of their stamp sway the soul by their
prestige, by their personal beauty and grandeur, by the concentrated intensity of their character, and by the fatality which seems to follow them.
To Achilles, to Alexander, to Napoleon, we cannot apply the rules of our
morality. It is, therefore, impossible for us, who must aim first at being
good citizens, careful in our generation, and subordinate to the laws of
society around us, to admire them without a reservation. Yet, after all
is said, a great and terrible glory does rest upon their heads ; and though
our sentiments of propriety may be offended by some of their actions, our
sense of what is awful and sublime is satisfied by the contemplation of
them.—J. A. Symonds, *Studies of the Greek Poets, Second Series.*

Upon many remarkable occasions Napoleon showed his contempt of
danger and how recklessly he could expose his own body when his doing
so was calculated to help him to success. He knew how to win the
imagination of Frenchmen and how with French armies to conquer ; but
he did not know how to die a hero's death. Why, oh why did he not end
his days with those gallant souls who, when everything was lost, tried in
his cause on the evening of that appalling overthrow to stem the overwhelming current of pursuit ? Why did he not die with those who died
for him upon that most eventful day of his life ? But as a patriot how
little worthy was he of all the reverence and devoted love bestowed upon
him by his brave, faithful, and loyal army ! It is as natural to die as to
be born, and it can matter little whether you fall like a soldier on the field
of battle when young and vigorous, or "sicken years away" to die in
your bed. . . . Bonaparte's march through the world was marked by the
blood-trail of tens of thousands of gallant soldiers who, had it not been for
his inordinate personal ambition, might have lived for years longer. Yet
it is not for this reason or because he wasted upon horrible war the means
of national prosperity and of individual enjoyment that men specially
loathe his memory. It is because his whole career, from childhood to
the day of his death, was one great untruth, and was made up of deceit,
treachery, and the most appalling and selfish indifference to the feelings
and wants of others—was, in fact, one great unholy deception.—Lord
Wolseley, *The Decline and Fall of Napoleon.*

The genius of war in the shape of Napoleon.—LORD ROSEBERY, *Life of Pitt.*

It is a peculiarity of great men that they have a tendency to wreck the throne on which they sit. . . . Take Napoleon—he differed from Frederic in that he did not find a throne, and had to construct one, but, being on it, one of his objects was to make it impossible for any one else to sit upon it. Combining the activity of a score of men with a mind embracing the largest questions and the smallest details, absorbing all, everything deriving light and guidance from him, so completely did he centralize everything, that had he died as Emperor his disappearance would have caused not a vacancy, but a gulf in which the whole apparatus of government would have disappeared.—*Id., Speech at the Cromwell Tercentenary, Queen's Hall, 14th Nov.,* 1899.

We have more chance of seeing the *man* Napoleon at St. Helena than at any other period of his career. In the first years of the consulate the man was revealed, but then he was undeveloped. On the throne he ceased to be human. At Elba he had no present existence; he was always in the past or the future. . . . Scavenger is a coarse word, yet it accurately represents Napoleon's first function as ruler. The volcano of the French Revolution had burned itself out. He had to clear away the cold lava ; the rubbish of past destruction ; the cinders and the scoriæ ; the fungus of corruption which had overgrown all, and was for the moment the only visible result. What he often said of the Crown of France is absolutely true of its government. " I found it in the gutter, and I picked it up on my sword's point." The gutter government he replaced by a new administrative machine, trim, pervading, and efficient ; efficient, that is to say, so long as the engineer was a man of extraordinary energy and genius. . . . Then he is a Scourge. He purges the floor of Europe with fire. As the Sword and Spirit of the Revolution, though in all the pomp of the purple, he visits the ancient monarchies, and compels them to set their houses in order. . . . Was Napoleon a good man ? The irresistible smile with which we greet the question proves, we think, not the proved iniquity, but the exceptional position of this unique personality. Ordinary measures and tests do not appear to apply to him. We seem to be trying to span a mountain with a tape. In such a creature we expect prodigious virtues and prodigious vices, all beyond our standard. We scarcely remember to have seen this question seriously asked with regard to Napoleon, though Metternich touches on it in a fashion ; it seems childish, discordant, superfluous. But asked nakedly in the ordinary sense, without reference to the circumstances of the time, it can admit but of one prompt reply. He was not, of course, good in the sense that Wilberforce or St. Francis was good. Nor was he one of the virtuous rulers : he was not a Washington or an Antonine. Somewhere or other he has said that he could not have achieved what he did had he been religious, and this is undoubtedly true. In England his name was a synonym for the author of all evil. He was, indeed, in our national judgment, a devil seven times worse than the others. But then we knew nothing at all about him. . . . To use a common vulgarism, he was not, we think, so black as he is painted. The tone of his age, the accepted and special latitude accorded to monarchs in the eighteenth century, the circumstances and temptations of his position must be taken into account. Men must judge men not absolutely but relatively, as they would themselves be judged. Circumstance, epoch, environment, training, temptation, must all be taken into account if you would test the virtues of mankind. . . . His lot was not cast in a monastery or in a pulpit. He came from Corsica a little Pagan, viewing the world as his oyster. He was reared in the life of camps and in the terrors of revolution. He was raised to rule a nation, which, in the horrors of a great convulsion, had formally renounced and practically abjured Christianity. He had to fight for his own hand against the whole world. It was breathless work which gave little time for reflection. . . . Was he a great man? That is a much simpler question, but it involves definitions. If by "great" be intended the combination of moral qualities with those of intellect, great he certainly was not. But that he was great in the sense of being extraordinary and supreme we can have no doubt. If greatness stands for natural power, for predominance, for something human beyond humanity, then Napoleon was assuredly great. Besides that indefinable spark which we call genius, he represents a combination of intellect and energy which has never perhaps been equalled, never certainly surpassed. He carried human faculty to the furthest point of which we have accurate knowledge. . . . But Napoleon lived under the modern microscope. Under the fiercest glare of scrutiny he enlarged indefinitely the limits of human conception and human possibility. Till he had lived, no one could realise that there could be so stupendous a combination of military and civil genius, such comprehension of view united to such grasp of detail, such prodigious vitality of body and mind. . . . The name of General Bonaparte—the young eagle that tore the very heart out of glory—is to our mind superior to the title of First Consul or of Emperor.—LORD ROSEBERY, *Napoleon, the Last Phase.*

HORATIO, VISCOUNT NELSON.

English Admiral : 1758-1805.

The vernal sun new life bestows
Even on the meanest flower that blows;
But vainly, vainly, may he shine
Where Glory weeps o'er NELSON's shrine.

—SIR WALTER SCOTT.

Nelson, Glory's favourite son.
—SOUTHEY, *The Lay of the Laureate : The Dream.*

Nelson was also there in the kingdom of peace, though his calling
While upon earth he dwelt, was to war and the work of destruction,
Not in him had that awful ministry deaden'd, or weaken'd
Quick compassion, and feelings that raise while they soften our nature.
Wise in council, and steady in purpose, and rapid in action,
Never thought of self from the course of his duty seduced him,
Never thought of the issue unworthily wrapt his intention,
Long shall his memory live, and while his example is cherished,
From the Queen of the Seas, the sceptre shall never be wrested.
—*Id., A Vision of Judgment : Worthies of the Georgian Age.*

The Sailor : " 'Tis there, the quarter-deck
On which brave Admiral Nelson stood—
A sight that would have roused your blood!

One eye he had, which, bright as ten,
Burnt like a fire among his men ;
Let this be land, and that be sea,
Here lay the French—and *thus* came we ! "
To Nelson, England's pride and treasure,
Her bulwark and her tower of strength.
　　　　　　—WORDSWORTH, *The Waggoner, Canto II.*

Here's to Nelson's memory !
'Tis the second time that I, at sea,
Right off Cape Trafalgar here,
Have drunk it deep in British beer.
Nelson for ever—any time
Am I his to command in prose or rhyme !
Give me of Nelson only a touch,
And I save it, be it little or much.
　　　　　　—ROBERT BROWNING, *Nationality in Drinks.*

Brave as a lion was our Nel,
And gentle as a lamb. . . .
" Not a great sinner." No, dear heart,
God grant in our death-pain,
We may have played as well our part,
And feel as free from stain.
We see the spots on such a star,
Because it burned so bright ;
But on the side next God they are
All lost in greater light.
　　　　　　—GERALD MASSEY, *Nelson.*

" Oh, brave Nelson, glorious Nelson, the liberator of Italy, the hope and tutelary angel of Naples ! "—QUEEN OF NAPLES.

My friend Nelson, whose spirit is equal to all undertakings, and whose resources are fitted to all occasions.—LORD COLLINGWOOD.

Lord Nelson was, in truth, the greatest naval officer of this or any other age or nation ; and if a veil could be drawn over the deeds at Naples, his public character might be deemed perfect.—SIR ARCHIBALD ALISON, *Epitome of History of Europe.*

The most triumphant death is that of the martyr ; the most splendid that of the hero in hour of victory ; and if the chariot and the horses of fire had been vouchsafed for Nelson's translation, he could scarcely have departed in a brighter blaze of glory. He has left us, not indeed his mantle of in-spiration, but a name and an example, which are at this hour inspiring thousands of the youth of England, a name which is our pride, and an example which will continue to be our shield and our strength.—SOUTHEY, *Life of Nelson.*

Lord Nelson was a great naval commander ; but for myself, I have not much opinion of a sea-faring life.—HAZLITT, *Table Talk.*

It is not every man who has the audacious ambition to measure the waves as a Scoresby, or to rule them as a Nelson.—LYTTON, *Essays : Knowledge of the World.*

The fame of Nelson has more than expiated the errors of his life.—
LAMARTINE, *Celebrated Characters (transl.)*, *Vol. I.*

The charm in Nelson's history is the unselfish greatness ; the assurance
of being supported to the uttermost by those whom he supports to the
uttermost.—EMERSON, *English Traits : Ability.*

No truer Englishman ever lived than Nelson. . . . Nelson was of the
same breed as Cromwell, though his shoulders were not so broad.—LESLIE
STEPHEN, *Hours in a Library*, *First Series.*

Wherever danger has to be faced or duty to be done, at cost to self, men
will draw inspiration from the name and deeds of Nelson.　Happy he who
lives to finish all his task.　The words, " I have done my duty," sealed the
closed book of Nelson's story with a truth broader and deeper than he himself could suspect.　His duty was done, and its fruit perfected. . . . To
use again St. Vincent's words, " There is but one Nelson ".—CAPT. A. T.
MAHAN, *Life of Nelson, Vol. II.*

NERO.

Emperor of Rome : 37-68.

Although that Nero were as vicious
As any send that lieth ful low adoun,
Yet he, as telleth us Suetonius,
This wide world had in subjectioun,
Both est and west, south and septentrioun.
　　　　　　　　　—CHAUCER, *The Monkes Tale.*

Like Nero, who, to raise his fancy higher
And finish the great work, set Rome on fire.
Such crimes make treason just, and might compel
Virginius, Vindex, Galba, to rebel ;
For what could Nero's self have acted worse
To aggravate the wretched nation's curse ?
　　　　　　　—GEORGE STEPNEY, *Juvenal, Satire VIII.*

　　　　Could height of power assuage
The mad excess of Nero's rage ?
Hard is the fate, when subjects find
The sword unjust to poison join'd !
　　　　　—DR. WILLIAM KING, *Nero : A Satire.*

When Nero perish'd by the justest doom,
Which ever the destroyer yet destroy'd,
Amidst the roar of liberated Rome,
Of nations freed, and the world overjoy'd,
Some hands unseen strew'd flowers upon his tomb ;
Perhaps the weakness of a heart not void
Of feeling for some kindness done, when power
Had left the wretch an uncorrupted hour.
　　　　　　　—BYRON, *Don Juan, Canto III.*

Nero is the most formidable figure of *ennui* that has ever appeared among men. The yawning monster that the ancients called Livor and the moderns call Spleen gives us this enigma to divine—Nero.—VICTOR HUGO, *William Shakespeare (transl.).*

JOHN HENRY NEWMAN.

Cardinal of the Roman Catholic Church : 1801-1890.

What are the laws of nature, not to bend
If the Church bid them ?—brother Newman asks.
Up with the Immaculate Conception, then—
On to the rack with faith !—is my advice.
            —ROBERT BROWNING, *Bishop Blougram's Apology.*

The history of our land will hereafter record the name of John Henry Newman among the greatest of our people, as a confessor for the faith, a great teacher of men, a preacher of justice, of piety, and of compassion. —CARDINAL MANNING in PURCELL'S *Life of Manning, Vol. II.*

It is hardly an overstrained inference to believe that, with that half-conscious aspiration which rises in the minds of most men, when they contemplate a life in which they recognise the embodiment of their own ideal, the John Henry Newman of those days sought to be the Ken of the nineteenth century, striving to lead the Church of England, and, through her, other Christian communities, to the doctrine and the worship of that undivided Church of the East and West, after which Ken yearned even to his dying hour.—DEAN PLUMPTRE, *Life of Thomas Ken, Vol. II.*

Newman knew well, and taught his followers, that no man can be said to *know* anything of religious importance till he has *done* something in consequence of it. So far as he imbued his party with this very practical truth he helped them to success. Whatever is *done* regularly, in the definite name of religion, drives a nail through the character, and fixes a man in his adherence to what he professes. . . . Newman has left us something to imitate, much more to avoid. Our debt to him is negative rather than positive. Not to despise God's facts, and not to be afraid of God's justice, are the two great lessons to be learned by all Englishmen, but especially by English theologians, from Newman's Anglican career. —E. A. ABBOTT, *Anglican Career of Cardinal Newman.*

If any man ever succeeded in anything, Cardinal Newman has succeeded in convincing all those who study his career with an approach to candour and discrimination, that the depth and luminousness of his conviction, that the true key to the enigma of life, is God's revelation of Himself in Christ and in His Church, are infinitely deeper in him, and more of the intimate essence of his mind and heart, than his appreciation, keen as it is, of the obstacles which stand in the way of those convictions and appear to bar the access to them. . . . No life known to me in the last century of our national history can for a moment compare with it, so far as we can judge of such deep matters, in unity of meaning and constancy of purpose. It has been carved, as it were, out of one solid block of spiritual substance, and though there may be weak and wavering lines here and there in the carving, it is not easy to detect any flaw in the material upon which the long indefatigable labour has been spent.—RICHARD H. HUTTON, *Life of Cardinal Newman.*

Far different from Keble, from my brother, from Dr. Pusey, from all the rest, was the true chief of the Catholic revival—John Henry Newman. Compared with him, they were all but as ciphers, and he the indicating number. . . . *Credo in Newmannum* was a common phrase at Oxford, and is still unconsciously the faith of nine-tenths of the English converts to Rome. . . . "Lead kindly Light" is the most popular hymn in the language. All of us, Catholic, Protestant, or such as can see their way to no positive creed at all, can here meet on common ground and join in a common prayer. . . . Two writers have affected powerfully the present generation of Englishmen. Newman is one, Thomas Carlyle is the other. But Carlyle has been at issue with all the tendencies of his age. Like a John the Baptist, he has stood alone preaching repentance in a world which is to him a wilderness. Newman has been the voice of the intellectual reaction of Europe, which was alarmed by an era of revolutions, and is looking for safety in the forsaken beliefs of the ages which it had been tempted to despise.—J. A. FROUDE, *Short Studies on Great Subjects, Vol. IV.*

Oh, Spirit of Truth, where wert thou, when the remorseless deep of superstition closed over the head of John Henry Newman, who surely deserved to be thy best loved son?—AUGUSTINE BIRRELL, *Obiter Dicta, First Series.*

Dr. Newman's style is pellucid, it is animated, it is varied; at times icy cold, it oftener glows with a fervid heat; it employs as its obedient and well-trained servant a vast vocabulary, and it does so always with the ease of the educated gentleman, who by a sure instinct ever avoids alike the ugly pedantry of the book-worm, the forbidding accents of the lawyer, and the stiff conceit of the man of scientific theory. Dr. Newman's sentences sometimes fall upon the ear like well-considered and final judgments, each word being weighed and counted out with dignity and precision; but at other times the demeanour and language of the judge are hastily abandoned, and, substituted for them, we encounter the impetuous torrent—the captivating rhetoric, the brilliant imagery, the frequent examples, the repetition of the same idea in different words, of the eager and accomplished advocate addressing men of like passions with himself. . . . Dr. Newman always aims at effect, and never misses it. He writes as an orator speaks, straight at you. His object is to convince by engaging your attention, exciting your interest, enlivening your fancy. It is not his general practice to address the pure reason. . . . Newman's books have long had a large and increasing sale. They stand on all sorts of shelves, and wherever they go a still, small voice accompanies them. They are speaking books; an air breathes from their pages.—*Id., Res Judicatæ.*

SIR ISAAC NEWTON.

English Mathematician: 1642-1727.

Nature and nature's laws lay hid in night;
God said "Let Newton be"; and all was light.
          —POPE, *Epitaph intended for Sir Isaac Newton.*

Let Newton, *pure intelligence*, from God
To mortals lent, to trace his boundless works
From laws sublimely simple, speak thy fame
In all philosophy.
—THOMSON, The Seasons : Summer.

Shall the great soul of Newton quit this earth
To mingle with his stars ; and every muse,
Astonish'd into silence, shun the weight
Of honours due to his illustrious name ?
But what can man ? Ev'n now the sons of light,
In strains high warbled to seraphic lyre,
Hail his arrival on the coast of bliss.
—Id., A Poem sacred to the Memory of Sir Isaac Newton.

These nations Newton made his own :
All *intimate* with him alone.
His mighty soul did, like a giant, run
To the vast volume's *closing* star ;
Decipher'd every character :
His reason pour'd new light upon the sun.
—YOUNG, The Merchant, Strain III.

And Newton, something more than man,
Div'd into nature's hidden springs,
Laid bare the principles of things,
Above the earth our spirits bore,
And gave us worlds unknown before.
—CHURCHILL, The Ghost, Book II.

See Newton chase conjecture's twilight ray,
And light up nature into certain day !
He wide creation's trackless mazes trod ;
And in each atom found the ruling God.
—DR. JOHN BROWN, On Honour.

Newton, who first th' Almighty's works display'd,
And smooth'd that mirror, in whose polish'd face
The great Creator now conspicuous shines ;
Who open'd Nature's adamantine gates,
And to our minds her secret powers expos'd.
—RICHARD GLOVER, Poem on Sir Isaac Newton.

And finishing at length his destin'd way,
To Newton he bequeath'd the radiant lamp of day.
—SOAME JENYNS, On the Immortality of the Soul, Book I.

Patient of contradiction as a child,
Affable, humble, diffident, and mild,
Such was Sir Isaac, and such Boyle and Locke,
Your blunderer is as sturdy as a rock.
—COWPER, Progress of Error.

Newton reaches heights unreach'd before.
—RICHARD SAVAGE, An Epistle to Sir R. Walpole.

O'er Nature's laws God cast the veil of night,
Out-blaz'd a Newton's soul—and all was light.
> —AARON HILL, *On Sir Isaac Newton.*

Lo! Newton, Priest of Nature, shines afar,
Scans the wide world, and numbers ev'ry star!
> —CAMPBELL.

There Priest of Nature! dost thou shine,
NEWTON! a King among the Kings divine.
> —SOUTHEY, *Translation of a Greek Ode on Astronomy.*

And Newton, exalted
There above those orbs whose motions from earth he had measured,
Through infinity ranging in thought.
> —*Id., A Vision of Judgment : The Elder Worthies.*

'Tis he—as I approach more near
The great Columbus of the skies I know!
'Tis Newton's soul, that daily travels here
In search of knowledge for mankind below.
O stay, thou happy spirit, stay,
And lead me on through all th' unbeaten wilds of day.
> —JOHN HUGHES, *The Ecstasy : An Ode.*

It is a Newton who sees himself in a child on the seashore, and his discoveries in the coloured shells.—R. A. WILLMOTT, *Advantages of Literature.*

A monument to Newton! a monument to Shakespeare! Look up to Heaven—look into the Human Heart. Till the planets and the passions—the affections and the fixed stars are extinguished—their names cannot die.—JOHN WILSON, *Noctes Ambrosianæ, Vol. III.*

Such men as Newton and Linnæus are incidental, but august, teachers of religion.—*Id., Essays : Education of the People.*

The contemplation of Newton's discoveries raises other feelings than wonder at his matchless genius. The light with which it shines is not more dazzling than useful. The difficulties of his course, and his expedients, alike copious and refined for surmounting them, exercise the faculties of the wise, while commanding their admiration ; but the results of his investigations, often abstruse, are truths so grand and comprehensive, yet so plain, that they both captivate and instruct the simple. . . . Nor when we recollect the Greek orator's exclamation, "The whole earth is the monument of illustrious men," can we stop short of declaring that the whole universe is Newton's.—LORD BROUGHAM, *Speech at the Inauguration of Statue at Grantham.*

To the highest powers of invention Newton added, what so seldom accompanies them, the talent of simplifying and communicating his profoundest speculations. In the economy of her distributions, Nature is seldom thus lavish of her intellectual gifts. The inspired genius which creates is rarely conferred along with the matured judgment which combines, and yet without the exertion of both, the fabric of human wisdom could never have been reared. Though a ray from heaven kindled the vestal fire, yet a humble priesthood was required to keep alive the flame.—SIR DAVID BREWSTER, *Life of Sir Isaac Newton.*

Newton and Laplace need myriads of ages and thick-strewn celestial areas. One may say a gravitating solar system is already prophesied in the nature of Newton's mind.—EMERSON, *Essays: History.*

No one since the creation has ever so clearly unfolded, as Newton has done, the laws by which the material World is regulated; or has done the work with more of that reverential and devout spirit of faith and love which is the fairest ornament of the Christian Philosopher.—BISHOP WORDSWORTH, *Miscellanies: Religion in Science.*

In Natural Philosophy, the airy fabrics of hypothetical visions ought not to claim the attention of a moment. The sun of Newton has absorbed the radiance of all other luminaries in this department. His works and those of his followers will, of course, supersede the infinite number of folios, which, to use the expressions of Horace, may be sent to wrap up frankincense and perfumes, the only way in which they can now be useful. —DR. VICESIMUS KNOX, *Essays: Cursory and General Hints on the Choice of Books.*

REV. JOHN NEWTON.

English Hymn Writer: 1725-1807.

If the section of the Church of England which usually bears that title [Evangelical] be properly so distinguished, there can be no impropriety in designating as her four Evangelists, John Newton, Thomas Scott, Joseph Milner and Henry Venn.—SIR JAMES STEPHEN, *Essays in Ecclesiastical Biography.*

Out of the profligate slave-dealer, John Newton, Methodism formed one of the purest and most unselfish of saints.—W. E. H. LECKY, *History of England, Vol. I.*

MOWBRAY, DUKE OF NORFOLK.

First Earl Marshal of England: (?)-1399.

Bishop: " Many a time hath banish'd Norfolk fought
For Jesu Christ in glorious Christian field,
Streaming the ensign of the Christian Cross
Against black pagans, Turks, and Saracens;
And, toil'd with works of war, retired himself
To Italy; and there, at Venice, gave
His body to that pleasant country's earth,
And his pure soul unto his captain Christ,
Under whose colours he had fought so long."
—SHAKSPERE, *King Richard II., Act IV., Scene I.*

DANIEL O'CONNELL.

Irish Orator and Agitator: 1775-1847.

The Political Apostle of the day.
—HARRIET MARTINEAU, *Biographical Sketches.*

See how triumphant in debate and in action O'Connell is! Why? because he asserts a broad principle and acts up to it, rests all his body on it and has faith in it.—S. T. COLERIDGE, *Table Talk.*

There is something almost awful in so dark a close of so brilliant a career. The more I dwell upon the subject, the more I am convinced of the splendour and originality of the genius and of the sterling character of O'Connell, in spite of the calumnies that surround his memory, and the many and grievous faults that obscured his life. But when to the great services he rendered to his country, we oppose the sectarian and class warfare that resulted from his policy, the fearful elements of discord he evoked, and which he alone could in some degree control, it may be questioned whether his life was a blessing or a curse to Ireland.—W. E. H. LECKY, *Leaders of Public Opinion in Ireland.*

ORIGEN.

Greek Father of the Church: 186-254.

Origen was a mystic, Tertullian a puritan. Origen was profound and speculative, Tertullian narrow and logical. Origen was gentle and tolerant, Tertullian bitter and exclusive. Nor do they differ less in their style. "The eloquence of the one," says Pressensé, "is large and limpid as his genius; it is a beautiful river, abundant and majestic; that of the other is a mountain torrent." Origen lightens, Tertullian thunders, Origen speaks to philosophers like a Christian philosopher; Tertullian is a tribune of the people who has gone down to the forum and the cross roads to kindle the passions of the crowd; he is the ancient orator with his unrestrained gestures, his vivid images, his grandiose pathos.—F. W. FARRAR, *Lives of the Fathers, Vol. I.*

OVID.

Roman Poet: B.C. 43-18 A.D.

O noble Ovide!

        —CHAUCER, *The Merchant's Tale.*

Venus' clerk, Ovid,
That hath sown wonder wide
The great god of love's name.

        —*Id., The House of Fame, Book III.*

The wanton Ovid, whose enticing rimes
Have with attractive wonder forc'd attention.

    —JOHN FLETCHER, *On Mr. Francis Beaumont's Imitations of Ovid.*

Wonder at Ovid, when he doth rehearse
The Change of Things. What mighty flame doth fill
His varied fancy to enrich his Quill!

        —GEORGE DANIEL, *An Essay Endeavouring to Ennoble our English Poesy.*

Familiar Ovid tender thoughts inspires,
And Nature seconds all his soft desires.

        —ROSCOMMON, *An Essay on Translated Verse.*

His tender accents pitying virgins move,
And charm the list'ning ear with tales of love.
—GAY, *To Bernard Lintott.*

Though Ovid was a merry man, love ever kept him sad;
He was as far from happiness, as one that is stark mad.
—SIR JOHN SUCKLING, *Love and Debt Alike Troublesome.*

Well sung sweet Ovid, in the days of yore,
What flight is that, which love will not explore?
—POPE, *January and May.*

THOMAS PAINE.

English Deist : 1737-1809.

Burke talked of " that digest of anarchy, called the Rights of Man ".—
SIR ARCHIBALD ALISON.

Even Paine, the most plausible and attractive of all popular theorists,
was scarcely known to any classes but the lowest, at the moment when
the government suddenly thought fit to toss him into celebrity on the
horns of a prosecution.—LYTTON, *England and the English.*

WILLIAM PALEY.

English Philosopher and Divine : 1743-1805.

It is a doubt whether mankind are most indebted to those who, like
Bacon and Butler, dig the gold from the mine of literature, or to those
who, like Paley, purify it, stamp it, fix its real value, and give it currency
and utility. For all the practical purposes of life, truth might as well be
in a prison as in the folio of a schoolman, and those who release her from
her cobwebbed shelf, and teach her to live with men, have the merit of
liberating, if not of *discovering* her.—REV. C. C. COLTON, *Bacon.*

Paley never was a bishop—nor, with all his great virtues and talents,
did he deserve to be one—for he was not orthodox either in his morality
or his religion. And we will never allow heterodoxy to wear the lawn
sleeves, and ominously squint on bench episcopal. But Paley was a
pellucid writer, and a bloody angler ; he was a ten-dozen-trout-a-day
man, dressed his own flies, and threw as far and fine a line as ever
dropped, gossamer-like, on deep or shallow.—JOHN WILSON, *Essays :
Anglomania.*

It is even yet more remarkable, that while Locke should be the great
metaphysician of a clerical University, so Paley should be its tutelary
moralist. Of all the systems of unalloyed and unveiled selfishness, which
human ingenuity ever devised, Paley's is, perhaps, the grossest and most
sordid.—LYTTON, *England and the English.*

Paley saw what he did see through an atmosphere of light. He seized
on the strong points of his subject with an intuitive sagacity, and has
given his clear bright thoughts in a style which has made them the property of his readers almost as perfectly as they were his own. In what,
then, did he fail? We have said that he was characterised by the dis-

tinctness of his vision. He was not, we think, equally remarkable for its extent. He was popular, rather than philosophical. He was deficient in that intellectual thirst which is a chief element of the philosophical spirit. He had no irrepressible desire to sound the depths of his own nature, or to ascend to wide and all-reconciling views of the works and ways of God. Moral philosophy he carried backward ; nor had he higher claims in religious than in ethical science.—W. E. CHANNING, *On the Character and Writings of Fénelon.*

VISCOUNT PALMERSTON.

English Statesman : 1784-1865.

Lord Palmerston, then, was a great man chiefly in the sense that he was so complete a man. His character deserves our attention more from its unusual combination of good qualities than from the marked presence of any one great quality or attribute. He had about him neither the glories nor the follies of a genius ; but he possessed in rare harmony characteristics which are generally in antagonism.—EVELYN ASHLEY, *Life of Viscount Palmerston, Vol. II.*

No one ever heard Lord Palmerston as the *Laudator temporis acti.* He had no feeble allusions to former triumphs, nor complacent recallings of the great deeds of yore. One could not tell, save from the striking maturity of his views and the firmness of his conclusions, that his experience had been greater than that of his audience. That which showed the true power of his mind was the lucid, well-balanced, rapid grasp with which he apprehended the question immediately to hand, shutting out entirely all others, and bringing to bear on the topic before him all the resources of his knowledge.—MARQUIS OF LORNE, *Life of Viscount Palmerston.*

There are men whose patriotism is loyal and single-minded, to whom politics is a creed and not a profession, and whose efforts to increase the prosperity of their country and the welfare of its people, are purely animated by honest and unselfish motives. To this class belonged Lord Palmerston. In the finest sense of the word he was a patriot. . . . The history of Lord Palmerston is that of a man who attained to power and kept it, not by a birth more illustrious than that of many of his contemporaries, nor by an industry which was insatiable, nor by talents of the very highest order ; but because his patriotism was loyal and undaunted, his honour and good faith undoubted, his tact consummate, his knowledge of the world accurate and varied, his sympathy with the people over whom he ruled ready, sincere, and never at fault—because in tastes and characteristics he was the most representative Englishman of his day. On the list of our Premiers he will be remembered as he himself would wish to be remembered, not as the greatest, but as the most English of our statesmen.—A. C. EWALD, *Representative Statesmen, Vol. II.*

PARACELSUS.

Swiss Physician, Alchemist, and Astrologer : 1493-1541.

The wondrous Paracelsus, life's dispenser,
Fate's commissary, idol of the schools.
                    —ROBERT BROWNING, *Paracelsus.*

The sixteenth century was fertile in men, like Paracelsus, full of arrogant pretensions, and eager to substitute their own dogmatism for that they endeavoured to overthrow.—HALLAM, *Literature of the Middle Ages, Vol. I.*

That medical Ishmael, Paracelsus. . . . Paracelsus gloried in grandiloquent shabbiness and boisterous vulgarity.—R. A. VAUGHAN, *Hours with the Mystics, Vol. II.*

Paracelsus was one of the most remarkable exemplars of knowledge and nonsense, wisdom and folly, science and ignorance, credulity and incredulity, honesty and dishonesty, religion and atheism, with which biography has made us acquainted. I say this, however, without any obstinacy, or attempt at accuracy. For his friends have been so lavish in his praise, and his enemies so unmeasured in their censures, that to acquire a true knowledge of his tenets, philosophy, morals, discoveries, and irregularities, would require more time than the subject is worth, and a skill that were better appropriated to other purposes. We may safely assert, however, that he was a quack of the first order, though his quackery did not command the greatest success.—CHARLES BUCKE, *Book of Human Character.*

CHARLES STEWART PARNELL.

Irish Statesman : 1846-1891.

The strength of Parnell was character rather than intellect. But the more you say in depreciation of the intellectual side, the more you at the same time raise the estimate of his strength of character. What that strength was, the whole world has learned to know. To bad ends and to self-destruction, the same terrible strength of will and tenacity of purpose were devoted, which formerly were given to noble and wise ends, but the qualities remained the same amid their diverse employment. Parnell defying and conquering the whole British Parliament, was not a more picturesque, or daring, or potent figure than Parnell fighting week after week his desperate and forlorn struggle against the Irish nation. . . . No, there is no doubt about Parnell's greatness. He was a portent, a great and tragic exception to Nature's ordinary laws, like an eclipse or an earthquake.—T. P. O'CONNOR, *Charles Stewart Parnell : A Memory.*

DR. THOMAS PARNELL.

English Poet : 1679-1717.

Admir'd and mourn'd !
With softest manners, gentlest Arts adorn'd !
Blest in each science, blest in ev'ry strain !
>   —POPE, *Epistle to Robert, Earl of Oxford.*

This tomb inscribed to gentle Parnell's name,
May speak our gratitude, but not his fame.
What heart but feels his sweetly-moral lay,
That leads to truth through pleasure's flowery way ?
Celestial themes confess'd his tuneful aid :
And Heaven, that lent him genius was repaid.
>   —GOLDSMITH, *Epitaph on Dr. Parnell.*

The correct and equable sweetness of Parnell.

—CAMPBELL.

A gentle wit was pure, polite Parnell,
By many praised, for many loved him well.
His muse glides on "with gentle swimming walk,"
And e'en while singing only seems to talk.
In fact she is an English gentlewoman,
Whom no one would believe a thing uncommon,
Till by experience taught, we find how rare
Such truly English gentlewomen are.
—HARTLEY COLERIDGE, *Parnell.*

BLAISE PASCAL.

French Philosopher and Mathematician : 1623-1662.

Pascal, by his Provincial Letters, did more to ruin the name of Jesuit than all the controversies of Protestantism, or all the fulminations of the parliament of Paris.—HALLAM, *Literature of the Middle Ages, Vol. IV.*

As it is easier to see the reflection of the great sphere in large globes, though defaced by some crack or blemish, than in drops of water, so men of large calibre, though with some eccentricity for madness, like Pascal or Newton, help us more than balanced mediocre minds.—EMERSON, *Swedenborg ; or, the Mystic.*

The chief accuser was Blaise Pascal. His powers of mind were such as have rarely been bestowed on any of the children of men ; and the vehemence of the zeal which animated him was but too well proved by the cruel penances and vigils under which his macerated frame sank into an early grave. His spirit was the spirit of St. Bernard : but the delicacy of his wit, the purity, the energy, the simplicity of his rhetoric, had never been equalled, except by the great masters of Attic eloquence. All Europe read and admired, laughed and wept. The Jesuits attempted to reply ; but their feeble answers were received by the public with shouts of mockery. —MACAULAY, *History of England, Vol. I., Chap. VI.*

When we read the *Provincial Letters* or the *Pensées*, we feel ourselves in communion with a living writer who knew how to light up with an immortal touch both the follies of ecclesiasticism and the struggles of a solitary spirit after truth. The tenderness of a genuine insight mingles with all the sublimity and severe reserve of the thought, and so we get close to a true soul, distant as Pascal himself in some respects remains to us. The play of human feeling which we miss in the man moves in his writings, and touches our hearts with an ineffable sympathy, even when we remain unconvinced or unenlightened.—DR. JOHN TULLOCH, *Life of Pascal.*

JOHN COLERIDGE PATTESON.

Missionary Bishop of Melanesia : 1827-1871.

The three highest titles that can be given to man are those of martyr, hero, saint ; and which of the three is there that in substance it would be irrational to attach to the name of John Coleridge Patteson?—GLADSTONE, *Gleanings, Vol. II.*

" He loved them all alike!" That was the secret of John Coleridge Patteson's history and his labours. Need more be said of him? Surely the simple islander's summary of his character is the honour he would prefer.—C. M. YONGE, *Life of J. C. Patteson, Vol. II.*

SIR ROBERT PEEL.

English Statesman: 1788-1850.

Sir Robert rides—he never rides at speed—
Careful his seat, and circumspect his gaze ;
And still the cautious trot the cautious mind betrays.
Wise is thy heed!—how stout soe'er his back,
Thy weight has oft proved fatal to thy hack ! . . .
From the starved wretch its own loved child we steal—
And " Free Trade " chirrups on the lap of Peel.
                                —LYTTON, *The New Timon.*

In all the course of my acquaintance with Sir Robert Peel, I never knew a man in whose truth and justice I had a more lively confidence, or in whom I saw a more invariable desire to promote the public service. In the whole course of my communication with him, I never knew an instance in which he did not show the strongest attachment to truth ; and I never saw in the whole course of my life the smallest reason for suspecting that he stated anything which he did not firmly believe to be the fact.—DUKE OF WELLINGTON, *Speech in House of Lords.*

In truth Sir Robert Peel is a remarkable man, confessedly a puissance in himself, confessedly the leading member of the representatives, yes, even of your reformed assembly ; he is worth our stopping in our progress for a moment, in order to criticise his merits.—LYTTON, *England and the English.*

Sir Robert Peel was a very circumspect statesman, and not the least so in those matters in which the public purse was concerned.—GLADSTONE.

No man knew better than Sir Robert Peel how evanescent and worthless a thing was the applause of the mob ; and at the same time, no man more ardently longed for applause than he did. Yet it must be said, that he looked far beyond the loud voices and the clapping of hands of to-day. He looked like " mighty Verulam," a man whose greatness he almost equalled, and whose virtues he far excelled—to foreign natio ns, and to posterity, to confirm the verdict of his own time, if it should happen to be favourable ; or to reserve it, if it should happen to be against him. As regards foreign nations, his wish was abundantly gratified before he died. His was the name that represented alike the common sense, the business tact, and the enlightened statesmanship of England. Europe rang with his fame ; and nations who never heard of his rivals or his enemies, were familiar with his actions, and respected England in his person.—CHARLES FITZHUGH, *Life and Character of Sir Robert Peel.*

His character has been termed an "enigma". It is no enigma to me. His apparent inconsistencies, for I think them apparent only, cause me no surprise. He is an enigma only in the sense in which all true, high and struggling nature is an enigma. The true life of thought is a life of struggle. His inconsistencies are the outward and visible signs of his struggles. Man has been termed a "bundle of habits"; he might be called also a bundle of inconsistencies. . . . Perhaps, when, in future times, the interest shall have subsided concerning some questions, which in his time so rent the world, and men speak of Peel as we now speak of Walpole, with calm approval of a wise and moderate statesman, it may be recorded of him as his highest honour, that whilst others spoke of his talents, his works, and his virtues too, Wellington, a man truthful himself above most men, in his old age, on the very brink of his own grave, spoke of one virtue which was particularly prominent in Peel, and praised him as one of the most truthful men he had ever known ; a golden key to unlock the "enigma" of his character.—SIR LAURENCE PEEL, *Life and Character of Sir R. Peel.*

Not that Sir Robert Peel was a theorist, a philosopher governed by general ideas and abstract principles. He was, on the contrary, a man of essentially practical mind, consulting facts at every step just as the mariner consults the face of heaven, seeking success above all things, and prudent even to circumspectness. But if he was not the servant of principles, neither was he their detractor ; he respected political philosophy without adoring it, believing it to be neither sovereign nor futile, and equally a stranger to the insane confidence of those who pretend to regulate all things according to the bent of their own mind, and to the impertinence of those who affect to despise the human mind, as if they themselves had some other. . . . God seldom accords to a man so many favours. He had endowed Sir Robert Peel, at his birth, with the gifts of intellect as well as the gifts of fortune. He had placed him in an age when his great qualities could be employed with success on great objects. When success was achieved, He recalled him suddenly to Himself, in the fulness of his strength and glory, like a noble workman who has performed his task before the close of the day, and who goes to receive his final reward from the master whom he has well served.—GUIZOT, *Memoirs of Sir Robert Peel.*

Peel was, undoubtedly, as Lord Beaconsfield has said, a great member of Parliament : but he was surely very much more than that ; he was a great statesman, a great Minister. He must always rank among the foremost of English Ministers. The proud boast of Heine is that, if any one names the best half-dozen of German poets his name must be brought in among them. If we name the best half-dozen of modern English Prime Ministers, we can hardly fail to bring in the name of Peel.—JUSTIN MCCARTHY, *Life of Sir Robert Peel.*

Peel has been deservedly praised for his sagacity. He saw clearly though he did not see far. He could thoroughly appreciate whatever lay within the range of his vision ; but his want of imagination prevented him from computing the issues of the future. He had an intellect exactly fitted to grasp details, and group them together with infallible accuracy ; but the bolder outlines of the picture generally escaped him. The valleys and the plains were his own ; but his eyes did not reach the sunlit mountain-peaks.

Take him all in all, he was emphatically a silent man ; but his silence was the silence of reflection passing into resolution—not like that of Napoleon the Third, the silence of doubt and hesitation.—W. H. DAVENPORT ADAMS, *English Party Leaders, Vol. II.*

In his last tenure of office Peel speaks of himself more than once as working seventeen hours a day. Even with that desperate diet of labour it seems difficult to understand how Peel accomplished all that he did at that time. . . . Aloof from his party he certainly was. In the Tom, Dick, and Harry business, as it may be called, he was certainly deficient: it is the charge brought against all great ministers. But he had one crowning merit which finds its place in any view of him as a parliamentary leader. He had disciples: he made men : he formed a school. Of no other minister since Pitt can this be said, and even of Pitt only in a lesser degree. What men he shaped! What a creed of honest work he left with them! What a tradition of public duty ! Graham, Gladstone, Hardinge, Dalhousie, Canning, Cardwell, Sidney Herbert, and Newcastle. These men stood together after his death like the last square of a broken army, firm in their faith, in their leader, in their cause. To be a Peelite was a distinction in itself: it denoted statesmanship, industry, conscience. . . . For then, and now, and for all time, above and beyond that Government and the perished passions of the time, there looms the great figure of the great Minister, with feet perhaps of clay as well as iron, but with a heart at least of silver, and a head of fine gold.—LORD ROSEBERY, *Sir Robert Peel.*

MARY, COUNTESS OF PEMBROKE.

Sister of Sir Philip Sidney : 1550-1621.

Underneath this marble hearse
Lies the subject of all verse,
Sidney's sister, Pembroke's mother ;
Death, ere thou hast slain another,
Learn'd and fair, and good as she,
Time shall throw a dart at thee.
—BEN JONSON, *Epitaph for Countess of Pembroke.*

WILLIAM PENN.

English Quaker : Founder of Pennsylvania : 1644-1718.

All who revere the memory of Penn
Grieve for the land on whose wild woods his name
Was fondly grafted with a virtuous aim,
Renounced, abandoned by degenerate Men
For state-dishonour black as ever came
To upper air from Mammon's loathsome den.
—WORDSWORTH, *To the Pennsylvanians.*

It should be sufficient for the glory of William Penn, that he stands upon record as the most humane, the most moderate, and the most pacific of all rulers. — LORD JEFFREY, *Essays.*

William Penn, the great legislator of the Quakers, had the success of a conqueror in establishing and defending his colony, among savage tribes, without ever drawing the sword; the goodness of the most benevolent rulers in treating his subjects as his own children; and the tenderness of an Universal Father, who opened his arms to all mankind, without distinction of sect or party. In his republic it was not the religious creed, but personal merit, that entitled every member of society to the protection and emoluments of the state.—FATHER O'LEARY, *Essay on Toleration.*

To speak the whole truth concerning Penn is a task which requires some courage; for he is rather a mythical than a historical person. Rival nations and hostile sects have agreed in canonizing him. England is proud of his name. A great commonwealth beyond the Atlantic regards him with a reverence similar to that which the Athenians felt for Theseus, and the Romans for Quirinus. The respectable society of which he was a member honours him as an apostle. By pious men of other persuasions, he is generally regarded as a bright pattern of Christian virtue. Meanwhile admirers of a very different sort have sounded his praises. The French philosophers of the eighteenth century pardoned what they regarded as his superstitious fancies in consideration of his contempt for priests, and of his cosmopolitan benevolence, impartially extended to all races and to all creeds. His name has thus become, throughout all civilised countries, a synonym for probity and philanthropy.—MACAULAY, *History of England, Vol. I., Chap. IV.*

SAMUEL PEPYS.

Diarist : 1632-1703.

Reading this book [Pepys' *Diary*], in short, seems to us to be quite as good as living with Mr. Samuel Pepys in his proper person.—LORD JEFFREY, *Essays.*

Samuel Pepys—the most confiding of diarists, the most harmless of turncoats, the most wondering of *quidnuncs.*—LEIGH HUNT, *Men, Women, and Books.*

Samuel Pepys stands incontestably at the head of the world's literature in his own department. . . . Pepys' *Diary* has been frequently compared with Boswell's *Life of Johnson*, and with justice in so far as the charm of each arises from the inimitable naïveté of the author's self-revelations. Boswell had a much greater character than his own to draw, but Pepys had to be his own Johnson. It is giving him no excessive praise to say that he makes himself as interesting as Johnson and Boswell together. . . . Another Milton is more likely to appear than another Pepys.—RICHARD GARNETT, *The Age of Dryden.*

Certainly Pepys was blest with the queerest and most omnivorous taste that ever fell to the lot of one man! . . . In S. Pepys, the understanding is *hypertrophied* to the necrosis or marasmus of the Reason and Imagination, while far-sighted (yet, ah! how short-sighted) Self-interest fills the place of Conscience. . . . Pepys was always a Commonwealth's man in his heart. N.B.—Not a Democrat; but, even more than the Constitutional Whigs, the very antipode of the modern Jacobins, or Tail-up Head-down Politicians. A Voluptuary, and without a spark of bigotry in his nature, he could not be a Puritan; but of his free choice he would have preferred Presbyterianism to Prelacy, and a mixed Aristocracy of Wealth and talent to a Monarchy, or even a mixed Government—such at least as the latter was in his time.—S. T. COLERIDGE, *Notes, Theological, Political, etc.*

Pepys has been likened to the barber of King Midas, who relieved his mind by communicating to a bundle of reeds the fact that his master had the ears of an ass; and assuredly no other writer has so unreservedly stripped his soul bare.—H. B. WHEATLEY, *Samuel Pepys and the World he lived in.*

PERICLES.

Athenian Statesman: B.C. 499-429.

Pericles, called half in derision by the comic poets the Zeus of Athens, called afterwards, with reverence, by Plutarch, the Olympian—Pericles expresses in himself the spirit of this age. He is the typical Athenian, who governed Athens during the years in which Athens governed Greece, who formed the taste of the Athenians at the time when they were educating the world by the production of immortal works of beauty. We have seen that the conquest of the Persians was the triumph of the spirit, and that after the conquest the spirit of Humanity found itself for the first time absolutely and consciously free in Athens. This spirit was, so to speak, incarnated in Pericles. *Verbum caro factum est*—the Word of the Greek genius was made flesh in him, and dwelt at Athens. In obedience to its dictates, he extended the political liberties of the Athenians to the utmost, while he controlled those liberties with the laws of his own reason. In obedience to the same spirit, he expended the treasures of the Ionian League upon the public works, which formed the subsequent glory of Hellas, and made her august even in humiliation.—J. ADDINGTON SYMONDS, *Studies of Greek Poets.*

PETER THE GREAT.

Emperor of Russia: 1672-1725.

Immortal Peter! first of monarchs! He
His stubborn country tam'd, her rocks, her fens,
Her floods, her seas, her ill-submitting sons!
And while the fierce barbarian he subdu'd,
To more exalted soul he rais'd the man.
                    —THOMSON, *The Seasons: Winter.*

    Illustrious Peter came.
Wise traveller he, who over Europe went,
    Marking the ways of men;
That so to his dear country, which then rose
Among the nations in uncultured strength,
    He might bear back the stores
        Of elder polity,
      Its sciences and arts.
      —SOUTHEY, *Ode to Emperor Alexander I. of Russia.*

The creative genius of Peter the Great added Russia to the list of civilised nations.—MAZZINI, *Life and Writings, Vol. II.*

What shall we say of him ?   The story of his life and works is his best monument.   Most remarkable is the energy of his vitality, the passion which he put into everything he did, work and play, humanity and cruelty. . . . Never answer " Presently " was his order.   The road of " To-morrow," he knew, leads to the house of " Never ".   He might have said, with Napoleon, " I may lose a battle, but I will never lose a minute ". Everything stuck fast when he was not there to push it.   He was no friend of luxury.   He slept on a plank, ate plainly and little, drank indeed too much, wore simple clothing, drove about in a gig.   Yet his simplicity was not free from parsimony.   His rough and boisterous horse-play has been already noticed.   Some of it belonged to his age.   He had a demonic side to his personality ; one might say that he was European in his intellect, Asiatic in his spirit, Savage in his wrath.   He possessed an extraordinary power of enjoyment.   His nature flowed out on all sides in an abundant stream.—OSCAR BROWNING, *Life of Peter the Great.*

Peter is Russia—her flesh and blood, her temperament and genius, her virtues and her vices.   With his various aptitudes, his multiplicity of effort, his tumultuous passions, he rises up before us, a collective being. This makes his greatness.   This raises him far above the pale shadows which our feeble historical evocation strives to snatch out of oblivion. There is no need to call his figure up.   He stands before us, surviving his own existence perpetuating himself—a continual actual fact.—K. WALISZEWSKI, *Life of Peter the Great (transl.), Vol. I.*

CHARLES MORDAUNT, EARL OF PETERBOROUGH.

English General : 1658-1735.

The English government had determined to send an expedition to Spain, under the command of Charles Mordaunt, Earl of Peterborough. This man was, if not the greatest, yet assuredly the most extraordinary character of that age, the King of Sweden himself not excepted.   Indeed, Peterborough may be described as a polite, learned, and amorous Charles the Twelfth.   His courage had all the French impetuosity, and all the English steadiness.   His fertility and activity of mind were almost beyond belief.   They appeared in everything that he did, in his campaigns, in his negociations, in his familiar correspondence, in his lightest and most unstudied conversation.   He was a kind friend, a generous enemy, and in deportment a thorough gentleman.   But his splendid talents and virtues were rendered almost useless to his country, by his levity, his restlessness, his irritability, his morbid craving for novelty and for excitement.   His weaknesses had not only brought him, on more than one occasion, into serious trouble ; but had impelled him to some actions altogether unworthy of his humane and noble nature.   Repose was insupportable to him.   He loved to fly round Europe faster than a travelling courier.   He was at the Hague one week, at Vienna the next. Then he took a fancy to see Madrid ; and he had scarcely reached Madrid, when he ordered horses and set off for Copenhagen.   No attendants could keep up with his speed.   No bodily infirmities could confine him.   Old age, disease, imminent death, produced scarcely any effect on his intrepid spirit. Just before he underwent the most horrible of surgical operations, his conversation was as sprightly as that of a young man in the full vigour of health. On the day after the operation, in spite of the entreaties of his medical advisers, he would set out on a journey. His figure was that of a skeleton. But his elastic mind supported him under fatigues and sufferings which seemed sufficient to bring the most robust man to his grave. Change of employment was as necessary to him as change of place. He loved to dictate six or seven letters at once.—MACAULAY, *Essays : War of the Succession in Spain.*

FRANCIS PETRARCH.

Italian Poet : 1304-1374.

Franceis Petrark, the Laureat poete,
Highte this clerk whos rethorike swete
Enlumined all Itaille of poetrie.
            —CHAUCER, *The Clerk's Prologue.*

        Therefore Petrark writeth
This storie, which with high stile he enditeth.
            —*Id., The Clerk's Tale.*

Or filch whole pages at a clap for need
From honest Petrarch, clad in English weed.
            —BISHOP HALL, *Satires, Book VI., Satire I.*

Then Petrarch follow'd, and in him we see
What rhyme improv'd in all its height can be.
            —DRYDEN, *Epistle V.: To the Earl of Roscommon.*

When wit and science trimm'd their wither'd bays,
At Petrarch's voice, and beam'd with half their rays.
        —JAMES CAWTHORN, *To Miss ——— of Horsemanden in Kent.*

          . . . Laura lies
In Petrarch's learned arms, drying those eyes
That did in such sweet smooth pac'd numbers flow,
As made the world enamour'd of his woe.
            —CAREW, *A Rapture.*

Hark yet again, like flute-tones mingling rare,
Comes the keen sweetness of Petrarca's moan.
Pass thou the lintel freely ; without fear
Feast on the music.
            —A. H. HALLAM.

For Petrarch's Laura still survives :
She died, but ne'er will die again.
    —BYRON, *Answer to a beautiful Poem entitled " The Common Lot ".*

        And the crown
Which Petrarch's laureate brow supremely wore.
            —*Id., Childe Harold's Pilgrimage, Canto IV.*

Petrarch! when we that name repeat,
Its music seems to fall
Like distant bells, soft voiced and sweet,
But sorrowful withal;—
That broken heart of love! that life
Of tenderness and tears!
So weak on earth—in earthly strife,—
So strong in holier spheres!
How in his boast of godlike pride,
While em'lous nations ran
To kiss his feet, he stept aside,
And wept the woes of man!

—LORD HOUGHTON.

That voice so sweet, which still enchants, inspires;
That voice, which sung of love, of liberty.
—SAMUEL ROGERS, *Italy : The Campagna of Florence.*

One whose verse shall live,
When the wave rolls o'er Venice.
—*Id., Italy : St. Mark's Place.*

Petrarch pale,
From whose brain-lighted heart were thrown
A thousand thoughts beneath the sun,
Each lucid with the name of One.
—E. B. BROWNING, *A Vision of Poets.*

Arise, O Petrarch, from th' Elysian bowers,
With never-fading myrtles twin'd,
And fragrant with ambrosial flowers,
Where to thy Laura thou again art join'd;
Arise, and hither bring the silver lyre,
Tun'd by thy skilful hand,
To the soft notes of elegant desire,
With which o'er many a land
Was spread the fame of thy disastrous love.
—LORD LYTTLETON, *To the Memory of Miss Lucy Fortescue.*

The ideal world in which Thou so long didst dwell was not disenchanted by thy Laura's death—it only lay in more pensive shade, more melancholy lustre. She who on earth had dwelt apart from thee in body, seemed not to be more remotely removed when she went to Heaven. Her spirit perhaps visited Thee more frequently than ever before did either her bodily presence, or the idea of her living. Lost at last utterly and for ever in the grave that Madonna-like countenance, which for so many long years shone on Thee but by glimpses, hurried and stealthy, and not without trouble and tears. But memory, strong as the eye in undying passion,

" Could give Thee back the dead,
Even in the loveliest looks she wore! "

That unengaged delight saved Thee from many sins, and thus

" Thy soul was like a star, and dwelt apart! "

and immortal fame came flying to thee on the wings of love!—JOHN WILSON, *Essays : The Loves of the Poets.*

The moral character of Petrarch was formed of dispositions peculiarly calculated for a poet. An enthusiast in the emotions of love and friendship, of glory, of patriotism, of religion, he gave the rein to all their impulses; and there is not perhaps a page in his Italian writing which does not bear the trace of one or other of these affections. By far the most predominant, and that which has given the greatest celebrity to his name, is his passion for Laura. Twenty years of unrequited and almost unaspiring love were lightened by song; and the attachment, which, having long survived the beauty of its object, seems to have at one time nearly passed from the heart to the fancy, was changed to an intenser feeling, and to a sort of celestial adoration, by her death. . . . The general excellences of Petrarch are his command over the music of his native language, his correctness of style, scarcely two or three words that he has used having been rejected by later writers, his exquisite elegance of diction, improved by the perpetual study of Virgil; but, far above all, that tone of pure and melancholy sentiment, which has something in it unearthly, and forms a strong contrast to the amatory poems of antiquity. . . . The great defect of Petrarch was his want of strong original conception, which prevented him from throwing off the affected and overstrained manner of the Provençal troubadours, and of the earlier Italian poets.—HALLAM, *Student's Middle Ages, Chap. IX., Part II.*

Petrarch appears to me a corollary from Dante; the same spirit in a different mould of individual character, and that a weaker mould; yet better adapted, by the circumstances of his position, to diffuse the great thought which possessed them both, and to call into existence so great a number of inferior recipients of it, as might affect insensibly, but surely, the course of general feeling.—A. H. HALLAM.

Petrarch introduced a more profound, liberal, and elegant scholarship, and communicated to his countrymen that enthusiasm for the literature, the history, and the antiquities of Rome, which divided his own heart with a frigid mistress and a more frigid Muse.—MACAULAY, *Essays: Machiavelli.*

Of all Italian writers, I prefer my much loved Petrarch. No poet in the whole world has ever surpassed him in depth and fervency of feeling, and its expression which goes straight to the heart. Therefore, I much prefer his sonnets, Trionfi and Canzoni, to the fantastic follies of Ariosto and horrid distortions of Dante. I find the natural flow of words which comes straight from the heart much more congenial than Dante's studied, even affected chariness of speech. He has always been, and will remain the poet of my heart.—SCHOPENHAUER (*transl.*).

One of the first and brightest luminaries which appeared in the literary horizon, after a long and dismal night, was the illustrious Francesco Petrarch. . . . Enough of his meaning and of his beauties has been understood by his own countrymen, to give him the title of the Father of the Tuscan poetry. The classical excellence of his language has contributed to give a name to the century in which he lived; for the Italians call it *the good age of their language*, and attribute the happy effect in a great measure to Petrarch. Sweet, indeed, are the greater part of his sonnets, sweet their language, and sweet their sentiments. Though criticism may point out quaintnesses and unnatural conceits, may censure one part as metaphysical, and another as affected, yet the sensible reader will not judge by parts, but by the whole effect of an entire piece; and if his feelings have been often finely touched, and his imagination delighted, he will give himself up to the magic of the poet, and joining in the general applause, leave the cold critic to whisper his detraction disregarded.—Dr. Vicesimus Knox, *Essays : Petrarch.*

Petrarch was great, not only by a bootless passion which his poetical genius clothed in imperishable language—the chaste language of tenderness and regret without a single line that can wound the most refined sensibility—but he was great by the love of letters to which he devoted a life of indefatigable industry; by his extraordinary learning and memory, which enabled him, we know not how, to acquire and retain a minute knowledge of classical literature and history, inconceivable in an age when every writer had to be studied in manuscript, and manuscripts themselves were scarce and costly; by his independence of character and love of truth, which made him the fearless advocate of every good and great cause, speaking his mind with an eloquence and energy then unknown to Europe, and without regard to consequences; and by his devoted and passionate adherence to the freedom and glory of Italy, which he sought to promote alike by imperial or aristocratic influence and by the democracy of Rome—the inspired herald of a struggle of five centuries, which has accomplished in our times and the liberation of united Italy.—Henry Reeve, *Life of Petrarch.*

But Petrarch's highest merit by no means consists in this new classic elegance; it consists in the fact that he was the first to write freely of all things in the same way that a man speaks. He was the first to throw aside all scholastic crutches, and prove how much more swiftly a man could walk without leaning upon them.—Pasquale Villari, *Machiavelli and his Times (transl.), Vol. I.*

The lines of Petrarch and Dante are woven like golden threads into the fabric of our conversation and literature.—H. R. Haweis, *Music and Morals.*

PINDAR.

Greek Lyric Poet : B.C. 522-442.

Here, like some furious prophet, Pindar rode,
And seem'd to labour with th' inspiring God.
Across the harp a careless hand he flings,
And boldly sinks into the sounding strings.
—Pope, The Temple of Fame.

O noblest, happiest age!
When Aristides rul'd, and Cimon fought;
When all the generous fruits of Homer's page
Exulting Pindar saw to full perfection brought.
O Pindar, oft shalt thou be hail'd of me:
Not that Apollo fed thee from his shrine;
Not that thy lips drank sweetness from the bee;
Nor yet that, studious of thy notes divine,
Pan danc'd their measure with the sylvan throng:
But that thy song was proud to unfold

What thy base rulers trembled to behold;
Amid corrupted Thebes was proud to tell
The deeds of Athens and the Persian shame:
Hence on thy head their impious vengeance fell.
—AKENSIDE, *Ode XVIII. : To Francis, Earl of Huntingdon.*

Pindar, that eagle, mounts the skies.
—PRIOR, *An English Ballad, etc.*

O thou Dircæan swan, on high,
Round whom familiar thunders fly,
While Jove attends a language like his own !
—YOUNG, *Imperium Palagi, Strain IV.*

Pindar's unnavigable Song
Like a swoln Flood from some steep Mountain pours along;
The Ocean meets with such a Voice
From his enlarged Mouth, as drowns the Ocean's Noise.
So Pindar does new Words and Figures roll
Down his impetuous Dithyrambic Tide,
Which in no Channel deigns t' abide,
Which neither Banks nor Dykes control.
Whether th' Immortal Gods he sings,
In a no less Immortal Strain,
Or the great Acts of God-descended Kings,
Who in his Numbers still survive and reign.
Each rich embroidered Line,
Which their triumphant Brows around,
By his sacred Hand is bound,
Does all their starry Diadems out-shine.
—COWLEY, *The Praise of Pindar, I., II.*

though he inherit
Nor the pride, nor ample pinion,
That the Theban Eagle bear
Sailing with supreme dominion
Thro' the azure deep of air.
—GRAY, *The Progress of Poesy.*

Bold
Electric Pindar, quick as fear,
With race-dust on his cheeks, and clear
Slant startled eyes that seem to hear
The chariot rounding the last goal,
To hurtle past it in his soul.
—E. B. BROWNING, *A Vision of Poets.*

Pindar unfortunately gave himself up to the turf, the prize-ring, and a
curious kind of Pagan high-church hagiology, much as if the editor of
Bell's Life, the author of *Boxiana*, and the poet of the *Christian Year*,
were all three gentlemen in one. The universal human vein shows itself,
however, here and there, with a strange gleam of tenderness, in stray
biographical allusions and moral reflections, interspersed with the main
subject in hand, which is always to celebrate some Derby event of that

21

old time, or to trace up the lineage of Hellenic game-chickens and White-headed Bobs to Hercules.—GEORGE BRIMLEY, *Essays.*

Here we must stop short in the front of Pindar—the Hamlet among these lesser actors, the Shakespeare among a crowd of inferior poets. To treat of Greek lyrical poetry and to omit Pindar is a paradox in action. Yet Pindar is so colossal, so much apart, that he deserves a separate study, and cannot be dragged in at the end of a bird's-eye view of a period of literature. At the time of Pindar, poetry was sinking into mannerism. He by the force of his native originality gave it a wholly fresh direction, and created a style as novel as it was inimitable. Like Athos, like Atlas, like the Matterhorn, like Monte Viso, like the Peak of Teneriffe, he stands alone, sky-piercing and tremendous in his solitary strength. . . . The grand pre-eminence of Pindar as an artist was due in a great measure to his personality. Frigid, austere, and splendid ; not genial like that of Simonides, not passionate like that of Sappho, not acrid like that of Archilochus ; hard as adamant, rigid in moral firmness, glittering with the strong keen light of snow ; haughty, aristocratic, magnificent—the unique personality of the man Pindar, so irresistible in its influence, so hard to characterise, is felt in every strophé of his odes. In his isolation and elevation Pindar stands like some fabled heaven-aspiring peak—a Matterhorn of solid gold, conspicuous from afar, girdled at the base with ice and snow, beaten by winds, wreathed round with steam and vapour, jutting a sharp and dazzling outline into cold blue ether. Few things that have life dare to visit him at this grand altitude. Glorious with sunlight and with stars, touched by rise and set of day with splendour, he shines when other lesser heights are dulled. Pindar among his peers is solitary. He had no communion with the poets of his day. He is the eagle, Simonides and Bacchylides are jackdaws. He soars to the empyrean ; they haunt the valley mists.

Reading his poetry is like quaffing wine that bubbles in a bowl of gold. . . . The splendour-loving Pindar is his name and title for all time. . . . To Pindar's soul splendour was as elemental as harmony to Milton's. Of the graces, Aglaia must have been his favourite. Nor, love as he did the gorgeousness of wealth, was it mere transitory pomp, the gauds and trappings of the world, which he admired. There must be something to stir the depths of his soul—beauty of person, or perfection of art, or moral radiance, or ideal grandeur. The blaze of real magnificence draws him as the sun attracts the eagle ; he does not flit moth-like about the glimmer of mere ephemeral lights. . . . In plain critical language, Pindar combines the strong flight of the eagle, the irresistible force of the torrent, the richness of Greek wine, the majestic pageantry of Nature in one of her sublimer moods.—J. ADDINGTON SYMONDS, *Studies of Greek Poets.*

Often in thinking over the best pieces of Pindar—the majestic organ-playing, the grave strong magic of language, the lightning-flashes of half-revealed mystery—one wonders why this man is not counted the greatest poet that ever lived, why he has not done more, mattered more. The answer perhaps is that he was a poet and nothing else. He thought in music ; he loved to live among great and beautiful images—Heracles, Achilles, Perseus, Iâson, the daughters of Cadmus. When any part of his beloved saga repelled his moral sensitiveness, he glided away from it, careful not to express scepticism, careful also not to speak evil of a god.

He loved poetry and music, especially his own. As a matter of fact, there was no poetry in the world like his, and when other people sang they jarred on him, he confesses, *like`crows.*—GILBERT MURRAY, *History of Ancient Greek Literature.*

WILLIAM PITT.

English Statesman: 1759-1806.

With more than mortal powers endowed,
How high they soared above the crowd!
Theirs was no common party race.
Jostling by dark intrigue for place;
Like fabled gods, their mighty war
Shook realms and nations in its jar:
Beneath each banner proud to stand,
Looked up the noblest of the land;
Till through the British world were known
The names of Pitt and Fox alone.

—-SIR WALTER SCOTT.

And thou, blest star of Europe's darkest hour,
Whose words were wisdom, and whose counsels power,
Whom earth applauded through her peopled shores;
Alas! whom earth too early lost deplores :
Young without follies, without rashness bold,
And greatly poor amidst a nation's gold;
In every veering gale of faction true,
Untarnish'd Chatham's genuine child adieu!
Unlike our common suns, whose gradual ray
Expands from twilight to intenser day;
Thy blaze broke forth in full meridian sway.

—HEBER.

In Pitt the genius withered the heart.—NAPOLEON BONAPARTE.

Nor were his political abilities his only talents : his eloquence was an era in the senate, peculiar and spontaneous ; familiarly expressing gigantic sentiments and instinctive wisdom : not like the torrent of Demosthenes, or the splendid conflagration of Tully, it resembled sometimes the thunder, and sometimes the music of the spheres. Like Murray, he did not conduct the understanding through the painful subtlety of argumentation ; nor was he, like Townshend, for ever on the rack of exertion ; but rather lightened upon the subject, and reached the point by the flashings of his mind ; which, like those of his eye, were felt, but could not be followed.— HENRY GRATTAN.

The greatest warrior of modern times is not Napoleon, it is Pitt. Napoleon carried on warfare, Pitt created it. It is Pitt who willed all the wars of the Revolution and of the Empire. They proceeded from him. Take away Pitt and put Fox in his place, there would then be no reason for that exorbitant battle of twenty-three years.—VICTOR HUGO, *William Shakespeare (transl.).*

Certainly no Minister ever better understood his time and country than the younger Pitt. The main cause of his precocious and enduring ascendency may be found in that remarkable sympathy with public opinion, which is the most incontestable proof of a statesman's comprehension of the spirit of his age and nation.—LYTTON, *Essays : Knowledge of the World.*

But separating the man from the policy, we find in Pitt statesmanship of the highest order. Though ruling by the sterner forms of command, he exercised the most complete sway over the House of Commons. Not even the tyrannical Chatham, who treated members of Parliament very much as the severe Dr. Busby treated his Westminster boys, was more implicitly obeyed. He was the greatest parliamentary minister that has ever been ; none knew better than he how to obtain a majority, how to quell opposition, and how to address the assembly. He had the great gift, which is often more allied with common sense than with genius, of seeing what was the right course to be pursued precisely at the right moment. . . . There have been on the beadroll of English ministers men more popular, more kindly, more generous, but none more able, more straightforward, or more worthy the high position he held, than the great, the disinterested, the severe William Pitt.—A. C. EWALD, *Representative Statesmen, Vol. I.*

We can well believe, from a perusal of Pitt's orations, that his contemporaries did not exaggerate when they compared his deportment and learning in debate to those of Marlborough in the field. If he descended into the arena it was as an acknowledged chief rather than as a combatant. It was for him to ride on the whirlwind and direct the storm. His courage was invincible, but it was not without fire or passion, deriving nothing from the ebullitions
        " Of mounting spirits, or fermenting blood."
He never lost his self-possession ; no tempest of opposition could shake his firmness.—W. H. DAVENPORT ADAMS, *English Party Leaders.*

William Pitt, that is, the second William Pitt, was a great Palliator ; insomuch, that, though of a high mind, personally, he defended almost every public delinquent, during the long period of his administration.— CHARLES BUCKE, *Book of Human Character.*

That is where we are ; on the one side, timid imbecility " waiting for instructions from the constituencies " ; furious imbecility on the other, looking out for party advantage. Oh ! for a few months of William Pitt ! —HUXLEY, *Letter to Sir J. Donnelly : Life and Letters, Vol. II.*

No country could have too many Pitts : the more she has the greater will she be.—LORD ROSEBERY, *Life of Pitt.*

FRANCIS PIZARRO.

Spanish Warrior, Conqueror of Peru : 1475-1541.

Pizarro here was born ; a greater name
The list of Glory boasts not. Toil and Pain,
Famine and hostile Elements, and Hosts
Embattled, fail'd to check him in his course,

Not to be wearied, not to be deterr'd,
Not to be overcome.   A mighty realm
He over-ran, and with relentless arm
Slew or enslaved its unoffending sons,
And wealth, and power, and fame, were his rewards.
There is another world, beyond the grave,
According to their deeds where men are judged.
>   —SOUTHEY, *For a Column at Truxillo.*

PLATO.

Greek Philosopher : B.C. 429-347.

Go, soar with Plato to th' empyreal sphere,
To the first good, first perfect, and first fair ;
Or tread the mazy round his followers trod,
And quitting sense call imitating God.
>   —POPE, *Essay on Man, Epistle II.*

The sum of Plato's wondrous wisdom is,
This is not that, and therefore, that not this.
>   —ROBERT DODSLEY, *Modern Reasoning.*

Like Plato, give us poetry in prose.
>   —CHURCHILL, *The Farewell.*

Form Plato's honey-dropping tongue distill'd
In copious streams, devolving o'er the sense
.   .   .   .
Its sweet regalement.
And Plato, for a heathen, nobler dreams
Than dream some modern poets.
>   —WILLIAM THOMPSON, *Sickness, a Poem.*

Then Plato's words of light in thee and me
Lingered like moonlight in the moonless east.
>   —SHELLEY, *Prince Athanase, Part II.*

What! are thy triumphs, sacred Truth, belied ?
Why then hath Plato liv'd—or Sydney died ?
>   —CAMPBELL.

>   The lunar beam
Of Plato's genius, from its lofty sphere,
Fell round him in the grave of Academe
Softening their inbred dignity austere.

>   —WORDSWORTH, *Dion.*

Every man is born an Aristotelian, or a Platonist. . . . Plato's works
are logical exercises for the mind. . . . I am sure no born Platonist can
ever change into an Aristotelian.—S. T. COLERIDGE, *Table Talk.*

Schools of real philosophy there are but two—best named by the arch-
philosopher of each, namely, Plato and Aristotle.—*Id., Notes on English
Divines, Vol. I.*

The writings of Plato, and Bishop Taylor, and the *Theoria Sacra* of Burnet, furnish undeniable proofs that poetry of the highest kind may exist without metre, and even without the contradistinguishing objects of a poem.—S. T. COLERIDGE, *Biographia Literaria.*

That Plato, more even than Pericles, saw the consummation of the Athenian intellect, and witnessed more than Pericles himself the civilisation wrought by Pericles. This consideration gives a value to every sentiment expressed by Plato. The Greek mind was then more intensely Greek than at any subsequent period.—DE QUINCEY, *Leaders in Literature.*

Plato is a gownsman : his garment though of purple, and almost sky-woven, is an academic robe, and hinders action with its voluminous folds. —EMERSON, *Swedenborg ; or, the Mystic.*

There are not in the world at any one time more than a dozen persons who read and understand Plato : never enough to pay for an edition of his works ; yet to every generation these come duly down, for the sake of those few persons, as if God brought them in his hand.—*Id., Spiritual Laws.*

Out of Plato come all things that are still written and debated about among men of thought. . . . Plato is philosophy, and philosophy, Plato, —at once the glory and the shame of mankind, since neither Saxon nor Roman have availed to add any idea to his categories. No wife, no children had he, and the thinkers of all civilized nations are his posterity, and are tinged with his mind.—How many great men Nature is incessantly sending up out of night, to be *his men,*—Platonists ! the Alexandrians, a constellation of genius ; the Elizabethans, not less ; Sir Thomas More, Henry More, John Hales, John Smith, Lord Bacon, Jeremy Taylor, Ralph Cudworth, Sydenham, Thomas Taylor ; Marcilius Ficinus, and Picus Mirandola. Calvinism is in his Phœdo ; Christianity is in it. Mahometanism draws all its philosophy, in its handbook of morals, the Akhlak-y-Jalaly, from him. Myticism finds in Plato all its texts.—*Id., Plato ; or the Philosopher.*

The delicious irony of Plato.—MACAULAY, *Essays: Lord Bacon.*

According to the opinions of the best judges, ancient and modern, the greatest master of the beauties of style whom the world ever saw was the divine Plato. The ancients hesitated not to assert, in the zeal of their admiration, that if Jupiter were to speak in the language of Greece, he would infallibly express himself in the diction of Plato. He possessed the art of combining severity with grace, and sweetness with grandeur.—DR. VICESIMUS KNOX, *Essays : On the Style of Xenephon and Plato.*

Plato himself, the supreme transcendentalist of antiquity, and to this day unapproached among mankind for the magnificent sweep of clear intellect and the beauty and gorgeousness of poetic expression with which he expounded Transcendentalism.—DAVID MASSON, *Life of Carlyle.*

Philosophers may be divided into seers on the one hand, and into gropers on the other. Plato, to use a contrast which is often used for other purposes, is the type of the first. On all subjects he seems to have before him a landscape of thought, with clear outline, and pure air, keen rocks and shining leaves, an Attic sky and crystal flowing-river, each detail which was as present, as distinct, as familiar to his mind as the view from the Acropolis, or the road to Decelea. As were his conceptions, so is his style.—WALTER BAGEHOT, *Literary Studies, Vol. II.*

Plato dies in the school to appear in the pulpit.—R. A. WILLMOTT, *Advantages of Literature.*

It is just this inconclusiveness of Plato's thought that has made it immortal. We get in him not a system but a spirit, and a spirit that no discoveries can supersede. It is a mistake to think of Plato as a dreamer; he was keen and even satirical in his insight, but he rises beyond his own satire, and, except in the *Gorgias* period, cares always more for the beauty he can detect in things than for the evil. It is equally a mistake to idealise him as a sort of Apolline hero, radiant and untroubled, or to take that triumphant head of the Indian Bacchus to be his likeness. He was known for his stoop and his searching eyes; the *Letters* speak often of illness; and Plato's whole tone towards his time is like Carlyle's or Mr. Ruskin's. He is the greatest master of Greek prose style, perhaps of prose style altogether, that ever lived. . . . If a man's life can be valued by what he thinks and what he lives for, Plato must rank among the saints of human history.—GILBERT MURRAY, *History of Ancient Greek Literature.*

PLUTARCH.

Greek Biographer and Moralist: 50-120.

Wise, honest Plutarch! to thy deathless praise
The sons of Rome this grateful statue raise:
For why? both Greece and Rome thy fame have shar'd;
Their heroes written, and their lives compar'd.
But thou thyself couldst never write thy own:
Their lives had parallels, but thine has none.
    —DRYDEN, *On Plutarch's Statue: From the Greek.*

First of thy votaries, peerless and alone,
Thy PLUTARCH shines, by moral beauty known;
Enchanting Sage! whose living lessons teach
What heights of virtue human efforts reach. . . .
    —R. A. WILLMOTT, *Advantages of Literature.*

Plutarch, by the general consent of Criticism, is the representative of popular Biography. . . .
Plutarch's *Lives* recall Titian's portraits. . . .
Plutarch stands between the Historian, the Poet, and the Romancer, and catches the beautiful lights of all.—*Id.*

If we explore the literature of Heroism, we shall quickly come to Plutarch, who is its doctor and historian. To him we owe the Brasidas, the Dion, the Epaminondas, the Scipio of old, and I must think we are more deeply indebted to him than to all the ancient writers.—EMERSON, *Essays: Heroism.*

We cannot read Plutarch without a tingling of the blood; and I accept the saying of the Chinese Mencius: "A sage is the instructor of a hundred ages".—*Id., Uses of Great Men.*

As a diligent collector of facts, as a warm friend to virtue, as an entertaining narrator, I venerate the name of Plutarch. His writings bear evident marks of extensive reading, and communicate much and multifarious knowledge. Theodore Gaza has said, that if all books were lost, and he might recover one, it should be Plutarch.—Dr. VICESIMUS KNOX, *Cursory Thoughts on Biography.*

One of the best of Greek books, once in everybody's hands, now, I fear, fallen considerably into the shade, is Plutarch. Here you have, whether for youth or manhood, in the shape of living examples of the most rich and various types, the very stuff from which human efficiency must ever be made. Our accurate critical historians have a small educational value when set against that fine instinct for all true human greatness, and that genial sympathy with all human weakness, which shine out so conspicuously in the classical picture-gallery of that rare old Bœotian.—J. STUART BLACKIE, *On Self-Culture.*

What is it that makes Plutarch's *Lives* " the pasture of great souls," as they were called by one who was herself a great soul? Because his aim was much less to tell a story than, as he says, " to decipher the man and his nature ; and in deciphering the man, to strike out pregnant and fruitful thoughts on all men ".—JOHN MORLEY, *Studies in Literature.*

EDGAR ALLAN POE.

American Poet and Novelist: 1809-1849.

There comes Poe, with his raven, like Barnaby Rudge,
Three-fifths of him genius and two-fifths sheer fudge.
—J. R. LOWELL, *A Fable for Critics.*

His was a music tender, strange, and wild ;
The ghost of many a weird, wan melody
Wailed from his lines ; wan faces through them smiled ;
The sense of horror there unceasingly
Haunts us, to terror and to awe beguiled
By what we know not—what we feel, not see.
—W. C. BENNETT, *Sonnet XLV.*

Behold ! within this narrow grave
Is shut the mortal part of him.
Behold ! he could not wholly dim
The gracious genius Heaven gave—

For strains of music here and there,
Weird murmurings, vague, prophetic tones,
Are blown across the silent zones
Forever in the midnight air.
—T. B. ALDRICH, *Poe.*

On the whole, it appears to us that, whether we regard the character of Poe's genius, or the nature of his career, we are looking upon as sad and strange a phenomenon as can be found in literary history. Principle he seems to have had none. Decision of character was entirely lacking. His envy of those more favoured by fortune than himself amounted to raging ferocity. He starved his wife and broke her heart. He estranged the friends who were most firmly resolved to hold by him. He foully slandered his best benefactors. He had no faith in man or woman. . . . And we carry with us from the contemplation of the entire subject the sad recollection of a powerful intellect, a most vivid imagination, an utterly evil heart, and a career of guilt, misery and despair.—A. K. H. BOYD, *Critical Thoughts of a Country Parson.*

Mr. Poe had that indescribable something which men have agreed to call *genius.* No man could ever tell us precisely what it is, and yet there is none who is not inevitably aware of its presence and its power. Let talent writhe and contort itself as it may, it has no such magnetism. Larger of bone and sinew it may be, but the wings are wanting. Talent sticks fast to earth, and its most perfect works have still one foot of clay. Genius claims kindred with the very workings of Nature herself, so that a sunset shall seem like a quotation from Dante or Milton, and if Shakespeare be read in the very presence of the sea itself, his verses shall seem but nobler for the sublime criticism of ocean. Talent may make friends for itself, but only genius can give to its creations the divine power of winning love and veneration. . . . To the eye of genius, the veil of the spiritual world is ever rent asunder, that it may perceive the ministers of good and evil who throng continually round it. No man of mere talent ever flung his inkstand at the devil.—J. R. LOWELL, *Poe's Works: Stoddard's Edition.*

The ancient fable of two antagonistic spirits imprisoned in one body, equally powerful and having the complete mastery by turns—of one man, that is to say, inhabited by both a devil and an angel—seems to have been realised, if all we hear is true, in the character of the extraordinary man whose name we have written above.—NATHANIEL P. WILLIS, *Ibid.*

Poe is a kind of Hawthorne and *delirium tremens.* . . . After reading some of Poe's stories one feels a kind of shock to one's modesty. We require some kind of spiritual ablution to cleanse our minds of his disgusting images.—LESLIE STEPHEN, *Hours in a Library, First Series.*

Edgar Allan Poe was fastidious—even morbidly fastidious—in his love of beautiful form ; but he had no root of humanity in him, and little passion for actual external nature. He was not an interpreter. He had no mission, save to create dreams. A greater dreamer in prose than in verse, he has yet added to American literature a few poems of the most striking originality ; but of deep spirituality he has none. His loftiest flights of imagination in verse, like his boldest efforts in prose fiction, rise into no more empyreal realm than the fantastic. His sense of beauty in language was usually fine. Like Gautier, he loved to work " in onyx and enamel ".—ERIC S. ROBERTSON, *Life of H. W. Longfellow.*

POMPEY THE GREAT.

Triumvir ; Roman General : B.C. 106-48.

Alas, Pompeie ! of the orient conquerour,
That Fortune unto swiche a sin thee brought.
                        —CHAUCER, *Monk's Tale.*

Knew you not Pompey ?   Many a time and oft
Have you climb'd up to walls and battlements,
To towers and windows, yea, to chimney-tops,
Your infants in your arms, and there have sat
The live-long day, with patient expectation,
To see great Pompey pass the streets of Rome.
—SHAKSPERE, *Julius Cæsar, Act I., Scene I.*

When the world bow'd to Rome's almighty sword,
Rome bow'd to Pompey, and confess'd her lord.
Yet one day lost, this deity below
Became the scorn and pity of his foe.
His blood a traitor's sacrifice was made,
And smok'd indignant on a ruffian's blade.
No trumpet's sound, no gasping army's yell,
Bid, with due horror, his great soul farewell.
—YOUNG, *The Last Day, Book II.*

ALEXANDER POPE.

English Poet: 1688-1744.

A voice there is, that whispers in my ear,
('Tis Reason's voice, which sometimes one can hear,)
" Friend Pope ! be prudent, let your Muse take breath,
And never gallop Pegasus to death :
Lest stiff and stately, void of fire or force,
You limp, like Blackmore on a Lord Mayor's horse."
—POPE, *Epistle I. of the First Book of Horace.*

Hail, happy Pope ! whose generous mind
Detesting all the statesmen kind,
Contemning courts, at courts unseen,
Refus'd the visits of a queen.
A soul with every virtue fraught,
By sages, priests, or poets taught ;
Whose filial piety excels
Whatever Grecian story tells ;
A genius for all stations fit,
Whose meanest talent is his wit ;
His heart too great, though fortune little,
To lick a rascal statesman's spittle ;
Appealing to the nation's taste,
Above the reach of want is plac'd :
By Homer dead was taught to thrive,
Which Homer never could alive ;
And sits aloft on Pindus' head,
Despising slaves that cringe for bread.
—SWIFT, *A Libel on Dr. Delany and Lord Carteret.*

When Pope's harmonious Muse with pleasure roves,
Amidst the plains, the murmuring streams, and groves,
Attentive echo, pleas'd to hear his songs,
Through the glad glade each warbling note prolongs ;

His various numbers charm our ravish'd ears,
His steady judgment far out-shoots his years,
And early in the youth the god appears.
   —GAY, *Epistle XIV., To Bernard Lintott.*

Like the young spreading laurel, Pope, thy name
Shoots up with strength, and rises into fame.
   —TICKELL, *A Poem on the Prospect of Peace.*

Smile all thy valleys in eternal spring,
Be hush'd, ye winds! while Pope and Virgil sing.
In English lays, and all sublimely great,
Thy Homer warms with all his ancient heat.
He shines in council, thunders in the fight,
And flames with every sense of great delight.
   —PARNELL, *To Mr. Pope.*

'Tis thine, O Pope, who choose the better part,
To tell how false, how vain, the Scholiast's art.
   —DAVID MALLET, *Of Verbal Criticism.*

O Pope! instructor of my studious day,
Who fix'd my steps in virtue's early ways:
On whom our labours, and our hopes depend,
Thou more than patron, and ev'n more than friend!
   —WALTER HARTE, *An Essay on Satire.*

O Pope! too great to copy, or to praise,
Whom envy sinks not, nor encomiums raise.
   —*Id., Macarius: or the Confessor*

All nature trembles! save the throne of Jove!
Have mercy, Pope, and kill me not with joy
'Tis tenfold rage, an agony of bliss!
Be less a god, nor force me to adore.
   —WILLIAM THOMPSON, *On Mr. Pope's Works.*

Others more daring, fix their hope
On rivalling the fame of Pope.
   —ROBERT LLOYD, *To * * *, Written in the Year* 1755.

Ere Pope refin'd the chink of rhyme.
   —*Ibid., Epistolary Verses to George Colman, Esq.*

And glow and warm in Pope's immortal line.
   —DR. JOHN BROWN, *On Honour.*

Through Pope's soft song though all the graces breathe,
And happiest art adorn his Attic page.
   —THOMAS WARTON, *The Pleasures of Melancholy.*

And Pope, the monarch of the tuneful train!
To whom be nature's, and Britannia's praise!
All their bright honours rush into his lays!
And all that glorious warmth his lays reveal,
Which only poets, kings, and patriots feel!
Though gay as mirth, as curious thought sedate,
As elegance polite, as power elate;

Profound as reason, and as justice clear ;
Soft as compassion, yet as truth severe ;
As bounty copious, as persuasion sweet,
Like Nature various, and like art complete ;
So fine her morals, so sublime her views,
His life is almost equall'd by his Muse.
                    —SAVAGE, *The Wanderer, Canto I.*

Then Pope, as harmony itself exact,
In verse well disciplined, complete, compact,
Gave virtue and morality a grace,
That, quite eclipsing pleasure's painted face,
Levied a tax of wonder and applause,
Even on the fools that trampled on their laws.
                    —COWPER, *Table Talk.*

And Cobham's groves and Windsor's green retreats,
When Pope describes them, have a thousand sweets.
                    —*Id., Retirement.*

    . . . Pope, with energy divine,
In one strong blaze bade wit and fancy shine ;
Whose verse by Truth in Virtue's triumph borne,
Gave knaves to infamy, and fools to scorn ;
Yet pure in manners, and in thought refined,
Whose life and lays adorned and blessed mankind.
                    —BEATTIE, *On the Report of a Monument, etc.*

'Squire Pope but busks his skinklin patches
            O' heathen tatters !
                    —BURNS, *Poem on Pastoral Poetry.*

Three times I've read your Iliad o'er ;
    The first time pleas'd me well ;
New beauties, unobserv'd before,
    Next pleas'd me better still.

Again I try'd to find a flaw ;
    Examin'd ilka line ;
The third time pleas'd me best of a',
    The labour seem'd divine.

Henceforward I'll not tempt my fate,
    On dazzling rays to stare,
Lest I shou'd tine dear self-conceit,
    And read and write nae mair.
                    —ALLAN RAMSAY, *To Mr. Pope.*

Better to err with Pope, than shine with Pye.
    .   .   .   .
Then in this happy isle, a Pope's pure strain
Sought the rapt soul to charm, nor sought in vain ;
A polish'd nation's praise aspired to claim,
And raised the people's, as the Poet's fame.
                    —BYRON, *English Bards and Scotch Reviewers.*

Where is that living language which could claim
Poetic more, as philosophic, fame,
If all our bards, more patient of delay,
Would stop, like Pope, to polish by the way?
—BYRON, *Hints from Horace.*

Pope was not content to satisfy; he desired to excel, and therefore always endeavoured to do his best; he did not court the candour, but dared the judgment of his reader, and expecting no indulgence from others, he showed none to himself. He examined lines and words with minute and punctilious observation, and retouched every part with indefatigable diligence, till he had left nothing to be forgiven. . . . Dryden knew more of man in his general nature, and Pope in his local manners. The notions of Dryden were formed by comprehensive speculation; and those of Pope by minute attention. There is more dignity in the knowledge of Dryden, and more certainty in that of Pope. Poetry was not the sole praise of either; for both excelled likewise in prose: but Pope did not borrow his prose from his predecessor. The style of Dryden is capricious and varied; that of Pope is cautious and uniform. Dryden observes the motions of his own mind; Pope constrains his mind to his own rules of composition. Dryden is sometimes vehement and rapid; Pope is always smooth, uniform, and gentle. Dryden's page is a natural field, rising into inequalities, and diversified by the varied exuberance of abundant vegetation; Pope's is a velvet lawn, shaven by the scythe, and levelled by the roller.—DR. JOHNSON, *Lives of the Poets: Pope.*

I will say nothing of his works, they speak sufficiently for themselves; they will live as long as letters and taste remain in this country, and be more and more admired as envy and resentment shall subside. But I will venture this piece of classical blasphemy, which is, that however he may be supposed to be obliged to Horace, Horace is more obliged to him.— LORD CHESTERFIELD.

Pope's poetry is full of nature, at least of what I have been in the constant habit of accounting nature for the last threescore and ten years. But leaving nature and art, and all that sort of thing, I wish to ask a single question: What poet of this age, with the exception perhaps of Byron, can be justly said, when put into close comparison with Pope, to have written the English language at all?—JOHN WILSON, *Noctes Ambrosianæ, Vol. I.*

The Nightingale of Twickenham.—*Id., Ibid., Vol. IV.*

Of all poets that have practised reasoning in verse, Pope is the one most inconsequential in the deduction of his thoughts, and the most severely distressed in any effort to effect or to explain the dependency of their parts. There are not ten consecutive lines in Pope unaffected by this infirmity. All his thinking proceeded by insulated and discontinuous jets; and the only resource for *him*, or chance of even seeming correctness, lay in the liberty of stringing his aphoristic thoughts like pearls, having no relation to each other but that of contiguity. To *set* them like diamonds was for Pope to risk distraction; to systematise was ruin. On the other hand, if this elliptical word *correctness*, for elliptical it must be until its subject of control is assigned, is to be understood with such a complimentary qualification as would restrict it to Pope's use of *language*, that construction is even more untenable than the other—more conspicuously untenable—for many are they who have erred by illogical thinking, or by distracted evolution of thoughts: but rare is the man amongst classical writers in any language who has disfigured his meaning more remarkably than Pope by imperfect expressions. We do not speak of plebeian phrases, of exotic phrases, of slang, from which Pope was not free, though *more* free than many of his contemporaries. From vulgarism indeed he was shielded, though imperfectly, by the aristocratic society he kept : *they* being right, *he* was right : and he erred only in the cases where they misled him : for even the refinement of that age was oftentimes coarse and vulgar. Still it is indisputable that a better model of diction and of grammar prevailed a century before Pope. In Spenser, in Shakespeare, in the Bible of King James's reign, and in Milton, there are very few grammatical errors. . . . It provokes fits of laughter, in a man who knows Pope's real nature, to watch him in the process of brewing the storm that spontaneously will not come : whistling, like a mariner, for a wind to fill his satiric sails ; and pumping up into his face hideous grimaces in order to appear convulsed with histrionic rages. Pope should have been counselled never to write satire, except on those evenings when he was suffering horribly from indigestion. By this means the indignation would have been ready-made. The rancour against all mankind would have been sincere ; and there would have needed to be no extra expense in getting up the steam. As it is the short puffs of anger, the uneasy snorts of fury in Pope's satires, give one painfully the feeling of a locomotive-engine with unsound lungs. Passion of any kind may become in some degree ludicrous, when disproportioned to its exciting occasions. But it is never entirely ludicrous, until it is self-betrayed as counterfeit. Sudden collapses of the manufactured wrath, sudden oblivion of the criminal, announce Pope's as *always* counterfeit. . . . If the question were asked, What ought to have been the best among Pope's poems ? most people would answer, the *Essay on Man.* If the question were asked, What *is* the worst ? all people of judgment would say, the *Essay on Man.* Whilst yet in its rudiments, this poem claimed the first place by the promise of its subject ; when finished, by the utter failure of its execution, it fell into the last.—DE QUINCEY, *Leaders in Literature.*

Where Horace is the poet of manners, as in the *Epistles* and *Satires* Pope may be said to surpass, in his paraphrases, the originals from which he draws inspiration. . . . But Pope can never approach Horace in the other and diviner side of the Roman's genius. He cannot pretend to the lyrical playfulness and fire, the mingled irony and earnestness, the tender pathos, the exquisite humanity, the wondrous felicity of expression, which render the Odes of Horace matchless in the power of *charm*. He cannot, in his Twickenham villa, seize and interpret the poetry of rural life and sylvan scenery like the recluse of the Sabine farm. Pope's genius, in short, is didactic, not lyrical.—LYTTON, *Essays : Knowledge of the World.*

I think of the works of young Pope as I do of the actions of young Bonaparte or young Nelson. In their common life you will find frailties and meannesses, as great as the vices and follies of the meanest men. But in the presence of the great occasion, the great soul flashes out, and conquers transcendent. In thinking of the splendour of Pope's young victories, of his merit, unequalled as his renown, I hail and salute the achieving genius, and do homage to the pen of a hero.—THACKERAY, *English Humourists of the Eighteenth Century.*

Pope, like Byron, suffered severely from the feuds and strifes of the literary world. Both poets also closely resembled each other in ambition and love of fame. Pope in his generation stood on the summit of Parnassus, like Byron in a later, and each with the weapons of his satire hurled down all aspirants from that height. Further, Pope was the poet of aristocratic society, in which he had gained a position, and was the acknowledged representative of the philosophy and the morality recognised by this society; he preached self-love as the basis of practical wisdom, and versified the philosophy of Shaftesbury and Bolingbroke.— KARL ELZE, *Life of Lord Byron (transl.).*

We talk of Pope, many of us, as the too-often cited *bourgeois gentilhomme* of Molière talked prose, without knowing it. There is hardly a line of *The Rape of the Lock* or *The Dunciad* that has not thus passed into the habitual conversation of our lives.—JUSTIN McCARTHY, *History of the Four Georges, Vol. II.*

In Pope's hands individuals became types; and his creative power in this respect surpasses that of the Roman satirists, and leaves Dryden himself behind.—A. W. WARD, *Memoir prefixed to Pope's Works.*

Admiration for the extraordinary literary talents, respect for the energy which, under all disadvantages of health and position, turned these talents to the best account; love of the real tender-heartedness which formed the basis of the man's character; pity for the many sufferings to which his morbid sensitiveness exposed him; contempt for the meannesses into which he was hurried; ridicule for the insatiable vanity which prompted his most degrading subterfuges; horror for the bitter animosities which must have tortured the man who cherished them even more than his victims—are suggested simultaneously by the name of Pope. As we look at him in one or other aspect, each feeling may come uppermost in turn.—LESLIE STEPHEN, *Life of Pope.*

As a banker's clerk can tell a bad coin by its ring on the counter, without need of a testing apparatus, the true critic can instinctively estimate the amount of bullion in Pope's epigrammatic tinsel.—*Id., Hours in a Library, First Series.*

When we turn from the man to the poet we have at once to change our key. A cleverer fellow than Pope never commenced author. He was in his own mundane way as determined to be a poet, and the best going, as John Milton himself. He took pains to be splendid—he polished and pruned. His first draft never reached the printer—though he sometimes said it did. This ought, I think, to endear him to us in these hasty days, when authors high and low think nothing of emptying the slops of their minds over their readers, without so much as a cry of " Heads below ". . . . Indifference, known by its hard heart and its callous temper, is the only unpardonable sin. Pope never committed it. He had much to put up with. We have much to put up with—in him. He has given enormous pleasure to generations of men, and will continue so to do. We can never give him any pleasure. The least we can do is

to smile pleasantly as we replace him upon his shelf, and say, as we truthfully may, "There was a great deal of human nature in Alexander Pope".
—AUGUSTINE BIRRELL, *Obiter Dicta, Second Series.*

RICHARD PORSON.

English Scholar and Critic : 1759-1808.

Whoever knew Richard Porson, felt that he knew a man of high and noble mind, who, with all his irregularities, and all his inclination to sarcasm and jest, had a sincere love of truth and honesty, and who, with an utter contempt for pretence and presumption, was ever ready to do justice to genuine worth. His life is an example, and an admonition, how much a man may injure himself by indulgence in one unhappy propensity, and how much an elevated mind may suffer by long association with those of an inferior order. A Porson cannot day after day descend to the level of a Hewardine, without finding it difficult at length to recover his original position above it.—REV. J. S. WATSON, *Life of Richard Porson.*

DR. JOSEPH PRIESTLEY.

English Chemist and Physicist : 1733-1804.

Dr. Priestley, who turns the whole dictionary of human nature into verbs impersonal with a perpetual *subauditur* of *Deus* for their common nominative case;—which said *Deus*, however, is but another *automaton*, self-worked indeed, but yet worked, not properly working, for he admits no more freedom or will to God than to man. The Lutheran leaves the free will whining with a broken back in the ditch; and Dr. Priestley put the poor animal out of his misery!—S. T. COLERIDGE, *Notes on English Divines, Vol. II.*

Some men, plunged into controversy, acquire fresh heat and life,—as fire-flies are said to regain their fading lustre on being immersed in hot water. Such a man was Priestley.—R. A. VAUGHAN, *Essays and Remains, Vol. II.*

MATTHEW PRIOR.

English Poet and Diplomatist : 1664-1721.

He merited much for his wit and his breeding.
                              —SWIFT, *News from Parnassus.*

Let Prior's muse with soft'ning accents move,
Soft as the strains of constant Emma's love :
Or let his fancy choose some jovial theme,
As when he told Hans Carvel's jealous dream ;
Prior th' admiring reader entertains,
With Chaucer's humour, and with Spenser's strains.
                              —GAY, *To Bernard Lintott.*

Dear Mat Prior's easy jingle.
                              —COWPER, *An Epistle to Robert Lloyd, Esq.*

While he of pleasure, power and wisdom sang,
My heart lap high, my lugs wi' pleasure rang:
These to repeat, braid-spoken I wad spill,
Altho' I should employ my utmost skill.
He towr'd aboon: but ah! what tongue can tell
How high he flew? how much lamented fell?
—ALLAN RAMSAY, *A Pastoral on the Death of M. Prior.*

Observe how easy Prior flows,
Then runs his numbers down to prose.
—ROBERT LLOYD, *To * * *, Written in the Year* 1755.

Though I have mention'd Prior's name,
Think not I aim at Prior's fame.
—*Id., Epistolary Verses to George Colman, Esq.*

The famed Mat Prior, it is said,
Oft bit his nails, and scratch'd his head,
And chang'd a thought a hundred times,
Because he did not like the rhymes.

—*Id., Ibid.*

CLAUDIUS PTOLEMY.

Alexandrian Astronomer and Geographer.

Of alle men yblessed mote he be
The wise astrologian Dan Ptholomee,
That sayth this proverbe in his Almageste,
Of alle men his wisdom is higheste
That rekketh not who hath the world in hond.
—CHAUCER, *Wife of Bath's Prologue.*

First Ptolemy his scheme celestial wrought,
And of machines a wild provision brought;
Orbs centric and eccentric he prepares,
Cycles and epicycles, solid spheres,
In order plac'd and with bright globes inlaid,
To solve the tow'rs by heavenly bodies made.
—SIR RICHARD BLACKMORE, *Creation.*

PULTENEY, EARL OF BATH.

English Statesman: 1682-1764.

Sing how a Pult'ney charms the list'ning throng,
While senates hang enraptur'd on his tongue;
With Tully's fire each oration glows,
In Tully's music how each period flows;
Instruct each babe to lisp the patriot's name,
Who in each bosom breathes a Roman flame.
—PAUL WHITEHEAD, *The State Dunces: a Satire.*

22

Henry Purcell.

English Musical Composer : 1658-1695.

So ceas'd the rival crew, when Purcell came ;
They sung no more, or only sung his fame :
Struck dumb, they all admir'd the god-like man :
    The god-like man
    Alas ! too soon retir'd,
    As he too late began.
The gods are pleas'd alone with Purcell's lays.
              —Dryden, *On the Death of Mr. Purcell.*

If human cares are lawful to the blest,
Already settled in eternal rest ;
Needs must he wish that Purcell only might
Have liv'd to set what he vouchsaf'd to write.
       —Sheffield, Duke of Buckingham, *Ode on the Death of
        Henry Purcell.*

Dr. Edward Bouverie Pusey.

English Theologian : 1800-1882.

If you knew my friend Dr. Pusey as well as I do—nay, as well as those generally who come tolerably near him—you would say, I am sure, that never was a man in this world on whom one should feel more tempted to bestow a name which belongs only to God's servants departed, the name of a saint.—Newman in Liddon's *Pusey, Vol. I.*

Remember, I am a Puseyite of the very deepest dye.—Keble, *Ibid., Vol. IV.*

Now that dearest Dr. Pusey is gone, the world is no longer the same world.—Dr. H. P. Liddon, *Ibid.*

No man was more variously judged, more sternly condemned, more tenderly loved.—Dean R. W. Church.

John Pym.

English Republican Statesman : 1584-1643.

Strafford : " Then join again, these paths ? For, huge in the dusk,
There's—Pym to face !
          Why then, I have a foe
To close with, and a fight to fight at last
Worthy my soul ! What do they beard the King ? "
        —Robert Browning, *Strafford, Act II., Scene II.*

Mr. Forster has shaped forth the large image of Pym, and has placed it on the height which its proportions demand. Pym was, in fact, not only the most popular man at that time in England, but, perhaps, as a practical politician, the ablest and most effective. What Mr. Disraeli said of the late Sir R. Peel may more accurately be said of Pym—" He was the greatest Member of Parliament that ever lived ". He thoroughly understood his audience and his theatre. No business was too large, none too small for him. . . . Pym more than Hampden, and far more than Vane, represents the House of Commons in its quarrel with Charles from the date of the Grand Remonstrance to the day when Pym himself was buried at Westminster amongst the monuments of kings, feebler and less despotic than himself. He was a chief who united most of the qualities that serve and adorn the leader of party : pre-eminent experience in public affairs, unrelaxing vigilance in the attention bestowed on them, profound mastery in those ready tactics by which occasions to weaken or wound an adversary are fearlessly seized and unscrupulously improved. . . . Pym can see nothing but deformity when he looks at an antagonist. It would be ludicrous, had the consequences been less tragic, to observe the gravity with which he accepts the absurdest rumours as the most con-clusive testimonies, if only those rumours affect the King or the King's friends ; and how, undisturbed by the substantial dangers in which his panic, real or assumed, involves his country, he keeps the public in con-stant terror by denunciations of visionary massacres and impracticable plots. In the casuistry which a subtle intellect adapts to the popular understanding, Pym was unsurpassed.—LYTTON, *Essays : Pym versus Falkland.*

The greatest member of parliament that ever lived, the greatest master of the convictions and the feelings of the House of Commons, was not Robert Peel, but John Pym. But if Pym, in modern garb and using modern phrase, could now rise in his old place, his words, though as practical as they are lofty, would, I fear, be thought " too clever for the House ". . . . Pym was a friend of constitutional monarchy in politics, a Protestant Episcopalian in religion ; against a despot, but for a king ; against the tyranny and the political power of the bishops, but satisfied with the form of Church government. He was no fanatic, and no ascetic. He was genial, social, even convivial. His enemies held him up to the hatred of the sectaries as a man of pleasure. As the statesman and orator of the less extreme party, and of the first period of the revolution, he is the English counterpart of Mirabeau, so far as a Christian patriot can be the counterpart of a Voltairean debauchee. . . . King Pym was the name given to Pym by the lampooners, and though in jest they spoke the truth.—GOLDWIN SMITH, *Three English Statesmen.*

Besides massive breadth of judgment, Pym had one of those luminous and discerning minds that have the rare secret in times of high contention of singling out the central issues and choosing the best battle-ground. Early he perceived and understood the common impulse that was uniting throne and altar against both ancient rights and the social needs of a new epoch. He was no revolutionist either by temper or principle. . . . Surrounded by men who were often apt to take narrow views, Pym, if ever English statesman did, took broad ones ; and to impose broad views upon the narrow is one of the things that a party leader exists for. He had the double gift, so rare even among leaders in popular assemblies, of being at once practical and elevated ; a master of tactics and organising arts, and yet the inspirer of solid and lofty principles. How can we measure the perversity of a King and counsellors who forced into opposi-tion a man so imbued with the deep instinct of Government, so whole-hearted, so keen of sight, so skilful in resource as Pym ?—JOHN MORLEY, *Oliver Cromwell.*

PYTHAGORAS.

Greek Philosopher: B.C. 580-500 (?).

No fool Pythagoras was thought ;
Whilst he his weighty doctrines taught,
He made his listening scholars stand,
Their mouth still cover'd with their hand :
Else, may be, some odd-thinking youth,
Less friend to doctrine than to truth,
Might have refus'd to let his ears
Attend the music of the spheres ;
Denied all transmigrating scenes,
And introduc'd the use of beans.

—PRIOR, *Alma, Canto III.*

Pythagoras, the learned sage,
As you may read in Pliny's page,
With much of thought, and pains, and care,
Found the proportions of a square,
Which threw him in such frantic fits
As almost robb'd him of his wits,
And made him, awful as his name was,
Run naked through the streets of Samos.

—JAMES CAWTHORN, *The Antiquarians : A Tale.*

Pythagoras must ever remain the perfect type of the philosopher, much though fable and myth may have mingled with the record of his astonishing career, and though we may be unable to distinguish what he himself propounded and instituted from what was set forth and established in his name. Travelling from land to land to add to the stores of his knowledge, seeking the divinest alike in his own deep soul and in the mysteries and symbols of the East ; never severing the vastest, loftiest ontological survey from the valiant glance at human destiny and duty ; beholding a poetry in numbers, a philosophy in poetry, a religion in music ; teaching the harmony of the spheres as the emblem of man's virtues ; enlarging, ennobling, transfiguring all sciences, all arts, demonstrating their concatenation, promoting their mutual relations ; making each science, each art a step in the march of the citizen to the godlike life ;—Plato, Archimedes, Moses, Pericles, Pestalozzi in one—and revealing no glory of the sky, picturing no sublime vision of the Deity that could not be turned to food and force for the education of our erring and suffering race.—WILLIAM MACCALL, *The Newest Materialism.*

In Pythagoras, and Socrates, and Plato—in Seneca, Epictetus, and Marcus Aurelius—we see the light of heaven struggling its impeded way through clouds of darkness and ignorance ; we thankfully recognise that the souls of men in the Pagan world, surrounded as they were by perplexities and dangers, were yet enabled to reflect as from the dim surface of silver, some image of what was divine and true ; we hail with the great and eloquent Bossuet, *The Christianity of Nature.*—F. W. FARRAR, *Seekers after God.*

Thomas de Quincey.

English Essayist and Critic : 1785-1859.

The *Selections Grave and Gay* of Thomas de Quincey will always be above criticism, and belong to the realm of rapture.—Augustine Birrell, *Essays about Men, Women, and Books.*

A De Quincey in a world where there was neither reading nor writing of books, would certainly either have committed suicide or gone mad.— Saintsbury, *Essays in English Literature.*

Quintilian.

Roman Rhetorician : 42-118.

In grave Quintilian's copious work we find
The justest rules and clearest method join'd.
>   —Pope, *Essay on Criticism.*

Though judgment in Quintilian's page,
Holds forth her lamp for ev'ry age ;
Yet *Hypercritics* I disdain,
A race of blockheads dull and vain,
And laugh at all those empty fools,
Who cramp a genius with dull rules.
>   —Robert Lloyd, *Epistle to J. B., Esq.,* 1757.

François Rabelais.

French Satirist : 1495-1553.

Then I went in-doors, brought out a loaf,
Half a cheese, and a bottle of Chablis ;
Lay on the grass and forgot the oaf
Over a jolly chapter of Rabelais.
>   —Robert Browning, *Garden Fancies.*

It is incomprehensible to me that this great and genial philosopher should have been a Frenchman, except on my hypothesis of a continued dilution of the Gothic blood from the reign of Henry IV. ; Descartes, Malébranches, Pascal and Molière being the *ultimi Gothorum*, the last in whom the Gothic predominates over the Celtic. . . . One cannot help regretting that no friend of Rabelais (and surely friends he must have had) has left an authentic account of him. His buffoonery was merely Brutus' rough stick, which contained a rod of gold ; it was necessary as an amulet against the monks and bigots. Beyond a doubt, he was amongst the deepest as well as the boldest thinkers of his age. Never was a more plausible, and seldom, I am persuaded, a less appropriate line than the thousand times quoted

" Rabelais laughing in his easy chair "

of Mr. Pope. The caricature of his filth and zanyism proves how fully he both knew and felt the danger in which he stood. I could write a treatise in proof and praise of the morality and moral elevation of

Rabelais' work which would make the Church stare and the conventicle groan, and yet should be the truth and nothing but the truth. I class Rabelais with the creative minds of the world, Shakespeare, Dante, Cervantes.—S. T. COLERIDGE, *Notes: Theological, Political, etc.* .

Rabelais, Pierre Leroux, and Ruskin. The first, were he seven times as unspeakably filthy as he is, I consider as priceless in wisdom, and often in true evangelic godliness—more of him hereafter.—KINGSLEY in KINGSLEY'S *Letters and Memories of his Life, Vol. I.*

Rabelais is the soul of Gaul; and who says Gaul says also Greece, for the Attic salt and the Gallic jest have at bottom the same flavour; and if anything, buildings apart, resembles the Pirœus, it is *La Rapée.* Aristophanes is distanced; Aristophanes is wicked. Rabelais is good— Rabelais would have defended Socrates. In the order of lofty genius, Rabelais chronologically follows Dante; after the stern face, the sneering visage. Rabelais is the wondrous mask of ancient comedy detached from the Greek proscenium, from bronze made flesh, henceforth a human living face, remaining enormous, and coming among us to laugh at us, and with us. Dante and Rabelais spring from the school of the Franciscan friars, as later Voltaire springs from the Jesuits; Dante the incarnate sorrow, Rabelais the parody, Voltaire the irony—they came from the Church against the Church. Every genius has his invention or his discovery; Rabelais has made this one, the belly. The serpent is in man, it is the intestines. It tempts, betrays, and punishes. Man, single being as a spirit and complex as man, has within himself for his earthly mission three centres—the brain, the heart, the stomach, each of these centres is august by one great function which is peculiar to it: the brain has thought, the heart has love, the belly has paternity and maternity. . . . Rabelais, doctor and priest, feels the pulse of papacy; he shakes his head and bursts out laughing. Is it because he has found life? No, it is because he has left death; it is, in reality, breathing its last. Whilst Luther reforms, Rabelais jests. Which tends best to the end? Rabelais ridicules the monk, the bishop, the pope; laughter and death-rattle together; fool's bell sounding the tocsin! Well, then, what? I thought it was a feast—it is agony: one may be deceived by the nature of the hiccup. Let us laugh all the same; death is at the table; the last drop toasts the last sigh. The agony feasting—it is superb. The inner colon is king; all that old world feasts and bursts; and Rabelais enthrones a dynasty of bellies—Grangousier, Pantagruel, and Gargantua. Rabelais is the Æschylus of morals.—VICTOR HUGO, *William Shakespeare* (transl.).

If we are to seek for an approximation to Aristophanic humour, we shall find it perhaps in Rabelais. Rabelais exhibits a similar disregard for decency, combining the same depth of purpose and largeness of insight with the same coarse fun. But in Aristophanes there is nothing quite grotesque and homely, whereas Rabelais is full of these qualities. Even the opening of the *Peace*, fantastic as it is in its absurdity, does not touch the note of grossness peculiar to French Pantagruelism.—J. A. SYMONDS, *Studies of Greek Poets.*

Alone among the great writers of the world, Rabelais can be appreciated by students only. To the general reader, to the young, to women in all ages, he is a closed book. For very shame he must be hidden away. His real features are only revealed to those who lift the veil with serious intent to study and not to laugh. To all others the man is a buffoon, and the book is what Voltaire called it in the early days before he understood it, *Un ramas des plus grossières ordures qu'un moine ivre puisse vomir.*—SIR WALTER BESANT, *Rabelais for English Readers.*

Rabelais, evangelist and prophet of the Resurrection of the Flesh (so long entombed, ignored, repudiated, misconstrued, vilified, by so many generations and ages of Galilean preachers and Pharisaic schoolmen)— Rabelais was content to paint the flesh merely, in its honest human reality—human at least, if also bestial; in its frank and rude reaction against the half brainless teachers whose doctrine he himself on the one hand, and Luther on the other, arose together to smite severally—to smite them hip and thigh, even till the going down of the sun ; the mock sun or marshy meteor that served only to deepen the darkness encompassing on every side the doubly dark ages—the ages of monarchy and theocracy, the ages of death and of faith.—SWINBURNE, *A Study of Shakespeare.*

JEAN RACINE.

French Dramatic Poet : 1639-1699.

Exact Racine, Corneille's noble fire,
Showed us that France had something to admire.
—POPE, *Imitations of Horace, Epistle I.*

In elegant Racine
How the more powerful though more humble voice
Of nature-painting Greece, resistless, breathed
The whole awakened heart.
—THOMSON, *Liberty, Part V.*

——classic judgment gained to sweet Racine
The temperate strength of Maro's chaster line.
—WILLIAM COLLINS, *Epistle to Sir Thomas Hanmer.*

So well are Racine's meanest persons taught,
But change a sentiment you make a fault.
—YOUNG, *Epistle : To Lord Lansdowne,* 1712.

The style of Racine is exquisite. Perhaps he is second only to Virgil among all poets.—HALLAM, *Literature of the Middle Ages, Vol. IV.*

ANN RADCLIFFE.

English Novelist : 1764-1823.

She makes her readers twice children ; and from the dim and shadowy veil which she draws over the objects of her fancy, forces us to believe all that is strange, and next to impossible, of their mysterious agency.— HAZLITT, *Lectures on the English Comic Writers.*

Sir Walter Raleigh.

English Navigator, Statesman, Courtier, Warrior: 1552-1618.

To thee, that art the summer's Nightingale,
　Thy sovereign Goddess's most dear delight,
Why do I send this rustic Madrigal,
　That may thy tuneful ear unseason quite?
Thou only fit this Argument to write,
　In whose high thoughts Pleasure hath built her bower,
And dainty love learned sweetly to indite.
　My rhymes I know unsavoury and sour.
To taste the streams that, like a golden shower,
　Flow from thy fruitful head, of thy love's praise;
Fitter, perhaps, to thunder Martial stour
　When so thee list thy lofty Muse to raise;
Yet, till that thou thy Poem wilt make known,
Let thy fair Cynthia's praises be thus rudely shown.
　　　　　　　—Spenser, *To Sir Walter Raleigh.*

Raleigh, with hopes of new discoveries fir'd,
And all the depths of human wit inspir'd,
Rov'd o'er the western world in search of fame,
Adding fresh glory to Eliza's name;
Subdued new empires, that will records be
Immortal of a queen's virginity.
　　　　　　　—Dr. William King, *Britain's Palladium.*

　　　　But who can speak
The numerous worthies of the maiden reign?
In Raleigh mark their every glory mix'd;
Raleigh, the scourge of Spain! whose breast with all
The sage, the patriot, and the hero burn'd.
Nor sunk his vigour, when a coward-reign
The warrior fetter'd, and at last resign'd,
To glut the vengeance of a vanquish'd foe.
Then, active still and unrestrain'd, his mind
Explor'd the vast extent of ages past,
And with his prison-hours enrich'd the world;
Yet found no times, in all the long research,
So glorious, or so base, as those he prov'd,
In which he conquer'd, and in which he bled.
　　　　　　　—Thomson, *The Seasons : Summer.*

Truth fairly must record, and, pleas'd to live
In league with mercy, justice may forgive
Kingdoms betray'd, and worlds resign'd to Spain,
But never can forgive a Raleigh slain.
　　　　　　　—Churchill, *Gotham, Book II.*

On Raleigh's grave, O strew the fairest flowers,
That on the bosom of the green vale blow!
There hang your vernal wreaths, ye village-maids!
Ye mountain nymphs, your crowns of wild thyme bring
To Raleigh's honour'd grave! There bloom the bay,

The virgin rose, that blushing to be seen,
Folds its fair leaves ; for modest worth was his :
A mind where truth, philosophy's first born,
Held her harmonious reign ; a Briton's breast,
That, careful still of freedom's holy pledge,
Disdain'd the mean arts of a tyrant's court,
Disdain'd and died ! Where was thy spirit then,
Queen of sea-crowning isles, when Raleigh bled ?
How well he serv'd thee, let Iberia tell !
Ask prostrate Cales, yet trembling at his name,
How well he serv'd thee ; when her vanquish'd hand
Held forth the base bribe, how he spurn'd it from him,
And cried, I fight for Britain ! History rise,
And blast the reigns that redden with the blood
Of those that gave them glory !
                              —Dr. John Langhorne, *Fragment*, 1762.

Raleigh, the soldier, the sailor, the scholar, the courtier, the orator, the poet, the historian, the philosopher, whom we picture to ourselves sometimes reviewing the Queen's guard, sometimes giving chase to a Spanish galleon, then answering the chiefs of the country party in the House of Commons, then again murmuring one of his sweet love-songs too near the ears of her Highness's maids of honour, and soon after poring over the *Talmud* or collating Polybius with Livy.—Macaulay, *Essays : Burleigh and His Times.*

The name of Sir Walter Raleigh is unquestionably one of the most renowned and attractive, and in some respects the most remarkable in English story. He acted a part in all the various functions of public life, military, naval, and civil ; and was illustrious in all. He was a projector on the grandest scale, an improver of naval architecture, a founder of colonies, a promotor of distant commerce. As the introducer or disseminator of two important articles of subsistence and luxury (potatoes and tobacco), he in a vast degree contributed to augment the food, and to modify the habits of all the nations of Europe. His fortunes were alike remarkable for enviable success and pitiable reverses. Raised to eminent station through the favour of the greatest female sovereign of England, he perished on the scaffold through the dislike and cowardly policy of the meanest of her kings. To crown all, his fame in letters as the author of that memorable work with which " his prison hours enriched the world," placed his name in glorious association with those of Bacon and Hooker, as it otherwise was with those of Essex and Vere, of Hawkins and Drake.
—Macvey Napier, *Lord Bacon and Sir Walter Raleigh.*

The variety of Raleigh's powers and tendencies, and of their exercise, is the distinctive note of him, and of the epoch which needed, fashioned, and used him. A whole band of faculties stood ready in him at any moment for action. Several generally were at work simultaneously. For the man to be properly visible, he should be shown flashing from more facets than a brilliant. Few are the pens which can vividly reflect versatility like his.—W. Stebbing, *Life of Sir Walter Raleigh.*

The Father of the United States.—A. P. Stanley.

I, for one, would rather take my stand with Raleigh, purged in the seven-times-heated furnace of affliction and forgiven for his Saviour's sake, than with millions of vulgar and every-day respectabilities, who have passed their life in the Pharisaism of false orthodoxies, and the pettiness of cheap observances.—F. W. FARRAR, *Social and Present-Day Questions.*

ALLAN RAMSAY.

Scottish Poet: 1685-1758.

Ramsay an' famous Ferguson
Gied Forth an' Tay a lift aboon ;
Yarrow an' Tweed, to monie a tune,
    Owre Scotland rings.
        —BURNS, *To William Simpson.*

Dear Ramsay, if I know thy soul aright,
Plain-dealing honesty's thy dear delight:
Not great, but candid born ; not rich, but free ;
Thinks kings most wretched, and most happy me.
    —WILLIAM HAMILTON, *Horace, Book I., Epistle XVIII., imitated.*

Or bonny RAMSAY please thee mo,
Who *sang sae* sweetly *aw* his woe.
    —ROBERT LLOYD, *The Poetry Professors.*

Like the poetry of Tasso and Ariosto, that of the Gentle Shepherd is engraven on the memory, and has sunk into the heart of its native country. Its verses have passed into proverbs ; and it continues to be the delight and solace of the peasantry whom it describes.—THOMAS CAMPBELL.

Ramsay hits with the hammer of Thor, when he should tap as lightly as 'twere reproof administered by a fair one with her fan. . . . But though I do not rate Burns the less, I value Ramsay the more, when I say that, had there been no Ramsay there might have been no Burns nor any Ferguson—at least, the genius of the two last named poets would not have found an adequate vehicle of expression lying ready-made to their hand. Ramsay it was who virtually rendered the Scots vernacular a possible medium for the use of Burns ; and this service, unconsciously rendered by the lesser genius to the greater, is generously acknowledged by the latter, who could not but be aware that, as his own star waxed higher and yet higher, from the horizon line of popularity, that of his elder rival waned more and more.—OLIVER SMEATON, *Life of Allan Ramsay.*

RAPHAEL.

Italian Painter: 1483-1520.

Long time the sister arts, in iron sleep,
A heavy sabbath did supinely keep :
At length in Raphael's age, at once they rise,
Stretch all their limbs, and open all their eyes.
    —DRYDEN, *To Sir Godfrey Kneller.*

Then sculpture and her sister-arts revive ;
Stones leap'd to form, and rocks began to live ;
With sweeter notes each rising temple rung ;
A Raphael painted, and a Vida sung.
                    —POPE, *Essay on Criticism.*

Fain would I Raphael's godlike art rehearse,
And show th' immortal labours in my verse,
Where from the mingled strength of shade and light,
A new creation rises to my sight ;
Such heavenly figures from his pencil flow,
So warm with life his blended colours glow,
From theme to theme with secret pleasures tost,
Amidst the soft variety I'm lost.
        —ADDISON, *A Letter from Italy to Lord Halifax,* 1701.

Raphael shall teach thee, friend, exalted thoughts
And intellectual bliss.   'Twas Raphael taught
The patriarch of our progeny th' affairs
Of heaven : (So Milton sings, enlightened bard !).
        —DR. WATTS, *To Mitio, my Friend, The Second Part.*

And, from the deeps of Raphael, rose
Celestial Love again.
                    —LYTTON, *Mazarin.*

Oh, their Rafael of the dear Madonnas,
Oh, their Dante of the dread Inferno,
Wrote one song—and in my brain I sing it,
Drew one angel—borne, see, on my bosom !
        —ROBERT BROWNING, *One Word More.*

Raphael would have been a great painter even if he had come into the world without hands.—LESSING *(transl.).*

Who would not prefer one Virgin and Child of Raphael, to all the pictures which Rubens, with his fat, frouzy Dutch Venuses, ever painted ? —J. STUART MILL, *Dissertations and Discussions, Vol. I.*

Three penstrokes of Raffaelle are a greater and a better picture than the most finished work that ever Carlo Dolci polished into inanity.— RUSKIN, *Modern Painters, Vol. I.*

The rich poets, as Homer, Chaucer, Shakespeare, and Raphael, have obviously no limits to their works, except the limits of their life-time, and resemble a mirror carried through the street, ready to render an image of every created thing.—EMERSON, *Essays : The Poet.*

When, however, Raphael's divine form still walked the earth, painting then stood above all as the highest acquisition to which the Romanic nations had ever attained ; the bond between religion and beauty, heaven and earth, was concluded.   And yet this glorious prime contained in itself even then the germs of its dissolution.   The soul of Italian art perished, when the noble author of that incomparable bond was snatched from earth.   Because he had summed up in himself all the perfections of former times, there was now only a fragmentary sundering of his universal aims left behind him on the field of art.   Raphael forms no school, because he is the end and close of an era in mental development; all that could be expressed within the sphere of art which he embraced, was expressed by him; his pupils are indeed only pupils, who cultivate his manner.—BARON VON WOLZOGEN, *Life of Raphael Santi (transl.).*

VAN RHYN PAUL REMBRANDT.

Dutch Painter and Engraver: 1608-1669.

Th' immortal Rembrandt all his pictures made
Soft as their union into light and shade:
Whene'er his colours wore too bright an air,
A kindred shadow took off all the glare ;
Whene'er that shadow, carelessly embrown'd,
Stole on the tints, and breath'd a gloom around.
        —JAMES CAWTHORN, *The Regulation of the Passions.*

I have seen an old head by Rembrandt at Burleigh House, and if I could produce a head at all like Rembrandt in a year, in my life-time, it would be glory and felicity, and wealth and fame enough for me.— HAZLITT, *Table Talk.*

SIR JOSHUA REYNOLDS.

English Painter: 1723-1792.

Here Reynolds is laid, and to tell you my mind,
He has not left a wiser or better behind ;
His pencil was striking, resistless and grand ;
His manners were gentle, complying and bland ;
Still born to improve us in every part,
His pencil our faces, his manners our heart ;
To coxcombs averse, yet more civilly steering,
When they judg'd without skill he was still hard of hearing :
When they talk'd of their Raphaels, Correggios, and stuff,
He shifted his trumpet, and only took snuff.
        —GOLDSMITH, *Retaliation.*

There, touch'd by Reynolds, a dull blank becomes
A lucid mirror, in which Nature sees
All her reflected features.
        —COWPER, *The Task : The Sofa.*

Dear President, whose art sublime
Gives perpetuity to time,
And bids transactions of a day,
That fleeting hours would waft away
To dark futurity, survive,
And in unfading beauty live.
        —*Id., To Sir Joshua Reynolds.*

Reynolds, with whom began that school of art which hath equall'd
Richest Italy's works, and the masterly labours of Belgium,
Came in that famous array.
        —SOUTHEY, *A Vision of Judgment: Worthies of the Georgian Age.*

Sir Joshua Reynolds was, on very many accounts, one of the most memorable men of his time. He was the first Englishman who added the praise of the elegant arts to the other glories of his country. In taste, in grace, in facility, in happy invention, and in the richness and harmony of colouring, he was equal to the great masters of the renowned ages. In portrait he went beyond them ; for he communicated to that description of the art, in which English artists are the most engaged, a variety, a fancy, and a dignity derived from the higher branches, which even those who professed them in a superior manner did not always preserve when they delineated individual nature. His portraits remind the spectator of the invention of history, and the amenity of landscape. In painting portraits he appeared not to be raised upon that platform ; but to descend to it from a higher sphere. His paintings illustrate his lessons, and his lessons seem to be derived from his paintings.—BURKE.

Sir Joshua Reynolds remains a memorable proof that it is possible for an artist to unite the highest genius and most imaginative power of mind to the wisdom of a philosopher, the liberality of a gentleman, the bene-volence of a Christian, and the simplicity of a child.—SIR ARCHIBALD ALISON, *Essays : Autobiography.*

It is related of Sir Joshua Reynolds, that " he took no other exercise than what he used in his painting room " : the writer means, in walking backwards and forwards to look at his picture.—WILLIAM HAZLITT.

We prefer a gipsy by Reynolds to his Majesty's head on a sign-post.— MACAULAY, *Essays : Moore's Life of Byron.*

Nearly every word that Reynolds wrote was contrary to his own practice ; he seems to have been born to teach all error by his precept, and all excellence by his example ; he enforced with his lips generalisation and idealism, while with his pencil he was tracing the patterns of the dresses of the belles of his day ; he exhorted his pupils to attend only to the invariable, while he himself was occupied in distinguishing every varia-tion of womanly temper ; and he denied the existence of the beautiful, at the same instant that he arrested it as he passed, and perpetuated it for ever.—RUSKIN, *Modern Painters, Vol. III.*

The work of other great men is hidden in its wonderfulness—you can-not see how it is done. But in Sir Joshua's there is no mystery : it is all amazement. No question but that the touch was so laid ; only that it *could* have been so laid, is a marvel for ever. So also there is no painting so majestic in sweetness. He is lily-sceptred ; his power blossoms, but burdens not. All other men of equal dignity paint more slowly ; all others of equal force paint less lightly. Tintoret lays his line like a king mark-ing the boundaries of conquered lands ; but Sir Joshua leaves it as a summer wind its trace on a lake ; he could have painted on a silken veil, where it fell free, and not bent it.—*Id., On the Old Road, Vol. I.*

I cannot separate the character of Reynolds—calm, simple, unfussy, amiable, and tolerant, prompt to kindly construction of words and things, keenly relishing life and character and social enjoyments, yet not over-valuing money or distinction—from the delightfulness of his pictures.— TOM TAYLOR, *Life and Times of Sir Joshua Reynolds, Vol. II.*

RICHARD I., CŒUR-DE-LION.

King of England: 1157-1199.

Was Cœur-de-lion blest with whiter days ?

. . . .

Of ten fair suns that roll'd their annual race,
Not one beheld him on his vacant throne.

—SHENSTONE, *The Ruined Abbey.*

Lion-hearted Richard was there, redoubtable warrior,
At whose irresistible presence the Saracen trembled ;
At whose name the Caliph exclaim'd in dismay on Mahommed,
Syrian mothers grew pale, and their children were scared into silence.
Born in a bloody age, did he in his prowess exulting
Run like a meteor his course, and fulfil the service assign'd him,
Checking the Mussulman power in the height of its prosperous fortune ;
But that leonine heart was with virtues humaner ennobled,
(Otherwhere else, be sure, his doom had now been appointed),
Friendship, disdain of wrong, and generous feeling redeem'd it,
Magnanimity there had its seat, and the love of the Muses.

—SOUTHEY, *A Vision of Judgment : The Sovereign.*

Redoubted king, of courage leonine,
I mark thee, Richard ! urgent to equip
Thy warlike person with the staff and scrip ;
I watch thee sailing o'er the midland brine ;
In conquered Cyprus see thy bride decline
Her blushing cheek, love-vows upon her lip,
And see love-emblems streaming from thy ship,
As thence she holds her way to Palestine.

—WORDSWORTH, *Richard I.*

His armour is made of the brass most strong,
But stronger still is his bosom ;
'Tis Cœur de Lion that's riding along,
That Christian chivalry's blossom.

—H. HEINE, *King Richard* (*transl.*).

Richard I. was rather a knight-errant than a king. His history is more that of a Crusade than of a Reign.—SIR JAMES MACKINTOSH, *History of England, Vol. I.*

Men called him " Lion-heart," not untruly; and the English as a people have prided themselves somewhat ever since on having every man of them the heart of a lion.—RUSKIN.

Cœur-de-Lion was not a theatrical popinjay with greaves and steel-cap on it, but a man living upon victuals.—CARLYLE, *Past and Present : Jocelin of Brakelond.*

RICHARD II.

King of England : 1366-1400.

Salisbury : " Ah, Richard, with the eyes of heavy mind,
I see thy glory, like a shooting star,

Fall to the base earth from the firmament !
Thy sun sets weeping in the lowly west,
Witnessing storms to come, woe, and unrest:
Thy friends are fled, to wait upon thy foes ;
And crossly to thy good all fortune goes."
                    —SHAKSPERE, *King Richard II., Act II., Scene IV.*

Richard II., a weak, vain, frivolous, inconstant prince ; without weight to balance the scales of government, without discernment to choose a good ministry ; without virtue to oppose the measures, or advice, of evil counsellors, even where they happened to clash with his own principles and opinion. He was a dupe to flattery, a slave to ostentation, and not more apt to give up his reason to the suggestion of sycophants and vicious ministers, than to sacrifice those ministers to his safety. He was idle, profuse, and profligate ; and, though brave by starts, naturally pusillanimous, and irresolute. His pride and resentment prompted him to cruelty and breach of faith : while his necessities obliged him to fleece his people, and degrade the dignity of his character and situation.— SMOLLETT.

RICHARD III.

King of England : 1450-1485.

For having rule and riches in our hand,
Who durst gaynsay the thing that we averde ?
Wyl was wysedome, our lust for lawe dyd stand,
In sorte so straunge, that who was not afeard
When he the sound but of Kyng Rychard heard ?
So hatefull wart the hearyng of his name,
That you may deeme the residewe by the same.

              .   .   .   .   .

So cruell seemde this Rychard Third to me,
That loe my selfe now loathde his crueltee.
                    —SACKVILLE, LORD BUCKHURST, *Complaynt of Duke of Buckinghame.*

So were his children young, being left to be protected
By Richard : who nor God, nor human laws respected.
This viper, this most vile devourer of his kind
(Whom his ambitious ends had struck so grossly blind)
From their dear mother's lap them seizing for a prey,
Himself in right the next, could they be made away
Most wrongfully usurp'd, and them in prison kept ;
Whom cruelly at last he smothered as they slept.
                    —DRAYTON, *Polyolbion, Song XVII.*

Robespierre vindicating, in the midst of massacre, the existence of a God of mercy, is like our own Richard III. issuing his Proclamation against Vice after the murder of his nephews. The sentiments professed by either may be admirable in themselves, but they only serve to deepen the general abhorrence of the character they contrast.—LYTTON, *Essays : The Reign of Terror.*

SAMUEL RICHARDSON.

English Novelist: 1689-1761.

Oh, Richardson, I dare pronounce that the most veritable history is full of fictions, and thy fictions are full of truths. History paints some individuals; thou paintest the human species. History attributes to some individuals what they have never said or done; all that thou attributest to man he has said and done. History embraces but a point of duration, a point on the surface of the globe; thou hast embraced all places and all times. The human heart, which has been and ever shall be the same, is the model which thou copiest. If we were severely to criticise the best historian, would he maintain his ground as thou? In this point of view, I can venture to say, that frequently history is a miserable romance; and romance, as thou hast composed it, is a good history. Painter of nature thou never liest! . . . Richardson is no more. His loss touches me as if my brother was no more. I love him as my brother without having seen him, and knowing him but by his works. He has not had all the reputation he merited. Richardson! if living thy merit has been disputed, how great wilt thou appear to our children's children, when they shall see thee at the distance we now see Homer! Then who will dare steal a line from thy sublime works? Thou hast more admirers amongst us than in thine own country—and at this I rejoice.—DIDEROT (*transl.*).

Richardson was well qualified to be the discoverer of a new style of writing, for he was a cautious, deep, and minute examinator of the human heart, and, like Cooke or Parry, left neither head, bay, nor inlet behind him, until he had traced its soundings, and laid it down in his chart, with all its minute sinuosities, its depths, and its shallows.—SIR WALTER SCOTT, *Prose Works, Vol. III.*

The great excellence of Richardson's novels consists, we think, in the unparalleled minuteness and copiousness of his descriptions, and in the pains he takes to make us thoroughly and intimately acquainted with every particular in the character and situation of the personages with whom we are occupied.—LORD JEFFREY, *Essays.*

The influence of Richardson upon the fiction and poetry of Europe was not only vast at the time, but, enduring still, it must endure for ever. In vain his language grows obsolete, in vain his minuteness has become wearisome, in vain the young race of novel-readers leave him on the shelf—to those somewhat tedious pages turns every genius who aspires to rise in fiction; from them, though with toil and study, can best be learned the art of extracting from the homeliest details the noblest pathos. In *Clarissa* is beheld that true spirit of tragedy which first dispensed with kings and heroes and the paraphernalia of the outward stage— teaching how the compass of all grandeur in fiction can be attained by him who can describe the affection, and comprehend the virtue, of one human being.—LYTTON, *Life of Schiller, Chap. II.*

As De Foe's novels are simply history *minus* the facts, so Richardson's are a series of letters *minus* the correspondents.—LESLIE STEPHEN, *Hours in a Library, First Series.*

Richardson was a woman's novelist, as Fielding was a man's. I sometimes think of Dr. Johnson's saying: "Claret for boys, port for men," and, smiling, "brandy for heroes". So one might fancy him saying: "Richardson for women, Fielding for men, Smollett for ruffians," though some of his rough customers were heroes too.—ANDREW LANG, *Letters on Literature.*

Richardson has always been exposed to a strong under-current of ridicule. I have known people to smile at the mention of his name, as if he were a sort of man-milliner—or, did the thing exist, as some day it may do, a male nursery governess. . . . Richardson, on the other hand, had his quiver full of new ideas ; he had his face to the east ; he was no mere inheritor, he was a progenitor. He is, in short, as has been often said, our Rousseau ; his characters were not stock characters.—AUGUSTINE BIRRELL, *Res Judicatæ.*

DUC DE RICHELIEU.

French Cardinal and Statesman : 1585-1642.

Ay, take the sword
To Cardinal Richelieu :—he gives gold for steel,
When worn by brave men.
Was ever lightning swifter, or more blasting,
Than Richelieu's forkèd guile ?

—LYTTON, *Richelieu.*

Let the world speak well or ill of the famous Cardinal, neither in my prose nor verse will I mention his name ; he has done me too much kindness to speak ill of him, and too much injury to speak well.—CORNEILLE.

Richelieu himself is still what he was in his own day—a man of two characters. If, on the one hand, he is justly represented as inflexible and vindictive, crafty and unscrupulous ; so, on the other, it cannot be denied that he was placed in times in which the long impunity of every licence required stern examples—that he was beset by perils and intrigues, which gave a certain excuse to the subtlest inventions of self-defence—that his ambition was inseparably connected with a passionate love for the glory of his country—and that, if he was her dictator, he was not less her benefactor.—LYTTON, *Preface to Richelieu.*

If Richelieu was pitiless, he was not, like most revengeful despots, either capricious or unjust. He did not strike the tool if he could reach the employer ; nor did he strike till guilt was obvious and incontestable ; his was no reckless reign of terror. His methods, though often arbitrary and contrary to legal custom and tradition, were always fearless and above-board. Political considerations sometimes made it impossible to inflict a fitting penalty upon men who richly deserved it, such as de Bouillon and the traitorous Gascon, but the motive that allowed them to escape was never terror nor a wish to curry favour.—RICHARD LODGE, *Life of Richelieu.*

Jean Paul Richter.

German Novelist: 1763-1825.

Once more,—once only,—we must stop so soon,—
What have we here? A GERMAN-SILVER SPOON;
A cheap utensil, which we often see
Used by the dabblers in æsthetic tea,
Of slender fabric, somewhat light and thin,
Made of mixed metal, chiefly lead and tin;
The bowl is shallow, and the handle small,
Marked in large letters with the name JEAN PAUL.
                —OLIVER WENDELL HOLMES, *An After-Dinner Poem.*

All who are acquainted with the writings of Jean Paul must be aware that, whatever is to be said of his genius as a whole or in comparison with that of his compatriot Goethe, in the single faculty of wild and rich prose-poesy he is the most astonishing even of German writers.—DAVID MASSON, *Wordsworth, Shelley, and Keats.*

Frederick William Robertson.

English Theologian: 1816-1853.

It is always to be borne in mind, that in the case of Robertson it is a unique phenomenon that we are witnessing, the making of thought; that in his case we are not witnessing the homogeneous perfected processes of mind, but are, as it were, admitted into the laboratory of the soul, and witness the gradual evolution of opinion and experience. . . . Robertson's great charm is that he goes straight to the human heart. The hearts of his people were swayed by him as the corn-fields are swept by a strong wind from heaven. We must believe with the heart.—FREDERICK ARNOLD, *Robertson of Brighton.*

He lies in a hollow of the Downs he loved so well. The sound of the waves may be heard there in the distance; and standing by his grave, it seems a fair and fitting requiem; for if the inquietude of the sea was the image of his outward life, its central calm is the image of his deep peace of activity in God. He sleeps well; and we, who are left alone with our love and his great result of work, cannot but rejoice that he has entered into his Father's rest. . . . He respected his conscience; believed in his own native force, and in the divine fire within him. He looked first at everything submitted to his judgment as if it were a new thing upon earth, and then permitted the judgments of the past to have their due weight with him. He endeavoured to receive, without the intervention of commentators, immediate impressions from the Bible.—STOPFORD BROOKE, *Life and Letters of F. W. Robertson, Vol. II.*

Maximilien Robespierre.

French Revolutionary Dictator: 1758-1794.

It would be difficult to point out within the whole range of history, ancient or modern, any person who played so great a part as Robespierre with so little genius.—LORD BROUGHAM, *Statesmen of the Reign of George III., Vol. III.*

These butchers so atrocious in the capital, were magnificent as statesmen and heroes the moment their mind flew to the borders of invaded France. There, the iron will of Robespierre, the savage genius of St. Just, the reckless daring of Danton, changed at once from vices into virtues. . . . The more, amidst that chaos of motives and actors, we regard the prominent individuals, the more we must perceive that the only INTELLIGENCE of the time was Maximilien Robespierre. He had objects and purposes beyond the hour ; he was ever looking forward to the time when the Reign of Blood was to cease ; he only desired to destroy his enemies in order to call into being the new state of things in which he could reduce to system the theories he cherished. . . . He firmly believed in all the principles he professed ;—a hypocrite in his conduct to men, but an enthusiast in his faith in dogmas.—LYTTON, *Essays : The Reign of Terror.*

Robespierre was a kind of spinster. Force of head did not match his spiritual ambition. He was not, we repeat, a coward in any common sense ; in that case he would have remained quiet among the croaking frogs of the Marsh, and by and by have come to hold a portfolio under the first Consul. He did not fear death, and he envied with consuming envy those to whom nature had given the qualities of initiative. But his nerves always played him false. The consciousness of having to resolve to take a decided step alone, was the precursor of a fit of trembling. His heart did not fail, but he could nor control the parched voice, nor the twitching features, nor the ghastly palsy of inner misgiving.—JOHN MORLEY, *Miscellanies, Vol. I.*

Had the reign of Robespierre lasted longer, multitudes would have thrown themselves under the guillotine : the love of life was extinct in every heart.—L. S. FRÉRON *(transl.)*.

FRANCIS, DUC DE LA ROCHEFOUCAULD.

French Moralist : 1613-1680.

As Rochefoucauld his maxims drew
From nature, I believe them true :
They argue no corrupted mind
In him ; the fault is in mankind.

—SWIFT, *On the Death of Dr. Swift.*

Man loves this sparkling satire on himself;
Gaze round—see Rochefoucauld on every shelf!

—LYTTON, *La Rochefoucauld and Condorcet.*

Don't *Rochefoucault* my motives.—BYRON in MOORE'S *Life of Byron.*

We are never to forget the extent to which the fashionable philosophy of France has operated on the intellect and action of Europe ; and Voltaire assures us, in his most celebrated work, that " the book which most contributed to form the taste of the French nation was the *Maxims* of François, Duc de Rochefoucauld ". That is true ;—not only the taste but the mode of thought. Helvetius, preceding the Revolution, is but a learned and lengthened expositor of the philosophy contained in the *Maxims*. Rochefoucauld was one of the founders of the Revolution, for his work was that of a leveller.—Lytton, *Essays: Knowledge of the World.*

Rochefoucault's precise and pregnant satire resolves every motive of man into self-interest. Self-interest does, indeed, seem to be the grand cement of social man. But, in telling this secret, Rochefoucault stripped the heart, as it were, naked, with all its deformities; careless of chances, and reckless of consequences. He presented poison in one hand, without administering an antidote in the other; like an unskilful surgeon, who, after laying open a deep wound, permits it to gangrene, with little or no solicitude as to the cure or subsequent contagious expansion.—Charles Bucke, *Book of Human Character.*

Samuel Rogers.

English Poet: 1763-1855.

And thou, melodious Rogers! rise at last,
Recall the pleasing memory of the past;
Arise! iet blest remembrance still inspire,
And strike to wonted tones thy hallow'd lyre;
Restore Apollo to his vacant throne,
Assert thy country's honour and thine own.
                    —Byron, *English Bards and Scotch Reviewers.*

Absent or present, still to thee,
  My friend, what magic spells belong!
As all can tell, who share like me,
  In turn thy converse and thy song.

But when the dreaded hour shall come
  By Friendship ever deem'd too nigh,
And " Memory " o'er her Druid's tomb
  Shall weep that aught of thee can die,

How fondly will she then repay
  Thy homage offer'd at her shrine,
And blend, while ages roll away,
  Her name immortally with *thine!*
        —*Id., Lines written on a blank leaf of " The Pleasures of Memory ".*

Two living Poets, however, it seems there are, who, according to Mr. Jeffrey, are never to be dead ones—two who are unforgetable, and who owe their immortality—to what think ye?—their *elegance!* That *Gracilis Puer*, Samuel Rogers, is one of the dual number. His perfect beauties will never be brought to decay in the eyes of an enamoured world. He is so polished, that time can never take the shine out of him—so classically correct are his charms, that to the end of time they will be among the principal Pleasures of Memory.—John Wilson, *Essays: Days Departed.*

Samuel Rogers has been spoken of, ever since anybody can remember, as " Rogers the Poet ". It is less as a poet, however, that his name will live than as a Patron of Literature—probably the last of that class who will in England be called a Mæcenas.—Harriet Martineau, *Biographical Sketches.*

George Romney.

English Painter: 1734-1802.

Romney, expert infallibly to trace,
On chart or canvas, not the form alone
And semblance, but however faintly shown
The mind's impression too on every face.
> —Cowper, *Sonnet to George Romney, Esq.*

Earl of Roscommon.

English Poet: 1633-1684.

The Muse's empire is restor'd again,
In Charles's reign, and by Roscommon's pen.
Yet modestly he does his work survey,
And calls a finish'd Poem an Essay.

. . . .

Roscommon, whom both court and camps commend,
True to his prince, and faithful to his friend ;
Roscommon, first in fields of honour known,
First in the peaceful triumphs of the gown ;
Who both Minerva justly makes his own.
> —Dryden, *To the Earl of Roscommon.*

Such was the muse whose rules and practice tell,
" Nature's chief master-piece is writing well."
Such was Roscommon, not more learn'd than good,
With manners gen'rous as his noble blood ;
To him the wit of Greece and Rome was known,
And ev'ry author's merit but his own.
> —Pope, *Essay on Criticism.*

In all Charles's days,
Roscommon only boasts unspotted bays.
> —*Id., Epistles of Horace imitated, Epistle I., Book II.*

Nor must Roscommon pass neglected by,
That makes ev'n rules a noble poetry :
Rules whose deep sense and heavenly numbers show
The best of critics, and of poets too.
> —Addison, *An Account of the Greatest English Poets.*

Dante Gabriel Rossetti.

English Poet and Painter: 1828-1882.

Yea, thou art dead, nor hast thou any care
That the first hawthorn swells in bud to-night,
Nor yet for our despair ;
Nor for the songs that once were thy delight,
Whose singing wings shall never cease to beat
In music strange and sweet,
And make a southern April in our air.
> —A. Mary F. Robinson, *In Memoriam : Dante Gabriel Rossetti.*

Spirit of Beauty tarry yet a-while! . . .
For One at least there is—He bears his name
  From Dante and the seraph Gabriel—
Whose double laurels burn with deathless flame
  To light thine altar.
              —OSCAR WILDE, *The Garden of Eros.*

Rossetti's luscious lines seldom fail to cast a spell.—AUGUSTINE
BIRRELL, *Obiter Dicta, First Series.*

With the choice of two media, in the use of both of which he was
equally proficient, Rossetti made naturally frequent experiments as to
which was the better adapted to his powers. To this moment the question remains unanswered. Unlike some poets, however, who have employed verse for the purpose of illustrating problems, polemical and
metaphysical, with the result that they are regarded as poets among
philosophers and as philosophers among poets, Rossetti has been received
with enthusiasm in both capacities by both poets and painters. It may,
indeed, be said that he is a painter's painter, and a poet's poet.—JOSEPH
KNIGHT, *Life of Dante Gabriel Rossetti* (1887).

Nowhere in Time's vista, where the forms of great men gather thickly,
do we see many shapes of those who, as painters and as poets, have been
alike illustrious. Among the few to whom, equally on both accounts,
conspicuous honours have been paid, none is superior to Rossetti, of whose
genius doubly exalted the artists say that in design he was pre-eminent,
while, on the other hand, the most distinguished poets of our age place
him in the first rank with themselves. As to this prodigious, if not unique,
distinction, of which the present age has not yet, perhaps, formed an
adequate judgment, there can be no doubt that with regard to the constructive portion of his genius Rossetti was better equipped in verse than
in design.—F. G. STEPHENS, *Dante Gabriel Rossetti* (1894).

JOACHIM ROSSINI.

Italian Musical Composer: 1792-1868.

Enough for us that the three great creative minds to whose exquisite
inventions all nations at this moment yield, Rossini, Meyerbeer, Mendelssohn, are of Hebrew race; and little do your men of fashion, your
muscadins of Paris, and your dandies of London, as they thrill into
raptures at the notes of a Pasta or a Grisi, little do they suspect that they
are offering their homage to the "sweet singers of Israel".—LORD
BEACONSFIELD, *Coningsby.*

LOUIS FRANÇOIS ROUBILLAC.

French Sculptor: 1695-1762.

Like statues made by Roubillac,
Though form'd beyond all skill antique,
They can't their marble silence break;
They only breathe, and think, and start,
Astonish'd at their master's art.
              —CHRISTOPHER SMART, *Fable IX., Madam and the Magpie.*

JEAN JACQUES ROUSSEAU.

French Philosopher and Writer: 1712-1778.

Corruption would not now thus much inherit
Of what was once Rousseau—nor this disguise
Stained that which ought to have disdained to wear it.
—SHELLEY, *The Triumph of Life.*

I do not know that I resemble Jean Jacques Rousseau. I have no ambition to be like so illustrious a madman—but this I know, that I shall live in my own manner, and as much alone as possible.—BYRON in MOORE'S *Life of Byron.*

The life of Rousseau neither requires so full a consideration as that of Voltaire, nor affords the materials for it. Mankind are not divided upon his character and his merits, nor ever were. That he was a person of rare genius within limited, nay, somewhat confined, bounds, of a lively imagination, wholly deficient in judgment, capable of great vices as well as virtues, and of a mind so diseased that it may possibly be doubted if he was accountable for his actions, is the opinion which his contemporaries formed of him during his life, which has ever since prevailed, and which, indeed, was formed by his own testimony, produced after his decease, and calculated to show that he would not have dissented from the sentence or even have hesitated to join in pronouncing it.—LORD BROUGHAM, *Men of Letters of the Time of George III., Vol. II.*

With Rousseau rose the great sect of HUMANITY; the school which seeks to lift human nature above convention; which would extract from social life all that is harsh and tyrannous; and (to use the phrase of Seneca) recognise a claim to kindness wherever it looks upon the face of a man.—LYTTON, *Life of Schiller, Vol. II.*

Of Rousseau's literary talents, greatly celebrated still among his countrymen, I do not say much. His books, like himself, are what I call unhealthy; not the good sort of books. There is a sensuality in Rousseau. Combined with such an intellectual gift as his, it makes pictures of a certain gorgeous attractiveness: but they are not genuinely poetical. Not white sunlight: something *operatic:* a kind of rosepink, artificial bedizenment. It is frequent, or rather it is universal, among the French since his time.—CARLYLE, *On Heroes and Hero-Worship.*

The interests which the loves of Petrarch excited in his own time, and the pitying fondness with which half Europe looked upon Rousseau, are well known. To readers of our age, the love of Petrarch seems to have been love of that kind which breaks no hearts, and the sufferings of Rousseau to have deserved laughter rather than pity, to have been partly counterfeited, and partly the consequences of his own perverseness and vanity.—MACAULAY, *Essays: Life of Byron.*

Every man has within himself an abyss, which he strives to conceal. Rousseau and Byron revealed theirs to the crowd, not as speaking of themselves only, but, to a certain extent, in the name and as the representative of society. Their moral defects they held up, like a Medusa's head, to the gaze of the world, with an unmistakably malignant pleasure, and they had no right to effect surprise if society, offended by the sight, averted its eyes from them.—KARL ELZE, *Life of Lord Byron (transl.).*

It was Rousseau who first in our modern time sounded a new trumpet note for one of the great battles of humanity. He makes the poor very proud, it was truly said. Some of his contemporaries followed the same view of thought, as we shall see, and he was only continuing work which others had prepared. But he alone had the gift of the golden mouth. It was in Rousseau that polite Europe first hearkened to strange voices and faint reverberation from out of the vague and cavernous shadow in which the common people move. . . . It was this spiritual part of him which made Rousseau a third great power in the century, between the encyclopædic party and the Church. He recognised a something in men, which the encyclopædists treated as a chimera imposed on the imagination by theologians and others for their own purposes; and he recognised this in a way which did not offend the rational feeling of the times, as the catholic dogmas offended it. In a word he was religious. In being so, he separated himself from Voltaire and his school, who did passably well without religion. Again, he was a puritan—a puritan of the eighteenth century, it will be understood.—JOHN MORLEY, *Life of Rousseau, Vol. I.*

In judging Rousseau, it would be unfair not to take note of the malarious atmosphere in which he grew up. The constitution of his mind was thus early infected with a serious taint that made him shiveringly sensitive to a temperature which hardier natures found bracing. To him this rough world was but too literally a rack. Good-natured Mother Nature commonly imbeds the nerves of her children in a padding of self-conceit that serves as a buffer against the ordinary shocks to which even a life of routine is liable, and it would seem at first sight as if Rousseau had been better cared for in this respect. . . . Rousseau has, in one respect, been utterly misrepresented and misunderstood. Even Chateaubriand most unfilially classes him and Voltaire together. It appears to me that the inmost core of his being was religious. Had he remained in the Catholic Church, he might have been a saint. Had he come earlier, he might have founded an order. He was precisely the nature on which religious enthusiasm takes the strongest hold—a temperament which finds a sensuous delight in spiritual things, and satisfies its craving for excitement with celestial debauch. He had not the iron temper of a great reformer and organiser like Knox, who, true Scotchman that he was, found a way to weld this world and the other together in a cast-iron creed; but he had as much as any man ever had that gift of a great preacher to make the oratorical fervour which persuades himself while it lasts into the abiding conviction of his hearers.—J. R. LOWELL, *Among My Books.*

The prince of all autobiographers in this full sense of the word—the man who represents the genuine type in its fullest realisation—is undoubtedly Rousseau. The *Confessions* may certainly be regarded not only as one of the most remarkable, but as in parts one of the most repulsive, books ever written. Yet, one must add, it is also one of the most fascinating. Rousseau starts by declaring that he is undertaking a task which has had no precedent, and will have no imitators—the task of showing a man in all the truth of nature, and that man himself. . . .

Rousseau represents the strange combination of a kind of sensual appetite for pure and simple pleasures. On one side he reminds us of Keats, by his intense appreciation of sensuous beauty; and, on the other, of Cowper, by his love of such simple pleasures as our English poet enjoyed when sitting at Mrs. Unwin's tea-urn. It is a strange, almost a contradictory mixture; but Rousseau's life is a struggle between antagonisms.— LESLIE STEPHEN, *Hours in a Library*, *Vol. III.*

The creed of Rousseau was not a faith but an emotion, capable of impelling, not of controlling or sustaining men.—GOLDWIN SMITH, *Three English Statesmen.*

Undoubtedly, Rousseau's extremely attractive and widely read writings did a great deal to give a colour of rationality to those principles of '89 which, even after the lapse of a century, are considered by a good many people to be the Magna Charta of the human race. " Liberty, Equality, and Fraternity " is still the war-cry of those, and they are many, who think, with Rousseau, that human sufferings must needs be the consequence of the artificial arrangements of society and can all be alleviated or removed by political changes.

The intellectual impulse which may thus be fairly enough connected with the name of the Genevese dreamer has by no means spent itself in the century and a half which has elapsed since it was given. On the contrary, after a period of comparative obscurity (at least outside France), Rousseauism has gradually come to the front again, and at present promises to exert once more a very grave influence on practical life. . . . The political lantern of Rousseauism is a mere corpse candle and will plunge those who follow it in the deepest of anarchic bogs. . . . Rousseau is not intelligible without Buffon.—HUXLEY, *Method and Results.*

DR. THOMAS RUNDLE.

Bishop of Derry : 1686-1743.

Make Rundle bishop ! fie for shame !
An Arian to usurp the name !
A bishop in the Isle of Saints !
How will his brethren make complaints !
       —SWIFT, *On Dr. Rundle, Bishop of Derry.*

And thou, O Rundle, lend thy strain,
Thou darling friend ! thou brother of his soul !
In whom the head and heart their stores unite ;
Whatever of fancy paints, invention gives,
Judgment digests, the well-tun'd bosom feels,
Truth natural, moral, or divine, has taught,
The Virtues dictate, or the Muses sing.
       —THOMSON, *A Poem to the Memory of the Right Hon. Lord Talbot.*

JOHN RUSKIN.

Art Critic and Political Economist : 1819-1900.

No true disciple of mine will ever be a Ruskinian ; he will follow, not me, but the instincts of his own soul, and the guidance of its Creator.— RUSKIN, *St. Mark's Rest.*

Note how colour enters into his style; and sound also—sound so conveyed in words that we hear what he writes of as though we were on the spot. Yes; even hear it more distinctly, because he calls our ear and interprets the harmonies. Again, there is the pulse-beat of his sentences —pulse-beats in which we feel the throb of a mighty soul, and which no literary enemic could yield. Take also the intermixture of Scripture. How he delicately, yet strikingly, interweaves the passages from the Bible, until a chapter on art or political economy becomes an exposition of many a text called in to finish a sentence or point a lesson! For interpreting life by Scripture, and Scripture by life, he stands unrivalled. But this presupposes a knowledge of Scripture that few have, and a sense of proportion that few possess.—MARSHALL MATHER, *John Ruskin, His Life and Teaching.*

Since Tennyson died no greater loss has been sustained by English literature than that of John Ruskin. Of all the men who have dominated the Art-world of Britain during the nineteenth century, Ruskin is beyond all question and beyond all comparison the greatest—by universal admission the most individual and most interesting. What his exact position as a critic and preacher of Art may be, what his rank as a scientist or a leader of thought, I make no pretence here of determining. But, by common consent, he has been the most distinguished figure in the arena of Art philosophy for half-a-century and more, the philanthropist-militant *par excellence.* He is the man who has admittedly moulded the taste of the public to a preponderating extent in æsthetic affairs and, apart from his labours outside the pale of Art, has exerted an influence so powerful that he has given a direction to the practice of painting and architecture that may still be traced in some of the happiest productions of the day. His death has given reason for mourning to many ; no one has more eloquently, more passionately, pleaded the cause of the poor than Ruskin ; no one (with the exception of Mr. Gladstone—his political *bête noire*) could boast so vast a number of friends amongst the great mass of the public. . . . If we had to define the main characteristics of Ruskin's mind, " and the keys to the secret of all he said or did," I think we could hardly do better than repeat the analysis he made of Turner's : " Uprightness, generosity, extreme tenderness of heart, sensuality, excessive obstinacy, irritability, infidelity " ; and, we should have to add, " impulsiveness, violent prejudice, kindliest sympathy, and profound piety ". But impulsiveness, and its offspring—prejudice—were at the root of too many of his acts and hastier judgments. He was supposed to hate Jews on principle, not from religious motives, but simply because some of the lowest and most contemptible of them practised the usury that persecution had schooled them in ; he despised all bishops, because some of them died rich. No one really deserves hanging, he says somewhere, save bankers and bishops. . . . Ruskin is and must be regarded, by friend and foe alike, as the great modern master of English prose—the Magician of Coniston Lake. . . . The sun has indeed gone down behind the Grand Old Man of Coniston ; while the sky is still all aglow with the fire of his words and the gold of his beneficent acts.—M. H. SPIELMANN, *John Ruskin.*

To read *Fors* is like being out in a thunderstorm. At first, you open the book with interest to watch the signs of the times. While you climb your mountain—shall we say the Old Man of Coniston ?—at unawares there is a darkening of the cloud upon you, and the tension of instinctive dread, as image after image arises of misery, and murder, and lingering death, with here and there a streak of sun in the foreground, only throwing the wildness of the scene into more rugged relief; and through the gaps you see broad fields of ancient history, like lands of promise left behind. By-and-by the gloom wraps you. The old thunder of the Ruskinian paragraph shortened now to whip-lash cracks, reverberates unremittingly from point to point, raising echoes, sounding deeps; allusions, suggestions, intimations, stirring the realm of chaos, that ordinarily we are glad to let slumber, but now terribly discern, by flashes of thought, most unexpectedly arriving. Fascinated by the hammer-play of Thor, berserking among Rime-giants—customs that " hang upon us, heavy as frost "—you begin to applaud; when a sudden stroke rolls your own standpoint into the abyss. But if you can climb forward, undismayed, to the summit, the storm drifts by ; and you see the world again, all new, beneath you—how rippling in Thor's laughter, how tenderly veiled in his tears! . . . A life which was a battle with adversities from the beginning. Over-stimulus in childhood ; intense application to work in youth and middle age, under conditions of discouragement, both public and private, which would have been fatal to many another man; and this, too, not merely hard work, but work of an intensely emotional nature, involving—in his view at least —wide issues of life and death, in which he was another Jacob wrestling with the angel in the wilderness, another Savonarola imploring reconciliation between God and man.—W. G. COLLINGWOOD, *Life and Work of John Ruskin.*

Ruskin's diction is noble in vigour and high in vitality in this work of impassioned intellect, *Fors Clavigera.* Not here does he force with difficulty the tired and inelastic common speech to explain his untired mind, as in some pages of the *Modern Painters :* not here are perorations of eloquence over-rich ; not here constructions after Hooker, nor signs of Gibbon. All the diction is fused in the fiery life, and the lesser beauties of eloquence are far transcended. During the publication of these letters the world told him, now that he could express himself but could not think, and now that he was effeminate. But he was giving to that world the words of a martyr of thought, and the martyr was a man.—MRS. MEYNELL, *John Ruskin.*

LORD WILLIAM RUSSELL.

Statesman and Patriot : 1639-1683.

Bring every sweetest flower, and let me strew
The grave where Russell lies ; whose temper'd blood,
With calmest cheerfulness for thee resign'd,
Stain'd the sad annals of a giddy reign.
—THOMSON, *The Seasons : Summer.*

Some men have found in a grateful posterity the guardians of an enviable renown, less by a remarkable excellence of their own, than by the wrongs they have suffered in a cause which is endeared to the interests of mankind. Thus, William Lord Russell and Algernon Sidney are hallowed to English freemen so long as our history shall last. But if they had not died on the scaffold, it may be reasonably doubted whether they could still live in fame.—LYTTON, *Essays : Posthumous Reputation.*

SAMUEL RUTHERFORD.

Scottish Theologian. 1600-1661.

Samuel Rutherford, . . . one of the uncanonized saints of the Church Universal.—A. B. GROSART, *Representative Nonconformists.*

DR. HENRY SACHEVERELL.

English Divine: 1672-1724.

States to embroil, and faction to display
In wild harangues, Sacheverell show'd the way.
—DODSLEY, *The Art of Preaching.*

Sacheverell charms with " Right Divine,"
Court preacher, and a Catiline !
—REV. JOHN DAVIES, *Historic Prologues.*

A sudden conflict rises from the swell
Of a proud slavery met by tenets strained
In liberty's behalf.   Fears true or feigned,
Spread through all ranks ; and lo ! the sentinel
Who loudest rang his pulpit 'larum bell,
Stands at the bar—absolved by female eyes,
Mingling their light with graver flatteries,
Lavished on *him* that England may rebel
Against her ancient virtue.   High and Low,
Watchwords of party, on all tongues are rife ;
As if a Church, though sprung from Heaven, must owe
To opposites and fierce extremes her life—
Not to the golden mean, and quiet flow
Of truths that soften hatred, temper, strife.
—WORDSWORTH, *Sacheverell.*

FRANCIS DE SALES.

French Roman-Catholic Prelate: 1567-1622.

What a difference, for instance, between Saint Bernard and Saint Francis de Sales : how much more human, natural, and universal is the one, how much more removed is the other from the largeness of the true type of manhood.—GLADSTONE, *Gleanings, Vol. III.*

" GEORGE SAND " (MME. A. L. A. DUDEVANT).

French Novelist and Dramatist: 1804-1876.

In George Sand's finest work there is a sweet spontaneity, almost as if she were an oracle of Nature uttering automatically the divine message. But, on the other hand, when the inspiration forsakes her, she drifts along on a windy current of words, the fatal facility of her pen often beguiling the writer into vague diffuseness and unsubstantial declamation.— MATHILDE BLIND, *Life of George Eliot.*

SAPPHO.

Greek Poetess: fl. B.C. 611-592.

When Sappho struck the quiv'ring wire,
The throbbing breast was all on fire :
And when she rais'd the vocal lay,
The captive soul was charm'd away!
> —SMOLLETT, *On a Young Lady Playing on a Harpsichord.*

At Sappho's woes we breathe a tender sigh,
And the soft sorrow steals from every eye.
> —WALTER HARTE, *To a Young Lady, with Fenton's Miscellanies.*

Among the ancients Sappho enjoyed a unique renown. She was called " The Poetess," as Homer was called " The Poet ". Aristotle placed her in the same rank as Homer and Archilochus. Plato in the *Phædrus* mentioned her as the tenth Muse. Solon, hearing one of her poems, prayed that he might not see death till he had learned it. Strabo speaks of her genius with religious awe. Longinus cites her love ode as a specimen of poetical sublimity. The epigrammatists call her Child of Aphrodite and Eròs, nursling of the Graces and Persuasion, pride of Hellas, peer of Muses, companion of Apollo. Nowhere is a hint whispered that her poetry was aught but perfect. As far as we can judge, these praises were strictly just. Of all the poets of the world, of all the illustrious artists of all literatures, Sappho is the one whose every word has a peculiar and unmistakable perfume, a seal of absolute perfection and inimitable grace. In her art she was unerring. Even Archilochus seems commonplace when compared with her exquisite rarity of phrase.—J. ADDINGTON SYMONDS, *Studies of Greek Poets.*

Sappho wrote in the most varied styles—there are fifty different metres in our scanty remains of her—but all bear a strong impress of personal character. By the side of Alcæus, one feels her to be a woman. Her dialect is more the native speech of Mitylene, where she lived; his the more literary. His interests cover war and drinking and adventure and politics; hers are all in personal feeling, mostly tender and introspective. Her suggestions of nature—the line, "*I heard the footfall of the flowery spring*"; the marvellously musical comparison, "*Like the one sweet apple very red, up high on the highest bough, that the apple-gatherers have forgotten; no, not forgotten, but could never reach so far*"—are perhaps more definitely beautiful than the love-poems which have made Sappho's name immortal. Two of these are preserved by accident; the rest of Sappho's poetry was publicly burned in 1073 at Rome and at Constantinople, as being too much for the shaky morals of the time. One must not overestimate the compliments of gallantry which Sappho had in plenty : she was "the Poetess" as Homer was "the Poet"; she was "the Tenth Muse," "the Pierian Bee "; the wise Solon wished to "learn a song of Sappho's and then die ".—GILBERT MURRAY, *History of Ancient Greek Literature.*

GIROLAMO SAVONAROLA.

Italian Dominican Monk and Reformer: 1452-1498.

Savonarola wore the martyr's shirt,
And gloried in the stake's encaustic robe.
For higher light—the Light not yet arrived.
> —ALFRED AUSTIN, *Human Tragedy.*

Have you boldly to rebuke vice ?   Read the life of Savonarola.—F. W.
FARRAR, *Social and Present-Day Questions.*

Savonarola was the first man of the fifteenth century to realise that the
human race was palpitating with the throes of a new life, and his words
were loudly echoed by that portion of the Italian people still left untainted
by the prevalent corruption.   He accordingly merits the title of the
prophet of the new civilisation. . . . Columbus discovered the paths of
the sea. Savonarola those of the soul ; when the one was mounting the
pulpit, the other had already set sail, and was cleaving with daring prow
the waves of an unknown deep.   The latter, while believing to have
found a new track to India, had discovered America instead ; the former
believed that he had found the way to reawaken faith and reconstitute
the religious unity of the human race, but his own martyrdom served to
prove that his purpose could only be attained after passing through a
period of schism and bloodshed.   Both believed themselves sent by the
Lord to diffuse Christianity on earth ; both beheld strange visions which
revived their ardour for the task ; both touched a new world with their
finger-tips, without being in a position to appreciate its immensity : the
one was rewarded with chains, the other with death at the stake. . . .
Accordingly, it were idle to inquire whether Savonarola upheld the
servum arbitrium of Martin Luther or the Calvinistic doctrine of pre-
destination !   He embraced a far vaster if much less definite world ; and,
although still shackled by the prejudices and superstitions of the past, looked
to a more remote aim.   He was the first, in his age, to urge humanity
towards the goal that even, at this day, is still unattained, but towards
which we are straining with redoubled effort.   He endeavoured to
conciliate reason with faith, religion with liberty.—PASQUALE VILLARI,
Life and Times of Girolamo Savonarola (transl.).

JULIUS CÆSAR SCALIGER.

Italian Philologist : 1484-1558.

Julius Cæsar Scaliger, who became a prodigy of learning, did not
commence the study of Greek till he was nearly forty.   He did not even
know the Greek characters till about that time ; nor did he devote himself
entirely to a life of letters till he was forty-seven.   His days till then had
been spent in an unsettled manner, chiefly in the army, with habits and
disposition unfavourable to study.   But he had a mind which, like that
of his namesake, the Roman conqueror, was formed to break down all
obstacles ; and age, instead of abating his vigour, served but to harden
and corroborate the sinews of his intellect.—DR. VICESIMUS KNOX,
Winter Evenings : Evening LXXIX.

FRIEDRICH VON SCHILLER.

German Poet and Historian : 1759-1805.

Schiller ! that hour I would have wish'd to die,
If through the shuddering midnight I had sent
From the dark dungeon of the tower time-rent
That fearful voice, a famished father's cry ;

Lest in some after moment aught more mean
Might stamp me mortal ! A triumphant shout
Black Horror scream'd, and all her goblin rout
Diminished shrunk from the more withering scene !
Ah ! Bard tremendous in sublimity !
Could I behold thee in thy loftier mood
Wandering at eve with finely frenzied eye
Beneath some vast old tempest-swinging wood !
Awhile with mute awe gazing I would brood ;
Then weep aloud in a wild ecstasy !
   —S. T. COLERIDGE, *To the Author of " The Robbers "*.

This is Goethe, with a forehead
 Like the fabled front of Jove ;
In its massive lines the tokens
 More of majesty than love.
This is Schiller, in whose features,
 With their passionate calm regard,
We behold the true ideal
 Of the higher heroic bard,
Whom the inward world of feeling
 And the outward world of sense
To the endless labour summon,
 And the endless recompense.
These are they, sublime and silent,
 From whose living lips have rung
Words to be remembered ever
 In the noble German tongue ;
Thoughts whose inspiration, kindling
 Into loftiest speech or song,
Still through all the listening ages
 Pours its torrent swift and strong.
   —W. ALLEN BUTLER, *The Busts of Goethe and Schiller.*

The poetry which would be produced by imagination, conversing intimately with human life, would be that of tragedy. But we have no tragic
poet. Schiller is, perhaps, the only great tragic poet who has lived in the
same day with ourselves. And wild and portentous as his shapes of life
often are, who is there that does not feel that the strange power by which
they hold us is derived from the very motions of our blood, and that the
breath by which we live breathes in them ? He has thrown back his
scenes into other times of the world : but we find *ourselves* there. It is
from real present life that he has borrowed that terrible spell of passion
by which he shakes so inwardly the very seat of feeling and thought.—
JOHN WILSON, *Essays : A Few Words on Shakespeare.*

Schiller was the best of friends—the best of fathers—the best of
husbands ; no quality was wanting to complete that gentle and peaceful
character, which was animated by the fire of genius alone. The love
of liberty, respect for the female sex, enthusiastic admiration of the fine
arts, inspired his mind ; and in the analysis of his works it would be
easy to point out to what particular virtue we owe the various productions of his masterly pen.—MADAME DE STAËL (*transl.*).

Schiller is a thousand times more *hearty* than Goethe. . . . Schiller's,
blank verse is bad.   He moves in it as a fly in a glue bottle.—S. T.
COLERIDGE, *Table Talk.*

No author ever had more earnestness than Schiller, his earnestness was
the real secret of his greatness ; this combination of philosophy and
poetry, this harmony between genius and conscience, sprang out of the
almost perfect, almost unrivalled equality of proportions which give symmetry to his various faculties.   With him the imagination and the intellect
were so nicely balanced, that one knows not which was the greater ;
owing, happily to the extensive range of his studies, it may be said that,
as the intellect was enriched, the imagination was strengthened.   Therefore, his philosophy, in strict accordance with his poetry, was designed
not so much to convince as to ennoble ; it addresses the soul rather than
the understanding.—LYTTON, *Life of Schiller.*

It is not the predominating force of any one faculty that impresses us
in Schiller ; but the general force of all.   Every page of his writings bears
the stamp of internal vigour ; new truths, new aspects of known truth,
bold thought, happy imagery, lofty emotion.   Schiller would have been
no common man, though he had altogether wanted the qualities peculiar
to poets.   His intellect is clear, deep, and comprehensive ; its deductions,
frequently elicited from numerous and distant premises, are presented
under a magnificent aspect, in the shape of theorems, embracing an immense multitude of minor propositions. . . .   To those who look on him
as we have wished to make them, Schiller will not need a further panegyric.   For the sake of Literature, it may still be remarked, that his
merit was peculiarly due to her.   Literature was his creed, the dictate of
his conscience ; he was an Apostle of the Sublime and Beautiful, and this
his calling made a hero of him.   For it was in the spirit of a true man he
received it, and undertook to cultivate it ; and its inspirations constantly
maintained the noblest temper in his soul. . . .   In another age, this
Schiller will stand forth in the foremost rank among the master-spirits of
his century, and be admitted to a place among the chosen of all centuries.
His works, the memory of what he did and was, will rise afar off like a
towering landmark in the solitude of the Past, when distance shall have
dwarfed into invisibility the lesser people that encompassed him, and hid
him from the near beholder.—CARLYLE, *Life of Friedrich Schiller.*

Schiller inspires us to noble action and to sacrifice.—MAZZINI, *Life and
Writings, Vol. II.*

The authority of the name of Schiller is too great for his books.   This
inequality of the reputation to the works or the anecdotes is not accounted
for by saying that the reverberation is longer than the thunder-clap ; but
somewhat resided in these men which begot an expectation that outran
all their performance.   The largest part of their power was latent.   This
is that which we call Character, a reserved force which acts directly by
presence, and without means.—EMERSON, *Essays : Character.*

But Schiller was not only a destroyer and liberator ; he fulfilled yet
another and more distinctive function of Apollo.   He was a purifier ; and
it was by his work of purification that his influence became most permanent.   It was this that made him a classic, and gave him a share in

moulding the language and thought of a great people. The purifiers of literature are, it is true, seldom popular ; they have " no cunning art to stir the blood " ; they seldom approach the themes that take the crown, the common sources of tears and laughter.—H. W. NEVINSON, *Life of Friedrich Schiller.*

ARTHUR SCHOPENHAUER.

German Philosopher: 1788-1860.

Schopenhauer's natural disposition was one of ill-tempered discontentment with things in general, joined to an immoderate self-esteem, and an abusive disdain of others ; and in spite of his own ethical precepts his conduct was marked by self-indulgence and ignoble fear. His unfortunate temperament was embittered by the long period of neglect which his doctrines had to encounter, and the predominance of those whom he regarded as sophists and charlatans ; his works are full of brilliant abuse of the professional philosophy of the universities.—ANDREW SETH, *Celebrities of the Century.*

Perhaps, however, his most interesting aspect is his character as a representative of the Indian intellect—a European Buddhist. The study of Indian wisdom, conducting by another path to conclusions entirely in harmony with the results of natural science, is destined to affect, and is affecting, the European mind in a degree not inferior to the modification accomplished by the renaissance of Hellenic philosophy ; but the process is retarded by the national peculiarities of the Indian sages, and the difficulty of naturalising them in Europe. It is, therefore, much to possess a writer like Arthur Schopenhauer, capable of imparting Western form to Eastern ideas, or rather to ideas once solely Eastern ; but which, like seeds wafted by the winds, have wandered far from their birthplace to germinate anew in the brain of Europe. . . . Schopenhauer may yet prove the Kapila of a new Buddha.—HELEN ZIMMERN, *Life of Arthur Schopenhauer.*

In thus keeping open and guarding that small door leading to the Unseen, Schopenhauer affords a grateful refuge to that love of the mysterious and unearthly, which lingers in many hearts, and refuses to be charmed away by the wisest and wittiest demonstration of the scientific masters that measurable matter is all, and in all. Wherever there lies an unsatisfied soul, longing for direct communication with the potency in universal nature, there is a possible disciple for Schopenhauer.—W. WALLACE, *Life of Arthur Schopenhauer.*

Schopenhauer, a man who hated much.—AUGUSTINE BIRRELL, *Essays about Men, Women, and Books.*

I must confess that I have not read Schopenhauer, and I decline to lower my spiritual temperature by reading a book which I am told is meant to convince one that " all things are for the worst in the worst of all possible worlds ".—THOMAS HODGKIN, *Society of Friends Conference,* 1895.

24

Franz Peter Schubert.

German Musical Composer : 1797-1828.

The cause of freedom, in music as elsewhere, is now very nearly triumphant ; but at a time when its adversaries were many and powerful, we can hardly imagine the sacred bridge of liberty kept by a more stalwart trio than Schubert the Armourer, Chopin the Refiner, and Liszt the Thunderer.—H. R. Haweis, *Music and Morals.*

Robert Schumann.

German Musical Composer : 1810-1856.

Schumann's our music-maker now ;
" Has his march-movement youth and mouth ? "
                            —Browning, *Dis aliter visum.*

Scipio Africanus.

Roman General : b.c. 234-183.

And thou Scipio, a myrrour mayst thou be
To all nobles, that they learn not too late,
Howe they once trust the unstable commontye,
Thou that recuredst the torne dismembred state,
Even when the conquerour was at the gate.
          —Lord Buckhurst, *Complaynt of Henrye, Duke of Buckingham.*

Bold Scipio, saviour of the Roman state ;
Great in his triumphs, in retirement great.
                            —Pope, *The Temple of Fame.*

Excess in youth made Scipio less rever'd.
                  —Prior, *Carmen Seculare, for the Year* 1700.

Scipio, the gentle chief, humanely brave,
Who soon the race of spotless glory ran
And, warm in youth to the poetic shade
With friendship and philosophy retir'd.
                            —Thomson, *The Seasons : Winter.*

Scipio, Milton called " the height of Rome " ; and all history resolves itself very easily into the biography of a few stout and earnest persons. . . . Every great man is a unique.   The Scipionism of Scipio is precisely that part he could not borrow.—Emerson, *Essays : Self-Reliance.*

Sir Walter Scott.

Scottish Novelist and Poet : 1771-1832.

. . . thou, with powers that mock the aid of praise,
Shouldst leave to humbler bards ignoble lays :
Thy country's voice, the voice of all the nine,
Demand a hallow'd harp—that harp is thine. . . .

Scotland! still proudly claim thy native bard,
And be thy praise his first, his best reward!
Yet not with thee alone his name should live,
But own the vast renown a world can give :
Be known, perchance, when Albion is no more,
And tell the tale of what she was before ;
To future times her faded fame recall,
And save her glory, though his country fall.
                    —BYRON, *English Bards and Scotch Reviewers.*

. . . the Ariosto of the North,
Sang ladye-love and war, romance and knightly worth.
                    —*Id., Childe Harold's Pilgrimage, Canto IV.*

Blessed be the act of sovereign grace
That raised thee 'bove the rhyming race ; . . .
Bootless the waste of empty words,
Thy pen is worth ten thousand swords.
                    —HOGG, *Lines to Sir Walter Scott, Bart.*

There too, old and young,
Gentle and simple, by Sir Walter's tales
Spell-bound, shall feel
Imaginary hopes and fears
Strong as realities,
And waking from the dream, regret its close.
                    —SOUTHEY, *Ode written after the King's Visit to Scotland.*

Great Minstrel of the Border.
                    —WORDSWORTH, *Yarrow Revisited.*

Lift up your hearts, ye Mourners! for the might
Of the whole world's good wishes with him goes ;
Blessings and prayers in nobler retinue
Than sceptred King or laurelled Conqueror knows,
Follow this wondrous Potentate.   Be true,
Ye winds of ocean, and the midland sea,
Wafting your charge to soft Parthenope.
                    —*Ibid., On Sir W. Scott's Departure for Naples.*

The trumpet-blast of Marmion never shook
The God-built walls of Ilion ; yet what shout
Of the Achaians swells the heart so high ?
                    —LANDOR, *To the Author of " Festus ".*

Of all that bloom in field or fell,
O Scott of Scots, how passing well
The Scottish flow'r, the wild Bluebell,
        May be assign'd to you.
On breezy heath it nods to greet
The happy rover's bounding feet,
Whose eye with welcome laughs to meet
        The glance of kindly blue ;
Or on some mouldering donjon tow'r
Waves in the wind its slender flow'r

> Where 'scutcheon'd banners flew—
> A bright existence, springing gay
> From time's despoil and power's decay.
>
> —W. ALLINGHAM, *Poets and Flowers.*

I belong to the Black Hussars of literature, who neither give nor receive criticism.—SIR WALTER SCOTT.

Sir Walter Scott! The man in Scotland I most wish to see!—KING GEORGE IV.

The poetically great Walter Scott came like a sunbeam to my dwelling.—ANNA SEWARD, *Letter to Mr. Cary.*

I see the *Lady of the Lake* advertised. Of course it is in his old ballad style and pretty. After all, Scott is the best of them. The end of all scribblement is to amuse, and he certainly succeeds there. I long to read his new romance. . . . He is undoubtedly the Monarch of Parnassus, and the most *English* of bards.—BYRON, in MOORE'S *Life of Byron.*

When I am very ill indeed, I can read Scott's novels, and they are almost the only books I can then *read.* I cannot at such times read the Bible; my mind reflects on it, but I can't bear the open page.—S. T. COLERIDGE, *Table Talk.*

Sir Walter Scott more nearly resembles Homer than any poet who has sung since the siege of Troy. Not that he has produced any poem which will for a moment bear a comparison with the *Iliad*—fine as the *Lady of the Lake* and *Marmion* are, it would be the height of national partiality to make any such comparison. But nevertheless Sir Walter's mind was cast in the same mould, and was in some respects of the same dimensions, as that of Homer. We see in him the same combination of natural sagacity with acquired information; of pictorial eye with dramatic capability; of observation of character with reflection and feeling; of graphic power with poetic fervour; of ardour of imagination with rectitude of principle; of warlike enthusiasm with domestic tenderness, which has rendered the Grecian bard immortal. . . . The battle in *Marmion* is beyond all question, as Jeffrey long ago remarked, the most Homeric strife which has been sung since the days of Homer.—SIR ARCHIBALD ALISON, *Essays : Homer, Dante, and M. Angelo.*

Scott burned with the soul of painting in his poetry and his prose.—Id., *Ibid.: British School of Painting.*

The King the other day made Sir Walter Scott a baronet, but not all the power of the Three Estates could make another Author of *Waverley.*—HAZLITT, *Table Talk.*

North : " Scott's poetry puzzles me—it is often very bad."
Tickler : " Very."
North : " Except when his martial soul is up, he is but a tame and feeble writer. His versification in general flows on easily—smoothly—almost sonorously—but seldom or never with impetuosity or grandeur. There is no strength, no felicity in his diction—and the substance of his poetry is neither rich nor rare. . . ."
Tickler : . . . " But then when his martial soul is up—and up it is at sight of a spear-point or a pennon—then indeed you hear the true poet

of chivalry. What care I, Kit, for all his previous drivelling—drivelling if it be—and God forbid I should deny drivelling to any poet, ancient or modern—for now he makes my very soul to burn within me—and, coward and civilian though I be—yes, a most intense and insuperable coward, prizing life and limb beyond all other earthly possessions, and loath to shed one single drop of blood either for my King or country—yet such is the trumpet-power of the song of that son of genius, that I start from my old elbow-chair, up with the poker, tongs, or shovel, no matter which, and flourishing it round my head, cry, ' Charge, Chester, charge ! On, Stanley, on !' and then dropping my voice, and returning to my padded bottom, whisper, ' Were the last words of Marmion !'

. . . .

" Therefore I say that Scott is a Homer of a poet, and so let him dose when he has a mind to it ; for no man I know is better entitled to an occasional half-canto of slumber."--JOHN WILSON, *Noctes Ambrosianæ*, *Vol. I.*

The Minstrel—the Magician—the Man.—*Id.*, *Ibid.*, *Vol. III.*

We believe that we speak the general voice when we place on a triple throne, Scott, Wordsworth, and Byron.

Though greatly inferior in many things to his illustrious brethren, Scott is perhaps, after all, the most unequivocally original. We do not know of any model after which the form of his principal Poems has been moulded. They bear no resemblance, and, we must allow, are far inferior to the heroic Poems of Greece ; nor do they, though he has been called the Ariosto of the North, seem to us to resemble, in any way whatever, any of the great Poems of modern Italy. He has given a most intensely real representation of the living spirit of the chivalrous age of his country. There is not much of all this in any modern poetry but his own ; and therefore it is, that, independently of all his other manifold excellences, we glory in him as the great modern National Poet of Scotland—in whom old times revive—whose Poetry prevents History from becoming that which, in times of excessive refinement, it is often too apt to become—a dead letter—and keeps the animating and heroic spectacles of the past moving brightly across our everyday world, and flashing out from them a kindling power over the actions and characters of our own age.—*Id.*, *Essays : Wordsworth.*

The principal merit of Walter Scott consists in his portraiture of times utterly distinct from the time in which he lived.—LYTTON, *Essays : The Moral Effect of Writers.*

And, first, it appears to me that one cause of Sir Walter Scott's unprecedented popularity as a novelist, among all classes and in all civilized lands, is to be found in the ease and the breadth of his knowledge of the world. He does not pretend too much metaphysical science or much vehement eloquence of passion. He troubles himself very little with the analysis of mind, with the struggle of conflicting emotions. For that reason, he could never have obtained, in the highest walks of the drama, a success correspondent to the loftiness of his fame as a tale-teller. The drama must bear to an audience the machinery of an intellect or the world of a heart. No mere interest of narrative, no mere skill of situation, can, for a play that is to retain a permanent hold on the stage, supply the want of that wondrous insight into motive and conduct which attests the philosophy of Shakespeare, or that fervent oratory of passion which exalts into eloquence almost superhuman the declamatory verse of Corneille. . . . Of all our great poets since Milton, Byron and Scott are at once those the most recognised by foreign nations, and who yet owe the least to foreign poets. They owed nothing to the French, yet of all our poets they are those whom the French most condescend to imitate. If the French now study Shakespeare, it is because Scott and Byron allured them to study English.—LYTTON, *Essays : Knowledge of the World.*

In the sense in which we are now using the word correctness, we think that Sir Walter Scott, Mr. Wordsworth, Mr. Coleridge, are far more correct poets than those who are commonly extolled as the models of correctness, Pope for example, and Addison.—MACAULAY, *Essays : Lord Byron.*

The most startling fault of the age being its faithlessness, it is necessary that its greatest man should be faithless. Nothing is more notable or sorrowful in Scott's mind than its incapacity of steady belief in anything. He cannot even resolve hardly to believe in a ghost, or a water-spirit ; always explains them away in an apologetic manner, not believing, all the while, even in his own explanation. He never can clearly ascertain whether there is anything behind the arras but rats ; never draws sword, and thrusts at it for life or death ; but goes on looking at it timidly, and saying, "It must be the wind". He is educated a Presbyterian and remains one, because it is the most sensible thing he can do if he is to live in Edinburgh ; but he thinks Romanism more picturesque, and profaneness more gentlemanly ; does not see that anything affects human life but love, courage and destiny ; which are, indeed, not matters of faith at all, but of sight. Any gods but those are very misty in outline to him ; and when the love is laid ghastly in poor Charlotte's coffin ; and the courage is no more of use ;—the pen having fallen from between the fingers ; and destiny is sealing the scroll,—the God-light is dim in the tears that fall on it. . . . He is in all the epitome of his epoch.—RUSKIN, *Modern Painters, Vol. III.*

Let Scott thank John Knox, for he owed him much, little as he dreamed of debt in that quarter ! No Scotchman of his time was more entirely Scotch than Walter Scott : the good and the not so good, which all Scotchmen inherit, ran through every fibre of him. . . . It can be said of Scott, when he departed he took a man's life along with him. No sounder piece of British manhood was put together in that eighteenth century of time. Alas, his fine Scotch face, with its shaggy honestness, sagacity, and goodness, when we saw it latterly on the Edinburgh streets, was all worn with care, the joy all fled from it, ploughed deep with labour and sorrow. We shall never forget it—we shall never see it again. Adieu, Sir Walter, pride of all Scotchmen ; take our proud and sad farewell.—CARLYLE.

The name of Scott is only less dear to Englishmen than the name of Shakespeare. . . . Scott is certainly the greatest of peaceful and beneficent conquerors in the world of letters.—SIR W. S. MAXWELL, *Miscellaneous Essays, Vol. VI.*

Scott is the other wonder of this age. Picturesque, interesting, and bard-like as are his narrative poems, the pathos, humour, description, character, and, above all, the marvellous fertility displayed in the novels, show far greater power: a whole region of the territory of Imagination is occupied by this extraordinary man alone and unapproachable.—LORD JOHN RUSSELL, *Introduction to Memoirs, Journal, and Correspondence of Thomas Moore, Vol. I.*

If Scott has contributed no great characters, like Hamlet, or Don Quixote, or Mephistopheles, to the world of fiction, he is the undisputed parent of a whole population full of enduring vitality, and, if rising to no ideal standard, yet reflecting with unrivalled clearness the characteristics of some of the strongest and sturdiest of the races of man.— LESLIE STEPHEN, *Hours in a Library, First Series.*

Possessing in a high degree the active and athletic frame, the robust health, the hardy training, the vigorous nerve, the bold spirit, the frank bearing, and the genial kindness of the gentlemen of the olden time, he could heartily appreciate and unhesitatingly approve all that time and revolution had spared of feudal dominion and territorial grandeur. The ancient loyalty, so happily tempering the firmness of a principle with the fervour of a feeling, never beat higher in the heart of a cavalier of the seventeenth than in that of the Scottish Advocate of the nineteenth century. Every one will remember that he refused to write a life of Mary Queen of Scots, because in reference to her conduct, his feelings were at variance with his judgment and in painting those old times in which his imagination delighted to revel, all that would most have revolted our modern mildness of manners, and shocked our modern sense of justice, was softened down or dropped out of sight, and the nobler features of those ages, their courage, their devotion, their strength and clearness of purpose, their marked individuality of character, their impulses of heroism and delicacy, their manly enterprise, their picturesque costumes and manners of life, were all brought into bold relief, and placed before the reader with such fulness of detail, in such grandeur of outline, in such bright and vivid colouring, as gave even to the unimaginative a more distinct conception of, and a more lively sympathy with, the past than they could gain for themselves of the present, as it was whirling and roaring round them, confusing them with its shifting of hues and forms, and stunning them with its hurricane of noises.—GEORGE BRIMLEY, *Essays.*

Scott's veneration for the past reached its highest and most shrewd and intelligent form in his Scotticism. It is a coincidence with more than the usual amount of verbal good luck in it that his name should have been Scott—generically and comprehensively *the* Scotchman.— DAVID MASSON, *British Novelists and their Styles.*

On the whole, and speaking roughly, these defects in the delineation which Scott has given us of human life are but two. He omits to give us a delineation of the soul. We have mind, manners, animation, but it is the stir of the world. We miss the consecrating power; and we miss it not only in its own peculiar sphere, which, from the difficulty of introducing the deepest elements into a novel, would have been scarcely matter for a harsh criticism, but in the place in which a novelist might most be expected to delineate it. . . . His heroes and heroines are well dressed for this world, but not for another; there is nothing even in their love which is suitable for immortality.—WALTER BAGEHOT, *Literary Studies, Vol. II.*

" This was a man ! " And Lockhart did not show us—would not let us see—what a man of men this was. But now that we know, we may say with Milton's Manoah, " Nothing is here for tears ". The very last days of all, as recorded by Lockhart, are painful indeed to read of, but not painfuller than would be the record of any other gradual and conscious decline and subsidence of spirit and body, overworked and overworn, towards the common end—" no rest for Sir Walter but in the grave ".—SWINBURNE, *Studies in Prose and Poetry.*

Sir Walter's influence on our fictitious literature will never disappear. He taught us *how* to tell those exquisite stories which now roll forth year by year, in hundreds from the presses, and will be a marvel to after ages. The ease and strength of the modern novel came from him. He showed writers how to construct plots devoid of the cumbrous machinery of *Paul Jones,* how to develop the graphic force of Defoe and to keep free from his twaddle, and how to put on paper a brilliant passage of repartee without the manifest effort of Sterne. He lived to see better novelists than himself in the field (and he had the noble-mindedness to acknowledge their excellence), but he had the satisfaction of observing that whatever new melodies and combinations of sound they produced it was his instruments they used.—J. C. JEAFFRESON, *Novels and Novelists from Elizabeth to Victoria, Vol. II.*

In Scott is broad health and freedom, breadth of sky, clearness of atmosphere, not less in the outlook and character of his own mind than in his presentation of artistic effects ; but nowhere does he show himself penetrated by any sense of the mystery and complexity of life. He writes with the good-natured ease of a man blessed with an excellent digestion and familiar with broad moors and sweet country air ; who, in his own life, has never sounded the deeper notes of tragedy and never known the bitter throes of anguish.—W. J. DAWSON, *Quest and Vision.*

Scott's biography is the true key to his art, and attracts us for reasons the exact opposite of those that lend fascination to the records of him who has brooded over the mystery of existence. He was not the chemist who analyses the contents of the cup of life, but he who quaffs them to the lees. There is no saner and more joyous youth than his told of in the annals of English literature ; though, were our knowledge more complete, it would probably be found that Shakespeare's equalled it in full-blooded gaiety.—P. A. GRAHAM, *Nature in Books.*

There was in Sir Walter, I think, at least as much of the Stoic as the Christian. But Stoic or Christian, he was a hero of the old, indomitable type. Even the last fragments of his imaginative power were all turned to account by that unconquerable will, amidst the discouragement of friends, and the still more disheartening doubts of his own mind. Like the headland stemming a rough sea, he was gradually worn away, but never crushed.—R. H. HUTTON, *Sir Walter Scott.*

For when Time, that old ravager, has done his very worst, there will be enough left of Sir Walter to carry down his name and fame to the remotest age.—AUGUSTINE BIRRELL, *Essays about Men, Women, and Books.*

Sir Walter's work has proved to be of so permanent a character, his insight into all things Scotch so deep and true, and his human worth and excellence so rare and noble, that it has hardly been worth while to re-member the froth and effervescence he at first occasioned; but that he did create a movement in the Oxford direction is certain. He made the old Catholic times interesting. He was not indeed, like the Tractarians, a man of " primitive " mind; but he was romantic, and it all told.—AUGUS-TINE BIRRELL, *Res Judicatæ.*

Scott, by the confession of all competent judges, save a very few, has created almost more men and women, undoubtedly real and life-like, than any other prose novelist. Now you cannot create a man or a woman without knowing whereof a man and a woman are made, though the converse proposition is unfortunately by no means so universally predicable. . . . There need be very little doubt that if we knew everything about Shake-speare, he would, as a man of mould might, come scatheless from the test. But we do know everything, or almost everything, about Scott, and he comes out nearly as well as any one but a faultless monster could. For all the works of the Lord in literature, as in other things, let us give thanks—for Blake and for Beddoes as well as for Shelley and for Swift. But let every one who by himself, or by his fathers, claims origin between Tol-Pedn-Penwith and Dunnet Head give thanks, with more energy and more confidence than in any other case save one, for the fact that his is the race and his the language of Sir Walter Scott.—SAINTSBURY, *Life of Sir Walter Scott.*

Concerning Scott, who will not agree with Lockhart's remark in the preface to his abridged edition of 1848: " I should have been more willing to produce an enlarged edition; for the interest of Sir Walter's history lies, I think, peculiarly in its minute details " ? You may explore here, and explore there, and still you find pure gold; for the man was gold right through. . . . To me, a southron, Scott is the most imaginative, and at the same time justest, writer of our language since Shakespeare died. To say this is not to suggest that he is comparable to Shakespeare. —A. T. QUILLER-COUCH, *Adventures in Criticism.*

Nowhere, else, perhaps, in modern literature could any one be found who, in an equal measure with Scott, has united these three conditions of a true spiritual analogy to Homer; living realisation of a past heroic age; a genius in native sympathy with the heroic; and a manner which joins the spontaneous impulse of the balladist to a higher order of art and intellect.—R. C. JEBB, *Introduction to the " Iliad " and " Odyssey ".*

JOHN SELDEN.

English Statesman and Jurist : 1584-1654.

Hayward and
Selden ! two names that so much understand !
On whom I could take up, and ne'er abuse,
The credit, what would furnish a tenth muse !
But here's no time nor place my wealth to tell,
You both are modest. So am I. Farewell.
—BEN JONSON, *An Epistle to Mr. John Selden.*

Mr. Selden was a person whom no character can flatter, or transmit in any expressions equal to his merit and virtue. He was of such stupendous

learning in all kinds and in all languages, as may appear from his excellent and transcendent writings, that a man would have thought he
had been entirely conversant among books, and had never spent an hour
but in reading or writing; yet his humanity, courtesy, and affability were
such, that he would have been thought to have been bred in the best courts,
but that his good-nature, charity, and delight in doing good, and communicating all he knew, exceeded that breeding.—CLARENDON.

It has been said that the *Table Talk* of Selden is worth all the Ana of
the Continent.—HALLAM, *Introduction to the Literature of Europe, Vol.
III.*

GEORGE AUGUSTUS SELWYN.

First Bishop of New Zealand: 1809-1878.

Seldom has such indomitable and courageous energy been witnessed
in any man, as was seen in Bishop Selwyn; never, perhaps, has such
determined energy been observed to issue forth from a character naturally
cautious and even nervous. Seldom has such a chastened delight been
felt by any man, as was felt by Bishop Selwyn, in handling the reins of
power; never, perhaps, has it been felt in equal degree by any one who
at the same time positively craved to be "under authority" and to whom
the habit of "obedience" formed the joy of his life.—G. H. CURTEIS,
Life of Bishop Selwyn.

George Selwyn was a heroic Christian soul—a rebuke to most of us.—
CARDINAL MANNING in PURCELL'S *Manning, Vol. I.*

SENECA.

Roman Stoic Philosopher and Moralist: 2-65.

Wel can Senek and many a philosophre
Bewailen time more than gold in coffre;
For losse of catel may recovered be,
But losse of time shendeth us, quod he.
                    —CHAUCER, *Man of Laws Prologue.*

This Seneka, of which that I devise,
Because Nero had of him swiche drede,
For he fro vices wold him ay chastise
Discretly, as by word, and not by dede.

                                        —*Id., Monk's Tale.*

He died not as the martyr dies,
Wrapped in his living shroud of flame;
He fell not as the warrior falls,
Gasping upon the field of fame;
A gentler passage to the grave,
The murderer's softened fury gave.
                    —OLIVER WENDELL HOLMES, *The Dying Seneca.*

Seneca wrote largely on natural philosophy, and magnified the importance of that study. But why? Not because it tended to assuage suffering

to multiply the conveniences of life, to extend the empire of man over the material world; but solely because it tended to raise the mind above low cares, to separate it from the body, to exercise its subtilty in the solution of very obscure questions. Thus natural philosophy was considered in the light merely of a mental exercise. It was made subsidiary to the art of disputation; and it consequently proved altogether barren of useful discoveries.—MACAULAY, *Essays: Lord Bacon.*

All that I here desire to say is, that in considering the life of Seneca we are not only dealing with a life which was rich in memorable incidents, and which was cast into an age upon which Christianity dawned as a new light in the darkness, but also the life of one who climbed the loftiest peaks of the moral philosophy of Paganism, and who in many respects may be regarded as the Coryphæus of what has been sometimes called a Natural Religion. . . . So died a Pagan philosopher, whose life must always excite our interest and pity, although we cannot apply to him the titles to great and good. He was a man of high genius, of great susceptibility, of an ardent and generous temperament, of far-sighted and sincere humanity. Some of his sentiments are so remarkable for their moral beauty and profundity that they forcibly remind us of the expressions of St. Paul. But Seneca fell infinitely short of his own high standard, and has contemptuously been called "the father of all them that wear shovel-hats". Inconsistency is written on the entire history of his life, and it has earned him the scathing contempt with which many writers have treated his memory. —F. W. FARRAR, *Seekers after God.*

ANTHONY ASHLEY COOPER, EARL OF SHAFTESBURY.

English Philanthropist: 1801-1885.

He took human suffering and human sorrow, and the helplessness of childhood, of the poor as the end for which to live. He spent and was spent for it, and his own life was a suffering life like the Man of Sorrows, going about doing good.—CARDINAL MANNING in PURCELL'S *Manning*, Vol. II.

The social reforms of the last century have not been mainly due to the Liberal party. They have been due mainly to the influence, character and perseverance of one man—Lord Shaftesbury.—DUKE OF ARGYLL.

If the Christian Socialists ever frame a Kalendar of Worthies (after the manner of Auguste Comte), it is to be hoped that they will mark among the most sacred of their anniversaries the day—28th April, 1801—which gave birth to Anthony Ashley, seventh Earl of Shaftesbury. His life of eighty-four years was consecrated, from boyhood till death, to the social service of humanity.—[G. W. E. RUSSELL], *Collections and Recollections.*

If "Christian Socialism" means the full and practical recognition of the duty to apply the word and will of the Saviour of man the sinner to the fullest present benefit of man the struggler and sufferer, leaving no relation and condition of life outside His government, Lord Shaftesbury, patrician of patricians, the perfect antithesis to the demagogue, totally free from that flattery of the masses which is as ignoble as any flattery of kings, was the ideal of a Christian Socialist.—DR. H. C. G. MOULE in *The "Record,"* 4th *Jan.,* 1901.

WILLIAM SHAKSPERE.

English Dramatist and Poet: 1564-1616.

He was not of an age, but for all Time . . .
Sweet Swan of Avon. . . .
            Soul of the age!
Th' applause! delight! the wonder of our stage!
My Shakespeare rise! I will not lodge thee by
Chaucer, or Spenser, or bid Beaumont lie
A little further, to make thee a room:
Thou art a monument without a tomb,
And art alive still, while thy book doth live,
And we have wits to read, and praise to give.
    —BEN JONSON, *To the Memory of my beloved Mr. Wm. Shakespeare.*

Renownèd Spenser, lie a thought more nigh
To learnèd Chaucer, and, rare Beaumont, lie
A little nearer Spenser, to make room
For Shakespeare in your threefold, fourfold Tomb.
To lodge all four in one bed make a shift
Until Doomsday, for hardly with a fifth
Betwixt this day and that by Fate be slain,
For whom your Curtains may be drawn again.
If your precedency in death doth bar
A fourth place in your sacred sepulchre,
Under this carvèd marble of thine own,
Sleep rare Tragedian, Shakespeare, sleep alone;
Thy unmolested peace, unsharèd Cave,
Possess as Lord, not Tenant, of thy Grave,
    That unto us and others it may be
    Honour hereafter to be laid by thee.
        —WILLIAM BASSE, *To Mr. Wm. Shakespeare.*

Hope to mend Shakespeare! or to match his style!
'Tis but a jest would make a Stoic smile.
    —DUKE OF BUCKINGHAM, *Prologue to the alteration of*
        Julius Cæsar.

Old mother Wit and Nature gave
Shakespeare and Fletcher all they have.
      —DENHAM, *On Mr. A. Cowley's Death and Burial.*

Or sweetest Shakespeare, Fancy's child,
Warble his native wood-notes wild.
              —MILTON, *L'Allegro.*

What needs my Shakespeare for his honor'd bones
The labor of an age in piled stones,
Or that his hallow'd reliques should be hid
Under a star-ypointing pyramid?
Dear son of memory! great heir of fame!
What need'st thou such weak witness of thy name?
Thou in our wonder and astonishment
Hast built thyself a live-long monument.
   .   .   .   .

And so sepulchred in such pomp dost lie,
That kings for such a tomb would wish to die.
—MILTON, *On Shakespeare.*

Shakespeare, who, taught by none, did first impart
To Fletcher wit, to labouring Jonson art;
He, monarch-like, gave those his subjects law,
And is that Nature which they paint and draw. . . .
But Shakespeare's magic could not copied be;
Within that circle none durst walk but he.
I must confess 'twas bold, nor would you now
That liberty to vulgar wits allow,
Which works by magic supernatural things;
But Shakespeare's power is sacred as a king's.
—DRYDEN, *Prologue to " The Tempest".*

Time, place, and action, may with pains be wrought;
But genius must be born, and never can be taught,
This is your portion; this your native store;
Heaven, that but once was prodigal before,
To Shakespeare gave as much; she could not give him more.
—*Id., Epistle X., To my dear Friend, Mr. Congreve.*

Shakespeare (whom you and ev'ry playhouse bill
Style the divine, the matchless, what you will)
For gain, not glory, wing'd his roving flight,
And grew immortal in his own despite.
     .   .   .   .   .   .
On Avon's banks where flow'rs eternal blow.
—POPE, *Epistles of Horace imitated, Epistle I., Book II.*

          For lofty sense,
Creative fancy, and inspection keen
Through the deep windings of the human heart,
Is not wild Shakespeare thine and Nature's boast?
—THOMSON, *The Seasons: Summer.*

          Shakespeare's muse aspires
Beyond the reach of Greece; with native fires,
Mounting aloft he wings his daring flight,
Whilst Sophocles below stands trembling at his height. . . .
Things of the noblest kind his genius drew,
And look'd through nature at a single view;
A loose he gave to his unbounded soul,
And taught new lands to rise, new seas to roll;
Call'd into being scenes unknown before,
And passing Nature's bounds, was something more.
—CHURCHILL, *The Rosciad.*

Shakespeare, thy gift, I place before my sight:
With awe, I ask his blessing ere I write;
With reverence look on his majestic face;
Proud to be less, but of his godlike race.
—*Id., Epistle XIV., To Sir Godfrey Kneller.*

Where Nature list'ning stood, whilst Shakespeare played,
And wonder'd at the work herself had made.
—CHURCHILL, The Author.

But is there then no honour due to age?
No reverence to great Shakespeare's noble page?
.   .   .   .
Pride of his own, and wonder of this age,
Who first created, and yet rules, the stage,
Bold to design, all-powerful to express,
Shakespeare each passion drew in every dress:
Great above rule, and imitating none;
Rich without borrowing, nature was his own.
—DAVID MALLET, Of Verbal Criticism.

To claim attention and the heart invade,
Shakespeare but *wrote* the play th' Almighty *made*.
.   .   .   .
None think of Shakespeare till the curtain falls.
.   .   .   .
And yet in Shakespeare something still I find,
Which makes me less esteem all humankind;
He made one nature, and another found,
Both in his page with master-strokes abound;
His witches, fairies, and enchanted isle,
Bid us no longer at our nurses smile;
Of lost historians we almost complain,
Nor think it the creation of his brain.
—YOUNG, Epistle to George, Lord Lansdowne.

Yet then shall Shakespeare's powerful art
O'er every passion, every heart,
Confirm his awful throne.
—AKENSIDE, Ode VII., On the Use of Poetry.

Say to each other: "This was Shakespeare's form;
Who walk'd in every path of human life,
Felt every passion; and to all mankind
Doth now, will ever, that experience yield
Which his own genius only could acquire."
—Id., Epistle IV.

    Far from the sun and summer-gale,
In thy green lap was Nature's Darling laid,
What time, where lucid Avon strayed,
    To him the mighty Mother did unveil
Her awful face.   The dauntless Child
Stretched forth his little arms, and smiled.
"This pencil take (she said) whose colours clear
Richly paint the vernal year;
Thine too these golden keys, immortal Boy!
This can unlock the gates of Joy;
Of Horror that, and thrilling Fears,
Or ope the sacred source of sympathetic Tears."
—GRAY, The Progress of Poesy, III., I.

We grant that Butler ravishes the heart,
As Shakespeare soar'd beyond the reach of art;
(For nature form'd those poets without rules,
To fill the world with imitating fools).
    —WALTER HARTE, *An Essay on Satire.*

When Shakespeare leads thy mind a dance,
From France to England, hence to France,
Talk not to me of time and place;
I own I'm happy in the chase.
Whether the drama's here or there,
'Tis nature, Shakespeare, everywhere.
    —ROBERT LLOYD, *Shakespeare.*

Next Shakespeare sat, irregularly great,
And in his hand a magic rod did hold,
Which visionary beings did create,
And turn the foulest dross to purest gold.
Whatever spirits rove in earth or air,
Or bad or good, obey his dread command;
To his behests these willingly repair,
Those aw'd by terrors of his magic wand,
The which not all their powers united might withstand.
    —*Id., The Progress of Envy.*

The name of King Shakespeare has charms
To rouse you to actions of glory.
.   .   .   .   .   .
What man but would Nature obey,
And fight for her Shakespeare for ever!
.   .   .   .   .   .
Thrice happy the nation that Shakespeare has charm'd!
More happy the bosoms his genius has warm'd!
Ye children of nature, of fashion, and whim,
He painted you all, all join to praise him.
    —DAVID GARRICK, *Song in Harlequin's Invasion.*

The garden of Shakespeare all fancies will suit,
With the sweetest of flowers, the fairest of fruit.
.   .   .   .   .   .
But law and the gospel in Shakespeare we find,
And he gives the best physic for body and mind.
.   .   .   .   .   .
The genius of Shakespeare outshines the bright day,
More rapture than wine to the heart can convey.
    —*Id., Shakespeare's Mulberry Tree.*

Æschylus' pen Will Shakespeare drives.
    —BURNS, *Poem on Pastoral Poetry.*

But happier Stratford, thou,
With incontested laurels deck thy brow:
Thy bard was thine unschool'd, and from thee brought
More than all Egypt, Greece, or Asia taught.

Not Homer's self such matchless honours won ;
The Greek has rivals, but thy Shakespeare none.

—ANNA SEWARD.

To Shakespeare, Sidney, Spenser and the rest
Who made our land an island of the blest.
Things wiser than were ever said in book,
Except in Shakespeare's wisest tenderness.

—SHELLEY, *Letter to Maria Gisborne.*

And Shakespeare, who in our hearts for himself has erected an empire
Not to be shaken by Time, nor e'er by another divided.

—SOUTHEY, *A Vision of Judgment : The Elder Worthies.*

Or warm with Fancy's energy, to glow,
And rival all but Shakespeare's name below !

—CAMPBELL.

We must be free or die, who speak the tongue
That Shakespeare spake ; the faith and morals hold
Which Milton held.   In everything we are sprung
Of earth's first blood, have titles manifold.

—WORDSWORTH, **Sonnets** *dedicated to Liberty.*

Shakespeare is not our poet, but the world's—
Therefore on him no speech !

—LANDOR.

And every human brow that veils a thought
Conceals the Castaly which Shakespeare sought.

—LYTTON, *The New Timon.*

. . . The wondrous pages
Of the great poet who foreruns the ages,
Anticipating all that shall be said ! . . .
The magic book, whose Syblline leaves have caught
The rarest essence of all human thought !

—LONGFELLOW, *On Mrs. Kemble's Readings from Shakespeare.*

If I'm a Shakespeare, let the well alone ;
Why should I try to be what now I am ?
If I'm no Shakespeare, as too probable,—
His power and consciousness and self-delight
And all we want in common, shall I find—
Trying for ever ?

—BROWNING, *Bishop Blougram's Apology.*

Shakespeare !—to such name's sounding, what succeeds
  Fitly as silence ?   Falter forth the spell,—
  Act follows word, the speaker knows full well,
Nor tampers with its magic more than needs.
Two names there are : That which the Hebrew reads
  With his soul only : if from lips it fell,
  Echo, back thundered by earth, heaven and hell,
Would own, " Thou didst create us ! "   Nought impedes
We voice the other name, man's most of might,
  Awesomely, lovingly : let awe and love

Mutely await their working, leave to sight
  All of the issue as below—above—
  Shakespeare's creation rises : one remove,
Though dread—this finite from that infinite.
                    —BROWNING, *Bishop Blougram's Apology.*

There Shakespeare, on whose forehead climb
The crowns o' the world ; oh, eyes sublime
With tears and laughter for all time.
              —ELIZABETH BARRETT BROWNING, *A Vision of Poets.*

  Seethed in mists of Penmenmawr,
Taught by Plinlimmon's Druid power,
England's genius filled all measure
Of heart and soul, of strength and pleasure,
Gave to the mind its emperor,
And life was larger than before :
Nor sequent centuries could hit
Orbit and sun of Shakespeare's wit.
The men who lived with him became
Poets, for the air was fame.

                              —EMERSON, *Solution.*

I see all human wits
  Are measured but a few
Unmeasured still my Shakspeare sits,
  Lone as the blessed Jew.

                      —*Id., Shakspeare.*

Shakespeare ! loveliest of souls,
Peerless in radiance, in joy.
              —MATTHEW ARNOLD, *Heine's Grave.*

Others abide our question.   Thou art free.
  We ask and ask—Thou smilest and art still,
  Out-topping knowledge.   For the loftiest hill,
Who to the stars uncrowns his majesty,
Planting his steadfast footsteps in the sea,
  Making the heaven of heavens his dwelling-place,
  Spares but the cloudy border of his base
To the foil'd searching of mortality ;
And thou, who didst the stars and sunbeams know,
Self-school'd, self-scann'd, self-honour'd, self-secure,
Didst tread on earth unguess'd at.—Better so !
All pains the immortal spirit must endure,
All weakness which impairs, all griefs which bow,
Find their sole speech in that victorious brow.
                      —*Id., Shakespeare.*

  It was said of Euripides, that every verse was a precept ; and it may be
said of Shakespeare, that from his works may be collected a system of
civil and economical prudence.   Yet his real power is not shown in the
splendour of particular passages, but by the progress of his fable, and the
tenor of his dialogue : and he that tries to recommend him by select
quotations, will succeed like the pedant in Hierocles, who, when he offered

25

his house to sale, carried a brick in his pocket as a specimen. . . . The sand heaped by one flood is scattered by another, but the rock always continues in its place. The stream of time, which is continually washing the dissoluble fabrics of other poets, passes without injury by the adamant of Shakespeare. . . . He needed not the spectacles of books to read nature : he looked inwards and found her there.—DR. JOHNSON, *Preface to Shakespeare.*

The genius of Shakespeare was an innate universality; wherefore he laid the achievements of human intellect prostrate beneath his indolent and kingly gaze: he could do easily men's utmost—his plan of tasks to come was not of this world. If what he proposed to do hereafter would not, in the idea, answer the aim, how tremendous must have been his conception of ultimates.—KEATS in LORD HOUGHTON'S *Life and Letters of John Keats.*

Shakespeare seems to have been a man of genius, raised above the definition of genius. " Born universal heir to all humanity." . . . If we wish to know the force of human genius, we should read Shakespeare. If we wish to see the insignificance of human learning, we may study his commentators.—HAZLITT, *Table Talk.*

Shakespeare is the Spinosistic deity—an omnipresent creativeness. . . . Our myriad-minded Shakespeare. . . . There's such a divinity doth hedge our Shakespeare round, that we cannot even imitate his style.—S. T. COLERIDGE, *Table Talk.*

In Shakespeare's Poems, the creative power and the intellectual energy wrestle as in a war embrace. Each in its excess of strength seems to threaten the extinction of the other. At length, in the drama they were reconciled, and fought each with its shield before the breast of the other. Or like two rapid streams that, at their first meeting within narrow and rocky banks, mutually strive to repel each other, and intermix reluctantly and in tumult, but soon finding a wider channel and more yielding shores, blend and dilate, and flow on in one current and with one voice.—*Id., Biographia Literaria.*

It is as nearly two centuries as possible since Shakespeare ceased to write, but when shall he cease to be read ? When shall he cease to give light and delight ? Yet even at this moment he is only receiving the first-fruits of that glory, which must continue to augment as long as our language is spoken. English has given immortality to him, and he has given immortality to English. Shakespeare can never die, and the language in which he wrote must with him live for ever. . . . In the plays of Shakespeare every man sees himself, without knowing that he does so: as in some of the phenomena of nature, in the mist of the mountain, the traveller beholds his own figure, but the glory round the head distinguishes it from a mere vulgar copy.—*Id., Lectures on Shakespeare and Milton.*

Shakespeare—that is, English tragedy—postulates the intense life of flesh and blood, of animal sensibility, of man and woman—breathing, waking, stirring, palpitating with the pulses of hope and fear. In Greek tragedy the very masks show the utter impossibility of these tempests or conflicts.—DE QUINCEY, *Leaders in Literature.*

Shakespeare came from heaven—and along with him a Tragedy that poured into one cup the tears of mirth and madness ; showed Kings one day crowned with jewelled diadems, and another day with wild wisps of straw ; taught the Prince who, in single combat,

> Had quench'd the flame of hot rebellion
> Even in the rebels' blood,

to moralise on the field of battle over the carcass of a fat buffoon wittily simulating death among the bloody corpses of English nobles ; nay, showed the son—and that son, prince, philosopher, paragon of men— jocularly conjuring to rest his Father's Ghost, who had revisited earth " by the glimpses of the moon, making night hideous ".—JOHN WILSON, *Noctes Ambrosianæ, Vol. II.*

Shakespeare is of no age. He speaks a language which thrills in our blood in spite of the separation of two hundred years. His thoughts, passions, feelings, strains of fancy, all are of this day, as they were of his own—and his genius may be contemporary with the mind of every generation for a thousand years to come. He, above all poets, looked upon men, and lived for mankind. His genius, universal in intellect and sympathy, could find, in no more bounded circumference, its proper sphere. It could not bear exclusion from any part of human existence. Whatever in nature and life was given to man, was given in contemplation and poetry to him also, and over the undimmed mirror of his mind passed all the shadows of our mortal world. . . . Of Shakespeare and Homer alone it may be averred, that we miss in them nothing of the greatness of nature. In all other poets we do ; we feel the measure of their power, and the restraint under which it is held ; but in Shakespeare and in Homer, all is free and unbounded as in nature ; and so we travel along with them, in a car drawn by celestial steeds, our view seems ever interminal as before, and still equally far off the glorious horizon.—*Id., Essays : A Few Words on Shakespeare.*

The Poet Laureate of the Court of Faery.—*Id., Ibid. : Cruickshank on Time.*

Highest among those who have exhibited human nature by means of dialogue, stands Shakespeare. His variety is like the variety of nature, endless diversity, scarcely any monstrosity. The characters of which he has given us an impression, as vivid as that which we receive from the characters of our own associates, are to be reckoned by scores. Yet in all these scores hardly one character is to be found which deviates widely from the common standard, and which we should call very eccentric if we met it in real life. The silly notion that every man has one ruling passion, and that this clue, once known, unravels all the mysteries of his conduct, finds no countenance in the plays of Shakespeare. There man appears as he is, made up of a crowd of passions, which contend for the mastery over him, and govern him in turn. What is Hamlet's ruling passion ? Or Othello's ? Or Harry the Fifth's ? Or Wolsey's ? Or Lear's ? Or Shylock's ? Or Benedict's ? Or that of Cassius ? Or that of Falconbridge ? But we might go on for ever.—MACAULAY, *Essays : Madame D'Arblay.*

I should like to have been Shakespeare's shoe-black—just to have lived in his house, just to have worshipped him—to have run on his errands, and seen that sweet serene face.—W. M. THACKERAY, *English Humourists of the Eighteenth Century.*

Of this Shakespeare of ours, perhaps the opinion one sometimes hears a little idolatrously expressed is, in fact, the right one; I think the best judgment not of this country only, but of Europe at large, is slowly pointing to the conclusion—That Shakespeare is the chief of all Poets hitherto; the greatest intellect who, in our recorded world, has left record of himself in the way of Literature. On the whole, I know not such a power of vision, such a faculty of thought, if we take all the characters of it, in any other man. Such a calmness of depth; placid joyous strength; all things imaged in that great soul of his so true and clear, as in a tranquil un-fathomable sea! It has been said, that in the constructing of Shakespeare's Dramas there is, apart from all other "faculties" as they are called, an understanding manifested, equal to that of Bacon's *Novum Organum.* That is true; and it is not a truth that strikes every one. It would become more apparent if we tried, any of us for himself, how, out of Shakespeare's dramatic materials, *we* could fashion such a result! . . . It is in what I called Portrait-painting, delineating of men and things, especially of men, that Shakespeare is great. All the greatness of the man comes out decisively here. It is unexampled, I think, that calm creative perspicacity of Shakespeare. The thing he looks at reveals not this or that face of it: but its inmost heart, and generic secret: it dissolves itself as in light before him, so that he discerns the perfect structure of it. Creative, we said: poetic creation, what is this too but *seeing* the thing sufficiently? . . . If I say therefore, that Shakespeare is the greatest of intellects, I have said all concerning him. But there is more in Shakespeare's intellect than we have yet seen. It is what I call an unconscious intellect; there is more virtue in it than he himself is aware of. Novalis beautifully remarks of him, that those Dramas of his are Products of Nature too, deep as Nature herself. I find a great truth in this saying. Shakespeare's Art is not Artifice; the noblest worth of it is not there by plan or precontrivance. It grows up from the deeps of Nature, through this noble sincere soul, who is a voice of Nature. . . . Here I say is an English King, whom no time or chance, Parliament or combination of Parliaments can dethrone! This King Shakespeare, does not he shine, in crowned sovereignty, over us all, as the noblest, gentlest, yet strongest of rallying-signs; *in*destructible; really more valuable in that point of view than any other means or appliance whatsoever? We can fancy him as radiant aloft over all the Nations of Englishmen, a thousand years hence. From Paramatta, from New York, wheresoever, under what sort of Parish Constable soever English men and women are, they will say to one another: "Yes, this Shakespeare is ours; we produced him, we speak and think by him; we are of one blood and kind with him".—CARLYLE, *On Heroes and Hero-Worship.*

Jesus and Shakespeare are fragments of the soul, and by love I conquer and incorporate them in my own conscious domain. His virtue,—is not that mine? His wit,—if it cannot be made mine, it is not wit.—EMERSON, *Essays: Compensation.*

Shakespeare is the only biographer of Shakespeare; and even he can tell nothing, except to the Shakespeare in us; that is, to our most apprehensive and sympathetic hour. He cannot step from off his tripod, and give us anecdotes of his inspirations. Read the antique documents extricated, analyzed, and compared by the assiduous Dyce and Collier; and now read one of those skyey sentences—aerolites—which seem to have fallen out of heaven, and which, not your experience, but the man within the breast, has accepted as words of fate; and tell me if they match; if the former account in any manner for the latter; or which gives the most historical insight into the man.—EMERSON, *Shakespeare; or, the Poet.*

When Shakespeare is charged with debts to his authors, Landor replies: "Yet he was more original than his originals. He breathed upon dead bodies and brought them into life."—*Id.*

Our love of Shakespeare, therefore, is not a *monomania* or solitary and unaccountable infatuation; but is merely the natural love which all men bear to those forms of excellence that are accommodated to their peculiar character, temperament, and situation.—LORD JEFFREY, *Essays.*

The name of Shakespeare is the greatest in our literature—it is the greatest in all literature. No man ever came near to him in the creative powers of the mind; no man had ever at once such strength, and such variety of imagination.—HALLAM, *Introduction to the Literature of Europe, Vol. III.*

Shakespeare's personages live and move as if they had just come forth from the hand of God.—MAZZINI, *Life and Writings, Vol. II.*

If it be said that Shakespeare wrote perfect historical plays on subjects belonging to the preceding centuries, I answer that they *are* perfect plays just because there is no care about centuries in them, but a life which all men recognise for the human life of all time; and this it is, not because Shakespeare sought to give universal truth, but because, painting honestly and completely from the men about him, he painted that human nature which is indeed constant enough—a rogue in the fifteenth century being, *at heart*, what a rogue is in the nineteenth and was in the twelfth; and an honest or a knightly man being, in like manner, very similar to other such at any other time. And the work of these great idealists is, therefore, always universal; not because it is *not portrait*, but because it is *complete* portrait down to the heart, which is the same in all ages; and the work of the mean idealists is *not* universal, not because it is portrait, but because it is *half* portrait—of the outside, the manners and the dress, not of the heart.—RUSKIN, *Modern Painters, Vol. III.*

The keen vision of the philosopher enlightens and directs the imagination of the poet; thus man appears to Shakespeare only when fully furnished with all that belongs to his nature. The truth is always there, before the eyes of the poet: he looks down and writes. . . . No one has ever combined, in an equal degree with Shakespeare, this double character of an impartial observer and a man of profound sensibility. Superior to all by his reason, and accessible to all by sympathy, he sees nothing without judging it, and he judges it because he feels it.—GUIZOT, *Shakespeare and his Times (transl.).*

Shakespeare, what is he? You might almost answer, he is the earth. Lucretius is the sphere, Shakespeare is the globe. There is more and less in the globe than in the sphere. In the sphere there is the whole; on the globe there is man. Here the outer, there the inner mystery.

Lucretius is the being, Shakespeare is the existence. Thence so much shadow in Lucretius; thence so much movement in Shakespeare. Space, the *blue*, as the Germans say, is certainly not forbidden to Shakespeare. The earth sees and surveys heaven; the earth knows heaven under its two aspects, darkness and azure, doubt and hope. . . . Shakespeare is a brother of Dante. The one completes the other. Dante incarnates all supernaturalism, Shakespeare all nature; and, as these two regions, nature and supernaturalism, which appear to us so different, are really the same unity, Dante and Shakespeare, however dissimilar, commingle outwardly, and are but one innately; there is something of the Alighieri, something of the ghost in Shakespeare. The skull passes from the hands of Dante into the hands of Shakespeare; Ugolino gnaws it, Hamlet questions it; and it shows perhaps even a deeper meaning and a loftier teaching in the second than in the first. Shakespeare shakes it and makes stars fall from it. . . . Shakespeare is Æschylus II. . . . Shakespeare is fertility, force, exuberance, the overflowing breast, the foaming cup, the brimful tub, the overrunning sap, the overflooding lava, the whirlwind scattering germs, the universal rain of life, everything by thousands, everything by millions, no reticence, no binding, no economy, the inordinate and tranquil prodigality of the creator. To those who feel the bottom of their pocket, the inexhaustible seems insane. Will it stop soon? Never, Shakespeare is the sower of dazzling wonders. At every turn, the image; at every turn, contrast: at every turn, light and darkness. . . . The depths of Shakespeare equal the gulfs of Chimborazo. . . . Art, like religion, has its *Ecce Homo.* Shakespeare is one of those of whom we may utter this grand saying: He is man.—VICTOR HUGO, *William Shakespeare (transl.).*

Shakespeare "glances from heaven to earth, from earth to heaven". All Nature ministers to him, as gladly as a mother to her child. Whether he wishes her to tune her myriad-voiced organ to Romeo's love, or to Miranda's innocence, or to Perdita's simplicity, or to Rosalind's playfulness, or to the sports of the Fairies, or to Timon's misanthropy, or to Macbeth's desolating ambition, or to Lear's heart-broken frenzy—he has only to ask, and she puts on every feeling and every passion with which he desires to invest her.—JULIUS C. HARE, *Guesses at Truth, First Series.*

One always fancies Shakespeare *in* his best verses, and Milton at the key-board of his organ. Shakespeare's language is no longer the mere vehicle of thought, it has become part of it, its very flesh and blood. The pleasure it gives us is unmixed, direct, like that from the smell of a flower or the flavour of a fruit.—J. R. LOWELL, *Among My Books.*

The works of Shakespeare . . . entirely unrivalled in all literature for largeness and variety, with depth.—GLADSTONE, *Gleanings, Vol. III.*

Certainly Shakespeare was a "million-minded man," if he was conscious of the innumerable philosophies and psychological truths which his million critics have found in every trifling word and sentence. I am heretic enough to think that Shakespeare was mind and dust, and that he can be very low and gross. Horace ventured to opine that now and then Homer nodded a little; he said it in a very gentlemanly way—for the friend of Mæcenas was a perfect gentleman—but I have no doubt he was reckoned a heretic for saying it. What I admire in Shakespeare, however, is that his loves are all human—no earthliness hiding itself from itself in sentimental transcendentalism—no loves of the angels, which are the least angelic things, I believe, that float in the clouds, though they do look down upon mortal feelings with contempt.—F. W. Robertson, *Life and Letters of F. W. Robertson, by Dr. Stopford Brooke.*

Surely, then, we may consider Shakespeare, as an ancient mythologist would have done, as "enskied" among "the invulnerable clouds," where no shaft, even of envy, can assail him. From this elevation we may safely predict that he never can be plucked. . . . We may compare the mind of Shakespeare to a diamond, pellucid, bright, and untinted, cut into countless polished facets, which, in constant movement, at every smallest change of direction or of angle, caught a new reflection, so that not one of its brilliant mirrors could be for a moment idle, but by a power beyond its control was ever busy with the reflection of innumerable images, either distinct or running into one another, or repeated each so clearly as to allow him, when he chose, to fix it in his memory.—Cardinal Wiseman, *William Shakespeare.*

Shakespeare is as astonishing for the exuberance of his genius in abstract notions, and for the depth of his analytic and philosophic insight, as for the scope and minuteness of his poetic imagination. It is as if into a mind poetical in *form* there had been poured all the *matter* that existed in the mind of his contemporary Bacon. In Shakespeare's plays we have thought, history, exposition, and philosophy, all within the round of the poet. The only difference between him and Bacon sometimes is that Bacon writes an essay and calls it his own, while Shakespeare writes a similar essay and puts it into the mouth of a Ulysses or a Polonius.— David Masson, *Wordsworth, Shelley, Keats, and other Essays.*

Take the entire range of English literature; put together our best authors, who have written upon subjects not professedly religious or theological, and we shall not find, I believe, in them *all united,* so much evidence of the Bible having been read and used, as we have found in Shakespeare *alone.* This is a *phenomenon* which admits of being looked at from several points of view; but I shall be content to regard it solely in connection with the undoubted fact, that of all our authors, Shakespeare is also, by general confession, the greatest and the best.—Bishop Charles Wordsworth, *On Shakespeare's Knowledge and Use of the Bible.*

The godlike equity of Shakespeare's judgment, his implacable and impeccable righteousness of instinct and of insight, was too deeply ingrained in the very core of his genius to be perverted by any provincial or pseudo-patriotic prepossessions; his patriotism was too national to be provincial. Assuredly no poet had more than he: not even the king of men and poets who fought at Marathon and sang of Salamis: much less had any or has any one of our own, from Milton on to Campbell and from Campbell even to Tennyson. . . . *Amica Britannia, sed magis amica veritas.* The master poet of England—all Englishmen may reasonably and honourably be proud of it—has not two weights and two measures for friend and foe. —Swinburne, *A Study of Shakespeare.*

From Shakespeare, no doubt, the world may learn, and has learnt, much, yet he professed so little to be a teacher, that he has often been represented as almost without personal opinions, as a mere undisturbed mirror, in which all Nature reflects herself.—J. R. SEELEY, *Goethe reviewed after Sixty Years.*

It is a favourite way with some eulogists of Shakespeare to deny him all individuality whatsoever. He was not one man, they say, but an epitome of all men. "His mind," says Hazlitt, "had no one peculiar bias or exclusive excellence more than another. He was just like any other man, but that he was like all other men. He was the least of an egotist that it was possible to be. He was nothing in himself; but he was all that others were or that they could become." Against such a degradation of Shakespeare's character, or of any man's character, it is our duty to protest. In trying to make Shakespeare more than human, the reckless panegyrist makes him considerably less than human : instead of the man whose prudence made him rich, whose affectionate nature made him loved almost to idolatry, and whose genius has been the wonder of the world, we are presented with plasticity in the abstract, an object not more interesting than a quarry of potter's clay.—WILLIAM MINTO, *Characteristics of English Poets.*

As a corollary to what has hitherto been said about the differences between the drama of Sophocles and that of Shakespeare, it follows that the former aims at depicting the destinies, and the latter the characters of men.—J. ADDINGTON SYMONDS, *Studies of the Greek Poets.*

Shakespeare illustrates every phase and variety of humour: a complete analysis of Shakespeare's humour would make a system of psychology.—R. G. MOULTON, *Shakespeare as a Dramatic Critic.*

Shakespeare's mind, as Hazlitt suggested, contained within itself the germs of all faculty and feeling. He knew intuitively how every faculty and feeling would develop in any conceivable change of fortune. Men and women—good or bad, old or young, wise or foolish, merry or sad, rich or poor—yielded their secrets to him, and his genius enabled him to give being in his pages to all the shapes of humanity that presents themselves on the highway of life. Each of his characters gives voice to thought or passion with an individuality and a naturalness that rouse in the intelligent play-goer and reader the illusion that they are over-hearing men and women speak unpremeditatingly among themselves, rather than that they are reading written speeches or hearing written speeches recited. The more closely the words are studied, the completer the illusion grows. Creatures of the imagination—fairies, ghosts, witches—are delineated with a like potency, and the reader or spectator feels instinctively that these supernatural entities could not speak, feel, or act otherwise than Shakespeare represents them. The creative power of poetry was never manifested to such effect as in the corporeal semblances in which Shakespeare clad the spirits of the air. . . . To Shakespeare the intellect of the world, speaking in divers accents, applies with one accord his own words : How noble in reason! how infinite in faculty! in apprehension how like a god!—SIDNEY LEE, *A Life of Shakespeare.*

PERCY BYSSHE SHELLEY.

English Poet: 1792-1822.

Sun-treader, life and light be thine for ever!
Thou art gone from us ; years go by and spring

'Gladdens and the young earth is beautiful,
Yet thy songs come not, other bards arise,
But none like thee : they stand, thy majesties,
Like mighty works which tell some spirit there
Hath sat regardless of neglect and scorn,
Till, its long task completed, it hath risen
And left us, never to return, and all
Rush in to peer and praise when all in vain. . . .
But thou art still for me who have adored
Tho' single panting, but to hear thy name
Which I believed a spell to me alone,
Scarce deeming thou wast as a star to men !

— BROWNING, *Pauline.*

What boots it, Shelley! that the breeze
Carried thy lovely wail away,
Musical through Italian trees
Which fringe thy soft blue Spezzian bay ?
Inheritors of thy distress
Have restless hearts one throb the less ?

— MATTHEW ARNOLD, *Stanzas from the Grand Chartreuse.*

He with the gleaming eyes,
And glances gentle and wild,
The angel eternal child ;
His heart could not throb with ours,
He could not see with our eyes
Dimm'd with the dulness of earth,
Blind with the bondage of hours ;
Yet none with diviner mirth
Hail'd what was noble and sweet ;
The blood-track'd journey of life,
        The way-sore feet
None have watch'd with more human eyes.

— PALGRAVE, *Two Graves at Rome.*

Slow from the shore the sullen waves retire ;
    His form a nobler element shall claim ;
Nature baptized him in ethereal fire,
    And death shall crown him with a wreath of flame.

.   .   .   .

Breathe for his wandering soul one passing sigh,
    O happier Christian, while thine eye grows dim,—
In all the mansions of the house on high,
    Say not that Mercy has not one for him !

— OLIVER WENDELL HOLMES, *After a Lecture on Shelley.*

Oh, not like ours that life was born,
    No mortal mother Shelley knew,
But kindled by some starry morn
    Lit like a snow-flake from the blue ;
Saw on some peak the lightnings gleam,
    The lingering soft auroras play ;
Then foamlike on a leaping stream

Sped downwards to the earthly day.
. . . .
So keen a wish had winged his flight—
 His heart was faint with such desire—
To bear from that supernal light
 A Promethean fount of fire:
His quivering thyrsus flashed with flame,
 He sang the spell long learnt above ;
With ardent eyes one only name
 He named ; the mountains echoed " Love ! "
     —F. W. H. MYERS, *Stanzas on Shelley.*

Thy voice is heard above the silent tomb,
And shall be heard until the end of days,
While Freedom lives, and whatsoever things
Are good and lovely—still thy spirit sings,
 And by thy grave to-day fresh violets bloom,
But on thy head imperishable bays.
     —WALTER CRANE, *At Shelley's Grave.*

When Keats died the Muses still had left
 One silver voice to sing his threnody,
But ah ! too soon of it we were bereft
 When on that riven night and stormy sea
Panthea claimed her singer as her own,
And slew the mouth that praised her. . . .
     —OSCAR WILDE, *The Garden of Eros.*

And in his gusts of song he brings
Wild odours shaken from strange wings,
And unfamiliar whisperings
  From far lips blown,
With all the rapturous heart of things
  Throbs through his own.
    —WILLIAM WATSON, *Shelley's Centenary* (*4th August,* 1892).

Brothers in Shelley, we this morn are strong:
 Our Heart of Hearts hath conquered—conquered those
Once fain to work the world and Shelley wrong ;
 Their pyre of hate now bourgeons with the rose—
 Their every fagot, now a sweet-brier, throws
Love's breath upon the breeze of Shelley's song !
     —THEODORE WATTS, *For the Shelley Centenary.*

Never did a fancy so teem with sensuous imagery as Shelley's. Words-worth economises an image, and detains it until he has distilled all the poetry out of it, and it will not yield a drop more : Shelley lavishes his with a profusion which is unconscious because it is inexhaustible.— J. STUART MILL, *Dissertations and Discussions, Vol. I.*

A dialogue between two qualities, in his dream, has more dramatic effect than a dialogue between two human beings in most plays. In this respect the genius of Bunyan bore a great resemblance to that of a man who had very little else in common with him, Percy Bysshe Shelley. The strong imagination of Shelley made him an idolater in his own despite. Out of the most indefinite terms of a hard, cold, dark, metaphysical system, he made a gorgeous Pantheon, full of beautiful, majestic, and life-like forms. He turned atheism itself into a mythology, rich with visions as glorious as the gods that live in the marble of Phidias, or the virgin saints that smile on us from the canvas of Murillo. The Spirit of Beauty, the Principle of Good, the Principle of Evil, when he treated of them, ceased to be abstractions. They took shape and colour. They were no longer mere words; but "intelligible forms," "fair humanities," objects of love, of adoration, or of fear. As there can be no stronger sign of a mind destitute of the poetical faculty than that tendency which was so common among the writers of the French school to turn images into abstractions, Venus, for example, into Love, Minerva into Wisdom, Mars into War, and Bacchus into Festivity, so there can be no stronger sign of a mind truly poetical than a disposition to reverse this abstracting process, and to make individuals out of generalities. Some of the metaphysical and ethical theories of Shelley were certainly most absurd and pernicious. But we doubt whether any modern poet has possessed in an equal degree some of the highest qualities of the great ancient masters. The words bard and inspiration, which seem so cold and affected when applied to other modern writers, have a perfect propriety when applied to him. He was not an author but a bard. His poetry seems not to have been an art, but an inspiration. Had he lived to the full age of man, he might not improbably have given to the world some great work of the very highest rank in design and execution. But, alas!—MACAULAY, *Essays: The Pilgrim's Progress.*

Shelley, with a more daring and dramatic genius, with great mastery of language, and the true Lucretian soul, for ever aspiring *extra flammantia moenia mundi*, is equally intellectual in his creations; and despite the young audacity which led him into denying a God, his poetry is of a remarkably ethereal and spiritualising cast. It is steeped in veneration—it is for ever thirsting for the Heavenly and the Immortal—and the Deity he questioned avenges Himself only by impressing His image upon all that the poet undertook. But Shelley at present has subjected himself to be misunderstood; he has become the apologist for would-be mystics, and dreamers of foolish dreams,—for an excellent master may have worthless disciples.—LYTTON, *England and the English.*

The greatest sinner of the oracular school was Shelley—because the only true poet. True poets admire his genius, but, in spite of love and pity for the dead, they disdain the voluntary darkness in which he perversely dallied with things of light that should never have been so enshrouded, and according to the command and law of nature should have been wooed, won, wedded, and enjoyed in the face of heaven.—JOHN WILSON, *Noctes Ambrosianæ, Vol. IV.*

A more crystalline heart than Shelley's has rarely throbbed in human bosom. He was incapable of an untruth, or of deceit in any form. . . . Whatever peculiarity there might have been in Shelley's religious faith, I have the best authority for believing that it was confined to the early period of his life. The *practical* result of its course of *action*, I am sure, had its source from the "Sermon on the Mount". There is not one clause in that Divine Code which his conduct towards his fellow mortals did not confirm and substantiate him to be—in action a follower of Christ. —CHARLES COWDEN CLARKE, *Recollections of Writers.*

What was the real character of the man whom critics and relatives, and the law, which stripped him of his children, and the self-righteous world, contrived to chase from society as a demon? a perfectly childlike and Christlike creature. If Christianity is love, and love of your neighbour especially, then was Shelley in heart and soul and daily deed a perfect Christian. He lamented his early errors, but found no forgiveness. " He was," says Captain Medwin, his relative, and one who knew him from childhood, " an enemy to all sensuality." The pleasures of the table, that form the *summum bonum* of the herd, were not his pleasures. His diet was that of a hermit, his drink water, and his principal and favourite food bread. His conversation was as chaste as his morals—all grossness he abominated.—WILLIAM HOWITT, *The Northern Heights of London.*

Shelley, with due admiration for his genius, is entirely mischievous.— RUSKIN.

Who that has read Shelley does not recollect scraps worthy to stand by Ariel's song—chaste, simple, unutterably musical? Yes, when he will be himself—Shelley the scholar and the gentleman and the singer—and leave philosophy and politics, which he does not understand, and shriekings and cursings, which are unfit for any civilised and self-respecting man, he is perfect. Like the American mocking-bird, he is harsh only when aping other men's tunes—his true power lies in his own " native woodnotes wild ".—CHARLES KINGSLEY, *Literary and General Lectures, etc.*

Shelleyism is very sublime, sublimer a good deal than God, for God's world is all wrong, and Shelley is all right—more pure than Christ, for Shelley can criticise Christ's heart and life—nevertheless Shelleyism is only atmospheric profligacy, to coin a Montgomeryism.—F. W. ROBERTSON, *Life and Letters of F. W. Robertson, Vol. I.*

We should regard Shelley as the poetical representative of those whose hopes and aspirations and affections rush forward to embrace the great Hereafter, and dwell in rapturous anticipation on the coming of the golden year, the reign of universal freedom, and the establishment of universal brotherhood. By nature and by circumstance he was marvellously fitted for his task—gentle, sensitive, and fervid, he shrank from the least touch of wrong, and hated injustice with the zeal and passion of a martyr. . . . With one exception, a more glorious poet has not been given to the English nation; and if we make one exception, it is because Shakespeare was a man of profounder insight, of calmer temperament, of wider experience, of more extensive knowledge; a greater philosopher, in fact, and a wiser man; not because he possessed more vital heat, more fusing, shaping power of imagination, or a more genuine poetic impulse and inspiration. After the passions and the theories which supplied Shelley with the subject-matter of his poems have died away and become mere matters of history, there will still remain a song, such as mortal man never sung before, of inarticulate rapture and of freezing pain—of a blinding light of truth and a dazzling weight of glory, translated into English speech, as coloured as a painted window, as suggestive, as penetrating, as intense as music.—GEORGE BRIMLEY, *Essays.*

Shelley had many merits and many defects. This is not the place for a complete or indeed for any estimate of him. But one excellence is most evident. His words are as flexible as any words; the rhythm of some modulating air seems to move them into their place without a struggle by the poet, and almost without his knowledge. This is the perfection of true art.—WALTER BAGEHOT, *Literary Studies, Vol. II.*

If ever any human being was gifted with " the vision and the faculty *divine,*" Shelley was so gifted.—P. G. PATMORE, *My Friends and Acquaintances, Vol. III.*

Perhaps there never was a man of more opulent religious phantasy, of more burning religious emotion, than Shelley; the same poet who called himself with boyish folly, Atheist, yet dreamed of and hymned the Spirit of Beauty. The Iconoclast, whether poet, or prophet, or satirist, may through the mere and earnest simplicity of contradiction, be, in certain barren or corrupt or Pharisaical ages, the True Adorer.—WILLIAM MACCALL, *The Newest Materialism.*

Shelley is pre-eminently the poet of what may be called meteorological circumstance. He is at home among winds, mists, rains, snows, clouds gorgeously coloured, glories of sunrise, nights of moonshine, lightnings, streamers, and falling stars; and what of vegetation and geology he brings in is but so much that might be seen by an aerial creature in its ascents and descents.—DAVID MASSON, *Wordsworth, Shelley, Keats, etc.*

Shelley, as pure a philanthropist as St. Francis or Howard, could forget mankind, and, like his Adonais, become one with nature.—JOHN NICHOL, *Life of Byron.*

The most truly spiritual of all English poets, Shelley. . . . We feel that Shelley transports the spirit to the highest bound and limit of the intelligible; and that with him thought passes through one superadded and more rarefying process than the other poet (Byron) is master of. If it be true, as has been written, that " Poetry is the breath and finer spirit of all knowledge," we may say that Shelley teaches us to apprehend that further something, the breath and finer spirit of poetry itself.—JOHN MORLEY, *Miscellanies, Vol. I.*

Who shall say that Shelley has not been " the trumpet of a prophecy " ? What matters it, though some of his poems should be disfigured by affectation, and others by a quixotic assault upon wind-mills of his own creation ?—there is yet a glamour over all his song, which proclaims him the great poet. Even in his translations—an important branch of his art —the same glamour shines. We understand the old aphorism, *poeta nascitur non fit,* when it is applied to him. The value and extent of his work, when placed in juxtaposition with the brevity of his life, leave us but astonishment and wonder. He was inspired, and has since been the source of inspiration in others. . . . His prophetic eyes shone with a glorified light from other suns than ours.—G. B. SMITH, *Shelley: A Critical Biography.*

Shelley seems to have sunk himself in Nature, and made himself the translator of Nature's mute emotions. To use one of his favourite phrases, his being became " inwoven " with the very life of the universe. We find it hard to realize him as a bodily presence; he is " as the air invulnerable ". He did not live prose and write poetry; he was poetry from the crown of his head to the sole of his foot; a creature of imagination all compact.— W. J. DAWSON, *Quest and Vision.*

Meanwhile, the thoughtful student of literature and history will not cease to ponder on the strange revenge of time which Shelley's life and works constitute. He whose mission it was to loosen traditional authority and untie worn-out convention was born in the very lap of that solid but exclusive comfort which the centuries had been building upon authority and convention. He who was more penetrable by ideas than any poet of his age came into the world among associations where every new idea was " God bless us ! a thing of naught ". . . . As Shelley the poet had been the supreme lord of song in a prosaic world, as Shelley the propogandist had been through faith the lord of hope, so Shelley the man had been, to those who hung upon him or needed him, the lord of love.—H. BUXTON FORMAN, *Memoir prefixed to Shelley's Poetical Works, Vol. I.*

Not for this set of readers nor for that, but for all who love what is loftiest and best in poetry, Shelley must always seem one of the highest enthroned among the kings of song. It can never be that the avarice of time shall take his name and his music from us. Even as " Adonais," of whom he wrote in deathless strains, he veritably wakes or sleeps with the enduring dead.—WILLIAM SHARP, *Life of Percy Bysshe Shelley.*

To illustrate Shelley would be as impossible as to paint a strain of music, unless indeed some of Turner's cloud scenery may be taken as representative of his incidental descriptions.—LESLIE STEPHEN, *Hours in a Library, Vol. III.*

Shelley is too great to serve as text for any sermon ; and yet we may learn from him as from a hero of Hebrew or Hellenic story. His life was a tragedy ; and like some protagonist of Greek Drama, he was capable of erring and of suffering greatly. . . . We have only to read Shelley's *Essay on Christianity*, in order to perceive what reverent admiration he felt for Jesus, and how profoundly he understood the true character of his teaching. That work, brief as it is, forms one of the most valuable extant contributions to a sound theology, and is morally far in advance of the opinions expressed by many who regard themselves as specially qualified to speak on the subject. It is certain that, as Christianity passes beyond its mediæval phase, and casts aside the husk of out-worn dogmas, it will more and more approximate to Shelley's exposition. Here and here only is a vital faith, adapted to the conditions of modern thought, indestructible because essential, and fitted to unite instead of separating minds of divers quality. It may sound paradoxical to claim for Shelley of all men a clear insight into the enduring element of the Christian creed ; but it was precisely his detachment from all its accidents which enabled him to discern its spiritual purity, and placed him in a true relation to its Founder. For those who would neither on the one hand relinquish what is permanent in religion, nor yet on the other deny the inevitable conclusions of modern thought, his teaching is indubitably valuable.—J. ADDINGTON SYMONDS, *Shelley : A Memoir.*

WILLIAM SHENSTONE.

English Poet : 1714-1763.

　　Nor Shenstone, thou
Shalt pass without thy meed, thou son of peace !
Who knew'st, perchance, to harmonize thy shades,

Still softer than thy song; yet was that song
Nor rude, nor inharmonious, when attun'd
To pastoral plaint, or tale of slighted love.
                              —W. MASON, *The English Garden*.

The pleasure of Shenstone was all in his eye; he valued what he
valued merely for its looks; nothing raised his indignation more than to
ask if there were any fishes in his water. His house was mean, and he
did not improve it; his care was of his grounds. When he came home
from his walks, he might find his floors flooded by a shower through the
broken roof; but could spare no money for its reparation. In time his
expenses brought clamours about him, that overpowered the lamb's bleat
and the linnet's song; and his groves were haunted by beings very
different from fauns and fairies.—DR. JOHNSON, *Lives of the Poets*:
Shenstone.

I have read, too, an octavo volume of Shenstone's Letters. Poor
man! he was always wishing for money, for fame, and other distinctions;
and his whole philosophy consisted in living against his will in retirement,
and in a place which his taste had adorned, but which he only enjoyed
when people of note came to see and commend it; his correspondence
is about nothing else but this place and his own writings, with two or
three neighbouring clergymen, who wrote verses too.—THOMAS GRAY.

RICHARD BRINSLEY SHERIDAN.

Irish Statesman, Orator, and Dramatist: 1751-1816.

Long shall we seek his likeness, long in vain,
And turn to all of him which may remain,
Sighing that Nature form'd but one such man,
And broke the die—in moulding Sheridan!
      —BYRON, *Monody on the Death of the Right Hon. R. B. Sheridan*.

Such was Sheridan! he could soften an attorney!
There has been nothing like it since the days of Orpheus.
                              —*Id*. in MOORE'S *Life of Byron*.

It was some Spirit! Sheridan! that breathed
O'er thy young mind such wildly various power!
My soul hath marked thee in her shaping hour,
Thy temples with Hymettian flow'rets wreathed:
And sweet thy voice, as when o'er Laura's bier
Sad music trembled through Vauclusa's glade;
Sweet, as at dawn the love-born Serenade
That wafts soft dreams to Slumber's listening ear.
Now patriot Rage and indignation high
Swell the full tones! And now thine eye-beams dance
Meanings of Scorn and Wit's quaint revelry!
Writhes inly from the bosom-probing glance
The apostate by the brainless rout adored,
As erst that elder Fiend beneath great Michael's sword.
                        —S. T. COLERIDGE, *Sonnet VI*.

Of Mr. Fox's adherents who have just been named, the most remarkable certainly was Mr. Sheridan, and with all his faults, and all his failings, and all his defects, the first in genius and greatest in power.—LORD BROUGHAM, *Statesmen of the Time of George III.*

Mr. Sheridan has been justly called "a dramatic star of the first magnitude"; and indeed among the comic writers of the last century he "shines like Hesperus among the lesser lights". . . . He had wit, fancy, sentiment at command, enabling him to place the thoughts of others in new lights of his own, which reflected back one added lustre on the originals: whatever he touched he adorned with all the ease, grace, and brilliancy of his style. If he ranks only as a man of second-rate genius, he was assuredly a man of first-rate talents.—HAZLITT, *Lectures on the English Comic Writers.*

Sheridan blazed and exploded from side to side in a reckless yet rigid course, like a gigantic and splendid piece of firework, his follies repeating themselves, his inability to follow up success, and careless abandonment of one way after another that might have led to a better and happier fortune. He had a fit of writing, a fit of oratory, but no impulse to keep him in either path long enough to make anything more than the dazzling but evanescent triumph of a day. His harvest was like a southern harvest, over early, while it was yet but May; but he sowed no seed for a second ingathering, nor was there any growth or richness left in the soon-exhausted soil.—MRS. OLIPHANT, *Life of Sheridan.*

THOMAS SHERLOCK.

Bishop of London : 1678-1761.

Rather verge
To Sherlock's plain compactness, that admits
No decorating figures, than o'erload
Thy lessons with the metaphor's crude mass.
            —RICHARD POLWHELE, *Pulpit Eloquence.*

Among the citizens be grave and slow;
Before the nobles let fine periods flow;
The Temple Church asks Sherlock's sense and skill ;
Beyond the Tow'r—no matter—what you will.
            —ROBERT DODSLEY, *The Art of Preaching.*

Sherlock staggered to and fro between Tritheism and Sabellianism.—S. T. COLERIDGE, *Table Talk.*

SIR PHILIP SIDNEY.

English Statesman and Poet : 1554-1586.

But that immortal spirit, which was deckt
With all the dowries of celestial grace,
By sovereign choice from th' heavenly quires select,

And lineally deriv'd from angels' race,
O what is now of it become? aread:
Aye me! can so divine a thing be dead?
> —SPENSER, *Upon the Death of Sir Philip Sidney.*

Immortal Sidney, glory of the field!
And glory of the Muses!
> —SAMUEL DANIEL, *A Funeral Poem, upon the Death of the
> Earl of Devonshire.*

Reason's sense and learning's sweeting
Where the Muses had their meeting,
Nature's grace and honour's glory,
Of the world the woful story;
That with bitter tears be read
Sweet Sir Philip Sidney dead.

Dead? Oh no! in heaven he liveth,
Whom the heavens such honour giveth,
That though here his body lie,
Yet his soul shall never die;
But as fame can perish never,
So his faith shall live for ever.
> —NICHOLAS BRETON, *Sir Philip Sidney's Epitaph.*

The noble Sidney, with this last arose,
That hero for numbers, and for prose.
That throughly pac'd our language as to show,
The plenteous English hand in hand might go
With Greek and Latin, and did first reduce
Our tongue from Lilly's writing then in use;
Talking of stones, stars, plants, of fishes, flies,
Playing with words, and idle similes.
> —MICHAEL DRAYTON, *Elegy to Henry Reynolds, Esq.*

Nor can the Muse the gallant Sidney pass,
The plume of war! with early laurels crown'd,
The lover's myrtle, and the poet's bay.
> —THOMSON, *The Seasons : Summer.*

O Britain, parent of illustrious names,
While o'er thy annals memory shoots her eye,
How the heart glows, rapt with high-wondering love,
And emulous esteem! hail, Sidney hail!
Whether Arcadian blithe, by fountain clear,
Piping thy love-lays wild, or Spartan bold,
In freedom's van distinguish'd, Sidney, hail!
Oft o'er thy laurell'd tomb from hands unseen
Fall flowers; oft in thy vale of Penshurst fair
The shepherd wandering from his nightly fold,
Listeneth strange music, by the tiny breath
Of fairy minstrels warbled.
> —JOHN LANGHORNE, *Fragment,* 1762.

Sidney, warbler of poetic prose.
> —COWPER, *The Task : The Winter Evening.*

> Sidney as he fought
> And as he fell, and as he lived and loved,
> Sublimely mild, a spirit without spot,
> Arose.
>
> —SHELLEY, *Adonais.*

> For a dearer life
> Never in battle hath been offered up,
> Since in like cause and in unhappy day,
> By Zutphen's walls the peerless Sidney fell.
>
> —SOUTHEY, *To the Memory of Major-General Mackinnon.*

> Arcadian Sidney—Nursling of the Muse,
> Flower of divine Romance, whose bloom was fed
> By daintiest Helicon's most silver dews,
> Alas! how soon thy lovely leaves were shed.
>
> —LYTTON, *The Last Days of Elizabeth.*

> Music bright as the soul of light, for wings an eagle, for notes a dove,
> Leaps and shines from the lustrous lines where through thy soul from afar above
> Shone and sang till the darkness rang with light whose fire is the fount of love.

> Love that led thee alive, and fed thy soul with sorrows and joys and fears,
> Love that sped thee, alive and dead, to fame's fair goal with thy peerless peers,
> Feeds the flame of thy quenchless name with light that lightens the rayless years.
>
> —SWINBURNE, *Astrophel, II.*

The life of Sir Philip Sidney was poetry put into action.—CAMPBELL.

Sir Philip Sidney is one of the patron saints of England, of whom Wotton said, " His wit was the measure of congruity ".—EMERSON, *English Traits : Manners.*

What English gentleman would not rejoice to bequeath a name like that of Sir Philip Sidney ?—LYTTON, *Essays: Posthumous Reputation.*

Sir Philip Sidney represented the popular sentiment in Elizabeth's day —Byron that in our own. Each became the poetry of a particular age put into action—each, incorporated with the feelings he addressed, attracted towards himself an enthusiasm which his genius alone did not deserve.—*Id., England and the English : Intellectual Spirit, etc.*

Personalities so unique as Sidney's exhale a perfume which evanesces when the lamp of life burns out. This the English nation felt when they put on mourning for his death. They felt that they had lost in Sidney, not only one of their most hopeful gentlemen and bravest soldiers, but something rare and beautiful in human life, which could not be recaptured, which could not even be transmitted, save by hearsay, to a future age. . . . When we review the life of Sir Philip Sidney, it is certain that one thought will survive all other thoughts about him in our mind. This man, we shall say, was born to show the world what goes to the making

of an English Gentleman.   But he belonged to his age; and the age of
Elizabeth differed in many essential qualities from the age of Anne and
from the age of Victoria.   Sidney was the typical English gentleman of
the modern era at the moment of transition from the mediæval period.
He was the hero of our Renaissance.—J. ADDINGTON SYMONDS, *Biography
of Sir Philip Sidney.*

SIMONIDES.

Greek Poet: B.C. 556-467.

O ye, who patiently explore
The wreck of Herculanean lore,
What rapture ! could ye seize
Some Theban fragment, or unroll
One precious, tender-hearted, scroll
Of pure Simonides.

—WORDSWORTH, *Departing Summer.*

The tenderest Poet that could be
Who sang in ancient Greece his loving lay.

—*Id.*

Of him who sang the Seasons as they roll,
With all a Hesiod's truth, a Homer's power,
And the pure feeling of Simonides.

—D. M. MOIR, *Thomson's Birthplace.*

In reviewing the life of Simonides, after admitting that he was greedy
of gain and not averse to flatter, we are bound to confess that, as a poet,
he proved himself adequate to the age of Marathon and Salamis.   He
was the voice of Hellas—the genius of Fame, sculpturing upon her
brazen shield with a pen of adamant, in austere letters of indelible gold,
the achievements to which the whole world owes its civilisation.   Happy
poet !   Had ever any other man so splendid a heritage of song allotted to
him ?   In style Simonides is always pure and exquisitely polished.   The
ancients called him the sweet poet—Melicertes —*par excellence*.   His
σωφροσύνη gives a mellow tone not merely to his philosophy and moral
precepts, but also to his art.   He has none of Pindar's rugged majesty,
volcanic force, gorgeous exuberance: he does not, like Pindar, pour
forth an inexhaustible torrent of poetical ideas, chafing against each
other in the eddies of breathless inspiration.   On the contrary, he works
up a few thoughts, a few carefully selected images, with patient skill,
producing a perfectly harmonious result, but one which is always border-
ing on the commonplace.   Like all correct poets, he is somewhat tame,
though tender, delicate, and exquisitely beautiful.—J. ADDINGTON SYMONDS,
Studies of Greek Poets.

SIXTUS IV.

Pope: 1414-1484.

Pope Sixtus IV., one of the worst men that ever sat in the chair of St.
Peter, praised himself immeasurably in the anathema he pronounced
against Lorenzo de Medici, whom he presumed to call "the Son of

Iniquity," and the " Heir of Perdition "; while he was himself all mild-ness, moderation, and gentleness. This was not self-delusion; but im-pudence, blended with the most astonishing hypocrisy. Sixtus was of an order, who, in their declamations against the crimes and vices of others, brave the discovery of their own crimes and defects. " They are them-selves the great sublime they draw."—CHARLES BUCKE, *Book of Human Character.*

ADAM SMITH.

English Political Economist : 1723-1790.

Adam Smith was nearly the first who made deeper reasonings and more exact knowledge popular among us.—LORD JEFFREY, *Essays.*

Adam Smith is, in an unobtrusive way, the apostle of Democracy as well as of Free Trade.—GOLDWIN SMITH, *Three English Statesmen.*

Adam Smith, one of the most distinguished positive thinkers in this negative century.—JOHN MORLEY, *Life of Edmund Burke.*

REV. SYDNEY SMITH.

Canon of St. Paul's ; Critic and Wit : 1771-1845.

Rare Sydney ! thrice honour'd the stall where he sits,
And be his every honour he deigneth to climb at !
Had England a hierarchy formed all of wits,
Whom, but Sydney, would England proclaim as its Primate ?
And long may he flourish, frank, merry, and brave,
A Horace to feast with, a Pascal to read !
While he *laughs* all is safe ; but when Sydney grows grave,
We shall then think the Church is in danger indeed.

—MOORE.

Tickler : " Yes—Sydney Smith has a rare genius for the grotesque. He is, with his quips and cranks, a formidable enemy to pomposity and pre-tension. No man can wear a big wig comfortably in his presence ; the absurdity of such enormous frizzle is felt ; and the dignitary would fain exchange all that horse-hair for a few scattered locks of another animal."—JOHN WILSON, *Noctes Ambrosianæ, Vol. I.*

As for Sydney Smith, to him fighting is fun, and he cuts as many capers in the ring as young Spring, the Conqueror. But he is formidable in his frolic—though rather too showy, yet a clean, straight, and even heavy hitter ; and most of his antagonists, though heavier men than himself, and deficient in neither science nor bottom, have, after a few rounds, in which their gravity was most amusingly, and to the infinite mirth of all beholders, contrasted with the antics of the Parson who kept hopping about like a mountebank, yet all the while dealing out right and left handers like lightning, been carried out of the ring deaf as a house, and blind as the pier of Leith, or the mole of Tyre. He has fought one or two drawn battles, especially one with the best man then in the ring, under the *nom de guerre* of Peter Plymley, which was brought to a wrangle, and ended in a draw—but he has never yet been fairly defeated ; and to accomplish that will require an out-and-outer.—*Idem., Essays : The Man of Ton.*

Mrs. Austin justly remarks that the reputation of Sydney Smith has risen since his death. It has risen, and it is to rise. Every year lessens the number of those who can remember the marvellous charm of his conversation, that diaphragm-shaking, fancy-chasing, oddity-piling, incongruity-linking, hyperbole-topping, wonder-working faculty of his, which a bookful of Homeric compound adjectives would still leave undescribed. But meanwhile, the true proportions of that large intellect have been growing upon the vision of men. Blinded with tears of laughter, they could not estimate his magnitude. Hands palsied by convulsive cachinnations were too unsteady to hold the measure and fit the colossus with a judgment. Now it is better understood how all that wit was only the efflorescence of his greatness—the waving wild flowers on the surface of a pyramid. Time may take from the edifice of his fame some of its lighter decorations, obliterate quaint carvings, decapitate some grotesque and pendant gargoyles, destroy some rich flamboyant word traceries; but that very spoliation will only display more completely the solid foundation, the broad harmonious plan of his life's structure, and exhibit the fine conscientiousness with which those parts of the building most remote from the public eye were finished, even as they most seem. . . . The wit of Sydney Smith was always under the control of good taste and good feeling. It was never mischievous to him by any unseemliness, impertinence, or vulgarity. Throughout his writings, so remarkable for natural flow and freedom of style, so simple and so idiomatic, you search in vain for anything slipshod, for triteness or chit-chat, for a single colloquial solecism. His style, like golden haired Pyrrha, is always *simplex munditiis.*—R. A. VAUGHAN, *Essays and Remains, Vol. II.*

We will not say that, like Goldsmith, he adorned everything he touched, but he compelled everything he touched to appear in its natural shape and genuine colours. In his hands the logical process called the *reductio ab absurdum* operated like the spear of Ithuriel. No form of sophistry or phase of bigotry could help throwing off its disguise at his approach; and the dogma which has been deemed questionable touching ridicule in general, may be confidently predicated of *his*, namely, that it was literally and emphatically the test of truth.—A. HAYWARD, *Biographical and Critical Essays, Vol. I.*

The reader of to-day who turns to refresh his mind with the mischievous sallies and sparkling common sense of Sydney Smith, hardly knows which to admire most—his vivacity or his vigour, and is equally delighted with the spontaneous flow of his humour and the honesty of purpose by which it is directed and curbed. His humour was genial, frolicsome, and healthy; it ran like a golden thread through all his articles, and lit up in the most unexpected manner subjects of the driest kind, and arguments of the most recondite description. His style is so clear and crisp that he who runs may read, and his illustrations are so felicitous that all who read must laugh. . . . Not a few of the noblest ministers of the Christian Church have not been cut after the regulation pattern, and, as a rule, such men have fared more hardly in the Church than in the world. All through the earlier years of Sydney Smith's ministry that was precisely his position. His ecclesiastical superiors looked coldly upon him; they were dazzled by his brilliant common sense, and alarmed at the freedom with which he applied it even to such venerable personages as themselves. He was regarded, in the prim and decorous circles of the day, as a dangerous man, and a dangerous man he certainly was to the end of the chapter, so far as all clerical, political, or social pretence and injustice were concerned. But straightforward people, high and low, from earls and marquesses to farm labourers and village children, opened their hearts to welcome a man who placed the precious things of his creed in circulation, not only in good words, but likewise in the more tangible coin of golden deeds.—S. J. REID, *Life and Times of the Rev. Sydney Smith.*

The history of the Liberal Movement in the English Church of the nineteenth century could not begin better than with Sydney Smith. He is the principal link between the Liberalism of the eighteenth and the Broad Churchism of the nineteenth century.—A. J. FITZROY, *Dogma and the Church of England.*

Sydney Smith was an ideal soldier of reform for his time, and in his way. He was not extraordinarily long-sighted—indeed (as his famous and constantly repeated advice to "take short views of life" shows) he had a distinct distrust of taking too anxious thought for political or any other morrows. But he had a most keen and, in many cases, a most just scent and sight for the immediate inconveniences and injustices of the day, and for the shortest and most effective ways of mending them. He was perhaps more destitute of romance and of reverence (though he had too much good taste to be positively irreverent) than any man who ever lived.—SAINTSBURY, *Essays in English Literature.*

I regard the admirable Sydney as not only the supreme head of all ecclesiastical jesters, but as, on the whole, the greatest humorist whose jokes have come down to us in an authentic and unmutilated form. Almost alone among professional jokers, he made his merriment—rich, natural, fantastic, unbridled as it was—subserve the serious purposes of his life and writing. Each joke was a link in an argument; each sarcasm was a moral lesson.—[G. W. E. RUSSELL], *Collections and Recollections.*

TOBIAS GEORGE SMOLLETT.

English Novelist and Historian: 1721-1771.

There are in the main only two divisions in the business of writing: the men who are themselves form one, and the men who are the echoes of somebody else form the other. In the first class there are gradations of merit, but its members are separated by a wide gulf, over which there is no passing, from the second order. Smollett was very distinctly on the right side of the gulf.—DAVID HANNAY, *Life of T. G. Smollett.*

Smollett seldom holds communication with his readers in his own person. He manages his delightful puppet-show without thrusting his head beyond the curtain, like Gines de Passamont, to explain what he is doing ; and hence, besides that our attention to the story remains unbroken, we are sure that the author, fully confident in the abundance of his materials, has no occasion to eke them out with intrinsic matter.—SCOTT, *Prose Works, Vol. III.*

Smo lett excels most as the lively caricaturist : Fielding as the exact painter and profound metaphysician.—HAZLITT, *Lectures on the English Comic Writers, Lecture VI : On the English Novelists.*

Faustus Socinus.

Founder of the Sect of the Socinians: 1539-1604.

Leave Socinus and the schoolmen,
Which Jack Bond swears do but fool men.
> —Suckling, *Upon my Lord Brohall's Wedding.*

Socrates.

Athenian Philosopher: b.c. 469-399.

Remembrith you of Socrates,
For he ne countith not thre strees
Of nought that Fortune coude ydo.
> —Chaucer, *The Dream of Chaucer.*

" Know," Socrates reply'd,
" I for the one true God a Martyr dy'd,
I knew great God by native Light,
And Conscience told me what was right."
> —Bishop Thomas Ken.

Then those who follow'd reason's dictates right,
Liv'd up, and lifted high their nat'ral light;
With Socrates may see their Maker's face,
While thousand rubric-martyrs want a place.
> —Dryden, *Religio Laici.*

Fair virtue's silent train: supreme of these
Here ever shines the godlike Socrates;
He whom ungrateful Athens could expel,
At all times just, but when he sign'd the shell.
> —Pope, *The Temple of Fame.*

First Socrates,
Who firmly good in a corrupted state,
Against the rage of tyrants single stood,
Invincible! calm reason's holy law,
That voice of God within th' attentive mind,
Obeying, fearless, or in life, or death:
Great moral teacher! wisest of mankind!
> —Thomson, *The Seasons: Winter.*

Socrates, for god-like virtue fam'd,
And wisest of the sons of men proclaim'd.
> —Falconer, *The Shipwreck.*

Yet here the mind of Socrates could soar ;
And, being less than man, he rose to more.
> —Walter Harte, *Boetius.*

Like Socrates or Antonine,
Or some auld pagan heathen,
The *moral man* he does define,
But ne'er a word o' *faith* in.
> —Burns, *The Holy Fair.*

The birth of that more subtle wisdom, which
Dawn'd in the world with Socrates, to bear
Its last most precious offspring in the rich
And genial soul of Shakespeare.

—LYTTON, *Euripides*.

Men love him [Euripides] not:
How should they? Nor do they much love his friend
Sokrates: but those two have fellowship:
Sokrates often comes to hear him read,
And never misses if he teach a piece.

—BROWNING, *Balaustion's Adventure*.

Socrates set the example of fixing the principles of virtue for private life.
—LORD JEFFREY, *Essays*.

What made Socrates the greatest of men? His moral truth—his ethics.
What proved Jesus Christ the Son of God hardly less than His miracles?
His moral precepts.—BYRON in MOORE's *Life of Byron*.

Socrates seems to have been continually oscillating between the good
and the useful.—S. T. COLERIDGE in T. ALLSOP's *Letters, Conversations,
and Recollections of S. T. Coleridge*.

Socrates himself wrote nothing; but " Socrates taught Xenophon and
Plato ". The minds of Xenophon and Plato were the works he left behind
him. It is only, however, a very superior genius in whom ideas thus
spontaneously cast off in familiar discourse can set into movement the
genius of great writers, and wing in others the words by which those ideas
are borne on through space. There is in this power something beyond
even the eloquence of public orators.—LYTTON, *Essays: Charles Lamb
and some of his Companions*.

He is a man, and partakes of humanity, even its weaknesses and doubts.
But he lived well, he spoke well, and he died well; that is to say, he performed the part in all its humility, and all its greatness, which Providence
imposes on every mortal, of thinking justly, leading an honest life, and
dying with hope. Such was Socrates, the purest incarnation of good
sense and practical philosophy, which Greece, the land of his birth, has
exhibited to antiquity.—LAMARTINE, *Celebrated Characters* (transl.),
Vol. II.

Socrates is now regarded as the greatest man in an age of great men.
The name of King has grown dim before that of Apostle. To teach,
whether by word or action, is the highest function on earth.—W. E.
CHANNING, *On Temperance*.

He was a cool fellow, adding to his humour a perfect temper, and a
knowledge of his man, be he who he might whom he talked with, which
laid the companion open to certain defeat in any debate,—and in debate
he immoderately delighted.—EMERSON, *Plato: or the Philosopher*.

In the face of the lofty affirmations of believers, Socrates had an un-
comfortable sly half-smile. There is something of Voltaire in Socrates.
Socrates denounced all the Eleusian philosophy as unintelligible and in-

discernible, and he said to Euripides that to understand Heraclitus and the old philosophers, "one required to be a swimmer of Delos"; in other words, a swimmer capable to land on an isle which was always receding from him.—VICTOR HUGO, *William Shakespeare (transl.).*

As to Socrates, it is about time we had done with him. We have all been betrayed into rhetoric regarding the most virtuous of Athenian sages, and the most gifted of Grecian sages. But was not Socrates, while attacking and ridiculing the sophists, an egregious sophist himself? Was not his mode of reasoning a clever, elaborate trickery, of which the frank tongue would be ashamed? Could a man intensely, irresistibly in earnest, have delighted so much in mere feats of intellectu-l legerdemain? Socrates unquestionably helped to slay the faith of his country, without attempting to put any more celestial faith in its place. Therefore he deserved the lash of Aristophanes; therefore he deserved the hemlock cup, the theatrical drinking of which by no means impresses us; therefore he ought not to be classed with the pure and puissant pleaders and fighters for eternal and immutable verities.—WILLIAM MACCALL, *The Newest Materialism.*

Socrates is, and has been for twenty centuries, reverenced among the great teachers and martyrs. But of the thousands who delight to honour his name how many would have honoured the man? how many would have seen divine significance in that ugly, unimposing figure *loafing* about the Agora, and teaching new disreputable doctrines? again, how many of those who have a distinct vision of the contrast between the aspect presented by Socrates, and the "ideal" foolishly demanded, would distrust their impressions if another Socrates were now in their company?— G. H. LEWES, *Introduction to A.* MAIN's *Life and Conversations of Dr. Samuel Johnson* (1874).

Socrates' positive doctrines amounted to little: he clung to a paradoxical belief that Virtue is Knowledge; a view refuted before him by Euripides, and after him by Aristotle—in its ordinary sense, at least: to him, of course, it meant something not ordinary. . . . He was working incessantly at a problem which he never really could frame to himself, which mankind never has been able to frame. He felt that the big truth he wanted must be visible everywhere, if we knew how to look for it. It is not more knowledge that we want: only the conscious realising of what is in us. . . . Socrates was never understood; it seems as if, for all his insistence on the need of self-consciousness, he never understood himself. . . . What was the source of Socrates' immense influence over all later philosophy, since in actual philosophic achievement he is not so great as Protagoras, not comparable with Democritus? It was largely the dæmonic, semi-inspired character of the man. Externally, it was the fact of his detachment from all existing bodies and institutions, so that in their wreck, when Protagoras, Pericles, Gorgias fell, he was left standing alone and undiscredited. And, secondly, it was the great fact that he sealed his mission with his blood. He had enough of the prophet in him to feel that it was well for him to die: that it was impossible to unsay a word of what he believed, or to make any promise he did not personally approve.—GILBERT MURRAY, *History of Ancient Greek Literature.*

The teaching of Socrates may be summed up in the injunction, *know thyself*, and in the formulas, *Virtue is knowledge ; Virtue may be taught ; No one wilfully goes wrong ; Virtue results in happiness ;* and all these maxims are first principles of Stoic dogma.—G. H. RENDALL, *Marcus Aurelius Antoninus to Himself.*

SOLON.

Athenian Legislator : B.C. 638-558.

Solon the next, who built his common-weal
On equity's wide base ; by tender laws
A lively people curbing, yet undamp'd
Preserving still that quick peculiar fire,
Whence in the laurel'd field of finer arts,
And of bold freedom, they unequal'd shone,
The pride of smiling Greece, and human-kind.
> —THOMSON, *The Seasons : Winter.*

Shall I, with Solon, form the moral plan,
And aim to mould a savage to a man ?
> —JAMES CAWTHORN, *The Equality of Human Conditions.*

SOPHOCLES.

Greek Tragic Poet : B.C. 495-405.

And Sophocles his last direction
Stamp'd with the signet of perfection.
> —ROBERT LLOYD, *Shakespeare : an Epistle.*

Born in a happier age, and happier clime,
Old Sophocles had merit, in his time.
> —WILLIAM WHITEHEAD, *A Charge to the Poets.*

Ours the great Dionusiac theatre,
And tragic triad of immortal fames,
Aischulos, Sophokles, Euripides !
> —BROWNING, *Balaustion's Adventure.*

Oh, our Sophocles, the royal
   Who was born to monarch's place,
And who made the whole word loyal
   Less by kingly power than grace !
> —E. B. BROWNING, *Wine of Cyprus.*

Be his
My special thanks, whose even-balanced soul,
From first youth tested up to extreme old age,
Business could not make dull, nor passion wild ;

Who saw life steadily, and saw it whole ;
The mellow glory of the Attic stage,
Singer of sweet Colonus, and its child.
> —MATTHEW ARNOLD, *To a Friend.*

Sophocles is sometimes—not seldom—sublime ; and perhaps his sublimity is the noblest of sublimities, for it seems to be but Beauty changing its character as it ascends the sky—even as one might think a Dove high up in the sunshine, and soaring so loftily that eye can no more discern her silver plumage—an Eagle ; nor in such heavenward flight would the Bird of Venus be not as sublime as the Bird of Jove.—JOHN WILSON, *Essays : Greek Drama.*

Sophocles attempted neither Cyclopean nor Praxitelean work. He attained to the perfection of Pheidias. Thus we miss in his tragedies the colossal scale and terrible effects of Æschylean art. His plays are not so striking at first sight, because it was his aim to put all the parts of his composition in their proper places, and to produce a harmony which should not agitate or startle, but which upon due meditation should be found complete. The σωφροσύνη, or moderation, exhibited in all his work, implies by its very nature the sacrifice of something—the sacrifice of passion and impetuosity to higher laws of equability and temper. So perfect is the beauty of Sophocles, that, as in the case of Raphael or Mozart, it seems to conceal the strength and fire which animate his art.—J. ADDINGTON SYMONDS, *Studies of the Greek Poets, Second Series.*

Sophocles shows at times one high power which but few of the world's poets share with him. He feels, as Wordsworth does, the majesty of order and well-being ; sees the greatness of God, as it were, in the untroubled things of life.—GILBERT MURRAY, *History of Ancient Greek Literature.*

DR. ROBERT SOUTH.

English Divine : 1633-1716.

Have I made South and Sherlock disagree,
And puzzle truth with learn'd obscurity ?
            —SIR SAMUEL GARTH, *The Dispensary, Canto V.*

                Idly might a South
His witty turns, his quaintnesses display,
Except to waken laughter.
            —RICHARD POLWHELE, *Pulpit Eloquence.*

He seems for a moment to tread on the verge of buffoonery, recovering himself by some stroke of vigorous sense and language ; such was the witty Dr. South, whom the courtiers delighted to hear.—HALLAM, *Literature of the Middle Ages, Vol. IV.*

South's sentences are gems, hard and shining : Voltaire's look like them, but are only French paste.—J. C. HARE, *Guesses at Truth, First Series.*

South has obtained a great and deserved reputation. Wit was his talent, yet he often reaches sublimity. He is, however, one of those authors who is to be admired and not imitated. To excite a laugh from the pulpit is to inspire the hearer with a levity of temper ill adapted to the indulgence of devotional feelings. The taste of the age in which South flourished gave countenance to a pulpit jocularity.—DR. VICESIMUS KNOX, *Essays : On Preaching and Sermon Writers.*

ROBERT SOUTHEY.

Poet Laureate : 1774-1843.

BOB SOUTHEY ! You're a poet—Poet-laureate,
And representative of all the race ;
Although 'tis true that you turn'd out a Tory at
Last,—yours has lately been a common case,—
And now, my Epic Renegade ! what are ye at ?
With all the Lakers, in and out of place ?
A nest of tuneful persons, to my eye
Like " four and twenty Blackbirds in a pye ".
　　　　　　　—BYRON, *Don Juan Dedication.*

Let Southey sing, although his teeming muse,
Prolific every spring, be too profuse.
　　　　—*Id., English Bards and Scotch Reviewers.*

Ye vales and hills whose beauty hither drew
The poet's steps, and fixed him here, on you
His eyes have closed ! And ye, loved books, no more
Shall Southey feed upon your precious lore,
To works that ne'er shall forfeit their renown,
Adding immortal labours of his own—
Whether he traced historic truth, with zeal
For the State's guidance, or the Church's weal,
Or Fancy, disciplined by studious art,
Informed his pen, or wisdom of the heart,
Or Judgments sanctioned in the Patriot's mind
By reverence for the rights of all mankind.
　　—WORDSWORTH, *Inscription for a Monument in Crossthwaite*
　　　　　　Church.

Southey was fain to pour forth his exuberant stream over regions
Near and remote : his command was absolute ; every subject,
Little or great, he controll'd ; in language, variety, fancy,
Richer than all his compeers.
　　　　　　　—LANDOR, *English Hexameters.*

Rare architect of many a wondrous tale
Which, till Helvellyn's head lie prostrate, shall remain !
　　　　　　　—*Id., To Southey,* 1833.

　　Southey, I have not seen much of. His appearance is *Epic ;* and he is
the only existing entire man of letters. All the others have some pursuit
annexed to their authorship. His manners are mild, but not those of a
man of the world, and his talents of the first order. His prose is perfect.
Of his poetry there are various opinions : there is, perhaps, too much of it
for the present generation ;—posterity will probably select. He has
passages equal to anything. At present, he has a *party,* but no *public*—
except for his prose writings. *The Life of Nelson* is beautiful.—BYRON
in MOORE's *Life of Byron.*

　　Crabbe's English is of course not upon a level with Southey's, which
is next door to faultless.—S. T. COLERIDGE, *Table Talk.*

It is, indeed, most extraordinary, that a mind like Mr. Southey's, a mind richly endowed in many respects by nature, and highly cultivated by study, a mind which has exercised considerable influence on the most enlightened generation of the most enlightened people that ever existed, should be utterly destitute of the power of discerning truth from falsehood. Yet such is the fact. Government is to Mr. Southey one of the fine arts. He judges of a theory, of a public measure, of a religion or a political party, of a peace or a war, as men judge of a picture or a statue, by the effect produced on his imagination. A chain of associations is to him what a chain of reasoning is to other men ; and what he calls his opinions are in fact merely his tastes.—MACAULAY, *Essays : Southey's Colloquies.*

Southey's rich taste and antique stateliness of mind. . . . The great charm of that simple verve which is so peculiarly Southeian. . . . But the most various, scholastic, and accomplished of such of our literary contemporaries as have written works as well as articles, and prose as well as poetry—is, incontestably, Mr. Southey. *The Life of Nelson* is acknowledged to be the best biography of the day. *The Life of Wesley* and *The Book of the Church*, however adulterated by certain prepossessions and prejudices, are, as mere compositions, characterized by an equal simplicity and richness of style,—an equal dignity and an equal ease. No writer blends more happily the academical graces of the style of the last century with the popular vigour of that which distinguishes the present.
—LYTTON, *England and the English.*

We may justly be proud of our late Laureate. Literature does not every day present us with so worthy a son ; students who forsake the trodden paths of life to earn their difficult crust by patient spinning of the brain cannot find a more illustrious example. The pursuit of letters was the business of Southey's life ; it was also the first and last joy of his heart. Rather than not at intervals breathe the pure air and partake of the golden light that await the worshipper on the topmost heights of Parnassus, he condescended to work as a bondman, through winter and summer from year to year, on its barren sides. Literature was his glory, and he her pride.—SAMUEL PHILLIPS, *Essays from " The Times," Vol. I.*

Southey, . . . like one of his best-known works, was only one long " Common-place Book ". His books were in reality dearer to him than the human species.—G. B. SMITH, *Shelley : a Critical Biography.*

EDMUND SPENSER.

English Poet : 1553-1599.

Spenser ! a jealous honourer of thine,
A forester deep in thy midmost trees,
Did, last eve, ask my promise to refine
Some English, that might strive thine ear to please.
But, Elfin-poet ! 'tis impossible
For an inhabitant of wintry earth
To rise, like Phœbus, with a golden quill. . . .
Of me no lines are loved nor letters are of price, . . .
Of all which speak our English tongue, but those of thy device.
—SIR WALTER RALEIGH, *Sonnet V.*

Farewell Judgment, with invention
To describe a heart's intention :
Farewell Wit, whose sound and sense
Show a poet's excellence.
    Farewell, all in one together,
    And with Spenser's garland, wither.
        —NICHOLAS BRETON, *An Epitaph upon Poet Spenser.*

Grave moral Spenser after these came on,
Than whom I am persuaded there was none
Since the blind Bard his Iliads up did make,
Fitter a task like that to undertake,
To set down boldly, bravely to invent,
In all high knowledge, surely excellent.
        —MICHAEL DRAYTON, *Elegy to Henry Reynolds, Esq.*

Divinest Spenser, heav'n-bred, happy muse !
Would any power into my brain infuse
Thy worth or all that poets had before,
I could not praise till thou deserv'st no more.
        —WILLIAM BROWNE, *Britannia's Pastoral, Book II., Song I.*

               . . . his memory yet green,
Lives in his well-tun'd songs, whose leaves immortal been.
Nor can I guess, whether his Muse divine
Or gives to those, or takes from them his grace. . . .
    Next to our Mantuan poet doth he rest ;
    There shall our Colin lives for ever blest. . . .
        —P. FLETCHER, *The Purple Island, Canto VI.,* 51, 52.

Old Spenser next, warm'd with poetic rage,
In ancient tales amus'd a barbarous age ;
An age that yet uncultivate and rude,
Where'er the poet's fancy led, pursued
Through pathless fields, and unfrequented floods,
To dens of dragons, and enchanted woods.
        —ADDISON, *An Account of the Greatest English Poets.*

When bright Eliza rul'd Britannia's state,
Widely distributing her high commands,
And boldly wise, and fortunately great,
Freed the glad nations from tyrannic bands ;
An equal genius was in Spenser found ;
To the high theme he match'd his noble lays ;
He travell'd England o'er on fairy ground,
In mystic notes to sing his monarch's praise :
Reciting wondrous truths in pleasing dreams,
He deck'd Eliza's head with Gloriana's beams.
        —MATTHEW PRIOR, *An Ode, Humbly Inscribed to the Queen.*

In Spenser native Muses play.
        —POPE, *Imitations of Horace, Part of the Ninth Ode of the
        Fourth Book.*

The gentle Spenser, fancy's pleasing son ;
Who, like a copious river, pour'd his song
O'er all the mazes of enchanted ground.
        —THOMSON, *The Seasons : Summer.*

Is this the land, where, on our Spenser's tongue,
Enamour'd of his voice, description hung ?

—CHURCHILL, *The Author.*

Sage Spencer wak'd his lofty lay
To grace Eliza's golden sway:
O'er the proud theme new lustre to diffuse,
He chose the gorgeous allegoric muse.

—THOMAS WARTON, *Ode on His Majesty's Birthday,*
4th June, 1787.

Fire-winged, and make a morning in his mirth.

—KEATS, *To Spenser.*

He whose green bays shall bloom for ever young,
And whose dear name whenever I repeat,
Reverence and love are trembling on my tongue;
Sweet Spenser, sweetest Bard; yet not more sweet
Than pure was he, and not more pure than wise,
High Priest of all the Muses' mysteries.

—SOUTHEY, *The Lay of the Laureate, Proem.*

Spenser, my master dear; with whom in boyhood I wander'd
Through the regions of Faeryland, in forest or garden
Spending delicious hours, or at tilt and tourney rejoicing;
Yea, by the magic of verse enlarged, and translated in spirit,
In the World of Romance free denizen I; till awakening,
When the spell was dissolved, this real earth and its uses
Seem'd to me weary, and stale, and flat.

—*Id., A Vision of Judgment : The Elder Worthies.*

Were I to name, out of the times gone by,
The poets dearest to me, I should say . . .
Spenser for luxury, and sweet, sylvan play . . .
But which take with me, could I take but one ?
Shakespeare, as long as I was unoppressed
With the world's weight, making sad thoughts intenser ;
But did I wish, out of the common sun,
To lay a wounded heart in leafy rest
And dream of things far off and healing,—Spenser.

—LEIGH HUNT, *His Poets (Examiner, 24th Dec.,* 1815).

. . . the lyre . . .
Among whose wires with light finger playing,
Our elder bard, Spenser, a gentle name,
The lady Muses' dearest darling child,
Elicited the deftest tunes yet heard
In hall or bower. . . .

—CHARLES LAMB, *To the Poet Cowper.*

. . . that gentle Bard,
Chosen by the Muses for their Page of State—
Sweet Spenser, moving through his clouded heaven
With the moon's beauty and the moon's soft pace,
I called him Brother, Englishman, and Friend !

—WORDSWORTH, *The Prelude, Book III.*

The palfrey pace and the glittering grace
    Of Spenser's magical song.
                    —ROBERT BUCHANAN, *Cloudland*.

Edmond Spenser, the Prince of Poets in his Tyme, whose Divine Spirrit needs noe othir witnesse than the works which he left behinde him.—*Spenser's Epitaph in Westminster Abbey*.

But Spenser I could have read for ever. Too young to trouble myself about the allegory, I considered all the knights and ladies and dragons and giants in their outward and exoteric sense, and God only knows how delighted I was to find myself in such society.—SIR WALTER SCOTT in LOCKHART'S *Life of Scott*.

The language of Spenser, like that of Shakespeare, is an instrument manufactured for the sake of the work it was to perform.—HALLAM, *Literature of the Middle Ages, Vol. II.*

Milton said, that he dared be known to think Spenser a better teacher than Scotus or Aquinas.—LEIGH HUNT, *Men, Women, and Books*.

Spenser, in whom philosophy, where found, as completely forgets its purpose, in allegorical fancies and melodious roundelays, as a bee may forget its hive amid the honeys of Hymettus.—LYTTON, *Essays : Knowledge of the World*.

That other, soft-burning, dewy, and almost twinkling star—now seeming to shine out into intenser beauty, and now almost dim, from no obscuring cloud or mist, but as if some internal spirit shaded the light for a moment, even as an angel may veil his countenance with his wings—that is the star of Spenser ! And of all the bright people of the skies, to fancy's gaze, thou, most lovely Planet, art the very Fairy Queen !—JOHN WILSON, *Essays : Old North and Young North*.

That which sets the Shepherd's Calendar and other of Spenser's earlier pieces above everything else that had preceded them in the language, what Chaucer had done only excepted, is the same thing the presence of which likewise we feel so strongly in the minor, and for the most part probably also earlier, poetry of Shakespeare,—the fulness and easy flow of the poetic vein, making the composition all life. The bright green herbage seems ready to burst forth everywhere, as from a soil of inexhaustible fertility and moisture. Whatever else may be wanting, whatever may be less carefully or less successfully executed, the spirit of poetry at least is always there, strong and abundant.—G. L. CRAIK, *Spenser and His Poetry*.

BENEDICT BARUCH SPINOZA.

Dutch Philosopher : 1632-1677.

Spinoza was truly, what Voltaire has with rather less justice called Clarke, a reasoning machine.—HALLAM, *Literature of the Middle Ages, Vol. IV.*

No vulgar sceptics can comprehend the ethereal scepticism of a Spinoza.
—LYTTON.

Let us not fall short of the truth through fear of falling into exaggeration :—Spinoza's life was of a beauty to which history can hardly find a parallel; on that Sunday afternoon of the 21st of February, two hundred years ago, there cracked as noble and as sweet a heart as ever beat in human breast.—A. B. LEE.

You may set out, like Spinoza, with all but the truth, and end with a conclusion which is altogether monstrous ; and yet the mere deduction shall be irrefragable.—S. T. COLERIDGE, *Table Talk.*

A god-intoxicated man.—NOVALIS (*transl.*).

Spinoza, the greatest and the most logical of all the descendants of Descartes.—J. P. MAHAFFY, *Life of Descartes.*

Bigotry does not like to confess its blunders, otherwise it would long have abandoned as a deplorable error and a flagrant injustice, the ignorant and stupid calumny which places Spinoza foremost among blasphemers and atheists. Those who reject popular idols are always classed by popular prejudice with such as deny God ; and few have suffered more from this cruel wrong than the great thinker whose career we propose to chronicle in all honesty and in no prejudiced or proselytising spirit, and whose holy deeds are the best indication of his sublime ideas. . . . Never was high thought so nobly embodied in every action, even the most insignificant, as in Spinoza ; which makes his path a fecund lesson and a blessed spectacle to many who feel nothing but distaste, and who express nothing but scorn for philosophy.—WILLIAM MACCALL, *Foreign Biographies, Vol. II.*

Whatever else Spinozism is, it is an attempt to find in the idea of God a principle from which the whole universe could be evolved by a necessity as strict as that by which, according to Spinoza's favourite illustration, the properties of a triangle follow from its definition. For the clear intelligence of Spinoza it was impossible to rest satisfied with a system in which metaphor plays the part of logical thought.—JOHN CAIRD, *Life of Spinoza.*

ARTHUR PENRHYN STANLEY.

Dean of Westminster : 1815-1881.

But to Arthur Stanley, as to all the best and truest men, the trappings and surroundings of life, all that makes the base cringe and kotow before the successful, were as nothing—F. W. FARRAR, *Social and Present-Day Questions.*

Every page of his many books teems with golden thoughts, happy illustrations, fervent piety. His whole life was a sermon. Seldom has the Christian religion been preached as attractively and healthily as in the words and deeds of Arthur Stanley.—A. J. FITZROY, *Dogma and the Church of England.*

SIR RICHARD STEELE.

English Essayist and Dramatic Writer : 1671-1729.

Thus Steele, who own'd what others writ,
And flourish'd by imputed wit,

27

From perils of a hundred jails,
Withdrew to starve, and die in Wales.
            —SWIFT, *A Libel on Dr. Delany and Lord Carteret.*

But allow me to speak what I honestly feel—
To a true poet-heart add the fun of Dick Steele,
Throw in all of Addison, *minus* the chill.
            —J. R. LOWELL, *A Fable for Critics.*

Steele seems to have gone into his closet to set down what he observed out of doors. Addison seems to have spent most of his time in his study, and to have spun out and wire-drawn hints which he borrowed from Steele, or took from nature, to the utmost. I am far from wishing to depreciate Addison's talents, but I am anxious to do justice to Steele, who was, I think, upon the whole, a less artificial and more original writer.—HAZLITT, *Lectures on the English Comic Writers.*

Alas! for poor Dick Steele! For nobody else, of course. There is no man or woman in *our* time who makes fine projects and gives them up from idleness or want of means. When duty calls upon *us*, we no doubt are always at home and ready to pay that grim tax-gatherer. When *we* are stricken with remorse and promise reform, we keep our promise, and are never angry, or idle, or extravagant any more. There are no chambers in *our* hearts, destined for family friends and affections, and now occupied by some Sin's emissary and bailiff in possession. There are no little sins, shabby peccadilloes, importunate remembrances, or disappointed holders of our promises to reform, hovering at our steps, or knocking at our door! Of course not. We are living in the nineteenth century; and poor Dick Steele stumbled and got up again, and got into jail and out again, and sinned and repented, and loved and suffered, and lived and died, scores of years ago. Peace be with him! Let us think gently of one who was so gentle: let us speak kindly of one whose own breast exuberated with human kindness.—THACKERAY, *English Humourists of the Eighteenth Century.*

There have been wiser, stronger, greater men. But many a strong man would have been stronger for a touch of Steel's indulgent sympathy; many a great man has wanted his genuine largeness of heart; many a wise man might learn something from his deep and wide humanity. His virtues redeemed his frailties. He was thoroughly amiable, kindly, and generous. *Faute d'archanges il faut aimer des créatures imparfaites.*— AUSTIN DOBSON, *Life of Richard Steele.*

LAURENCE STERNE.

English Parson and Novelist: 1713-1768.

Shall pride a heap of sculptur'd marble raise,
Some worthless, unmourn'd titled fool to praise,
And shall we not by one poor grave-stone learn
Where genius, wit, and humour, sleep with Sterne?
            —DAVID GARRICK, *Epitaph on Sterne.*

Sterne is our best example of the plagiarist whom none dare make ashamed.—AUGUSTINE BIRRELL, *Essays about Men, Women, and Books.*

Sterne's morals are bad, but I don't think they can do much harm to any one whom they would not find bad enough before.—S. T. COLERIDGE, *Table Talk*.

This illustrious Irishman (I have a Shandean reason for speaking of him under that title) is Rabelais reborn at a riper period of the world, and gifted with sentiment. To accuse him of cant and sentimentality is itself a cant or an ignorance ; or at least, if neither of these, it is but to misjudge him from *an excess of manner here and there*. The matter always contains the solidest substance of truth and duty. Among passages which are supposed to be connected with coarseness, but really are not so, are some which are yet destined to be of important service.—LEIGH HUNT.

What lavish and riotous beauty beyond that of mere prose, and dispensing with the interest of mere fiction, sporting with the Muse like a spoiled darling of the Graces, charms poets and thinkers in the wayward genius of Sterne ! Though his most exquisite characters are but sketches and outlines, Mr. Shandy, Uncle Toby, Corporal Trim, and the mysterious, shadowy Yorick,—though his finest passages in composition are marred and blurred by wanton conceit, abrupt impertinence, audacious levity, ribald indecorum,—still how the lively enchanter enforces and fascinates our reluctant admiration !—LYTTON, *Essays : Knowledge of the World*.

The life of literary men is often a kind of sermon in itself; for the pursuit of fame, when it is contrasted with the grave realities of life, seems more absurd and trifling than most pursuits, and to leave less behind it. Mere *amusers* are never respected. It would be harsh to call Sterne a mere amuser, he is much more ; but so the contemporary world regarded him. They laughed at his jests, disregarded his death-bed, and neglected his grave.—WALTER BAGEHOT, *Literary Studies, Vol. II*.

Sterne has been called the English Rabelais, and was apparently more ambitious himself of being considered as an English Cervantes. To a modern English reader he is certainly far more amusing than Rabelais, and he can be appreciated with less effort than Cervantes. But it is impossible to mention these great names without seeing the direction in which Sterne falls short of the highest excellence. We know that, on clearing away the vast masses of buffoonery and ribaldry under which Rabelais was forced, or chose, to hide himself we come to the profound thinker and powerful satirist. Sterne represents a comparatively shallow vein of thought.—LESLIE STEPHEN, *Hours in a Library, Vol. III*.

Even now the grace, the insinuating delicacy, the light lucidity, the diamond-like sparkle of Sterne's style make reading him a peculiar literary pleasure.—DAVID MASSON, *British Novelists and their Styles*.

What did Sterne contribute to the English novel ? Quite a new element, and an unmistakable one. Scarcely a novel issued from the Minerva press, scarcely one comes from the incomparable novelists of Europe and America in our own day, in which "the Sterne art" is not immediately to be recognised. Prolix and tedious as Sterne could be when it was his whim, he showed us how to tell stories gracefully. No writer previous to him was so skilful a narrator ; knew so well how to arrest the attention ; by the repetition of what notes to work the charm. Dealing largely in bad grammar and obscure and careless expressions, he had a delicate acquaintance with and ready command of words when the nicety of his subject required them. In him we find no vast creations, no original forms of architecture, but a rare variety of tracery and ornament with which every later builder has decorated his structures.—J. C. JEAFFRESON, *Novels and Novelists, Vol. I.*

To talk of "the style" of Sterne is almost to play one of those tricks with language of which he himself was so fond. For there is hardly any definition of the word which can make it possible to describe him as having any style at all. It is not only that he manifestly recognized no external canons whereto to conform the expression of his thoughts, but he had apparently no inclination to invent and obscure, except indeed in the most negative of senses, any style of his own. The "style of Sterne," in short, is as though one should say "the form of Proteus". He was determined to be uniformly eccentric, regularly irregular, and that was all. —H. D. TRAILL, *Life of Sterne.*

The English Rabelais.—PERCY FITZGERALD, *Life of Laurence Sterne, Vol. II.*

Sterne has given us a thousand occasions to laugh, but never an occasion to laugh on the wrong side of the mouth. For savagery or bitterness you will search his works in vain. He is obscene, to be sure. But who, pray, was ever the worse for having read him? Alas, poor Yorick! He had his obvious and deplorable failings. I never heard that he communicated them. Good humour he has been communicating now for a hundred and fifty years.—A. T. QUILLER-COUCH, *Adventures in Criticism.*

THOMAS WENTWORTH, EARL OF STRAFFORD.

Statesman : 1593-1641.

Great Strafford! worthy of that name, though all
Of thee could be forgotten but thy fall,
Crush'd by imaginary treason's weight,
Which too much merit did accumulate.
As chemists gold from brass by fire would draw,
Pretexts are into reason forg'd by law.
His wisdom such at once it did appear
Three kingdoms wonder, and three kingdoms fear,
Whilst single he stood forth, and seem'd, although
Each had an army, as an equal foe.
Such was his force of eloquence, to make
The hearers more concern'd than he that spake.
Each seem'd to act that part he came to see,
And none was more a looker-on than he.
So did he move our passions, some were known
To wish, for the defence, the crime their own.
    —SIR JOHN DENHAM, *On the Earl of Strafford's Life and Death.*

But what is man at enmity with truth?
What were the fruits of Wentworth's copious mind
When (blighted all the promise of his youth)
The patriot in a tyrant's league had join'd?
    Let Ireland's loud-lamenting plains,

Let Tyne's and Humber's trampled swains,
Let menac'd London tell
How impious guile made wisdom base ;
How generous zeal to cruel rage gave place ;
And how unbless'd he liv'd, and how dishonour'd fell.
—AKENSIDE, *Ode IV. : To the Hon. Charles Townshend.*

Charles : "Strafford, my friend, there may have been reports,
Vain rumours. Henceforth touching Strafford is
To touch the apple of my sight : why gaze
So earnestly."
—ROBERT BROWNING, *Strafford.*

But Wentworth, who ever names him without thinking of those harsh dark features, ennobled by their expression into more than the majesty of an antique Jupiter ; of that brow, that eye, that cheek, that lip, wherein, as in a chronicle, are written the events of many stormy and disastrous years, high enterprise accomplished, frightful dangers braved, power unsparingly exercised, suffering unshrinkingly borne ; of that fixed look, so full of severity, of mournful anxiety, of deep thought, of dauntless resolution, which seems at once to forebode and to defy a terrible fate, as it lowers on us from the living canvas of Vandyke ? Even at this day the haughty earl overawes posterity as he overawed his contemporaries, and excites the same interest when arraigned before the tribunal of history which he excited at the bar of the House of Lords. In spite of ourselves, we sometimes feel towards his memory a certain relenting similar to that relenting which his defence, as Sir John Denham tells us, produced in Westminster Hall. —MACAULAY, *Essays : John Hampden.*

It is said of Salvator Rosa, that everything in his pictures was of a piece : his rocks, trees, mountains, and skies, having the same wild character that animated his figures. Well had it been for Lord Strafford had he exhibited the same consistency. For, had he adhered to the advice he gave to Charles I.—*viz.*, to let his ministers serve him according to the laws and statutes of the realm ; had he done this, he had not perished on a scaffold. He had been, in fact, one of the noblest men of his age.— CHARLES BUCKE, *Book of Human Character.*

Strafford was born to command. The maxim, Thorough—that was his guiding-star through life—fitly represents his actions. Everything he undertook he did with his might, and knew no rest till Thorough had been accomplished. . . . Save from the King he brooked neither control nor interference, and those who crossed his path found in him an enemy as pitiless as a Richelieu or a Napoleon. If he could not be Cæsar he would be Cæsar's first lieutenant, and none should dare oust him from the post.—A. C. EWALD, *Representative Statesmen, Vol. I.*

Ireland in all its ranks and classes having through its parliament applauded him as a benefactor, now with strange versatility cursed him as a tyrant. It was the weight of all these converging animosities that destroyed him. "Three whole kingdoms," says a historian of the time, " were his accusers, and eagerly sought in one death a recompense of all their sufferings."—JOHN MORLEY, *Oliver Cromwell.*

DAVID FRIEDRICH STRAUSS.

German Rationalistic Theologian: 1808-1874.

As well be Strauss as swing 'twixt Paul and him.
It's not worth having, such imperfect faith,
No more available to do faith's work
Than unbelief like mine.   Whole faith, or none!
.   .   .   .
Then add there's still that plaguy hundredth chance
Strauss may be wrong.   And so a risk is run.
    —ROBERT BROWNING, *Bishop Blougram's Apology.*

SIR JOHN SUCKLING.

English Poet, Dramatist, Courtier: 1609-1641.

Had I the pen of Sir John Suckling,
And could find out a rhyme for duckling,
Why dearest madam, in that case,
I would invite you to a brace.
    —CHRISTOPHER SMART, *An Invitation to Mrs. Tyler, etc.*

    O Suckling, O gallant Sir John,
Thou gentleman poet, first plume of the *ton ;* . . .
Fresh painter of " Weddings," great author of rare
" Poet Sessions." . . .
O *facile princeps* of " wit about town ". . . .
    —LEIGH HUNT, *The Feast of the Violets, Canto III.*

The blithest throat that ever carolled love
 In music made of morning's merriest heart,
Glad Suckling. . . .
    —SWINBURNE, *James Shirley.*

Sir John Suckling is acknowledged to have left far behind him all former
writers of song in gaiety and ease ; it is not equally clear that he has ever
since been surpassed.—HALLAM, *Introduction to the Literature of Europe,
Vol. III.*

EMANUEL SWEDENBORG.

Swedish Philosopher and Theosophist: 1688-1772.

 Great minds—Swedenborg's for instance—are never in the wrong, but
in consequence of being in the right, but imperfectly.—S. T. COLERIDGE,
Table Talk.

 This (*De Cultu et Amore Dei*) would of itself serve to mark Swedenborg
as a man of philosophic genius, indicative and involent.   Much of what is
most valuable in the philosophic works of Schelling, Schubert, and Escher-
mayer is to be found anticipated in this supposed Dementato, or madman.
Oh! thrice happy should we be if the learned and the teachers of the present age were gifted with a similar madness.   A madness indeed celestial,
and flowing from a divine mind!—*Id., Notes : Theological, Political and
Miscellaneous.*

Swedenborg styles himself, in the title-page of his books, " Servant of the Lord Jesus Christ " ; and by force of intellect, and in effect, he is the last Father in the Church, and is not likely to have a successor. No wonder that his depth of ethical wisdom should give him influence as a teacher. To the withered traditional Church yielding dry catechisms, he let in nature again, and the worshipper, escaping from the vestry of verbs and texts, is surprised to find himself a party to the whole of his religion : his religion thinks for him, and is of universal application : he turns it on every side ; it fits every part of life, interprets and dignifies every circumstance.—EMERSON, *Swedenborg ; or, the Mystic.*

The most remarkable step in the religious history of recent ages is that made by the genius of Swedenborg, who describes the moral faculties and affections of man, with the hard realism of an astronomer describing the suns and planets of our system, and explained his opinion of the history and destiny of souls in a narrative form, as of one who had gone in a trance into the society of other worlds.—*Id., Immortality.*

DR. JONATHAN SWIFT.

Irish Satirist ; Dean of St. Patrick's : 1667-1745.

O Swift ! if fame be life (as well we know
That bards and heroes have esteem'd it so),
Thou canst not wholly die. Thy works will shine
To future times, and life in fame be thine.
     —PARNELL, *To Dr. Swift on his Birthday.*

Thou too, my Swift, dost breathe Bœotian air ;
When wilt thou bring back wit and humour here ?
     —GAY, *Epistle VI.: To Mr. Pope.*

Let Ireland tell, how wit upheld her cause,
Her trade supported, and supplied her laws :
And leave on Swift this grateful verse engrav'd :
" The rights a court attack'd, a poet sav'd ".
     —POPE, *Epistles of Horace imitated, Epistle I., Book II.*

Let Swift be Swift, nor e'er demean
The sense and humour of the Dean.
     —ROBERT LLOYD, *The Two Rubric Posts.*

Those doctors in the laughing school,
Those giant sons of Ridicule,
Swift, Rab'lais.
     —*Id., A Familiar Epistle.*

Swift too, thy tale is told : a sound, a name,
No more than Lucian, Butler, or Scarron.
Fantastic humour drop'd the feeling sense,
Her empire less'ning by his fall. The shades
Of frolic Rabelais, and HIM of Spain,
Madrid's facetious glory, joins his ghost ;
Triumvirate of laughter !
     —WILLIAM THOMPSON, *Sickness, a Poem : The Recovery.*

And Swift expires a driv'ler and a show.
　　　　　　—Dr. Johnson, *The Vanity of Human Wishes.*

Nature imparting her satiric gift,
Her serious mirth, to Arbuthnot and Swift,
With droll sobriety they raise a smile
At folly's cost, themselves unmoved the while.
That constellation set, the world in vain,
Must hope to look upon their like again.
　　　　　　　　　　　—Cowper, *Table Talk.*

But (I might instance in St. Patrick's dean)
Too often rails to gratify his spleen.
Most satirists are indeed a public scourge;
Their mildest physic is a farrier's purge;
Their acrid temper turns, as soon as stirr'd,
The milk of their good purpose all to curd.
　　　　　　　　　　—*Id., Charity.*

Yes, friend! for thee I'll quit my cynic cell,
And bear Swift's motto, " Vive la bagatelle ".
　　.　　.　　.　　.　　.　　.
The dirty language, and the noisome jest,
Which pleased in Swift of yore, we now detest,
Proscribed not only in the world polite,
But even too nasty for a city knight!

Peace to Swift's faults! his wit hath made them pass,
Unmatch'd by all, save matchless Hudibras!
　　　　　　—Byron, *Hints from Horace.*

When Swift is considered as an author, it is just to estimate his powers by their effects. In the reign of Queen Anne he turned the stream of popularity against the Whigs, and must be confessed to have dictated for a time the political opinions of the English nation. In the succeeding reign he delivered Ireland from plunder and oppression; and showed that wit, confederated with truth, had such force as authority was unable to resist. He said truly of himself, that Ireland " was his debtor ". It was from the time when he first began to patronize the Irish, that they may date their riches and prosperity. He taught them first to know their own interest, their weight and their strength, and gave them spirit to assert that equality with their fellow-subjects to which they have ever since been making vigorous advances, and to claim those rights which they have at last established. Nor can they be charged with ingratitude to their benefactor; for they reverenced him as a guardian, and obeyed him as a dictator. . . . It was said, in a Preface to one of his Irish editions, that Swift had never been known to take a single thought from any writer, ancient or modern. This is not literally true; but perhaps no writer can easily be found that has borrowed so little, or that in all his excellences and all his defects, has so well maintained his claim to be considered as original.—Dr. Johnson, *Lives of the Poets: Swift.*

When these articles of his political tenets are examined, they will leave no room for any one particular party to assume the honour of having had him in their alliance.   He was neither Whig nor Tory, neither Jacobite nor Republican.   He was DOCTOR SWIFT.—EARL OF ORRERY, *An Essay upon Dr. Swift*.

M. Swift est Rabelais dans son bon sens, et vivant en bonne compagnie. Il n'a pas, à la verité, la gaîté du premier, mais il a toute la finesse, la raison, le choix, le bon goût qui manquent à notre curé de Meudon.   Ses vers sont d'un goût singulier, et presque inimitable ; la bonne plaisanterie est son partage en vers et en prose ; mais pour le bien entendre il faut faire un petit voyage dans son pays.—VOLTAIRE, *Lettres sur les Anglais, Let.* 22.

The other day, mention was made of a "Dean of St. Patrick's" *now living :* as if there was, or ever could be, more than one Dean of St. Patrick's.—LEIGH HUNT, *Men, Women, and Books.*

Swift was *anima Rabellaisii habitans in sicco*,—the soul of Rabelais dwelling in a dry place.—S. T. COLERIDGE, *Table Talk.*

In humour and in irony, and in the talent of debasing and defiling what he hated, we join with all the world in thinking the Dean of St. Patrick's without a rival.—LORD JEFFREY, *Essays.*

The master-Mocker of Mankind.—LYTTON, *The Souls of Books.*

How realistic or materialistic in treatment of his subject is Swift.   He describes his fictitious persons as if for the police.—EMERSON, *English Traits : Literature.*

The manner of Swift is the very opposite to this.   He moves laughter, but never joins in it.   He appears in his works such as he appeared in society.   All the company are convulsed with merriment, while the Dean, the author of all the mirth, preserves an invincible gravity, and even sourness of aspect, and gives utterance to the most eccentric and ludicrous fancies, with the air of a man reading the commination service. . . . Severity, gradually hardening and darkening into misanthropy, characterises the works of Swift. . . . The mirth of Swift is the mirth of Mephistopheles.—MACAULAY, *Essays : Addison.*

Little did Temple imagine that the coarse exterior of his dependent concealed a genius equally suited to politics and to letters, a genius destined to shake great kingdoms, to stir the laughter and the rage of millions, and to leave to posterity memorials which can perish only with the English language.—*Id., Ibid. : Sir William Temple.*

As fierce a beak and talon as ever struck—as strong a wing as ever beat, belonged to Swift.   I am glad, for one, that fate wrested the prey out of his claws, and cut his wings and chained him.   One can gaze, and not without awe and pity, at the lonely eagle chained behind the bars. . . . Ah man ! you, educated in Epicurean Temple's library, you whose friends were Pope and St. John—what made you to swear to fatal vows, and bind yourself to a life-long hypocrisy before the Heaven which you adored with such real wonder, humility, and reverence ?   For Swift was a reverent, was a pious spirit—for Swift could love and could pray.   Through the storms and tempests of his furious mind, the stars of religion and love break out in the blue, shining serenely, though hidden by the driving clouds and the maddened hurricane of his life.—THACKERAY, *English Humourists of the Eighteenth Century*.

The rule of measuring what is knowable of a famous man by the inverse ratio of what has been said about him, is applicable to Swift in a marked degree. Few men who have been talked about so much are known so little. His writings and his life are connected so closely, that to judge of either fairly with an imperfect knowledge of the other is not possible.—JOHN FORSTER, *Life of Swift, Vol. I*.

On this gloom one luminary rose, and Ireland worshipped it with Persian idolatry; her true patriot—her first—almost her last. Sagacious and intrepid, he saw—he dared; above suspicion, he was trusted; above envy, he was beloved; above rivalry, he was obeyed. His wisdom was practical and prophetic—remedial for the present, warning for the future. He first taught Ireland that she might become a nation, and England that she must cease to become a despot. But he was a churchman; his gown impeded his course, and entangled his efforts. Guiding a senate, or heading an army, he had been more than Cromwell, and Ireland not less than England. As it was, he saved her by his courage, improved her by his authority, adorned her by his talents, and exalted her by his fame. His mission was but of ten years, and for ten years only did his personal power mitigate the government; but though no longer feared by the great, he was not forgotten by the wise; his influence, like his writings, has survived a century; and the foundations of whatever prosperity we have since erected are laid in the disinterested and magnanimous patriotism of Swift.—J. W. CROKER, *A Sketch of Ireland*.

Greater men than Dean Swift may have lived. A more remarkable man never left his impress upon the age, immortalized by his genius. To say that English history supplies no narrative more singular and original than the career of Jonathan Swift, is to assert little. We doubt whether the histories of the world can furnish, for example and instruction, for wonder and pity, for admiration and scorn, for approval and condemnation, a specimen of humanity at once so illustrious and so small. Before the eyes of his contemporaries, Swift stood a living enigma. To posterity he must continue for ever a distressing puzzle. One hypothesis—and one alone—gathered from a close and candid perusal of all that has been transmitted to us upon this interesting subject, helps us to account for a whole life of anomaly, but not to clear up the mystery in which it is shrouded. From the beginning to the end of his days Jonathan Swift was more or less MAD.—SAMUEL PHILLIPS, *Essays from "The Times," Vol. I*.

One may dislike such a man as Swift, but one cannot set him aside. His amazing intellectual vigour, the power with which he states some of the great problems of life, and the trenchant decision of his answer, give him a right to be heard. We may shudder, but we are forced to listen.— LESLIE STEPHEN, *Hours in a Library, Vol. III*.

Swift at Dublin recalls Napoleon at Elba. The duties of a deanery are not supposed, I believe, to give absorbing employment for all the faculties of the incumbent; but an empire, however small, may be governed; and Swift at an early period set about establishing his supremacy within his small domains.—*Id., Life of J. Swift*.

At the same time, while it must be admitted that Swift was far from being a model clergyman, it is, I conceive, a misapprehension to regard him as a secret disbeliever in Christianity. He was admirably described by St. John as "a hypocrite reversed". He disguised as far as possible both his religion and his affections, and took a morbid pleasure in parading the harsher features of his nature. If we bear this in mind, the facts of his life seem entirely incompatible with the hypothesis of habitual concealed unbelief.—W. E. H. LECKY, *Biographical Introduction to the Prose Works of Jonathan Swift, Vol. I.*

Swift, in his fictions, as in the rest of his writings, is the British satirist of his age. His prototype, in as far as he had any, was Rabelais. In Swift first the mad, the obscene, the ghastly, the all but infernal and yet infinitely sorrowful humour of the French satirist of the sixteenth century appears in full measure in the literature of Britain. That he was a reader of Rabelais cannot be doubted. He adopts his style and the whimsicalities of his method so openly as almost to court the name of his imitator. But it was as a man of original genius, who would have gone near to be the Rabelais of his time and country, even had no Rabelais been in France before him.—DAVID MASSON, *British Novelists and their Styles.*

THOMAS SYDENHAM.

English Doctor of Medicine : 1624-1689.

If we may adapt the simple but sublime saying of Sir Isaac Newton, Sydenham, though diligent beyond most other "children" in gathering his pebbles and shells on the shore of the great deep, and in winning for mankind some things of worth from the vast and formless infinite, was not unconscious of the mighty presence beside which he was at work ; he was not deaf to the strong music of that illimitable sea. He recognised in the midst of the known, a greater, an infinite, a divine unknown ; behind everything certain and distinct, he beheld something shadowy and unsearchable, past all finding out ; and he did not, as many of his class have too often done, and still do, rest in the mere contemplation and recognition of the τὶ θεῖον. This was to him but the shadow of supreme substance, ὁ θεὸς.—JOHN BROWN, *Horæ Subsecivæ, First Series.*

CAIUS CORNELIUS TACITUS.

Roman Historian : 55-117.

Wise Tacitus, of penetration deep,
Each secret spring reveal'd.
> —SOMERVILLE, *Hobbinol, Canto II.*

The object of Tacitus was to demonstrate the desperate consequences of the loss of liberty on the minds and hearts of men.—S. T. COLERIDGE, *Table Talk.*

The greatest man who has as yet given himself to the recording of human affairs is, beyond question, Cornelius Tacitus.—J. A. FROUDE, *Short Studies, Vol, II.*

In Tacitus, Stoicism has left an external evidence how grand a creature man may be, though unassisted by conscious dependence on external spiritual help, through steady disdain of what is base, steady reverence for all that deserves to be revered, and inflexible integrity in word and deed. —*Id., Calvinism.*

Men like Tacitus are unhealthy subjects for authority. Tacitus applies his style to the shoulder of an emperor, and the mark remains. Tacitus always makes his thrust at the required spot. A deep thrust . . . Tacitus has the conciseness of red iron.—VICTOR HUGO, *William Shakespeare (transl.).*

Tacitus belongs to a different class among the great writers of the world. He had, beyond almost any author of the front rank that has ever lived, the art of condensing his thought and driving it home to the mind of the reader with a flash.—JOHN MORLEY, *Studies in Literature.*

That gloomy moralist, Tacitus—the Carlyle of his day.—C. LORING BRACE, *The Unknown God.*

TORQUATO TASSO.

Italian Poet : 1544-1595.

In scenes like these, which, daring to depart
   From sober truth, are still to nature true,
   And call forth fresh delight to fancy's view,
The heroic muse employed her Tasso's art ! . . .
Prevailing poet ! whose undoubting mind
   Believed the magic wonders which he sung !
Hence, at each sound, imagination glows !
   Hence, at each picture, vivid life starts here !
Hence his warm lay with softest sweetness flows !
   Melting it flows, pure, murmuring, strong, and clear,
   And fills the impassioned heart, and wins the harmonious ear !
      —W. COLLINS, *Ode on the Popular Superstitions of the High-*
         lands of Scotland, XII.

Peace to Torquato's injured shade ! 'twas his
In life and death to be the mark where Wrong
Aim'd with her poison'd arrows—but to miss.
Oh, victor unsurpass'd in modern song !
Each year brings forth its millions ; but how long
The tide of generations shall roll on,
And not the whole combined and countless throng
Compose a mind like thine ? Though all in one
Condensed their scatter'd rays, they would not form a sun.
      —BYRON, *Childe Harold's Pilgrimage.*

I honour every man and each man's merit ;
To Tasso I am only just. His eye
Scarce rests upon this earth ; his eye perceives
The harmony of nature ; while his breast
Accepts, at once and gladly, every gift
Of history's records, or that life bestows :
Things widely scattered can his mind collect,
His heart on lifeless things true life bestow.
What we thought common he ennobles oft,

While what we prized before him turns to nought.
In such peculiar magic circle wanders
The marvellous man, and makes us wander with him.
—GOETHE, Torquato Tasso (transl.).

His to drink deep of sorrow, and, through life,
To be the scorn of them that knew him not,
Trampling alike the giver and his gift,
The gift a pearl precious, inestimable,
A lay divine, a lay of love and war,
To charm, ennoble, and, from age to age,
Sweeten the labour when the oar was plied
Or on the Adrian or the Tuscan sea.
—ROGERS, Italy : Amalfi.

He, whose song beguiles
The day of half its hours ; whose sorcery
Dazzles the sense, turning our forest-glades
To lists that blaze with gorgeous armoury,
Our mountain-caves to regal palaces.
—Id., Ibid. : Banditti.

Tasso's ardent numbers
  Float along the pleased air,
Calling youth from idle slumbers,
  Rousing them from Pleasure's lair :—
Then o'er the strings his fingers gently move,
And melt the soul to pity and to love.
—KEATS, Ode to Apollo.

She that reads Tasso or Malherbe,
Chooses a step that is superb.
—DR. WILLIAM KING, The Art of Love, Part XII.

Considered as a work of imagination, the *Gerusalemme Liberata*, is one of the most exquisite conceptions of human fancy, and will for ever command the admiration of romantic and elevated minds. But it wants that yet higher, or, at least, more popular quality, which arises from a thorough knowledge of human nature—a graphic delineation of actual character, a faithful picture of the real passions and sufferings of mortality. It is the most perfect example of poetic *fancy :* but the highest species of the epic poem is to be found, not in poetic fancy, but *poetic history.*—SIR ARCHIBALD ALISON, *Essays : The Crusades.*

Tasso is not one of my favourites, either as a man or a poet. There is too little of the fine frenzy in his verses, and too much in his life.—MACAULAY, *Life and Letters, Vol. II.*

A thousand romantic associations cling round the very name of Torquato Tasso. His strange and eventful story, his genius, above all, his misfortunes, encompass his image with a halo of interest denied to common men, and even to greater poets than himself; and have made his woes the theme of other bards, and his form the central figure of dramas, such as those of Goldoni and of Goethe. Variously estimated by his own contemporaries according to their differing powers of insight—a madman to some, a sage to others—they yet all agree that he was good—they all in some sense acknowledge that he was great.—E. J. HASELL, *Life of Tasso.*

Jeremy Taylor.

Bishop of Down and Connor and Dromore: 1613-1667.

Taylor too was there, from whose mind of its treasures redundant
Streams of eloquence flow'd, like an inexhaustible fountain.
—Southey, *A Vision of Judgment: The Elder Worthies.*

Jeremy Taylor is an excellent author for a young man to study, for
the purpose of imbibing noble principles.—S. T. Coleridge, *Table
Talk.*

The writings of Bishop Jeremy Taylor are a perpetual feast to me.   His
hospitable board groans under the weight and multitude of viands.   Yet I
seldom rise from the perusal of his works without repeating or recollecting
the excellent observation of Minucius Felix : *Fabulas et errores ale imperitis
parentibus discimus ; et quod est gravius, ipsis studiis et disciplinis elabor-
amus.—Id., Notes : Theological, Political, and Miscellaneous.*

There is a great distinction between the art of style and what the phren-
ologists call "the organ of language".   In Jeremy Taylor, for instance,
we are dazzled by the opulent splendour of diction with which the preacher
comes in state to our souls.   High priest of eloquence, to his sacred tiara
the many royalties of genius contribute the richest gems of their crowns.
But no teacher of style would recommend as a safe model to his pupil the
style of Jeremy Taylor.—Lytton, *Essays : On Style and Diction.*

From amongst the ranks of the people rose Taylor, the Milton of the
Church, whose power and pathos, and "purple grandeur ' of eloquence,
beautified even piety itself.—*Id., England and the English.*

The gentleman, the orator, the poet, and the Christian !   Such are the
titles of Bishop Taylor to the regard of posterity ; consummate in every
character, unapproachable in many of the qualities that go to form the instructor of the people, and the enunciator of the holy messages of Heaven.
In the pulpit he captivated and enravished his listeners by the richness of
a fancy which found food in all that nature could supply or erudition bring.
In his works the acuteness of the schoolman, the depth of the philosopher,
the piety of a saint, meet you at every turn.—Samuel Phillips, *Essays
from " The Times," Vol. II.*

The ethereal tincture that pervades the style of Jeremy Taylor, making
it, as Burke said of Sheridan's eloquence, "neither prose nor poetry, but
something better than either ".—J. R. Lowell, *Among My Books.*

I doubt whether we shall not as soon see another Shakespeare as another
Jeremy Taylor.—F. W. Farrar, *Masters in English Theology : Jeremy
Taylor.*

Even the mighty rhetoric of . . . Jeremy Taylor, to whom only it has
been granted to open the trumpet-stop on that great organ of passion,
oftentimes leaves behind it the sense of sadness which belongs to beautiful
apparitions starting out of darkness upon the morbid eye, only to be re-
claimed by darkness in the instant of their birth, or which belongs to
pageantries in the clouds.—De Quincey, *Leaders in Literature.*

David Teniers.

Flemish Painter: 1610-1694.

Never did any one paint air, the thin air, the absolutely apparent vacancy between object and object, so admirably as Teniers.—S. T. Coleridge, *Table Talk.*

Alfred Lord Tennyson.

Poet Laureate: 1809-1892.

Poet! I come to touch thy lance with mine;
  Not as a knight, who on the listed field
  Of tourney touched his adversary's shield
  In token of defiance, but in sign
Of homage to the mastery, which is thine,
  In English song; nor will I keep concealed,
  And voiceless as a rivulet frost-congealed,
  My admiration for thy verse divine.
Not of the howling dervishes of song,
  Who craze the brain with their delirious dance,
  Art thou, O sweet historian of the heart!
Therefore to thee the laurel-leaves belong,
  To thee our love and our allegiance,
For thy allegiance to the poet's art.
            —Longfellow, *Wapentake: To Alfred Tennyson.*

Tennyson's enchanted reverie. . . .
            —E. B. Browning, *Lady Geraldine's Courtship.*

Then cried the King, and smote the oak,
  " Love, Truth, and Beauty, one, but three,
  This is the Artist's Trinity!"
And lo, 'twas Tennyson who spoke.
  For this shall be through endless time
  The burden of the golden rhyme
    Of Tennyson, our Laureate.
            —W. C. Monkhouse, *Recollections of Alfred Tennyson: A Day Dream* (1869).

Fairer far than the morning star, and sweeter far than the songs that rang
Loud through Heaven from the choral Seven when all the stars of the
    morning sang,
Shines the song that we loved so long—since first such love in us flamed
    and sprang.
            —Swinburne, *Threnody.*

Thy song can girdle hill and mead
  With choirs, more pure, more fair,
Their locks with wild flower dressed and weed,
  Than ever Hellas bare:
Theocritus, we cry, once more
Treads his beloved Trinacrin shore!
            —Aubrey de Vere, *Ode (The Golden Mean).*

Long may your green maturity maintain
Its universal season ; and your voice,
A household sound, be heard about our hearths,
Now as a Christmas carol, now as the glee
Of vernal Maypole, now as harvest song.
And when, like light withdrawn from earth to heaven,
Your glorious gloaming fades into the sky,
We, looking upward, shall behold you there,
Shining amid the young unageing stars.
—ALFRED AUSTIN, *A Poet's Eightieth Birthday* (*6th August*, 1889).

Thy place is with the Immortals. Who shall gauge
Thy rank among thy peers of world-wide song ?
Others, it may be, touched a note more strong,
Scaled loftier heights, or glowed with fiercer rage ;
But who like thee could slay our modern Doubt ?
Or soothe the sufferers with a tenderer heart ?
Or dress gray legends with such perfect grace ?
Or nerve life's world-worn pilgrims for their part ?
Who, since our English tongue first grew, has stirred
More souls to noble effort by his word ?
More reverent who of Man, of God, of Truth ?
More piteous of the sore-tried strength of Youth ?
Thy chaste, white Muse, loathing the Pagan rout,
Would drive with stripes the goatish Satyr out.
Thy love of Righteousness preserved thee pure,
Thy lucid genius scorned to lurk obscure,
And all thy jewelled Art and native Grace
Were consecrate to God and to the Race.
—LEWIS MORRIS, *6th October*, 1892.

From Alfred Tennyson—although in perfect sincerity I regard him as
the noblest poet that ever lived—I have left myself time to cite only a very
brief specimen. I call him, and *think* him the noblest of poets—*not* because the impressions he produces are, at *all* times, the most profound—
not because the poetical excitement which he produces is, at *all* times, the
most intense—but because it *is*, at all times, the most ethereal—in other
words, the most elevating and the most pure. No poet is so little of the
earth, earthy.—POE, *Works of Edgar A. Poe, Vol. I.*

Tennyson is endowed precisely in points where Wordsworth wanted.
There is no finer ear than Tennyson's, nor more command of the keys of
language. Colour, like the dawn, flows over the horizon from his pencil,
in waves so rich that we do not miss the central form. Through all his
refinements, too, he has reached the public—a certificate of good sense and
general power, since he who aspires to be the English poet must be as
large as London, not in the same kind as London, but in his own kind.
—EMERSON, *English Traits : Literature.*

Tennyson should speak of the sea so as to rouse the souls of sailors,
rather than the soles of tailors—the enthusiasm of the deck, rather than of
the board. Unfortunately, he seems never to have seen a ship, or, if he
did, to have forgotten it. The vessel in which the land-lubbers were drifting, when the Sea-Fairies salute them with a song, must have been an old
tub of a thing, unfit even for a transport. Such a jib ! In the cut of her

mainsail you smoke the old table-cloth. To be solemn—Alfred Tennyson
is as poor on the sea as Barry Cornwall—and of course, calls him a serpent.
They both write like people who, on venturing upon the world of waters
in a bathing-machine, would insure their lives by a cork-jacket. Barry
swims on the surface of the Great Deep like a feather; Alfred dives less
after the fashion of a duck than a bell; but the one sees few lights, the
other few shadows, that are not seen just as well by an oyster-dredger.
But the soul of the true sea-poet doth undergo a sea-change, soon as he
sees Blue Peter; and he is off in the gig,

> "While bending back, away they pull,
> With measured strokes most beautiful "—
> There goes the Commodore!
> —JOHN WILSON, *Essays : Tennyson's Poems.*

Lately I have been reading again some of Alfred Tennyson's second
volume, and with profound admiration of his truly lyric and idyllic genius.
There seems to me to have been more epic power in Keats, that fiery,
beautiful meteor; but they are two most true and great poets. When we
think of the amount of recognition they have received, one may well bless
God that poetry is in itself strength and joy, whether it be crowned by all
mankind or left alone in its own magic hermitage.—JOHN STERLING,
Essays and Tales.

Tennyson, finding himself in a world where sorrow alternates with joy,
and in a nation whose humour, even, has been supposed to have a serious
and Saturnine cast,—having heard, too, we may presume, of a text in a
certain book which says, "Blessed are they that mourn, for they shall be
comforted,"—and having himself lost a friend who was as the light of his
eyes and the joy of his heart, has not thought it an unworthy employment
of his poetic gifts to bestow them in erecting a monument to his friend,
upon which he has carved bas-reliefs of exceeding grace and beauty, and
has worked delicate flowers into the cornices, and adorned the capitals of
the columns with emblematic devices ; and upon the summit he has set
the statue of his friend, and about the base run the sweetest words of love
with the mournfullest accents of grief—the darkest doubts with the sub-
imest hopes.—GEORGE BRIMLEY, *Essays.*

Should our noble Tennyson survive as a constant writer till his black locks
have grown grey, one sees qualities in him that predict for him more than
a Wordsworth's fame.—DAVID MASSON, *Wordsworth, Shelley, and Keats.*

Tennyson, among the poets of the nineteenth century, owes much to
the Greek idyllists. His genius appears to be in many respects akin to
theirs, and the age in which he lives is not unlike the Ptolemaic period.
Unfitted, perhaps, by temperament for the most impassioned lyrics, he
delights in minutely finished pictures, in felicities of expression and in
subtle harmonies of verse. Like Theocritus, he finds in nature and in the
legends of past ages subjects congenial to his muse. *Œnone* and *Tithonus*
are steeped in the golden beauty of Syracusan art.—J. A. SYMONDS,
Studies in the Greek Poets.

In Tennyson and Browning we have veritable fountain-heads of the
spiritual energy of our time. "Ranging and ringing thro' the minds of
men," their words are linked in many a memory with what life has held of
best.—F. W. H. MYERS, *Science and a Future Life.*

The melodious languors of Tennyson's early poems soon gave way to the deep-centred activities of thought which were everywhere rending men's lives apart, and the golden clime in which the poet was born was speedily vexed with the rolling cloud and tempest of the great upheaval. The *In Memoriam* is the nineteenth century's Book of Job, and is inseparably inwoven with the history of the century because it is woven out of the sentiment of the century.—W. J. Dawson, *Quest and Vision.*

Lord Tennyson's poetry is the newspaper of his era, and he the supreme journalist of the time.   It is not that he has been the mere reporter or chronicler of passing events, but he has been an assiduous commentator on them.   He has filled his place without aspiring to leadership. . . . His first *Locksley Hall* was the Nicene creed of a party. . . . The elaborately painted flowers, laburnum, and tulip, and marigold, that occur in the verse of Tennyson like illuminations in a mediæval manuscript.—P. G. Graham, *Nature in Books.*

The death of Tennyson was worthy of his life.   He died with the sim,-plicity which marked his life, and yet with a certain conscious stateliness which was all his own ; and these two, simplicity and stateliness, were also vital in the texture of his poetry.   But his dying hour, though it has left a noble picture on the mind of England, is not the important thing.   His life and poetry are the real matter of use and interest, and its death gains its best import from its being the beautiful and fitting end of all the work that had gone before it.   It became an artist, it became a Christian, it became a man.—Stopford Brooke, *Tennyson.*

Both Tennyson and Browning are full of hope.   But it is a sober hope —a hope that has to justify itself at every turn, to fight its way at every step, against possible challenge or denial ; essentially a reasoned, not an instinctive hope.—C. E. Vaughan in *Browning Notes.*

William Makepeace Thackeray.

English Novelist and Satirist : 1811-1863.

Mr. Thackeray's humour does not mainly consist in the creation of oddities of manner, habit, or feeling ; but in so representing actual men and women as to excite a sense of incongruity in the reader's mind—a feeling that the follies and vices described are deviations from an ideal of humanity always present to the writer.   The real is described vividly, with that perception of individuality which constitutes the artist ; but the description implies and suggests a standard higher than itself, not by any direct assertion of such a standard, but by an unmistakable irony.   The moral antithesis of actual and ideal is the root from which springs the peculiar charm of Mr. Thackeray's writings ; that mixture of gaiety and seriousness, of sarcasm and tenderness, of enjoyment and cynicism, which reflects so well the contradictory consciousness of man as a being with senses and passions and limited knowledge, yet with a conscience and a reason speaking to him of eternal laws and a moral order of the universe. It is this that makes Mr. Thackeray a profound moralist, just as Hogarth showed his knowledge of perspective by drawing a landscape throughout in violation of its rules.   So, in Mr. Thackeray's picture of society as it is, society as it ought to be is implied. He could not have painted *Vanity Fair* as he has, unless Eden had been shining brightly in his inner eyes. The historian of "snobs" indicates in every touch his fine sense of a gentleman or a lady. No one could be simply amused with Mr. Thackeray's descriptions or his dialogues. A shame at one's own defects, at the defects of the world in which one was living, was irresistibly aroused along with the reception of the particular portraiture. But while he was dealing with his own age, his keen perceptive faculty prevailed, and the actual predominates in his pictures of modern society.—GEORGE BRIMLEY, *Essays.*

Whatever Thackeray says, the reader cannot fail to understand; and whatever Thackeray attempts to communicate, he succeeds in conveying. —ANTHONY TROLLOPE, *Life of Thackeray.*

Thackeray, like Sterne, looked at everything—at nature, at life, at art—from a sensitive aspect. His mind was to some considerable extent like a woman's mind. It could comprehend abstractions when they were unrolled and explained before it, but it never naturally created them ; never of itself, and without external obligation, devoted itself to them. The visible scene of life—the streets—the servants, the clubs, the gossip, the West End—fastened on his brain. They were to him reality. They burnt in upon his brain ; they pained his nerves ; their influence reached him through many avenues, which ordinary men do not feel much, or to which they are altogether impervious. He had distinct and rather painful sensations where most men have but confused and blurred ones.—WALTER BAGEHOT, *Literary Studies, Vol. II.*

Thackeray's success is almost solely owing to his moral influence. Much as we respect his intellectual powers, we have a far higher admiration of his heart—that noble courageous generosity for which language has no word. He is emphatically the true gentleman of our generation, who has appealed to our best and most chivalric sympathies, and raising us from the slough and pollution of the Regency has made us once more " a nation of gentlemen ".—J. C. JEAFFRESON, *Novels and Novelists from Elizabeth to Victoria, Vol. II.*

For myself, I honestly confess that I never could learn anything from Thackeray ; there is a certain feeble amiability even about his best characters, which, if it is free from the depressing influence of his bad ones, is certainly anything but bracing.—J. STUART BLACKIE, *On Self-Culture.*

William Makepeace Goliath, white waistcoat and all.—A. T. QUILLER-COUCH, *Adventures in Criticism.*

Thackeray, with a fine and sympathetic soul, had a creative imagination that was far stronger on the darker and fouler sides of life than it was on the brighter and pure side of life. He saw the bright and pure side : he loved it, he felt with it, he made us love it. But his artistic genius worked with more free and consummate zest when he painted the dark and the foul. His creative imagination fell short of the true equipoise, of that just vision of *chiaroscuro*, which we find in the greatest masters of the human heart. This limitation of his genius has been visited upon Thackeray with a heavy hand. And such as it is, he must bear it.—FREDERIC HARRISON, *Studies in Early Victorian Literature.*

THEOCRITUS.

Greek Poet: fl. 3rd cent. B.C.

Our Theocritus, our Bion,
  And our Pindar's shining goals!—
These were cup-bearers undying,
  Of the wine that's meant for souls.
                        —E. B. BROWNING, *Wine of Cyprus.*

The names and shades adored of all of us,
  The nurslings of the brave world's earlier brood,
Grown gods for us themselves: Theocritus
  First, and more dear Catullus, names bedewed
      With blessings bright like tears
      From the old memorial years,
And loves and lovely laughters, every mood
      Sweet as the drops that fell
      Of their own venomel
From living lips to clear the multitude
      That feeds on words divine.
      —SWINBURNE, *Song for the Centenary of Walter Savage Landor.*

Shepherd: " The Allan Ramsay o' Sicily, as I hae heard ; and the best pastoral poet o' the ancient warld."—JOHN WILSON, *Noctes Ambrosianæ, Vol. I.*

Theocritus is perhaps the most universally attractive of all Greek poets. It is common to find young students who prefer him to Homer, and most people are conscious of a certain delighted surprise when they first make his acquaintance.   In his own sweet and lowly domain he is absolute monarch ; one might almost say that there is hardly anything beautiful in the pastoral poetry of the world that does not come from Theocritus.— GILBERT MURRAY, *History of Ancient Greek Literature.*

SAINT THERESA.

Spanish Carmelite Nun: 1515-1582.

Ah! rather would I forget myself, than forget the writings of Teresa.— MADAME GUYON (*transl.*).

Teresa's image still stands in the Castilian churches.   The faithful crowd about her with their offerings, and dream that they leave behind them their aches and pains ; but her words were forgotten, and her rules sank again into neglect.   The Church of Rome would have done better in keeping alive Teresa's spirit than in converting her into a goddess.   Yet the Church of Rome is not peculiarly guilty, and we all do the same thing in our own way.   When a great teacher dies who has told us great truths which it would be disagreeable to act upon, we write adoring lives of him, we place him in the intellectual pantheon ; but we go on as if he had never lived at all.   We put up statues to him as if that would do as well, and the prophet who has denounced idols is made an idol himself.—J. A. FROUDE, *The Spanish Story of the Armada and other Essays.*

Wherever the tears of Theresa fell, new weeds of superstition sprang up.—R. A. VAUGHAN, *Hours with the Mystics, Vol. II.*

James Thomson.

Scottish Poet : 1700-1748.

See Thomson loitering near some limpid well,
For Britain's friend the verdant wreath prepare,
Or studious of revolving seasons, tell,
How peerless Lucia made all seasons fair.
　　　— Shenstone, *Elegy XXIII.*

O favour'd stream ! where thy fair current flows,
The child of nature, gentle Thomson rose.
Young as he wander'd on thy flowery side,
With simple joy to see thy bright waves glide,
Thither, in all their native charms array'd,
From climes remote the sister seasons stray'd.
Long each in beauty boasted to excel,
(For jealousies in silver-bosoms dwell)
But now, delighted with the liberal boy,
Like heaven's fair rivals in the groves of Troy,
Yield to a humble swain their high debate,
And from his voice the palm of beauty wait.
　　　—Dr. J. Langhorne, *Genius and Valour.*

To paint with Thomson's landscape-glow. . . .
　　　—Burns, *The Vision, II.*

The warblings of the blackbird, clear and strong,
Are musical enough in Thomson's song.
　　　—Cowper, *Retirement.*

　　　. . . the poet well you know :
Oft has he touch'd your hearts with tender woe :
Oft in this crowded house, with just applause
You heard him teach fair Virtue's purest laws ;
For his chaste muse employ'd her heaven-taught lyre
None but the noblest passions to inspire,
Not one immortal, one corrupted thought,
One line, which dying he could wish to blot.
　　　—Lord Lyttleton, *Prologue to Thomson's " Coriolanus ".*

　　　. . . the strain my Thomson sung,
Delicious dreams inspiring by his note.
What time to Indolence his harp he strung. . . .
　　　—Scott, *Introduction to " Harold the Dauntless ".*

In other climates, youths and maidens there
Shall learn from Thomson's verse in what attire
The various seasons, bringing in their change
　　　Variety of good,
Revisit their beloved English ground.
　　　—Southey, *Ode written after the King's visit to Scotland.*

As a writer, he is entitled to one praise of the highest kind : his mode
of thinking, and expressing his thoughts, is original. His blank verse is
no more the blank verse of Milton, or of any other poet, than the rhymes
of Prior are the rhymes of Cowley. His numbers, his pauses, his diction,

are of his own growth, without transcription, without imitation. He thinks in a peculiar train, and he thinks always as a man of genius ; he looks round on Nature and on Life with the eye which Nature bestows only on a poet ; the eye that distinguishes in everything presented to its view, whatever there is on which imagination can delight to be detained, and with a mind that at once comprehends the vast, and attends to the minute. The reader of the *Seasons* wonders that he never saw before what Thomson shows him, and that he never yet has felt what Thomson impresses. His is one of the works in which blank verse seems properly used.—DR. JOHNSON, *Lives of the Poets : Thomson.*

Thomson breathed landscape beauty in the *Seasons.*—SIR ARCHIBALD ALISON, *Essays : British School of Painting.*

HENRY DAVID THOREAU.

Transcendentalist : 1817-1862.

Thoreau's Mysticism, though born out of due time, is pure Darwinian. In that Walden wood he stands as the most wonderful and sensitive register of phenomena, finer and more exact than any cunningly devised measure. He is vision and learning, touch, smelling, and taste incarnate. Not only so, but he knows how to preserve the flashing forest colours in unfading light, to write down the wind's music in a score that all may read, to glean and garner every sensuous impression.—P. A. GRAHAM, *Nature in Books.*

LORD EDWARD THURLOW.

Lord Chancellor of England : 1732-1806.

Round Thurlow's head in early youth,
    And in his sportive days,
Fair Science pour'd the light of truth,
    And genius shed its rays.
            —COWPER, *On the Promotion of Edward Thurlow, Esq.*

I wonder whether any one ever was so wise as Thurlow looks.—C. J. FOX.

JOHN TILLOTSON.

Archbishop of Canterbury : 1630-1694.

We with pride may own
Our Tillotson ; and Rome, her Fénelon.
            —RICHARD SAVAGE, *Character of the Rev. James Foster.*

I have frequently heard him (Dryden) own with pleasure, that if he had any talent for English prose it was owing to his having often read the writings of the great Archbishop Tillotson.—WILLIAM CONGREVE.

Tillotson is always of a tolerant and catholic spirit ; enforcing right actions rather than orthodox opinions.—HALLAM, *Literature of the Middle Ages, Vol. IV.*

The gentle Tillotson, once the standard of all pulpit persuasion. —LYTTON, *England and the English : Survey of Education.*

Of all the members of the Low Church party Tillotson stood highest in general estimation. As a preacher he was thought by his contemporaries to have surpassed all rivals living or dead. Posterity has reversed this judgment. Yet Tillotson still keeps his place as a legitimate English classic. . . . His style is not brilliant ; but it is pure, transparently clear, and equally free from the levity and from the stiffness which disfigure the sermons of some eminent divines of the seventeenth century. He is always serious, yet there is about his manner a certain graceful ease which marks him as a man who knows the world, who has lived in populous cities and in splendid courts, and who has conversed, not only with books, but with lawyers and merchants, wits and beauties, statesmen and princes.—MACAULAY, *History of England, Vol. II., Chap. XIV.*

Tillotson, who was long the great model of English preachers, was latitudinarian in his opinions, and singularly mild and tolerant in his disposition.—W. E. H. LECKY, *History of England, Vol. I.*

Unlike South's, the character of John Tillotson is no matter for controversy. With the possible exception of Archbishop Herring, he was the most amiable man that ever filled the See of Canterbury, and was pronounced by the discerning and experienced William III. the best friend he had ever had and the best man he had ever known. To the meekness of the pastor, Tillotson added the qualities of the statesman, and happy was it for the Church of England that such a man could be found to fill the primacy at such a time.—RICHARD GARNETT, *The Age of Dryden.*

TITIAN (TIZIANO VECELLIO).

Venetian Painter : 1477-1576.

But how should any sign-post dauber know
The worth of Titian or of Angelo ?
Hard features every bungler can command ;
To draw true beauty, shows a master's hand.
                    —DRYDEN, *To Mr. Lee, on his Alexander.*

Titian glowing paint the canvas warm'd.
                              —GAY, *Trivia, Book II.*

Titian's warmth divine.
                    —POPE, *Epistle to Mr. Jervas.*

Rarely a Titian, or a Pope appears,
The forming glory of a thousand years !

.   .   .   .

Exact correctness Titian's hand bestow'd.
                    —WALTER HARTE, *An Essay on Painting.*

So when great Titian rose, immortal man !
With rural scenes his pencil first began ;
Employ'd all genial nature's laws to trace.
And copy from her ever-blooming face.
                    —SAMUEL BOYSE, *To Mr. Thomson.*

The golden scenes of Titian and Raphael. . . . Names that make us hear the music of their owners.—LEIGH HUNT, *Men, Women, and Books.*

There is no greater name in Italian art—therefore no greater in art— than that of Titian. If the Venetian master does not soar as high as Leonardo da Vinci or Michelangelo, those figures so vast, so mysterious, that clouds even now gather round their heads and half veil them from our view; if he has not the divine suavity, the perfect balance, not less of spirit than of answering hand, that makes Raphael an appearance unique in art, since the palmiest days of Greece; he is wider in scope, more glowing with the life-blood of humanity, more the poet-painter of the world and the world's fairest creatures, than any one of these.—CLAUDE PHILLIPS, *The Earlier Work of Titian.*

FLAVIUS SABINUS VESPASIANUS TITUS.

Roman Emperor : 40-81.

This world, 'tis true,
Was made for Cæsar—but for Titus too ;
And which more blest ? who chain'd his country, say,
Or he whose virtue sigh'd to lose a day ?
                                        —POPE, *Essay on Man.*

MARCUS ULPIUS NERVA TRAJANUS.

Emperor of Rome : 52-117.

I gladly commune with the mind and heart
Of him who thus survives by classic art,
His actions witness, venerate his mien,
And study Trajan as by Pliny seen ;
Behold how fought the chief whose conquering sword
Stretched far as earth might own a single lord.
In the delight of moral prudence schooled,
How feelingly at home the sovereign ruled ;
Best of the good—in pagan faith allied
To more than man by virtue deified.
                                        —WORDSWORTH, *The Pillar of Trajan.*

HENRI, VICOMTE DE TURENNE.

Marshal of France : 1611-1675.

Louis Fourteenth's Marshals are a kind of poetical men withal ; the things Turenne says are full of sagacity and geniality, like sayings of Samuel Johnson.—CARLYLE, *On Heroes and Hero-Worship.*

JOSEPH MALLORD WILLIAM TURNER.

English Painter : 1775-1851.

Of pictures, I should like to own
Titians and Raphaels three or four,—
I love so much their style and tone,—

One Turner, and no more,
(A landscape—foreground golden dirt,—
The sunshine painted with a squirt).
—OLIVER WENDELL HOLMES, Contentment.

Turner was once without a rival; all that his fancy whispered, his skill executed. Of late, he has forsaken the beautiful and married the fantastic. His genius meant him for the Wordsworth of description, he has spoilt himself to the Cowley! he no longer sympathizes with Nature, he coquets with her.—LYTTON, *England and the English: Intellectual Spirit, etc.*

But the original make and frame of Turner's mind being not vulgar, but as nearly as possible a combination of the minds of Keats and Dante, joining capricious waywardness, and intense openness to every fine pleasure of sense; and hot defiance of formal precedence, with a quite infinite tenderness, generosity, and desire of justice and truth—this kind of mind did not become vulgar, but very tolerant of vulgarity, even fond of it in some forms; and on the outside, visibly infected by it, deeply enough; the curious result, in its combination of elements, being to most people wholly incomprehensible. It was as if a cable had been woven of blood-crimson silk, and then tarred on the outside. People handled it, and the tar came off on their hands; red gleams were seen through the black underneath, at the places where it had been strained. Was it ochre?—said the world—or red lead?—RUSKIN, *Modern Painters, Vol. III.*

J. M. W. Turner's vagueness and extravagance, so much complained of by common folk, is another example of the transformation of thoughts into emotion. Mr. Ruskin has observed that Turner painted the *souls* of pictures. Even Turner's opponents will agree that in many of his pictures most of the distinct images have evaporated; while others perceive that these have only vanished to make way for emotions of transcendent force and beauty.—H. R. HAWEIS, *Music and Morals.*

SIR ANTHONY VANDYCK.

Flemish Painter: 1599-1641.

Vandyck is dead; but what bold Muse shall dare
(Tho' poets in that word with painters share)
T' express her sadness? Poesy must become
An art, like painting here, an art that's dumb.
Let's all our solemn grief in silence keep,
Like some sad picture which he made to weep.
—COWLEY, On the Death of Sir Anthony Vandyck.

That picture there your eyes does strike;
It is the work of great Van Dyck,
Which by a Roman would be sainted:
What was't but canvas till 'twas painted?
—DR. WILLIAM KING, The Art of Love, Part XII.

Sir Henry Vane.

English Statesman : 1589-1654.

Lady Carlisle : "You'll vanquish Pym ?
  Old Vane
Can vanquish you. And Vane you think to fly ?
Rush on the Scots ! Do nobly ! Vane's slight sneer
Shall test success, adjust the praise, suggest
The faint result : Vane's sneer shall reach you there."
     —Robert Browning, *Act II., Scene II.*

Sir Henry Vane, The Younger.

Republican Statesman : 1612-1662.

Vane, young in years, but in sage counsel old,
Than whom a better senator ne'er held
The helm of Rome, when gowns not arms repell'd
The fierce Epirot and the African bold,
Whether to settle peace, or to uphold
The drift of hollow states hard to be spell'd,
Then to advise how War may best upheld
Move by her two main nerves, iron and gold.
 . . . . . .
Therefore on thy firm hand Religion leans
In peace, and reckons thee her eldest son.
   —Milton, *Sonnet to Sir Henry Vane, The Younger.*

O for one hour of that undaunted stock
That went with Vane and Sydney to the block !
       —J. R. Lowell.

Hampden : "You may grow one day,
A steadfast light to England, Henry Vane !"
   —Robert Browning, *Strafford, Act II., Scene I.*

The Lord deliver me from Sir Harry Vane.—Oliver Cromwell.

We need not sneer at the high aspirations of Vane and the Republicans. If some men did not aspire too high, the world in general would fall too low.—Goldwin Smith, *Three English Statesmen.*

Andreas Vesalius.

Dutch Anatomist : 1514-1564.

If Vesalius was not quite to anatomy what Copernicus was to astronomy, he has yet been said, a little hyperbolically, to have discovered a new world.—Hallam, *Literature of the Middle Ages, Vol. I.*

Let the astronomers vaunt their Copernicus, the natural philosophers their Galileo and Torricelli, the mathematicians their Pascal, the geographers their Columbus, I shall always place Vesalius above all their heroes.—Baron de Portal.

LEONARDO DA VINCI.

Florentine Painter : 1452-1519.

Four great walls in the New Jerusalem,
Meted on each side by the angel's reed,
For Leonard, Rafael, Agnolo and me
To cover—the three first without a wife,
While I have mine !
                    —ROBERT BROWNING, *Andrea del Sarto.*

Like Vinci's strokes, the verses we behold,
Correctly graceful, and with labour bold.

                              —WALTER HARTE.

VIRGIL.

Roman Poet : B.C. 70-19

Glorie and honour, Virgile Mantuan,
Be to thy name, and I shal as I can
Folowe thy lanterne as thou goest beforne.
                    —CHAUCER, *The Legend of Dido.*

        The Mantuan,
As Sweet in fields, as stately in Troy's fire.
                    —G. DANIEL, *A Vindication of Poesy.*

Homer and Virgil !—with what sacred awe
Do those mere sounds the world's attention draw !
    .   .   .   .
Whose just discernment, Virgil-like is such,
Never to say too little or too much.
                    —DUKE OF BUCKINGHAM, *An Essay on Poetry.*

How many ages since has Virgil writ !
How few are they who understand him yet !
Approach his altars with religious fear :
No vulgar deity inhabits there.
Heaven shakes not more at Jove's imperial nod,
Than poets should before their Mantuan God.
                    —ROSCOMMON, *An Essay on Translated Verse.*

First from the green retreats and lowly plains,
Her Virgil soar'd sublime in epic strains ;
His theme so glorious, and his flight so true,
She with Mæonian garlands grac'd his brow.
                    —ELIJAH FENTON, *An Epistle to Mr. Southerne.*

Two shepherds most I love with just adoring ;
That Mantuan swain, who chang'd his slender reed
To trumpet's martial voice, and war's loud roaring,
From Corydon to Turnus' dering-deed ;
    And next our home-bred Colin's sweetest firing ;
    That steps not following close, but far admiring ;
To lackey one of these is all my pride's aspiring.
                    —PHINEAS FLETCHER, *The Purple Island, Canto VI.*

Welcome the Mantuan swan! Virgil the wise,
Whose verse walks highest, but not flies;
Who brought green Poesy to her perfect age,
And made that art which was a rage.

—COWLEY, *The Motto.*

Hence mighty Virgil's said of old,
From dung to have extracted gold.

—SAMUEL BUTLER, *Satire upon Plagiaries.*

In fame's fair temple, o'er the boldest wits
Inshrin'd on high the sacred Virgil sits.

—PARNELL, *To Mr. Pope.*

O had I Virgil's force, to sing the man,
Whose learned lines can millions raise *per ann.*

—GAY, *Epistle XI.*

Amongs the Lotyns Vyrgilius
Was beste of poets founde.

—CHATTERTON, *Song to Œlla.*

Melodious swells
The sweet majestic tone of Maro's lyre:
The soul delighted on each accent dwells,—
Enraptured dwells. . . .

—KEATS, *Ode to Apollo.*

Virgil: shade of Mantuan beech
Did help the shade of bay to reach
And knit around his forehead high;
For his gods wore less majesty
Than his brown bees hummed deathlessly.

—E. B. BROWNING, *A Vision of Poets.*

Landscape-lover, lord of language
    More than he that sang the Works and Days,
All the chosen coin of fancy
    Flashing out from many a golden phrase;
Thou that singest wheat and woodland,
    Tilth and vineyard, hive and horse and herd;
All the charm of all the Muses
    Often flowering in a lonely word;
Poet of the happy Tityrus
    Piping underneath his beechen bowers;
Poet of the poet-satyr
    Whom the laughing shepherd bound with flowers; . . .
Light among the vanish'd ages;
    Star that gildest yet this phantom shore;
Golden branch amid the shadows,
    Kings and realms that pass to rise no more; . . .
I salute thee, Mantovano,
    I that loved thee since my day began,
Wielder of the stateliest measure
    Ever moulded by the lips of man.

—TENNYSON, *To Virgil.*

Even the grandiloquent Virgil cannot get through his epic without a strong spice of love, and pious Æneas vindicates for himself the English as well as the Latin force of the stereotyped epithet by behaving like a scoundrel to a woman, and sneaking off without even saying good-bye, or leaving a christening-cup for the possible Tyrian Julus. That episode has saved the *Æneid* from becoming a mere scholar's poem, in spite of its magnificent versification.—GEORGE BRIMLEY, *Essays.*

Virgil had been Dante's guide in the three kingdoms of the unseen world; Virgil is Petrarch's guide in the study of nature.—PASQUALE VILLARI, *Niccolò Macchiavelli and his Times (transl.), Vol. I.*

Virgil and Horace lived nearly two thousand years ago, and belonged to a society of which the outward form and fashion have utterly perished. But Virgil and Horace do not grow old, because while society changes, men continue, and we recognise in reading them that the same heart beat under the toga which we feel in our own breasts.—J. A. FROUDE, *Short Studies on Great Subjects, Vol. IV.*

FRANÇOIS MARIE AROUET DE VOLTAIRE.

French Philosopher, Poet, Historian : 1694-1778.

The Frenchman, first in literary fame,
(Mention him, if you please. Voltaire? The same.)
With spirit, genius, eloquence supplied,
Lived long, wrote much, laugh'd heartily, and died ;
The Scripture was his jest-book, whence he drew
Bon-mots to gall the Christian and the Jew ;
An infidel in health, but what when sick ?
Oh—then a text would touch him to the quick ;
View him at Paris in his last career,
Surrounding throngs the demigod revere :
Exalted on his pedestal of pride,
And fumed with frankincense on every side,
He begs their flattery with his latest breath,
And smother'd in't at last, is praised to death.

—COWPER, *Truth.*

Voltaire ! long life's the greatest curse
That mortals can receive,
When they imagine the chief end
Of living is to live.

—YOUNG, *Resignation.*

And a light on the brow of the bronze Voltaire
Like the ghost of a cynical joke.

—OWEN MERIDITH, *Two out of the Crowd.*

In Voltaire, as in most men, there was a double self—the one sickened to cynicism by the iniquity and folly which he saw around him—the other, hungering after a nobler life.—KINGSLEY, *Historical Lectures and Essays.*

The mention of Voltaire at once presents to every one the idea, not so much of a philosopher whose early inquiries have led him to doubt upon the foundations of religion, or even to disbelieve its truths, as of a bitter enemy to all belief in the evidence of things unseen—an enemy whose assaults were directed by malignant passions, aided by unscrupulous contrivances, and above all, pressed by the unlawful weapon of ridicule, not the fair armoury of argument; in a word, he is regarded as a scoffer, not a reasoner.—LORD BROUGHAM, *Men of Letters, Vol. II.*

The most figuring person in the work, and indeed of the age to which it belongs, was beyond all question Voltaire. . . . He receives no other name throughout the book, than "The Patriarch" of the Holy Philosophical Church.—LORD JEFFREY, *Essays.*

Voltaire is the prince of buffoons. His merriment is without disguise or restraint. He gambols; he grins; he shakes his sides; he points the finger; he turns up the nose; he shoots out the tongue. . . . The nature of Voltaire was, indeed, not inhuman; but he venerated nothing. Neither in the masterpieces of art nor in the purest examples of virtue, neither in the Great First Cause nor in the awful enigma of the grave, could he see anything but subjects for drollery. The more solemn and august the theme, the more monkey-like was his grimacing and chattering.— MACAULAY, *Essays: Addison.*

In truth, of all the intellectual weapons which have ever been wielded by man, the most terrible was the mockery by Voltaire. Bigots and tyrants, who had never been moved by the wailing and cursing of millions, turned pale at his name. Principles unassailable by reason, principles which had withstood the fiercest attacks of power, the most valuable truths, the most generous sentiments, the noblest and most graceful images, the purest reputations, the most august institutions, began to look mean and loathsome as soon as that withering smile was turned upon them. To every opponent, however strong in his cause and his talents, in his station and in his character, who ventured to encounter the great scoffer, might be addressed the caution which was given of old to the Archangel:—

> "I forewarn thee shun
> His deadly arrow; neither vainly hope
> To be invulnerable in those bright arms
> Though temper'd heavenly; for that fatal dint,
> Save Him who reigns above, none can resist."

We cannot pause to recount how often that rare talent was exercised against rivals worthy of esteem; how often it was used to crush and torture enemies worthy only of silent disdain; how often it was perverted to the more noxious purpose of destroying the last solace of earthly misery, and the last restraint on earthly power. Neither can we pause to tell how often it was used to vindicate justice, humanity, and toleration, the principles of sound philosophy, the principles of free government.— *Id., Ibid.: Frederic the Great.*

This singular man, who was a freethinker at London, a Cartesian at Versailles, a Christian at Nancy, and an infidel at Berlin. In society, he was alternately an Aristippus and a Diogenes. He made pleasure the object of his researches: he enjoyed it, and made it the object of his praise; he grew weary of it, and turned it into ridicule.—ALEXANDER CHALMERS, *Biographical Dictionary.*

Of all the many kinds of knowledge possessed by Voltaire, knowledge of the world was, perhaps, that for which he was most remarkable. It was that knowledge which secured to him so vast an audience and so lofty a position; and the aptitude for such kind of knowledge was inborn with him—made three parts of his *ingenium* or native genius. . . . Voltaire's knowledge of this world, as exhibited whether in his life or his writings, was exceedingly keen and sharp; and for any knowledge of a world beyond this, Voltaire is the last guide a man of bold genius would follow, or a man of calm judgment consult.—LYTTON, *Essays: Knowledge of the World.*

The withered Pontiff of Encyclopedism. . . . The unbelieving French believe in their Voltaire; and burst out round him into very curious Hero-worship, in that last act of his life when they "stifle him under roses". It has always seemed to me extremely curious this of Voltaire. Truly, if Christianity be the highest instance of Hero-worship, then we may find here in Voltaireism one of the lowest! He whose life was that of a kind of Antichrist, does again on this side exhibit a curious contrast. No people were ever so little prone to admire at all as those French of Voltaire. *Persiflage* was the character of their whole mind; adoration had nowhere a place in it. Yet see! The old man of Ferney comes up to Paris; an old, tottering, infirm man of eighty-four years. They feel that he too is a kind of Hero; that he has spent his life in opposing error and injustice, delivering Calases, unmasking hypocrites in high places; in short, that *he* too, though in a strange way, has fought like a valiant man. They feel withal that, if *persiflage* be the great thing, there never was such a *persifleur*. He is the realised ideal of every one of them; the thing they are all wanting to be; of all Frenchmen the most French. *He* is properly their god, such god as they are fit for. Accordingly all persons, from the Queen Antoinette to the Douanier at the Porte St. Denis, do they not worship him?—CARLYLE, *On Heroes and Hero-Worship.*

The fertility of Voltaire is wonderful, but great part of what he has written is so objectionable on the score of religion or humanity, that even his wit does not furnish salt enough to keep from corruption the intellectual food he has lavished in such abundance.—LORD JOHN RUSSELL, *Introduction to Memoirs, Journal, and Correspondence of Thomas Moore, Vol. I.*

However this may be, it is chiefly as a literary phenomenon that Voltaire is now interesting to us. In that light it appears to the present writer that no inconsiderable part of his extraordinary fame was owing to the circumstances of the period, and the conditions in which he wrote, and has reasonably vanished with the lapse of time. That he still retains so eminent a position in France is due, in great measure, to those gifts of expression which do not much aid in extending a writer's reputation beyond his own country. But, after the winnowings of generations, a wide and deep repute still remains to him; nor will any diminution which it may have suffered be without compensation, for, with the fading of old prejudices, and with better knowledge, his name will be regarded with increased liking and respect. Yet it must not be supposed that he is here held up as a pattern man. He was, indeed, an infinitely better one than the religious bigots of the time. He believed, with far better effect on his practice than they could boast, in a Supreme Ruler. He was the untiring and eloquent advocate, at the bar of the Unseen, of the rights of humanity. He recognised and lamented all the evils permitted by Providence. But he forgot, except sometimes in theory, to return thanks for the blessings which are showered along with those evils on the earth, and thus the great intellect and the high purpose are left without the crowning grace of reverence.—COLONEL HAMLEY, *Life of Voltaire.*

The rays from Voltaire's burning and far-shining spirit no sooner struck upon the genius of the time, seated dark and dead like the black stone of Memnon's statue, than the clang of the breaking chord was heard through Europe, and men awoke in new day and more spacious air. The sentimentalist has proclaimed him a mere mocker. To the critic of the schools, ever ready with compendious label, he is the revolutionary destructive. To each alike of the countless orthodox sects his name is the symbol for the prevailing of the gates of hell. Erudition figures him as shallow and a trifler ; culture condemns him for pushing his hatred of spiritual falsehood much too seriously ; Christian charity feels constrained to unmask a demon from the depths of the pit. . . . Voltaire was ever in the front and centre of the fight. His life was not a mere chapter in a history of literature. He never counted truth a treasure to be discreetly hidden in a napkin. He made it a perpetual war-cry and emblazoned it on a banner that was many a time rent, but was never out of the field. . . . Voltaire was the very eye of modern illumination. It was he who conveyed to his generation in a multitude of forms the consciousness at once of the power and the rights of human intelligence. Another might well have said of him what he magnanimously said of his famous contemporary, Montesquieu, that humanity had lost its title-deeds, and he had recovered them.—JOHN MORLEY, *Life of Voltaire.*

Voltaire is never so good as when he is ridiculing the cruel folly which crimps a number of ignorant and innocent peasants, dresses them up in uniform, teaches them to march and wheel, and sends them off to kill and be killed by another army of peasants, ignorant and innocent like themselves, as a sacrifice to what is called the honour of kings.—GOLDWIN SMITH, *Three English Statesmen.*

Voltaire, so great in the eighteenth century, is still greater in the nineteenth. The grave is a crucible. That earth, thrown on a man, sifts his name, and allows that name to pass forth only purified. Voltaire has lost his false glory and retained the true. To lose the false is to gain. Voltaire is neither a lyric poet, nor a comic poet, nor a tragic poet ; he is the indignant yet tender critic of the old world ; he is the mild reformer of manners ; he is the man who softens men. Voltaire, who has lost ground as a poet, has risen as an apostle. He has done what is good, rather than what is beautiful. . . . Voltaire is common sense in a continual stream. Excepting in literature, he is a good judge in everything. Voltaire was, in spite of his insulters, almost adored during his lifetime ; he is in our days admired, now that the true facts of the case are known. The eighteenth century saw his mind : we see his soul.—VICTOR HUGO, *William Shakespeare (transl.).*

SIR WILLIAM WALLACE.

Scotch Patriot : 1270-1305.

All this may be, the people's voice is odd ;
The Scots will fight for Wallace as for God.
—POPE.

At WALLACE'S name, what Scottish blood,
But boils up in a spring-tide flood !
Oft have our fearless fathers strode
      By WALLACE'S side.
Still pressing onward, red-wat-shod,
      Or glorious dy'd !
—BURNS, *To William Simpson.*

Is there no daring bard will rise, and tell
How glorious Wallace stood, how hapless fell ?
—Id., *Scots Prologue.*

But never in all her annals were found together Shame and Scotland.
Sir William Wallace has not left Shame one single dark cavern wherein
to hide her head.—JOHN WILSON, *Essays : Old North and Young North.*

Wallace's name stands brightly forward among the foremost of men,
with Vasa, with the two Williams of Orange, with Washington, with
Kosciusko, with his own more fortunate but less pure successor, Robert
Bruce.—SIR JAMES MACKINTOSH, *History of England, Vol. I.*

The instinct of the Scotch people has guided it aright in choosing
Wallace for its national hero. He was the first to assert freedom as a
national birthright, and amidst the despair of nobles and priests to call
the people itself to arms.—J. R. GREEN, *History of England.*

EDMUND WALLER.

English Poet : 1605-1687.

Parent of harmony in English verse,
Whose tuneful Muse in sweetest accents flows,
In couplets first taught straggling sense to close.
—CHURCHILL, *The Apology.*

Waller by Nature for the Bays design'd,
With force and fire, and fancy unconfin'd,
In panegyric does excel mankind.
—ROCHESTER, *An Allusion.*

Waller had numbers, fancy, wit, and fire ;
And Saccharissa was his fond desire.
—HALIFAX, *Written at Althrop in a blank leaf of Waller's Poems.*

The courtly Waller next commands thy lays:
Muse, tune thy verse, with art, to Waller's praise.
While tender airs and lovely dames inspire
Soft melting thoughts, and propagate desire :
So long shall Waller's strains our passions move,
And Saccharissa's beauty kindle love.
—ADDISON, *An Account of the Greatest British Poets.*

29

Waller, the Muse with heavenly verse supplies,
Smooth as the fair, and sparkling as their eyes.
　　　　—ELIJAH FENTON, *An Epistle to Mr. Southerne.*

O Waller! Petrarch! you who tun'd the lyre
To the soft notes of elegant desire.
　　　　—LORD LYTTLETON, *Elegy.*

Of the praise of Waller, though much may be taken away, much will remain; for it cannot be denied that he added something to our elegance of diction, and something to our propriety of thought; and to him may be applied what Tasso said, with equal spirit and justice, of himself and Guarini, when, having perused the Pastor Fido, he cried out, "If he had not read Aminta, he had not excelled it".—DR. JOHNSON, *Lives of the Poets: Waller.*

HORACE WALPOLE.

Earl of Orford: 1717-1797.

The faults of Horace Walpole's head and heart are indeed sufficiently glaring. His writings, it is true, rank as high among the delicacies of intellectual epicures as the Strasburg pies among the dishes described in the *Almanach des Gourmands*. But as the *pâté-de-fois-gras* owes its excellence to the diseases of the wretched animal which furnishes it, and would be good for nothing if it were not made of livers preternaturally swollen, so none but an unhealthy and disorganised mind could have produced such literary luxuries as the works of Walpole. . . . He was, unless we have formed a very erroneous judgment of his character, the most eccentric, the most artificial, the most fastidious, the most capricious of men. His mind was a bundle of inconsistent whims and affectations. . . . The conformation of his mind was such that whatever was little seemed to him great, and whatever was great seemed to him little. Serious business was a trifle to him, and trifles were his serious business. . . . What then is the charm, the irresistible charm, of Walpole's writings? It consists, we think, in the art of amusing without exciting. He never convinces the reason, or fills the imagination, or touches the heart; but he keeps the mind of the reader constantly attentive, and constantly entertained.— MACAULAY, *Essays: Walpole.*

Our own Horace Walpole's knowledge of the world is much more expansive than that of St. Simon or Rochefoucauld, and is much less deep in proportion to its width. It takes a more varied survey of manner and humours, embracing more of the active and serious employments of that life which is not spent in patrician salons and royal anterooms.—LYTTON, *Essays: Knowledge of the World.*

Horace Walpole was a man of the world and a courtier; he had quick natural parts and much acquired discernment. No elevated thoughts, no lofty aspirations, no patristic resolves, are visible in his writings. Political *insouciance* was his prevailing habitude of mind; an invincible tendency to *laissez-aller* the basis of his character. But he did not lie by and observe events, like Metternich and Talleyrand, to become imbued with their tendency, and ultimately gain the mastery of them; he let them take their course, and in reality cared very little for the result. He was an epicurean, not a stoic, in politics. His character approaches very nearly to that which common report has assigned to Lord Melbourne.—SIR ARCHIBALD ALISON, *Essays : British History, etc.*

The history of England throughout a very large segment of the eighteenth century, is simply a synonym for the works of Horace Walpole. . . . Walpole, in fact, represents a common creed amongst comfortable but clear-headed men of his time. It was the strange mixture of scepticism and conservatism which is exemplified in such men as Hume and Gibbon. He was at heart a Voltairian, and, like his teacher, confounded all religious and political beliefs under the name of superstition. —LESLIE STEPHEN, *Hours in a Library, Second Series.*

SIR ROBERT WALPOLE.

Earl of Orford : 1676-1745.

See Britain, see thy Walpole shine from far,
His azure ribbon, and his radiant star ;
A star that, with auspicious beams, shall guide
Thy vessel safe, through fortune's roughest tide.
—YOUNG, *The Instalment.*

Few men ever reached and maintained for so many years the highest station which the citizen of a free state can hold, who have enjoyed more power than Sir Robert Walpole, and have left behind them less just cause of blame, or more monuments of the wisdom and virtue for which his country has to thank him.—LORD BROUGHAM, *Statesmen of the Time of George III., Vol. II.*

Lord Dover seems to have been enthusiastic on the same side, and goes so far as to call Sir Robert " the glory of the Whigs ". Sir Robert deserved this high eulogium, we think, as little as he deserved the abusive epithets which have often been coupled with his name. A fair character of him still remains to be drawn : and, whenever it shall be drawn, it will be equally unlike the portrait by Coxe and the portrait by Smollett. He had, undoubtedly, great talents and great virtues. He was not, indeed, like the leaders of the party which opposed his Government, a brilliant orator. He was not a profound scholar, like Carteret, or a wit and a fine gentleman, like Chesterfield. In all these respects his deficiencies were remarkable. His literature consisted of a scrap or two of Horace and an anecdote or two from the end of the Dictionary. His knowledge of history was so limited that, in the great debate on the Excise Bill, he was forced to ask the Attorney-General Yorke who Empson and Dudley were. His manners were a little too coarse and boisterous even for the age of Westerns and Topehalls. When he ceased to talk of politics, he could talk of nothing but women : and he dilated on his favourite theme with a freedom which shocked even that plain-spoken generation, and which was quite unsuited to his age and station.—MACAULAY, *Essays : Horace Walpole.*

No English minister had a sounder judgment in emergencies or a greater skill in reading and in managing men.—W. E. H. LECKY, *History of England, Vol. I.*

For the greater part of his life Walpole had been behind the scenes; he had seen the actresses paint and powder and storm at each other; he had seen the actors learn their parts, pad their limbs and set their features; he had seen the mechanism of the performances, and how the art had been acquired which was to hide the art; and therefore we cannot expect from him the same opinion of the play and of the players as from the audience which watches the stage from the front of the house. It is only those in power who can really know the heights to which man can rise, and the depths into which he can fall. . . . Human nature was to Walpole what the human body is to the anatomist—he dissected its different component parts, and knew the exact value and comparative merits of each. During his leadership of the House of Commons no statesman ever better succeeded in commanding the adhesion of his followers and in suppressing the spite of personal feuds. High principles, a sound morality, greatness of sentiment, he did not possess; he bribed, he cajoled, he intrigued, he resorted to every political trick within the compass of parliamentary tactics, and the result was that his tenure of office is among the longest and most successful on record. Yet lax as we should now consider his political dealings, his personal honour throughout his career was unsullied.—A. E. EWALD, *Representative Statesmen, Vol. I.*

IZAAC WALTON.

English Author: 1593-1683.

Methinks their very names shine still and bright;
Apart, like glow-worms on a summer night;
Or lonely tapers when from far they fling
A guiding ray; or seen, like stars on high,
Satellites burning in a lucid ring
Around meek Walton's heavenly memory.
                    —WORDSWORTH, *Walton's Book of Lives.*

NEVILL, EARL OF WARWICK.

English Courtier: 1420-1471.

We might not, however, hold for ourselves that the State is a church-maker as the Earl of Warwick was a king-maker.—GLADSTONE, *Gleanings, Vol. III.*

GEORGE WASHINGTON.

First President of the United States: 1732-1799.

Where may the wearied eye repose
When gazing on the Great,
Where neither guilty glory glows,
Nor despicable state?
Yes—one—the first—the last—the best—
The Cincinnatus of the West,
Whom envy dared not hate,
Bequeath'd the name of WASHINGTON,
To make man blush there was but one!

                    —BYRON, *Ode to Napoleon.*

While Washington's a watchword, such as ne'er
Shall sink while there's an echo left to air.
>—BYRON, *The Age of Bronze.*

Where Washington hath left
His aweful memory
A light for after time!
>—SOUTHEY, *Ode written during the War with America.*

Washington! said the Monarch, well hast thou spoken and truly,
Just to thyself and to me. On them is the guilt of the contest,
Who, for wicked ends, with foul arts of faction and falsehood,
Kindled and fed the flame: but verily they have their guerdon.
Thou and I are free from offence. And would that the nations,
Learning of us, would lay aside all wrongful resentment,
All injurious thought, and honouring each in the other
Kindred courage and virtue, and cognate knowledge and freedom,
Live in brotherhood wisely conjoin'd. We set the example.
>—*Id., A Vision of Judgment.*

Vain is Empire's mad temptation!
Not for him an earthly crown!
He whose sword hath freed a nation!
Strikes the offered sceptre down.
See the throneless Conqueror seated,
Ruler by a people's choice;
See the Patriot's task completed;
Hear the Father's dying voice.
>—OLIVER W. HOLMES, *Ode for Washington's Birthday.*

Surely Washington was the greatest man that ever lived in this world uninspired by divine wisdom and unsustained by supernatural virtue.—LORD BROUGHAM, *Statesmen of the Reign of George III., Vol. III.*

England missed the sobriety, the self-command, the perfect soundness of judgment, the perfect rectitude of intention, to which the history of revolutions furnishes no parallel, or furnishes a parallel in Washington alone.—MACAULAY, *Essays: John Hampden.*

Washington, the perfect citizen.—EMERSON, *Society and Solicitude: Old Age.*

Washington served us chiefly by his sublime moral qualities. To him belonged the proud distinction of being the leader in a revolution, without awakening one doubt or solicitude as to the spotless purity of his purpose. His was the glory of being the brightest manifestation of the spirit which reigned in his country; and in this way he became a source of energy, a bond of union, the centre of an enlightened people's confidence.

In such a revolution as that of France, Washington would have been nothing; for that sympathy which subsisted between him and his fellow-citizens, and which was the secret of his power, would have been wanting. By an instinct which is unerring, we call Washington, with grateful reverence, the Father of his country, but not its Saviour. A people which wants a saviour, which does not possess an earnest and pledge of freedom in its own heart, is not yet ready to be free.—DR. W. E. CHANNING, *On the Life and Character of Napoleon.*

Washington is to my mind the purest figure in history.—GLADSTONE.

In Washington, America . . . found a leader who could be induced by no earthly motive to tell a falsehood, or to break an engagement, or to commit any dishonourable act.—W. E. H. LECKY, *History of England, Vol. I.*

DR. ISAAC WATTS.

Nonconformist Divine and Author: 1674-1748.

Thy soul, great Watts! forsakes the earth,
  And scorns the glitt'ring toy;
While conscious of her higher birth
    She seeks immortal joy.
      —SAMUEL BOYSE, *Written in Mr. Watts' Horæ Lyricæ.*

Few men have left behind such purity of character, or such monuments of laborious piety. He has provided instruction for all ages; from those who are lisping their first lessons, to the enlightened readers of Malebranche and Locke; he has left neither corporeal nor spiritual nature unexamined; he has taught the art of reasoning, and the science of the stars. His character, therefore, must be formed from the multiplicity and diversity of his attainments, rather than from any single performance; for it would not be safe to claim for him the highest rank in any single denomination of literary dignity; yet perhaps there was nothing in which he would not have excelled, if he had not divided his powers to different pursuits. . . . It is sufficient for Watts to have done better than others what no man has done well.—DR. JOHNSON, *Lives of the Poets: Watts.*

ARTHUR WELLESLEY, DUKE OF WELLINGTON.

Field Marshal and Statesman: 1769-1852.

     Such fearful odds
Were balanced by Sir Arthur's master mind
And by the British heart.
      —SOUTHEY, *Inscription: Talavera.*

Next with loose rein and careless canter view
Our man of men, the Prince of Waterloo;
O'er the firm brow the hat as firmly prest,
The firm shape rigid in the button'd vest;
Within—the iron which the fire has proved,
And the close Sparta of a mind unmoved!
      —LYTTON, *The New Timon.*

Bury the Great Duke
With an empire's lamentation,
Let us bury the Great Duke
To the noise of the mourning of a mighty nation.
   .   .   .   .   .
So great a soldier taught us there,
What long-enduring hearts could do
In that world-earthquake, Waterloo!
      —TENNYSON, *Ode on the Death of the Duke of Wellington.*

How could a thousand words of all the names that could be named speak so powerfully, and even if I spoke with the tongue of an angel—as if I mention one word—Sir Arthur Wellesley, Duke of Wellington, the hero of a hundred fields, in all of which his banner was raised in triumph! Who never—bear witness, Europe! bear witness, Asia!—advanced but to cover his arms with glory; the captain who never advanced but to be victorious; the mightier captain who never retreated, but to eclipse the glory of his advances, by the yet harder task of unwearied patience, indomitable to lassitude—by the inexhaustible resources of transcendent skill, showing the wonders, the marvels of a moral courage never yet subdued.—LORD BROUGHAM, *Speech at Banquet to the Duke of Welling-ton, August,* 1839.

Wellington belongs to the latter, and by far the highest class of illustrious characters. He was not a great man because he was a great general, but a great general because he was a great man. He would have been equally great in anything else which he undertook. It is reported that he has said "that the native bent of his mind was towards finance and civil government rather than military affairs". It is certain that when he took his seat at the board of the cabinet council, it was the vigour of thought and perfect command of every subject which came before them, even more than his military fame, which won such general respect, and ultimately raised him, in difficult times, to the highest place in the government. . . . Napoleon placed himself at the head of Europe, and desolated it for fifteen years with his warfare: Europe placed Wellington at the head of its armies, and he gave it thirty years of unbroken peace. The former was in the end led to ruin while blindly following the meteor of worldly greatness; the latter was unconsciously led to final greatness while only following the star of public duty. Wellington was a warrior, but he was so only to become a pacificator: he has seen shed the blood of men, but it was only to stop the shedding of human blood: he has borne aloft the sword of conquest, but it was only to plant in its stead the emblems of mercy.—SIR ARCHIBALD ALISON, *Essays : Wellington.*

THE DUKE OF WELLINGTON! . . . May my tongue cleave to the roof of my mouth—or wag in mumbling palsy—if ever my breath seek to stain the lustre of that glorious name. He saved England. . . . Till the day of my death will I raise up my feeble voice in honour of the Hero of Waterloo. He saved Europe—the world. Twin-stars in England's sky, immortally shall burn the deified spirits of Nelson and Wellington. . . . In war, Wellington, the Gaul-humbler, is a greater name, immeasurably greater, than Alfred, the Dane-destroyer.—JOHN WILSON, *Noctes Ambro-sianæ, Vol. II.*

Wellington, the perfect soldier.—EMERSON, *Society and Solicitude : Old Age.*

Of all the Heroes of Duty whose names history proudly cherishes none occupies a more conspicuous position on the list than England's greatest General. With Wellington duty was the absorbing principle of his life. It was the guiding star of all his actions. When he said it was "his duty" to proceed in any particular course, men knew it to be worse than useless to endeavour to turn him from his purpose. Throughout his dispatches, throughout his orders, throughout his vast private correspondence, it is curious to observe how often the word "duty" occurs. Nor was there in this love of Wellington for duty anything of the courtier or the aspirant: he did not set before him fame, glory, or reward; he did his duty because it was his duty—simply because it was the right thing to do. . . . In summing up the biography of the Duke of Wellington, both as soldier and as statesman, we can arrive at no other conclusion than that he was a great Englishman—haughty, proud with all the faults and virtues of his orders, but the pink of honour, most just in the disposal of his patronage, indifferent to public applause or public hate, yet ever sensitive to the verdict of his own conscience, brave, truthful, straightforward, patriotic.— A. C. EWALD, *Representative Statesmen, Vol. II.*

The more deeply and thoroughly, we examine the Duke's character, the more we admire it.   To those who have the fatal gift of idealization such a character as the Duke of Wellington's offers repose.   For once they find their Ideal exists.   To those who have the sad talent of minute and perspicuous observation, the Duke's conduct is also satisfactory.   To those, and they are but few, who have the misfortune to possess both these qualities; who " walk in a region that they find almost uninhabited "; it is a consolation to believe that Human Nature has for once reached such perfection. . . . This Globe has produced three beings, whose names will only perish when the Earth itself shall be dissolved into its elements; a POET, an ARTIST, and a MAN: of these BRITAIN claims two; ITALY one: SHAKESPEARE the POET; MICHAEL ANGELO the ARTIST; WELLINGTON the MAN.—SIR WILLIAM FRASER, *Words on Wellington.*

The place I should be inclined to assign to Wellington as a general would be one in the very first rank—equal, if not superior, to that given to Napoleon.   In estimating the comparative merits of these illustrious rivals, it may be conceded that the schemes of the French Emperor were more comprehensive, his genius more dazzling, and his imagination more vivid than Wellington's.   On the other hand, the latter excelled in that coolness of judgment which Napoleon himself described as " the foremost quality in a general ".—GENERAL LORD ROBERTS, *The Rise of Wellington.*

JOHN WESLEY.

Founder of Methodism : 1703-1791.

Reverend in comely mien, of aspect mild and benignant,
There, too, Wesley I saw and knew, whose zeal apostolic,
Though with error alloy'd, hath on earth its merited honour,
As in Heaven its reward.
        —SOUTHEY, *A Vision of Judgment : Worthies of the Georgian Age.*

I look upon the whole world as my parish.—JOHN WESLEY.

I hear my son John has the honour of being styled the Father of the Holy Club.   If it be so, I am sure I must be the grandfather of it, and I need not say that I had rather any of my sons should be so dignified and distinguished than have the title His Holiness.—REV. SAMUEL WESLEY.

Mr. Wesley's conversation is good.   He talks well on any subject.   I could converse with him all night.—DR. JOHNSON in BOSWELL'S *Life.*

The history of men who have been prime agents in those great moral and intellectual revolutions which from time to time take place among mankind, is not less important than that of statesmen and conquerors. If it has not to treat of actions wherewith the world has rung from side to side, it appeals to the higher part of our nature, and may perhaps excite more salutary feelings, a worthier interest, and wiser meditations. The Emperor Charles V., and his rival of France, appear at this day infinitely insignificant, if we compare them with Luther and Loyola ; and there may come a time when the name of Wesley will be more generally known, and in remoter regions of the globe, than that of Frederick or of Catharine. For the works of such men survive them, and continue to operate, when nothing remains of worldly ambition but the memory of its vanity and its guilt.—ROBERT SOUTHEY, *Life of Wesley, Vol. I.*

John Wesley, the Ignatius Loyola of the English Church. . . . If Louis XIV. could say with truth *L'État c'est moi*, with even greater accuracy could Wesley claim the Methodist body as his own.—FRANCIS HITCHMAN, *Eighteenth Century Essays : The Father of Methodism.*

An institution is the lengthened shadow of one man ; . . . Methodism of Wesley.—EMERSON, *Essays : Self-Reliance.*

The *Life of Wesley* (Southey's) will probably live. Defective as it is, it contains the only popular account of a most remarkable moral revolution, and of a man whose eloquence and logical acuteness might have made him eminent in literature, whose genius for government was not inferior to that of Richelieu, and who, whatever his errors may have been, devoted all his powers, in defiance of obloquy and derision, to what he sincerely considered as the highest good of his species.—MACAULAY, *Essays : Southey's Colloquies.*

He was an enthusiast of no vulgar kind : as Nelson was an enthusiast for his country, so was John Wesley for religion. Where the highest interests of men were concerned, Wesley made no account of precedent, or public opinion, or maxims of human or even of ecclesiastical precedence.—ALEXANDER KNOX.

The robust energy of Wesley and Whitfield.—W. E. H. LECKY, *History of England, Vol. I.*

In the beginnings of Methodism there was something of the grandeur and simplicity of Early Christianity, or if that is too strong a comparison, of the foundation of the Mendicant Orders.—FRANCIS DE PRESSENSÉ, *Cardinal Manning (transl.).*

If ever a good Protestant has been practically *canonised*, it has been John Wesley ! It would be strange indeed if his name was not well known. . . . Let us thank God for what John Wesley *was*, and not keep poring over his deficiencies, and only talking of what he *was not*. Whether we like it or not, John Wesley was a mighty instrument in God's hand for good ; and, next to George Whitfield, was the first and foremost evangelist of England a hundred years ago.—BISHOP J. C. RYLE, *English Leaders of the Last Century.*

Not Mark Anthony, not Charles the Twelfth, not Napoleon, ever went through such physical suffering for the love of war, or for the conqueror's ambition, as Wesley was accustomed to undergo for the sake of preaching at the right time and in the right place to some crowd of ignorant and obscure men, the conversion of whom could bring him neither fame nor fortune. . . . Wesley was as completely in command of his body of missionaries as the general of the order of Jesuits is of those over whom he is called to exercise control. The humblest of the Wesleyan preachers caught something, caught indeed very much, of the energy, the courage, the devotion, the self-sacrifice, of their great leader.—JUSTIN McCARTHY, *History of the Four Georges, Vol. II.*

How truly it has been said by a writer in the *British Quarterly*, that the most romantic lives of the saints of the Roman Catholic calendar do not present a more startling succession of incidents than those which meet us in the life and labours of Wesley. Blessed Raymond, of Pegna-fort, spread his cloak upon the sea to transport him across the water, sailing one hundred and sixty miles in six hours, and entering the convent through closed doors! The devout and zealous Francis Xavier spent three whole days in two different places at the same time, preaching all the while! Rome shines out in transactions like these : Wesley does not ; but he seems to have been almost ubiquitous, and he moves with a rapidity reminding us of that flying angel who had the everlasting Gospel to preach, and he shines alike in his conflicts with nature and the still wilder tempests caused by the passions of men. We read of his travelling, through the long wintry hours, two hundred and eighty miles on horseback in six days ; it was a wonderful feat in those times. When Wesley first began his itinerancy there were no turnpikes in the country ; but before he closed his career, he had probably paid more, says Dr. Southey, for turnpikes than any other man in England, for no other man in England travelled so much.—E. PAXTON HOOD, *Vignettes of the Great Revival.*

What deathful torpor would have succeeded the shamelessness of the Restoration epoch in the eighteenth century but for John Wesley!—F. W. FARRAR, *Social and Present-Day Questions.*

The heart religion of John Wesley, the everlasting yea of Carlyle.—W. S. LILLY, *Four English Humourists.*

The Christ of the Cross and of the Throne has received gifts of men for men, some apostles and prophets, and some pastors and evangelists. And of those men He has in His grace bestowed in these later centuries, John Wesley holds a place as primary as it is arresting, and as unchallenged as it is immeasurably and prophetically fruitful. He is the chief prophet of the eighteenth century. The Prophetism of the New Testament in all its sublime qualities and successes reaches its maximum in him, and places him at the spring head of the spiritual life of our modern England. . . . No man with an eye for spiritual facts can look into Wesley's history without seeing God ; and he who looks continuously is likely to feel, as Newton did after looking at the sun, that the image of God is so burned into his soul that he can see nothing else.—DR. JOHN CLIFFORD, *Sermon preached at the Wesley Centenary* (1891).

Two great men in the eighteenth century were contemporaries. There is not much interval between the dates of their respective deaths,—Voltaire and Wesley. You trace the influence of Voltaire through the French Revolution—for that Revolution was practically originated by him—that influence is seen to-day in the legislation, in the government, in the morals, in the irreligion of France. The same description can be applied to Wesley. We trace his history through the same period of time, and we see his influence to-day in the legislation, the government, the morals, and the religion of Great Britain.—Sir Henry H. Fowler, *Address at the Wesley Centenary* (1891).

The Rev. John Wesley was a distinguished man, if ever there was one, and his name is associated with a movement certainly as remarkable as, and a great deal more useful than, the one connected with the name of Newman. Wesley's great missionary tours in Devon and Cornwall, and the wild, remote parts of Lancashire, lack no single element of sublimity. To this day the memories of those apostolic journeys are green and precious, and a source of strength and joy: the portrait of the eager preacher hangs up in almost every miner's cottage, whilst his name is pronounced with reverence by a hundred thousand lips.—Augustine Birrell, *Res Judicatæ*.

WILLIAM WHISTON.

English Theologian and Mathematician : 1667-1752.

Whiston perhaps in Euclid may succeed,
But shall I trust him to reform my creed?
—Elijah Fenton, *An Epistle to Thomas Lombard, Esq*

HENRY KIRKE WHITE.

English Poet : 1785-1806.

Unhappy White! while life was in its spring,
And thy young muse just waved her joyous wing,
The spoiler swept the soaring lyre away
Which else had sounded an immortal lay.
Oh! what a noble heart was here undone,
When Science' self destroy'd her favourite son!
Yes, she too much indulged thy fond pursuit ;
She sow'd the seeds but death has reap'd the fruit.
—Byron, *English Bards and Scotch Reviewers.*

Not alone of the Muses
But by the Virtues loved, his soul in its youthful aspirings
Sought by the Holy Hill, and his thirst was for Siloa's waters.
—Southey, *A Vision of Judgment.*

GEORGE WHITFIELD.

English Preacher and Revivalist : 1714-1770.

Leuconomus (beneath well-sounding Greek
I slur the name a poet must not speak)
Stood pilloried on infamy's high stage,
And bore the pelting scorn of half an age ;
The very butt of slander, and the blot
For every dart that malice ever shot.
.   .   .   .

Now, Truth, perform thine office ; waft aside
The curtain drawn by prejudice and pride,

Reveal (the man is dead) to wondering eyes
This more than monster in his proper guise.
He loved the world that hated him; the tear
That dropp'd upon his Bible was sincere.
Assail'd by scandal and the tongue of strife,
His only answer was a blameless life,
And he that forged and he that threw the dart
Had each a brother's interest in his heart.
Paul's love of Christ, and steadiness unbribed,
Were copied close in him, and well transcribed;
He follow'd Paul; his zeal a kindred flame,
His apostolic charity the same,
Like him, cross'd cheerfully tempestuous seas,
Forsaking country, kindred, friends, and ease;
Like him, he labour'd, and like him, content
To bear it, suffer'd shame where'er he went.

—COWPER, *Hope.*

God sent his two servants Whitfield and Wesley; were they prophets?
Or were they idiots and madmen? " Show us Miracles? "
Can you have greater Miracles than these? Men who devote
Their life's whole comfort to entire scorn, injury, and death?

—W. BLAKE.

Let the name of George Whitfield perish, if God be glorified. . . .
Lord Jesus, I am weary in Thy work, but not of Thy work.—GEORGE
WHITFIELD.

The quarterings of Whitfield are entitled to a conspicuous place in the
" Evangelical " scutcheon; and they who bear it are not wise in being
ashamed of the blazonry. . . . If ever philanthropy burned in the human
heart with a pure and intense flame, embracing the whole family of man
in the spirit of universal charity, it was in the heart of George Whitfield.
He loved the world that hated him. He had no preferences but in favour
of the ignorant, the miserable, and the poor.—SIR JAMES STEPHEN, *Essays
in Ecclesiastical Biography.*

The first and foremost whom I will name is the well-known George
Whitfield. Though not the first in order, if we look at the date of his
birth, I place him first in the order of merit, without any hesitation. Of
all the spiritual heroes of a hundred years ago none saw so soon as
Whitfield what the times demanded, and none were so forward in the
great work of spiritual aggression. I should think I committed an act of
injustice if I placed any name before his. . . . That any human frame
could so long endure the labours that Whitfield went through does indeed
seem wonderful. That his life was not cut short by violence, to which
he was frequently exposed, is no less wonderful. But he was immortal
till his work was done. . . . The Arabians have a proverb which says,
" He is the best orator who can turn men's ears into eyes ". Whitfield
seems to have had a peculiar faculty of doing this. He dramatised his
subject so thoroughly that it seemed to move and walk before your eyes.
He used to draw such vivid pictures of the things he was handling, that
his hearers could believe they actually saw and heard them.—BISHOP J.
C. RYLE, *English Leaders of the Last Century.*

Whitfield must be allowed to occupy the luminous centre upon the field of Methodism. Besides his personal claim to this distinction, which we think is clear, there is a ground on which those who would award this position to Wesley might be content to relinquish it in his behalf; for, if it be true that *his* ministerial course furnishes peculiar evidence of the reality of the Gospel which he preached, and of the presence of Him who " worketh all in all "—if it be true that Wesley's glory was, as one may say, an effulgence of Christianity itself, the same may more emphatically be affirmed as to Whitfield, whose natural endowments were fewer, and whose success as a preacher of the Gospel was not less, perhaps greater. —Isaac Taylor, *Wesley and Methodism.*

He lived perpetually in the sight of eternity, and a desire to save souls was the single passion of his life.—W. E. H. Lecky, *History of England, Vol. I.*

We do not exaggerate in speaking of him as the very Orpheus of the pulpit. Assuredly, as it has been said, Orpheus, by the power of his music, drew trees, stones, the frozen mountain-tops, and the floods to bow to his melody, so men, " stockish, hard, and full of rage," felt a change pass over their nature as they came under the spell of Whitfield.—E. Paxton Hood, *Vignettes of the Great Revival.*

Walt Whitman.

American Poet : 1819-1892.

Good-bye, Walt!
Good-bye from all you loved on earth—
Rock, tree, dumb creature, man and woman—
    To you their comrade human.
        The last assault
Ends now ; and now in some great world has birth
A minstrel whose strong soul finds broader wings,
    More brave imaginings.
Stars crown the hill-tops where your dust shall lie,
    Even as we say good-bye,
        Good-bye old Walt !
            —E. C. Stedman (*Read at Whitman's Burial*).

Friend Whitman! wert thou less serene and kind,
    Surely thou mightest (like our Bard sublime,
Scorn'd by a generation deaf and blind)
    Make thine appeal to the avenger, Time ;
    For thou art none of those who upward climb,
Gathering roses with a vacant mind ;
Ne'er have thy hands for jaded triflers twined
    Sick flowers of rhetoric and weeds of rhyme.
Nay, thine hath been a Prophet's stormier fate
While Lincoln and the martyred legions wait
    In the yet widening blue of yonder sky,
On the great strand below them thou art seen,
Blessing, with something Christ-like in thy mien,
    A sea of turbulent lives that break and die !
            —Robert Buchanan, *Walt Whitman.*

The term *poet* does not fully describe Walt Whitman : the word *prophet* would come nearer ; but that might be misunderstood. Schopenhauer has been well described as "the great prophet of the world's despair". Walt Whitman may be termed conversely the great prophet of the world's hope. . . . He sounds all the chords of human feeling with the depth and urgency of one who has suffered, in his own person and by sympathy, all woes and agonies, but whose spirit is too great to be turned by any suffering from the clear faith that "*all is* well".—H. BUXTON FORMAN in *Celebrities of the Century*.

Whitman has seldom struck a note of thought and speech so just and so profound as Blake has now and then touched upon ; but his work is generally more frank and fresh, smelling of sweeter air, and readier to expound or expose its message than this of the prophetic books. Nor is there among these any poem or passage of equal length so faultless and so noble as his "Voice out of the Sea," or as his dirge over President Lincoln—the most sweet and sonorous nocturn ever chanted in the church of the world.—SWINBURNE, *William Blake : A Critical Essay*.

The voluminous and incoherent effusions of Walt Whitman. . . . He has said wise and noble things upon such simple and eternal subjects as life and death, pity and enmity, friendship and fighting ; and even the intensely conventional nature of its elaborate and artificial simplicity should not be allowed, by a magnanimous and candid reader too absolutely to eclipse the genuine energy and the occasional beauty of his feverish and convulsive style of writing. . . . Mr. Whitman's Eve is a drunken apple-woman, indecently sprawling in the slush and garbage of the gutter amid the rotten refuse of her overturned fruit-stall : but Mr. Whitman's Venus is a Hottentot wench under the influence of cantharides and adulterated rum. Cotyto herself would repudiate the ministration of such priestesses as these.—*Id., Ibid.*

Walt Whitman is American among the Americans, untamable as a fowl of the Atlantic, rude in his strength, contemptuous of authority, hopeful of a new cycle of great national histories to be acted on this little earth, and "sounding his barbaric yaup over the roof of the world" in an ecstasy of healthy animalism. Notwithstanding this animalism, he reveals the deepest spirituality at times. His tuneless songs are full of noble thought. It is impossible to describe Whitman without searching for the language of exaggeration. He is a Hebrew bard translated to the American backwoods, where he has turned himself inside out, thence going on to study pantheism on the quays of New York.—ERIC S. ROBERTSON, *Life of H. W. Longfellow*.

JOHN GREENLEAF WHITTIER.

American Poet : 1807-1892.

O thou, whose daily life anticipates
The life to come, and in whose thought and word
The spiritual world preponderates,

Hermit of Amesbury! thou too hast heard
  Voices and melodies from beyond the gates,
  And speakest only when thy soul is stirred!
        —LONGFELLOW, *The Three Silences of Molinos.*
                (*To John Greenleaf Whittier.*)

The faith that lifts, the courage that sustains,
  These thou wert sent to teach:
Hot blood of battle, beating in thy veins.
  Is turned to gentle speech.

Not less, but more, than others hast thou striven;
  Thy victories remain;
The scars of ancient hate, long since forgiven,
  Have lost their power to pain.

Apostle pure of Freedom and of Right,
  Thou had'st thy one reward:
Thy prayers were heard, and flashed upon thy sight
  The Coming of the Lord!

Now, sheathed in myrtle of thy tender songs,
  Slumbers the blade of Truth;
But Age's wisdom, crowning thee, prolongs
  The eager hope of Youth!
        —BAYARD TAYLOR, *A Friend's Greeting.*

There is Whittier, whose swelling and vehement heart
Strains the strait-breasted drab of the Quaker apart,
And reveals the live Man, still supreme and erect,
Underneath the bemummying wrappers of sect.
        —J. R. LOWELL, *A Fable of Critics*

And he, so serene, so majestic, so true,
Whose temple hypœthral the planets shine through,
Let us catch but five words from that mystical pen,
We should know our one sage from all children of men.

 .   .   .   .

So fervid, so simple, so loving, so pure,
We hear but one strain and our verdict is sure,
Thee cannot elude us, no further we search,
"'Tis Holy George Herbert cut loose from his church!
        —OLIVER WENDELL HOLMES, *Whittier's Birthday.*

In Whittier with his special themes—(his out-cropping love of heroism and war, for all his Quakerdom, his verses at times like the measured step of Cromwell's old veterans)—in Whittier lives the zeal, the moral energy, that founded New England—the splendid rectitude and ardour of Luther, Milton, George Fox—I must not, dare not, say the wilfulness and narrowness—though doubtless the world needs now, and always will need, almost above all, just such narrowness and wilfulness.—WALT WHITMAN, *Specimen Days.*

John G. Whitter, a man whose genius and virtues would do honour to any city, whose poetry bursts from the soul with the fire and indignant energy of an ancient prophet, and whose noble simplicity of character is said to be the delight of all who know him. — DR. W. E. CHANNING, *Remarks on the Slavery Question.*

JOHN WICLIF.

English Reformer : 1324-1384.

The returning light,
That first through Wickliff streak'd the priestly gloom,
Now burst in open day.   Bar'd to the blaze,
Forth from the haunts of superstition crawl'd
Her motly sons, fantastic figures all ;
And wide-dispers'd, their useless fetid wealth
In graceful labour bloom'd, and fruits of peace.
—THOMSON, *Liberty.*

Hail, honour'd Wickliff ! enterprising sage !
An Epicurus in the cause of truth !
For 'tis not radiant suns, the jovial hours
Of youthful spring, an ether all serene,
Nor all the verdure of Campania's vales,
Can chase religious gloom !   'Tis reason, thought,
The light, the radiance that pervades the soul,
And sheds its beams on heav'n's mysterious sway !
—SHENSTONE, *The Ruin'd Abbey.*

Once more the Church is seized with sudden fear,
And at her call is Wicliffe disinhumed ;
Yea, his dry bones to ashes are consumed,
And flung into the brook that travels near ;
Forthwith that ancient voice which streams can hear,
Thus speaks, (that voice which walks upon the wind,
Though seldom heard by busy human kind,)
" As thou these ashes, little brook ! wilt bear
Into the Avon, Avon to the tide
Of Severn, Severn to the narrow seas,
Into main ocean they, this deed accurst
An emblem yields to friends and enemies
How the bold teacher's doctrine, sanctified
By truth shall spread throughout the world dispersed."
—WORDSWORTH, *Wicliffe.*

Not least art thou, thou little Bethlehem
In Judah, for in thee the Lord was born ;
Nor thou in Britain, little Lutterworth,
Least, for in thee the word was born again.

.   .   .   .

Rather to thee, thou living water, drawn
By this good Wiclif mountain down from heaven,
And speaking clearly in thy native tongue—
No Latin—He that thirsteth, come and drink.
—TENNYSON, *To Sir John Oldcastle, Lord Cobham.*

Wiclif was in religion, what Bacon was afterwards in science ; the
great detecter of those arts and glosses, which the barbarism of ages had
drawn together to obscure the mind of man.   To this intuitive genius
Christendom was unquestionably more obliged than to any name in the
list of reformers.   He explored the regions of darkness, and let in not a

feeble and glimmering ray; but such an effulgence of light, as was never afterwards obscured. He not only loosened prejudices; but advanced such clear, incontestable proofs, as, having once obtained footing, still kept their ground, and even in an age of reformation wanted little amendment.—W. GILPIN, *Lives of the Reformers, Vol. I.*

Such was this great pioneer of the Reformation. That he was apt to ply the axe with indiscriminate violence, it would be scarcely reasonable to deny; with such violence, indeed, that he, *occasionally*, seems to work like one, who was rather making a *clearance* for the foundation of new edifices, than ridding the earth of the rubbish which encumbered and deformed the old.—CHARLES WEBB LE BAS, *Life of Wiclif.*

Wicliffe's genius was, perhaps, not equal to Luther's; but really the more I know of him . . . I think him as extraordinary a man as Luther upon the whole.—S. T. COLERIDGE, *Table Talk.*

Wickliffe's testimony was a shaking of the papacy: Luther's, an establishment of the Gospels. At the approach of Wickliffe the minions of Rome trembled, as if a strong man armed had burst into their house at night. When Luther spoke, they slunk into corners, as do creatures of darkness at the breaking of the day. . . . Wickliffe stands as the representative of the class of practical reformers. The constitution of his mind was characteristically English, more distinguished by a straightforward good sense than by intellectuality, richness, or refinement;—impatient of subterfuges, indignant at abuses, he arrived at truth as a consequence of his rejection of error. . . . The ship of the Church, to resume our figure, needs a Wickliffe, from time to time, to trim the rigging, to clear the decks, to pack the ballasts; but she must look to men of another mould to steer her in the storm, and to work her in the hour of battle. Luther and his colleagues were such men.—ISAAC TAYLOR, *Introduction to G. Pfizer's " Life of Luther ".*

The slowness and limitation of Wiclif's work, when compared with Luther's, may be explained to a large extent by the fact that Wiclif's only instrument was the pen, whilst Luther sowed the living seed with the press.—REV. W. L. WATKINSON, *Life of John Wicklif.*

John Wycliffe may be justly accounted one of the greatest men that our country has produced. He is one of the very few who have left the impress of their minds, not only on their own age but on all time.—DEAN W. F. HOOK.

The first and perhaps the greatest of the reformers, John Wickliffe.—MACAULAY, *Essays : Burleigh and His Times.*

It was the misfortune of Wycliffe, as it was his greatest glory, that he anticipated by almost two centuries the principles of a more enlightened generation, and scattered his lessons on a soil not yet prepared to give them maturity. Therefore it was wisely determined by this admirable Christian to send forth along with them the sacred volume itself. This was the life of the system, the treasure which he bequeathed to future ages for their immortal inheritance. —DEAN G. WADDINGTON.

Wickliffe was the Daniel of his era,—he dared to be singular, and to offend even to exasperation a power the most dreadful and overwhelming and implacable that then existed. . . . To the Romish hierarchy, Wickliffe was more mischievous when dead than when alive.   His books conferred on him a spiritual omnipresence, for by those he spoke at once in a multitude of places, and to tens of thousands.   When the Romanists could do no more, they bestowed an epitaph on their arch-opponent. This singular article was expressed as follows :—" The devil's instrument, church's enemy, people's confusion, heretic's idol, hypocrite's mirror, schism's broacher, hatred's sower, lie's forger, flattery's sink—who, at his death, despaired like Cain, and stricken by the terrible judgment of God, breathed forth his wicked soul to the dark mansion of the black devil ! "— G. G. CUNNINGHAM, *Lives of Illustrious Englishmen.*

WILLIAM WILBERFORCE.

Philanthropist : 1759-1833.

Thy country, Wilberforce, with just disdain,
Hears thee by cruel men and impious call'd
Fanatic, for thy zeal to loose the inthrall'd
From exile, public sale, and slavery's chain.
Friend of the poor, the wrong'd, the fetter-gall'd,
Fear not lest labour such as thine be vain.
—COWPER, *Sonnet to William Wilberforce, Esq.*

          And one, I ween,
Is Wilberforce, placed rightly at his side.
Whose eloquent voice in that great cause was heard
So oft and well.
—SOUTHEY, *The Poet's Pilgrimage : The Hopes of Man.*

The basis of the natural or indigenous character of Mr. Wilberforce was laid in this quick fellow-feeling with other men.   All the restless vivacity of Voltaire, and a sensibility more profound than that of Rousseau, met in him and mutually controlled each other.—SIR JAMES STEPHEN, *Essays in Ecclesiastical Biography.*

Few persons have ever either reached a higher and more enviable place in the esteem of their fellow-creatures, or have better deserved the place they had gained, than William Wilberforce.—LORD BROUGHAM, *Statesmen of the Time of George III., Vol. I.*

JOHN WILKES.

English Politician : 1727-1797.

Next Wilkes appear'd, vain hoping the reward,
A glorious patriot, an inglorious bard,
Yet erring, shot far wide of Freedom's mark,
And rais'd a flame in putting out a spark.
—CUTHBERT SHAW, *The Race.*

The celebrated John Wilkes is said to have explained to King George III. that he himself, amid his full tide of popularity, was never a Wilkite. —SIR WALTER SCOTT.

Wilkes was one of the worst specimens of a popular leader.—Dr. Arnold, *Introductory Lectures on Modern History.*

John Wilkes, member of Parliament for Aylesbury, was singled out for persecution. Wilkes had, till very lately, been known chiefly as one of the most profane, licentious, and agreeable rakes about town. He was a man of taste, reading, and engaging manners. His sprightly conversation was the delight of green rooms and taverns, and pleased even grave hearers when he was sufficiently under restraint to abstain from detailing the particulars of his amours, and from breaking jests on the New Testament. His expensive debaucheries forced him to have recourse to the Jews. He was soon a ruined man, and determined to try his chance as a political adventurer. In parliament he did not succeed. His speaking, though pert, was feeble, and by no means interested his hearers so much as to make them forget his face, which was so hideous that the caricaturists were forced, in their own despite, to flatter him. As a writer he made a better figure.—Macaulay, *Essays : The Earl of Chatham,* 1844.

The turbulent democracy of Wilkes.—Lord Rosebery, *Life of Pitt.*

Sir David Wilkie.

Scotch Painter : 1785-1841.

Wilkie is the Goldsmith of painters, in the amiable and pathetic humour, in the combination of smiles and tears, of the familiar and the beautiful ; but he has a stronger hold, both over the more secret sympathies and the springs of a broader laughter than Goldsmith himself. If the Drama could obtain a Wilkie, we should hear no more of its decline. He is the exact illustration of the doctrine I have advanced—of the power and dignity of the popular school, in the hands of a master ; dignified, for truth never loses a certain majesty, even in her most familiar shapes. . . . Who does not feel that the pathos and the humour of that most remarkable painter have left on him recollections as strong and enduring as the *chef-d'œuvres* of literature itself ; and that every new picture of Wilkie—in Wilkie's own view—constitutes an era in enjoyment ? More various, more extensive in his grasp than even Hogarth, his genius sweeps from the dignity of history to the verge of caricature itself.—Lytton, *England and the English : Intellectual Spirit.*

William I.

King of England : 1027-1087.

For first, the Norman conqu'ring all by might,
By might was forc'd to keep what he had got;
Mixing our customs and the form of right
With foreign constitutions he had brought.
Mast'ring the mighty, humbling the poorer wight,
By all severest means that could be wrought.
—Samuel Daniel, *History of the Civil Wars, Book I.*

From the first William, our great Norman king,
The bold Plantagenets and Tudors bring
Illustrious virtues.
                    —Prior, *Carmen Seculare, for the Year* 1700.

Proud Nimrod first the bloody chase began,
A mighty hunter, and his prey was man:
Our haughty Norman boasts that barbarous name,
And makes his trembling slaves the royal game.
                    —Pope, *Windsor Forest.*

The haughty Norman seiz'd at once an isle,
For which, through many a century in vain,
The Roman, Saxon, Dane, had toil'd in vain,
Of Gothic nations this the final burst;
And, mix'd the genius of these people all,
These virtues mix'd in one exalted stream,
Here the rich tide of English blood grew full.

                    —Thomson, *Liberty.*

The Son of Love and Lord of War I sing;
Him who bade England bow to Normandy,
And left the name of the Conqueror more than King
To his unconquerable dynasty.
                    —Byron, *The Conquest.*

Rage enough was in this Willelmus Conquæstor, rage enough for his occasions:—and yet the essential element of him, as of all such men, is not scorching *fire* but shining illuminative *light.* Fire and light are strangely interchangeable; nay, at bottom, I have found them different forms of the same most godlike "elementary substance" in our world: a thing worth stating in these days. The essential element of the Conquæstor is, first of all, the most sun-eyed perception of what is really what on this God's-Earth;—which, thou wilt find, does mean at bottom, "Justice," and "Virtues" not a few: *Conformity* to what the Maker has seen good to make. . . . I have a certain indestructible regard for Willelmus Conquæstor. A resident House-Surgeon, provided by Nature for her beloved English People, and even furnished with the requisite fees, as I said; for he by no means felt himself doing Nature's work, this Willelmus, but his own work exclusively! And his own work withal it was; informed *par la Splendeur de Dieu.*—Carlyle, *Past and Present: Democracy.*

As long as William lived, ruthless as he was to all rebels, he kept order and did justice with a strong and steady hand; for he brought with him from Normandy the instincts of a truly great statesman.— Kingsley, *Historical Lectures and Essays.*

That the history of England for the last eight hundred years has been what it has been has come of the personal character of a single man. That we are what we are to this day comes of the fact that there was a moment when our national destiny might be said to hang on the will of a single man, and that that man was William, surnamed at different stages of his life and memory, the Bastard, the Conqueror, and the Great. . . . As far as mortal man can guide the course of things when he is gone, the course of our national history since William's day has been the result of

William's character and of William's acts.   Well may we restore to him the surname that men gave him in his own day.   He may worthily take his place as William the Great alongside of Alexander, Constantine, and Charles.—E. A. FREEMAN, *William the Conqueror : A Memoir.*

WILLIAM II.

King of England : 1056-1100.

King Rufus,—a man of rough ways, in whom the " inner Lightbeam " shone very fitfully.—CARLYLE, *Past and Present.*

Deep as is the importance of the reign of William Rufus in so many ways, there is a certain way of looking at things in which the reign of William Rufus is a kind of episode.   Or rather it is an attempt at a certain object which, when tried in the person of Rufus, failed, and which had to be again tried with better luck, in the person of Henry.   The problem was to reconcile the English nation to the Norman Conquest, to nationalize, so to speak, the Conquest and the dynasty which the Conquest had brought in.   The means thereto was to find a prince of the foreign stock who should reign as an English king, with the good will of the English people, in the interests of the English people.   William Rufus might have held that place, if he had been morally capable of it.—E. A. FREEMAN, *The Reign of William Rufus, Vol. II.*

WILLIAM III.

King of England : 1650-1702.

And here, perhaps, by fate's unerring doom,
Some mighty bard lies hid in years to come,
That shall in William's godlike acts engage,
And with his battles warm a future age.

The race of Nassau was by heaven design'd
To curb the proud oppressors of mankind.
—ADDISON, *A Poem to His Majesty*, 1695.

And yet, O Muse, remains the noblest theme ;
The first of men, mature for endless fame.
Thy future songs shall grace, and all thy lays,
Thenceforth, alone shall wait on William's praise.
—CONGREVE, *The Birth of the Muse.*

Hopes after hopes of pious Papists fail'd,
While mighty William's thundering arm prevail'd.
—POPE, *Imitations of Horace, Book II., Epistle II.*

To save Britannia, lo ! my darling son,
Than hero more ! the patriot of mankind !
Immortal Nassau came.
—THOMSON, *Liberty.*

For William's praise can ne'er expire,
Though nature's self at last must die,
And all this fair-erected sky
Must sink with earth and sea, and melt away in fire.
                    —JOHN HUGHES, *The House of Nassau.*

William, the scourge of tyrants past,
And awe of princes yet unborn.
                    —DR. WATTS, *An Epitaph on King William III.*

Such Nassau is, the fairest, gentlest mind,
In blooming youth the Titus of mankind.
                    —DAVID MALLET, *Verses presented to the Prince of Orange.*

Calm as an under-current—strong to draw
Millions of waves into itself, and run,
From sea to sea, impervious to the sun
And ploughing storm—the spirit of Nassau.
                    —WORDSWORTH, *William the Third.*

The reign of William the Third, as Mr. Hallam happily says, was the nadir of the national prosperity. It was also the nadir of the national character. It was the time when the rank harvest of vices sown during thirty years of licentiousness and confusion was gathered in; but it was also the seed-time of great virtues.—MACAULAY, *Essays: Hallam.*

Few English sovereigns have ever sunk to the tomb less regretted by the mass of the English nation than William III.—W. E. H. LECKY, *History of England, Vol. I.*

William was self-contained, proud, and ambitious as Lucifer; a statesman, a diplomatist, and yet, above all things, a devoted patriot. So able was he as a negociator, that his allies, it was said, reaped as much benefit from his diplomacy as his own subjects. His courage was rather of the Wellington than of the Cæsar type, for as a leader, he lacked that depth of human sympathy, that sense of comradeship, which some masterminds inspire, and which cause them to be followed with blind devotion. There was none of that animal magnetism about him, with which some leaders are so charged as to infect all who come within the zone of their influence.—LORD WOLSELEY, *Life of Marlborough, Vol. I.*

JAMES WOLFE.

English General: 1726-1759.

            They have fallen
Each in his field of glory: one in arms,
And one in council—Wolfe upon the lap
Of smiling Victory that moment won.

      .   .   .   .   .   .
            Wolfe, where'er he fought,
Put so much of his heart into his act,
That his example had a magnet's force,
And all were swift to follow whom all loved.
                    —COWPER, *The Task: The Time-Piece.*

So long as the pulses of men's hearts do answer to any martial music, so long men will say of Wolfe that he died well as became a soldier, a hero, and a gentleman.—JUSTIN McCARTHY, *History of the Four Georges, Vol. II.*

THOMAS WOLSEY.

English Cardinal and Statesman : 1471-1530.

King Henry : " Who's there ? my good Lord Cardinal ?   O, my Wolsey.
The quiet of my wounded conscience ;
Thou art a cure fit for a king."
                —SHAKSPERE, *King Henry VIII., Act II., Scene II.*

Wolsey : " Cromwell, I did not think to shed a tear
In all my miseries; but thou hast forced me,
Out of thy honest truth, to play the woman.
Let's dry our eyes : and thus far hear me, Cromwell ;
And, when I am forgotten, as I shall be,
And sleep in dull cold marble, where no mention
Of me more must be heard of, say, I taught thee,
Say, Wolsey, that once trod the ways of glory,
And sounded all the depths and shoals of honour,
Found thee a way, out of his wreck, to rise in ;
A sure and safe one, though thy master miss'd it.
Mark but my fall, and that that ruin'd me.
Cromwell, I charge thee, fling away ambition ;
By that sin fell the angels ; how can man, then,
The image of his Maker, hope to win by it ?
Love thyself last : cherish those hearts that hate thee ;
Corruption wins not more than honesty.
Still in thy right hand carry gentle peace,
To silence envious tongues.   Be just, and fear not :
Let all the ends thou aim'st at be thy country's,
Thy God's, and truth's ; then if thou fall'st, O Cromwell,
Thou fall'st a blessèd martyr ! Serve the king ;
And, prithee, lead me in :
There take an inventory of all I have,
To the last penny ; 'tis the king's : my robe,
And my integrity to heaven, is all
I dare now call mine own. O Cromwell, Cromwell !
Had I but served my God with half the zeal
I served my king, he would not in mine age
Have left me naked to mine enemies."
                —*Id., Ibid., Act III., Scene II.*

In full-blown dignity, see Wolsey stand,
Law in his voice, and fortune in his hand :
To him the church, the realm, their pow'rs consign,
Thro' him the rays of regal bounties shine ;
Turn'd by his nod the stream of honour flows,
His smile alone security bestows :
Still to new heights his restless wishes tow'r ;
Claim leads to claim, and pow'r advances pow'r ;

Till conquest unresisted ceas'd to please,
And rights submitted left him none to seize.
At length his sov'reign frowns—the train of state
Mark the keen glance, and watch the sign to hate.
Where'er he turns he meets a stranger's eye,
His suppliants scorn him, and his followers fly :
Now drops at once the pride of awful state,
The golden canopy, the glitt'ring plate,
The regal palace, the luxurious board,
The liv'ried army, and the menial lord.
With age, with cares, with maladies opprest,
He seeks the refuge of monastic rest.
Grief aids disease, remember'd folly stings,
And his last sighs reproach the faith of kings.
Speak thou, whose thoughts at humble peace repine,
Shall Wolsey's wealth with Wolsey's end be thine ?
Or liv'st thou now, with safer pride content,
The wisest justice on the banks of Trent ?
For why did Wolsey near the steeps of fate,
On weak foundations raise th' enormous weight ?
Why but to sink, beneath misfortune's blow,
With louder ruin to the gulphs below ?
                    —DR. JOHNSON, *The Vanity of Human Wishes.*

Then Wolsey rose, by nature form'd to seek
Ambition trophies, by address to win,
By temper to enjoy—whose humbler birth
Taught the gay scenes of pomp to dazzle more.
                    —SHENSTONE, *The Ruin'd Abbey.*

WILLIAM WORDSWORTH.

Poet Laureate : 1770-1850.

Let Wordsworth weave, in mystic rhyme,
Feelings ineffably sublime,
And sympathies unknown ;
Yet so our yielding breasts enthral,
His Genius shall possess us all,
His thoughts become our own,
And, strangely pleased, we start to find
Such hidden treasures in *our* mind.
                    —JAMES MONTGOMERY, *A Theme for a Poet.*

And Wordsworth, in a rather long " Excursion,"
(I think the quarto holds five hundred pages)
Has given a sample from the vasty version
Of his new system to perplex the sages ;
'Tis poetry—at least by his assertion,
And may appear so when the dog-star rages—
And he who understands it would be able
To add a story to the Tower of Babel.
          .   .   .   .   .   .
We learn from Horace, " Homer sometimes sleeps " ;
We feel without him, Wordsworth sometimes wakes,—

To show with what complacency he creeps,
With his dear *Waggoners*, around his lakes.
He wishes for " a boat " to sail the deeps—
Of ocean ?—No, of air : and then he makes
Another outcry for " a little boat,"
And drivels seas to set it well afloat.
—BYRON, *Don Juan : Dedication and Third Canto.*

Poet of Nature, thou has wept to know
That things depart which never may return :
Childhood and youth, friendship, and love's first glow,
Have fled like sweet dreams, leaving thee to mourn.
These common woes I feel.   One loss is mine,
Which thou too feel'st, yet I alone deplore.
Thou wert as a lone star whose light did shine
On some frail bark in winter's midnight roar :
Thou hast like to a rock-built refuge stood
Above the blind and battling multitude :
In honoured poverty thy voice did weave
Songs consecrate to truth and liberty.
Deserting these, thou leavest me to grieve,
Thus, having been, that thou shouldst cease to be.
—SHELLEY, *To Wordsworth.*

This be the meed, that thy song creates a thousand-fold echo !
Sweet as the warble of woods ; that awakes at the gale of the morning !
List ! the Hearts of the Pure, like caves in the ancient mountains
Deep, deep *in* the Bosom, and *from* the Bosom resound it,
Each with a different tone, complete or in musical fragments—
All have welcomed thy Voice, and receive and retain and prolong it !
—S. T. COLERIDGE, *Ad Vilmum Axiologum* (*To William Wordsworth*).

　　　　Then (last strain)
Of duty, chosen laws controlling choice,
Action and joy !—An Orphic song indeed,
A song divine of high and passionate thoughts,
To their own music chanted !
　　　　O great Bard
Ere yet that last strain dying awed the air,
With steadfast eye I view'd thee in the choir
Of ever-enduring men.   The truly great
Have all one age, and from one visible space
Shed influence !   They, both in power and act,
Are permanent, and Time is not with them,
Save as it worketh for them, they in it.
Nor less a sacred roll than those of old,
And to be placed, as they, with gradual fame,
Among the archives of mankind, thy work
Makes audible a linked lay of truth,
Of truth profound a sweet continuous lay,
Not learnt, but native, her own natural notes !
—*Id.,* *To William Wordsworth* (*Composed on the Night
after his Recitation of " The Prelude "*).

Man in his simple grandeur, which can take
　From power but poor increase; the Truth which lies
Upshining in "the Well of homely Life";
　The Winds, the Waters, and their Mysteries—
The Morn and moted Noon, the Stars which make
　Their mirror in the heart; the Earth all rife
With warnings and with wisdom; the deep lore
　Which floateth air-like over lonely places—
These made thy study and thy theme; and o'er
　The Beauty of thy Soul no Paphian Graces,
But a religious and a reverent Awe,
　Breathed Sanctity and Music—inspiration,
Not from the dark Obscure of priestly law,
　But that which burns—the Centre of Creation—
A Love, a Mystery, and a Fear—the unseen
Source of all worship since the world hath been!
—LYTTON, To Wordsworth.

I spake of Wordsworth, of that lofty mind,
Enthronised in a little monarchy
Of hills and waters, where no one thing is,
Lifeless, or pulsing fresh with mountain strength,
But pays a tribute to his shaping spirit!
—ARTHUR H. HALLAM, Meditative Fragments.

Others, perchance, as keenly felt,
As musically sang as he;
To Nature as devoutly knelt,
Or toil'd to serve humanity:
But none with those ethereal notes,
That star-like sweep of self-control;
The insight into worlds unseen,
The lucid sanity of soul.
The fever of our fretful life,
The autumn poison of the air,
The soul with its own self at strife.
He saw and felt, but could not share:
With eye made clear by pureness, pierced
The life of Man and Nature through;
And read the heart of common things,
Till new seem'd old, and old was new.
—F. T. PALGRAVE, William Wordsworth.

The last poetic voice is dumb—
We stand to-day by Wordsworth's tomb. . . .
But where will Europe's latter hour
Again find Wordsworth's healing power?
—MATTHEW ARNOLD, Memorial Verses.

Too fast we live, too much are tried,
Too harass'd, to attain
Wordsworth's sweet calm.
—Id., In Memory of the Author of "Obermann".

How welcome to our ears, long pained
  By strife of sect and party noise,
The brook-like murmur of his song
  Of nature's simple joys!
The violet by its mossy stone,
  The primrose by the river's brim,
And chance-sown daffodil, have found
  Immortal life through him.
The sunrise on his breezy lake,
  The rosy tints his sunset brought,
World-seen, are gladdening all the vales
  And mountain-peaks of thought.

            —WHITTIER, *Wordsworth.*

From Shelley's dazzling glow or thunderous haze,
  From Byron's tempest-anger, tempest-mirth,
Men turned to thee and found—not blast and blaze,
  Tumult of tottering heavens, but peace on earth.
Nor peace that grows by Lethe, scentless flower,
  There in white languors to decline and cease;
But peace whose names are also rapture, power,
  Clear sight, and love: for these are parts of peace.

      —WILLIAM WATSON, *Wordsworth's Grave.*

Man and nature as they appear through the telescope of Wordsworth assume no ideal grace, no visionary excellence; but they wear a comeliness which engenders optimism. The age is not yet prepared to appreciate the poet in his fulness—who in winning accents of sweetly uttered knowledge convinces us that the humblest object which can attract our gaze, though seemingly inanimate, is yet an instrument of design in the laboratory of the Lord of all.—KEATS, *Lord Houghton's Life and Letters of John Keats.*

I think Wordsworth possessed more of the genius of a great philosophic poet than any man I ever knew, or, as I believe, has existed in England since Milton.—S. T. COLERIDGE, *Table Talk.*

Mr. Wordsworth is the last man to "look abroad into universality," if that alone constituted genius: he looks at home into himself, and is "content with riches fineless".—HAZLITT, *Table Talk.*

Wordsworth—with his eternal—Here we go up, and here we go down, down, and here we go roundabout, roundabout!—Look at the nerveless laxity of his *Excursion!*—What interminable prosing!—The language is out of condition:—fat and fozy, thick-winded, purpled and plethoric. Can he be compared with Pope?—Fie on't! no, no, no!—Pugh, pugh! . . . I confess that the *Excursion* is the worst poem, of any character, in the English language. It contains about two hundred sonorous lines, some of which appear to be fine, even in the sense, as well as the sound. The remaining seven thousand three hundred are quite ineffectual. Then, what labour the builder of that lofty rhyme must have undergone! It is,—in its own way, a small tower of Babel, and all built by a single man!—JOHN WILSON, *Noctes Ambrosianæ, Vol I.*

Wordsworth, the High Priest of Nature's joy.—*Id., Essays: Greek Drama.*

We believe that Wordsworth's genius has had a greater influence on the spirit of poetry in Britain, than was ever before exercised by any individual mind. He was the first man who impregnated all his descriptions of external nature with sentiment or passion. In this he has been followed —often successfully—by other true poets. He was the first man that vindicated the native dignity of human nature, by showing that all her elementary feelings were capable of poetry—and in that too he has been followed by other true poets, although here he stands, and probably ever will stand, unappoached. He was the first man that stripped thought and passion of all vain or foolish disguises, and showed them in their just proportions and unencumbered power. He was the first man who in poetry knew the real province of language, and suffered it not to veil the meanings of the spirit. In all these things,—and in many more,—Wordsworth is indisputably the most ORIGINAL POET OF THE AGE ; and it is impossible, in the very nature of things, that he can ever be eclipsed. From his golden urn other orbs may draw light ; but still it will be said of him—

> " Then shone the firmament
> With living sapphires. HESPERUS, WHO LED
> THE STARRY HOST, RODE BRIGHTEST."
> —JOHN WILSON, *Essays : Wordsworth.*

Wordsworth is the apostle, the spiritualiser of those who cling to the most idealised part of things that are – Religion and her houses, Loyalty and her monuments—the tokens of the Sanctity which overshadows the Past : these are of him, and he of them.—LYTTON, *Essays : Intellectual Spirit of the Time.*

In Wordsworth, the poetry is almost always the mere setting of a thought. The thought may be more valuable than the setting, or it may be less valuable, but there can be no question as to which was first in his mind : what he is impressed with, and what he is anxious to impress, is some proposition, more or less distinctly conceived ; some truth, or something which he deems such. He lets the thought dwell in his mind, till it excites, as in the nature of thought, other thoughts, and also such feelings as the measure of his sensibility is adequate to supply.—J. STUART MILL, *Dissertations and Discussions, Vol. I.*

The exceptional fact of the period is the genius of Wordsworth. He had no master but nature and solitude. " He wrote a poem," says Landor, " without the aid of war." His verse is the voice of sanity in a worldly and ambitious age. One regrets that his temperament was not more liquid and musical. He has written longer than he was inspired. But for the rest he has no competitor.—EMERSON, *English Traits : Literature.*

The works of genius of our age breathe a spirit of universal sympathy. The great poet of our times, Wordsworth—one of the few who are to live— has gone to common life, to the feelings of our universal nature, to the obscure and neglected portions of society, for beautiful and touching themes. Nor ought it to be said that he has shed over these the charms of his genius, as if in themselves they had nothing grand or lovely. Genius is not a creator, in the sense of fancying or feigning what does not exist. Its distinction is to discern more of truth than common minds. It sees under disguises and humble forms everlasting beauty. . . . This it is the prerogative of Wordsworth to discern and reveal in the ordinary walks of life, in the common human heart. He has revealed the loveliness of the primitive feelings, of the universal affections of the human soul. The grand truth which pervades his poetry is that the beautiful is not confined to the rare, the new, the distant—to scenery and modes of life open only to the few; but that it is poured forth profusely on the common earth and sky, that it gleams from the loneliest flower, that it lights up the humblest sphere, that the sweetest affections lodge in lowly hearts, that there is sacredness, dignity, and loveliness in lives which few eyes rest on—that, even in the absence of all intellectual culture, the domestic relations can quietly nourish that disinterestedness which is the element of all greatness, and without which intellectual power is a splendid deformity. . . . Wordsworth is the poet of humanity; he teaches reverence for our universal nature; he breaks down the factitious barriers between human hearts.—DR. W. E. CHANNING, *The Present Age.*

Next to Byron, there is no poet whose writings have had so much influence on the taste of the age as Wordsworth. Byron drove on through the upper air till the thunder of his wheels died on the ear. Wordsworth drove to Parnassus by the lower road, got sometimes lost in bushes and lowland fogs, and was much molested by mosquito critics.—LONGFELLOW, *Samuel Longfellow's Life of H. W. Longfellow, Vol. I.*

Wordsworth is more like Scott, and understands how to be happy, but yet cannot altogether rid himself of the sense that he is a philosopher, and ought always to be saying something wise. He has also a vague notion that Nature would not be able to get on well without Wordsworth; and finds a considerable part of his pleasure in looking at himself as well as at her.—RUSKIN, *Modern Painters, Vol. III.*

Look at the self-confidence of Wordsworth, stiffening every other sentence of his prefaces into defiance; there is no more of it than was needed to enable him to do his work, yet it is not a little ungraceful here and there.—*Id., On the Old Road, Vol. I.*

Tennyson says of the laureate wreath which he so deservedly wears, that it is

> " Greener than the brows
> Of him who uttered nothing base ".

And this, which seems at first sight negative praise, is, in reality, a proof of exquisite discernment; for it is just that which constitutes the marked distinction between Wordsworth and the other really original poets who are likely to share with him the honour of representing poetically to posterity the early part of the nineteenth century. In their crowns there is alloy, both moral and intellectual. His may not be of so imperial a fashion; the gems that stud it may be less dazzling; but the gold is of ethereal temper, and there is no taint upon his robe. Weakness, incompleteness, imperfection, he had, for he was a mortal man of limited faculties, but spotless purity is not to be denied him—he uttered nothing base.—GEORGE BRIMLEY, *Essays.*

That we would assign to Wordsworth a high place among the poets of England the whole tenor of our observations hitherto will have made clear. At the same time, that he falls short of the very highest rank, that he does not stand on the very top of our English Parnassus, where

Chaucer, Milton, and Spenser keep reverent company with Shakespeare, but rather on that upper slope of the mountain whence these greatest are visible, and where various other poets hold perhaps as just, if not so fixed, a footing: this also we have sought to convey as part of our general impression. . . . The ink of Wordsworth is rarely his own blood.—DAVID MASSON, *Wordsworth, Shelley, Keats, and other Essays.*

Wordsworth was, and felt himself to be, a discoverer, and like other great discoverers, his victory was in seeing by faith things which were not yet seen, but which were obvious, or soon became so, when once shown. He opened a new world of thought and enjoyment to Englishmen; his work formed an epoch in the intellectual and moral history of the race. But for that very reason he had, as Coleridge said, like all great artists, to create the taste by which he was to be relished, to teach the art by which he was to be seen and judged. And people were so little prepared for the thorough and systematic way in which he searched out what is deepest or highest or subtlest in human feeling under the homeliest realities, that not being able to understand him they laughed at him. Nor was he altogether without fault in the misconceptions which occasioned so much ridicule and scorn.—DEAN R. W. CHURCH, *Dante, and other Essays.*

For those to whom the mission of Wordsworth appears before all things as a religious one, there is something solemn in the spectacle of the seer standing at the close of his own apocalypse, with the consciousness that the stiffening brain would never permit him to drink again that overflowing sense of glory and revelation; never, till he should drink it new in the kingdom of God. He lived, in fact, through another generation of men, but the vision came to him no more.

> " Or if some vestige of those gleams
> Survived, 'twas only in his dreams." . . .

Surely of him, if of any one, we may think as of a man who was so in accord with Nature, so at one with the very soul of things, that there can be no Mansion of the Universe which shall not be to him a home, no Governor who will not accept him among His servants, and satisfy him with love and peace.—F. W. H. MYERS, *Life of Wordsworth.*

The influence of Wordsworth upon his time has been the influence of the Gulf-Stream; it has flowed silently and surely, and has conquered. . . . He is in the great apostolic succession of truth, and his diocese is as wide as the walls of heaven. . . . If poetry is, as some one has beautifully described it, the Sabbath influence of literature, Wordsworth breathes upon us the very Sabbath of poetry—its rest, its devotion, and its healing calm.—W. J. DAWSON, *Quest and Vision.*

If Wordsworth is pleasant to read it is on account neither of his direct religious and moral teaching, nor by reason of his expression, but because he has like no other entered deeply into the joy of earth. Indeed the very odour of newly dug soil seems to hang about his verse; when most dull and tiresome he suggests at worst the weariness of a long journey over a dull landscape. At his best the charm he wields is comparable only to that of sunlight on waving corn, of birds singing on flowery hawthorn, of the brook chattering round its ferny islets.—P. A. GRAHAM, *Nature in Books.*

Wordsworth has exercised more influence over English poetry than any other man of this century. He has done so mainly by virtue of his originality, for he is pre-eminently original. It is, of course, true that we find among his predecessors, and especially in Burns, anticipations of his style, and, at times, of his mode of thought. It is also true that the spirit of Wordsworth gives a poetic exposition of the cry of Rousseau for a return to nature, and in making it less a theory makes it much more profoundly true. But it is just in this that his originality consists. He gives a clear exposition to tendencies which before his day had been vague and undefined. To do so he breaks boldly with the past, and enters upon a path of his own, a path which had been missed just because it is so very obvious. Wordsworth's great principle is to be in all things natural, natural in thought, natural in language; to avoid far-fetched ingenuities of fancy and expression, and to trust for success to the force of simple truth.—HUGH WALKER in *Celebrities of the Century.*

SIR CHRISTOPHER WREN.

English Architect: 1632-1723.

Stone-masons collected the dome of St. Paul's, but Wren hung it in air.—R. A. WILLMOTT, *Advantages of Literature.*

WILLIAM WYCHERLEY.

English Dramatist: 1640-1715.

The standard of thy style let Etherege be ;
For wit, th' immortal spring of Wycherley ;
Learn, after both, to draw some just design,
And the next age will learn to copy thine.
—DRYDEN, To Mr. Southerne.

Thou, whom the Nine with Plautus' wit inspire,
The art of Terence, and Menander's fire ;
Whose sense instructs us, and whose humour charms,
Whose judgment sways us, and whose spirit warms.
—POPE, Pastorals.

Wycherley earns hard whate'er he gains ;
He wants no Judgment and he spares no Pains :
He frequently excels ; and at the least
Makes fewer Faults than any of the rest.
—ROCHESTER, An Allusion to the Tenth Satire of the First
Book of Horace.

In sense and numbers if you would excel,
Read Wycherley, consider Dryden well.
In one, what vigorous turns of fancy shine !
In th' other, Syrens warble in each line.
—GARTH, The Dispensary, Canto IV.

Wycherley was a worse Congreve. There was, indeed, a remarkable analogy between the writings and lives of these two men. Both were gentlemen liberally educated. Both led town lives, and knew human nature only as it appears between Hyde Park and the Tower.   Both were men of wit.   Neither had much imagination.   Both at an early age produced lively and profligate comedies.   Both retired from the field while still in early manhood, and owed to their youthful achievements in literature whatever consideration they enjoyed in later life.   Both, after they had ceased to write for the stage, published volumes of miscellanies which did little credit either to their talents or to their morals.   Both, during their declining years, hung loose upon society; and both, in their last moments, made eccentric and unjustifiable dispositions of their estates.—MACAULAY, *Essays: Leigh Hunt.*

FRANCIS XAVIER.

Jesuit Missionary ; The Apostle of the Indies: 1506-1552.

The "God-in-us" enthusiasm of Francis Xavier. . . . Xavier the magnanimous, the holy, and the gay ; the canonised saint, not of Rome only, but of universal Christendom ; who, if at this hour there remained not a solitary Christian to claim and to rejoice in his spiritual ancestry, should yet live in hallowed and everlasting remembrance, as the man who has bequeathed to these later ages, at once the clearest proof and the most illustrious example, that even amidst the enervating arts of our modern civilisation the apostolic energy may still burn with all its primeval ardour in the human soul, when animated and directed by a power more than human.—SIR JAMES STEPHEN, *Essays in Ecclesiastical Biography.*

XENOPHON.

Athenian General, Historian and Philosopher: B.C. 445-355.

And Attic Xenophon unfolds
Rich honey from Lycéum's flow'rs.
  —J. G. COOPER, *Epistle I.: The Retreat of Aristippus.*

Was the retreat of the Ten Thousand under Xenophon, or his work of that name, the most consummate performance ?—HAZLITT, *Table Talk.*

Xenophon, the Attic bee, presents us with a style flowing with honey.—DR. VICESIMUS KNOX, *Essays: Cursory Thoughts on Biography.*

XERXES I.

King of Persia: B.C. 485-465.

Great Xerxes comes to seize the certain prey,
And starves exhausted regions on his way ;
Attendant Flatt'ry counts his myriads o'er,
Till counted myriads soothe his pride no more ;
Fresh praise is tried till madness fires his mind,
The waves he lashes, and enchains the wind ;
New pow'rs are claim'd, new pow'rs are still bestow'd,
Till rude resistance lops the spreading god ;
The daring Greeks deride the martial show,

And heap their valleys with the gaudy foe ;
Th' insulted sea with humbler thoughts he gains,
A single skiff to speed his flight remains :
Th' encumber'd oar scarce leaves the dreaded coast
Through purple billows and a floating host.
> —DR. JOHNSON, *The Vanity of Human Wishes.*

Xerxes the Percian kyng yet sawe I there,
⸺ With his huge host that dranke the rivers drye,
Dismounted hilles, and made the vales uprere,
His hoste and all yet sawe I slayne perdye.
> —LORD BUCKHURST, *Induction to a Mirror for Magistrates.*

DR. EDWARD YOUNG.

English Poet : 1684-1765.

And kindle the brisk-sallying fire of Young.
> —DR. JOHN BROWN, *On Honour.*

What Young, satiric and sublime, has writ,
Whose life is virtue, and whose muse is wit.
> —SAVAGE, *The Wanderer, Canto* I.

Night's seraphic bard, immortal Young !
> —MICHAEL BRUCE, *Lochleven.*

To crown the hoary bard of night,
The muses and the virtues all unite.
> —BEATTIE, *On the Report of a Monument.*

. . . the Bard
Whose genius spangled o'er a gloomy theme
With fancies thick as his inspiring stars. . . .
> —WORDSWORTH, *The Prelude.*

Young's works are as devout, as satirical, sometimes as merry, as those of Cowper ; and, undoubtedly, more witty.—LORD JEFFREY, *Essays.*

A later satirist, Dr. Young, is still read with pleasure. But he has the fault of Seneca, of Ovid, of Cowley : a profuse and unseasonable application of wit. His satires have been justly called a string of epigrams. A lover of originality, he did not regard models. Had he endeavoured to imitate Juvenal or Persius, he would have avoided this fault. Those great masters were too much engrossed by the importance of their subjects to fall into the puerility of witticism. There is also something in Young's versification which a good ear does not approve.—DR. VICESIMUS KNOX, *Essays : Cursory Thoughts on Satire and Satirists.*

ZENO.

Emperor of the East : 474-491.

More just the prescience of the eternal goal,
Which gleam'd 'mid Cyprian shades, on Zeno's soul.

Or shone to Plato in the lonely cave;
God in all space, and life in every grave!
>—LYTTON, *The New Timon.*

See how nations and races flit by on the sea of time, and leave no ripple to tell where they floated or sunk, and one good soul shall make the name of Moses, or of Zeno, or of Zoroaster reverent for ever.—EMERSON, *An Address, 15th July,* 1838.

ZOROASTER.

Ancient Persian Philosopher.

There, in long robes, the royal Magi stand;
Grave Zoroaster waves the circling wand.
>—POPE, *The Temple of Fame.*

Oh Persic Zoroaster, lord of stars
—Who said these old renowns, dead long ago,
Could make me overlook the living world
To gaze through gloom at where they stood, indeed.
>—ROBERT BROWNING, *Paracelsus.*

The grave and time-worn sentences of Zoroaster may all be parsed, though we do not parse them. . . . Therefore, when we speak of the Poet in any high sense, we are driven to such examples as Zoroaster and Plato, St. John and Menu, with their moral burdens.—EMERSON, *Poetry and Imagination.*

Zoroaster, like Moses, saw behind the physical forces into the deeper laws of right and wrong. He supposed himself to discover two antagonist powers contending in the heart of man as well as in the outward universe—a spirit of light and a spirit of darkness, a spirit of truth and a spirit of falsehood, a spirit life-giving and beautiful, a spirit poisonous and deadly. To one or other of these powers man was necessarily in servitude. As the follower of Ormuzd, he became enrolled in the celestial armies, whose business was to fight against sin and misery, against wrong-doing and impurity, against injustice and lies and baseness of all sorts and kinds; and every one with a soul in him to prefer good to evil was summoned to the holy wars, which would end at last after ages in the final overthrow of Ahriman. . . . The Persians caught rapidly Zoroaster's spirit. Uncorrupted by luxury, they responded eagerly to a voice which they recognised as speaking truth to them. They have been called the Puritans of the Old World. Never any people, it is said, hated idolatry as they hated it, and for the simple reason that they hated lies.—J. A. FROUDE, *Calvinism: An Address.*